POLITICAL IDEOLOGIES

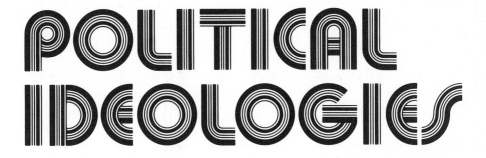

POLITICAL IDEOLOGIES

James A. Gould
University of South Florida

Willis H. Truitt
University of South Florida

Macmillan Publishing Co., Inc.
New York

Macmillan Publishing Co., Inc.
866 Third Avenue, New York, New York 10022

Collier-Macmillan Canada, Ltd., Toronto, Ontario

Library of Congress catalog card number: 72-81653

Printing: 3 4 5 6 7 8   Year: 4 5 6 7 8 9

We wish to acknowledge the research support of
Thomas D. Raymond.

For Francesca—

J. A. G.

For Steve and Julie—

W. H. T.

Contents

Introduction

The Theory of Ideology

The Ideology of Democratic Liberalism

The Ideology of Fascism

Conservatism

The Ideology of the Radical Right

Traditional Marxist and Marxist-Leninist Ideology

The Ideology of Democratic Socialism

New Left Ideologies

Third-World Ideologies

Anarchism, Neoanarchism, and Counterculture

The End of Ideology

Introduction

The word *ideology* has become closely associated with political views, programs, and rationalizations. It does, however, have a more general meaning, or perhaps several more general meanings. These are discussed in the first section, on theories of ideology.

It would seem that "ideology" was first used by the Frenchman de Tracy as meaning the science of ideas. By this he meant the study of the natural origin of ideas, how they are formed in the mind (brain), and how they are caused by sensations. De Tracy's conception of ideology, then, was not too different in its aims from empirical psychology. He wanted to rid the science of ideas of all its supernaturalistic and religious elements. But he also hoped that by establishing a science of ideas (an ideology with perhaps the same status as, say, physiology) he could discover what constituted human nature (as distinct from animal, nonthinking nature). And once he was in possession of this knowledge he hoped to determine further the kinds of social laws, institutions, and practices best suited to meet natural human needs.

Therefore, even the earliest conception of ideology had political implications, its ultimate goal being the creation of those social and political norms best suited to the human species. In this book we have for the most part concentrated on presenting political ideologies. The selections are chosen as being representative of the main classes of political ideologies, extending from the extreme right to the extreme left of the political spectrum.

Since these ideologies compete for adherents and because they frequently appear to contradict one another on important social, ethical, and scientific questions, some must accurately reflect political and social realities while others fail. Perhaps it was because of obvious discrepancies such as these that many people, especially the Marxists, became suspicious of all political ideologies. Indeed Marx and Engels are the originators of what became a widely accepted theory of ideology—that ideologies are interrelated systems of false ideas, false consciousness. The question for Marx and Engels, as we shall see in their writings, was that of scientifically investigating the causes of false political consciousness or of disclosing the origins of ideologies. Marx and Engels thought that political ideologies were for the most part post facto justifications or rationalizations for the existing material or economic organization of society. A principal question for Marxists thus became: What interest groups does a political ideology support

1

and what interest groups does it try to subvert or discredit? They (the Marxists) tended to conclude that all political ideologies served the interests of the ruling classes either directly or indirectly.

The ideology of liberalism and liberal democracy that characterizes most of the political beliefs of the noncommunist Western countries is somewhat diffuse, but it still forms a recognizable pattern of political attitudes. Within the framework of the institutions of private ownership of the means of production and limited constitutional government, liberals are inclined to advocate doctrines such as majority rule but minority rights, political representation, a party system of loyal opposition, relative freedom of speech and press, relative freedom of assembly, religious toleration, and equality of opportunity (as opposed to socialist equality of access to all goods and services produced within society).

Fascist ideology has assumed several forms. The most significant forms, however, were those that developed in Italy, Germany, and Spain between the end of World War I and the beginning of World War II. There are a number of ways in which the content of Fascist ideology can be understood. The most sympathetic approach suggests that Fascist ideas are an outgrowth of the response to the disintegration of the traditional community and family under the influence of industrialization and urbanization. In this light Fascism is seen to be a "calling forth" of the tight-knit, racially and culturally homogeneous preindustrial community, relying on such concepts as common traditions, nationalistic feelings, and racial solidarity. Another way of looking at the rise of Fascist ideology is to suppose that it springs from certain irrationalistic tendencies in late eighteenth- and nineteenth-century European philosophy: notably the racialisms of Comte de Gobineau, and Huston Stewart Chamberlain, the organicism and statism of Hegel, the Will theories of Nietzsche and his followers, the doctrines of Social Darwinists like Spencer, and the racial anthropological views of such men as F. K. Günther. These elements, it is then argued, were fused into political programs as a result of the economic and social crises following World War I. The Marxists argue that such attempts to understand Fascist ideology are too vague and offer instead a more concrete analysis of its rise. Most Marxists contend that the ruling business classes, finding that it was difficult and perhaps impossible to sustain capitalism with liberal institutions and liberal ideas, simply reversed the teachings of liberalism so as to maintain the status quo and secure the capitalist system by force. This interpretation is often thought convincing because it did in fact occur in Germany in the years between the wars when many of the big industrialists backed Hitler's rise to power. Another reason this interpretation appears credible is that Fascist ideological values do appear to be the very reverse of liberal ideological values: constitutional and representative government gives way to dictatorship, minority rights give way to persecution of minorities, the party system gives way to one-party domination, freedom of speech gives way to oppressive censorship, religious toleration is suspended, and throughout this broad transformation capitalist control of the means of production is retained.

Conservatism as a political ideology has a great deal in common with liberalism. In fact, the conservative often calls himself a classical liberal. The main difference between liberal and conservative ideologies is that the conservative places far more emphasis on economic free enterprise and individualism. Therefore, even though he agrees with the liberal that constitutional and representative government is good, he will argue that it is only good to the extent that it stays out of the affairs of individuals' private lives. Governments, he says, have no right to legislate matters of social equality, housing, education, and so forth. With great stress on individual self-determination, the conservative often believes that social injustice and inequality will best be overcome by means of personal initiative and hard work. Even the lowliest of individuals on the social scale, it is maintained, are capable of improving themselves within the institutions of capitalism and economic free enterprise. The radical conservative will often add that those who fail to achieve equality are intellectually, morally, and physically inferior and that they deserve no more than they get (this is a variant of Social Darwinism). The radical conservative may also stress what he calls the "republican form" of government as opposed to democracy, which he may consider socialistic or at least incipiently socialist. Also, the radical conservative may not be as tolerant as the liberal or the ordinary conservative on such issues as free speech, free press, free assembly, and the right to protest. He often believes that such rights if carried to an extreme may undermine "republican form" and free enterprise.

The Marxist ideology and the teachings of Marxism-Leninism are revolutionary in their very nature. This is because the programmatic side of Marxism-Leninism requires, first, the transformation of control of the means of production from the private to the public sector and, second, the eventual abolition of "political" (as opposed to social-managerial) institutions. It is not surprising, then, that one party often dominates in communist countries because an ultimate goal of the communist party and the socialist revolution is the liquidation of all political parties—parties by their nature serve vested interests. In fact, Marx and Engels, as was mentioned above, felt that all political ideologies are forms of false consciousness and that the teachings of scientific socialism (Marxism) were not ideological but rather objective descriptions of social relations. Lenin, on the other hand, seems to have thought that Marxist theory was incomplete, that it required supplementation and extension. Therefore, he found no difficulty in referring to Marxist theory and practice as ideology—the Marxist ideology. This ideology is viewed by Lenin as progressive and revolutionary. It is designed to combat other political ideologies, which are reactionary or static. The main objective of Marxist ideology and political practice is always the establishment of socialism, which is true democracy. And in the struggle to achieve socialism it may be necessary to subordinate liberal political ideals such as freedom of speech, press, and assembly to the exigencies and requirements of the struggle. After all, it is Lenin's argument that these ideals were not and cannot be realized in class societies. Thus their temporary suspension under the dictatorship of the proletariat during the transition from capitalism to socialism is no great loss to the masses. It is a loss only to those who would seek to foment a counterrevolution to restore the capitalist order.

In very recent times a number of new radical and revolutionary ideologies have proliferated. Most of the new ideologies are leftist or socialistic in content. The new leftists have no doubt drawn heavily from traditional Marxism and Marxism-Leninism in framing their own ideology. But they have also incorporated other sources. The main Marxist component of their writings is taken from the early humanistic essays of Marx, which were largely preoccupied with alienation. In addition, there has been an infusion of such Freudian concepts as repression and sublimation in the works of new-Marxists like Herbert Marcuse, Erich Fromm, and Norman Brown. The general result has been that the critical ideology of traditional Marxism was expanded by the New Left so that the focus goes far beyond an examination of the conditions of the working classes to encompass a general critique of the total culture. This critique occupies itself especially with issues of life quality. It attacks the widespread intellectual, aesthetic, and moral deprivation, which it construes as a consequence of the logic of advanced capitalism: a logic that subjects all activities and interests to the criterion of profitability (exchange value) in place of the criterion of meeting human and social needs (use value). The New Left has also called for a reevaluation and reinterpretation of the economic situation in an era of affluence. This requires an analysis that explains why it is that revolutionary consciousness is most intense among middle-class students and academics and peripheral minority groups and is lowest among the traditional working classes. If there is a deterioration of the New Left, it may well be a result of its formulating a political ideology that is intelligible only to the initiated young intellectuals, in this way cutting itself off from the working masses.

Other new revolutionary groupings have developed ideologies that meet their own special needs. Thus colonial peoples throughout the world and "colonized" minorities within capitalist countries advocate doctrines of anti-imperialism and third-world solidarity. Often inspired by the revolutionary writings of Mao Tse-tung and Che Guevarra, these movements are primarily concerned with the achievement of self-determination and liberation from external domination, both political and economic. For the most part such movements and their ideologies are socialistic or variants of Marxism-Leninism which have been creatively reworked to meet the specific needs of an emerging country or class.

The women's liberation movement, to the extent that it has become politicized, has also tended to adapt critical leftist ideology to the special problems of women. Here again the ideology must be reformulated in such a way that it is capable of dealing with nonclass problems such as sexism and discrimination. Much creative energy has been channeled into the recasting of traditional revolutionary doctrines so that they can be made to combat institutions and practices that perpetuate the subjugation of women.

There is a strong anarchist component in the new revolutionary consciousness. In this book we chose to consider this component alongside the more traditionalist doctrines of cooperationism and the abolition of state power. Since anarchism is so often mistakenly identified with violence, we have deliberately omitted the violence-prone teachings of Sorel and Bakunin in favor of the less violently oriented theory of Kropotkin. The continuity between traditional anarchist ideology and that of the neoanarchists is evident and can be seen in typical anti-ideological and antitheoretical positions. This in turn leads to a deemphasis of political organization, an antiprogrammatic defense of "doing one's thing." The neoanarchists in the radical youth culture espouse communitarian values with emphasis on individual moral commitment. Still there is a trace of violence in certain sectors of the movement and it issues in sporadic terrorism: bombings, arson, assassination.

In the concluding chapter of the book some attention is given to a debate that recent history has passed by. That is to say, this debate, which began in the early 1960s, has been settled by events. It began with the claim, on the part of some political and social scientists, that the age of ideology had come to an end in the static, affluent social equilibrium and the international coexistence era of the late 1950s and early 1960s. Almost as soon as the doctrine was enunciated, the world, the society, the culture, exploded. It became clear that the present and the future would witness the combat of warring ideologies. Some even argued that the view that the age of ideology had come to an end was simply another ideology which acted to protect the status quo and sustain existing social arrangements. We have presented some main participants and principal ideas of this controversy and we suggest that the controversy itself be taken as a significant theoretical confrontation between opposing ideologies.

The Theory of Ideology

INTRODUCTION

The earliest consistent use of the term "ideology," by Destutt de Tracy, referred to the investigation of the natural sensory origin of ideas, how ideas come to be formed in the mind, and how a general science of ideas (an ideology) could be developed. Also included in de Tracy's conception of ideology was the determination of human nature based on the study of thought, since man alone is a thinking being. This determination, it was hoped, would provide a means for defining general social laws and institutions most conducive for human betterment. The early French conception of ideology was critical and revolutionary in that it was aimed at undermining the traditional religious and idealistic conception of mind with its belief in the soul and its claim that man was essentially a spiritual being. De Tracy advocated a materialistic and biological method that would rid the philosophy of mind of all its metaphysical and supernaturalistic elements.

The rise of Hegelian philosophy, however, had the effect of "idealizing" the critical, materialistic thrust of ideology. This was not altogether a regressive influence, for even though Hegel's treatment of ideology was idealistic, and in his later work even reactionary in a political sense, he recognized that ideas (ideologies) were as much the product of historical, cultural, and social conditioning as they were the result of sensory stimulation and cerebral mechanics. The problem with the Hegelianization of the concept of ideology lay in Hegel's assumption that the thoughts of real historical men issued ultimately from an absolute mind the presence of which would assure the consolidation and preservation of legal, political, cultural, philosophical, artistic, and religious institutions. Hegel, in his late work, accepted existing conditions in all these areas as finally worked out, as rational. Thus, his ideology, which became the officially sanctioned German ideology, turned out to be a reaction against the critical tendencies of de Tracy's thought.

What was required, then, was a critique of Hegelian ideological idealism and political reactionism that would preserve the insights of Hegel (that ideas are historically and socially conditioned as well as being conditioned by the sensory apparatus) and at the same time turn ideology again in a critical and progressive direction. And this is precisely the significance of Marx's several critiques of Hegel and of Marx's and Engels's analysis of the *German ideology*.

So it is that the Marxist conception of ideology is borne on the Marxist critique of the Hegelian (German) ideology. The materialist element of de Tracy's theory of ideology is restored by Marx. But at the same time it is broadened to encompass not just the biological faculties of men (their brains, senses, and so on) but also their social institutions, which are equally real and material and equally influential (probably even decisive) in determining what men think.

Hence in the *German ideology*, and other works, Marx and Engels argue, against the idealism of Hegel, that it is not some absolute mind that determines the content of human thought.

The production of ideas, of conceptions, of consciousness is at first directly interwoven with the material activity and the material intercourse of men.

According to this view, all thought, all politics, law, morality, religion, metaphysics are reflections of the productive forces and the productive relations of society. In a word, man's conscious life is a product of his real material existence. What appears to be reason embodied in legal and political institutions, in philosophy and religion, is merely a rationalization of the prevailing arrangement of social productive forces and the social relations that these forces give rise to.

Mannheim, in his book *Ideology and Utopia*, calls our attention to the fact that ideology can best be understood in the unfolding historical process. Thus in order to understand it critically we must observe how one conception, say that of de Tracy, gives way to the Hegelian view, and how in turn the Marxist view arises out of a critique of Hegel.

It is in this light that Habermas's contribution is of interest. Whereas Marx and Engels, following de Tracy, thought that scientific understanding was objective and free from the distortion they reserved for legal, political, and social theories, Habermas argues that science and technology have become a form of ideology, a distortion of reality, which serves vested interests and prevailing institutions. In other words, science has become itself a social institution which no longer serves the interests of men but instead makes men its servants, enslaving their critical faculties, perpetuating the existing state of affairs.

The Material Basis of Ideology
Karl Marx
Friedrich Engels

Karl Marx (1818-1883) collaborated with Friedrich Engels on *The Communist Manifesto* (1848) and wrote *Das Kapital* (1867-1888). Marx is the most important single figure in the development of the philosophy of modern communism.

Friedrich Engels (1820-1895), in addition to his coauthorship with Karl Marx, was active in the English working-class movement and an agitator for revolutionary reform. He helped to found the First International. His influential writings also include *Anti-Duhring* (1878); *The Origin of the Family, Property and the State* (1884); and *Feuerbach and the End of Classical German Philosophy* (1888).

The production of ideas, of conceptions, of consciousness is at first directly interwoven with the material activity and the material intercourse of men, the language of real life. Conceiving, thinking, the mental intercourse of men appear at this stage as the direct efflux of their material behavior. The same applies to mental production as expressed in the language of the politics, laws, morality, religion, metaphysics of a people. Men are the producers of their conceptions, ideas, etc.—real, active men, as they are conditioned by a definite development of their productive forces and of the intercourse corresponding to these, up to its furthest forms. Consciousness can never be anything else than conscious existence, and the existence of men is their actual life process. If in all ideology men and their circumstances appear upside down, as in a *camera obscura*, this phenomenon arises just as much from their historical life process as the inversion of objects on the retina does from their physical life process.

In direct contrast to German philosophy, which descends from heaven to earth, here we ascend from earth to heaven. That is to say, we do not set out from what men say, imagine, conceive, nor from men as narrated, thought of, imagined, conceived, in order to arrive at men in the flesh. We set out from real, active men, and on the basis of their real life process we demonstrate the development of the ideological reflexes and echoes of this life process. The phantoms formed in the human brain are also, necessarily, sublimates of their material life process, which is empirically verifiable and bound to material premises. Morality, religion, metaphysics, all the rest of ideology and their corresponding forms of consciousness, thus no longer retain the semblance of independence. They have no history, no development; but men, developing their material production and their material intercourse, alter, along with this, their real existence, their thinking, and the products of their thinking. Life is not determined by consciousness, but consciousness by life. In the first method of approach the starting point is

From Karl Marx and Friedrich Engels, *The German Ideology* (Moscow: Foreign Languages Publishing House, 1947), pp. 247-255.

consciousness taken as the living individual; in the second it is the real, living individuals themselves, as they are in actual life, and consciousness is considered solely as *their* consciousness.

This method of approach is not devoid of premises. It starts out from the real premises, and does not abandon them for a moment. Its premises are men, not in any fantastic isolation or abstract definition, but in their actual, empirically perceptible process of development under definite conditions. As soon as this active life process is described, history ceases to be a collection of dead facts, as it is with the empiricists (themselves still abstract), or an imagined activity of imagined subjects, as with the idealists.

Where speculation ends—in real life—there real, positive science begins: the representation of the practical activity, of the practical process of development of men. Empty talk about consciousness ceases, and real knowledge has to take its place. When reality is depicted, philosophy as an independent branch of activity loses its medium of existence. At best, its place can be taken only by a summing up of the most general results, abstractions which arise from the observation of the historical development of men. Viewed apart from real history, these abstractions have in themselves no value whatsoever. They can only serve to facilitate the arrangement of historical material, to indicate the sequence of its separate strata. But they by no means afford a recipe or schema, as does philosophy, for neatly trimming the epochs of history. On the contrary, our difficulties begin only when we set about the observation and the arrangement—the real depiction—of our historical material, whether of a past epoch or of the present. The removal of these difficulties is governed by premises which it is quite impossible to state here, but which only the study of the actual life process and the activity of the individuals of each epoch will make evident. We shall select here some of these abstractions, which we use to refute the ideologists, and shall illustrate them by historical examples.

HISTORY

Since we are dealing with the Germans, who do not postulate anything, we must begin by stating the first premise of all human existence, and therefore of all history, the premise, namely, that men must be in a position to live in order to be able to "make history." But life involves, before everything else, eating and drinking, a habitation, clothing, and many other things. The first historical act is thus the production of the means to satisfy these needs, the production of material life itself. And indeed this is a historical act, a fundamental condition of all history, which today, as thousands of years ago, must daily and hourly be fulfilled merely in order to sustain human life. . . . The first necessity therefore in any theory of history is to observe this fundamental fact in all its significance and all its implications, and to accord it its due importance. This, as is notorious, the Germans have never done, and they have never, therefore, had an earthly basis for history and consequently never a historian. The French and the English, even if they have conceived the relation of this fact with so-called history only in an extremely one-sided fashion, particularly as long as they remained in the toils of political ideology, have nevertheless made the first attempts to give the writing of history a materialistic basis by being the first to write histories of civil society, of commerce and industry. . . .

The second fundamental point is that as soon as a need is satisfied (which implies the action of satisfying, and the acquisition of an instrument), new needs are made; and this production of new needs is the first historical act. Here we recognize immediately the spiritual ancestry of the great historical wisdom of the Germans, who, when they run out of positive material and when they can serve up neither theological nor political nor literary rubbish, do not write history at all but invent the "prehistoric era." They do not, however, enlighten us as to how we proceed from this nonsensical "prehistory" to history proper; although, on the other hand, in their historical speculation they seize upon this "prehistory" with especial eagerness because they imagine themselves safe there from interference on the part of "crude facts," and, at the same time, because there they can give full rein to their speculative impulse and set up and knock down hypotheses by the thousand.

The third circumstance which, from the very first, enters into historical development is that men, who daily remake their own life, begin to make other men, to propagate their kind: the relation between man and wife, parents and children, the *family*. The family, which to begin with is the only social relationship, becomes later, when increased needs create new social relations and the increased population new needs, a subordinate one (except in Germany) and must then be treated and analyzed according to the existing empirical data,[1] not according to "the concept of the family," as is the custom in Germany. These three aspects of social activity are not of course to be taken as three different stages, but just, as I have said, as three aspects or, to make it clear to the Germans, three "moments," which have existed simultaneously since the dawn of history and the first men, and still assert themselves in history today.

The production of life, both of one's own in labor and of fresh life in procreation, now appears as a double relationship: on the one hand as a natural, on the other as a social relationship. By social we understand the co-operation of several individuals, no matter under what conditions, in what manner, and to what end. It follows from this that a certain mode of production or industrial stage is always combined with a certain mode of co-operation, or social stage, and this mode of co-operation is itself a "productive force." Further, that the multitude of

[1] The building of houses. With savages each family has of course its own cave or hut like the separate family tent of the nomads. This separate domestic economy is made only the more necessary by the further development of private property. With the agricultural peoples a communal domestic economy is just as impossible as a communal cultivation of the soil. A great advance was the building of towns. In all previous periods, however, the abolition of individual economy, which is inseparable from the abolition of private property, was impossible for the simple reason that the material conditions governing it were not present. The setting up of a communal domestic economy presupposes the development of machinery, of the use of natural forces and of many other productive forces—e.g., of water supplies, of gas lighting, steam heating, etc., the removal of the antagonism of town and country. Without these conditions a communal economy would not in itself form a new productive force; lacking any material basis and resting on a purely theoretical foundation, it would be a mere freak and would end in nothing more than a monastic economy. What was possible can be seen in the formation of towns and the erection of communal buildings for various definite purposes (prisons, barracks, etc.). That the abolition of individual economy is inseparable from the abolition of the family is self-evident.

productive forces accessible to men determines the nature of society, hence that the "history of humanity" must always be studied and treated in relation to the history of industry and exchange. But it is also clear how in Germany it is impossible to write this sort of history, because the Germans lack not only the necessary power of comprehension and the material but also the "evidence of their senses," for across the Rhine you cannot have any experience of these things since history has stopped happening. Thus it is quite obvious from the start that there exists a materialistic connection of men with one another, which is determined by their needs and their mode of production and which is as old as men themselves. This connection is ever taking on new forms and thus presents a "history" independently of the existence of any political or religious nonsense which would hold men together on its own.

Only now, after having considered four moments, four aspects of the fundamental historical relationships, do we find that man also possesses "consciousness"; but, even so, not inherent, not "pure" consciousness. From the start the "spirit" is afflicted with the curse of being "burdened" with matter, which here makes its appearance in the form of agitated layers of air, sounds—in short, of language. Language is as old as consciousness; language is practical consciousness, as it exists for other men, and for that reason is really beginning to exist for me personally as well; for language, like consciousness, arises only from the need, the necessity, of intercourse with other men. Where there exists a relationship, it exists for me: the animal has no "relations" with anything, cannot have any. For the animal, its relation to others does not exist as a relation. Consciousness is therefore from the very beginning a social product and remains so as long as men exist at all. Consciousness is at first, of course, merely consciousness concerning the immediate sensuous environment and consciousness of the limited connection with other persons and things outside the individual who is growing self-conscious. At the same time it is consciousness of nature, which first appears to men as a completely alien, all-powerful, and unassailable force, with which men's relations are purely animal and by which they are overawed like beasts; it is thus a purely animal consciousness of nature (natural religion).

We see here immediately: this natural religion or animal behavior toward nature is determined by the form of society and vice versa. Here, as everywhere, the identity of nature and man appears in such a way that the restricted relation of men to nature determines their restricted relation to one another, and their restricted relation to one another determines men's restricted relation to nature, just because nature is as yet hardly modified historically; and, on the other hand, man's consciousness of the necessity of associating with the individuals around him is the beginning of the consciousness that he is living in society at all. This beginning is as animal as social life itself at this stage. It is mere herd-consciousness, and at this point man is only distinguished from sheep by the fact that with him consciousness takes the place of instinct or that his instinct is a conscious one.

This sheeplike or tribal consciousness receives its further development and extension through increased productivity, the increase of needs, and, what is fundamental to both of these, the increase of population. With these there develops the division of labor, which was originally nothing but the division of labor in the sexual act, then that division of labor which develops spontaneously or "naturally" by virtue of natural predisposition (e.g., physical strength), needs, accidents, etc., etc. Division of labor becomes truly such only from the moment when a division of material and mental labor appears. From this moment onward consciousness *can* really flatter itself that it is something other than consciousness of existing practice, that it is *really* conceiving something without conceiving something *real*; from now on consciousness is in a position to emancipate itself from the world and to proceed to the formation of "pure" theory, theology, philosophy, ethics, etc. But even if this theory, theology, philosophy, ethics, etc., comes into contradiction with the existing relations, this can occur only as a result of the fact that existing social relations have come into contradiction with existing forces of production; this, moreover, can also occur in a particular national sphere of relations through the appearance of the contradiction, not within the national orbit, but between this national consciousness and the practice of other nations; i.e., between the national and the general consciousness of a nation.

Moreover, it is quite immaterial what consciousness starts to do on its own: out of all such muck we get only the one inference that these three moments, the forces of production, the state of society, the consciousness, can and must come into contradiction with one another, because the division of labor implies the possibility—nay, the fact—that intellectual and material activity—enjoyment and labor, production and consumption—devolve on different individuals and that the only possibility of their not coming into contradiction lies in the negation in its turn of the division of labor. It is self-evident, moreover, that "specters," "bonds," "the higher being," "concept," "scruple" are merely the idealistic, spiritual expression, the conception apparently of the isolated individual, the image of very empirical fetters and limitations, within which the mode of production of life and the form of intercourse coupled with it move.

With the division of labor, in which all these contradictions are implicit and which in its turn is based on the natural division of labor in the family and the separation of society into individual families opposed to one another, is given simultaneously the distribution, and indeed the unequal distribution (both quantitative and qualitative), of labor and its products, hence property: the nucleus, the first form, of which lies in the family, where wife and children are the slaves of the husband. This latent slavery in the family, though still very crude, is the first property, but even at this early stage it corresponds perfectly to the definition of modern economists who call it the power of disposing of the labor power of others. Division of labor and private property are, moreover, identical expressions: in the one the same thing is affirmed with reference to activity as is affirmed in the other with reference to the product of the activity.

Further, the division of labor implies the contradiction between the interest of the separate individual or the individual family and the communal interest of all individuals who have intercourse with one another. And indeed, this communal interest does not exist merely in the imagination, as "the general good," but first of all in reality, as the mutual interdependence of the individuals among whom the labor is divided. And finally, the division of labor offers us the first example of how, as long as man remains in natural society—that is, as long as a cleavage exists between the particular and the common interest—as long, therefore, as activity is not voluntarily but naturally divided, man's own deed becomes an alien power opposed to him, which enslaves him instead of being controlled by him. For as soon as labor is distributed, each man has a particular, exclusive sphere of activity which is forced upon him and from which he cannot escape. He is a hunter, a fisherman, a shepherd, or a critical critic, and must remain so if he does not want to lose his means of livelihood; while in communist society, where nobody has one exclusive sphere of activity but each can become accomplished in any branch he wishes, society regulates the general production and thus makes it possible for me to do one thing today and another tomorrow, to hunt in the morning, fish in the afternoon, rear cattle in the evening, criticize after dinner, just as I have a mind, without ever becoming hunter, fisherman, shepherd, or critic.

This crystallization of social activity, this consolidation of what we ourselves produce into an objective power above us, growing out of our control, thwarting our expectations, bringing to naught our calculations, is one of the chief factors in historical development up till now. And out of this very contradiction between the interest of the individual and that of the community the latter takes an independent form as the state, divorced from the real interests of individual and community, and at the same time as an illusory communal life, always based, however, on the real ties existing in every family and tribal conglomeration (such as flesh and blood, language, division of labor on a larger scale, and other interests) and especially, as we shall enlarge upon later, on the classes, already determined by the division of labor, which in every such mass of men separate out, and of which one dominates all the others. It follows from this that all struggles within the state, the struggle between democracy, aristocracy, and monarchy, the struggle for the franchise, etc., etc., are merely the illusory forms in which the real struggles of the different classes are fought out among one another (of this the German theoreticians have not the faintest inkling, although they have received a sufficient introduction to the subject in *The German-French Annals* and *The Holy Family*). . . .

Differing Conceptions of Ideology
Karl Mannheim

Karl Mannheim (1893-1947) was a German emigrant whose academic career was cut short by Nazism, which had an important influence on his theories of social science. He was the author of *Diagnosis of Our Time* (1943); *Essays on the Sociology of Culture* (1956); and *Freedom, Power, and Democratic Planning* (1950).

THE CONCEPT IDEOLOGY IN HISTORICAL PERSPECTIVE

Just as the particular and total conceptions of ideology can be distinguished from one another on the basis of their differences in meaning, so the historical origins of these two concepts may also be differentiated even though in reality they are always intertwined. We do not as yet possess an adequate historical treatment of

From *Ideology and Utopia* by Karl Mannheim. Reprinted by permission of Harcourt Brace Jovanovich, Inc., and Routledge & Kegan Paul Ltd.

the development of the concept of ideology, to say nothing of a sociological history of the many variations[1] in its meaning. Even if we were in a position to do so, it would not be our task, for the purposes we have in mind, to write a history of the changing meanings in the concept of ideology. Our aim is simply to present such facts from the scattered evidence as will most clearly exhibit the distinction between the two terms made in the previous chapter, and to trace the process which gradually led to the refined and specialized meaning which the terms have come to possess. Corresponding to the dual meaning of the term ideology which we have designated here as the particular and total conceptions, respectively, are two distinct currents of historical development.

The distrust and suspicion which men everywhere evidence towards their adversaries, at all stages of historical development, may be regarded as the immediate precursor of the notion of ideology. But it is only when the distrust of man toward man, which is more or less evident at every stage of human history, becomes explicit and is methodically recognized, that we may properly speak of an ideological taint in the utterances of others. We arrive at this level when we no longer make individuals personally responsible for the deceptions which we detect in their utterances, and when we no longer attribute the evil that they do to their malicious cunning. It is only when we more or less consciously seek to discover the source of their untruthfulness in a social factor, that we are properly making an ideological interpretation. We begin to treat our adversary's views as ideologies only

[1] As a partial bibliography of the problem, the author indicates the following of his own works:—

Mannheim, K., "Das Problem einer Soziologie des Wissens," *Archiv für Sozialwissenschaft und Sozialpolitik*, 1925, vol. 54.

Mannheim, K., "Ideologische und soziologische Interpretation der geistigen Gebilde," *Jahrbuch für Soziologie*, edited by Gottfried Salomon, ii (Karlsruhe, 1926), pp. 424 ff.

Other relevant materials are to be found in:—

Krug, W. T., *Allgemeines Handwörterbuch der philosophischen Wissenschaften nebst ihrer Literatur und Geschichte*, 2nd edit., Leipzig, 1833.

Eisler's *Philosophisches Wörterbuch*.

Lalande, *Vocabulaire de la philosophie* (Paris, 1926).

Salomon, G., "Historischer Materialismus und Ideologienlehre," *Jahrbuch für Soziologie*, ii, pp. 386 ff.

Ziegler, H. O., "Ideologienlehre," *Archiv für Sozialwissenschaft und Sozialpolitik,* vol. 57, pp. 657 ff.

The majority of the studies of ideology never reach the level of attempting a systematic analysis, confining themselves usually to historical references or to the most general considerations. As examples, we cite the well-known works of Max Weber, Georg Lukács, Carl Schmitt, and more recently—

Kelsen, Hans, "Die philosophischen Grundlagen der Naturrechtslehre und der Rechtspositivismus," No. 31 of the *Vorträge der Kant Gesellschaft*, 1928.

The standard works of W. Sombart, Max Scheler, and Franz Oppenheimer are too widely known to require detailed reference.

In a wider connection the following studies are of especial interest:—

Reizler, K., "Idee und Interesse in der politischen Geschichte," *Die Dioskuren*, vol. iii (Munich, 1924).

Szende, Paul, *Verhüllung und Enthüllung* (Leipzig, 1922).

Adler, Georg, *Die Bedeutung der Illusionen für Politik und soziales Leben* (Jena, 1904).

Jankelevitch, "Du rôle des idées dans l'évolution des sociétés," *Revue philosophique*, vol. 66, 1908, pp. 256 ff.

Millioud, M., "La formation de l'idéal," ibid., pp. 138 ff.

Dietrich, A., "Kritik der politischen Ideologien," *Archiv für Geschichte und Politik*, 1923.

when we no longer consider them as calculated lies and when we sense in his total behaviour an unreliability which we regard as a function of the social situation in which he finds himself. The particular conception of ideology therefore signifies a phenomenon intermediate between a simple lie at one pole, and an error, which is the result of a distorted and faulty conceptual apparatus, at the other. It refers to a sphere of errors, psychological in nature, which, unlike deliberate deception, are not intentional, but follow inevitably and unwittingly from certain causal determinants.

According to this interpretation, Bacon's theory of the *idola* may be regarded to a certain extent as a forerunner of the modern conception of ideology. The "idols" were "phantoms" or "preconceptions," and there were, as we know, the idols of the tribe, of the cave, of the market, and of the theatre. All of these are sources of error derived sometimes from human nature itself, sometimes from particular individuals. They may also be attributed to society or to tradition. In any case, they are obstacles in the path to true knowledge.[2] There is certainly some connection between the modern term "ideology" and the term as used by Bacon, signifying a source of error. Furthermore, the realization that society and tradition may become sources of error is a direct anticipation of the sociological point of view.[3] Nevertheless, it cannot be claimed that there is an actual relationship, directly traceable through the history of thought, between this and the modern conception of ideology.

It is extremely probable that everyday experience with political affairs first made man aware of and critical toward the ideological element in his thinking. During the Renaissance, among the fellow citizens of Machiavelli, there arose a new adage calling attention to a common observation of the time—namely that the thought of the palace is one thing, and that of the public square is another.[4] This was an expression of the increasing degree to which the public was gaining access to the secrets of politics. Here we may observe the beginning of the process in the

[2] A characteristic passage from Bacon's *Novum Organum*, § 38. "The idols and false notions which have already preoccupied the human understanding and are deeply rooted in it, not only so beset men's minds that they become difficult of access, but even when access is obtained will again meet, and trouble us in the instauration of the sciences, unless mankind when forewarned guard themselves with all possible care against them," *The Physical and Metaphysical Works of Lord Bacon* (including the *Advancement of Learning* and *Novum Organum*). Edited by Joseph Devey, p. 389. G. Bell and Sons (London, 1891).

[3] "There are also idols formed by the reciprocal intercourse and society of man with man, which we call idols of the market from the commerce and association of men with each other; for men converse by means of language, but words are formed at the will of the generality, and there arises from a bad and unapt formation of words a wonderful obstruction to the mind." Bacon, op. cit., p. 390, § 43. Cf. also § 59.

On "the idol of tradition" Bacon says:—

"The human understanding, when any proposition has once been laid down (either from general admission and belief, or from the pleasure it affords), forces everything else to add fresh support and confirmation: and although most cogent and abundant instances exist to the contrary, yet either does not observe or despises them or gets rid of and rejects them by some distinction, with violent and injurious prejudice, rather than sacrifice the authority of its first conclusion." Op. cit., § 46, p. 392.

That we are confronted here with a source of error is evinced by the following passage:—

"The human understanding resembles not a dry light, but admits a tincture of the will and passions, which generate their own system accordingly, for man always believes more readily that which he prefers." Op. cit., § 49, pp. 393-4. Cf. also § 52.

[4] Machiavelli, *Discorsi*, vol. ii, p. 47. Cited by Meinecke, *Die Idee der Staatsräson* (Munich and Berlin, 1925), p. 40.

course of which what had formerly been merely an occasional outburst of suspicion and scepticism toward public utterances developed into a methodical search for the ideological element in all of them. The diversity of the ways of thought among men is even at this stage attributed to a factor which might, without unduly stretching the term, be denominated as sociological. Machiavelli, with his relentless rationality, made it his special task to relate the variations in the opinions of men to the corresponding variations in their interests. Accordingly when he prescribes a *medicina forte* for every bias of the interested parties in a controversy,[5] he seems to be making explicit and setting up as a general rule of thought what was implicit in the common-sense adage of his time.

There seems to be a straight line leading from this point in the intellectual orientation of the Western world to the rational and calculating mode of thought characteristic of the period of the Enlightenment. The psychology of interests seems to flow from the same source. One of the chief characteristics of the method of rational analysis of human behaviour, exemplified by Hume's *History of England*, was the presupposition that men were given to "feigning"[6] and to deceiving their fellows. The same characteristic is found in contemporary historians who operate with the particular conception of ideology. This mode of thought will always strive in accordance with the psychology of interests to cast doubt upon the integrity of the adversary and to deprecate his motives. This procedure, nevertheless, has positive value as long as in a given case we are interested in discovering the genuine meaning of a statement that lies concealed behind a camouflage of words. This "debunking" tendency in the thought of our time has become very marked.[7] And even though in wide circles this trait is considered undignified and disrespectful (and indeed in so far as "debunking" is an end in itself, the criticism is justified), this intellectual position is forced upon us in an era of transition like our own, which finds it necessary to break with many antiquated traditions and forms.

FROM THE PARTICULAR TO THE TOTAL CONCEPTION OF IDEOLOGY

It must be remembered that the unmasking which takes place on the psychological level is not to be confused with the more radical scepticism and the more thoroughgoing and devastating critical analysis which proceeds on the ontological and noological levels. But the two cannot be completely separated. The same historical forces that bring about continuous transformations in one are also operative in the other. In the former, psychological illusions are constantly being undermined, in the latter, ontological and logical formulations arising out of given world-views and modes of thought are dissolved in a conflict between the interested parties. Only in a world in upheaval, in which fundamental new values are being

[5] Cf. Meinecke, ibid.

[6] Meusel, Fr., *Edmund Burke und die französische Revolution* (Berlin 1913), p. 102, note 3.

[7] Carl Schmitt analysed this characteristic contemporary manner of thought very well when he said that we are in continual fear of being misled. Consequently we are perpetually on guard against disguises, sublimations, and refractions. He points out that the word *simulacra*, which appeared in the political literature of the seventeenth century, may be regarded as a forerunner of the present attitude (*Politische Romantik*, 2nd edit., (Munich and Leipzig, 1925), p. 19).

created and old ones destroyed, can intellectual conflict go so far that antagonists will seek to annihilate not merely the specific beliefs and attitudes of one another, but also the intellectual foundations upon which these beliefs and attitudes rest.

As long as the conflicting parties lived in and tried to represent the same world, even though they were at opposite poles in that world, or as long as one feudal clique fought against its equal, such a thoroughgoing mutual destruction was inconceivable. This profound disintegration of intellectual unity is possible only when the basic values of the contending groups are worlds apart. At first, in the course of this ever-deepening disintegration, naïve distrust becomes transformed into a systematic particular notion of ideology, which, however, remains on the psychological plane. But, as the process continues, it extends to the noological-epistemological sphere. The rising bourgeoisie which brought with it a new set of values was not content with merely being assigned a circumscribed place within the old feudal order. It represented a new "economic system" (in Sombart's sense), accompanied by a new style of thought which ultimately displaced the existing modes of interpreting and explaining the world. The same seems to be true of the proletariat today as well. Here too we note a conflict between two divergent economic views, between two social systems, and, correspondingly, between two styles of thought.

What were the steps in the history of ideas that prepared the way for the total conception of ideology? Certainly it did not merely arise out of the attitude of mistrust which gradually gave rise to the particular conception of ideology. More fundamental steps had to be taken before the numerous tendencies of thought moving in the same general direction could be synthesized into the total conception of ideology. Philosophy played a part in the process, but not philosophy in the narrow sense (as it is usually conceived) as a discipline divorced from the actual context of living. Its role was rather that of the ultimate and fundamental interpreter of the flux in the contemporary world. This cosmos in flux is in its turn to be viewed as a series of conflicts arising out of the nature of the mind and its responses to the continually changing structure of the world. We shall indicate here only the principal stages in the emergence of the total conception of ideology on the noological and ontological levels.

The first significant step in this direction consisted in the development of a philosophy of consciousness. The thesis that consciousness is a unity consisting of coherent elements sets a problem of investigation which, especially in Germany, has been the basis of monumental attempts at analysis. The philosophy of consciousness has put in place of an infinitely variegated and confused world an organization of experience the unity of which is guaranteed by the unity of the perceiving subject. This does not imply that the subject merely reflects the structural pattern of the external world, but rather that, in the course of his experience with the world, he spontaneously evolves the principles of organization that enable him to understand it. After the objective ontological unity of the world had been demolished, the attempt was made to substitute for it a unity imposed by the perceiving subject. In the place of the medieval-Christian objective and ontological unity of the world, there emerged the subjective unity of the absolute subject of the Enlightenment—"consciousness in itself."

Henceforth the world as "world" exists only with reference to the knowing mind, and the mental activity of the subject determines the form in which the world appears. This constitutes in fact the embryonic total conception of ideology, though it is, as yet, devoid of its historical and sociological implications.

At this stage, the world is conceived as a structural unity, and no longer as a plurality of disparate events as it seemed to be in the intermediate period when the breakdown of the objective order seemed to bring chaos. It is related in its entirety to a subject, but in this case the subject is not a concrete individual. It is rather a fictitious "consciousness in itself." In this view, which is particularly pronounced in Kant, the noological level is sharply differentiated from the psychological one. This is the first stage in the dissolution of an ontological dogmatism which regarded the "world" as existing independently of us, in a fixed and definitive form.

The second stage in the development of the total conception of ideology is attained when the total but super-temporal notion of ideology is seen in historical perspective. This is mainly the accomplishment of Hegel and the Historical school. The latter, and Hegel to an even greater degree, start from the assumption that the world is a unity and is conceivable only with reference to a knowing subject. And now at this point, what is for us a decisive new element is added to the conception—namely, that this unity is in a process of continual historical transformation and tends to a constant restoration of its equilibrium on still higher levels. During the Enlightenment the subject, as carrier of the unity of consciousness, was viewed as a wholly abstract, super-temporal, and super-social entity: "consciousness in itself." During this period the *Volksgeist*, "folk spirit," comes to represent the historically differentiated elements of consciousness, which are integrated by Hegel into the "world spirit." It is evident that the increasing concreteness of this type of Philosophy results from the more immediate concern with the ideas arising from social interaction and the incorporation of historical-political currents of thought into the domain of philosophy. Thenceforth, however, the experiences of everyday life are no longer accepted at face value, but are thought through in all their implications and are traced back to their presuppositions. It should be noted, however, that the historically changing nature of mind was discovered not so much by philosophy as by the penetration of political insight into the everyday life of the time.

The reaction following upon the unhistorical thought of the period of the French Revolution revitalized and gave new impetus to the historical perspective. In the last analysis, the transition from the general, abstract, world-unifying subject ("consciousness in itself") to the more concrete subject (the nationally differentiated "folk spirit") was not so much a philosophical achievement as it was the expression of a transformation in the manner of reacting to the world in all realms of experience. This change may be traced to the revolution in popular sentiment during and after the Napoleonic Wars when the feeling of nationality was actually born. The fact that more remote antecedents may be found for both the historical perspective and the *Volksgeist* does not detract from the validity of this observation.[8]

The final and most important step in the creation of the total conception of ideology likewise arose out of the historical-social process. When "class" took the

[8] For future reference, we state here that the sociology of knowledge, unlike the orthodox history of ideas, does not aim at tracing ideas back to all their remote historical prototypes. For if one is bent on tracing similar *motifs* in thought to their ultimate origins, it is always possible to find "precursors" for every idea. There is nothing which has been said, which has not been said before (*Nullum est iam dictum, quod non sit dictum prius*). The proper theme of our study is to observe how and in what form intellectual life at a given historical moment is related to the existing social and political forces. Cf. my study, "Das konservative Denken," loc. cit., p. 103, note 57.

place of "folk" or nation as the bearer of the historically evolving consciousness, the same theoretical tradition, to which we have already referred, absorbed the realization which meanwhile had grown up through the social process, namely—that the structure of society and its corresponding intellectual forms vary with the relations between social classes.

Just as at an earlier time, the historically differentiated "folk spirit" took the place of "consciousness as such," so now the concept of *Volksgeist*, which is still too inclusive, is replaced by the concept of class consciousness, or more correctly class ideology. Thus the development of these ideas follows a two-fold trend—on the one hand, there is a synthesizing and integrating process through which the concept of consciousness comes to furnish a unitary centre in an infinitely variable world; and on the other, there is a constant attempt to make more pliable and flexible the unitary conception which has been too rigidly and too schematically formulated in the course of the synthesizing process.

The result of this dual tendency is that instead of a fictional unity of a timeless, unchanging "consciousness as such" (which was never actually demonstrable) we get a conception which varies in accordance with historic periods, nations, and social classes. In the course of this transition, we continue to cling to the unity of consciousness, but this unity is now dynamic and in constant process of becoming. This accounts for the fact that despite the surrender of the static conception of consciousness, the growing body of material discovered by historical research does not remain an incoherent and discontinuous mass of discrete events. This latest conception of consciousness provides a more adequate perspective for the comprehension of historical reality.

Two consequences flow from this conception of consciousness: first we clearly perceive that human affairs cannot be understood by an isolation of their elements. Every fact and event in an historical period is only explicable in terms of meaning, and meaning in its turn always refers to another meaning. Thus the conception of the unity and interdependence of meaning in a period always underlies the interpretation of that period. Secondly, this interdependent system of meanings varies both in all its parts and in its totality from one historical period to another. Thus the re-interpretation of that continuous and coherent change in meaning becomes the main concern of our modern historical sciences. Although Hegel has probably done more than anyone else in emphasizing the need for integrating the various elements of meaning in a given historical experience, he proceeded in a speculative manner, while we have arrived at a stage of development where we are able to translate this constructive notion, given us by the philosophers, into empirical research.

What is significant for us is that although we separated them in our analysis, the two currents which led to the particular and total conceptions of ideology, respectively, and which have approximately the same historical origin, now begin to approach one another more closely. The particular conception of ideology merges with the total. This becomes apparent to the observer in the following manner: previously, one's adversary, as the representative of a certain political-social position, was accused of conscious or unconscious falsification. Now, however, the critique is more thoroughgoing in that, having discredited the total structure of his consciousness, we consider him no longer capable of thinking correctly. This simple observation means, in the light of a structural analysis of thought, that in earlier attempts to discover the sources of error, distortion was uncovered only on the psychological plane by pointing out the personal roots of intellectual bias. The annihiliation is now more thoroughgoing since the attack is made on the noological level and the validity of the adversary's theories is undermined by showing that they are merely a function of the generally prevailing social situation. Herewith a new and perhaps the most decisive stage in the history of modes of thought has been reached. It is difficult, however, to deal with this development without first analysing some of its fundamental implications. The total conception of ideology raises a problem which has frequently been adumbrated before, but which now for the first time acquires broader significance, namely the problem of how such a thing as the "false consciousness" (*falsches Bewusstsein*)—the problem of the totally distorted mind which falsifies everything which comes within its range— could ever have arisen. It is the awareness that our total outlook as distinguished from its details may be distorted, which lends to the total conception of ideology a special significance and relevance for the understanding of our social life. Out of this recognition grows the profound disquietude which we feel in our present intellectual situation, but out of it grows also whatever in it is fruitful and stimulating.

OBJECTIVITY AND BIAS

The suspicion that there might be such a thing as "false consciousness," every cognition of which is necessarily wrong, where the lie lay in the soul, dates back to antiquity. It is of religious origin, and has come down to us as part of our ancient intellectual heritage. It appears as a problem whenever the genuineness of a prophet's inspiration or vision is questioned either by his people or by himself.[9]

Here we seem to have an instance where an age-old conception underlies a modern epistemological idea, and one is tempted to assert that the essence of the observation was already present in the older treatment; what is new is only its form. But here, too, as elsewhere, we must maintain, in opposition to those who attempt to derive everything from the past, that the modern form taken by the idea is much more important than its origin. Whereas formerly, the suspicion that there might be such a thing as "false consciousness" was only a statement of observed fact, to-day, working with clearly defined analytical methods, we have been able to make a more fundamental attack on the problems of consciousness. What was formerly a mere traditional anathema, has in our time been transformed into a methodical procedure resting upon scientific demonstration.

Of even greater importance is the change which we are about to discuss. Since the problem has been torn out of its purely religious context, not only have the methods of proof, of demonstrating the falsity or truth of an insight changed, but even the scale of values by which we measure truth and falsity, reality and unreality have been profoundly transformed. When the prophet doubted the genuiness of his vision it was because he felt himself deserted by God, and his disquietude was based upon a transcendental source of reference. When, on the contrary, we, of to-day, become critical of our own ideas, it is because we fear that they do not measure up to some more secular criterion.

---

[9] "Beloved, believe not every spirit, but try the spirits whether they are of God, because many false prophets are gone out into the world." 1 John, iv, 1.

To determine the exact nature of the new criterion of reality which superseded the transcendental one, we must subject the meaning of the word "ideology" also in this respect to a more precise historical analysis. If, in the course of such an analysis, we are led to deal with the language of everyday life, this simply indicates that the history of thought is not confined to books alone, but gets its chief meaning from the experiences of everyday life, and even the main changes in the evaluations of different spheres of reality as they appear in philosophy eventually go back to the shifting values of the everyday world.

The word "ideology" itself had, to begin with, no inherent ontological significance; it did not include any decision as to the value of different spheres of reality, since it originally denoted merely the theory of ideas. The ideologists,[10] were, as we know, the members of a philosophical group in France who, in the tradition of Condillac, rejected metaphysics and sought to base the cultural sciences on anthropological and psychological foundations.

THE RISE OF POLITICAL IDEOLOGY

The modern conception of ideology was born when Napoleon, finding that this group of philosophers was opposing his imperial ambitions, contemptuously labelled them "ideologists." Thereby the word took on a derogatory meaning which, like the word "doctrinaire," it has retained to the present day. However, if the theoretical implications of this contempt are examined, it will be found that the depreciative attitude involved is, at bottom, of an epistemological and ontological nature. What is depreciated is the validity of the adversary's thought because it is regarded as unrealistic. But if one asked further, unrealistic with reference to what?—the answer would be, unrealistic with reference to practice, unrealistic when contrasted with the affairs that transpire in the political arena. Thenceforth, all thought labelled as "ideology" is regarded as futile when it comes to practice, and the only reliable access to reality is to be sought in practical activity. When measured by the standards of practical conduct, mere thinking or reflection on a given situation turns out to be trivial. It is thus clear how the new meaning of the term ideology bears the imprint of the position and the point of view of those who coined it, namely, the political men of action. The new word gives sanction to the specific experience of the politician with reality,[11] and it lends support to that practical irrationality which has so little appreciation for thought as an instrument for grasping reality.

[10] Cf. Picavet, *Les idéologues, essai sur l'histoire des idées et des théories scientifiques, philosophiques, religieuses en France depuis 1789* (Paris, Alcan, 1891).

Destutt de Tracy, the founder of the above-mentioned school, defines the science of ideas as follows: "The science may be called ideology, if one considers only the subject-matter; general grammar, if one considers only the methods; and logic, if one considers only the purpose. Whatever the name, it necessarily contains these three subdivisions, since one cannot be treated adequately without also treating the two others. Ideology seems to me to be the generic term because the science of ideas subsumes both that of their expression and that of their derivation." *Les éléments de l'idéologie*, 1st edit. (Paris, 1801), cited from the 3rd edit., the only one available to me (Paris, 1817), p. 4 n.

[11] From the conclusions of Part III it would be possible to define more exactly, according to the social position he occupies, the type of politician whose conception of the world and whose ontology we are here discussing, for not every politician is addicted to this irrational ontology. (Cf. pp. 119 ff.).

During the nineteenth century, the term ideology, used in this sense, gained wide currency. This signifies that the politician's feeling for reality took precedence over and displaced the scholastic, contemplative modes of thought and of life. Henceforward the problem implicit in the term ideology—what is really real?—never disappeared from the horizon.

But this transition needs to be correctly understood. The question as to what constitutes reality is by no means a new one; but that the question should arise in the arena of public discussion (and not just in isolated academic circles) seems to indicate an important change. The new connotation which the word ideology acquired, because it was redefined by the politician in terms of his experiences, seems to show a decisive turn in the formulation of the problem of the nature of reality. If, therefore, we are to rise to the demands put upon us by the need for analysing modern thought, we must see to it that a sociological history of ideas concerns itself with the actual thought of society, and not merely with self-perpetuating and supposedly self-contained systems of ideas elaborated within a rigid academic tradition. If erroneous knowledge was formerly checked by appeal to divine sanction, which unfailingly revealed the true and the real, or by pure contemplation, in which true ideas were supposedly discovered, at present the criterion of reality is found primarily in an ontology derived from political experience. The history of the concept of ideology from Napoleon to Marxism, despite changes in content, has retained the same political criterion of reality. This historical example shows, at the same time, that the pragmatic point of view was already implicit in the accusation which Napoleon hurled at his adversaries. Indeed we may say that for modern man pragmatism has, so to speak, become in some respects, the inevitable and appropriate outlook, and that philosophy in this case has simply appropriated this outlook and from it proceeded to its logical conclusion.

We have called attention to the nuance of meaning which Napoleon gave to the word ideology in order to show clearly that common speech often contains more philosophy and is of greater significance for the further statement of problems than academic disputes which tend to become sterile because they fail to take cognizance of the world outside the academic walls.[12]

We are carried a step farther in our analysis, and are able to bring out another aspect of this problem by referring to the example just cited in another connection. In the struggle which Napoleon carried on against his critics, he was able, as we have seen, by reason of his dominant position to discredit them by pointing out the ideological nature of their thinking. In later stages of its development, the word ideology is used as a weapon by the proletariat against the dominant group. In short, such a revealing insight into the basis of thought as that offered by the notion of ideology cannot, in the long run, remain the exclusive privilege of one class. But it is precisely this expansion and diffusion of the ideological approach which leads finally to a juncture at which it is no longer possible for one point of view and interpretation to assail all others as ideological without itself being placed in the position of having to meet that challenge. In this manner we arrive

---

[12] Concerning the structure and peculiarities of scholastic thought, and, for that matter, every type of thought enjoying a monopolistic position, cf. the author's paper delivered in Zürich at the Sixth Congress of the Deutsche Gesellschaft für Soziologie, "Die Bedeutung der Konkurrenz im Gebiete des Geistigen," *Verhandlungen des sechsten deutschen Soziologentages in Zürich* (J. C. B. Mohr, Tübingen, 1929).

inadvertently at a new methodological stage in the analysis of thought in general.

There were indeed times when it seemed as if it were the prerogative of the militant proletariat to use the ideological analysis to unmask the hidden motives of its adversaries. The public was quick to forget the historical origin of the term which we have just indicated, and not altogether unjustifiably, for although recognized before, this critical approach to thought was first emphasized and methodically developed by Marxism. It was Marxist theory which first achieved a fusion of the particular and total conceptions of ideology. It was this theory which first gave due emphasis to the role of class position and class interests in thought. Due largely to the fact that it originated in Hegelianism, Marxism was able to go beyond the mere psychological level of analysis and to posit the problem in a more comprehensive, philosophical setting. The notion of a "false consciousness"[13] hereby acquired a new meaning.

Marxist thought attached such decisive significance to political practice conjointly with the economic interpretation of events, that these two became the ultimate criteria for disentangling what is mere ideology from those elements in thought which are more immediately relevant to reality. Consequently it is no wonder that the conception of ideology is usually regarded as integral to, and even identified with, the Marxist proletarian movement.

But in the course of more recent intellectual and social developments, however, this stage has already been passed. It is no longer the exclusive privilege of socialist thinkers to trace bourgeois thought to ideological foundations and thereby to discredit it. Nowadays groups of every standpoint use this weapon against all the rest. As a result we are entering upon a new epoch in social and intellectual development.

In Germany, the first beginnings in this direction were made by Max Weber, Sombart, and Troeltsch—to mention only the more outstanding representatives of this development. The truth of Max Weber's words becomes more clear as time goes on: "The materialistic conception of history is not to be compared to a cab that one can enter or alight from at will, for once they enter it, even the revolutionaries themselves are not free to leave it." The analysis of thought and ideas in terms of ideologies is much too wide in its application and much too important a weapon to become the permanent monopoly of any one party. Nothing was to prevent the opponents of Marxism from availing themselves of the weapon and applying it to Marxism itself.

[13] The expression "false consciousness" (*falsches Bewusstsein*) is itself Marxist in origin. Cf. Mehring, Franz, *Geschichte der deutschen Sozialdemokratie*, i, 386; cf. also Salomon, op. cit., p. 147.

Technology and Science as "Ideology"

Jurgen Habermas

Jurgen Habermas (1929-   ) studied at the universities of Gottingen, Zurich, and Bonn. He was a research fellow and professor at the universities of Frankfurt am Main, Marburg, and Heidelberg before occupying his present position as Professor of Philosophy and Sociology at Frankfurt. *Toward a Rational Society* (1970) is the first of three books by Habermas to be published by Beacon Press. Others are *Knowledge and Human Interests* (1971) and *Theory and Practice* (forthcoming).

Max Weber introduced the concept of "rationality" in order to define the form of capitalist economic activity, bourgeois private law, and bureaucratic authority. Rationalization means, first of all, the extension of the areas of society subject to the criteria of rational decision. Second, social labor is industrialized, with the result that criteria of instrumental action also penetrate into other areas of life (urbanization of the mode of life, technification of transport and communication). Both trends exemplify the type of purposive-rational action, which refers to either the organization of means or choice between alternatives. Planning can be regarded as purposive-rational action of the second order. It aims at the establishment, improvement, or expansion of systems of purposive-rational action themselves.

The progressive "rationalization" of society is linked to the institutionalization of scientific and technical development. To the extent that technology and science permeate social institutions and thus transform them, old legitimations are destroyed. The secularization and "disenchantment" of action-orienting world-views, of cultural tradition as a whole, is the obverse of the growing "rationality" of social action.

Herbert Marcuse has taken these analyses as a point of departure in order to demonstrate that the formal concept of rationality—which Weber derived from the purposive-rational action of the capitalist entrepreneur, the industrial wage laborer, the abstract legal person, and the modern administrative official and based on the criteria of science as well as technology—has specific substantive implications. Marcuse is convinced that what Weber called "rationalization" realizes not rationality as such but rather, in the name of rationality, a specific form of unacknowledged political domination. Because this sort of rationality extends to the correct choice among strategies, the appropriate application of technologies, and the efficient establishment of systems (with *presupposed* aims in *given* situations), it removes the total social framework of interests in which strategies are chosen, technologies applied, and systems established, from the scope of reflection and rational reconstruction. Moreover, this rationality extends only to relations of possible technical control and therefore requires a type of action that implies domination, whether of nature or of society. By virtue of its structure, purposive-rational action is the exercise of control. That is why, in accordance with this rationality, the "rationalization" of the conditions of life is synonymous with the institutionalization of a form of domination whose political character becomes unrecognizable: the technical reason of a social system of purposive-rational action does not lose its political content. Marcuse's critique of Weber comes to the conclusion that

the very concept of technical reason is perhaps ideological. Not only the application of technology but technology itself is domination (of nature and men)—methodical, scientific, calculated, calculating control. Specific purposes and interests of domination are not foisted upon technology "subsequently" and from the outside; they enter the very construction of the technical apparatus. Technology is always a historical-social project: in it is projected what a society and its ruling interests intend to do with men and things. Such a "purpose" of domination is "substantive" and to this extent belongs to the very form of technical reason.

As early as 1956 Marcuse referred in a quite different context to the peculiar phenomenon that in industrially advanced capitalist societies domination tends to lose its exploitative and oppressive character and become "rational," without political domination thereby disappearing: "domination is dependent only on the capacity and drive to maintain and extend the apparatus as a whole." Domination is rational in that a system can be maintained which can allow itself to make the growth of the forces of production, coupled with scientific and technical progress, the basis of its legitimation although, at the same time, the level of the productive forces constitutes a potential in relation to which "the renunciations and burdens placed on individuals seem more and more unnecessary and irrational." In Marcuse's judgment, the objectively superfluous repression can be recognized in the "intensified subjection of individuals to the enormous apparatus of production and distribution, in the deprivatization of free time, in the almost indistinguishable fusion of constructive and destructive social labor." Paradoxically, however, this repression can disappear from the consciousness of the population because the legitimation of domination has assumed a new character: it refers to the "constantly increasing productivity and domination of nature which keeps individuals . . . living in increasing comfort."

The institutionalized growth of the forces of production following from scientific and technical progress surpasses all historical proportions. From it the institutional framework draws its opportunity for legitimation. The thought that relations of production can be measured against the potential of developed productive forces is prevented because the existing relations of production present themselves as the technically necessary organizational form of a rationalized society. Here "rationality," in Weber's sense, shows its Janus face. It is no longer only a critical standard for the developmental level of the forces of production in relation to which the objectively superfluous, repressive character of historically obsolete relations of production can be exposed. It is also an apologetic standard through which these same relations of production can be justified as a functional institutional framework. Indeed, in relation to its apologetic serviceability, "rationality" is weakened as a critical standard and degraded to a corrective *within* the system: what can still be said is at best that society is "poorly programmed." At the stage of their scientific-technical development, then, the forces of production appear to enter a new constellation with the relations of production. Now they no longer function as the basis of a critique of prevailing legitimations in the interest of political enlightenment, but become instead the basis of legitimation. *This* is what Marcuse conceives of as world-historically new.

But if this is the case, must not the rationality embodied in systems of purposive-rational action be understood as specifically limited? Must not the rationality of science and technology, instead of being reducible to unvarying rules of logic and method have absorbed a substantive, historically derived, and therefore transitory a priori structure? Marcuse answers in the affirmative:

The principles of modern science were a priori structured in such a way that they could serve as conceptual instruments for a universe of self-propelling, productive control; theoretical operationalism came to correspond to practical operationalism. The scientific method which led to the ever-more-effective domination of nature thus came to provide the pure concepts as well as the instrumentalities for the ever-more-effective domination of man by man through the domination of nature ... Today, domination perpetuates and extends itself not only through technology but as technology, and the latter provides the great legitimation of the expanding political power, which absorbs all spheres of culture.

In this universe, technology also provides the great rationalization of the unfreedom of man and demonstrates the "technical" impossibility of being autonomous, of determining one's own life. For this unfreedom appears neither as irrational nor as political, but rather as submission to the technical apparatus which enlarges the comforts of life and increases the productivity of labor. Technological rationality thus protects rather than cancels the legitimacy of domination and the instrumentalist horizon of reason opens on a rationally totalitarian society.

Weber's "rationalization" is not only a long-term process of the transformation of social structures but simultaneously "rationalization" in Freud's sense: the true motive, the perpetuation of objectively obsolete domination, is concealed through the invocation of purposive-rational imperatives. This invocation is possible only because the rationality of science and technology is immanently one of control: the rationality of domination.

Suggested Readings

Aiken, Henry D., *The Age of Ideology* (New York: Mentor Books, 1956).

Apter, David, *Ideology and Discontent* (New York: The Free Press, 1964).

Ladd, E. C., *Ideology in America* (Ithaca, N.Y.: Cornell University Press, 1969).

Lukacs, George, *History and Class Consciousness* (Cambridge, Mass.: The M.I.T. Press, 1971).

Mannheim, Karl, *Ideology and Utipia* (New York: Harcourt Brace Jovanovich, Inc., 1936).

Marcuse, Herbert, *Reason and Revolution* (Boston: Beacon Press, 1960).

Marx, Karl, *Contribution to the Critique of Political Economy* (Chicago: Charles Kerr, 1904).

Marx, Karl, and Friedrich Engels, *The German Ideology* (New York: International Publishers Company, Inc., 1965).

Merton, Robert, *Social Theory and Social Structure* (New York: The Free Press, 1968).

Plamenetz, John, *Ideology* (New York: Praeger Publishers, Inc., 1970).

The Ideology of Democratic Liberalism

INTRODUCTION

For most people, the term *democracy* is a political concept, and when so considered is, of course, independent of economic concepts. When it is looked upon only as a political concept, then such statements as "government by the people," "a form of government in which the ultimate power is invested in the people and exercised by them or by their elected representatives in a free electoral system," and so on, are often suggested as definitions.

It has not always been considered to be a desirable system. As Wollheim points out, it was a political system that was rejected in Greece and Rome by nearly all famous political philosophers. Since the eighteenth century, however, some form of political democracy has become favored in the world, especially in the Western world. Many of these ideas came from Locke, whose philosophy gave rise to much of the political ideas and framework of England and the United States. He believed in a government in which the power ultimately lay with the people through their representatives. He also believed that if the representatives did not carry out the will of the people, then the people had a right to violently revolt against them.

The Greeks had an economic system in which their particular political systems existed—a slave economy, and Locke conceived his democratic system in a laissez-faire world. Because property was so readily available for almost anyone, he believed, in fact, that property was an ultimate value. The next sections are from the writings of John Stuart Mill, who strongly and more ably than anyone else spoke out for the value of liberty, of free speech and thought, of freedom from the tyranny of the ideas of the majority of people in a society. He, too, believed in a laissez-faire economic system but a more restricted one than that of Locke's.

It was John Dewey who best stated the intimate connection between the political and economic, and his philosophies took on the name "democratic liberalism" because his economic position was quite liberal. What most Americans conceive to be democracy is really a representative political theory plus a modified economic system related to the ideas of Locke and Mill. One can, of course, talk of the political system independent of the economic system, as is done in some sections of the writings of Wollheim, Dahl, and Benn, but this separation is never found in practice.

Democracy: Its History
Richard Wollheim

Richard Wollheim (1923-   ) is Grote Professor of Philosophy of Mind and Logic at the University of London. His books include *F. H. Bradley* (1959), *Socialism and Culture* (1961), *Art and Its Objects* (1968), and *A Family Romance* (1969).

A

The Ancient Greeks are generally regarded as the founders of Democracy. And rightly so, for it is to them that we are indebted for the earliest examples of Democracy in practice and in theory, and indeed for the word itself.

It needs to be remembered, however, that, ultimately, Antiquity rejected Democracy.[1] As a form of government it lacked permanence even in Athens, and in the realm of speculation, the most famous thinkers both of Greece and Rome—Plato and Aristotle, Cicero and Seneca—were against it. One consequence of this is that our knowledge and understanding of classical democratic thought is of necessity partial and limited; and some of its finest expressions—such as the Funeral Oration of Pericles—have been influential more through successive misinterpretations than in virtue of what they actually say.

Both the practice and the theory of Democracy appear to be somewhat older than the word itself. It is convenient to regard Cleisthenes as the creator of Athenian democratic government (c. 508 B.C.), but it is most unlikely that either he or his contemporaries used the term δημοκρατία.[2] Equally, it seems that many of the arguments later to be used in favor of Democracy had already been voiced in

From Richard Wollheim, "Democracy," *Journal of the History of Ideas*, Vol. 19 (1958), pp. 225-242. Reprinted by permission.

[1] J. A. O. Larsen, "Judgment of Antiquity on Democracy," *Classical Philology*, 49 (1954), 1-4.

[2] A. Debrunner, "Δημοκρατία," *Festschrift für E. Tièche* (Bern, 1947), 11-24; Victor Ehrenberg, "Origins of Democracy," *Historia* (1950), 515-48; J. A. O. Larsen, "Cleisthenes and the Development of the Theory of Democracy at Athens," *Essays in Political Theory Presented to George H. Sabine* (Ithaca, 1948), 1-16.

an earlier controversy: that between the supporters of the unfettered rule of one man and those who believed in a system under which all were equal before the law (ἰσονομια).[3] This controversy we glimpse in the works of Aeschylus (*Pers.* 213-4; *Pr. Bound* 323-4; *Suppliants, passim*) and, more liberally, in the famous account given by Herodotus (*Hist.* III 80-4) of a debate between a number of Persian nobles immediately upon the death of the Magian usurper in 522 B.C. They discuss what kind of government should be adopted, and in the course of the debate—which though clearly apocryphal as a piece of Persian history is most probably a good index of 'progressive' Athenian thought of the period just after the Persian War [491-79 B.C.]—Otanes, the supporter of ἰσονομια, not merely puts forward what are to be the main democratic arguments but also lays down the terms within which most future discussion of the subject is to be contained. These deserve examination:

In the first place, the discussion about Democracy is primarily a discussion about forms of government, not one about forms of society. Of course, it was a commonplace of Greek political thinking that constitutional forms have an all-important effect on the manners or ways (τρόποι) of the citizens. So, for instance, Pericles in the Funeral Oration (Thuc. *Hist.* II. 35-46) claims that Athenian Democracy was an education for all its members; and Plato, in asserting a complete parallelism between the organization of a Polis and the organization of the souls of those who live in it, was only generalizing popular conceptions. But, for all that, Democracy was not associated in the classical mind with any clear-cut form of society in the sense of specific social structure. To Pericles, for instance, Democracy is perfectly compatible with differences of wealth; what it is not compatible with is that these differences should carry with them any political influence. In Demosthenes' Fourth Philippic (*Orationes* X. 44) we find the same conception. Even Aristotle, the most sociologically minded of ancient thinkers, who talks of Democracy as the natural product of a particular form of society (*Pol.* III. 1286b), has yet nothing serious to say about it as an active agent in society. Moreover it must be remembered that the advocates of Democracy (with the exception of a few radical sophists, e.g., Antiphon) regarded it as perfectly consistent with the exclusion of slaves, foreigners, and women from political life; and even, it would seem, with an oppressive régime over subject territory (cf. Pericles' Funeral Oration).

Secondly, Democracy as a form of government is rigorously connected with, if not identified by, certain specific political institutions. Otanes refers to the selection of officials by lot, the scrutiny at the end of a term of office, and the decision of policy by popular assembly. In practice democrats recognized that certain offices of state, e.g., the command of the army, called for special skill and in consequence were prepared to allow that such posts should be removed from the sphere of lottery. But apart from this and similar minor modifications, the list of essential democratic institutions remains fairly constant throughout the classical period.

Thirdly, the superiority or otherwise of forms of government is to be determined by a criterion that is, after all, essentially *practical*—if in the very highest sense of the word; namely, the capacity to provide rational and harmonious government, both rationality and harmony being conceived of as empirically verifiable

[3] Gregory Vlastos, "Isonomia," *American Journal of Philology*, 74 (1953), 337-66.

phenomena. As an application of this criterion the superiority of Democracy is held to rest on the surer wisdom of the many. Those to whom Democracy gives power may individually vary in intelligence and goodwill, but collectively they are bound to be superior. This view which is suggested by Otanes reappears in the Funeral Oration, though its classical formulation is in Aristotle (*Pol.* III. 1281b) who, however, recounts it more as a good and established argument than as one that he personally accepts. Behind this argument there lies the great issue in Greek political philosophy: whether government is an expert skill, like medicine and navigation, or a matter in which all are equally competent. This issue finds its most philosophical expression in the *Republic*, where the argument is between government based on mere Opinion (δόξα), which is the possession of the many, and government grounded in Truth (ἀλήθεια), which is the prerogative of the few. Plato claims to 'prove' the superiority of philosophical rule, and Democracy is in consequence condemned.

Neither of two famous modern arguments for Democracy—i.e., the moral argument that all men have the right to govern themselves, and the sceptical argument that since men can never know what is right, they should be governed in accordance with their wishes—is much heard of as far as we know in antiquity. Aristotle at one point mentions one established 'democratic' argument which might seem to have a sceptical ring—i.e., that 'the diner, not the cook, will be the best judge of a feast' (*Pol.* 1282a). However, Aristotle in this passage is not maintaining that there is no certain method of judging good government, but rather is suggesting that hitherto this method may have been misconceived.

In classical thought—and so ultimately in later thought based directly upon it—Democracy is seldom considered in isolation. Constitutional discussion generally takes the form of drawing up a list of all possible forms of government and then contrasting, favorably or unfavorably, the merits of each with each. Not only do different thinkers vary in their estimates of Democracy, but they tend to disagree on the meaning that they attach to the concept according to the way they have drawn up their initial lists. For the list being intended as exhaustive, each item in it draws its meaning negatively from the other items, i.e., it means what they don't mean. In the *Republic* the classification of states (i.e., imperfect states) is fourfold—Timocracy, Oligarchy, Democracy, Tyranny; in Xenophon's *Memorabilia* it is fivefold—Kingship, Tyranny, Aristocracy, Plutocracy, Democracy; in the *Politicus* it is sixfold—Kingship, Aristocracy and Democracy by consent, and Tyranny, Oligarchy and Democracy by violence; in the *Politics* it is again sixfold—Kingship, Aristocracy and Polity, and Tyranny, Oligarchy and Democracy. This rather sterile method of discussing government—as though all possible forms of organization were timelessly laid open to inspection and History had nothing to teach—was unfortunately the feature of classical speculation that medieval thinkers found easiest to assimilate. In consequence it disfigures much of their speculation. Significantly, however, the real and permanent contribution of the Middle Ages to the history of Democracy was made in the field not of theory but of practice: in the development of representation. Representational institutions, though not unknown in antiquity—as some historians have claimed—were nearly everywhere of far less importance than the 'primary assemblies' in which all the citizens participated.[4]

[4] J. A. O. Larsen, *Representative Government in Greek and Roman History* (Berkeley-Los Angeles, 1955).

B

The development of the concept of Democracy in Anglo-American discussions is hard to trace. In the first place, it is extremely complex. Secondly, it is intertwined with the history of related concepts such as Equality, Liberty, Toleration, etc.; to separate them out is almost impossible, to leave them involved is disastrous. And thirdly, there is no clear dividing line between the history of Democracy and the present condition of Democracy with all the problems and controversies that surround it. Accordingly, the best that can be done is to isolate the most important single incidents in this long history.

The Puritans. It was in the course of the English Civil War, amongst the more militant Puritan sects, that the modern notion of Democracy originated. It was the product of two dominant ideas of Puritanism. First, the belief in the separation of church and state. The original Calvinist doctrine of passive obedience gave way under the impact of official hostility and persecution to a vociferous separatism. This made possible for the first time in modern history a purely secular political theory. Secondly, there was the belief in 'the priesthood of all believers.' According to this doctrine, man should be left free to follow his own vocation, and in doing so he stood in no need of the mediation of either priest or presbyter. Transposed into political terms the idea of freedom meant that man had no obligation to any government that sought to control him for anything but his own benefit, and the idea of self-sufficiency meant that man had no need of any government that sought to control him for his own benefit—he could do that for himself. These views, which are particularly associated with the Levellers (John Lilburne, John Wildman, Overton and Walwyn) crystallized in the course of the long discussions on the type of constitution that England was to have after the Civil War, and they received their most specific formulation in the Agreement of the People presented at the Putney Debates (Nov.-Dec. 1647).[5]
　　The central thesis of Puritan Democracy is that the basis of all legitimate government is *consent*. But this notion of consent suffers gradual dilution the closer the argument comes to practical politics. At its most extreme it means that everyone should consent to every single law that commands his obligation—a view which leads to what might be called the 'market' view of Democracy as a permanently functioning mechanism for registering the popular will: more moderately the notion means that everyone should consent to those who make laws for him, while at its weakest it is held to involve no more than that everyone should 'have a voice in electing.'

The Revolution of 1688. The next stage in the history of Democracy is recorded in John Locke's *Second Treatise of Civil Government* (1689), a document which has always been regarded as a justification of the Glorious Revolution of 1688 though it was probably written and its leading ideas certainly laid down some years before. Here the political theory of the Puritans is taken up but with its revolutionary implications neutralized. The 'birthright' of every English citizen, on which the Levellers had insisted, is exchanged for a fixed list of 'natural rights.' Significantly, these rights do not include any specifically political rights, i.e., rights to exercise or

---

[5] A. S. P. Woodhouse, *Puritanism and Liberty* (London, 1948).

control political power. Natural rights give man only what might be called an indirect interest in government, in that the government is responsible for safeguarding these natural rights. This responsibility is expressed in Locke's *Treatise* by means of the old metaphor of a *social contract* to which the people and the government are the two parties; the people pledge their obligation to the government, and in return the government undertakes to protect the people's rights. If the government fails to keep its side of the contract, the people automatically can revoke theirs. In other words, the right of everyone to a share in the government on which the Puritans had laid such stress has now been whittled down to no more than the right to revolt against the government if things go too far.

The American Revolution. The prevailing theory of the American Revolution is Lockean. Both Jefferson and Madison explicitly declared themselves to be democrats—though at this period the 'democratic form of government' and the 'republican form of government' seem to have been used as synonyms. Democracy, however, is to be contrasted not so much with other and specific types of government, as with any kind of arbitrary or tyrannical rule. To Madison the real danger is 'the spirit of faction,' i.e., the spirit that leads one part of the community to try and rule the rest in its own sectional interests, and he welcomed representation in some form or another as a good method of curbing this spirit. However, it was not the only method, nor even a particularly sacrosanct method. For it had in the first place to be supplemented by a series of constitutional checks and balances; and secondly, it introduced dangers of its own—in Madison we hear for the first time of the 'tyranny of the majority.'

Amongst the American revolutionaries there was also a more radical democratic theory.[6] This finds classical expression in Tom Paine's *Common Sense* (1776). Paine believed that all government was an evil, but that it could be a justified evil. To be justified it had to concur with the will of the majority, and Paine supported representation as the method of assuring that it did so. Paine's significance in the history of democratic thought is twofold. In the first place—as he himself said of the French Revolution—he 'grafted representation upon democracy.' Prior to Paine there had been a tendency on the part of more radical thinkers to regard representation with suspicion as masking the true expression of popular consent, whereas it was the more conservatively minded thinkers who welcomed it, at any rate in a modified form, as one of the various elements in a 'balanced' constitution. Secondly, in Paine we see the growing awareness that Democracy involves a great deal in the way of social reform and economic redistribution.

Despite the support that the more radical democrats received in, for example, Massachusetts and Pennsylvania, they were unsuccessful in their program, and even their political objectives were unrealized.

The Utilitarians. The Utilitarian democratic theory is the product of two general principles—one psychological, the other moral—both of which derive directly from the thought of the Enlightenment. The first principle is that all men pursue their own happiness. The second is that the only justification of any action is that, compared with alternatives, it produces the greatest happiness of the greatest

[6] Elisha P. Douglass, *Rebels and Democrats* (Chapel Hill, 1955).

number. From the first principle it follows that some government is necessary; from a combination of the two principles it follows that Democracy is the best form of government. For if everyone pursues his own happiness and government ought to pursue the happiness of the greatest number, then government must be in the hands of the greatest number. Democracy is no longer claimed as a right—Bentham dismissed the doctrine of Natural Rights as 'a pomposity on stilts'—but is advocated as the only possible means to a self-evidently desirable end.

It is indicative of the Utilitarians' detached scientific attitude to forms of government that the early Utilitarians avoided the democratic conclusion from their premises, either because they believed in the natural harmony of interests (a belief popularized by the political economists of the day), or because they believed that properly trained intellectuals might by their superior intelligence transcend the ordinary egotistic condition of humanity and act as altruistic legislators. It seems that it was James Mill who converted Bentham to democratic beliefs,[7] and certainly the best statement of the position of democratic Utilitarianism or Philosophical Radicalism is his *Essay on Government* (1820). Even he, however, advocates not universal suffrage but only a suffrage wide enough to secure the representation of all interests and to make the predominance of sinister interests impossible.

The Struggle for Majority Rule. In America the struggle for Democracy—in the fullest sense of unqualified rule by the majority—was resumed in the early part of the nineteenth century. The debates in the Massachusetts Convention of 1820, the New York Convention of 1821, and the Virginia Convention of 1829-30, the prolonged controversy in South Carolina, and the bitter struggle in Rhode Island culminating in the 'Dorr War' of 1842, mark the various phases in the struggle of limited v. universal suffrage. The arguments of the conservatives vary: sometimes they appeal to a view of government as a balance of interests, sometimes to the rights of property, sometimes to fears of majority tyrrany, sometimes to the absurdity of general political principles and rights, sometimes to local circumstances. By comparison the reformers are of one voice. To them it seemed absurd to concede suffrage *to a certain extent* and then stop; any good reason one had for going so far, was a reason for going further, for wherever one drew the line must be arbitrary. Gradually the logic of this position triumphed.

In Great Britain the position was different. The constitution not being in the first place an artefact, the creature of debate and choice, there was no original *ratio decidendi* to which appeal could be made. In consequence each time the suffrage was extended—in 1832, in 1867, and in 1884—the liberals tended to stress the practical necessity of the measure, while the conservatives emphasized its practical dangers. On neither side do we find much theoretical discussion apart from John Stuart Mill's *Representative Government* (1861) which combined Utiltarianism with a profound sense of minority rights.

The peculiar contribution of Great Britain to the spread of Democracy consisted not so much in any theoretical justification of the extension of the suffrage as in practical measures for making this extension effective. The history of this consists of two distinct processes. The first process was the growing dependence of government upon the representative assembly. This meant on the one hand that no government could survive without a majority in, or at any rate the confidence of,

[7] Elie Halévy, *The Growth of Philosophical Radicalism* (London, 1928).

the House of Commons, and secondly that it was not enough for the government to present and defend its policy before the House of Lords.[8] The second process was the gradual development of party organization. In its modern form this dates from the 1830s, but the vital event is the formation of the Birmingham 'Caucus' after 1867.[9] For all its possible drawbacks, the development of political parties has had a threefold significance for Democracy: in the first place, they serve to formulate clearly the policies that are presented to the electorate; secondly, they arouse the interest of the electorate in these policies; and thirdly they ensure that the victorious policy is in fact binding on the ensuing government. This second process culminates in the theory of 'the mandate.'

It has been observed by political writers that the second process when complete has succeeded to some extent in undoing or reversing the first process. For though the life of the government continues to depend upon the will of the Commons, during its life the government now manages to enforce its will upon the Commons; and it manages to do so because it is in effect the organ of party leadership.

The Fears of Democracy. The constant feature that runs through nineteenth-century thought, both conservative and liberal, is the fear of Democracy. For the most part this is of an entirely *a priori* kind. All arguments, for instance, about Democracy as the cause of lower cultural standards (Carlyle, Lecky, Henry Adams) are necessarily of this kind since then, as now, there was not even a rudimentary sociology of art. Some of the arguments, however, are more empirical in character. In the middle of the century, the great source-book for those who were rationally frightened of democratic excesses was Alexis de Tocqueville's *De la démocratie en l'Amérique* (1835). Tocqueville has, however, been much misunderstood. He was not an enemy of Democracy: he was, rather, so convinced of its coming victory that he passed over the advantages and concentrated on its defects and dangers. Towards the end of the century and at the beginning of the twentieth century, most anxiety about Democracy finds fresh sustenance in the finding of the new science of psychology. Originally these findings were the preserve of those who were openly and actively hostile to Democracy, but gradually they were taken up by a considerable body of thinkers who were basically favorable to Democracy and wanted to find a way of reconciling their beliefs with the new science. These range from optimistic thinkers like Graham Wallas to more pessimistic thinkers like Walter Lippmann.

Democracy and Economics. To eighteenth- and early nineteenth-century democrats the natural corollary of their political beliefs seemed to be the economic doctrine of laissez-faire. A few radical voices were raised in protest against this prevailing orthodoxy, but to no great effect. However, from the middle of the nineteenth century onwards the traditional view of the correct economic implications of democratic belief was increasingly called in doubt. It became apparent that Democracy implied laissez-faire only on certain further assumptions, largely of a psychological and economic character, that were not themselves justified. The main psychological assumption was a thoroughgoing egoism inherited from eighteenth-century mechanistic theory, but which found little support in empirical psychol-

---

[8] Sir Ivor Jennings, *Cabinet Government* (Cambridge, England, 1937).
[9] M. Ostrogorsky, *Democracy and the Organization of Political Parties* (London, 1902).

ogy. The most significant economic assumption was that the theoretical requirements of perfect competition were in fact satisfied under ordinary conditions;
increasingly did it become apparent to orthodox economists that in practice
monopolistic and semi-monopolistic conditions are inevitable.[10] . . .

[10] J. M. Keynes, *The End of Laissez-Faire* (London, 1927).

"A Priori" Liberalism
John Locke

John Locke (1632-1704) was a physician, political theorist, and philosopher who
exercised considerable and lasting influence in two branches of thought—epistemo-
logy and political theory. His *Essay Concerning Human Understanding* (1689)
initiated the philosophical tradition known as modern British empiricism. His *Two
Treatises of Government* (1690) and *Letters Concerning Toleration* (1689), both of
which he published anonymously, contain ideas—on democracy, religious freedom,
natural rights, and the status and structure of government—that inspired the founders
of the American republic and influenced the political philosophy of the French
encyclopedists.

To understand political power right, and derive it from its original, we must
consider what state all men are naturally in, and that is, a state of perfect freedom
to order their actions and dispose of their possessions and persons, as they think fit,
within the bounds of the law of nature; without asking leave, or depending upon
the will of any other man.

A state also of equality, wherein all the power and jurisdiction is reciprocal, no
one having more than another; there being nothing more evident, than that
creatures of the same species and rank, promiscuously born to all the same
advantages of nature, and the use of the same faculties, should also be equal one
amongst another without subordination or subjection; unless the lord and master of
them all should, by any manifest declaration of his will, set one above another, and
confer on him, by an evident and clear appointment, an undoubted right to
dominion and sovereignty. . . .

But though this be a state of liberty, yet it is not a state of licence: though man in
that state has an uncontrollable liberty to dispose of his person or possessions, yet
he has not liberty to destroy himself, or so much as any creature in his possession,
but where some nobler use than its bare preservation calls for it. The state of nature
has a law of nature to govern it, which obliges every one: and reason, which is that
law, teaches all mankind, who will but consult it, that being all equal and

From *Second Treatise of Government*, 1690.

independent, no one ought to harm another in his life, health, liberty, or possessions: for men being all the workmanship of one omnipotent and infinitely wise Maker; all the servants of one sovereign Master, are sent into the world by His order, and about His business; they are His property, Whose workmanship they are, made to last during His, not another's pleasure: and being furnished with like faculties, sharing all in one community of nature, there cannot be supposed any such subordination among us, that may authorise us to destroy another, as if we were made for one another's uses, as the inferior ranks of creatures are for ours. Every one, as he is bound to preserve himself, and not to quit his station wilfully, so by the like reason, when his own preservation comes not in competition, ought he, as much as he can, to preserve the rest of mankind, and may not, unless it be to do justice to an offender, take away or impair the life, or what tends to the preservation of life, the liberty, health, limb, or goods of another.

And that all men may be restrained from invading others' rights, and from doing hurt to one another, and the law of nature be observed, which willeth the peace and preservation of all mankind, the execution of the law of nature is, in that state, put into every man's hands, whereby every one has a right to punish the transgressors of that law to such a degree as may hinder its violation: for the law of nature would, as all other laws that concern men in this world, be in vain, if there were nobody that in the state of nature had a power to execute that law, and thereby preserve the innocent and restrain offenders. And if any one in the state of nature may punish another for any evil he has done, every one may do so: for in that state of perfect equality, where naturally there is no superiority or jurisdiction of one over another, what any may do in prosecution of that law, every one must needs have a right to do.

And thus, in the state of nature, 'one man comes by a power over another'; but yet no absolute or arbitrary power, to use a criminal, when he has got him in his hands, according to the passionate heats, or boundless extravagancy of his own will; but only to retribute to him, so far as calm reason and conscience dictate, what is proportionate to his transgression; which is so much as may serve for reparation and restraint: for these two are the only reasons, why one man may lawfully do harm to another, which is that we call punishment.

Men being, as has been said, by nature, all free, equal, and independent, no one can be put out of this estate, and subjected to the political power of another, without his own consent. The only way, whereby any one divests himself of his natural liberty, and puts on the bonds of civil society, is by agreeing with other men to join and unite into a community, for their comfortable, safe, and peaceable living one amongst another, in a secure enjoyment of their properties, and a greater security against any, that are not of it. This any number of men may do, because it injures not the freedom of the rest; they are left as they were in the liberty of the state of nature. When any number of men have so consented to make one community or government, they are thereby presently incorporated, and make one body politic, wherein the majority have a right to act and conclude the rest.

For when any number of men have, by the consent of every individual, made a community, they have thereby made that community one body, with a power to act as one body, which is only by the will and determination of the majority: for that which acts any community, being only the consent of the individuals of it, and it being necessary to that which is one body to move one way; it is necessary the body should move that way whither the greater force carries it, which is the consent of the majority: or else it is impossible it should act or continue one body, one community, which the consent of every individual that united into it, agreed that it should; and so every one is bound by that consent to be concluded by the majority. And therefore we see, that in assemblies, empowered to act by positive laws, where no number is set by that positive law which empowers them, the act of the majority passes for the act of the whole, and of course determines; as having, by the law of nature and reason, the power of the whole.

And thus every man, by consenting with others to make one body politic under one government, puts himself under an obligation, to every one of that society, to submit to the determination of the majority, and to be concluded by it.

The great end of men's entering into society being the enjoyment of their properties in peace and safety, and the great instrument and means of that being the laws established in that society; the first and fundamental positive law of all commonwealths is the establishing of the legislative power; as the first and fundamental natural law, which is to govern even the legislative itself, is the preservation of the society, and (as far as will consist with the public good) of every person in it. This legislative is not only the supreme power of the commonwealth, but sacred and unalterable in the hands where the community have once placed it; nor can any edict of any body else, in what form soever conceived, or by what power soever backed, have the force and obligation of a law, which has not its sanction from that legislative which the public has chosen and appointed; for without this the law could not have that, which is absolutely necessary to its being a law, the consent of the society; over whom nobody can have a power to make laws, but by their own consent, and by authority received from them. And therefore all the obedience, which by the most solemn ties any one can be obliged to pay, ultimately terminates in this supreme power, and is directed by those laws which it enacts; nor can any oaths to any foreign power whatsoever, or any domestic subordinate power, discharge any member of the society from his obedience to the legislative, acting pursuant to their trust; nor oblige him to any obedience contrary to the laws so enacted, or farther than they do allow; it being ridiculous to imagine one can be tied ultimately to obey any power in the society, which is not supreme.

Though the legislative, whether placed in one or more, whether it be always in being, or only by intervals, though it be the supreme power in every common-wealth; yet first, it is not, nor can possibly be absolutely arbitrary over the lives and fortunes of the people: for it being but the joint power of every member of the society given up to that person, or assembly, which is legislator; it can be no more than those persons had in a state of nature before they entered into society, and gave up to the community: for nobody can transfer to another more power than he has in himself; and nobody has an absolute arbitrary power over himself, or over any other, to destroy his own life, or take away the life or property of another. A man, as has been proved, cannot subject himself to the arbitrary power of another; and having in the state of nature no arbitrary power over the life, liberty, or possession of another, but only so much as the law of nature gave him for the preservation of himself and the rest of mankind; this is all he doth, or can give up to the commonwealth, and by it to the legislative power, so that the legislative can have no more than this. Their power, in the utmost bounds of it, is limited to the public good of the society. It is a power, that hath no other end but preservation, and therefore can never have a right to destroy, enslave, or designedly to impoverish the subjects. The obligations of the law of nature cease not in society, but only in many cases are drawn closer, and have by human laws known penalties annexed to them, to enforce their observation. Thus the law of nature stands as an eternal rule to all men, legislators as well as others. The rules that they make for other men's actions, must, as well as their own and other men's actions, be conformable to the laws of nature, *i.e.* to the will of God, of which that is a declaration; and the 'fundamental law of nature being the preservation of mankind', no human sanction can be good, or valid against it.

Though in a constituted commonwealth, standing upon its own basis, and acting according to its own nature, that is, acting for the preservation of the community, there can be but one supreme power, which is the legislative, to which all the rest are and must be subordinate; yet the legislative being only a fiduciary power to act for certain ends, there remains still 'in the people a supreme power to remove or alter the legislative', when they find the legislative act contrary to the trust reposed in them: for all power given with trust for the attaining an end, being limited by that end; whenever that end is manifestly neglected or opposed, the trust must necessarily be forfeited, and the power devolve into the hands of those that gave it, who may place it anew where they shall think best for their safety and security. And thus the community perpetually retains a supreme power of saving themselves from the attempts and designs of any body, even of their legislators, whenever they shall be so foolish, or so wicked, as to lay and carry on designs against the liberties and properties of the subject.

Of the Ends of Political Society and Government

If man in the state of nature be so free as has been said; if he be absolute lord of his own person and possessions, equal to the greatest, and subject to nobody, why will he part with his freedom, why will he give up his empire, and subject himself to the dominion and control of any other power? To which it is obvious to answer that though in the state of nature he has such a right, yet the enjoyment of it is very uncertain, and constantly exposed to the invasion of others; for all being kings as much as he, every man his equal, and the greater part no strict observers of equity and justice, the enjoyment of the property he has in this state is very unsafe, very unsecure. This makes him willing to quit a condition which, however free, is full of fears and continual dangers, and it is not without reason that he seeks out and is willing to join in society with others who are already united, or have a mind to

From *Second Treatise of Government*, 1690.

unite, for the mutual preservation of their lives, liberties, and estates, which I call by the general name "property."

The great and chief end, therefore, of men's uniting into commonwealths and putting themselves under government is the preservation of their property. To which in the state of nature there are many things wanting:

First, there wants an established, settled, known law, received and allowed by common consent to be the standard of right and wrong, and the common measure to decide all controversies between them; for though the law of nature be plain and intelligible to all rational creatures, yet men being biased by their interest, as well as ignorant for want of studying it, are not apt to allow of it as a law binding to them in the application of it to their particular cases.

Secondly, in the state of nature there wants a known and indifferent judge, with authority to determine all differences according to the established law; for everyone in that state being both judge and executioner of the law of nature, men being partial to themselves, passion and revenge is very apt to carry them too far and with too much heat in their own cases, as well as negligence and unconcernedness to make them too remiss in other men's.

Thirdly, in the state of nature there often wants power to back and support the sentence when right, and to give it due execution. They who by any injustice offend, will seldom fail, where they are able, by force to make good their injustice; such resistance many times makes the punishment dangerous, and frequently destructive to those who attempt it.

Thus mankind, notwithstanding all the privileges of the state of nature, being but in an ill condition while they remain in it, are quickly driven into society. Hence it comes to pass that we seldom find any number of men live any time together in this state. The inconveniences that they are therein exposed to, by the irregular and uncertain exercise of the power every man has of punishing the transgressions of others, make them take sanctuary under the established laws of government and therein seek the preservation of their property. It is this makes them so willingly give up every one his single power of punishing, to be exercised by such alone as shall be appointed to it among them; and by such rules as the community, or those authorized by them to that purpose, shall agree on. And in this we have the original right of both the legislative and executive power, as well as of the governments and societies themselves.

For in the state of nature, to omit the liberty he has of innocent delights, a man has two powers:

The first is to do whatsoever he thinks fit for the preservation of himself and others within the permission of the law of nature, by which law, common to them all, he and all the rest of mankind are one community, make up one society, distinct from all other creatures. And, were it not for the corruption and viciousness of degenerate men, there would be no need of any other, no necessity that men should separate from this great and natural community, and by positive agreements combine into smaller and divided associations.

The other power a man has in the state of nature is the power to punish the crimes committed against that law. Both these he gives up when he joins in a private, if I may so call it, or particular politic society and incorporates into any commonwealth separate from the rest of mankind.

The first power, viz., of doing whatsoever he thought fit for the preservation of himself and the rest of mankind, he gives up to be regulated by laws made by the society, so far forth as the preservation of himself and the rest of that society shall require; which laws of the society in many things confine the liberty he had by the law of nature.

Secondly, the power of punishing he wholly gives up, and engages his natural force (which he might before employ in the execution of the law of nature, by his own single authority, as he thought fit) to assist the executive power of the society, as the law thereof shall require; for being now in a new state, wherein he is to enjoy many conveniences from the labor, assistance, and society of others in the same community as well as protection from its whole strength, he is to part also with as much of his natural liberty, in providing for himself, as the good, prosperity, and safety of the society shall require, which is not only necessary, but just, since the other members of the society do the like.

But though men when they enter into society, give up the equality, liberty, and executive power they had in the state of nature, into the hands of the society, to be so far disposed of by the legislative as the good of the society shall require; yet it being only with an intention in everyone the better to preserve himself, his liberty and property (for no rational creature can be supposed to change his condition with an intention to be worse), the power of the society, or legislative constituted by them, can never be supposed to extend farther than the common good, but is obliged to secure everyone's property by providing against those three defects above-mentioned that made the state of nature so unsafe and uneasy. And so whoever has the legislative or supreme power of any commonwealth is bound to govern by established standing laws, promulgated and known to the people, and not by extemporary decrees; by indifferent and upright judges who are to decide controversies by those laws; and to employ the force of the community at home only in the execution of such laws, or abroad to prevent or redress foreign injuries, and secure the community from inroads and invasion. And all this to be directed to no other end but the peace, safety, and public good of the people. . . .

On Property

Whether we consider natural reason, which tells us, that men, being once born, have a right to their preservation, and consequently to meat and drink, and such other things as nature affords for their subsistence; or revelation, which gives us an account of those grants God made of the world to Adam, and to Noah, and his sons; it is very clear, that God, as king David says, Psal. cxv. 16. "Has given the earth to the children of men;" given it to mankind in common. But this being supposed, it seems to some a very great difficulty how any one should ever come to have a property in any thing: I will not content myself to answer, that if it be difficult to make out property, upon a supposition, that God gave the world to Adam, and his posterity in common, it is impossible that any man, but one universal monarch, should have any property upon a supposition, that God gave the world to Adam, and his heirs in succession, exclusive of all the rest of his posterity.

From John Locke, *The Works of John Locke*, Vol. 5 (London: T. Davison, 1812).

But I shall endeavour to show, how men might come to have a property in several parts of that which God gave to mankind in common, and that without any express compact of all the commoners.

God, who hath given the world to men in common, hath also given them reason to make use of it to the best advantage of life, and convenience. The earth, and all that is therein, is given to men for the support and comfort of their being. And though all the fruits it naturally produces, and beasts it feeds, belong to mankind in common, as they are produced by the spontaneous hand of nature; and nobody has originally a private dominion, exclusive of the rest of mankind, in any of them, as they are thus in their natural state; yet being given for the use of men, there must of necessity be a means to appropriate them some way or other, before they can be of any use, or at all beneficial to any particular man. The fruit, or venison, which nourishes the wild Indian, who knows no enclosure, and is still a tenant in common, must be his, and so his, i.e. a part of him, that another can no longer have any right to it, before it can do him any good for the support of his life.

Though the earth, and all inferior creatures, be common to all men, yet every man has a property in his own person: this nobody has any right to but himself. The labour of his body, and the work of his hands, we may say, are properly his. Whatsoever then he removes out of the state that nature hath provided, and left it in, he hath mixed his labour with, and joined to it something that is his own, and thereby makes it his property. It being by him removed from the common state nature hath placed it in, it hath by this labour something annexed to it, that excludes the common right of other men. For this labour being the unquestionable property of the labourer, no man but he can have a right to what that is once joined to, at least where there is enough, and as good, left in common for others.

He that is nourished by the acorns he picked up under an oak, or the apples he gathered from the trees in the wood, has certainly appropriated them to himself. Nobody can deny but the nourishment is his. I ask then, when did they begin to be his? when he digested? or when he eat? or when he boiled? or when he brought them home? or when he picked them up? and it is plain, if the first gathering made them not his, nothing else could. That labour put a distinction between them and common: that added something to them more than nature, the common mother of all, had done; and so they became his private right. And will any one say, he had no right to those acorns or apples he thus appropriated, because he had not the consent of all mankind to make them his? was it a robbery thus to assume to himself what belonged to all in common? If such a consent as that was necessary, man had starved, notwithstanding the plenty God had given him. We see in commons, which remain so by compact, that it is the taking any part of what is common, and removing it out of the state nature leaves it in, which begins the property; without which the common is of no use. And the taking of this or that part does not depend on the express consent of all the commoners. Thus the grass my horse has bit; the turfs my servant has cut; and the ore I have digged in any place, where I have a right to them in common with others; become my property, without the assignation or consent of any body. The labour that was mine, removing them out of that common state they were in, hath fixed my property in them.

By making an explicit consent of every commoner necessary to any one's appropriating to himself any part of what is given in common, children or servants could not cut the meat, which their father or master had provided for them in common, without assigning to every one his peculiar part. Though the water running in the fountain be every one's, yet who can doubt, but that in the pitcher is his only who drew it out? His labour hath taken it out of the hands of nature, where it was common, and belonged equally to all her children, and hath thereby appropriated it to himself.

Thus this law of reason makes the deer that Indian's who hath killed it; it is allowed to be his goods, who hath bestowed his labour upon it, though before it was the common right of every one. And amongst those who are counted the civilized part of mankind, who have made and multiplied positive laws to determine property, this original law of nature, for the beginning of property, in what was before common, still takes place; and by virtue thereof, what fish any one catches in the ocean, that great and still remaining common of mankind; or what ambergrise any one takes up here, is by the labour that removes it out of that common state nature left it in, made his property, who takes that pains about it. And even amongst us, the hare that any one is hunting, is thought his who pursues her during the chace: for being a beast that is still looked upon as common, and no man's private possession; whoever has employed so much labour about any of that kind, as to find and pursue her, has thereby removed her from the state of nature, wherein she was common, and hath begun a property.

It will perhaps be objected to this, that "if gathering the acorns, or other fruits of the earth, &c. makes a right to them, then any one may engross as much as he will." To which I answer, Not so. The same law of nature, that does by this means give us property, does also bound that property too. "God has given us all things richly," I Tim. vi. 17. is the voice of reason confirmed by inspiration. But how far has he given it us? To enjoy. As much as any one can make use of to any advantage of life before it spoils, so much he may by his labour fix a property in: whatever is beyond this, is more than his share, and belongs to others. Nothing was made by God for man to spoil or destroy. And thus, considering the plenty of natural provisions there was a long time in the world, and the few spenders; and to how small a part of that provision the industry of one man could extend itself, and engross it to the prejudice of others; especially keeping within the bounds, set by reason, of what might serve for his use; there could be then little room for quarrels or contentions about property so established.

But the chief matter of property being now not the fruits of the earth, and the beasts that subsist on it, but the earth itself; as that which takes in, and carries with it all the rest; I think it is plain, that property in that too is acquired as the former. As much land as a man tills, plants, improves, cultivates, and can use the product of, so much is his property. He by his labour does, as it were, enclose it from the common. Nor will it invalidate his right, to say everybody else has an equal title to it, and therefore he cannot appropriate, he cannot enclose, without the consent of all his fellow commoners, all mankind. God, when he gave the world in common to all mankind, commanded man also to labour, and the penury of his condition required it of him. God and his reason commanded him to subdue the earth, i.e. improve it for the benefit of life, and therein lay out something upon it that was his own, his labour. He that, in obedience to this command of God, subdued, tilled, and sowed any part of it, thereby annexed to it something that was his property, which another had no title to, nor could without injury take from him.

Nor was this appropriation of any parcel of land, by improving it, any prejudice to any other man, since there was still enough, and as good left; and more than the yet unprovided could see. So that, in effect, there was never the less left for others because of his enclosure for himself: for he that leaves as much as another can make use of, does as good as take nothing at all. Nobody could think himself injured by the drinking of another man, though he took a good draught, who had a whole river of the same water left him to quench his thirst; and the case of land and water, where there is enough for both, is perfectly the same.

God gave the world to men in common; but since he gave it them for their benefit, and the greatest conveniencies of life they were capable to draw from it, it cannot be supposed he meant it should always remain common and uncultivated. He gave it to the use of the industrious and rational, (and labour was to be his title to it) not to the fancy or covetousness of the quarrelsome and contentious. He that had as good left for his improvement, as was already taken up, needed not complain, ought not to meddle with what was already improved by another's labour: if he did, it is plain he desired the benefit of another's pains, which he had no right to, and not the ground which God had given him in common with others to labour on, and whereof there was as good left, as that already possessed, and more than he knew what to do with, or his industry could reach to.

It is true, in land that is common in England, or any other country, where there is plenty of people under government, who have money and commerce, no one can enclose or appropriate any part, without the consent of all his fellow-commoners; because this is left common by compact, i.e. by the law of the land, which is not to be violated. And though it be common, in respect of some men, it is not so to all mankind, but is the joint property of this country, or this parish. Besides, the remainder, after such enclosure, would not be as good to the rest of the commoners, as the whole was when they could all make use of the whole; whereas in the beginning and first peopling of the great common of the world, it was quite otherwise. The law man was under, was rather for appropriating. God commanded, and his wants forced him to labour. That was his property which could not be taken from him wherever he had fixed it. And hence subduing or cultivating the earth, and having dominion, we see are joined together. The one gave title to the other. So that God, by commanding to subdue, gave authority so far to appropriate: and the condition of human life, which requires labour and materials to work on, necessarily introduces private possessions.

The measure of property nature has well set by the extent of men's labour, and the conveniencies of life: no man's labour could subdue, or appropriate all; nor could his enjoyment consume more than a small part; so that it was impossible for any man, this way, to entrench upon the right of another, or acquire to himself a property, to the prejudice of his neighbour, who would still have room for as good, and as large a possession (after the other had taken out his) as before it was appropriated. This measure did confine every man's possession to a very moderate proportion, and such as he might appropriate to himself, without injury to any body, in the first ages of the world, when men were more in danger to be lost, by wandering from their company, in the then vast wilderness of the earth, than to be straitened for want of room to plant in. And the same measure may be allowed still without prejudice to any body, as full as the world seems: for supposing a man, or family, in the state they were at first peopling of the world by the children of Adam, or Noah; let him plant in some inland, vacant places of America, we shall find that the possessions he could make himself, upon the measures we have given, would not be very large, nor, even to this day, prejudice the rest of mankind, or give them reason to complain, or think themselves injured by this man's encroachment; though the race of men have now spread themselves to all the corners of the world, and do infinitely exceed the small number was at the beginning. Nay, the extent of ground is of so little value, without labour, that I have heard it affirmed, that in Spain itself a man may be permitted to plough, sow, and reap, without being disturbed, upon land he has no other title to, but only his making use of it. But, on the contrary, the inhabitants think themselves beholden to him, who, by his industry on neglected, and consequently waste land, has increased the stock of corn, which they wanted. But be this as it will, which I lay no stress on; this I dare boldly affirm, that the same rule of propriety, (viz.) that every man should have as much as he could make use of, would hold still in the world, without straitening any body; since there is land enough in the world to suffice double the inhabitants, had not the invention of money, and the tacit agreement of men to put a value on it, introduced (by consent) larger possessions, and a right to them; which, how it has done, I shall by and by show more at large.

This is certain, that in the beginning, before the desire of having more than man needed had altered the intrinsic value of things, which depends only on their usefulness to the life of man; or had agreed, that a little piece of yellow metal, which would keep without wasting or decay, should be worth a great piece of flesh, or a whole heap of corn; though men had a right to appropriate, by their labour, each one to himself as much of the things of nature as he could use: yet this could not be much, nor to the prejudice of others, where the same plenty was still left to those who would use the same industry. To which let me add, that he who appropriates land to himself by his labour, does not lessen, but increase the common stock of mankind: for the provisions serving to the support of human life, produced by one acre of enclosed and cultivated land, are (to speak much within compass) ten times more than those which are yielded by an acre of land of an equal richness lying waste in common. And therefore he that encloses land, and has a greater plenty of the conveniences of life from ten acres, than he could have from an hundred left to nature, may truly be said to give ninety acres to mankind: for his labour now supplies him with provisions out of ten acres, which were by the product of an hundred lying in common. I have here rated the improved land very low, in making its produce but as ten to one, when it is much nearer an hundred to one: for I ask, whether in the wild woods and uncultivated waste of America, left to nature, without any improvement, tillage, or husbandry, a thousand acres yield the needy and wretched inhabitants as many conveniencies of life, as ten acres equally fertile land do in Devonshire, where they are well cultivated.

Before the appropriation of land, he who gathered as much of the wild fruit, killed, caught, or tamed, as many of the beasts as he could; he that so employed his pains about any of the spontaneous products of nature, as any way to alter them from the state which nature put them in, by placing any of his labour on them, did thereby acquire a propriety in them: but if they perished, in his possession, without their due use; if the fruits rotted, or the venison putrified, before he could spend it; he offended against the common law of nature, and was liable to be punished: he invaded his neighbour's share, for he had no right, farther than his use called for any of them, and they might serve to afford him conveniencies of life. . . .

Thus labour, in the beginning, gave a right of property, wherever any one was pleased to employ it upon what was common, which remained a long while the far greater part, and is yet more than mankind makes use of. Men, at first, for the most part, contented themselves with what unassisted nature offered to their necessities: and though afterwards, in some parts of the world, (where the increase of people and stock, with the use of money, had made land scarce, and so of some value) the several communities settled the bounds of their distinct territories, and by laws within themselves regulated the properties of the private men of their society, and so, by compact and agreement, settled the property which labour and industry began: and the leagues that have been made between several states and kingdoms, either expressly or tacitly disowning all claim and right to the land in the others possession, have, by common consent, given up their pretences to their natural common right, which originally they had to those countries, and so have, by positive agreement, settled a property amongst themselves, in distinct parts and parcels of the earth; yet there are still great tracts of ground to be found, which (the inhabitants thereof not having joined with the rest of mankind, in the consent of the use of their common money) lie waste, and are more than the people who dwell on it do, or can make use of, and so still lie in common; though this can scarce happen amongst that part of mankind that have consented to the use of money.

The greatest part of things really useful to the life of man, and such as the necessity of subsisting made the first commoners of the world look after, as it doth the Americans now, are generally things of short duration; such as, if they are not consumed by use, will decay and perish of themselves: gold, silver, and diamonds, are things that fancy or agreement hath put the value on, more than real use, and the necessary support of life. Now of those good things which nature hath provided in common, every one had a right, (as hath been said) to as much as he could use, and property in all that he could effect with his labour; all that his industry could extend to, to alter from the state nature had put it in, was his. He that gathered a hundred bushels of acorns or apples, had thereby a property in them, they were his goods as soon as gathered. He was only to look, that he used them before they spoiled, else he took more than his share, and robbed others. And indeed it was a foolish thing, as well as dishonest, to hoard up more than he could make use of. If he gave away a part to any body else, so that it perished not uselessly in his possession, these he also made use of. And if he also bartered away plums, that would have rotted in a week, for nuts that would last good for his eating a whole lear, he did no injury; he wasted not the common stock; destroyed no part of the portion of the goods that belonged to others, so long as nothing perished uselessly in his hands. Again, if he would give his nuts for a piece of metal, pleased with its colour; or exchange his sheep for shells, or wool for a sparkling pebble or a diamond, and keep those by him all his life, he invaded not the right of others, he might heap as much of these durable things as he pleased; the exceeding of the bounds of his just property not lying in the largeness of his possession, but the perishing of any thing uselessly in it.

And thus came in the use of money, some lasting thing that men might keep without spoiling, and that by mutual consent men would take in exchange for the truly useful, but perishable supports of life.

And as different degrees of industry were apt to give men possessions in different proportions, so this invention of money gave them the opportunity to continue and enlarge them: for supposing an island, separate from all possible commerce with the rest of the world, wherein there were but an hundred families, but there were sheep, horses, and cows, with other useful animals, wholesome fruits, and land enough for corn for a hundred thousand times as many, but nothing in the island, either because of its commonness, or perishableness, fit to supply the place of money; what reason could any one have there to enlarge his possessions beyond the use of his family and a plentiful supply to its consumption, either in what their own industry produced, or they could barter for like perishable, useful commodities with others? Where there is not something, both lasting and scarce, and so valuable to be hoarded up, there men will not be apt to enlarge their possessions of land, were it ever so rich, ever so free for them to take: for I ask, what would a man value ten thousand, or an hundred thousand acres of excellent land, ready cultivated and well stocked too with cattle, in the middle of the inland parts of America, where he had no hopes of commerce with other parts of the world, to draw money to him by the sale of the product? It would not be worth enclosing, and we should see him give up again to the wild common of nature, whatever was more than would supply the conveniencies of life to be had there for him and his family.

Thus in the beginning all the world was America, and more so than that is now; for no such thing was any where known. Find out something that hath the use and value of money amongst his neighbours, you shall see the same man will begin presently to enlarge his possessions.

But since gold and silver, being little useful to the life of man in proportion to food, raiment, and carriage, has its value only from the consent of men, whereof labour yet makes, in great part, the measure; it is plain, that men have agreed to a disproportionate and unequal possession of the earth, they having, by a tacit and voluntary consent, found out a way how a man may fairly possess more land than he himself can use the product of, by receiving in exchange for the overplus, gold and silver, which may he hoarded up without injury to any one; these metals not spoiling or decaying in the hands of the possessor. This partage of things in an inequality of private possessions, men have made practicable out of the bounds of society, and without compact; only by putting a value on gold and silver, and tacitly agreeing in the use of money: for in governments, the laws regulate the right of property, and the possession of land is determined by positive constitutions.

And thus, I think, it is very easy to conceive, "how labour could at first begin a title of property" in the common things of nature, and how the spending it upon our uses bounded it. So that there could then be no reason of quarrelling about title, nor any doubt about the largeness of possession it gave. Right and conveniency went together; for as a man had a right to all he could employ his labour upon, so he had no temptation to labour for more than he could make use of. This left no room for controversy about the title, nor for encroachment on the right of others; what portion a man carved to himself, was easily seen; and it was useless, as well as dishonest, to carve himself too much, or take more than he needed.

On the Dissolution of Government

He that will with any clearness speak of the dissolution of government, ought in the first place to distinguish between the dissolution of the society and the dissolution of the government. That which makes the community and brings men out of the loose state of nature into one politic society is the agreement which everyone has with the rest to incorporate and act as one body, and so be one distinct commonwealth. The usual, and almost only, way whereby this union is dissolved is the inroad of foreign force making a conquest upon them; for in that case (not being able to maintain and support themselves as one entire and independent body) the union belonging to that body which consisted therein must necessarily cease, and so everyone return to the state he was in before, with a liberty to shift for himself and provide for his own safety, as he thinks fit, in some other society. Whenever the society is dissolved, it is certain the government of that society cannot remain. Thus conquerors' swords often cut up governments by the roots and mangle societies to pieces, separating the subdued or scattered multitude from the protection of, and dependence on, that society which ought to have preserved them from violence. The world is too well instructed in, and too forward to allow of, this way of dissolving of governments to need any more to be said of it; and there wants not much argument to prove, that where the society is dissolved, the government cannot remain—that being as impossible as for the frame of a house to subsist when the materials of it are scattered and dissipated by a whirlwind, or jumbled into a confused heap by an earthquake.

Besides this overturning from without, governments are dissolved from within.

First, when the legislative is altered. Civil society being a state of peace among those who are of it, from whom the state of war is excluded by the umpirage which they have provided in their legislative for the ending all differences that may arise among any of them; it is in their legislative that the members of a commonwealth are united and combined together into one coherent living body. This is the soul that gives form, life, and unity to the commonwealth; from hence the several members have their mutual influence, sympathy, and connection; and, therefore, when the legislative is broken or dissolved, dissolution and death follows; for the essence and union of the society consisting in having one will, the legislative, when once established by the majority, has the declaring and, as it were, keeping of that will. The constitution of the legislative is the first and fundamental act of society, whereby provision is made for the continuation of their union under the direction of persons and bonds of laws made by persons authorized thereunto by the consent and appointment of the people, without which no one man, or number of men, among them can have authority of making laws that shall be binding to the rest. When any one, or more, shall take upon them to make laws, whom the people have not appointed so to do, they make laws without authority, which the people are not therefore bound to obey; by which means they come again to be out of subjection and may constitute to themselves a new legislative as they think best,

From *Second Treatise of Government*, 1690.

being in full liberty to resist the force of those who without authority would impose anything upon them. Everyone is at the disposure of his own will when those who had, by the delegation of the society, the declaring of the public will are excluded from it, and others usurp the place, who have no such authority or delegation. . . .

There is therefore, secondly, another way whereby governments are dissolved, and that is when the legislative or the prince, either of them, act contrary to their trust.

First, the legislative acts against the trust reposed in them, when they endeavor to invade the property of the subject, and to make themselves, or any part of the community, masters or arbitrary disposers of the lives, liberties, or fortunes of the people.

The reason why men enter into society is the preservation of their property; and the end why they choose and authorize a legislative is that there may be laws made, and rules set, as guards and fences to the properties of all the members of the society, to limit the power, and moderate the dominion of every part and member of the society; for since it can never be supposed to be the will of the society that the legislative should have a power to destroy that which everyone designs to secure by entering into society, and for which the people submitted themselves to legislators of their own making. Whenever the legislators endeavor to take away and destroy the property of the people, or to reduce them to slavery under arbitrary power, they put themselves into a state of war with the people, who are thereupon absolved from any further obedience, and are left to the common refuge which God has provided for all men against force and violence. Whensoever therefore the legislative shall transgress this fundamental rule of society, and either by ambition, fear, folly, or corruption, endeavour to grasp themselves, or put into the hands of any other, an absolute power over the lives, liberties, and estates of the people, by this breach of trust they forfeit the power the people had put into their hands for quite contrary ends, and it devolves to the people, who have a right to resume their original liberty, and, by the establishment of a new legislative, such as they shall think fit, provide for their own safety and security, which is the end for which they are in society. What I have said here concerning the legislative in general holds true also concerning the supreme executor, who having a double trust put in him, both to have a part in the legislative and the supreme execution of the law, acts against both when he goes about to set up his own arbitrary will as the law of the society. He acts also contrary to his trust when he either employs the force, treasure, and offices of the society to corrupt the representatives and gain them to his purposes, or openly pre-engages the electors and prescribes to their choice such whom he has by solicitations, threats, promises, or otherwise won to his designs, and employs them to bring in such who have romised beforehand what to vote and what to enact. Thus to regulate candidates and electors, and new-model the ways of election, what is it but to cut up the government by the roots, and poison the very fountain of public security? For the people having reserved to themselves the choice of their representatives, as the fence to their properties, could do it for no other end but that they might always be freely chosen, and, so chosen, freely act and advise as the necessity of the commonwealth and the public good should, upon examination and mature debate, be judged to require. This, those who give their votes before they hear the debate and have weighed the reasons on all sides are not capable of doing. To prepare such an assembly as this, and endeavor to set up the declared abettors of his own will for the true representatives of the people and the lawmakers of the society, is certainly as great a breach of trust and as perfect a declaration of a design to subvert the government as is possible to be met with. To which if one shall add rewards and punishments visibly employed to the same end, and all the arts of perverted law made use of to take off and destroy all that stand in the way of such a design, and will not comply and consent to betray the liberties of their country, it will be past doubt what is doing. What power they ought to have in the society, who thus employ it contrary to the trust that went along with it in its first institution, is easy to determine; and one cannot but see that he who has once attempted any such thing as this cannot any longer be trusted.

To this perhaps it will be said, that the people being ignorant, and always discontented, to lay the foundation of government in the unsteady opinion and uncertain humor of the people, is to expose it to certain ruin; and no government will be able long to subsist if the people may set up a new legislative, whenever they take offense at the old one. To this I answer: Quite the contrary. People are not so easily got out of their old forms as some are apt to suggest. They are hardly to be prevailed with to amend the acknowledged faults in the frame they have been accustomed to. And if there be any original defects, or adventitious ones introduced by time or corruption, it is not an easy thing to get them changed, even when all the world sees there is an opportunity for it. This slowness and aversion in the people to quit their old constitutions has, in the many revolutions which have been seen in this kingdom, in this and former ages, still kept us to, or after some interval of fruitless attempts still brought us back again to, our old legislative of king, lords, and commons; and whatever provocations have made the crown be taken from some of our princes' heads, they never carried the people so far as to place it in another line.

But it will be said this hypothesis lays a ferment for frequent rebellion. To which I answer.

First, no more than any other hypothesis; for when the people are made miserable, and find themselves exposed to the ill-usage of arbitrary power, cry up their governors as much as you will for sons of Jupiter, let them be sacred or divine, descended or authorized from heaven, give them out for whom or what you please, the same will happen. The people generally ill-treated, and contrary to right, will be ready upon any occasion to ease themselves of a burden that sits heavy upon them. They will wish and seek for the opportunity, which in the change, weakness, and accidents of human affairs seldom delays long to offer itself. He must have lived but a little while in the world who has not seen examples of this in his time, and he must have read very little who cannot produce examples of it in all sorts of governments in the world.

Secondly, I answer, such revolutions happen not upon every little mismanagement in public affairs. Great mistakes in the ruling part, many wrong and inconvenient laws, and all the slips of human frailty will be borne by the people without mutiny or murmur. But if a long train of abuses, prevarications, and artifices, all tending the same way, make the design visible to the people, and they cannot but feel what they lie under, and see whither they are going, it is not to be wondered that they should then rouse themselves and endeavor to put the rule into such hands which may secure to them the ends for which government was at first erected, and without which ancient names and specious forms are so far from being better than they are much worse than the state of nature or pure anarchy—the inconveniences being all as great and as near, but the remedy further off and more difficult.

Thirdly, I answer that this doctrine of a power in the people of providing for their safety anew by a new legislative, when their legislators have acted contrary to their trust by invading their property, is the best fence against rebellion, and the probablest means to hinder it; for rebellion being an opposition, not to persons, but authority which is founded only in the constitutions and laws of the government, those, whoever they be, who by force break through, and by force justify their violation of them, are truly and properly rebels; for when men, by entering into society and civil government, have excluded force and introduced laws for the preservation of property, peace, and unity among themselves, those who set up force again in opposition to the laws do *rebellare*, that is, bring back again the state of war, and are properly rebels; which they who are in power (by the pretense they have to authority, the temptation of force they have in their hands, and the flattery of those about them), being likeliest to do, the properest way to prevent the evil is to show them the danger and injustice of it who are under the greatest temptation to run into it.

In both the forementioned cases, when either the legislative is changed, or the legislators act contrary to the end for which they were constituted, those who are guilty are guilty of rebellion; for if anyone by force takes away the established legislative of any society, and the laws of them made pursuant to their trust, he thereby takes away the umpirage which everyone had consented to for a peaceable decision of all their controversies, and a bar to the state of war among them. They who remove or change the legislative take away this decisive power which nobody can have but by the appointment and consent of the people, and so destroying the authority which the people did, and nobody else can, set up, and introducing a power which the people has not authorized, they actually introduce a state of war which is that of force without authority; and thus, by removing the legislative established by the society (in whose decisions the people acquiesced and united as to that of their own will), they untie the knot and expose the people anew to the state of war. And if those, who by force take away the legislative, are rebels, the legislators themselves, as has been shown, can be no less esteemed so, when they who were set up for the protection and preservation of the people, their liberties and properties, shall by force invade and endeavor to take them away; and so they putting themselves into a state of war with those who made them the protectors and guardians of their peace, are properly, and with the greatest aggravation, *rebellantes*, rebels.

But if they who say "it lays a foundation for rebellion" mean that it may occasion civil wars or intestine broils, to tell the people they are absolved from obedience when illegal attempts are made upon their liberties or properties, and may oppose the unlawful violence of those who were their magistrates when they invade their properties contrary to the trust put in them, and that therefore this doctrine is not to be allowed, being so destructive to the peace of the world; they may as well say, upon the same ground, that honest men may not oppose robbers or pirates because this may occasion disorder or bloodshed. If any mischief come in such cases, it is not to be charged upon him who defends his own right, but on him that invades his neighbor's. If the innocent honest man must quietly quit all he has, for peace's sake, to him who will lay violent hands upon it, I desire it may be considered, what a kind of peace there will be in the world, which consists only in violence and rapine, and which is to be maintained only for the benefit of robbers and oppressors. Who would not think it an admirable peace betwixt the mighty and the mean when the lamb without resistance yielded his throat to be torn by the imperious wolf? Polyphemus' den gives us a perfect pattern of such a peace and such a government, wherein Ulysses and his companions had nothing to do but quietly to suffer themselves to be devoured. And no doubt Ulysses, who was a prudent man, preached up passive obedience, and exhorted them to a quiet submission by representing to them of what concernment peace was to mankind, and by showing the inconveniences which might happen if they should offer to resist Polyphemus, who had now the power over them.

The end of government is the good of mankind. And which is best for mankind: that the people should be always exposed to the boundless will of tyranny, or that the rulers should be sometimes liable to be opposed when they grow exorbitant in the use of their power and employ it for the destruction and not the preservation of the properties of their people?

Nor let anyone say that mischief can arise from hence as often as it shall please, a busy head, or turbulent spirit, to desire the alteration of the government. It is true such men may stir whenever they please, but it will be only to their own just ruin and perdition; for till the mischief be grown general, and the ill designs of the rulers become visible, or their attempts sensible to the greater part, the people, who are more disposed to suffer than right themselves by resistance, are not apt to stir. The examples of particular injustice or oppression of here and there an unfortunate man moves them not. But if they universally have a persuasion, grounded upon manifest evidence, that designs are carrying on against their liberties, and the general course and tendency of things cannot but give them strong suspicions of the evil intention of their governors, who is to be blamed for it? Who can help it if they who might avoid it bring themselves into this suspicion? Are the people to be blamed if they have the sense of rational creatures and can think of things no otherwise than as they find and feel them? And is it not rather their fault who put things into such a posture that they would not have them thought to be as they are? I grant that the pride, ambition, and turbulence of private men have sometimes caused great disorders in commonwealths, and factions have been fatal to states and kingdoms. But whether the mischief has oftener begun in the people's wantonness and a desire to cast off the lawful authority of their rulers, or in the rulers' insolence and endeavors to get and exercise an arbitrary power over the people—whether oppression or disobedience gave the first rise to the disorder, I leave it to impartial history to determine. This I am sure: whoever, either ruler or subject, by force goes about to invade the rights of either prince or people and lays the foundation for overturning the constitution and frame of any just government is highly guilty of the greatest crime I think a man is capable of—being to answer for all those mischiefs of blood, rapine, and desolation, which the breaking to pieces of governments bring on a country. And he who does it is justly to be esteemed the common enemy and pest of mankind, and is to be treated accordingly.

That subjects or foreigners, attempting by force on the properties of any people, may be resisted with force, is agreed on all hands. But that magistrates doing the same thing may be resisted, has of late been denied; as if those who had the greatest privileges and advantages by the law, had thereby a power to break those laws by which alone they were set in a better place than their brethren; whereas their offense is thereby the greater, both as being ungrateful for the greater share they have by the law, and breaking also that trust which is put into their hands by their brethren.

Whosoever uses force without right, as everyone does in society who does it without law, puts himself into a state of war with those against whom he so uses it; and in that state all former ties are canceled, all other rights cease, and everyone has a right to defend himself and to resist the aggressor. . . .

Here, it is like, the common question will be made: Who shall be judge whether the prince or legislative act contrary to their trust? This, perhaps, ill-affected and factious men may spread among the people, when the prince only makes use of his due prerogative. To this I reply: The people shall be judge; for who shall be judge whether his trustee or deputy acts well and according to the trust reposed in him, but he who deputes him, and must, by having deputed him, have still a power to discard him when he fails in his trust? If this be reasonable in particular cases of private men, why should it be otherwise in that of the greatest moment, where the welfare of millions is concerned, and also where the evil, if not prevented, is greater, and the redress very difficult, dear, and dangerous?

But further, this question, "Who shall be judge?" cannot mean that there is no judge at all; for where there is no judicature on earth, to decide controversies among men, God in heaven is Judge. He alone, it is true, is Judge of the right. But every man is judge for himself, as in all other cases, so in this, whether another has put himself into a state of war with him, and whether he should appeal to the Supreme Judge, as Jephthah did.

If a controversy arise betwixt a prince and some of the people in a matter where the law is silent or doubtful, and the thing be of great consequence, I should think the proper umpire, in such a case, should be the body of the people; for in cases where the prince has a trust reposed in him and is dispensed from the common ordinary rules of the law, there, if any men find themselves aggrieved, and think the prince acts contrary to or beyond that trust, who so proper to judge as the body of the people (who, at first, lodged that trust in him) how far they meant it should extend? But if the prince, or whoever they be in the administration, decline that way of determination, the appeal then lies nowhere but to Heaven; force between either persons who have no known superior on earth, or which permits no appeal to a judge on earth, being properly a state of war, wherein the appeal lies only to Heaven; and in that state the injured party must judge for himself, when he will think fit to make use of that appeal, and put himself upon it.

To conclude, the power that every individual gave the society when he entered into it can never revert to the individuals again as long as the society lasts, but will always remain in the community, because without this there can be no community, no commonwealth, which is contrary to the original agreement; so also when the society has placed the legislative in any assembly of men, to continue in them and their successors, with direction and authority for providing such successors, the legislative can never revert to the people while that government lasts; because having provided a legislative with power to continue forever, they have given up their political power to the legislative and cannot resume it. But if they have set limits to the duration of their legislative, and made this supreme power in any person or assembly, only temporary, or else, when by the miscarriages of those in authority it is forfeited, upon the forfeiture, or at the determination of the time set, it reverts to the society, and the people have a right to act as supreme and continue the legislative in themselves, or erect a new form, or under the old form place it in new hands, as they think good.

The History of Liberty
John Stuart Mill

John Stuart Mill (1806-1873) was the most influential British philosopher of the nineteenth century. His major works include *On Liberty* (1859), *Considerations on Representative Government* (1861), *Utilitarianism* (1863), and *The Subjection of Women* (1869).

The struggle between Liberty and Authority is the most conspicuous feature in the portions of history with which we are earliest familiar, particularly in that of Greece, Rome, and England. But in old times this contest was between subjects, or some classes of subjects, and the Government. By liberty, was meant protection against the tyranny of the political rulers. The rulers were conceived (except in some of the popular governments of Greece) as in a necessarily antagonistic position to the people whom they ruled. They consisted of a governing One, or a governing tribe or caste, who derived their authority from inheritance or conquest, who, at all events, did not hold it at the pleasure of the governed, and whose supremacy men did not venture, perhaps did not desire, to contest, whatever precautions might be taken against its oppressive exercise. Their power was regarded as necessary, but also as highly dangerous; as a weapon which they would attempt to use against their subjects, no less than against external enemies. To prevent the weaker members of the community from being preyed upon by innumerable vultures, it was needful that there should be an animal of prey stronger than the rest, commissioned to keep them down. But as the king of the vultures would be no less bent upon preying on the flock than any of the minor harpies, it was indispensable to be in a perpetual attitude of defence against his beak and claws. The aim, therefore, of patriots was to set limits to the power which the ruler should be suffered to exercise over the community; and this limitation was what they meant by liberty. It was attempted in two ways. First, by obtaining a recognition of certain immunities, called political liberties or rights, which it was to be regarded as a breach of duty in the ruler to infringe, and which if he did infringe, specific resistance, or general rebellion, was held to be justifiable. A second, and generally a later expedient, was the establishment of constitutional checks, by which the consent of the community, or of a body of some sort, supposed to represent its interests, was made a necessary condition to some of the more important acts of the governing power. To the first of these modes of limitation, the ruling power, in most European countries, was compelled, more or less, to submit. It was not so with the second; and, to attain this, or when already in some degree possessed, to attain it more completely, became everywhere the principal object of the lovers of liberty. And so long as mankind were content to combat one enemy by another, and to be ruled by a master, on condition of being guaranteed more or less efficaciously against his tyranny, they did not carry their aspirations beyond this point.

A time, however, came, in the progress of human affairs, when men ceased to

From *On Liberty*, 1859.

think it a necessity of nature that their governors should be an independent power, opposed in interest to themselves. It appeared to them much better that the various magistrates of the State should be their tenants or delegates, revocable at their pleasure. In that way alone, it seemed, could they have complete security that the powers of government would never be abused to their disadvantage. By degrees this new demand for elective and temporary rulers became the prominent object of the exertions of the popular party, wherever any such party existed; and superseded, to a considerable extent, the previous efforts to limit the power of rulers. As the struggle proceeded for making the ruling power emanate from the periodical choice of the ruled, some persons began to think that too much importance had been attached to the limitation of the power itself. That (it might seem) was a resource against rulers whose interests were habitually opposed to those of the people. What was now wanted was, that the rulers should be identified with the people; that their interest and will should be the interest and will of the nation. The nation did not need to be protected against its own will. There was no fear of its tyrannizing over itself. Let the rulers be effectually responsible to it, promptly removable by it, and it could afford to trust them with power of which it could itself dictate the use to be made. Their power was but the nation's own power, concentrated, and in a form convenient for exercise. This mode of thought, or rather perhaps of feeling, was common among the last generation of European Liberalism, in the Continental section of which it still apparently predominates. Those who admit any limit to what a government may do, except in the case of such governments as they think ought not to exist, stand out as brilliant exceptions among the political thinkers of the Continent. A similar tone of sentiment might by this time have been prevalent in our own country, if the circumstances which for a time encouraged it, had continued unaltered.

But, in political and philosophical theories, as well as in persons, success discloses faults and infirmities which failure might have concealed from observation. The notion, that the people have no need to limit their power over themselves, might seem axiomatic, when popular government was a thing only dreamed about, or read of as having existed at some distant period of the past. Neither was that notion necessarily disturbed by such temporary aberrations as those of the French Revolution, the worst of which were the work of a usurping few, and which, in any case, belonged, not to the permanent working of popular institutions, but to a sudden and convulsive outbreak against monarchical and aristocratic despotism. In time, however, a democratic republic came to occupy a large portion of the earth's surface, and made itself felt as one of the most powerful members of the community of nations; and elective and responsible government became subject to the observations and criticisms which wait upon a great existing fact. It was now perceived that such phrases as "self-government", and "the power of the people over themselves", do not express the true state of the case. The "people" who exercise the power are not always the same people with those over whom it is exercised; and the "self-government" spoken of is not the government of each by himself, but of each by all the rest. The will of the people, moreover, practically means the will of the most numerous or the most active *part* of the people; the majority, or those who succeed in making themselves accepted as the majority; the people, consequently *may* desire to oppress a part of their number; and precautions are as much needed against this as against any other abuse of power. The limitation, therefore, of the power of government over individuals loses none of its importance when the holders of power are regularly accountable to the community, that is, to the strongest party therein. This view of things, recommending itself equally to the intelligence of thinkers and to the inclination of those important classes in European society to whose real or supposed interests democracy is adverse, has had no difficulty in establishing itself; and in political speculations "the tyranny of the majority" is now generally included among the evils against which society requires to be on its guard.

Like other tyrannies, the tyranny of the majority was at first, and is still vulgarly, held in dread, chiefly as operating through the acts of the public authorities. But reflecting persons perceived that when society is itself the tyrant—society collectively over the separate individuals who compose it—its means of tyrannizing are not restricted to the acts which it may do by the hands of its political functionaries. Society can and does execute its own mandates: and if it issues wrong mandates instead of right, or any mandates at all in things with which it ought not to meddle, it practises a social tyranny more formidable than many kinds of political oppression, since, though not usually upheld by such extreme penalties, it leaves fewer means of escape, penetrating much more deeply into the details of life, and enslaving the soul itself. Protection, therefore, against the tyranny of the magistrate is not enough: there needs protection also against the tyranny of the prevailing opinion and feeling; against the tendency of society to impose, by other means than civil penalties, its own ideas and practices as rules of conduct on those who dissent from them; to fetter the development, and, if possible, prevent the formation, of any individuality not in harmony with its ways, and compels all characters to fashion themselves upon the model of its own. There is a limit to the legitimate interference of collective opinion with individual independence: and to find that limit, and maintain it against encroachment, is as indispensable to a good condition of human affairs, as protection against political despotism.

. . .

We have now recognized the necessity to the mental well-being of mankind (on which all their other well-being depends) of freedom of opinion, and freedom of the expression of opinion, on four distinct grounds; which we will now briefly recapitulate.

First, if any opinion is compelled to silence, that opinion may, for aught we can certainly know, be true. To deny this is to assume our own infallibility.

Secondly, though the silenced opinion be an error, it may, and very commonly does, contain a portion of truth; and since the general or prevailing opinion of any subject is rarely or never the whole truth, it is only by the collision of adverse opinions that the remainder of the truth has any chance of being supplied.

Thirdly, even if the received opinion be not only true, but the whole truth; unless it is suffered to be, and actually is, vigorously and earnestly contested, it will, by most of those who receive it, be held in the manner of a prejudice, with little comprehension or feeling of its rational grounds. And not only this, but, fourthly, the meaning of the doctrine itself will be in danger of being lost, or enfeebled, and deprived of its vital effect on the character and conduct: the dogma becoming a mere formal profession, inefficacious for good, but cumbering the ground, and preventing the growth of any real and heartfelt conviction, from reason or personal experience.

Before quitting the subject of freedom of opinion, it is fit to take some notice of those who say, that the free expression of all opinions should be permitted, on condition that the manner be temperate, and do not pass the bounds of fair discussion. Much might be said on the impossibility of fixing where these supposed bounds are to be placed; for if the test be offense to those whose opinion is attacked, I think experience testifies that this offense is given whenever the attack is telling and powerful, and that every opponent who pushes them hard, and whom they find difficult to answer, appears to them, if he shows any strong feeling on the subject, an intemperate opponent. But this, though an important consideration in a practical point of view, merges in a more fundamental objection. Undoubtedly the manner of asserting an opinion, even though it be a true one, may be very objectionable, and may justly incur severe censure. But the principal offenses of the kind are such as it is mostly impossible, unless by accidental self-betrayal, to bring home to conviction. The gravest of them is, to argue sophistically, to suppress facts or arguments, to misstate the elements of the case, or misrepresent the opposite opinion. But all this, even to the most aggravated degree, is so continually done in perfect good faith, by persons who are not considered, and in many other respects may not deserve to be considered, ignorant or incompetent, that it is rarely possible on adequate grounds conscientiously to stamp the misrepresentation as morally culpable; and still less could law presume to interfere with this kind of controversial misconduct. With regard to what is commonly meant by intemperate discussion, namely invective, sarcasm, personality, and the like, the denunciation of these weapons would deserve more sympathy if it were ever proposed to interdict them equally to both sides; but it is only desired to restrain the employment of them against the prevailing opinion: against the unprevailing they may not only be used without general disapproval, but will be likely to obtain for him who uses them the praise of honest zeal and righteous indignation. Yet whatever mischief arises from their use, is greatest when they are employed against the comparatively defenseless; and whatever unfair advantage can be derived by any opinion from this mode of asserting it, accrues almost exclusively to received opinions. The worst offense of this kind which can be committed by a polemic, is to stigmatize those who hold the contrary opinion as bad and immoral men. To calumny of this sort, those who hold any unpopular opinion are peculiarly exposed, because they are in general few and uninfluential, and nobody but themselves feels much interested in seeing justice done them; but this weapon is, from the nature of the case, denied to those who attack a prevailing opinion: they can neither use it with safety to themselves, nor, if they could, would it do anything but recoil on their own cause. In general, opinions contrary to those commonly received can only obtain a hearing by studied moderation of language, and the most cautious avoidance of unnecessary offense, from which they hardly ever deviate even in a slight degree without losing ground: while unmeasured vituperation employed on the side of the prevailing opinion, really does deter people from professing contrary opinions, and from listening to those who profess them. For the interest, therefore, of truth and justice, it is far more important to restrain this employment of vituperative language than the other; and, for example, if it were necessary to choose, there would be much more need to discourage offensive attacks on infidelity, than on religion. It is, however, obvious that law and authority have no business with restraining either, while opinion ought, in every instance, to determine its verdict by the circumstances of the individual case; condemning everyone, on whichever side of the argument he places himself, in whose mode of advocacy either want of candor, or malignity, bigotry, or intolerance of feeling manifest themselves; but not inferring these vices from the side which a person takes, though it be the contrary side of the question to our own: and giving merited honor to everyone, whatever opinion he may hold, who has calmness to see and honesty to state what his opponents and their opinions really are, exaggerating nothing to their discredit, keeping nothing back which tells, or can be supposed to tell, in their favor. This is the real morality of public discussion: and if often violated, I am happy to think that there are many controversialists who to a great extent observe it, and a still greater number who conscientiously strive towards it.

Individuality

It is desirable that in things which do not primarily concern others, individuality should assert itself. Where, not the person's own character, but the traditions or customs of other people are the rule of conduct, there is wanting one of the principal ingredients of human happiness, and quite the chief ingredient of individual and social progress.

In maintaining this principle, the greatest difficulty to be encountered does not lie in the appreciation of means towards an acknowledged end, but in the indifference of persons in general to the end itself. If it were felt that the free development of individuality is one of the leading essentials of well-being; that it is not only a co-ordinate element with all that is designated by the terms civilization, instruction, education, culture, but is itself a necessary part and condition of all those things; there would be no danger that liberty should be undervalued, and the adjustment of the boundaries between it and social control would present no extraordinary difficulty. But the evil is, that individual spontaneity is hardly recognized by the common modes of thinking as having any intrinsic worth, or deserving any regard on its own account. The majority, being satisfied with the ways of mankind as they now are (for it is they who make them what they are), cannot comprehend why those ways should not be good enough for everybody; and what is more, spontaneity forms no part of the ideal of the majority of moral and social reformers, but is rather looked on with jealousy, as a troublesome and perhaps rebellious obstruction to the general acceptance of what these reformers, in their own judgement, think would be best for mankind. Few persons, out of Germany, even comprehend the meaning of the doctrine which Wilhelm von Humboldt, so eminent both as a *savant* and as a politician, made the text of a treatise—that "the end of man, or that which is prescribed by the eternal or immutable dictates of reason, and not suggested by vague and transient desires, is the highest and most harmonious development of his powers to a complete and consistent whole"; that, therefore, the object "towards which every human being must ceaselessly direct his efforts, and on which especially those who design to

From *On Liberty*, 1859.

influence their fellow-men must ever keep their eyes, is the individuality of power and development"; that for this there are two requisites, "freedom, and variety of situations"; and that from the union of these arise "individual vigour and manifold diversity", which combine themselves in "originality".

Little, however, as people are accustomed to a doctrine like that of von Humboldt, and surprising as it may be to them to find so high a value attached to individuality, the question, one must nevertheless think, can only be one of degree. No one's idea of excellence in conduct is that people should do absolutely nothing but copy one another. No one would assert that people ought not to put into their mode of life, and into the conduct of their concerns, any impress whatever of their own judgement, or of their own individual character. On the other hand, it would be absurd to pretend that people ought to live as if nothing whatever had been known in the world before they came into it; as if experience had as yet done nothing towards showing that one mode of existence, or of conduct, is preferable to another. Nobody denies that people should be so taught and trained in youth as to know and benefit by the ascertained results of human experience. But it is the privilege and proper condition of a human being, arrived at the maturity of his faculties, to use and interpret experience in his own way. It is for him to find out what part of recorded experience is properly applicable to his own circumstances and character. The traditions and customs of other people are, to a certain extent, evidence of what their experience has taught *them*; presumptive evidence, and as such, have a claim to his deference: but, in the first place, their experience may be too narrow; or they may not have interpreted it rightly. Secondly, their interpretation of experience may be correct, but unsuitable to him. Customs are made for customary circumstances and customary characters; and his circumstances or his character may be uncustomary. Thirdly, though the customs be both good as customs, and suitable to him, yet to conform to custom, merely *as* custom, does not educate or develop in him any of the qualities which are the distinctive endowment of a human being. The human faculties of perception, judgement, discriminative feeling, mental activity, and even moral preference, are exercised only in making a choice. He who does anything because it is the custom makes no choice. He gains no practice either in discerning or in desiring what is best. The mental and moral, like the muscular powers, are improved only by being used. The faculties are called into no exercise by doing a thing merely because others do it, no more than by believing a thing only because others believe it. If the grounds of an opinion are not conclusive to the person's own reason, his reason cannot be strengthened, but is likely to be weakened, by his adopting it: and if the inducements to an act are not such as are consentaneous to his own feelings and character (where affection, or the rights of others, are not concerned) it is so much done towards rendering his feelings and character inert and torpid, instead of active and energetic. . . .

But society has now fairly got the better of individuality; and the danger which threatens human nature is not the excess, but the deficiency, of personal impulses and preferences. Things are vastly changed since the passions of those who were strong by station or by personal endowment were in a state of habitual rebellion against laws and ordinances, and required to be rigorously chained up to enable the persons within their reach to enjoy any particle of security. In our times, from the highest class of society down to the lowest, every one lives as under the eye of a hostile and dreaded censorship. Not only in what concerns others, but in what concerns only themselves, the individual or the family, do not ask themselves—what do I prefer? or, what would suit my character and disposition? or, what would allow the best and highest in me to have fair play, and enable it to grow and thrive? They ask themselves, what is suitable to my position? what is usually done by persons of my station and pecuniary circumstances? or (worse still) what is usually done by persons of a station and circumstances superior to mine? I do not mean that they choose what is customary in preference to what suits their own inclination. It does not occur to them to have any inclination, except for what is customary. Thus the mind itself is bowed to the yoke: even in what people do for pleasure, conformity is the first thing thought of; they like in crowds; they exercise choice only among things commonly done: peculiarity of taste, eccentricity of conduct, are shunned equally with crimes: until by dint of not following their own nature they have no nature to follow: their human capacities are withered and starved: they become incapable of any strong wishes or native pleasures, and are generally without either opinions or feelings of home growth, or properly their own. Now is this, or is it not, the desirable condition of human nature?

The Limits of Social Authority

What, then, is the rightful limit to the sovereignty of the individual over himself? Where does the authority of society begin? How much of human life should be assigned to individuality, and how much to society?

Each will receive its proper share, if each has that which more particularly concerns it. To individuality should belong the part of life in which it is chiefly the individual that is interested; to society, the part which chiefly interests society.

Though society is not founded on a contract, and though no good purpose is answered by inventing a contract in order to deduce social obligations from it, every one who receives the protection of society owes a return for the benefit, and the fact of living in society renders it indispensable that each should be bound to observe a certain line of conduct towards the rest. This conduct consists, first, in not injuring the interests of one another; or rather interests, which, either by express legal provision or by tacit understanding, ought to be considered as rights; and secondly, in each person's bearing his share (to be fixed on some equitable principle) of the labours and sacrifices incurred for defending the society or its members from injury and molestation. These conditions society is justified in enforcing, at all costs to those who endeavour to withhold fulfilment. Nor is this all that society may do. The acts of an individual may be hurtful to others, or wanting in due consideration for their welfare, without going to the length of violating any of their constituted rights. The offender may then be justly punished by opinion, though not by law. As soon as any part of a person's conduct affects prejudicially the interests of others, society has jurisdiction over it, and the question whether the

From *On Liberty*, 1859.

general welfare will or will not be promoted by interfering with it, becomes open to discussion. But there is no room for entertaining any such question when a person's conduct affects the interests of no persons besides himself, or needs not affect them unless they like (all the persons concerned being of full age, and the ordinary amount of understanding). In all such cases, there should be perfect freedom, legal and social, to do the action and stand the consequences.

It would be a great misunderstanding of this doctrine to suppose that it is one of selfish indifference, which pretends that human beings have no business with each other's conduct in life, and that they should not concern themselves about the well-doing or well-being of one another, unless their own interest is involved. Instead of any diminution, there is need of a great increase of disinterested exertion to promote the good of others. But disinterested benevolence can find other instruments to persuade people to their good than whips and scourges, either of the literal or the metaphorical sort. I am the last person to undervalue the self-regarding virtues; they are only second in importance, if even second, to the social. It is equally the business of education to cultivate both. But even education works by conviction and persuasion as well as by compulsion, and it is by the former only that, when the period of education is passed, the self-regarding virtues should be inculcated. Human beings owe to each other help to distinguish the better from the worse, and encouragement to choose the former and avoid the latter. They should be for ever stimulating each other to increased exercise of their higher faculties, and increased direction of their feelings and aims toward wise instead of foolish, elevating instead of degrading, objects and contemplations. But neither one person, nor any number of persons, is warranted, in saying to another human creature of ripe years, that he shall not do with his life for his own benefit what he chooses to do with it. He is the person most interested in his own well-being: the interest which any other person, except in cases of strong personal attachment, can have in it, is trifling, compared with that which he himself has; the interest which society has in him individually (except as to his conduct to others) is fractional, and altogether indirect; while with respect to his own feelings and circumstances, the most ordinary man or woman has means of knowledge immeasurably surpassing those that can be possessed by any one else. The interference of society to overrule his judgement and purposes in what only regards himself must be grounded on general presumptions, which may be altogether wrong, and even if right, are as likely as not to be misapplied to individual cases, by persons no better acquainted with the circumstances of such cases than those are who look at them merely from without. In this department, therefore, of human affairs, Individuality has its proper field of action. In the conduct of human beings towards one another it is necessary that general rules should for the most part be observed, in order that people may know what they have to expect: but in each person's own concerns his individual spontaneity is entitled to free exercise. Considerations to aid his judgement, exhortations to strengthen his will, may be offered to him, even obtruded on him, by others: but he himself is the final judge. All errors which he is likely to commit against advice and warning are far outweighed by the evil of allowing others to constrain him to what they deem his good. . . .

The distinction here pointed out between the part of a person's life which concerns only himself, and that which concerns others, many persons will refuse to admit. How (it may be asked) can any part of the conduct of a member of society be a matter of indifference to the other members? No person is an entirely isolated being; it is impossible for a person to do anything seriously or permanently hurtful to himself, without mischief reaching at least to his near connections, and often far beyond them. If he injures his property, he does harm to those who directly or indirectly derived support from it, and usually diminishes, by a greater or less amount, the general resources of the community. If he deteriorates his bodily or mental faculties, he not only brings evil upon all who depended on him for any portion of their happiness, but disqualifies himself for rendering the services which he owes to his fellow-creatures generally; perhaps becomes a burthen on their affection or benevolence; and if such conduct were very frequent, hardly any offence that is committed would detract more from the general sum of good. Finally, if by his vices or follies a person does no direct harm to others, he is nevertheless (it may be said) injurious by his example; and ought to be compelled to control himself, for the sake of those whom the sight or knowledge of his conduct might corrupt or mislead.

And even (it will be added) if the consequences of misconduct could be confined to the vicious or thoughtless individual, ought society to abandon to their own guidance those who are manifestly unfit for it? If protection against themselves is confessedly due to children and persons under age, is not society equally bound to afford it to persons of mature years who are equally incapable of self-government? If gambling, or drunkenness, or incontinence, or idleness, or uncleanliness, are as injurious to happiness, and as great a hindrance to improvement, as many or most of the acts prohibited by law, why (it may be asked) should not law, so far as is consistent with practicability and social convenience, endeavour to repress these also? And as a supplement to the unavoidable imperfections of law, ought not opinion at least to organize a powerful police against these vices, and visit rigidly with social penalties those who are known to practise them? There is no question here (it may be said) about restricting individuality, or impeding the trial of new and original experiments in living. The only things it is sought to prevent are things which have been tried and condemned from the beginning of the world until now; things which experience has shown not to be useful or suitable to any person's individuality. There must be some length of time and amount of experience after which a moral or prudential truth may be regarded as established; and it is merely desired to prevent generation after generation from falling over the same precipice which has been fatal to their predecessors.

I fully admit that the mischief which a person does to himself may seriously affect, both through their sympathies and their interests, those nearly connected with him and, in a minor degree, society at large. When, by conduct of this sort, a person is led to violate a distinct and assignable obligation to any other person or persons, the case is taken out of the self-regarding class, and becomes amenable to moral disapprobation in the proper sense of the term. If, for example, a man, through intemperance or extravagance, becomes unable to pay his debts, or, having undertaken the moral responsibility of a family, becomes from the same cause incapable of supporting or educating them, he is deservedly reprobated, and might be justly punished; but it is for the breach of duty to his family or creditors, not for the extravagance. If the resources which ought to have been devoted to them, had been diverted from them for the most prudent investment, the moral culpability would have been the same. George Barnwell murdered his uncle to get money for his mistress, but if he had done it to set himself up in business, he would equally have been hanged. Again, in the frequent case of a man who causes grief to his family by addiction to bad habits, he deserves reproach for his unkindness or ingratitude; but so he may for cultivating habits not in themselves vicious, if they are painful to those with whom he passes his life, or who from personal ties are dependent on him for their comfort. Whoever fails in the consideration generally due to the interests and feelings of others, not being compelled by some more imperative duty, or justified by allowable self-preference, is a subject of moral disapprobation for that failure, but not for the cause of it, nor for the errors, merely personal to himself, which may have remotely led to it. In like manner, when a person disables himself, by conduct purely self-regarding, from the performance of some definite duty incumbent on him to the public, he is guilty of a social offence. No person ought to be punished simply for being drunk; but a soldier or a policeman should be punished for being drunk on duty. Whenever, in short, there is a definite damage, or a definite risk of damage, either to an individual or to the public, the case is taken out of the province of liberty, and placed in that of morality or law.

But with regard to the merely contingent, or, as it may be called, constructive injury which a person causes to society, by conduct which neither violates any specific duty to the public, nor occasions perceptible hurt to any assignable individual except himself; the inconvenience is one which society can afford to bear, for the sake of the greater good of human freedom. If grown persons are to be punished for not taking proper care of themselves, I would rather it were for their own sake, than under pretence of preventing them from impairing their capacity or rendering to society benefits which society does not pretend it has a right to exact. But I cannot consent to argue the point as if society had no means of bringing its weaker members up to its ordinary standard of rational conduct, except waiting till they do something irrational, and then punishing them, legally or morally, for it. Society has had absolute power over them during all the early portion of their existence: it has had the whole period of childhood and nonage in which to try whether it could make them capable of rational conduct in life. The existing generation is master both of the training and the entire circumstances of the generation to come; it cannot indeed make them perfectly wise and good, because it is itself so lamentably deficient in goodness and wisdom; and its best efforts are not always, in individual cases, its most successful ones; but it is perfectly well able to make the rising generation, as a whole, as good as, and a little better than, itself. If society lets any considerable number of its members grow up mere children, incapable of being acted on by rational consideration of distant motives, society has itself to blame for the consequences. Armed not only with all the powers of education, but with the ascendancy which the authority of a received opinion always exercises over the minds who are least fitted to judge for themselves; and aided by the *natural* penalties which cannot be prevented from falling on those who incur the distaste or the contempt of those who know them; let not society pretend that it needs, besides all this, the power to issue commands and enforce obedience in the personal concerns of individuals, in which, on all principles of justice and policy, the decision ought to rest with those who are to abide the consequences. Nor is there anything which tends more to discredit and frustrate the better means of influencing conduct than a resort to the worse. If there be among those whom it is attempted to coerce into prudence or temperance any of the material of which vigorous and independent characters are made, they will infallibly rebel against the yoke. No such person will ever feel that others have a right to control him in his concerns, such as they have to prevent him from injuring them in theirs; and it easily comes to be considered a mark of spirit and courage to fly in the face of such usurped authority, and do with ostentation the exact opposite of what it enjoins; as in the fashion of grossness which succeeded, in the time of Charles II, to the fanatical moral intolerance of the Puritans. With respect to what is said of the necessity of protecting society from the bad example set to others by the vicious or the self-indulgent; it is true that bad example may have a pernicious effect, especially the example of doing wrong to others with impunity to the wrong-doer. But we are now speaking of conduct which, while it does no wrong to others, is supposed to do great harm to the agent himself: and I do not see how those who believe this can think otherwise than that the example, on the whole, must be more salutary than hurtful, since, if it displays the misconduct, it displays also the painful or degrading consequences which, if the conduct is justly censured, must be supposed to be in all or most cases attendant on it.

But the strongest of all the arguments against the interference of the public with purely personal conduct is that, when it does interfere, the odds are that it interferes wrongly, and in the wrong place. On questions of social morality, of duty to others, the opinion of the public, that is, of an overruling majority, though often wrong, is likely to be still oftener right; because on such questions they are only required to judge of their own interests; of the manner in which some mode of conduct, if allowed to be practised, would affect themselves. But the opinion of a similar majority, imposed as a law on the minority, on questions of self-regarding conduct, is quite as likely to be wrong as right; for in these cases public opinion means, at the best, some people's opinion of what is good or bad for other people; while very often it does not even mean that; the public, with the most perfect indifference, passing over the pleasure or convenience of those whose conduct they censure, and considering only their own preference. There are many who consider as an injury to themselves any conduct which they have a distaste for, and resent it as an outrage to their feelings; as a religious bigot, when charged with disregarding the religious feelings of others, has been known to retort that they disregard his feelings, by persisting in their abominable worship or creed. But there is no parity between the feeling of a person for his own opinion, and the feeling of another who is offended at his holding it; no more than between the desire of a thief to take a purse, and the desire of the right owner to keep it. And a person's taste is as much his own peculiar concern as his opinion or his purse. It is easy for any one to imagine an ideal public which leaves the freedom and choice of individuals in all uncertain matters undisturbed, and only requires them to abstain from modes of conduct which universal experience has condemned. But where has there been seen a public which set any such limit to its censorship? or when does the public trouble itself about universal experience? In its interferences with personal conduct it is seldom thinking of anything but the enormity of acting or feeling differently from itself; and this standard of judgement, thinly disguised, is held up to mankind as the dictate of religion and philosophy, by nine-tenths of all moralists and speculative writers. These teach that things are right because they are right; because we feel them to be so. They tell us to search in our own minds and hearts for laws of conduct binding on ourselves and on all others. What can the poor public do but apply these instructions, and make their own personal feelings of good and evil, if they are tolerably unanimous in them, obligatory on all the world?

That the Ideally Best Form of Government Is Representative Government

It has long (perhaps throughout the entire duration of British freedom) been a common saying, that if a good despot could be ensured, despotic monarchy would be the best form of government. I look upon this as a radical and most pernicious misconception of what good government is; which, until it can be got rid of, will fatally vitiate all our speculations on government.

The supposition is, that absolute power, in the hands of an eminent individual, would ensure a virtuous and intelligent performance of all the duties of government. Good laws would be established and enforced, bad laws would be reformed; the best men would be placed in all situations of trust; justice would be as well administered, the public burthens would be as light and as judiciously imposed, every branch of administration would be as purely and as intelligently conducted, as the circumstances of the country and its degree of intellectual and moral cultivation would admit. I am willing, for the sake of the argument, to concede all this; but I must point out how great the concession is; how much more is needed to produce even an approximation to these results than is conveyed in the simple expression, a good despot. Their realization would in fact imply, not merely a good monarch, but an all-seeing one. He must be at all times informed correctly, in considerable detail, of the conduct and working of every branch of adminis-tration, in every district of the country, and must be able, in the twenty-four hours per day which are all that is granted to a king as to the humblest labourer, to give an effective share of attention and superintendence to all parts of this vast field; or he must at least be capable of discerning and choosing out, from among the mass of his subjects, not only a large abundance of honest and able men, fit to conduct every branch of public administration under supervision and control, but also the small number of men of eminent virtues and talents who can be trusted not only to do without that supervision, but to exercise it themselves over others. So extraordinary are the faculties and energies required for performing this task in any supportable manner, that the good despot whom we are supposing can hardly be imagined as consenting to undertake it, unless as a refuge from intolerable evils, and a transitional preparation for something beyond. But the argument can do without even this immense item in the account. Suppose the difficulty vanquished. What should we then have? One man of superhuman mental activity managing the entire affairs of a mentally passive people. Their passivity is implied in the very idea of absolute power. The nation as a whole, and every individual composing it, are without any potential voice in their own destiny. They exercise no will in respect to their collective interests. All is decided for them by a will not their own, which it is legally a crime for them to disobey. What sort of human beings can be formed under such a regimen? What development can either their thinking or their active

From *Considerations on Representative Government*, 1861.

faculties attain under it? On matters of pure theory they might perhaps be allowed to speculate, so long as their speculations either did not approach politics, or had not the remotest connection with its practice. On practical affairs they could at most be only suffered to suggest; and even under the most moderate of despots, none but persons of already admitted or reputed superiority could hope that their suggestions would be known to, much less regarded by, those who had the management of affairs. A person must have a very unusual taste for intellectual exercise in and for itself, who will put himself to the trouble of thought when it is to have no outward effect, or qualify himself for functions which he has no chance of being allowed to exercise. The only sufficient incitement to mental exertion, in any but a few minds in a generation, is the prospect of some practical use to be made of its results. It does not follow that the nation will be wholly destitute of intellectual power. The common business of life, which must necessarily be performed by each individual or family for themselves, will call forth some amount of intelligence and practical ability, within a certain narrow range of ideas. There may be a select class of *savants*, who cultivate science with a view to its physical uses, or for the pleasure of the pursuit. There will be a bureaucracy, and persons in training for the bureaucracy, who will be taught at least some empirical maxims of government and public administration. There may be, and often has been, a systematic organization of the best mental power in the country in some special direction (commonly military) to promote the grandeur of the despot. But the public at large remain without information and without interest on all the greater matters of practice; or, if they have any knowledge of them, it is but a *dilettante* knowledge, like that which people have of the mechanical arts who have never handled a tool. Nor is it only in their intelligence that they suffer. Their moral capacities are equally stunted. Wherever the sphere of action of human beings is artificially circumscribed, their sentiments are narrowed and dwarfed in the same proportion. The food of feeling is action: even domestic affection lives upon voluntary good offices. Let a person have nothing to do for his country, and he will not care for it. It has been said of old, that in a despotism there is at most but one patriot, the despot himself; and the saying rests on a just appreciation of the effects of absolute subjection, even to a good and wise master. Religion remains: and here at least, it may be thought, is an agency that may be relied on for lifting men's eyes and minds above the dust at their feet. But religion, even supposing it to escape perversion for the purposes of despotism, ceases in these circumstances to be a social concern, and narrows into a personal affair between an individual and his Maker, in which the issue at stake is but his private salvation. Religion in this shape is quite consistent with the most selfish and contracted egoism, and identifies the votary as little in feeling with the rest of his kind as sensuality itself.

A good despotism means a government in which, so far as depends on the despot, there is no positive oppression by officers of state, but in which all the collective interests of the people are managed for them, all the thinking that has relation to collective interests done for them, and in which their minds are formed by, and consenting to, this abdication of their own energies. Leaving things to the government, like leaving them to Providence, is synonymous with caring nothing about them, and accepting their results, when disagreeable, as visitations of Nature. With the exception, therefore, of a few studious men who take an intellectual interest in speculation for its own sake, the intelligence and sentiments of the whole people are given up to the material interests, and, when these are provided for, to the amusement and ornamentation, of private life. But to say this is to say, if the whole testimony of history is worth anything, that the era of national decline has arrived: that is, if the nation had ever attained anything to decline from. If it has never risen above the condition of an Oriental people, in that condition it continues to stagnate. But if, like Greece or Rome, it had realized anything higher, through the energy, patriotism, and enlargement of mind, which as national qualities are the fruits solely of freedom, it relapses in a few generations into the Oriental state. And that state does not mean stupid tranquillity, with security against change for the worse; it often means being overrun, conquered, and reduced to domestic slavery, either by a stronger despot, or by the nearest barbarous people who retain along with their savage rudeness the energies of freedom.

Such are not merely the natural tendencies, but the inherent necessities of despotic government; from which there is no outlet, unless in so far as the despotism consents not to be despotism; in so far as the supposed good despot abstains from exercising his power, and, though holding it in reserve, allows the general business of government to go on as if the people really governed themselves. However little probable it may be, we may imagine a despot observing many of the rules and restraints of constitutional government. He might allow such freedom of the press and of discussion as would enable a public opinion to form and express itself on national affairs. He might suffer local interests to be managed, without the interference of authority, by the people themselves. He might even surround himself with a council or councils of government, freely chosen by the whole or some portion of the nation; retaining in his own hands the power of taxation, and the supreme legislative as well as executive authority. Were he to act thus, and so far abdicate as a despot, he would do away with a considerable part of the evils characteristic of despotism. Political activity and capacity for public affairs would no longer be prevented from growing up in the body of the nation; and a public opinion would form itself not the mere echo of the government. But such improvement would be the beginning of new difficulties. This public opinion, independent of the monarch's dictation, must be either with him or against him; if not the one, it will be the other. All governments must displease many persons, and these having now regular organs, and being able to express their sentiments, opinions adverse to the measures of government would often be expressed. What is the monarch to do when these unfavourable opinions happen to be in the majority? Is he to alter his course? Is he to defer to the nation? If so, he is no longer a despot, but a constitutional king; an organ or first minister of the people, distinguished only by being irremovable. If not, he must either put down opposition by his despotic power, or there will arise a permanent antagonism between the people and one man, which can have but one possible ending. Not even a religious principle of passive obedience and "right divine" would long ward off the natural consequences of such a position. The monarch would have to succumb, and conform to the conditions of constitutional royalty, or give place to some one who would. The despotism, being thus chiefly nominal, would possess few of the advantages supposed to belong to absolute monarchy; while it would realize in a very imperfect degree those of a free government; since however great an amount of liberty the citizens might practically enjoy, they could never forget that they held it on sufferance, and by a concession which under the existing constitution of the state might at any moment be resumed; that they were legally slaves, though of a prudent, or indulgent, master.

It is not much to be wondered at if impatient or disappointed reformers, groaning under the impediments opposed to the most salutary public improvements by the ignorance, the indifference, the intractableness, the perverse obstinacy of a people, and the corrupt combinations of selfish private interests armed with the powerful weapons afforded by free institutions, should at times sigh for a strong hand to bear down all these obstacles, and compel a recalcitrant people to be better governed. But (setting aside the fact, that for one despot who now and then reforms an abuse, there are ninety-nine who do nothing but create them) those who look in any such direction for the realization of their hopes leave out of the idea of good government its principal element, the improvement of the people themselves. One of the benefits of freedom is that under it the ruler cannot pass by the people's minds, and amend their affairs for them without amending them. If it were possible for the people to be well governed in spite of themselves, their good government would last no longer than the freedom of a people usually lasts who have been liberated by foreign arms without their own co-operation. It is true, a despot may educate the people; and to do so really, would be the best apology for his despotism. But any education which aims at making human beings other than machines, in the long run makes them claim to have the control of their own actions. The leaders of French philosophy in the eighteenth century had been educated by the Jesuits. Even Jesuit education, it seems, was sufficiently real to call forth the appetite for freedom. Whatever invigorates the faculties, in however small a measure, creates an increased desire for their more unimpeded exercise; and a popular education is a failure, if it educates the people for any state but that which it will certainly induce them to desire, and most probably to demand.

I am far from condemning, in cases of extreme exigency, the assumption of absolute power in the form of a temporary dictatorship. Free nations have, in times of old, conferred such power by their own choice, as a necessary medicine for diseases of the body politic which could not be got rid of by less violent means. But its acceptance, even for a time strictly limited, can only be excused, if, like Solon or Pittacus, the dictator employs the whole power he assumes in removing the obstacles which debar the nation from the enjoyment of freedom. A good despotism is an altogether false ideal, which practically (except as a means to some temporary purpose) becomes the most senseless and dangerous of chimeras. Evil for evil, a good despotism, in a country at all advanced in civilization, is more noxious than a bad one; for it is far more relaxing and enervating to the thoughts, feelings, and energies of the people. The despotism of Augustus prepared the Romans for Tiberius. If the whole tone of their character had not first been prostrated by nearly two generations of that mild slavery, they would probably have had spirit enough left to rebel against the more odious one.

There is no difficulty in showing that the ideally best form of government is that in which the sovereignty, or supreme controlling power in the last resort, is vested in the entire aggregate of the community; every citizen not only having a voice in the exercise of that ultimate sovereignty, but being, at least occasionally, called on to take an actual part in the government, by the personal discharge of some public function, local or general.

To test this proposition, it has to be examined in reference to the two branches into which the inquiry into the goodness of a government conveniently divides itself, namely, how far it promotes the good management of the affairs of society by means of the existing faculties, moral, intellectual, and active, of its various members, and what is its effect in improving or deteriorating those faculties.

The ideally best form of government, it is scarcely necessary to say, does not mean one which is practicable or eligible in all states of civilization, but the one which, in the circumstances in which it is practicable and eligible, is attended with the greatest amount of beneficial consequences, immediate and prospective. A completely popular government is the only polity which can make out any claim to this character. It is pre-eminent in both the departments between which the excellence of a political constitution is divided. It is both more favourable to present good government, and promotes a better and higher form of national character, than any other polity whatsoever.

Its superiority in reference to present well-being rests upon two principles, of as universal truth and applicability as any general propositions which can be laid down respecting human affairs. The first is, that the rights and interests of every or any person are only secure from being disregarded when the person interested is himself able, and habitually disposed, to stand up for them. The second is, that the general prosperity attains a greater height, and is more widely diffused, in proportion to the amount and variety of the personal energies enlisted in promoting it.

Putting these two propositions into a shape more special to their present application; human beings are only secure from evil at the hands of others in proportion as they have the power of being, and are, self-*protecting*; and they only achieve a high degree of success in their struggle with Nature in proportion as they are self-*dependent*, relying on what they themselves can do, either separately or in concert, rather than on what others do for them.

The former proposition—that each is the only safe guardian of his own rights and interests—is one of those elementary maxims of prudence, which every person, capable of conducting his own affairs, implicitly acts upon, wherever he himself is interested. Many, indeed, have a great dislike to it as a political doctrine, and are fond of holding it up to obloquy, as a doctrine of universal selfishness. To which we may answer, that whenever it ceases to be true that mankind, as a rule, prefer themselves to others, and those nearest to them to those more remote from that moment Communism is not only practicable, but the only defensible form of society; and will, when that time arrives, be assuredly carried into effect. For my own part, not believing in universal selfishness, I have no difficulty in admitting that Communism would even now be practicable among the *élite* of mankind, and may become so among the rest. But as this opinion is anything but popular with those defenders of existing institutions who find fault with the doctrine of the general predominance of self-interest, I am inclined to think they do in reality believe that most men consider themselves before other people. It is not, however, necessary to affirm even thus much in order to support the claim of all to participate in the sovereign power. We need not suppose that when power resides in an exclusive class, that class will knowingly and deliberately sacrifice the other classes to themselves: it suffices that, in the absence of its natural defenders, the interest of the excluded is always in danger of being overlooked; and, when looked at, is seen with very different eyes from those of the persons whom it directly concerns. In this country, for example, what are called the working classes may be considered as excluded from all direct participation in the government. I do not believe that the classes who do participate in it have in general any intention of sacrificing the working classes to themselves. They once had that intention; witness the persevering attempts so long made to keep down wages by law. But in the present day their ordinary disposition is the very opposite: they willingly make considerable sacrifices, especially of their pecuniary interest, for the benefit of the working classes, and err rather by too lavish and indiscriminating beneficence; nor do I believe that any rulers in history have been actuated by a more sincere desire to do their duty towards the poorer portion of their countrymen. Yet does Parliament, or almost any of the members composing it, ever for an instant look at any question with the eyes of a working man? When a subject arises in which the labourers as such have an interest, is it regarded from any point of view but that of the employers of labour? I do not say that the working men's view of these questions is in general nearer to the truth than the other: but it is sometimes quite as near; and in any case it ought to be respectfully listened to, instead of being, as it is, not merely turned away from, but ignored. . . .

It is an adherent condition of human affairs that no intention, however sincere, of protecting the interests of others can make it safe or salutary to tie up their own hands. Still more obviously true is it, that by their own hands only can any positive and durable improvement of their circumstances in life be worked out. Through the joint influence of these two principles, all free communities have both been more exempt from social injustice and crime, and have attained more brilliant prosperity, than any others, or than they themselves after they lost their freedom. Contrast the free states of the world, while their freedom lasted, with the contemporary subjects of monarchical or oligarchical despotism: the Greek cities with the Persian satrapies; the Italian republics and the free towns of Flanders and Germany, with the feudal monarchies of Europe; Switzerland, Holland, and England, with Austria or ante-revolutionary France. Their superior prosperity was too obvious ever to have been gainsaid: while their superiority in good government and social relations is proved by the prosperity, and is manifest besides in every page of history. If we compare, not one age with another, but the different governments which co-existed in the same age, no amount of disorder which exaggeration itself can pretend to have existed amidst the publicity of the free states can be compared for a moment with the contemptuous trampling upon the mass of the people which pervaded the whole life of the monarchical countries, or the disgusting individual tyranny which was of more than daily occurrence under the systems of plunder which they called fiscal arrangements, and in the secrecy of their frightful courts of justice.

It must be acknowledged that the benefits of freedom, so far as they have hitherto been enjoyed, were obtained by the extension of its privileges to a part only of the community; and that a government in which they are extended impartially to all is a desideratum still unrealized. But though every approach to this has an independent value, and in many cases more than an approach could not, in the existing state of general improvement, be made, the participation of all in these benefits is the ideally perfect conception of free government. In proportion as any, no matter who, are excluded from it, the interests of the excluded are left without the guarantee accorded to the rest, and they themselves have less scope and encouragement than they might otherwise have to that exertion of their energies for the good of themselves and of the community, to which the general prosperity is always proportioned.

Thus stands the case as regards present well-being; the good management of the affairs of the existing generation. If we now pass to the influence of the form of government upon character, we shall find the superiority of popular government over every other to be, if possible, still more decided and indisputable.

This question really depends upon a still more fundamental one, viz., which of two common types of character, for the general good of humanity, it is most desirable should predominate—the active, or the passive type; that which struggles against evils, or that which endures them; that which bends to circumstances, or that which endeavours to make circumstances bend to itself.

The commonplaces of moralists, and the general sympathies of mankind, are in favour of the passive type. Energetic characters may be admired, but the acquiescent and submissive are those which most men personally prefer. The passiveness of our neighbours increases our sense of security, and plays into the hands of our wilfulness. Passive characters, if we do not happen to need their activity, seem an obstruction the less in our own path. A contented character is not a dangerous rival. Yet nothing is more certain than that improvement in human affairs is wholly the work of the uncontented characters; and, moreover, that it is much easier for an active mind to acquire the virtues of patience than for a passive one to assume those of energy. . . .

The only government which can fully satisfy all the exigencies of the social state is one in which the whole people participate; that any participation, even in the smallest public function, is useful; that the participation should everywhere be as great as the general degree of improvement of the community will allow; and that nothing less can be ultimately desirable than the admission of all to a share in the sovereign power of the state. But since all cannot, in a community exceeding a single small town, participate personally in any but some very minor portions of the public business, it follows that the ideal type of a perfect government must be representative.

The Nature of Democracy
John Dewey

John Dewey (1859-1952), one of America's outstanding philosophers, wrote upon topics in all the major fields of philosophy and was widely influential for his treatment of problems in education, social psychology, and politics. His major works include *Democracy and Education* (1916), *Reconstruction in Philosophy* (1920), *Liberalism and Social Action* (1935), and *Freedom and Culture* (1939).

. . . Democracy is much broader than a special political form, a method of conducting government, of making laws and carrying on governmental administration by means of popular suffrage and elected officers. It is that, of course. But it is something broader and deeper than that. The political and governmental phase of

From an address delivered to the National Education Association, February 22, 1937, and published under the title "Democracy and Educational Administration" in *School and Society*, 45 (April 3, 1937), 457-467.

democracy is a means, the best means so far found, for realizing ends that lie in the wide domain of human relationships and the development of human personality. It is, as we often say, though perhaps without appreciating all that is involved in the saying, a way of life, social and individual. The key-note of democracy as a way of life may be expressed, it seems to me, as the necessity for the participation of every mature human being in formation of the values that regulate the living of men together: which is necessary from the standpoint of both the general social welfare and the full development of human beings as individuals.

Universal suffrage, recurring elections, responsibility of those who are in political power to the voters, and the other factors of democratic government are means that have been found expedient for realizing democracy as the truly human way of living. They are not a final end and a final value. They are to be judged on the basis of their contribution to end. It is a form of idolatry to erect means into the end which they serve. Democratic political forms are simply the best means that human wit has devised up to a special time in history. But they rest back upon the idea that no man or limited set of men is wise enough or good enough to rule others without their consent; the positive meaning of this statement is that all those who are affected by social institutions must have a share in producing and managing them. The two facts that each one is influenced in what he does and enjoys and in what he becomes by the institutions under which he lives, and that therefore he shall have, in a democracy, a voice in shaping them, are the passive and active sides of the same fact.

The development of political democracy came about through substitution of the method of mutual consultation and voluntary agreement for the method of subordination of the many to the few enforced from above. Social arrangements which involve fixed subordination are maintained by coercion. The coercion need not be physical. There have existed, for short periods, benevolent despotisms. But coercion of some sort there has been; perhaps economic, certainly psychological and moral. The very fact of exclusion from participation is a subtle form of suppression. It gives individuals no opportunity to reflect and decide upon what is good for them. Others who are supposed to be wiser and who in any case have more power decide the question for them and also decide the methods and means by which subjects may arrive at the enjoyment of what is good for them. This form of coercion and suppression is more subtle and more effective than is overt intimidation and restraint. When it is habitual and embodied in social institutions, it seems the normal and natural state of affairs. The mass usually become unaware that they have a claim to a development of their own powers. Their experience is so restricted that they are not conscious of restriction. It is part of the democratic conception that they as individuals are not the only sufferers, but that the whole social body is deprived of the potential resources that should be at its service. The individuals of the submerged mass may not be very wise. But there is one thing they are wiser about than anybody else can be, and that is where the shoe pinches, the troubles they suffer from.

The foundation of democracy is faith in the capacities of human nature; faith in human intelligence and in the power of pooled and cooperative experience. It is not belief that these things are complete but that if given a show they will grow and be able to generate progressively the knowledge and wisdom needed to guide collective action. Every autocratic and authoritarian scheme of social action rests on a belief that the needed intelligence is confined to a superior few, who because of inherent natural gifts are endowed with the ability and the right to control the conduct of others; laying down principles and rules and directing the ways in which they are carried out. It would be foolish to deny that much can be said for this point of view. It is that which controlled human relations in social groups for much the greater part of human history. The democratic faith has emerged very, very recently in the history of mankind. Even where democracies now exist, men's minds and feelings are still permeated with ideas about leadership imposed from above, ideas that developed in the long early history of mankind. After democratic political institutions were nominally established, beliefs and ways of looking at life and of acting that originated when men and women were externally controlled and subjected to arbitrary power, persisted in the family, the church, business and the school, and experience shows that as long as they persist there, political democracy is not secure.

Belief in equality is an element of the democratic credo. It is not, however, belief in equality of natural endowments. Those who proclaimed the idea of equality did not suppose they were enunciating a psychological doctrine, but a legal and political one. All individuals are entitled to equality of treatment by law and in its administration. Each one is affected equally in quality if not in quantity by the institutions under which he lives and has an equal right to express his judgment, although the weight of his judgment may not be equal in amount when it enters into the pooled result to that of others. In short, each one is equally an individual and entitled to equal opportunity of development of his own capacities, be they large or small in range. Moreover, each has needs of his own, as significant to him as those of others are to them. The very fact of natural and psychological inequality is all the more reason for establishment by law of equality of opportunity, since otherwise the former becomes a means of oppression of the less gifted.

While what we call intelligence be distributed in unequal amounts, it is the democratic faith that it is sufficiently general so that each individual has something to contribute, whose value can be assessed only as enters into the final pooled intelligence constituted by the contributions of all. Every authoritarian scheme, on the contrary, assumes that its value may be assessed by some *prior* principle, if not of family and birth or race and color or possession of material wealth, then by the position and rank a person occupies in the existing social scheme. The democratic faith in equality is the faith that each individual shall have the chance and opportunity to contribute whatever he is capable of contributing and that the value of his contribution be decided by its place and function in the organized total of similar contributions, not on the basis of prior status of any kind whatever.

I have emphasized in what precedes the importance of the effective release of intelligence in connection with personal experience in the democratic way of living. I have done so purposely because democracy is so often and so naturally associated in our minds with freedom of *action*, forgetting the importance of freed intelligence which is necessary to direct and to warrant freedom of action. Unless freedom of individual action has intelligence and informed conviction back of it, its manifestation is almost sure to result in confusion and disorder. The democratic idea of freedom is not the right of each individual to *do* as he pleases, even if it be qualified by adding "provided he does not interfere with the same freedom on the part of others." While the idea is not always, not often enough, expressed in words, the basic freedom is that of freedom of *mind* and of whatever degree of freedom of action and experience is necessary to produce freedom of intelligence. The modes of freedom guaranteed in the Bill of Rights are all of this nature: Freedom of belief and conscience, of expression of opinion, of assembly for discussion and conference, of the press as an organ of communication. They are guaranteed because without them individuals are not free to develop and society is deprived of what they might contribute.

It is a disputed question of theory and practice just how far a democratic political government should go in control of the conditions of action within special groups. At the present time, for example, there are those who think the federal and state governments leave too much freedom of independent action to industrial and financial groups, and there are others who think the government is going altogether too far at the present time. I do not need to discuss this phase of the problem, much less to try to settle it. But it must be pointed out that if the methods of regulation and administration in vogue in the conduct of secondary social groups are non-democratic, whether directly or indirectly or both, there is bound to be unfavorable reaction back into the habits of feeling, thought and action of citizenship in the broadest sense of that word. The way in which any organized social interest is controlled necessarily plays an important part in forming the dispositions and tastes, the attitudes, interests, purposes and desires, of those engaged in carrying on the activities of the group. For illustration, I do not need to do more than point to the moral, emotional and intellectual effect upon both employers and laborers of the existing industrial system. Just what the effects specifically are is a matter about which we know very little. But I suppose that every one who reflects upon the subject admits that it is impossible that the ways in which activities are carried on for the greater part of the waking hours of the day; and the way in which the share of individuals are involved in the management of affairs in such a matter as gaining a livelihood and attaining material and social security, can not but be a highly important factor in shaping personal dispositions; in short, forming character and intelligence.

In the broad and final sense all institutions are educational in the sense that they operate to form the attitudes, dispositions, abilities and disabilities that constitute a concrete personality. The principle applies with special force to the school. For it is the main business of the family and the school to influence directly the formation and growth of attitudes and dispositions, emotional, intellectual and moral. Whether this educative process is carried on in a predominantly democratic or non-democratic way becomes, therefore, a question of transcendent importance not only for education itself but for its final effect upon all the interests and activities of a society that is committed to the democratic way of life.

. . . there are certain corollaries which clarify the meaning of the issue. Absence of participation tends to produce lack of interest and concern on the part of those shut out. The result is a corresponding lack of effective responsibility. Automatically and unconsciously, if not consciously, the feeling develops, "This is none of our affair; it is the business of those at the top; let that particular set of Georges do what needs to be done." The countries in which autocratic government prevails are just those in which there is least public spirit and the greatest indifference to matters of general as distinct from personal concern.

. . . Where there is little power, there is correspondingly little sense of positive responsibility. It is enough to do what one is told to do sufficiently well to escape flagrant unfavorable notice. About larger matters, a spirit of passivity is engendered. In some cases, indifference passes into evasion of duties when not directly under the eye of a supervisor; in other cases, a carping, rebellious spirit is engendered. . . . habitual exclusion has the effect of reducing a sense of responsibility for what is done and its consequences. What the argument for democracy implies is that the best way to produce initiative and constructive power is to exercise it. Power, as well as interest, comes by use and practice. . . . It is also true that incapacity to assume the responsibilities involved in having a voice in shaping policies is bred and increased by conditions in which that responsibility is denied. I suppose there has never been an autocrat, big or little, who did not justify his conduct on the ground of the unfitness of his subjects to take part in government.

. . . I conclude by saying that the present subject is one of peculiar importance at the present time. The fundamental beliefs and practices of democracy are now challenged as they never have been before. In some nations they are more than challenged. They are ruthlessly and systematically destroyed. Everywhere there are waves of criticism and doubt as to whether democracy can meet pressing problems of order and security. The causes for the destruction of political democracy in countries where it was nominally established are complex. But of one thing I think we may be sure. Wherever it has fallen it was too exclusively political in nature. It had not become part of the bone and blood of the people in daily conduct of its life. Democratic forms were limited to Parliament, elections and combats between parties. What is happening proves conclusively, I think, that unless democratic habits of thought and action are part of the fiber of a people, political democracy is insecure. It can not stand in isolation. It must be buttressed by the presence of democratic methods in all social relationships. The relations that exist in educational institutions are second only in importance in this respect to those which exist in industry and business, perhaps not even to them.

The Future of Liberalism

The emphasis of earlier liberalism upon individuality and liberty defines the focal points in discussion of the philosophy of liberalism today. This earlier liberalism was itself an outgrowth, in the late eighteenth and nineteenth centuries, of the earlier revolt against oligarchical government, one which came to its culmination in the "glorious revolution" of 1688. The latter was fundamentally a demand for freedom of the taxpayer from government arbitrary action in connection with a demand for confessional freedom in religion by the Protestant churches. In the later liberalism, expressly so called, the demand for liberty and individual freedom of action came primarily from the rising industrial and trading class and was directed against restrictions placed by government, in legislation, common law and judicial action, and other institutions having connection with the political state, upon freedom of economic enterprise. In both cases, governmental action and the desired freedom were placed in antithesis to each other. This way of conceiving liberty has

From John Dewey, "The Future of Liberalism," *The Journal of Philosophy*, April 25, 1935, pp. 225-230. Reprinted by permission.

persisted; it was strengthened in this country by the revolt of the colonies and by pioneer conditions.

Nineteenth-century philosophic liberalism added, more or less because of its dominant economic interest, the conception of natural laws to that of natural rights of the Whig movement. There are natural laws, it held, in social matters as well as in physical, and these natural laws are economic in character. Political laws, on the other hand, are man-made and in that sense artificial. Governmental intervention in industry and exchange was thus regarded as a violation not only of inherent individual liberty but also of natural laws—of which supply and demand is a sample. The proper sphere of governmental action was simply to prevent and to secure redress for infringement by one, in the exercise of his liberty, of like and equal liberty of action on the part of others.

Nevertheless, the demand for freedom in initiation and conduct of business enterprise did not exhaust the content of earlier liberalism. In the minds of its chief promulgators there was included an equally strenuous demand for the liberty of mind, freedom of thought and its expression in speech, writing, print, and assemblage. The earlier interest in confessional freedom was generalized, and thereby deepened as well as broadened. This demand was a product of the rational enlightenment of the eighteenth century and of the growing importance of science. The great tide of reaction that set in after the defeat of Napoleon, the demand for order and discipline, gave the agitation for freedom of thought and its expression plenty of cause and plenty of opportunity.

The earlier liberal philosophy rendered valiant service. It finally succeeded in sweeping away, especially in its home, Great Britain, an innumerable number of abuses and restrictions. The history of social reforms in the nineteenth century is almost one with the history of liberal social thought. It is not, then, from ingratitude that I shall emphasize its defects, for recognition of them is essential to an intelligent statement of the elements of liberal philosophy for the present and any nearby future. The fundamental defect was lack of perception of historic relativity. This lack is expressed in the conception of the individual as something given, complete in itself, and of liberty as a ready-made possession of the individual, only needing the removal of external restrictions in order to manifest itself. The individual of earlier liberalism was a Newtonian atom having only external time and space relations to other individuals, save that each social atom was equipped with inherent freedom. These ideas might not have been especially harmful if they had been merely a rallying cry for practical movements. But they formed part of a philosophy and of a philosophy in which these particular ideas of individuality and freedom were asserted to be absolute and eternal truths; good for all times and all places.

This absolutism, this ignoring and denial of temporal relativity, is one great reason why the earlier liberalism degenerated so easily into pseudo-liberalism. For the sake of saving time, I shall identify what I mean by this spurious liberalism, the kind of social ideas represented by the "Liberty League" and ex-President Hoover. I call it a pseudo-liberalism because it ossified and narrowed generous ideas and aspirations. Even when words remain the same, they mean something very different when they are uttered by a minority struggling against repressive measures and when expressed by a group that, having attained power, then uses ideas that were once weapons of emancipation as instruments for keeping the power and wealth it has obtained. Ideas that at one time are means of producing social change assume another guise when they are used as means of preventing further social change. This fact is itself an illustration of historic relativity, and an evidence of the evil that lay in the assertion by earlier liberalism of the immutable and eternal character of their ideas. Because of this latter fact, the *laissez-faire* doctrine was held by the degenerate school of liberals to express the very order of nature itself. The outcome was the degradation of the idea of individuality, until in the minds of many who are themselves struggling for a wider and fuller development of individuality, individualism has become a term of hissing and reproach, while many can see no remedy for the evils that have come from the use of socially unrestrained liberty in business enterprise, save change produced by violence. The historic tendency to conceive the whole question of liberty as a matter in which individual and government are opposed parties has borne bitter fruit. Born of despotic government, it has continued to influence thinking and action after government had become popular and *in theory* the servant of the people.

I pass now to what tne social philosophy of liberalism becomes when its inheritance of absolutism is eliminated. In the first place such liberalism knows that an individual is nothing fixed, given ready-made. It is something achieved, and achieved not in isolation, but the aid and support of conditions, cultural and physical, including in "cultural" economic, legal, and political institutions as well as science and art. Liberalism knows that social conditions may restrict, distort, and almost prevent the development of individuality. It therefore takes an active interest in the working of social institutions that have a bearing, positive or negative, upon the growth of individuals who shall be rugged in fact and not merely in abstract theory. It is as much interested in the positive construction of favorable institutions, legal, political, and economic, as it is in the work of removing abuses and overt oppressions.

In the second place, liberalism is committed to the idea of historic relativity. It knows that the content of the individual and freedom change with time; that this is as true of social change as it is of individual development from infancy to maturity. The positive counterpart of opposition to doctrinal absolutism is experimentalism. The connection between historic relativity and experimental method is intrinsic. Time signifies change. The significance of individuality with respect to social policies alters with change of the conditions in which individuals live. The earlier liberalism in being absolute was also unhistoric. Underlying it there was a philosophy of history which assumed that history, like time in the Newtonian scheme, means only modification of external relations; that is quantitative, not equalitative and internal. The same thing is true of any theory that assumes, like the one usually attributed to Marx, that temporal changes in society are inevitable—that is to say, are governed by a law that is not itself historical. The fact is that the historicism and the evolutionism of nineteenth-century doctrine were only half-way doctrines. They assumed that historical and developmental processes were subject to some law or formula outside temporal processes.

The commitment of liberalism to experimental procedure carries with it the idea of continuous reconstruction of the ideas of individuality and of liberty in intimate connection with changes in social relations. It is enough to refer to the changes in productivity and distribution since the time when the earlier liberalism was formulated, and the effect of these transformations, due to science and technology, upon the terms on which men associate together. An experimental method is the recognition of this temporal change in ideas and policies so that the latter shall coördinate with the facts instead of being opposed to them. Any other view maintains a rigid conceptualism and implies that facts should conform to concepts that are framed independently of temporal or historical change.

The two things essential, then, to thorough-going social liberalism are, first, realistic study of existing conditions in their movement, and, secondly, leading ideas, in the form of policies for dealing with these conditions in the interest of development of increased individuality and liberty. The first requirement is so obviously implied that I shall not elaborate it. The second point needs some amplification. Experimental method is not just messing around nor doing a little of this and a little of that in the hope that things will improve. Just as in the physical sciences, it implies a coherent body of ideas, a theory, that gives direction to effort. What is implied, in contrast to every form of absolutism, is that the ideas and theory be taken as methods of action tested and continuously revised by the consequences they produce in actual social conditions. Since they are operational in nature, they modify conditions, while the first requirement, that of basing them upon realistic study of actual conditions, brings about their continuous reconstruction.

It follows finally that there is no opposition in principle between liberalism as social philosophy and radicalism in action, if by radicalism is signified the adoption of policies that bring about drastic instead of piece-meal social changes. It is all a question of what kind of procedures the intelligent study of changing conditions discloses. These changes have been so tremendous in the last century, yes, in the last forty years, that it looks to me as if radical methods were now necessary. But all that the argument here requires is recognition of the fact that there is nothing in the nature of liberalism that makes it a milk-water doctrine, committed to compromise and minor "reforms." It is worth noting that the earlier liberals were regarded in their day as subversive radicals.

What has been said should make it clear that the question of method in formation and execution of policies is the central thing in liberalism. The method indicated is that of maximum reliance upon intelligence. This fact determines its opposition to those forms of radicalism that place chief dependence upon violent overthrow of existing institutions as the method of effecting desired social change. A genuine liberal will emphasize as crucial the complete correlation between the means used and the consequences that follow. The same principle which makes him aware that the means employed by pseudo-liberalism only perptetuate and multiply the evils of existing conditions, makes him also aware that dependence upon sheer massed force as the means of social change decides the kind of consequences that actually result. Doctrines, whether proceeding from Mussolini or from Marx, which assume that because certain ends are desirable therefore those ends and nothing else will result from the use of force to attain them is but another example of the limitations put upon intelligence by any absolute theory. In the degree in which mere force is resorted to, actual consequences are themselves so compromised that the ends originally in view have in fact to be worked out afterwards by the method of experimental intelligence.

In saying this, I do not wish to be understood as meaning that radicals of the type mentioned have any monopoly of the use of force. The contrary is the case. The reactionaries are in possession of force, in not only the army and police, but in the press and the schools. The only reason they do not advocate the use of force is the fact that they are already in possession of it, so their policy is to cover up its existence with idealistic phrases—of which their present use of individual initiative and liberty is a striking example.

Democracy as Polyarchy
Robert A. Dahl

Robert A. Dahl (1915-) is a Professor of Political Science at Yale. He has been President of the American Political Science Association. He is the author of *Who Governs?* (1961); *Modern Political Analysis* (1963); and *Politics, Economics, and Welfare* (1953).

Polyarchy is defined loosely as a political system in which the following conditions exist to a relatively high degree:

DURING THE VOTING PERIOD

1. Every member of the organization performs the acts we assume to constitute an expression of preference among the scheduled alternatives, e.g., voting.
2. In tabulating these expressions (votes), the weight assigned to the choice of each individual is identical.
3. The alternative with the greatest number of votes is declared the winning choice.

DURING THE PREVOTING PERIOD

4. Any member who perceives a set of alternatives, at least one of which he regards as preferable to any of the alternatives presently scheduled, can insert his preferred alternative(s) among those scheduled for voting.
5. All individuals possess identical information about the alternatives.

DURING THE POSTVOTING PERIOD

6. Alternatives (leaders or policies) with the greatest number of votes displace any alternatives (leaders or policies) with fewer votes.
7. The orders of elected officials are executed.

DURING THE INTERELECTION STAGE

8.1. Either all interelection decisions are subordinate or executory to those arrived at during the election stage, i.e., elections are in a sense controlling.
8.2. Or new decisions during the interelection period are governed by the

preceding seven conditions, operating, however, under rather different institutional circumstances.

8.3. Or both.

I think it may be laid down dogmatically that no human organization—certainly none with more than a handful of people—has ever met or is ever likely to meet these eight conditions. It is true that the second, third, and sixth conditions are quite precisely met in some organizations, although in the United States corrupt practices sometimes nullify even these; the others are, at best, only crudely approximated.

As to the first, evidently in all human organizations there are significant variations in participation in political decisions—variations which in the United States appear to be functionally related to such variables as degree of concern or involvement, skill, access, socioeconomic status, education, residence, age, ethnic and religious identifications, and some little understood personality characteristics. As is well known, in national elections on the average something like half of all adults in the United States go to the polls; only a quarter do anything more than vote: write to their congressmen, for example, or contribute to campaigns, or attempt to persuade others to adopt their political views. In the 1952 election, of one nationwide sample only 11 per cent helped the political parties financially, attended party gatherings, or worked for one of the parties or candidates; only 27 per cent talked to other people to try to show them why they should vote for one of the parties or candidates. The effective political elites, then, operate within limits often vague and broad, although occasionally narrow and well defined, set by their expectations as to the reaction of the group of politically active citizens who go to the polls. Other organizations, such as trade-unions, where political equality is prescribed in the formal charter, operate in much the same way, although the elites and the politically active members are often even a smaller proportion of the total.

In no organization of which I have any knowledge does the fourth condition exist. Perhaps the condition is most closely approximated in very small groups. Certainly in all large groups for which we have any data, control over communication is so unevenly distributed that some individuals possess considerably more influence over the designation of the alternatives scheduled for voting than do others. I do not know how to quantify this control, but if it could be quantified I suppose that it would be no exaggeration to say that Mr. Henry Luce[1] has a thousand or ten thousand times greater control over the alternatives scheduled for debate and tentative decision at a national election than I do. Although we have here a formidable problem that so far as I know has never been adequately analyzed, it is a reasonable preliminary hypothesis that the number of individuals who exercise significant control over the alternatives scheduled is, in most organizations, only a tiny fraction of the total membership. This seems to be the case even in the most democratic organizations if the membership is at all large.

Much the same remarks apply to the fifth condition. The gap in information between the political elites and the active members—not to say the inactive members—no doubt is almost always great. In recent times the gap has been further widened in national governments by growing technical complexities and the rapid spread of security regulations. As every student of bureaucracy knows, the seventh

[1] Recent owner of Time-Life, Inc. [Ed.]

condition is the source of serious difficulties; however the extent to which this condition is achieved is perhaps the most puzzling of all to measure objectively.

If elections, like the market, were continuous, then we should have no need of the eighth condition. But of course elections are only periodic. It is sometimes suggested that the interelection pressures on decision processes are a kind of election, but this is at best only a deceptive metaphor. . . .

Because human organizations rarely and perhaps never reach the limit set by these eight conditions, it is necessary to interpret each of these conditions as one end of a continuum or scale along which any given organization might be measured. Unfortunately there is at present no known way of assigning meaningful weights to the eight conditions. However, even without weights, if the eight scales could each be metricized, it would be possible and perhaps useful to establish some arbitrary but not meaningless classes of which the upper chunk might be called "polyarchies."

It is perfectly evident, however, that what has just been described is no more than a program, for nothing like it has, I think, ever been attempted. I shall simply set down here, therefore, the following observations. Organizations do in fact differ markedly in the extent to which they approach the limits set by these eight conditions. Furthermore, "polyarchies" include a variety of organizations which Western political scientists would ordinarily call democratic, including certain aspects of the governments of nation states such as the United States, Great Britain, the Dominions (South Africa possibly excepted), the Scandinavian countries, Mexico, Italy, and France; states and provinces, such as the states of this country and the provinces of Canada; numerous cities and towns; some trade-unions; numerous associations such as Parent-Teachers' Associations, chapters of the League of Women Voters, and some religious groups; and some primitive societies. Thus it follows that the number of polyarchies is large. (The number of egalitarian polyarchies is probably relatively small or perhaps none exists at all.) The number of polyarchies must run well over a hundred and probably well over a thousand. Of this number, however, only a tiny handful has been exhaustively studied by political scientists, and these have been the most difficult of all, the governments of national states, and in a few instances the smaller governmental units.

The Nature, Conditions, and Justification of Democracy

Richard Wollheim

Richard Wollheim (1923-) is Grote Professor of Mind and Logic in The University of London. He has written widely in the fields of social philosophy, logic, and aesthetics. He is the author of *F. H. Bradley* (1969) and *Art and Its Objects* (1968).

Contemporary discussion of Democracy may be brought under four rough headings: the *meaning* of Democracy, the *conditions* of Democracy, the *justification* of Democracy, and the *relation of Democracy to other political concepts and principles*.

1. The problem of the meaning of Democracy arises as soon as one considers with any degree of literalness the word itself: *democracy*, the 'rule of the people.' For contrast this with other similar words, such as *plutocracy*, 'rule of the rich,' and *theo-cracy*, the 'rule of the priests.'[1] Immediately two questions assert themselves. In the first place, how can the people rule in the way in which the rich or the priests clearly can? For surely there are too many of them for it to be a practical possibility. And secondly, if the people rule, who is there left to be ruled? (It is to be observed that in the classical world neither of these two questions arose with the force that they do for us. For in the first place, the City State was generally small enough to permit the people to participate directly in government. Secondly, to most classical thinkers the word 'demos' meant the people in the sense of 'the common people' or 'the ordinary man,' or, more simply, 'the poor,' not in the modern sense of 'the people as a whole,' or 'every member of society': in consequence if the demos ruled, this left the rich and the noble to be ruled over.)

Two traditions of democratic thought can be identified by the way in which they treat this problem. One tradition, stemming ultimately from Rousseau, insists on taking this problem very literally and proposing to it a radical and peculiar solution. To begin with, all the members of society are said to possess two wills or selves: a 'true' or 'real' self, and an 'arbitrary' or 'fitful' self. All the true selves in any community are harmonious in their demands, whereas it is a mark of the arbitrary selves that they are discordant. In terms of this para-psychological assumption the two questions outlined above—or the 'paradox of self-government,' as a thinker of this school, Bernard Bosanquet called it—are readily solved. For to the first question, how can the people rule, being so many and so diverse?, the reply comes that it is their better selves that rule, and these selves, though naturally diverse, are necessarily harmonious. Secondly, to the question, who remains to be ruled if everyone rules?, the answer is given that though in a Democracy the ruled are certainly different from the rulers as much as they are in a plutocracy or in a

From Richard Wollheim, "Democracy," *Journal of the History of Ideas,* 19 (1958), pp. 225-242. Reprinted by permission.

[1] G. A. Paul, "Democracy," *Chambers Encyclopaedia,* 4 (1944), 430-1.

theocracy, they are however different, not in being different people, but in being different parts of the same people—that is, the ruled are the arbitrary or fitful selves of those whose real or true selves are the rulers.[2]

This tradition of thought, for all its metaphysical neatness, would appear to raise as many problems as it solves; and these further problems to be debarred of solution. For no empirical method is suggested whereby we can recognize or pick out the dictates of the true or real selves as opposed to those of the arbitrary selves. Indeed, when, as usually happens in this tradition of thought, the true self is further identified with the moral self, it is clear that no such method could be provided without falling into the errors of ethical Naturalism. From all this one might well assume that this 'idealist' tradition of democratic thought would lead to a total and barren scepticism about democratic practice. In fact the result has been rather different. Idealist thinkers have been led to support the notion of a supreme legislator or leader who would be able to penetrate the surface of conflicting individual desires and intuit the underlying rational and harmonious will of the community. Such a conception has been called "Totalitarian Democracy."[3] If in Anglo-American political thought, little or no attention has ever been paid by "idealist" thinkers to this very difficult problem of the practical interpretation of their theory, such self-denial though saying something for their political wisdom, scarcely redounds to their intellectual credit.

A different answer to this problem is provided by a school of thought, more empiricist in outlook, which seeks to remove the so-called paradox at an earlier stage. On this view, though in a Democracy the people rule, they do not rule in the sense in which the rich might rule in a plutocracy or the priests in a theocracy; that is to say, they do not rule in the sense of holding in their own hands and wielding directly the supreme legislative and executive powers. They rule in a modified sense in that they exercise some control over the use of these powers. And in this sense of ruling, the argument continues, there can be no difficulty in seeing how the people, many of them though there may be, can rule. Equally, on this view, there is no difficulty in seeing how the people can at once rule and be ruled. For the supreme legislative and executive powers, like any other external force or instrument, can be controlled *by* a group of people and yet also exercised *over* that group. This empiricist solution differs from the idealist solution above in that the paradox that is supposed to arise from the fact that the rulers and the ruled are in a Democracy identical, is disposed of, not by any dialectical legerdemain leading to a radical reinterpretation of political experience, but by an analysis which seeks to understand the concept of "rule" or "government" as it appears in the context of democratic thought, without in any way altering it.

However, it would be a mistake to assume that this empiricist view does not also give rise to further problems. For though it may answer the difficulties connected with the size or vastness of the ruling group in a Democracy, it still leaves unsettled those which arise or are alleged to arise out of its diversities and disharmonies. If the people do not agree upon how the supreme legislative and executive powers of the community are to be used—as they most likely will not—how can they control the use of these powers? Such difficulties certainly exist. It is, however, error to regard these as metaphysical or logical, rather than practical, difficulties. For there is no absurdity or inconsistency or self-contradiction in

[2] Bernard Bosanquet, *The Philosophical Theory of the State* (London, 1899).
[3] J. L. Talmon, *The Origins of Totalitarian Democracy* (London, 1952).

supposing the people to exert control over policy even when the policy pursued is not to the taste of all. The only issue is whether the method employed for selecting policy by aggregating tastes is "reasonable" or "fair," and this issue is practical.

In Anglo-Saxon countries the usual method employed for ensuring popular control is that of representative institutions with a composition determined by specific electoral procedures, and these methods have over the years been found to satisfy the natural or intuitive demands of "reasonableness" and "fairness." However, it needs to be emphasized that all these devices are no more than well-tried means of securing democratic control: none of them logically guarantees such control.

Though much of the criticism levelled at representative institutions is grossly exaggerated in that it assimilates the abuses of the system to its necessary concomitants, it does provide certain healthy reminders of how the system can go wrong. These may be brought under four headings:

(a) The society may be so sunk in apathy or swept away by hysteria that the majority vote is untypical of the considered ideas and desires of the majority of the society. To guard against apathy certain democratic countries have introduced compulsory voting (Australia, Belgium, Switzerland, etc.). In spite of the arguments that can be put forward in favor of this measure—most of which were raised in the debates in the Australian Parliament on its introduction in 1924—it has generally been regarded as "undemocratic" in itself. Against mass hysteria no plausible constitutional safeguard has yet been proposed.

(b) The society may be entirely reasonable and balanced in its voting habits, and yet, through some technical aspect of the electoral procedure, it may be impossible to arrive at a decision that can properly be said to represent the wishes of the majority. The limiting case which arises for any electoral procedure is where each of the alternatives voted upon attracts an equal number of voters, for then no decision whatsoever is forthcoming. A more difficult case is where a decision is forthcoming, but this clearly does not tally with what ordinarily or intuitively would be thought to be the majority will. It can be demonstrated that for every known 'reasonable' method of voting if the alternatives are three or more there is a situation in which this is bound to happen.[4] The only absolutely foolproof system is where every elector votes in turn on every pair of alternatives—a scarcely practical method.[5] (Proportional representation, often at this stage recommended as a panacea, merely transfers these difficulties from the electoral stage to the legislative stage.)

(c) The society may know its own mind, express it unequivocally through the electoral procedure, and then the majority so established may enforce its policy with a complete disregard for the desires, interests or rights of the minority. Fears of the 'tyranny of the majority' were a constant theme in the nineteenth century, the great age of democratic thought. In the twentieth century, the great age of democratic practice, these fears have not on the whole been realized—though, significantly, where they have been, the reality has been on a scale far exceeding the worst envisaged. It would seem that the problem here is sociological rather than political, in that social conditioning is more likely to be an effective remedy than a system of constitutional checks and balances.

[4] E. J. Nanson, "Methods of Election," *Transactions and Proceedings of the Royal Society of Victoria*, 19 (1883), 197-240; Kenneth Arrow, *Social Choices and Individual Values* (New York, 1951).

[5] Robert A. Dahl, *A Preface to Democratic Theory* (Chicago, 1956).

(d) The majority may know its own mind, express it through the electoral mechanism, and the majority so constituted so far from tyrannizing over the minority, may fail even to exert rule over it. For power can fall into the hands of a minority within the majority. Some thinkers have indeed claimed that any machinery of majority rule is bound to put effective control into the hands of a minority. But this would seem to be exaggeration. Since the end of the last century, increasing attention has, however, been paid to the oligarchic tendencies implicit in democratic machinery: in particular, those relating to party organization and program construction.

Perhaps the most important single lesson to be learnt from these objections is that Democracy cannot be self-guaranteeing. It is exposed to risks, in the first place, from the mechanism that is devised to implement it, and secondly, from the other elements in society. It has been called justifiably, a 'calculated risk.'[6]

2. The question of the conditions of Democracy, i.e., what must exist for Democracy to exist, is one of the great problems of the age. Unfortunately, a great deal of contemporary discussion of it is bedevilled by an essential ambiguity in the nature of the question. It is often unclear whether the question is *logical*, i.e., what conditions must be satisfied for us to say correctly that Democracy exists, or *empirical*, i.e., what conditions must exist elsewhere in society for Democracy to come into existence and to survive.[7] Such ambiguity is common in theoretical arguments, but in this context there are two additional factors to account for its persistence. One is the absence of any developed sociology of politics; and the other is the extreme prestige attached to the word 'Democracy,' so that writers tend to take over any concomitant of Democracy that they like and write about it as if it were part of Democracy.

In contemporary discussions of the conditions of Democracy, three issues have been singled out for particular attention:

(a) The connection between Democracy and Socialism. Those who assert that there is a real connection between the two may be divided into three groups.

First, there are the Marxists. These are sometimes taken to assert that Democracy is incomplete without socialism. This, however, is a misunderstanding of their true position. For what they wish to do is not so much to extend the concept of Democracy as to transpose it completely. Believing in what has been called the 'impotence of politics,'[8] they are indifferent to constitutional and political organization, but at the same time want to secure the full prestige of this concept for their own preference in what they consider to be the truly important field—that of economic organization. It is significant that the use of the word 'Democracy' as a word of praise in Marxist thought dates from the time when it became a universally honorific word.

Secondly, there are the Democratic Socialists. Of these the Guild Socialists used to argue that a society could not truly be called 'democratic' unless all the institutions in it were themselves democratic. Amongst these institutions were to be numbered factories and other industrial plants, and the democratization of such institutions necessarily involves workers' control, i.e., Socialism.[9] Nowadays, most Socialists would prefer to use less *a priori* arguments. Some would use a pragmatic

[6] Robert A. Dahl and Charles Lindblom, *Politics, Economics and Welfare* (New York, 1953).
[7] Joseph A. Schumpeter, *Capitalism, Socialism and Democracy* (New York, 1947).
[8] Karl R. Popper, *The Open Society and Its Enemies* (London, 1945).
[9] G. D. H. Cole, *Guild Socialism Re-Stated* (London, 1920).

argument, namely that political Democracy cannot be truly safe without economic reorganization: and again others would prefer a moral argument to the effect that there is an inconsistency in applying the principle of equality in the field of politics and denying it in the field of economics.

Thirdly, there are the conservatives who argue that Democracy is in its nature incompatible with Socialism. There are a number of arguments raised in current discussion to this effect: they are differentiated according to the feature of Democracy that they hold to be the ground of this incompatibility. Some have held this to be competition, others tolerance, others the existence of property. A recent argument that has attracted attention is that which maintains that Democracy requires freedom, freedom requires the Rule of Law, and Socialism in its advocacy of bureaucratic planning has to dispense with the Rule of Law.[10] Against this it has been urged in the first place, that the Rule of Law guarantees security, not freedom; and secondly, that even if economic planning does contract freedom in some directions, it extends it in others and the overall effect may well be an increase rather than a diminution.[11]

(b) The connection between Democracy and the belief in Democracy. Since John Stuart Mill who claimed (ironically enough) that Democracy was not suitable for 'Malays and Bedouins,' it has been generally conceded by even the most fervent democrats that there are some conditions that a population must satisfy for it to be fit for Democracy. However, despite the practical urgency of this problem with the break-up of the old colonial empires, our knowledge of what these conditions are has not increased. On one condition—which to some appears to have a certain intuitive obviousness—controversy has been bitter: viz., the belief in, or acceptance of Democracy. Now if this condition is taken as applying to society as a whole it is obviously true, perhaps logically so. But it does not follow from this that it is therefore true of every single member of a society. Society to be democratic must believe in Democracy; but how many members it can successfully contain who do not themselves believe in Democracy, is a question incapable of any *a priori* answer. It depends on the restraints that these dissidents are prepared to put upon their own behavior, on the moral or spiritual authority that they wield over others, and on the extent to which their behavior can be neutralized by other factors in society (free speech, the press, education, etc.).

(c) The connection between Democracy and Constitutionalism. It would be common ground to nearly all supporters of Democracy that there are certain laws or regulations that ought not to be passed even if the greater part or indeed the whole of the people favor them. To some it has seemed desirable to inscribe these 'moral limitations' of Democracy in a charter or Constitution. Some English thinkers have gloried in the fact that liberties enjoyed in Great Britain are to be found not in any Constitution but in the accumulated precedents of common law.[12] It would seem, however, that though this may well be something to be grateful for, it is not a matter for pride, and it is perfectly natural that other, and in particular younger, Democracies should prefer to express their ideals in a more systematic if necessarily more 'artificial' fashion.

However, the issue somewhat changes when the Constitution is regarded not

[10] F. A. von Hayek, *The Road to Serfdom* (London, 1944).
[11] Hans Kelsen, "Democracy and Socialism," *Conference on Jurisprudence and Politics* (Chicago, 1954), 63-87.
[12] A. V. Dicey, *Introduction to the Study of the Law of the Constitution* (London, 1885).

merely as a systematic statement of the liberties recognized in society but as a method of guaranteeing them. In such cases the Constitution is accompanied by some mechanism for enforcing provisions like that of judicial review. To certain thinkers this has seemed the obvious requirement of Democracy; by others it has been regarded as inequitable, incompetent, and unnecessary. It is inequitable because it tries to limit the power of the living majority by means of the 'the dead hand' of the past: it is incompetent because the only cases where it is likely to arise are just those where the Constitution itself will require 'interpretation'; and it is unnecessary because a society that is likely to accept the findings of such a mechanism is unlikely seriously to offend against the spirit of its Constitution. These strictures are sometimes supported by a historical examination of the record of actual mechanisms, e.g., the history of 'judicial review' in the U.S. as an instrument of Democracy.[13]

3. There are in circulation in Anglo-Saxon thought a number of arguments, all purporting to justify Democracy. These arguments vary greatly in acceptability according to the number and validity of the principles they invoke, the truth of the factual assumptions they make use of, and the relevance of the kind of Democracy for which they argue to the kind that we experience.

(a) To exercise rule or to enjoy any form of political authority is a kind of moral education. On egalitarian grounds the opportunity for such self-improvement should be extended to as many as possible. In Democracy it is extended to all: therefore Democracy is the best of all forms of government. This argument, which is originally to be found in Aristotle (*Pol.* III. 1277b), may have had some application within the confines of the Polis, but applied to the conditions of the modern world it seems hopelessly unrealistic. Significantly enough, it is the characteristic argument of a kind of Liberalism which is or was peculiarly associated with a classical education.

(b) The second argument is that true opinion on political and moral matters is the privilege of the common man. Accordingly, power in a community should reside with him: and this it does only in a Democracy. Hence the superiority of Democracy. As we have seen, this argument is central to the Greek conception of Democracy. In modern thought it has received reinforcement from a certain sentimental theory of the goodness of human nature uncorrupted by wealth, luxury and education. In contrast to this, Democracy has come in for much criticism based on the so-called discovery of man's 'irrationality' by modern psychology. Much of this criticism is confused, and, if it proves anything, proves not so much the weakness of Democracy as the weakness of this particular argument for it.

(c) A more materialistic version of the preceding argument makes the ordinary man the best judge not of what is right for the community but of his own interests. In consequence, if the people are allowed to control the government, then the interests of the people will be dominant. Democracy is identified with popular control, and therefore vindicated. This argument is the argument of the Utilitarians, supported in their case by a thoroughgoing psychological egoism. It also has been subjected to a great deal of empirical criticism. Recent sociology has, for instance, cast doubt on the classical notions of class by bringing out what has been called (perhaps misleadingly) the 'subjective' element in class determination. Nevertheless the argument has considerable weight.

[13] Henry S. Commager, *Majority Rule and Minority Rights* (New York-London, 1943).

(d) A further retreat from the positions maintained in the two previous arguments leads to the completely sceptical argument for Democracy. According to this argument, it is impossible for anyone to discover what is the right course of action for the community, or where the true interests of its inhabitants reside. From this it follows that everyone in the community should be allowed to do what he wants to do as far as is socially possible. The only society in which this can happen is the one in which everyone has some control in the government: therefore Democracy is favored. As a variant of this argument, it may be maintained that even if one can discover what is ideally the right course of action to pursue, it would be wrong to insist on it unless everyone in the community recognized its rightness. Accordingly in practice one must adopt a sceptical attitude towards government and allow people to have the laws, institutions, etc., that they want: hence Democracy.

It seems to be certainly the case that scepticism does involve Democracy—even if the link is not as rigorous or as formal as some would believe. It does not follow from this, though—as certain critics of Democracy would have us believe—that Democracy involves scepticism.

(e) At the opposite end of the scale it is maintained that everyone has a natural right to control government and that this right is recognized only in Democracy: therefore Democracy is the best form of government. This argument has been subjected to two lines of criticism, both of which are misguided. The first is that the conception of 'a natural right' is metaphysical. Now natural rights are capable of, and often receive, a metaphysical interpretation, but this is not necessary. To say that something is a natural right may merely be a way of saying that it is an ultimate value. Secondly, it has been urged that it is absurd to allow that everyone has a natural right to exercise control over government when in fact not everyone can do so. But this argument assumes that the right in question is, in the terminology of jurisprudence, 'a right proper' (i.e., correlative to duty) whereas it seems more natural to assume that it is a liberty or privilege.[14]

(f) Finally, it may be maintained that it is irrelevant whether Democracy does in fact maximize welfare, safeguard rights, accord with natural law, etc., for the fact is that under modern conditions it is the only working possibility. No member of an emancipated industrial society will put up with political tutelage. He insists on having a fair chance of influencing the government in accordance with his own desires and ideas; and by a 'fair' chance he means a chance 'as good as the next man's.' This argument was succinctly summarized in the nineteenth century by the conservative James Fitz-James Stephen who said that in Democracy we count heads to avoid breaking them; and it remains to-day one of the best arguments in favor of Democracy on account of its extreme economy.

[14] Richard Wollheim and Isaiah Berlin, "Equality," *Proceedings of the Aristotelian Society*, 30 (1956), 281-326.

Some Problems of Democracy
Stanley I. Benn

Stanley I. Benn (1933-   ) is a Senior Fellow at the University of London. He has published *Social Principles and the Democratic State* (1953).

"Democracy" is difficult to define, not only because it is vague, like so many political terms, but more importantly, because what one person would regard as a paradigm case another would deny was a democracy at all. The word has acquired a high emotive charge in the last hundred years; it has become good tactics to apply it to one's own favored type of regime and to deny it to rivals. The most diverse systems have been claimed as democracies of one sort or another, and the word has been competitively redefined, to match changes in extension by appropriate changes in intention. However, there is still this much agreement: democracy consists in "government by the people" or "popular self-government." As such it would still be universally distinguished from, say, a despotism that made no pretense of popular participation—the despotism of Genghis Khan or of Louis XIV, for instance—or from a theocracy, like the Vatican. There remains plenty of room for disagreement, however, about the conditions under which the people can properly be said to rule itself.

In the first place, what is "the people"? In ancient Greece, the *demos* was the poorer people; democracy meant rule of the poor over the rich. This is still the usage of those who identify the people with the proletariat and democracy with the rule of the working class. However, the word "people" is often used to differentiate the subject mass from the ruling elite, as, for instance, when Locke speaks of a tyrannical government putting itself into a state of war with the people. In this sense, "the people" necessarily means the ruled. Can the people, however, be said *to rule itself* in the same sense as it is said to be ruled by monarchs, oligarchs, and priests? To rule is, generally, to prescribe conduct for someone else. There is a sense, it is true, in which moralists speak of ruling oneself, when by a kind of metaphor they speak of reason governing the passions. Again, a former colony becomes self-governing when its people is no longer ruled by outsiders; but this is not inconsistent with its still being ruled by *native* masters.

The usual paradigm of a people governing itself is the direct democracy of ancient Athens. Admittedly, citizenship was a hereditary privilege, excluding slaves and metics, and it is very doubtful whether, without this limitation, the citizen body would have been small enough for it to have operated as it did. Aside from this, however, the Athenian people governed itself in the sense that every individual could participate personally in policy decisions by discussion and voting, in a face-to-face situation. Athenian procedures are held to have been democratic in the sense that everyone was supposed to have an equal opportunity to state a case and

From "Democracy" by Stanley I. Benn. Reprinted with permission of the Publisher from *The Encyclopedia of Philosophy*, Paul Edwards, Editor in Chief. Volume Two, pages 338-341. Copyright © 1967 by Crowell Collier and Macmillan, Inc.

influence decisions, even if, in some cases, individuals had ultimately to accept decisions that they had previously resisted. So today, in a similar sense, if a school or a department is said to be democratically run, we should expect its head to consult his staff on important issues and to concur in decisions to which he himself is opposed when the weight of opinion is against him. Self-government for a small group consists in general participation in the deliberative process, in which each person's voice carries a weight appropriate not to his status but to the merits, in the judgment of others, of what he has to say. If, despite continuing disagreement, a decision is essential, then it must be arrived at by majority vote. For it is not consistent with equal participation in decision making for any one individual to be privileged to say in advance that regardless of the distribution of opinions, his own or that of his group must prevail. That privilege excluded, decisions may be reached by lot or by vote; and if by vote, the opinion of either the lesser or the greater number may prevail. Deciding by lot was in fact used in Athens to fill certain public offices; it is a way of giving everyone an equal chance where advantages or privileges cannot be equally and simultaneously enjoyed, but to decide policy by lot would make nonsense of the procedure of public discussion, which is as integral to the democratic process as the idea of equality. The same would apply to a rule whereby whatever opinion received the fewest votes would prevail; for what point would there be in persuasion if it had no effect on the outcome or, still worse, if it actually reduced the chance of one's view being implemented? If a democratic decision is thought of, then, as the result of a fair confrontation of opinions, it must, at best, be generally agreed upon, and at worst, agreed upon by the majority.

CONDITIONS OF POLITICAL DEMOCRACY

Obviously, the conditions of face-to-face democracy, with direct participation, cannot be fulfilled within the political structure of modern states, both because of the size of their populations and because of the specialized knowledge needed to govern them. So although everyone may agree on what makes a small group democratic, when it comes to applying the concept to mass organizations, there is plenty of room for different interpretations of the principles to be applied and of the way to realize them under these very different conditions. Democracy now becomes representative government, that is, government by persons whom the people elect and thereby authorize to govern them.

"Election" and "representation" are themselves complex notions, however. In one sense to be representative of a group may mean no more than to possess salient characteristics common to and distinctive of most of its members. In another, quasi-legal sense, one person may be said to represent another if, according to some code of rules, the consequences attached to an act of the representative are precisely those that would be attached to the act had it been performed by the principal himself; the representative can, in this case, *commit* the represented. In yet a third sense, one may represent another by looking after his interests, with or without his authorization (for example, the representation of infants in law). Now, democratic representation need not imply representation in the first sense, that of resemblance. Since an elected member of a legislature is taken to represent those who voted against as much as those who voted for him, he need not resemble those he represents, even in his opinions. Nor does he commit them as if they themselves had acted; the fact of their having legal duties does not depend on the fiction that, if their representative votes for a law, they have personally agreed to it. Their legal duties remain even if their representative voted against it. Nor must we necessarily accept moral responsibility for what is done by those who politically represent us, for in voting against them, we may have done the only thing open to us to disavow them.

Political representation is closer to the third sense of the term—the representation of interests; a democratic representative is usually thought to have the duty to watch over either the interests of his constituents or, as a member of an assembly representing the whole people, the interests of the people at large. Nevertheless, he could still represent the interests of a group of people without their having had any part in choosing him. Some members of colonial legislatures in Africa used to be nominated by the governor to represent the interests of the unenfranchised native population. Precisely analogous, from the standpoint of the liberal democrat, is the case of a single-party system, where the ruling party invites the electors to endorse the candidate it has chosen to represent them. No matter how zealously the representative watched their interests, this would not count as democratic representation, precisely because the electors had had no part in selecting him. This view of democracy, therefore, is not compatible with tutelage; it implies the possibility not only of rejecting but also of freely proposing candidates, if none put forward by others is acceptable. Choosing and rejecting representatives is, indeed, the central act of participation by the citizens of a mass democracy, from which any effectiveness that they might have in other respects derives.

Closely related to election is the notion of the *responsibility* of the democratic representative. This means, in practice, that representatives must submit themselves periodically for re-election and, as a corollary, that they must be prepared to justify their actions and to attend to the experience and needs of their constituents, whose good will they must retain so long as they wish to remain in office.

DEMOCRACY AND POPULAR SOVEREIGNTY

It is often said that in a democracy the people's will is sovereign. But can the people be said to have a will? Opinions are divided on most things; there may be ignorance and apathy; on many questions only sectionally interested groups may have any clear opinions at all. Small groups, like committees, may reach agreed policies to which everyone feels committed; or in time of grave national danger, whole nations may discover a collective devotion to a single objective, overriding all conflicts in interest. However, although it might be intelligible to speak of a collective will in such cases, they are too limited or too rare to provide a framework for a general theory of democratic government. Such cases apart, one may speak of action, will, or decision in relation to collectivities only if their collective acts can be identified by some more or less formal procedure or if there are rules authorizing some identifiable individual to act *in the name of* the whole group. Thus, "Parliament has decided . . ." presupposes rules determining who are members of Parliament, defining their roles, and giving their several actions a collective significance and validity as "legislation." Are there analogous procedures, by virtue of which the people can be said to act or to express a will? Only by voting and by applying the majority principle in elections and referenda. And of course, applied to any particular collection of individual votes, different systems of voting or different arrangements of constituency boundaries can yield quite different results, each in its own rule context expressing "the people's will." Nevertheless, some people consider a system democratic to the extent that it approximates to government by referendum, though they would agree that this could not work as a day-to-day procedure. The doctrine that a government ought not to initiate policy changes without putting them to a vote in a general election (or, in a stronger form, that having done so, it is entitled—or obliged—to implement them forthwith) is a practical application of the popular-sovereignty view of democracy. A possible corollary sometimes derived from this last view is that it is undemocratic to oppose or impede any government acting with the people's mandate. Moreover, since the people is sovereign, the traditionally important safeguards against the abuse of power become otiose; for, in Rousseau's words, "the sovereign, being formed wholly of the individuals who compose it, neither has nor can have any interest contrary to theirs." Popular-sovereignty theory is always, therefore, on the brink of totalitarianism, since—as the French Jacobin party showed—it is only a short step from proclaiming the sovereignty of the people to claiming the unlimited authority of its elected representatives, to proscribing opposition, and to denying individuals any rights other than those which the government with majority support deems fit.

There is, of course, another view, closer to the tradition of liberal individualism, which sees democracy as a way of safeguarding and reconciling individual and group interests. For James Madison, the virtue of the new constitution of the United States was that it permitted no faction, not even a majority, to deprive minorities of their natural rights, since it demanded the concurrence in action of independent authorities. The constitution was designed to balance diverse interests against one another, so that none might ever become a dominant and entrenched majority. Recent pluralistic accounts of democracy (or of what R. A. Dahl calls "polyarchy"), while more sophisticated, follow a similar approach. To be democratic, policy-making agencies must be sensitive to a wide range of pressures, so that no interest significantly affected by a decision will be left out of account. Popular participation consists not merely in voting, but also in wide consultation with interest groups and in the whole process of public criticism and governmental self-justification. Democracy, according to this view, requires the dispersal, not the concentration, of power; every voter has his quantum, making him worth the attention of those who want to govern. The people is not homogeneous, but a highly diversified complex of interest groups with crisscrossing memberships. It rarely makes sense to talk of the majority, except with reference to the result of a particular election or referendum, to describe how the votes were cast. A sectional majority, if there were one, would have no intrinsic claim to rule. To govern, a party would have to piece together an electoral majority; but every elector would have his own reasons for voting as he did, and no party could say in advance that, since it had no potential supporters among the members of some particular group, that group could, therefore, be safely neglected. Admittedly, wherever group divisions coincide over a wide range of interests (as, for instance, in many polyethnic societies), these conditions might not be fulfilled, and there might be a built-in majority and minority. In such a case, no party aiming at majority support could afford to uphold a minority interest, and democracy would tend to give way to majority tyranny. Thus, where popular-sovereignty theorists see the majority as the expression of the supreme will of the people, writers like Madison, Alexis de

Tocqueville, J. S. Mill and, more recently, Walter Lippmann and the pluralists have seen it as either a myth or a potential tyrant.

THE POSSIBILITY OF DEMOCRACY

According to elitist sociologists like Vilfredo Pareto, Gaetano Mosca, and Robert Michels, there is always, behind the democratic facade, an oligarchy, even though its members take turns at playing the key governing roles. Now obviously, in every organization leaders initiate action and followers concur, but the power relations between leader and led are not on that account always the same. Precisely because democracy is a form of political organization, it *must* also be a pattern of leadership; nevertheless, the way leaders gain and retain their authority; the extent to which their initiatives respond to the interests of those they lead; their need to listen to and answer criticism—these things distinguish a democracy in important ways from what we usually mean by an oligarchy.

For the Marxist, bourgeois democracy is a sham because equal political rights cannot equalize political power where economic power is unequal. This does not amount to saying that democracy is *necessarily* impossible, only that economic equality and a classless society are necessary conditions for it.

According to other critics, popular self-government is delusory because government calls for expertise which few voters possess. Most accept the directions of some party, to whose image they are irrationally committed, and are incapable of a rational choice of policy. However, except in the popular-sovereignty variant, democracy does not require the electors to choose policies. Their role is merely to choose governors whom they trust to deal fairly and efficiently with problems as they emerge, and to look for new governors when they are disillusioned. A party's public image need not be an irrational construct; it may accurately epitomize deep-rooted tendencies and traditional preferences and be a reliable guide to the spirit in which the party would govern.

JUSTIFICATION OF DEMOCRACY

Democracy, it is sometimes said, asks too much of ordinary men, who would never be prepared to maintain the lively and informed interest in politics that ideally it demands. This however, presupposes a particular view of the purpose and justification of democratic government. For some writers, as J. S. Mill, men and women cannot be fully responsible, adult, moral persons unless they are "self-determining," that is, concerned about the ways in which their lives are to be controlled. This view is a development from an older natural-rights theory of democracy, according to which (in the words of Colonel Rainborough, the Leveller), "Every man that is to live under a government ought first by his own consent put himself under that government," this being a condition for preserving his natural autonomy as a rational being. Or again, for democrats in the tradition of Rousseau, men achieve moral fulfillment only as participants in the collective self-governing process, helping to give expression to the "General Will" for the "Common Good"; failure in this constitutes failure in one's moral duty as a citizen.

There is, however, a more strictly utilitarian theory, sketched by Bentham and

James Mill and implicit in a good deal of the work of democratic political scientists today. According to this view, the test of the adequacy of a political system is whether it tends to provide for the interests of the governed and protect them against the abuse of power. Democracy, they maintain, is likely to do this better than other systems. Active participation has no intrinsic virtue. James Mill would have limited the franchise to men over 40, on the grounds that the interests of women and younger men would be adequately safeguarded by their husbands and fathers, and therefore universal suffrage would be an unnecessary expense. For many modern writers, politics is a second-order activity: if things are going well, there is really no reason for people who prefer to spend their time on other things to devote it to politics. Political activity, indeed, is often most vigorous, as in Germany before 1933, when passions are high and democracy is in imminent danger of collapse. Apathy may be a sign of political health, indicating that there are no irreconcilable conflicts nor serious complaints. If there is ground for disquiet, it is only that apathy may become so habitual that democracy's defenses may be found unmanned in the face of some future attack.

This is a prudential model of democracy, in which satisfaction is maximized and conflicts reconciled by pressures bringing countervailing pressures into operation. It leaves out of account, perhaps, the sense in which democracy moralizes politics. Because decisions have to be publicly justified, political debate is conducted in moral terms, reviewing the impact of decisions of all interests affected, not just on this or that pressure group. Moreover, the quantum of power one has as a citizen can be represented not simply as a lever for personal or sectional protection or advantage, but also as a public responsibility; for even when one'e own interests are not affected, one is still a member of a court of appeal. The bystanders in a democracy are, in a sense, the guarantors that a political decision shall not simply register the strongest pressure but shall be a reasoned response to diverse claims, each of which has to be shown to be *reasonable*, in the light of whatever standards are widely accepted in the community.

The End of Laissez-faire
John Maynard Keynes

John Maynard Keynes (1883-1946) was one of the creators of the modern economic world. Among his books are *Economic Consequences of the Peace* (1919); *A Treatise on Probability* (1921); *A Revision of the Treaty* (1922); *A Short View of Russia, The End of Laissez-faire* (1926); *A Treatise on Money* (1930); *Essays in Biography* (1933); *The General Theory of Employment, Interest and Money*, (1936); and *How to Pay for the War* (1940).

Let us clear from the gound the metaphysical or general principles upon which, from time to time, *laissez-faire* has been founded. It is *not* true that individuals possess a prescriptive "natural liberty" in their economic activities. There is *no* "compact" conferring perpetual rights on those who Have or on those who Acquire. The world is *not* so governed from above that private and social interest always coincide. It is *not* so managed here below that in practice they coincide. It is *not* a correct deduction from the Principles of Economics that enlightened self-interest always operates in the public interest. Nor is it true that self-interest generally *is* enlightened; more often individuals acting separately to promote their own ends are too ignorant or too weak to attain even these. Experience does *not* show that individuals, when they make up a social unit, are always less clear-sighted than when they act separately.

We cannot, therefore, settle on abstract grounds, but must handle on its merits in detail, what Burke termed "one of the finest problems in legislation, namely, to determine what the State ought to take upon itself to direct by the public wisdom, and what it ought to leave, with as little interference as possible, to individual exertion." We have to discriminate between what Bentham, in his forgotten but useful nomenclature, used to term *Agenda* and *Non-Agenda*, and to do this without Bentham's prior presumption that interference is, at the same time, "generally needless" and "generally pernicious."[1] Perhaps the chief task of Economists at this hour is to distinguish afresh the *Agenda* of Government from the *Non-Agenda*; and the companion task of Politics is to devise forms of Government within a Democracy which shall be capable of accomplishing the *Agenda*. I will illustrate what I have in mind by two examples.

1. I believe that in many cases the ideal size for the unit of control and organization lies somewhere between the individual and the modern State. I suggest, therefore, that progress lies in the growth and the recognition of semi-autonomous bodies within the State—bodies whose criterion of action within their own field is solely the public good as they understand it, and from whose deliberations motives of private advantage are excluded, though some place it may

[1] Bentham's *Manual of Political Economy*, published posthumously, in Bowring's edition (1843).

still be necessary to leave, until the ambit of men's altruism grows wider, to the separate advantage of particular groups, classes, or faculties—bodies which in the ordinary course of affairs are mainly autonomous within their prescribed limitations, but are subject in the last resort to the sovereignty of the democracy expressed through Parliament.

I propose a return, it may be said, towards mediaeval conceptions of separate autonomies. But, in England at any rate, corporations are a mode of government which has never ceased to be important and is sympathetic to our institutions. It is easy to give examples, from what already exists, of separate autonomies which have attained or are approaching the mode I designate—the Universities, the Bank of England, the Port of London Authority, even perhaps the Railway Companies.

But more interesting than these is the trend of Joint Stock Institutions, when they have reached a certain age and size, to approximate to the status of public corporations rather than that of individualistic private enterprise. One of the most interesting and unnoticed developments of recent decades has been the tendency of big enterprise to socialise itself. A point arrives in the growth of a big institution—particularly a big railway or big public utility enterprise, but also a big bank or a big insurance company—at which the owners of the capital, *i.e.* the shareholders, are almost entirely dissociated from he management, with the result that the direct personal interest of the latter in the making of great profit becomes quite secondary. When this stage is reached, the general stability and reputation of the institution are more considered by the management than the maximum of profit for the shareholders. The shareholders must be satisfied by conventionally adequate dividends; but once this is secured, the direct interest of the management often consists in avoiding criticism from the public and from the customers of the concern. This is particularly the case if their great size or semi-monopolistic position renders them conspicuous in the public eye and vulnerable to public attack. The extreme instance, perhaps, of this tendency in the case of an institution, theoretically the unrestricted property of private persons, is the Bank of England. It is almost true to say that there is no class of persons in the Kingdom of whom the Governor of the Bank of England thinks less when he decides on his policy than of his shareholders. Their rights, in excess of their conventional dividend, have already sunk to the neighbourhood of zero. But the same thing is partly true of many other big institutions. They are, as time goes on, socialising themselves.

Not that this is unmixed gain. The same causes promote conservatism and a waning of enterprise. In fact, we already have in these cases many of the faults as well as the advantages of State Socialism. Nevertheless we see here, I think, a natural line of evolution. The battle of Socialism against unlimited private profit is being won in detail hour by hour. In these particular fields—it remains acute elsewhere—this is no longer the pressing problem. There is, for instance, no so-called important political question so really unimportant, so irrelevant to the reorganisation of the economic life of Great Britain, as the Nationalisation of the Railways.

It is true that many big undertakings, particularly Public Utility enterprises and other business requiring a large fixed capital, still need to be semi-socialised. But we must keep our minds flexible regarding the forms of this semi-socialism. We must take full advantage of the natural tendencies of the day, and we must probably prefer semi-autonomous corporations to organs of the Central Government for which Ministers of State are directly responsible.

I criticise doctrinaire State Socialism, not because it seeks to engage men's altruistic impulses in the service of Society, or because it departs from *laissez-faire*, or because it takes away from man's natural liberty to make a million, or because it has courage for bold experiments. All these things I applaud. I criticise it because it misses the significance of what is actually happening; because it is, in fact, little better than a dusty survival of a plan to meet the problems of fifty years ago, based on a misunderstanding of what some one said a hundred years ago. Nineteenth-century State Socialism sprang from Bentham, free competition, etc., and is in some respects a clearer, in some respects a more muddled, version of just the same philosophy as underlies nineteenth-century individualism. Both equally laid all their stress on freedom, the one negatively to avoid limitations on existing freedom, the other positively to destroy natural or acquired monopolies. They are different reactions to the same intellectual atmosphere.

2. I come next to a criterion of *Agenda* which is particularly relevant to what it is urgent and desirable to do in the near future. We must aim at separating those services which are *technically social* from those which are *technically individual*. The most important *Agenda* of the State relate not to those activities which private individuals are already fulfilling, but to those functions which fall outside the sphere of the individual, to those decisions which are made by *no one* if the State does not make them. The important thing for Government is not to do things which individuals are doing already, and to do them a little better or a little worse; but to do those things which at present are not done at all.

It is not within the scope of my purpose on this occasion to develop practical policies. I limit myself, therefore, to naming some instances of what I mean from amongst those problems about which I happen to have thought most.

Many of the greatest economic evils of our time are the fruits of risk, uncertainty, and ignorance. It is because particular individuals fortunate in situation or in abilities, are able to take advantage of uncertainty and ignorance, and also because for the same reason big business if often a lottery, that great inequalities of wealth come about; and these same factors are also the cause of the Unemployment of Labour, or the disappointment of reasonable business expectations, and of the impairment of efficiency and production. Yet the cure lies outside the operations of individuals; it may even be to the interest of individuals to aggravate the disease. I believe that the cure for these things is partly to be sought in the deliberate control of the currency and of credit by a central institution, and partly in the collection and dissemination on a great scale of data relating to the business situation, including the full publicity, by law if necessary, of all business facts which it is useful to know. These measures would involve Society in exercising directive intelligence through some appropriate organ of action over many of the inner intricacies of private business, yet it would leave private initiative and enterprise unhindered. Even if these measures prove insufficient, nevertheless they will furnish us with better knowledge than we have now for taking the next step.

My second example relates to Savings and Investment. I believe that some co-ordinated act of intelligent judgement is required as to the scale on which it is desirable that the community as a whole should save, the scale on which these savings should go abroad in the form of foreign investments, and whether the present organisation of the investment market distributes savings along the most nationally productive channels. I do not think that these matters should be left entirely to the chances of private judgement and private profits, as they are at present.

My third example concerns Population. The time has already come when each country needs a considered national policy about what size of Population, whether larger or smaller than at present or the same, is most expedient. And having settled this policy, we must take steps to carry it into operation. The time may arrive a little later when the community as a whole must pay attention to the innate quality as well as to the mere numbers of its future members.

These reflections have been directed towards possible improvements in the technique of modern Capitalism by the agency of collective action. There is nothing in them which is seriously incompatible with what seems to me to be the essential characteristic of Capitalism, namely the dependence upon an intense appeal to the money-making and money-loving instincts of individuals as the main motive force of the economic machine. Nor must I, so near to my end, stray towards other fields. Nevertheless, I may do well to remind you, in conclusion, that the fiercest contests and the most deeply felt divisions of opinion are likely to be waged in the coming years not round technical questions, where the arguments on either side are mainly economic, but round those which, for want of better words, may be called psychological or, perhaps, moral.

In Europe, or at least in some parts of Europe—but not, I think, in the United States of America—there is a latent reaction, somewhat widespread, against basing Society to the extent that we do upon fostering, encouraging, and protecting the money-motives of individuals. A preference for arranging our affairs in such a way as to appeal to the money-motive as little as possible, rather than as much as possible, need not be entirely *a priori*, but may be based on the comparison of experiences. Different persons, according to their choice of profession, find the money-motive playing a large or a small part in their daily lives, and historians can tell us about other phases of social organisation in which this motive has played a much smaller part than it does now. Most religions and most philosophies deprecate, to say the least of it, a way of life mainly influenced by considerations of personal money profit. On the other hand, most men to-day reject ascetic notions and do not doubt the real advantages of wealth. Moreover it seems obvious to them that one cannot do without the money-motive, and that, apart from certain admitted abuses, it does its job well. In the result the average man averts his attention from the problem, and has no clear idea what he really thinks and feels about the whole confounded matter.

Confusion of thought and feeling leads to confusion of speech. Many people, who are really objecting to Capitalism as a way of life, argue as though they were objecting to it on the ground of its inefficiency in attaining its own objects. Contrariwise, devotees of Capitalism are often unduly conservative, and reject reforms in its technique, which might really strengthen and preserve it, for fear that they may prove to be first steps away from Capitalism itself. Nevertheless a time may be coming when we shall get clearer than at present as to when we are talking about Capitalism as an efficient or inefficient technique, and when we are talking about it as desirable or objectionable in itself. For my part, I think that Capitalism, wisely managed, can probably be made more efficient for attaining economic ends than any alternative system yet in sight, but that in itself it is in many ways extremely objectionable. Our problem is to work out a social organisation which shall be as efficient as possible without offending our notions of a satisfactory way of life.

The next step forward must come, not from political agitation or premature experiments, but from thought. We need by an effort of the mind to elucidate our own feelings. At present our sympathy and our judgement are liable to be on different sides, which is a painful and paralysing state of mind. In the field of action reformers will not be successful until they can steadily pursue a clear and definite object with their intellects and their feelings in tune. There is no party in the world at present which appears to me to be pursuing right aims by right methods. Material Poverty provides the incentive to change precisely in situations where there is very little margin for experiments. Material Prosperity removes the incentive just when it might be safe to take a chance. Europe lacks the means, America the will, to make a move. We need a new set of convictions which spring naturally from a candid examination of our own inner feelings in relation to the outside facts.

Suggested Readings

Benn, S. I., and R. S. Peters, *Social Principles and the Democratic State* (London: George Allen & Unwin, Ltd., 1959).

Clover, T. R., *Democracy in the Ancient World* (New York: Cambridge University Press, 1927). "Foundations of Democracy." *The Monist*, Vol. 55, No. 1 (January 1971). Entire issue diverted to "Democracy."

Dahl, R. A., *Preface to Democratic Theory* (Chicago: University of Chicago Press, 1956).

DeGrazia, A., *Public and Republic* (New York: Alfred A. Knopf, Inc., 1951).

Gooch, G. P., *English Democratic Ideas in the Seventeenth Century*, H. J. Laski, Ed. (New York: Cambridge University Press, 1927).

Hartz, Friedrich A. Von, *The Constitution of Liberty* (Chicago: Chicago University Press, 1960).

Konvitz, M. R., and C. L. Rossiter, Eds., *Aspects of Liberty* (Ithaca, N.Y.: Cornell University Press, 1958).

Laski, Harold, J., *The Rise of European Liberalism* (New York: Harper & Row, Publishers, 1936).

Neill, T. P., *Rise and Decline of Liberalism* (New York: Bruce Books, 1953).

Pennock, J. R., *Liberal Democracy: Its Merits and Prospects* (New York: Holt, Rinehart and Winston, Inc., 1950).

Spitz, D., *Patterns of Antidemocratic Thought* (New York: The Macmillan Company, 1949).

Woodhouse, A. S. P., *Puritanism and Liberty* (Chicago: University of Chicago Press, 1951).

The Ideology of Fascism

INTRODUCTION

In its narrowest sense, Fascism was only an Italian movement which existed in Italy during the period 1922 to 1945. Although the term has been used by some to apply to all military dictatorships, its strict use should be limited to the Mussolini years of Italy and perhaps to Nazi Germany. Other countries, such as present-day Greece and Spain as well as many South American countries, are military dictatorships that should have a name of their own. Even though an appropriate name has not been developed, liberals and Marxists often call such governments Fascist.

The term Fascism itself comes from the word *fasciare*, which means to bind. Fascism was hoped to bind the Italian nation into an organic entity, which would continue to develop the traditions and glories of ancient Rome. In fact, its symbol, the "fasces," was the two-headed ancient Roman axe noting authority.

Mussolini founded the Italian Fascist Party in 1919, and he came to power in 1922 at the time of his famous "March on Rome." Although there are still slight elements of Fascism in Italy, the movement died with Mussolini upon his assassination in 1945. According to Fascist doctrine, the state or nation is the central entity. It becomes a mystical entity armed with a historical mission. It is the duty of the individual to raise himself to the national consciousness and to lose his own identity in it. Mussolini's essay "The Doctrine of Fascism" sets forth his organic theory of the state and his antidemocratic tenets.

With regard to the economic life of the state, Mussolini opposed the *laissez-faire* economics of capitalism as well as the bourgeois way of life. Fascism also opposed Socialism because of its doctrines of class war and trade unionism, views that did not help to bind a nation together. Fascism set up corporations that were meant to integrate the interest of the various segments of the nation. Essentially, this meant that the private industry remained, but whenever private interests were not able to adequately deal with an economic problem, the state could step in. Most significantly this corporate state affected labor groups.

Strikes were outlawed and hence arbitration was mandatory. Labor associations existed but without the power of normal unions. There were many foreigners who believed that Mussolini ran the country efficiently. For example, it was said that the "Italian trains ran on time." This was a myth. The truth was that economic growth was minimal, as was efficiency, but through his dictatorship he was able to hide manifestations of economic disorder.

Giovanni Gentile, a philosopher, became Minister of Education under Mussolini. Heavily influenced by pragmatism, he argues in his essay against philosophies that are not practical. He also maintains that individual liberty can only be realized through the State. Mario Palmeri argues that one's life can only acquire meaning through the institutions of the Church, the Family, the Nation (the people), and the State. Such a life must realize the unity of the peoples and the basic duties one has to the leader, to the nation and state, and to God.

Fascism differs from Marxism in that Marx saw history as the history of conflict between classes; Fascists see history in terms of conflict between nations. Marxists are materialists; Fascists are spiritualists. Marxists are economic determinists; Fascists are nationalistic determinists. Marxists believe that class struggle is inevitable; Fascists believe in the organic unity of a nation. Marxism professes to be scientific; Fascism glorifies the irrational.

The Fascist movements in Italy and Germany existed during the same decades. Philosophically the two states were very similar, but they had a few differences. Mussolini maintained that the state created the nation; Hitler argued that the state was an instrument of the nation or the people. Racism played a greater role in Nazism than in Italian Fascism, and this emphasis by the Nazis was partly responsible for unmatched persecution of the Jews and other minorities.

The Doctrine of Fascism
Benito Mussolini

Benito Mussolini (1883-1945) was the dictator of Italy from 1922 to 1943 and founder of the Fascist Party. In 1932 he published *The Doctrine of Fascism.*

FUNDAMENTAL IDEAS

1. Like every sound political conception, Fascism is both practice and thought; action in which a doctrine is immanent, and a doctrine which, arising out of a given system of historical forces, remains embedded in them and works there from within. Hence it has a form correlative to the contingencies of place and time, but it has also a content of thought which raises it to a formula of truth in the higher level of the history of thought. In the world one does not act spiritually as a human will

From Michael Oakeshott, *Social and Political Doctrines of Contemporary Europe* (London: Cambridge University Press, 1950), pp. 164-168, 180-181. Reprinted by permission.

dominating other wills without a conception of the transient and particular reality under which it is necessary to act, and of the permanent and universal reality in which the first has its being and its life. In order to know men it is necessary to know man; and in order to know man it is necessary to know reality and its laws. There is no concept of the State which is not fundamentally a concept of life: philosophy or intuition, a system of ideas which develops logically or is gathered up into a vision or into a faith, but which is always, at least virtually, an organic conception of the world.

2. Thus Fascism could not be understood in many of its practical manifestations as a party organization, as a system of education, as a discipline, if it were not always looked at in the light of its whole way of conceiving life, a spiritualized way. The world seen through Fascism is not this material world which appears on the surface, in which man is an individual separated from all others and standing by himself, and in which he is governed by a natural law that makes him instinctively live a life of selfish and momentary pleasure. The man of Fascism is an individual who is nation and fatherland, which is a moral law, binding together individuals and the generations into a tradition and a mission, suppressing the instinct for a life enclosed within the brief round of pleasure in order to restore within duty a higher life free from the limits of time and space: a life in which the individual, through the denial of himself, through the sacrifice of his own private interests, through death itself, realizes that completely spiritual existence in which his value as a man lies.

3. Therefore it is a spiritualized conception, itself the result of the general reaction of modern times against the flabby materialistic positivism of the nineteenth century. Anti-positivistic, but positive: not sceptical, nor agnostic, nor pessimistic, nor passively optimistic, as are, in general, the doctrines (all negative) that put the centre of life outside man, who with his free will can and must create his own world. Fascism desires an active man, one engaged in activity with all his energies: it desires a man virilely conscious of the difficulties that exist in action and ready to face them. It conceives of life as a struggle, considering that it behoves man to conquer for himself that life truly worthy of him, creating first of all in himself the instrument (physical, moral, intellectual) in order to construct it. Thus for the single individual, thus for the nation, thus for humanity. Hence the high value of culture in all its forms (art, religion, science), and the enormous importance of education. Hence also the essential value of work, with which man conquers nature and creates the human world (economic, political, moral, intellectual).

4. This positive conception of life is clearly an ethical conception. It covers the whole of reality, not merely the human activity which controls it. No action can be divorced from moral judgement; there is nothing in the world which can be deprived of the value which belongs to everything in its relation to moral ends. Life, therefore, as conceived by the Fascist, is serious, austere, religious: the whole of it is poised in a world supported by the moral and responsible forces of the spirit. The Fascist disdains the "comfortable" life.

5. Fascism is a religious conception in which man is seen in his immanent relationship with a superior law and with an objective Will that transcends the particular individual and raises him to conscious membership of a spiritual society. Whoever has seen in the religious politics of the Fascist regime nothing but mere opportunism has not understood that Fascism besides being a system of government is also, and above all, a system of thought.

6. Fascism is an historical conception, in which man is what he is only in so far as he works with the spiritual process in which he finds himself, in the family or social group, in the nation and in the history in which all nations collaborate. From this follows the great value of tradition, in memories, in language, in customs, in the standards of social life. Outside history man is nothing. Consequently Fascism is opposed to all the individualistic abstractions of a materialistic nature like those of the eighteenth century; and it is opposed to all Jacobin utopias and innovations. It does not consider that "happiness" is possible upon earth, as it appeared to be in the desire of the economic literature of the eighteenth century, and hence it rejects all teleological theories according to which mankind would reach a definitive stabilized condition at a certain period in history. This implies putting oneself outside history and life, which is a continual change and coming to be. Politically, Fascism wishes to be a realistic doctrine; practically, it aspires to solve only the problems which arise historically of themselves and that of themselves find or suggest their own solution. To act among men, as to act in the natural world, it is necessary to enter into the process of reality and to master the already operating forces.

7. Against individualism, the Fascist conception is for the State; and it is for the individual in so far as he coincides with the State, which is the conscience and universal will of man in his historical existence. It is opposed to classical Liberalism, which arose from the necessity of reacting against absolutism, and which brought its historical purpose to an end when the State was transformed into the conscience and will of the people. Liberalism denied the State in the interests of the particular individual; Fascism reaffirms the State as the true reality of the individual. And if liberty is to be the attribute of the real man, and not of that abstract puppet envisaged by individualistic Liberalism, Fascism is for liberty. And for the only liberty which can be a real thing, the liberty of the State and of the individual within the State. Therefore, for the Fascist, everything is in the State, and nothing human or spiritual exists, much less has value, outside the State. In this sense Fascism is totalitarian, and the Fascist State, the synthesis and unity of all values, interprets, develops and gives strength to the whole life of the people.

8. Outside the State there can be neither individuals nor groups (political parties, associations, syndicates, classes). Therefore Fascism is opposed to Socialism, which confines the movement of history within the class struggle and ignores the unity of classes established in one economic and moral reality in the State; and analogously it is opposed to class syndicalism. Fascism recognizes the real exigencies for which the socialist and syndicalist movement arose, but while recognizing them wishes to bring them under the control of the State and give them a purpose within the corporative system of interests reconciled within the unity of the State.

9. Individuals form classes according to the similarity of their interests, they form syndicates according to differentiated economic activities within these interests; but they form first, and above all, the State, which is not to be thought of numerically as the sum-total of individuals forming the majority of a nation. And consequently Fascism is opposed to Democracy, which equates the nation to the majority, lowering it to the level of that majority; nevertheless it is the purest form of democracy if the nation is conceived, as it should be, qualitatively and not quantitatively, as the most powerful idea (most powerful because most moral, most coherent, most true) which acts within the nation as the conscience and the will of a few, even of One, which ideal tends to become active within the conscience and

the will of all—that is to say, of all those who rightly constitute a nation by reason of nature, history or race, and have set out upon the same line of development and spiritual formation as one conscience and one sole will. Not a race,[1] nor a geographically determined region, but as a community historically perpetuating itself, a multitude unified by a single idea, which is the will to existence and to power: consciousness of itself, personality.

10. This higher personality is truly the nation in so far as it is the State. It is not the nation that generates the State, as according to the old naturalistic concept which served as the basis of the political theories of the national States of the nineteenth century. Rather the nation is created by the State, which gives to the people, conscious of its own moral unity, a will and therefore an effective existence. The right of a nation to independence derives not from a literary and ideal consciousness of its own being, still less from a more or less unconscious and inert acceptance of a *de facto* situation, but from an active consciousness, from a political will in action and ready to demonstrate its own rights: that is to say, from a state already coming into being. The State, in fact, as the universal ethical will, is the creator of right.

11. The nation as the State is an ethical reality which exists and lives in so far as it develops. To arrest its development is to kill it. Therefore the State is not only the authority which governs and gives the form of laws and the value of spiritual life to the wills of individuals, but it is also a power that makes its will felt abroad, making it known and respected, in other words, demonstrating the fact of its universality in all the necessary directions of its development. It is consequently organization and expansion, at least virtually. Thus it can be likened to the human will which knows no limits to its development and realizes itself in testing its own limitlessness.

12. The Fascist State, the highest and most powerful form of personality, is a force, but a spiritual force, which takes over all the forms of the moral and intellectual life of man. It cannot therefore confine itself simply to the functions of order and supervision as Liberalism desired. It is not simply a mechanism which limits the sphere of the desired. It is not simply a mechanism which limits the sphere of the supposed liberties of the individual. It is the form, the inner standard and the discipline of the whole person; it saturates the will as well as the intelligence. Its principle, the central inspiration of the human personality living in the civil community, pierces into the depths and makes its home in the heart of the man of action as well as of the thinker, of the artist as well as of the scientist: it is the soul of the soul.

13. Fascism, in short, is not only the giver of laws and the founder of institutions, but the educator and promoter of spiritual life. It wants to remake, not the forms of human life, but its content, man, character, faith. And to this end it requires discipline and authority that can enter into the spirits of men and there govern unopposed. Its sign, therefore, is the Lictors' rods, the symbol of unity, of strength and justice.

---

[1] "Race; it is an emotion, not a reality; ninety-five per cent of it is emotion." Mussolini.

THE FASCIST DECALOGUE

1. Know that the Fascist and in particular the soldier, must not believe in perpetual peace.

2. Days of imprisonment are always deserved.

3. The nation serves even as a sentinel over a can of petrol.

4. A companion must be a brother, first, because he lives with you, and secondly because he thinks like you.

5. The rifle and cartridge belt, and the rest, are confided to you not to rust in leisure, but to be preserved in war.

6. Do not ever say "The Government will pay . . ." because it is *you* who pay; and the Government is that which you willed to have, and for which you put on a uniform.

7. Discipline is the soul of armies; without it there are no soldiers, only confusion and defeat.

8. Mussolini is always right.

9. For a volunteer there are no extenuating circumstances when he is disobedient.

10. One thing must be dear to you above all: the life of the Duce.

1934

1. Remember those who fell for the revolution and for the empire march at the head of your columns.

2. Your comrade is your brother. He lives with you, thinks with you, and is at your side in the battle.

3. Service to Italy can be rendered at all times, in all places, and by every means. It can be paid with toil and also with blood.

4. The enemy of Fascism is your enemy. Give him no quarter.

5. Discipline is the sunshine of armies. It prepares and illuminates the victory.

6. He who advances to the attack with decision has victory already in his grasp.

7. Conscious and complete obedience is the virtue of the Legionary.

8. There do not exist things important and things unimportant. There is only duty.

9. The Fascist revolution has depended in the past and still depends on the bayonets of its Legionaries.

10. Mussolini is always right.

1938

The Philosophic Basis of Fascism
Giovanni Gentile

Giovanni Gentile (1875-1944) was a neo-Hegelian philosopher and one of the leaders of intellectual affairs in pre-Fascist Italy. He became Minister of Education in the Mussolini government and the chief Fascist theoretician. The following passage underscores the totalitarian and anti-intellectual character of the fascist philosophy.

. . . In the definition of Fascism, the first point to grasp is the comprehensive, or as the Fascists say, the "totalitarian" scope of its doctrine, which concerns itself not only with political organization and political tendency, but with the whole will and thought and feeling of the nation.

There is a second and equally important point. Fascism is not a philosophy. Much less is it a religion. It is not even a political theory which may be stated in a series of formulae. The significance of Fascism is not to be grasped in the special theses which it from time to time assumes. When on occasion it has announced a program, a goal, a concept to be realized in action, Fascism has not hesitated to abandon them when in practice these were found to be inadequate or inconsistent with the principle of Fascism. Fascism has never been willing to compromise its future. Mussolini has boasted that he is a *tempista*, that his real pride is in "good timing." He makes decisions and acts on them at the precise moment when all the conditions and considerations which make them feasible and opportune are properly matured. This is a way of saying that Fascism returns to the most rigorous meaning of Mazzini's "Thought and Action," whereby the two terms are so perfectly coincident that no thought has value which is not already expressed in action. The real "views" of the *Duce* are those which he formulates and executes at one and the same time.

Is Fascism therefore "anti-intellectual," as has been so often charged? It is eminently anti-intellectual, eminently Mazzinian, that is, if by intellectualism we mean the divorce of thought from action, of knowledge from life, of brain from heart, of theory from practice. Fascism is hostile to all Utopian systems which are destined never to face the test of reality. It is hostile to all science and all philosophy which remain matters of mere fancy or intelligence. It is not that Fascism denies value to culture, to the higher intellectual pursuits by which thought is invigorated as a source of action. Fascist anti-intellectualism holds in scorn a product peculiarly typical of the educated classes in Italy: the *leterato*—the man who plays with knowledge and with thought without any sense of responsibility for the practical world. It is hostile not so much to culture as to bad culture, the culture which does not educate, which does not make men, but rather creates pedants and aesthetes, egotists in a word, men morally and politically indifferent. It has no use, for instance, for the man who is "above the conflict" when his country or its important interests are at stake.

From Giovanni Gentile, "The Philosophic Basis of Fascism," from *Readings on Fascism and National Socialism* © 1952, reprinted by permission of The Swallow Press, Inc., Chicago.

By virtue of its repugnance for "intellectualism," Fascism prefers not to waste time constructing abstract theories about itself. But when we say that it is not a system or a doctrine we must not conclude that it is a blind praxis or a purely instinctive method. If by system or philosophy we mean a living thought, a principle of universal character daily revealing its inner fertility and significance, then Fascism is a perfect system, with a solidly established foundation and with a rigorous logic in its development; and all who feel the truth and the vitality of the principle work day by day for its development, now doing, now undoing, now going forward, now retracing their steps, according as the things they do prove to be in harmony with the principle or to deviate from it.

And we come finally to a third point.

The Fascist system is not a political system, but it has its center of gravity in politics. Fascism came into being to meet serious problems of politics in post-war Italy. And it presents itself as a political method. But in confronting and solving political problems it is carried by its very nature, that is to say by its method, to consider moral, religious, and philosophical questions and to unfold and demonstrate the comprehensive totalitarian character peculiar to it. It is only after we have grasped the political character of the Fascist principle that we are able adequately to appreciate the deeper concept of life which underlies that principle and from which the principle springs. The political doctrine of Fascism is not the whole of Fascism. It is rather its more prominent aspect and in general its most interesting one.

The politic of Fascism revolves wholly about the concept of the national State; and accordingly it has points of contact with nationalist doctrines, along with distinctions from the latter which it is important to bear in mind.

Both Fascism and nationalism regard the State as the foundation of all rights and the source of all values in the individuals composing it. For the one as for the other the State is not a consequence—it is a principle. But in the case of nationalism, the relation which individualistic liberalism, and for that matter socialism also, assumed between individual and State is inverted. Since the State is a principle, the individual becomes a consequence—he is something which finds an antecedent in the State: the State limits him and determines his manner of existence, restricting his freedom, binding him to a piece of ground whereon he was born, whereon he must live and will die. In the case of Fascism, State and individual are one and the same things, or rather, they are inseparable terms of a necessary synthesis.

Nationalism, in fact, founds the State on the concept of nation, the nation being an entity which transcends the will and the life of the individual because it is conceived as objectively existing apart from the consciousness of individuals, existing even if the individual does nothing to bring it into being. For the nationalist, the nation exists not by virtue of the citizen's will, but as datum, a fact, of nature.

For Fascism, on the contrary, the State is a wholly spiritual creation. It is a national State, because, from the Fascist point of view, the nation itself is a creation of the mind and is not a material presupposition, is not a datum of nature. The nation, says the Fascist, is never really made; neither, therefore, can the State attain absolute form, since it is merely the nation in the latter's concrete, political manifestation. For the Fascist, the State is always *in fieri*. It is in our hands, wholly; whence our very serious responsibility towards it.

But this State of the Fascists which is created by the consciousness and the will of the citizen, and is not a force descending on the citizen from above or from without, cannot have toward the mass of the population the relationship which was presumed by nationalism.

Nationalism identified State with Nation, and made of the nation an entity preexisting, which needed not to be created but merely to be recognized or known. The nationalists, therefore, required a ruling class of an intellectual character, which was conscious of the nation and could understand, appreciate and exalt it. The authority of the State, furthermore, was not a product but a presupposition. It could not depend on the people—rather the people depended on the State and on the State's authority as the source of the life which they lived and apart from which they could not live. The nationalistic State was, therefore, an aristocratic State, enforcing itself upon the masses through the power conferred upon it by its origins.

The Fascist State, on the contrary, is a people's state, and, as such, the democratic State *par excellence*. The relationship between State and citizen (not this or that citizen, but all citizens) is accordingly so intimate that the State exists only as, and in so far as, the citizen causes it to exist. Its formation therefore is the formation of a consciousness of it in individuals, in the masses. Hence the need of the Party, and of all the instruments of propaganda and education which Fascism uses to make the thought and will of the *Duce* the thought and will of the masses. Hence the enormous task which Fascism sets itself in trying to bring the whole mass of the people, beginning with the little children, inside the fold of the Party.

On the popular character of the Fascist State likewise depends its greatest social and constitutional reform—the foundation of the Corporations of Syndicates. In this reform Fascism took over from syndicalism the notion of the moral and educational function of the syndicate. But the Corporations of Syndicates were necessary in order to reduce the syndicates to State discipline and make them an expression of the State's organism from within. The Corporations of Syndicates are a device through which the Fascist State goes looking for the individual in order to create itself through the individual's will. But the individual it seeks is not the abstract political individual whom the old liberalism took for granted. He is the only individual who can ever be found, the individual who exists as a specialized productive force, and who, by the fact of his specialization, is brought to unite with other individuals of his same category and comes to belong with them to the one great economic unit which is none other than the nation.

This great reform is already well under way. Toward it nationalism, syndicalism, and even liberalism itself, were already tending in the past. For even liberalism was beginning to criticize the older forms of political representation, seeking some system of organic representation which would correspond to the structural reality of the State.

The Fascist conception of liberty merits passing notice. The *Duce* of Fascism once chose to discuss the theme of "Force or consent?"; and he concluded that the two terms are inseparable, that the one implies the other and cannot exist apart from the other; that, in other words, the authority of the State and the freedom of the citizen constitute a continuous circle wherein authority presupposes liberty and liberty authority. For freedom can exist only within the State, and the State means authority. But the State is not an entity hovering in the air over the heads of its citizens. It is one with the personality of the citizen. Fascism, indeed, envisages the contrast not as between liberty and authority, but as between a true, a concrete liberty which exists, and an abstract, illusory liberty which cannot exist.

Liberalism broke the circle above referred to, setting the individual against the State and liberty against authority. What the liberal desired was liberty as against the State, a liberty which was a limitation of the State; though the liberal had to resign himself, as the lesser of the evils, to a State which was a limitation on liberty. The absurdities inherent in the liberal concept of freedom were apparent to liberals themselves early in the Nineteenth Century. It is no merit of Fascism to have again indicated them. Fascism has its own solution of the paradox of liberty and authority. The authority of the State is absolute. It does not compromise, it does not bargain, it does not surrender any portion of its field to other moral or religious principles which may interfere with the individual conscience. But on the other hand, the State becomes a reality only in the consciousness of its individuals. And the Fascist corporative State supplies a representative system more sincere and more in touch with realities than any other previously devised and is therefore freer than the old liberal State.

The Fascist State
Mario Palmieri

Mario Palmieri (1900-1941) published *The Philosophy of Fascism* in Chicago in 1936. Unlike the short essays and speeches of some Italian Fascists, it is a volume of considerable scope. The following passages present the Fascist position on some matters not touched upon in the preceding selections.

Without State there is no Nation. These words reverse the commonly accepted principle of modern political science that without Nation there is no State. They seem at first to run counter to all evidence, but they represent, instead, for Fascism, the expression of a fundamental truth, one of those truths which are at the very basis of the social life of mankind.

To say, in fact, that in the State and through the State a Nation first rises to the consciousness of itself, means that the State gives to the people that political, social and moral unity without which there is no possibility of a true national life. Furthermore, the State is the only organ through which the anonymous will of the people can find the expression of will of a single personality, conscious of its aims, its purposes and its needs.

The State becomes thus invested with the dignity, the attributes and the power of an ethical personality which exists and lives, and develops and progresses or decays, and, finally dies.

Compared to this personality of the State with its characteristics of transcendent

From Mario Palmieri, *The Philosophy of Fascism, 1936.*

values and its problems of momentous magnitude, the personality of the single individual loses all of that importance which it had assumed in the modern times.

It is possible thus for a Fascist writer, G. Corso, to write:

... the liberal idea, the democratic idea and the socialist idea, start from the common presupposition that the individual must be free because only the individual is real. To such a conception Fascism opposes the other that the individual is to be considered as a highly transitory and apparent thing, when compared to the ethnic reality of the race, the spiritual reality of the Nation, the ethical reality of the State.

Or for Mussolini to state:

... Liberalism denied the State in the interest of the particular individual; Fascism, instead reaffirms the State as the true reality of the individual.

In this shifting of emphasis from the individual to the State, the very functions of the one become part of the life of the other. The State must, therefore, concern itself not only with social order, political organization and economic problems, but with morality and religion as well.

The Fascist State is, in other words, not only the social, political and economic organization of the people of one nation, but is also the outward manifestation of their moral and religious life, and, as such, is therefore an Ethical State.

The Fascist State presupposes that man beside being an individual is also a social being, and therefore, willing and compelled to come under some form of disciplinary authority for the good of the whole.

It presupposes also that the highest law for man is the moral law, and that right or wrong, good or evil, have well defined meanings in this moral law and are beyond the pale of individual likes or dislikes or individual judgment.

It presupposes, finally, that the Nation-State is gifted with an organic life of its own, which far transcends in meaning the life of the individual, and whose development, growth and progress, follow laws which man cannot ignore or modify, but only discover and obey.

Henceforth the State is no longer a word denoting the authority underlying a complex system of relationships between individuals, classes, organizations, etc., but something of far greater import, far greater meaning than that; it is a living entity, it is the highest spiritual entity of the political world. . . .

To bring mankind back to the true vision of the relative worth of the individual and of the nation, that organism of which the single individual is an integral, although accidental and infinitesimal part, needs a truly superhuman effort.

Gone is forever the time when it was possible to find a way to the heart of man through his devotion to higher things than his personal affairs; gone is the time when it was possible to appeal to the mystic side of his nature through a religious commandment; gone, finally, is the time when it was possible to illuminate the reasoning powers of his mind with the light of ideals whose existence and whose reason of being cannot be proved through the powers of reason.

All that remains is an appeal to force, to compulsion; intellectual as well as physical, an appeal to what lies outside of man, to what he fears and with what he must of necessity abide.

Such a forceful appeal is made at present by Fascism which, compelling the elder or educating the younger, is slowly but surely bringing the Italian people to the comprehension of the worth, the beauty and the significance of the National Ideal.

But if the Fascist State is an Ethical State, it is also, and above all, a Sovereign State. Its power, therefore, is not conditional to the will of the people, the parliament, the King, or any other of its constituent elements: it is rather immanent in its very essence.

Once more we find Individualism with its offsprings: the liberal, democratic and radical doctrines, in antithetic contrast to Fascism on an issue of paramount importance for the whole world of man.

Passing from the Liberal doctrine, which had conceded the sovereignty of the State to the people as a whole, to the democratic doctrine, which this sovereignty gave away to the numerical majority and to the socialistic, communistic doctrine which invested it in one small particular class, we find an always greater abdication of the sovereign attributes to an always more restricted constituent element of the nation.

To affirm instead, as Fascism does, that "All is in the State and for the State; nothing outside the State, nothing against the State," means to affirm that the Ideal State is the one which is above individuals, organizations, castes or classes; or above all particularized interests, needs or ambitions.

The rise of Fascism destroys forever, thus, that Gordian Knot of apparently insoluble social problems born from the clash of conflicting interests of individuals within the State. It destroys also the subjection of the welfare of the State to the welfare of any individual, or any group of individuals, or even the totality of all the people. And, as the resort to the Will of God as final authority in all matters which may affect the welfare of the State has lost all meaning in our modern, individualistic, materialistic Society, in the same way the demagogic appeal to the will of the people is to lose all significance in the coming Fascist Society.

The triumph of Fascism means, in fact, that the role of the people is finally brought back to that secondary importance which it assumes when considered in its proper relation to the other elements of the Nation-State.

National Socialism: Twenty-five Points

Adolf Hitler

Adolph Hitler (1889-1945) was appointed Chancellor of Germany in 1933, but very soon he assumed absolute power. He was one of the world's foremost dictators. He was admired by most of the German citizens, who were inspired by his impassioned oratory. His book, *Mein Kampf* was written while he was in prison during the 1920's. It expresses his philosophy.

The programme of the German Workers' Party[1] is limited as to period. The leaders have no intention, once the aims announced in it have been achieved, of setting up fresh ones, so as to ensure the continued existence of the Party by the artificially increased discontent of the masses.

1. We demand, on the basis of the right of national self-determination, the union of all Germans to form one Great Germany.

2. We demand juridical equality for the German people in its dealings with other nations, and the abolition of the Peace Treaties of Versailles and St Germain.

3. We demand territory and soil (colonies) for the nourishment of our people and for settling our surplus population.

4. None but members of the nation may be citizens of the State. None but those of German blood, whatever their creed, may be members of the nation. No Jew, therefore, may be considered a member of the nation.

5. Anyone who is not a citizen of the State may live in Germany only as a guest and must be regarded as subject to the laws governing aliens.

6. The right to determine the leadership and laws of the State is to be enjoyed by the citizens of the State alone. We demand, therefore, that all official appointments of whatever kind, whether in the Reich, in the one or other of the federal states, or in the municipalities, shall be held by citizens of the State alone.

We oppose the corrupt Parliamentary custom of filling public offices merely with a view to party considerations, and without reference to character or capacity.

7. We demand that the State shall make it one of its chief duties to provide work and the means of livelihood for the citizens of the State. If it is not possible to provide for the entire population living within the confines of the State, foreign nationals (non-citizens of the State) must be excluded (expatriated).

8. All further non-German immigration must be prevented. We demand that all non-Germans who have entered Germany subsequently to 2 August 1914 shall be required forthwith to depart from the Reich.

From Michael Oakeshott, *Social and Political Doctrines of Contemporary Europe* (London: Cambridge University Press, 1950), pp. 190-193. Reprinted by permission.

[1] The National Socialist German Workers' Party announced their programme in these Twenty-Five Points at a mass-meeting of the Party in the Hofbrauhausfestsaal in Munich, on 25 February 1920.

9. All citizens of the State shall be equal as regards rights and duties.

10. It must be the first duty of every citizen of the State to work with his mind or with his body. The activities of the individual must not clash with the interests of the whole, but must be pursued within the framework of the national activity and must be for the general good.

11. We demand, therefore, the abolition of incomes unearned by work, and emancipation from the slavery of interest charges.

12. Because of the enormous sacrifice of life and property demanded of a nation by every war, personal profit through war must be regarded as a crime against the nation. We demand, therefore, the complete confiscation of all war profits.

13. We demand the nationalization of all business combines (trusts).

14. We demand that the great industries shall be organized on a profit-sharing basis.

15. We demand an extensive development of provision for old age.

16. We demand the creation and maintenance of a healthy middle class; the immediate communalization of the big department stores and the lease of the various departments at a low rate to small traders, and that the greatest consideration shall be shown to all small traders supplying goods to the State, the federal states or the municipalities.

17. We demand a programme of land reform suitable to our national requirements, the enactment of a law for confiscation without compensation of land for communal purposes, the abolition of ground rents, the prohibition of all speculation in land.[2]

18. We demand a ruthless campaign against all whose activities are injurious to the common interest. Oppressors of the nation, usurers, profiteers, etc., must be punished with death, whatever their creed or race.

19. We demand that the Roman Code, which serves the materialistic world order, shall be replaced by a system of German Common Law.

20. The State must undertake a thorough reconstruction of our national system of education, with the aim of giving to every capable and industrious German the benefits of a higher education and therewith the capacity to take his place in the leadership of the nation. The curricula of all educational establishments must be brought into line with the necessities of practical life. With the first dawn of intelligence, the schools must aim at teaching the pupil to know what the State stands for (instruction in citizenship). We demand educational facilities for specially gifted children of poor parents, whatever their class or occupation, at the expense of the State.

21. The State must concern itself with raising the standard of health in the nation by exercising its guardianship over mothers and infants, by prohibiting child labour, and by increasing bodily efficiency by legally obligatory gymnastics and sports, and by the extensive support of clubs engaged in the physical training of the young.

---

[2] "It is necessary to reply to the false interpretation on the part of our opponents of Point 17 of the programme of the N.S.D.A.P. Since the N.S.D.A.P. admits the principle of private property, it is obvious that the expression 'confiscation without compensation' merely refers to possible legal powers to confiscate, if necessary, land illegally acquired, or not administered in accordance with the national welfare. It is directed in the first instance against Jewish companies which speculate in land." Adolf Hitler, Munich, 13 April 1928.

22. We demand the abolition of a paid army and the foundation of a national army.

23. We demand legal measures against intentional political lies and their dissemination in the Press. In order to facilitate the creation of a German national Press, we demand:

(*a*) that all editors of newspapers and all contributors, employing the German language, shall be members of the nation;

(*b*) that special permission from the State shall be necessary before non-German newspapers may appear. These must not be printed in the German language;

(*c*) that non-Germans shall be prohibited by law from participation financially in, or from influencing German newspapers, and that the penalty for contravention of this law shall be suppression of any such newspaper and the immediate deportation of the non-German concerned in it.

It must be forbidden to publish newspapers which do not conduce to the national welfare. We demand the legal prosecution of all tendencies in art and literature of a kind calculated to disintegrate our national life, and the suppression of institutions which militate against the above-mentioned requirements.

24. We demand liberty for all religious denominations in the State, in so far as they are not a danger to it and do not militate against the moral sense of the German race.

The Party, as such, stands for a positive Christianity, but does not bind itself in the matter of creed to any particular confession. It is strenuously opposed to the Jewish-materialist spirit within and without the Party, and is convinced that our nation can only achieve permanent well-being from within on the principle of placing the common interests before self-interest.

25. That all the foregoing demands may be realized, we demand the creation of a strong central power of the Reich; the unconditional authority of the central Parliament over the entire Reich and its organization; the formation of Diets and vocational Chambers for the purpose of administering in the various federal States the general laws promulgated by the Reich.

The leaders of the Party swear to proceed regardless of consequences—if necessary to sacrifice their lives—in securing the fulfilment of the foregoing points.

.   .   .

[The following passages are from speeches by Adolph Hitler.]

Selected Speeches

THE STRONG OVER THE WEAK

... It is evident that the stronger has the right before God and the world to enforce his will. History shows that the right as such does not mean a thing, unless it is backed up by great power. If one does not have the power to enforce his right, that right alone will profit him absolutely nothing. The stronger have always been victorious. The whole of nature is a continuous struggle between strength and weakness, an eternal victory of the strong over the weak. All nature would be full of decay if it were otherwise. And the states which do not wish to recognize this law will decay. If you need an example of this kind of decay, look at the present German Reich. (Munich, April 13, 1923; *Völkischer Boebachter*, April 15/16, 1923.)

ONLY FORCE RULES

The fundamental motif through all the centuries has been the principle that force and power are the determining factors. All development is struggle. Only force rules. Force is the first law. A struggle has already taken place between original man and his primeval world. Only through struggle have states and the world become great. If one should ask whether this struggle is gruesome, then the only answer could be: For the weak, yes, for humanity as a whole, no.

World history proves that in the struggle between nations, that race has always won out whose drive for self-preservation was the more pronounced, the stronger. ... Unfortunately, the contemporary world stresses internationalism instead of the innate values of race, democracy and the majority instead of the worth of the great leader. Instead of everlasting struggle the world preaches cowardly pacifism, and everlasting peace. These three things, considered in the light of their ultimate consequences, are the causes of the downfall of all humanity. The practical result of conciliation among nations is the renunciation of a people's own strength and their voluntary enslavement. (Essen, Nov. 22, 1926; *Völkischer Beobachter*, Nov. 26, 1926.)

THE NONSENSE OF HUMANITARIANISM

The inventions of mankind are the result of eternal struggle. Never would aviation have progressed so remarkably had it not been for the war, had not countless thousands sacrificed their lives in this cruel struggle against nature. The struggle against the great beasts is ended, but it is being inexorably carried on against the

This and the following selections are from *Hitler's Words, the Speeches of Adolph Hitler from 1923-1943*, edited by G. Prange and reprinted by permission of the Public Affairs Press, Washington, D.C.

tiny creatures—against bacteria and bacilli. There is no Marxian reconciliation on this score; it is either you or I, life or death, either extermination or servitude.

From [various] examples we arrive at the fundamental conclusion that there is no humanitarianism but only an eternal struggle, a struggle which is the prerequisite for the development of all humanity.

The borderline between man and the animal is established by man himself. The position which man enjoys today is his own accomplishment. We see before us the Aryan race which is manifestly the bearer of all culture, the true representative of all humanity. All inventions in the field of transportation must be credited to the members of a particular race. Our entire industrial science is without exception the work of the Nordics. All great composers from Beethoven to Richard Wagner are Aryans, even though they were born in Italy or France. Do not say that art is international. The tango, the shimmy, and the jazzband are international but they are not art. Man owes everything that is of any importance to the principle of struggle and to one race which has carried itself forward successfully. Take away the Nordic Germans and nothing remains but the dance of apes. . . . Because we recognize the fact that our people can endure only through struggle, we National Socialists are fighters. (Munich, April 2, 1927; *Völkischer Beobachter*, April 5, 1927.)

STRUGGLE—THE SOURCE OF STRENGTH

Politics is nothing else than the struggle of a people for its existence in this world; it is the eternal battle of a people, for better or for worse, for its existence on this planet. How does this struggle take place? Great men of world history have described it. Frederick the Great said that politics is the art of serving one's people with all the means at one's disposal; according to Bismarck, politics is the art of the possible. . . . Clemenceau decleared that the politics of peace was nothing else than the continuation of war with other means. Clausewitz asserted that war was nothing else than the continuation of politics with other weapons. In reality, then, politics is the struggle of a people with all weapons to the limit of its power for its existence on this earth.

With what question is struggle primarily related? It is the drive for self-preservation which leads to struggle—that is, the question of love and hunger. These are the two fundamental primitive forces around which everything on this earth centers. The total space on which life is carried on is circumscribed. This leads to a struggle of one against the other for this limited area. In addition, this area is more restricted for certain groups than for others so that their existence is dependent upon the preservation of the particular region which they inhabit.

Thus, the struggle for daily bread becomes in reality a struggle for the soil which produces this daily bread; that is, for space itself. It is an iron principle: the weak fall in order that the strong may live. . . . From all the innumerable creatures a complete species rises and becomes the master of the rest. Such a one is man—the most brutal, the most resolute creature on earth. He knows nothing but the extermination of his enemies in the world. . . . This struggle, this battle has not been carried on by all men in the same way. Certain species stand out, and at the top of the list is the Aryan. The Aryan has forged the weapons with which mankind has made itself master of the animal world. There is scarcely anything in existence which when traced back to its origin cannot claim an Aryan as its creator. . . . Never have votes and majorities added one iota to the culture of mankind. Every accomplishment is solely the result of the work and energy of great men, and as such, a flaming protest against the inertia of the masses.

How does this process then take place? It is an eternal struggle. Every achievement is nothing else than the result of a struggle of give-and-take. Every new invention is a triumph over an old one. Every record is a struggle against that which exists. Every championship performance is a conquest of that which prevailed previously.

Hence the following principles result: The value of man is determined in the first place by his inner racial virtues; second, by the ability of the race to bring forth men who in turn become leaders in the struggle for advancement, third, this entire process takes place in the form of eternal struggle. As a consequence struggle is the father of all things in this world. (Munich, Nov. 21, 1927; *Völkischer Beobachter*, Nov. 23, 1927.)

ORIGINALITY PLUS BRUTALITY

The will to live leads beyond the limitations of the present to the struggle for the prerequisites of life. Struggle is the impulse of self-preservation in nature. Man has become great through struggle.

The first fundamental of any rational *Weltanschauung* is the fact that on earth and in the universe force alone is decisive. Whatever goal man has reached is due to his originality plus his brutality. Whatever man possesses today in the field of culture is the culture of the Aryan race. The Aryan has stamped his character on the whole world. The basis for all development is the creative urge of the individual, not the vote of majorities. The genius of the individual is decisive, not the spirit of the masses. All life is bound up in three theses: Struggle is the father of all things, virtue lies in blood, leadership is primary and decisive. (Chemnitz, April 2, 1928; *Völkischer Beobachter*, April 7, 1928.)

MAN MUST KILL

If men wish to live, then they are forced to kill others. The entire struggle for survival is a conquest of the means of existence which in turn results in the elimination of others from these same sources of subsistence. As long as there are peoples on this earth, there will be nations against nations and they will be forced to protect their vital rights in the same way as the individual is forced to protect his rights.

There is in reality no distinction between peace and war. Life, no matter in what form, is a process which always leads to the same result. Self-preservation will always be the goal of every individual. Struggle is ever-present and will remain. This signifies a constant willingness on the part of man to sacrifice to the utmost. Weapons, methods, instruments, formations, these may change, but in the end the struggle for survival remains. . . .

One is either the hammer or the anvil. We confess that it is our purpose to prepare the German people again for the role of the hammer. . . . We confess further that we will dash anyone to pieces who should dare to hinder us in this undertaking. . . . Our rights will never be represented by others. Our rights will be protected only when the German Reich is again supported by the point of the German dagger. (Munich, March 15, 1929; *Völkischer Beobachter*, March 17, 1929.)

LONG LIVE FANATICAL NATIONALISM

Our entire work consists of enlightening our people, of reshaping its mentality. It consists in the creation of a new Movement which will reform our people from top to bottom even reaching into the soul of the common German man, a new Movement which establishes three great postulates without which foreign policy cannot be carried out in the future.

In the first place, our people must be delivered from the hopeless confusion of international convictions, and educated consciously and systematically to fanatical nationalism. We will not declare that our goal is to have the German people sing German songs again in the future. No, our goal is that the German people should again acquire honor and conviction, that it should again bow in adoration before its own history, that it should respect those things which formerly gave it significance, and that it should curse that which damaged its honor. We recognize only two Gods: A God in Heaven and a God on earth and that is our Fatherland.

Second, insofar as we educate the people to fight against the delirium of democracy and bring it again to the recognition of the necessity of authority and of leadership, we tear it away from the nonsense of parliamentarianism; thereby we deliver it from the atmosphere of irresponsibility and lead it to responsibility and to a recognition of duty on the part of the individual person.

Third, insofar as we deliver the people from the atmosphere of pitiable belief in possibilities which lie outside the bounds of one's own strength—such as the belief in reconciliation, understanding, world peace, the League of Nations, and international solidarity—we destroy these ideas. There is only one right in this world and this right is one's own strength.

The people must recognize that its future will not be molded through cowardly belief in the help of others but through faithful devotion to one's own task. Out of this devotion deliverance must one day come—freedom and happiness and life. (Munich, Sept. 22, 1968; *Völkischer Beobachter*, Sept. 23, 1928.)

RACIAL AND NATIONAL REGENERATION

Racial degeneration continues apace. The bastardization of great states has begun. The Negroization of culture, of customs—not only of blood—strides forward. The world becomes democratized. The value of the individual declines. The masses apparently are gaining the victory over the idea of the great leader. Numbers are chosen as the new God.

The poison of pacifism is again scattered about. The world forgets that struggle is the father of all things. State upon state is becoming intoxicated with ideas that must lead to the obliteration of a people. When the bastard, however, stands against the thoroughbred, and the Negro stands against the white man, the one who from the racial standpoint is the strongest, will be victorious. The individual is creative and has given culture to the world. When cowardice is pitted against courage and pacifism against daring, courage and daring gain the victory. That state will be victorious which does not fall prey to the vice of cowardice and pacifism. The people who opposed pacifism with the idea of struggle will with mathematical certainty become the master of its fate.

A people who opposes the bastardization of its spirit and its blood can be saved. The German people has its specific value and cannot be placed on the same level as 70,000,000 Negroes. If the German people will recognize its value it can mold the forces which will lead to victory.

Negro music is now the rage. But if we put the shimmy alongside a Beethoven symphony, then the triumph is clear. Let us think about the German soul, and then faith, creative power, and tenacity will not fail. Our people has always found men who conquered distress. Now it is believed, however, that leaders can be dispensed with; and at present world history is not being made, but, rather, the history of submission. Out of our strong faith will come the strength to help ourselves against this bastardization.

Racism: Nordic Europe
Alfred Rosenberg

Alfred Rosenberg (1893-1946) was the leading apologist for German racism, elaborating at length upon the myth of blood, and Volk, and Aryan superiority. After a lengthy trial at Nurnberg in 1946 he was convicted and hanged as a war criminal. Appropriately, his chief work was entitled *The Myth of the Twentieth Century* (1930).

RACE AND HISTORY

Racial history is thus at the same time natural history and soul-*mystique*. The history of the religion of blood is, conversely, the great world-narrative of the rise and decline of peoples, their heroes and thinkers, their inventors and artists. . . .

The "meaning of world history" has radiated out from the north over the whole world, borne by a blue-eyed blond race which in several great waves determined the spiritual face of the world. . . . These wander-periods were the legendary migration of the Atlantides across north Africa, the migration of the Aryans into India and Persia; the migration of the Dorians, Macedonians, Latins; the migration of the Germanic tribes; the colonization of the world by the Germanic occident. . . .

From A. Rosenberg, *The Myth of the Twentieth Century*, 1930. These passages are reprinted from selections appearing in *National Socialism*, a report prepared by the Division of European Affairs, U.S. Department of State, United States Government Printing Office, Washington, D.C., 1943.

THE MYTH OF NORDIC BLOOD

We stand today before a definitive decision. Either through a new experience and cultivation of the old blood, coupled with an enhanced fighting will, we will rise to a purificatory action, or the last Germanic-western values of morality and state-culture shall sink away in the filthy human masses of the big cities, become stunted on the sterile burning asphalt of a bestialized inhumanity, or trickle away as a morbific agent in the form of emigrants, bastardizing themselves in South America, China, Dutch East India, Africa. . . .

A *new* faith is arising today: the myth of the blood, the faith, to defend with the blood the divine essence of man. The faith, embodied in clearest knowledge, that the Nordic blood represents that *mysterium* which has replaced and overcome the old sacraments. . . .

The new real struggle today is concerned not so much with external changes in power, along with an internal compromise as hitherto, but, conversely, with the new rebuilding of the soul-cells of the Nordic peoples, for the sake of the re-institution in their sovereign rights [*Herrscherrechte*] of those ideals and values from which originates everything which signifies culture to us, and for the sake of the preservation of the racial substance itself. . . .

GERMAN NATIONAL HONOR

A German religious movement, which would like to develop into a folk-church, will have to declare that the ideal of neighborly love is unconditionally to be subordinated to the idea of national honor, that no act of a German church may be approved which does not primarily serve the safeguarding of the *Volkstum*. . . .

The idea of honor, national honor, is for us the beginning and end of our entire thinking and doing. It does not admit of any equal-valued center of force alongside of it, no matter of what kind, neither Christian love, nor the Masonic humanity, nor the Roman philosophy. . . .

The essence of the contemporary world revolution lies in the awakening of the racial types. Not in Europe alone but on the whole planet. This awakening is the organic counter movement against the last chaotic remnants of the liberal economic fulfillment of the demanded values lies on a line with the highest values of this blood. With the others the inheritance, which exhibits itself in actions, outweighs personal appearance. . . .

STATE AND FOLK

The state is nowadays no longer an independent idol, before which everything must bow down; the state is not even an end but is only a means for the preservation of the folk. . . Forms of the state change, and the laws of the state pass away; the folk remains. From this alone follows that the nation is the first and *last*, that to which everything else has to be subordinated. . . .

The new thought puts folk and race higher than the state and its forms. It declares protection of the folk more important than protection of a religious denomination, a class, the monarchy, or the republic; it sees in treason against the folk a greater crime than high treason against the state. . . .

No folk of Europe is racially unified, including Germany. In accordance with the newest researches, we recognize five races, which exhibit noticeably different types. Now it is beyond question true that the Nordic race primarily has borne the genuine cultural fruits of Europe. The great heroes, artists, founders of states have come from this race. . . . Nordic blood created *German* life above all others. Even those sections, in which only a small part today is pure Nordic, have their basic stock from the Nordic race. Nordic is German and has functioned so as to shape the culture and human types of the *westisch, dinarisch* and *ostisch-Baltisch* races. Also a type which is predominantly *dinarisch* has often been innerly formed in a Nordic mode. This emphasis on the Nordic race does not mean a sowing of "race-hatred" in Germany but, on the contrary, the conscious acknowledgement of a kind of racial cement within our nationality. . . . On the day when Nordic blood should completely dry up, Germany would fall to ruin, would decline into a characterless chaos. That many forces are consciously working toward this, has been discussed in detail. For this they rely primarily on the Alpine lower stratum, which, without any value of its own, has remained essentially superstitious and slavish despite all Germanization. Now that the external bond of the old idea of the Reich has fallen away, this blood is active, together with other bastard phenomena, in order to put itself in the service of a magic faith or in the service of the democratic chaos, which finds its herald in the parasitic but energetic Judaism. . . .

The foundation for the arising of a *new aristocracy* lies in those men who have stood—in a spiritual, political, and military sense—in the foremost positions in the struggle for the coming Reich. It will appear thereby with inner necessity that up to 80 percent of these men will also externally approach the Nordic type, since the fulfillment of the demanded values lies on a line with the highest values of this blood. With the others the inheritance, which exhibits itself in actions, outweighs personal appearance. . . .

NORDIC EUROPE

Europe's states have all been founded and preserved by the Nordic man. This Nordic man through alcohol, the World War, and Marxism has partially degenerated, partially been uprooted. . . . In order to preserve Europe, the Nordic energies of Europe must first be revitalized, strengthened. That means then Germany, Scandinavia with Finland, and England. . . .

Nordic Europe is the fated future, with a *German* central Europe. Germany as racial and national state, as central power of the continent, safeguarding the south and southeast; the Scandinavian states with Finland as a second group, safeguarding the northeast; and Great Britain, safeguarding the west and overseas at those places where required in the interest of the Nordic man. . . .

The People, the Führer, and the Reich

Ernst R. Huber

Ernst R. Huber (1903-   ) was one of the foremost philosophers of the Third German Reich. In the following passages he develops the three central concepts of German fascism: the people, the Führer, and the Nazi party, which represents the state.

THE PEOPLE

There is no people without an objective unity, but there is also none without a common consciousness of unity. A people is determined by a number of different factors: by racial derivation and by the character of its land, by language and other forms of life, by religion and history, but also by the common consciouness of its solidarity and by its common will to unity. For the concrete concept of a people, as represented by the various peoples of the earth, it is of decisive significance which of these various factors they regard as determinants for the nature of the people. The new German Reich proceeds from the concept of the political people, determined by the natural characteristics and by the historical idea of a closed community. The political people is formed through the uniformity of its natural characteristics. Race is the natural basis of the people. . . . As a political people the natural community becomes conscious of its solidarity and strives to form itself, to develop itself, to defend itself, to realize itself. "Nationalism" is essentially this striving of a people which has become conscious of itself toward self-direction and self-realization, toward a deepening and renewing of its natural qualities.

This consciousness of self, springing from the consciousness of a historical idea, awakens in a people its will to historical formation: the will to action. The political people is no passive, sluggish mass, no mere object for the efforts of the state at government or protective welfare work. . . . The great misconception of the democracies is that they can see the active participation of the people only in the form of plebiscites according to the principle of majority. In a democracy the people does not act as a unit but as a complex of unrelated individuals who form themselves into parties. . . . The new Reich is based on the principle that real action of a self-determining people is only possible according to the principle of leadership and following. . . .

In the theory of the nationalistic [*völkisch*] Reich, people and state are conceived as an inseparable unity. The people is the prerequisite for the entire political order; the state does not form the people but the people molds the state out of itself as the form in which it achieves historical permanence. . . . The state is

From E. R. Huber, *Constitutional Law of the Greater German Reich*, 1939. These passages are reprinted from selections appearing in *National Socialism*, a report prepared by the Division of European Affairs, U.S. Department of State, U.S. Government Printing Office, Washington, D.C., 1943.

a function of the people, but it is not therefore a subordinate secondary machine which can be used or laid aside at will. It is the form in which the people attains to historical reality. It is the bearer of the historical continuity of the people which remains the same in the center of its being in spite of all changes, revolutions, and transformations. . . .

THE FÜHRER

The Führer Reich of the [German] people is founded on the recognition that the true will of the people cannot be disclosed through parliamentary votes and plebiscites but that the will of the people in its pure and uncorrupted form can only be expressed through the Führer. Thus a distinction must be drawn between the supposed will of the people in a parliamentary democracy, which merely reflects the conflict of the various social interests, and the true will of the people in the Führer-state, in which the collective will of the real political unit is manifested. . . .

The Führer is the bearer of the people's will; he is independent of all groups, associations, and interests, but he is bound by laws which are inherent in the nature of his people. In this twofold condition: independence of all factional interests but unconditional dependence of the people, is reflected the true nature of the Führer principle. Thus the Führer has nothing in common with the functionary, the agent, or the exponent who exercises a mandate delegated to him and who is bound to the will of those who appoint him. The Führer is no "representative" of a particular group whose wishes he must carry out. He is no "organ" of the state in the sense of a mere executive agent. He is rather himself the bearer of the collective will of the people. In his will the will of the people is realized. He transforms the mere feelings of the people into a conscious will. . . . Thus it is possible for him, in the name of the true will of the people which he serves, to go against the subjective opinions and convictions of single individuals within the people if these are not in accord with the objective destiny of the people. . . . He shapes the collective will of the people within himself and he embodies the political unity and entirety of the people in opposition to individual interests. . . .

But the Führer, even as the bearer of the people's will, is not arbitrary and free of all responsibility. His will is not the subjective, individual will of a single man, but the collective national will is embodied within him in all its objective, historical greatness. . . . Such a collective will is not a fiction, as is the collective will of the democracies, but it is a political reality which finds its expression in the Führer. The people's collective will has its foundation in the political idea which is given to a people. It is present in the people, but the Führer raises it to consciousness and discloses it. . . .

In the Führer are manifested also the natural laws inherent in the people: It is he who makes them into a code governing all national activity. In disclosing these natural laws he sets up the great ends which are to be attained and draws up the plans for the utilization of all national powers in the achievement of the common goals. Through his planning and directing he gives the national life its true purpose and value. This directing and planning activity is especially manifested in the lawgiving power which lies in the Führer's hand. The great change in significance which the law has undergone is characterized therein that it no longer sets up the limits of social life, as in liberalistic times, but that it drafts the plans and the aims of the nation's actions. . . .

The Führer principle rests upon unlimited authority but not upon mere outward force. It has often been said, but it must constantly be repeated, that the Führer principle has nothing in common with arbitrary bureaucracy and represents no system of brutal force, but that it can only be maintained by mutual loyalty which must find its expression in a free relation. The Führer-order depends upon the responsibility of the following, just as it counts on the responsibility and loyalty of the Führer to his mission and to his following. . . . There is no greater responsibility than that upon which the Führer principle is grounded. . . .

The office of the Führer developed out of the National Socialist movement. It was originally not a state office; this fact can never be disregarded if one is to understand the present legal and political position of the Führer. The office of the Führer first took root in the structure of the Reich when the Führer took over the powers of the Chancellor, and then when he assumed the position of the Chief of State. But his primary significance is always as leader of the movement; he has absorbed within himself the two highest offices of the political leadership of the Reich and has created thereby the new office of "Führer of the people and the Reich." That is not a superficial grouping together of various offices, functions, and powers. . . . It is not a union of offices but a unity of office. The Führer does not unite the old offices of Chancellor and President side by side within himself, but he fills a new, unified office. . . .

The Führer unites in himself all the sovereign authority of the Reich; all public authority in the state as well as in the movement is derived from the authority of the Führer. We must speak not of the state's authority but of the Führer's authority if we wish to designate the character of the political authority within the Reich correctly. The state does not hold political authority as an impersonal unit but receives it from the Führer as the executor of the national will. The authority of the Führer is complete and all-embracing; it unites in itself all the means of political direction; it extends into all fields of national life; it embraces the entire people, which is bound to the Führer in loyalty and obedience. The authority of the Führer is not limited by checks and controls, by special autonomous bodies or individual rights, but it is free and independent, all-inclusive and unlimited. It is not, however, self-seeking or arbitrary and its ties are within itself. It is derived from the people; that is, it is entrusted to the Führer by the people. It exists for the people and has its justification in the people; it is free of all outward ties because it is in its innermost nature firmly bound up with the fate, the welfare, the mission, and the honor of the people. . . .

.   .   .

[THE INDIVIDUAL AND THE REICH]

Not until the nationalistic political philosophy had become dominant could the liberalistic idea of basic rights be really overcome. The concept of personal liberties of the individual as opposed to the authority of the state had to disappear; it is not to be reconciled with the principle of the nationalistic Reich. There are no personal liberties of the individual which fall outside of the realm of the state and which must be respected by the state. The member of the people, organically connected with the whole community, has replaced the isolated individual; he is included in the totality of the political people and is drawn into the collective action. There can no longer be any question of a private sphere, free of state influence, which is sacred and untouchable before the political unity. The constitution of the nationalistic Reich is therefore not based upon a system of inborn and inalienable rights of the individual. . . .

The legal position of the individual member of the people forms an entirely new concept which is indispensable for the construction of a nationalistic order. The legal position of the individual is always related to the community and conditioned by duty. It is developed not for the sake of the individual but for the community, which can only be filled with life, power, and purpose when a suitable field of action is insured for the individual member. Without a concrete determination of the individual's legal position there can be no real community.

This legal position represents the organic fixation of the individual in the living order. Rights and obligations arise from the application of this legal position to specific individual relationships. . . . But all rights must be regarded as duty-bound rights. Their exercise is always dependent upon the fulfillment by the individual of those duties to which all rights are subordinate. . . .

It is a mistake to claim that the citizen of the Reich has no rights but only duties; that there is no right of choice but only a duty of acclamation. There are, of course, no inborn, inalienable political rights which are inherent in the individual himself and which would tend to limit and hamper the leadership of the Reich. But in every true political community the individual has his legal position which he receives from the Führer and which makes him a true follower. . . .

This Time the World
George Lincoln Rockwell

George Lincoln Rockwell (1918-1967) was the Nazi leader of the National Socialist White People's Party. The slogan for the party is "White Power." Killed by a sniper in Arlington, Virginia.

. . . Above all, I had to make sure that all of our people understood that Communism is not an economic plot and not even just part of the Jewish scheme for dominating the earth although it is both of these.

Communism is a mutiny of the world's inferiors against the elite.

Since man first fashioned a rude stone implement, he has fought a never-ending battle with the forces of nature which have overwhelmed him. Death in childbirth, death in earthquakes, volcanic eruptions, plagues, tidal waves, droughts, famines, and death at the claws and fangs of ferocious animals have been the lot of a great portion of humanity for tens of thousands of years.

In order to have one or two surviving children, parents had to have ten or twelve born. Only the strongest, wiliest and toughest survived human existence for unnumbered ages. This always seemed cruel and most unfortunate.

From George Lincoln Rockwell, *This Time the World* (New York: Parliment House, 1961), pp. 401-404, 407-410, 413-414. Reprinted by permission.

But the very severity of this unequal battle with nature insured that ONLY the smartest and strongest individuals rose to leadership; ONLY the best organized and most excellent families rose to leadership of the group; and ONLY the strongest, smartest and best organized of the groups rose to preeminence in a desperately struggling world.

Weaklings and fools did not last long. Especially, they could not swindle the strong and wise men who had survived the awful struggle of existence into accepting fools, demagogues and weaklings as "great leaders." Thus, from the dawn of human history, with rare exceptions (caused by inheritance of power, which did not last, relatively speaking) only leaders who could lead attained REAL, permanent leadership, and only races (groups) which were TRULY superior could dominate.

Under these conditions the group of humanity loosely called "Aryan white men" inevitably rose to complete domination of the civilized world, and civilized much of the savage world. And within this elite human group, or breed,—Ceasars, Pericles, Fredericks and Washingtons rose to personal leadership.

The natural enemies of humanity, such as disease, wild beasts and brutal elements forced the naturally inferior groups to accept the domination and leadership of the superior white group. And the same cruel struggle within the white group forced the masses of inferiors to accept and even seek the leadership and domination of the naturally superior and elite minority. "People's Revolutions" were always relatively temporary, and power and leadership sooner or later was back in the hands of the biologically superior humans who had REAL capacity and force to LEAD.

As a result, the world was benefited by the civilizing drive of the exceptional whites of England, Germany, France, Spain, Portugal, Italy, etc.—but most of all by NORDICS.

While the "subjects" of colonization might have chafed and complained under the yoke, millions of inferior savages who had lived for thousands of years in prehistoric squalor, ignorance and savagery were relatively suddenly taught the rudimentary technical methods of controlling natural forces so that many more of them could survive and become, in their own way, more powerful than their savage, uncolonized brothers.

During all of these eons of history, it was highly advantageous to the subjects—inferior races and even to the inferior individuals among the white race, to seek and accept the leadership of the best races and best individuals even if this involved some tyranny. Nature herself was a still crueler tyrant and only with the leadership and organization supplied by the superior white race and the superior individuals within the white race could humanity hold its own or advance in the battle with nature.

The weapon of the superior white man and the superior individual who led the white men was never physical strength alone but always the power of ORGANIZA-TION—which is the supreme form of THE HUMAN WILL in action.

In applying his intellect to the cruel forces of nature which tyrannized over him. the white man inevitably cast aside superstition, religious myths, old wives' tales and wishful thinking. He discovered what we now call the "scientific method"—the power of organized, scrupulously LOGICAL thinking.

With the full understanding and use of this intellectual tool MAN SUDDENLY GAINED TERRIFIC POWER TO CONTROL MANY OF THE WILD FORCES OF

NATURE WHICH HAD BEEN BEATING HIM FOR THOUSANDS OF YEARS. With this method there is almost no thing or action which cannot be somehow dominated, controlled and used by mankind.

Man has penetrated outer space and the atom itself. He has controlled one natural killer and disease after another and even developed artificial human organs to replace those destroyed or decayed. He is, perhaps, on the verge of discovering the secrets of life itself.

Utterly astounded at his own genius and accomplishment through the use of the scientific method, MAN THEN MADE WHAT MAY YET BE HIS *FATAL* ERROR.

From the discovery that he could USE natural laws he jumped to the conclusion that he could CONQUER NATURE and FLAUNT HER IRON LAWS.

Bursting with conceit over his scientific and material accomplishments he forgot that HE, TOO, IS A PART OF NATURE, AN ANIMAL.

He proceeded to "conquer" EVOLUTION. He has now REVERSED it. THAT is the supreme danger of our chaotic times.

Where nature had for countless centuries culled humanity until the best individuals and the best group (speaking of the average) dominated humanity, he now applies scientific method to EVERYTHING ELSE BUT HIS OWN BREED-ING. He allowed anthropomorphism—conceit—to enter the picture and control him just as it did his most savage and stupid ancestors 10,000 years ago in the form of superstition. Science showed him the secrets of heredity and how to use these secrets to breed better cattle, dogs, horses and even bugs. But when it came to his own heredity man was loathe to admit the perhaps "unfair" but brutally true fact that there is no scientific reason why all individuals and groups of the species homo sapiens should be equally valuable and have equal natural abilities any more than that all horses or dogs should be of the same quality whether by breeds or by individuals.

As a matter of fact, during the 18th and 19th century MAN FELL IN LOVE WITH BOTH THE SCIENTIFIC METHOD AND HIS OWN INTELLECT. With his medical knowledge he largely conquered the natural forces which had so long SELECTED the best individuals and groups alone for survival, thus utterly reversing the process of evolution which produced the superior white man and the very brains of the geniuses among the white men who discovered these scientific wonders.

With this sort of worship of the intellect went a concomitant degradation of physical force. Where once the white man had not only out-thought and out-manoeuvred the savage races but also kept them in meek submission by naked force and even terror, when necessary, the white man now began to delude himself with the soothing "liberal" idea that force could be dispensed with and man could maintain and extend his accomplishments by sheer intellect alone. He laid down his knotty club, bent over his books and began to fancy himself as "above" the rest of the animal world which still had to copulate, deficate, urinate—and FIGHT to survive. And as he did this, there was one human group which had been schooled and especially selected in this super intellectualism for thousands of years: the Jews.

Naturally weak, unaggressive and lacking in creative force, this human group had survived solely by its wits as a sort of parasite and had even developed a "religion" which codified and even glorified intellectual paranoiaism and physical cowardice as the "way of God."

When the forceful, domineering and driving white man laid aside his club, forgot that he also was an animal, and allowed his scientific method and medical knowledge to reverse evolution, HE SET UP HUMANITY FOR DOMINATION BY THE JEW.

Instinctively the Jew perceived the white man's growing unwillingness to FIGHT, and realized that in a battle of words and mutual swindling his thousands of years of experience would be more than a match for the less subtle Aryan white man. The JEW THUS BECAME THE LEADING AND LOUDEST EXPONENT OF INTELLECTUALISM AND THE SCIENTIFIC METHOD. AND AT THE SAME TIME HE INSTINCTIVELY DEPRECATED ALL IDEAS OF HEREDITY, BREEDING, RACE OR INDIVIDUAL LEADERSHIP. It is the Jew who would be master in a mongrelised world.

A wolf pack is led by the strongest and smartest wolf by a sort of mutual consent based on force. This arrangement benefits the entire pack because the wise and tough old wolf leader is the best guarantee for the rest of the pack that they will be led in an organized and successful manner toward food and safety, etc.

Humanity until the seventeen and eighteen hundreds was much in the position of such a wolf pack, beset as it was with natural dangers and human enemies.

But with the rise of intellectualism and pacifism the Jew was able to approach the members of the "wolf pack" of humanity and say, in effect, "Why should we be bossed around by the leader, 'the tyrant' when we outnumber him so greatly? Let us set up a DEMOCRACY and we will VOTE him out of business."

If the "pack" can be sold on this swindle it will mutiny against its natural leader and the resulting "democracy" will actually be run by the smartest demagogue or smooth talker, usually a Jew, once the strong leader is eliminated by sheer numbers.

This is what we saw in the French Revolution, Oliver Cromwell's uprising, and a hundred other similar "people's revolutions" against the naturally superior leaders of humanity, the so-called "aristocrats", who had lost their FORCE and became decadent.

About 1850 the Jew, Karl Marx, organized and codified this mutiny of the inferiors against their natural leaders in the name of intellectualism, science and democracy. Organized by the Jews in the form of COMMUNISM, this "mutiny" by the massed millions of the earth's inferiors against the naturally superior races and individuals threatens to overwhelm humanity.

Today, in the name of "humanitarianism" and "progress", man has selfishly and stupidly stopped or even reversed every one of the mechanisms by which Nature kept him vigorous and evolving as a species. Where he once had twelve or thirteen children, so that only the strongest and fittest survived, he now cruelly limits his offspring to one, two, three, or, at the most, four. Of these, he hamstrings the strong and vigorous with the frustrating doctrines of "pacifism" and brotherhood with human trash, while he mobilizes the entire forces of society and science to keep alive the sorriest kind of creatures—from drooling idiots down to two-headed monsters. Daily grows the number of high-powered appeals for contributions to this or that foundation for the preservation of the lives and therefore the ability to procreate of the most miserable and unhappy little human mistakes, whom Nature would mercifully put out of their suffering, were it not for the soft-headed "humanitarianism" of short-sighted men and women, of whom Eleanor Roosevelt is perhaps the most disgusting example.

While the white race is thus emasculating and extinguishing itself by severely limiting its offspring and then keeping the most unfit individuals alive at the expense of the species, it is also actively helping and even forcing the numberless hordes of colored humanity to proliferate at such a staggering rate that the result is nothing less than a population explosion of the lowest kind of human mongrels. There are already SEVEN colored people for every white person in the world, and the ratio is becoming more overwhelmingly black every day. If we really believe in "democracy", as our leaders would have us, then, with one vote per person, we are already only a tiny minority about to be washed away in a tidal wave of colored and black "equality". The United Nations is already giving even the stupidest whites an inkling of this development, as cannibals and the most improbable spear-toters from the Congo are treated as "statesmen" by our liberal toadies, even as these minstral "statesmen" are picking morsels of their late political opponents from their pointed teeth.

Even the diminishing number of high quality white human beings, if they are able to get born and then survive a world being increasingly rigged for the benefit of the unfit and lazy, are still not permitted to survive in our insane world. Twice in my own lifetime, the same vicious forces which promote the unlimited breeding of the poorest and darkest of humanity, in the name of "democracy", have promoted horrible mutual massacres called "World Wars", in which the BEST of the Whites on one side slaughter the BEST of the Whites on the other "side"—although neither of these "sides" ever "wins". Always it is the Jews, the colored races and the Marxists who "win" these nightmarish butcherings, while the cream of our people, the bravest, most idealistic, unselfish and self-sacrificing young men go off to murder each other as VOLUNTEERS. The 4-Fs and the mercantile princes stay home to provide the band-music, the bullets, the fine uniforms, and the rest of the machinery for inflaming "patriotic" youth to go and kill each other to "make the world safe for democracy", or go "put down tyranny", etc.—although these same lads are cautioned not to get excited about RED tyranny, or BLACK tyranny—which is really "democracy" at work. Every thirty years or so, it seems, the decreasing number of the white elite of the world are set at each other's throats, while they are taught to work and struggle to make the world a better place to breed more Jews and Negroes.

Our people NEVER see this cruel and suicidal process, and, even now, the BEST of our people, the most patriotic, are whooping and war dancing to go and murder the RUSSIANS—who are also White People—instead of realizing that it is the COMMUNISTS who are the enemies of humanity, not the miserable, uneducated and helpless Russian white men and women who are prisoners of these world-fiends, just as, in a sense, we are here in America.

And, in between these planet-wide butcheries of the biological cream of humanity, the Jews give the elite no respite. "Liberalism" castrates our intellectual youth, makes them actually LOVE their destroyers and every process of their own disintegration. The resulting moral depravity finally produces the ultimate disgrace of civilization,—pansies,—queers! The Jewish-dominated fields of medicine would have us look with compassion and tolerance on this abomination because the people are "sick." But then, so are mad killers in the street. The Jews say Hitler was "sick" too, but there were no recommendations to let him work his poor, frustrated little will. They say I am sick, but they do not seem anxious to permit me my little pecadillos. It is always and ONLY for disintegrative moral depravity that they bring out the "let-him-alone-he's-just-sick" bit.

Our great-grandfathers would probably have risen in overpowering and natural wrath to slaughter, left and right, the unspeakable crawling, filthy things we excuse as "beats." Doped up with narcotics, physically dirty, ostentatiously anti-social and repulsive, "crazy" with the orgiastic rythyms of Africa's lowest cannibals, full of the phoniest imaginable Jewish "intellectualism," (Ginsberg) and sleeping interchangeably with male and female Negroes,—these degraded and pitiful creatures are the inevitable result of putting "democracy" and "liberalism" into working practice.

In short, every force of "modern" society, scientific, cultural, moral and intellectual has short-sightedly forgotten the RACE, the GROUP,—in the wild "liberal" scramble to pamper the INDIVIDUAL AT THE EXPENSE OF THE SPECIES. Every NATURAL process of selection and breeding has been violently REVERSED, and humanity is breeding itself back to the jungles and caves out of which our ancestors once battled in thousands and thousands of years of bitter struggle with a merciless but healthy environment.

The idiocy of despising their own hereditary genius and strength has been made the fashion among young college "intellectuals" all over the world and, unless the white man becomes aware that the intellectualism and scientific method he so much admires must be applied TO HIMSELF AND HIS BREEDING AS AN ANIMAL humanity will be destroyed by social chaos and the reversal of biological evolution. In fact this process is already far along, and, like hypnotized birds before snakes, the white men and nations all over the world are cringing in abject cowardice before mutinous gangs of inferior people and black savages, inflamed and led by Jews.

National Socialism is, above all things, the doctrine that it is not only for the good of humanity but absolutely essential for the survival of humanity that scientific method be applied not only to the breedings of animals and bugs but also to the breeding of human beings. National Socialism does not wish to destroy inferior races or individuals any more than a wolf leader wants to destroy the pack but only to organize them into a productive ORDER which alone can enable them to survive and enjoy some degree of human felicity.

National Socialism deplores the reversal of human evolution being accelerated by welfare-ism, brotherhood-ism, race-mixing and the unlimited breeding of the inferior races and individuals while the superior limit themselves to few offspring or

To accomplish these utterly fundamental and vital aims, National Socialism declares its goal to be nothing less than the absolute domination of the white, civilized areas of the earth by the Aryan white man and the leadershp of the Aryan white man by the strongest and wisest individuals of the race rather than the largest number of weaklings, mediocrities and selfish private interests.

To achieve this goal National Socialism recognizes that power must be won legally, first in the strategic center of the world, the United States, and then in all the other white Aryan areas of the earth. National Socialism does not recognize the imaginary geographic boundaries of nations as being as important as the very real boundaries set by nature in RACE.

We therefore declare our intention eventually to incorporate all Nordic and Aryan white peoples into a single political entity so that never again will white men fight and kill each other on behalf of such silly things as imaginary geographic boundaries or such vicious things as Jewish economic swindles,—either Communism or Capitalism.

We further declare that we do not seek to murder or destroy any race but only that we intend to establish separate areas within which each race will be at liberty to achieve its own destiny so long as it does not encroach upon or attack the areas or members of another race.

Finally, we declare our intention of utterly destroying all individuals, OF WHATEVER RACE, who are guilty of organizing, planning, or carrying out the criminal Communist conspiracy and mutiny against humanity and the laws of Nature. We recognize a great proportion of Jews have been, and are the leaders of this criminal Bolshevik mutiny and conspiracy against the race of humanity and will not shrink from the task of utterly destroying such poisonous human bacteria.

But this is only the negative part of our ideals and aims. The goal of National Socialism is and always will be a felicitous human ORDER in which each human being will be able to develop and express his contributions to humanity to the maximum possible extent and, by the application of scientific method to human breeding itself, to insure that this world is peopled, not with more and more negroid degenerates, but with human beings who increasingly approximate the lordly ideal expressed in the ancient Nordic sagas by the Gods and Goddesses of Valhalla.

Suggested Readings

Deakin, Frederick W., *The Brutal Friendship: Mussolini, Hitler and the Fall of Italian Fascism* (New York: Harper & Row, Publishers, 1962).

Green, Nathanael, *Fascism: An Anthology* (New York: Thomas Y. Crowell Company, 1968).

Gregor, A. J., *The Ideology of Fascism* (New York: The Free Press, 1969).

Kedward, H. R., *Fascism in Western Europe* (New York: New York University Press, 1971).

Laquer, W. Z., and G. L. Mosse, *International Fascism: 1920-1945* (New York: Harper & Row, Publishers, 1966).

Mosse, G. L., *The Crises of German Ideology: Intellectual Origins of the Third Reich* (New York: Grosset & Dunlap, Inc., 1964).

Neumann, F., *Behemoth* (New York: Octagon Books, 1944).

Nolte, E., *Three Faces of Fascism* (New York: The New American Library, Inc., 1969).

Rogger, H., and E. Weber, *The European Right* (Berkeley: University of California Press, 1965).

Stern, F., *The Politics of Cultural Despair* (Berkeley: University of California Press, 1961).

Viereck, Peter, *Metapolitics: The Roots of the Nazi Mind* (New York: G. P. Putnam's Sons, 1961).

Weiss, J., *Fascist Tradition* (New York: Holt, Rinehart and Winston, Inc., 1967).

Wiskemann, E., *Fascism in Italy* (New York: St. Martin's Press, Inc., 1971).

Conservatism

INTRODUCTION

One usually marks the beginning of conservative philosophy with the publication of Edmund Burke's *Reflections on the Revolution in France* in 1790. Of course, there was conservative political theory before that. Lord Cecil once wrote that "before the Reformation it is impossible to distinguish conservatism in politics, not because there was none but because there was nothing else." Nonetheless, Burke is usually considered to be not only the originator of conservatism but, by many, its high point.

Among the beliefs of Burkean conservatism are the following: First, it definitely argues that radical social change is wrong, especially radical change that is instigated by force. Second, the conservatives believe that it is the main function of government to maintain peace and order. It should do little else. Third, conservatives view human nature as complex, unpredictable, and often immoral. Regarding this last point, they contend that such immoral characteristics as cruelty and greed are inevitably present in human existence. Consequently, political and social institutions cannot be perfected. We must accept their necessary inadequacies. Related to this is the belief of conservatives that institutions as well as people can only become adequate for society through historical development. Individuals learn how to govern others by practice and example. Hence those best suited to rule come from the members of a long-established ruling class. Such aristocrats, it is argued, have had the tradition, have had the education, and have had the experience of living with successful rulers. It is the same with institutions. Only those institutions that have survived the many decades and centuries—such as the state, the church, and the family—are those society should want. Those institutions that have long existed must be workable, successful institutions. Finally, these conservatives are usually quite religious. They usually believe in God and God's role in history. Not all conservatives agree with each of these tenets. Many reject Burke's autocratic element. Others support change, that is, those changes which will preserve the fundamental elements of their society. Burke's theory is called *aristocratic*. Other versions, called *autonomous* and *situational*, emphasize the values of balance and moderation or valuable existing institutions, respectively. Hence there is no single ideology of conservatism.

133

Yet in the articles, note how many of the following themes appear: the need of a ruling aristocracy, the uncertainty of progress, the primary role of private property, the necessity of social classes and orders, the natural inequality of men in their mental abilities, the imperfect and sinful nature of men, the existence of God and the need for organized religion, the limitations of human reason, and the inadequacy of majority rule and its potentiality for a tyranny.

Government, Aristocracy, and Representation
Edmund Burke

Edmund Burke (1730-1797) was an Irish-English philosopher and stateman. He has been held to be, by many, the greatest writer setting forth the conservative ideology. He was greatly upset by the excesses of the French revolution. His ideal system was a representative government whose representatives would use their own judgment rather than simply express the wishes of their constituents, and one in which the government exhibited the well-functioning institutions worked out through long tradition.

THE LIMITS OF GOVERNMENTAL INTERFERENCE[1]

It is one of the finest problems of legislation, and what has often engaged my thoughts while I followed that profession: What the state ought to take upon itself to direct by the public wisdom, and what it ought to leave, with as little interference as possible, to individual direction. Nothing, certainly, can be laid down on the subject that will not admit of exceptions, many permanent, some occasional. But the clearest line of distinction which I could draw, while I had my chalk to draw any line, was this: That the State ought to confine itself to what regards the State, or the creatures of the State—namely, the exterior establishment of its religion; its magistracy, its revenue, its military force by sea and land, the corporations that owe their existence to its fiat—in a word, to everything that is *truly and properly* public, to the public peace, to the public safety, to the public order, to the public prosperity. In its preventive police it ought to be sparing of its efforts, and to employ means rather few, infrequent, and strong, than many and frequent; and, of course (as they multiply their puny political race and dwindle), small and feeble. Statesmen who know themselves will, with the dignity which belongs to wisdom, proceed only in this, the superior orb and first mover of their duty, steadily, vigilantly, severely, courageously; whatever remains will, in a manner, provide for itself. But as they descend from the State to a province, from a province to a parish, and from a parish to a private house, they go on accelerated to

[1] Part of an essay entitled "Thoughts and Details on Scarcity," 1795.

their fall. They *cannot* do the lower duty; and, in proportion as they try it, they will certainly fail in the higher. They ought to know the different departments of things; what belongs to laws, and what manners alone can regulate. To these great politicians may give a leaning, but they cannot give a law. Our Legislature has fallen into this fault as well as other Governments: all have fallen into it more or less. I can never quote France without a foreboding sigh. My dear departed friend, whose loss is even greater to the public than to me, had often remarked that the leading vice of the French Monarchy (which he had well studied) was in good intention ill-directed and a restless desire of governing too much. The hand of authority was seen in everything and in every place. All, therefore, that happened amiss in the course even of domestic affairs was attributed to the Government; and, as it always happens in this kind of officious universal interference, what began in odious power ended always, I may say without exception, in contemptible imbecility.

AN ARISTOCRACY ESSENTIAL TO THE CONSTITUTION OF A STATE[2]

A true natural aristocracy is not a separate interest in the State, or separable from it. It if formed out of a class of legitimate presumptions, which, taken as generalities, must be admitted for actual truths. To be bred in a place of estimation; to see nothing low and sordid from one's infancy; to be taught to respect one's self; to be habituated to the censorial inspection of the public eye; to look early to public opinion; to stand upon such elevated ground as to be enabled to take a large view of the widespread and infinitely diversified combinations of men and affairs in a large society; to have leisure to read, to reflect, to converse; to be enabled to draw the court and attention of the wise and learned wherever they are to be found; to be habituated in armies to command and to obey; to be taught to despise danger in the pursuit of honour and duty; to be formed to the greatest degree of vigilance, foresight, and circumspection, in a state of things in which no fault is committed with impunity, and the slightest mistakes draw on the most ruinous consequences; to be led to a guarded and regulated conduct from a sense that you are considered as an instructor of your fellow-citizens in their highest concerns, and that you act as a reconciler between God and man; to be employed as an administrator of law and justice, and to be thereby among the first benefactors to mankind; to be a professor of high science, or of liberal and ingenious art; to be among rich traders, who, from their success, are presumed to have sharp and vigorous understandings, and to possess the virtues of diligence, order, constancy, and regularity, and to have cultivated an habitual regard to commutative justice—these are the circumstances of men that form what I should call a *natural* aristocracy, without which there is no nation. The state of civil society, which necessarily generates this aristocracy, is a state of nature; and much more truly so than a savage and incoherent mode of life. For man is, by nature, reasonable; and he is never perfectly in his natural state but when he is placed where reason may be best cultivated and most predominates. Art is man's nature. We are as much, at least, in a state of nature in formed manhood as in immature and helpless infancy. Men, qualified in the manner I have just described, form in Nature, as she operates in the common modification of society,

[2] From *Appeal from the New to the Old Whigs*, 1791.

the leading, guiding, and governing part. It is the soul to the body, without which the man does not exist. To give, therefore, no more importance, in the social order, to such descriptions of men than that of so many units is a horrible usurpation.

"THE PEOPLE." MAJORITY RULE[3]

When the supreme authority of the people is in question, before we attempt to extend or to confine it, we ought to fix in our minds, with some degree of distinctness, an idea of what it is we mean when we say the PEOPLE.

In a state of *rude* nature there is no such thing as people. A number of men in themselves have no collective capacity. The idea of a people is the idea of a corporation. It is wholly artificial, and made, like all other legal fictions, by common agreement. What the particular nature of that agreement was is collected from the form into which the particular society has been cast. Any other is not *their* covenant. When men, therefore, break up the original compact or agreement which gives its corporate form and capacity to a State, they are no longer a people; they have no longer a corporate existence; they have no longer a legal coactive force to bind within, nor a claim to be recognised abroad. They are a number of vague, loose individuals, and nothing more. With them all is to begin again. . . .

. . . To enable men to act with the weight and character of a people, and to answer the ends for which they are incorporated into that capacity, we must suppose them (by means immediate or consequential) to be in that state of habitual social discipline in which the wiser, the more expert, and the more opulent conduct, and, by conducting, enlighten and protect the weaker, the less knowing, and the less provided with the goods of fortune. Numbers in a State are always of consideration; but they are not the whole consideration.

When great multitudes act together under that description of nature I recognize the PEOPLE; I acknowledge something that perhaps equals, and ought always to guide, the sovereignty of convention. In all things the voice of this grand chorus of national harmony ought to have a mighty and decisive influence. But when you disturb this harmony, when you break up this beautiful order, this array of truth and nature, as well as of habit and prejudice; when you separate the common sort of men from their proper chieftains, so as to form them into an adverse army, I no longer know that venerable object called the people in such a disbanded race of deserters and vagabonds. For a while they may be terrible indeed; but in such a manner as wild beasts are terrible. The mind owes them no sort of submission. They are, as they have always been reputed, rebels. They may lawfully be fought with, and brought under, whenever an advantage offers.

A PARLIAMENTARY REPRESENTATIVE NOT A MERE DELEGATE[4]

It ought to be the happiness and glory of a representative to live in the strictest union, the closest correspondence, and the most unreserved communication with

[3] From *Appeal from the New to the Old Whigs*, 1791.
[4] From a speech delivered (in 1774) to the citizens of Briston, while campaigning for election to Parliament from that constituency.

his constituents. Their wishes ought to have great weight with him; their opinion, high respect; their business, unremitted attention. It is his duty to sacrifice his repose, his pleasures, his satisfactions, to theirs; and, above all, ever and in all cases to prefer their interest to his own. But his unbiased opinion, his mature judgment, his enlightened conscience, he ought not to sacrifice to you, to any man, or to any set of men living. These he does not derive from your pleasure, no, nor from the law and the Constitution. They are a trust from Providence, for the abuse of which he is deeply answerable. Your representative owes you, not his industry only, but his judgment; and he betrays, instead of serving you, if he sacrifices it to your opinion.

My worthy colleague says his will ought to be subservient to yours. If that be all, the thing is innocent. If government were a matter of will upon any side, yours, without question, ought to be superior. But government and legislation are matters of reason and judgment, and not of inclination; and what sort of reason is that in which the determination precedes the discussion; in which one set of men deliberate and another decide; and where those who form the conclusion are perhaps three hundred miles distant from those who hear the arguments?

To deliver an opinion is the right of all men; that of constituents is a weighty and respectable opinion, which a representative ought always to rejoice to hear, and which he ought always most seriously to consider. But *authoritative* instructions, *mandates* issued, which the member is bound blindly and implictly to obey, to vote, and to argue for, though contrary to the clearest conviction of his judgment and conscience; these are things utterly unknown to the laws of this land, and which arise from a fundamental mistake of the whole order and tenour of our constitution.

Parliament is not a *congress* of ambassadors from different and hostile interests; which interests each must maintain, as an agent and advocate against other agents and advocates; but Parliament is a *deliberative* assembly of *one* nation, with *one* interest, that of the whole. You choose a member indeed; but when you have chosen him, he is not member of Bristol, but he is a member of *Parliament.* If the local constituent should have an interest, or should form a hasty opinion, evidently opposite to the real good of the rest of the community, the members for that place ought to be as far as any other from any endeavour to give it effect.... Your faithful friend, your devoted servant, I shall be to the end of my life; a flatterer you do not wish for.

The Principles of Conservatism
F. J. C. Hearnshaw

F. J. C. Hearnshaw (1869-1946) taught at Kings College in London. His books include *Conservatism in England (1932), The Social and Political Ideas of Some Great French Thinkers of the Age of Reason (1934), Some Great Political Idealists of the Christian Era (1937),* and *Political Principles of Some Notable Prime Ministers of the 19th Century (1940).*

If I were called upon to enumerate in summary fashion and tabular form the general principles of conservatism, particularly as it exists and displays itself in the world of modern national states, I should be disposed to say that conservatism stands for (1) reverence for the past, (2) the organic conception of society, (3) communal unity, (4) constitutional continuity, (5) opposition to revolution, (6) cautious or evolutionary reform, (7) the religous basis of the state, (8) the divine source of legitimate authority, (9) the priority of duties to rights, (10) the prime importance of individual and communal character, (11) loyalty, (12) common sense, realism, and practicality. A few words concerning each must suffice.

REVERENCE FOR THE PAST

The conservative reveres the past, not for its own sake, but for the sake of the present and the future. He feels instinctively that the accumulated wisdom and experience of the countless generations gone is more likely to be right than the passing fashion of the moment. He believes that, even though each successive generation of his ancestors was in its day no more intellectually sane or morally sound than the silly and sentimental generation to which he himself belongs, nevertheless a long process of trial and rejection has purified their creations from error and made them fit for their appointed work. He realises, moreover, that it is much easier to destroy than to construct; that a cathedral that took a century to build can be burnt down in a night; that an institution that has evolved during a thousand years can be ruined by a single injudicious reform. He recognises as one of the soundest of conservative maxims the rule, already quoted, that "unless it is necessary to change, it is necessary not to change." He tends to faith in the great motto "Securus judicat orbis terarum." He stands for the universal and permanent things of life; for the ancient traditions of the race; for the fundamental laws of his people; for established customs; for the family; for property; for the church; for the constitution; for the great heritage of Christian civilisation in general.

From F. J. C. Hearnshaw, *Conservatism in England* (London and Basingstoke: The Macmillan Company, 1933), pp. 22-33. Reprinted by permission.

THE ORGANIC CONCEPTION OF SOCIETY

One main reason why he values and strives to conserve the past is that he feels that in a real sense it is one with the present. He has an organic or biological conception of society, as opposed to the inorganic or legal conception prevalent among the philosophical radicals. To him the great community to which he belongs—e.g., the national state—is a living entity, albeit of a psychological rather than a physical type; a spiritual organism to which every individual of the community belongs. He feels with St. Paul that we are all members one of another; all joined together in the large and enduring life of a mystical body, whose abode is a mother-country or a fatherland. Hence he is impressed by the need to preserve the integrity of this communal life, which is larger and more enduring than his own brief individual existence; he strives to safeguard the body politic from injury at the hands both of malignant enemies and injudicious friends; he struggles to maintain the communal identity amid all the changes that time inevitably brings. He studies with loving care the records of the past growth of his people and of their institutions, in order that he may to the extent of his power help to keep the necessary new developments along the old lines of progress.

COMMUNAL UNITY

An all-important corollary to the conservative conception of society as an organism is the fine and inspiring idea of the essential oneness of the community. Conservatism is utterly opposed to the horrible dogma of the class-war which is one of the most damnable features of Marxian socialism or bolshevism. It denies the existence of any irreconcilable antagonisms in a healthy body politic. It holds, on the contrary, that the efficiency and prosperity of each class—upper, middle, lower, each with its countless internal gradations—is essential for the wellbeing of the community as a whole. It recognises the distinction between the classes as natural, fundamental, and beneficial; the same sort of distinction as exists between the head, the body, and the limbs of a man or an animal. But it regards the distinction as one of function mainly, and not necessarily one of honour or emolument. And it realises that if any one of the three great classes suffers or is diseased, the whole organism is weakened and incapacitated. "We may say," exclaims Mr. Harold Begbie, "that at the centre of conservative thinking is the idea of unity."[1] Similarly Lord Irwin, with his noble and catholic spirit, maintains that "the conservative stands for the unity of the nation, and of all interests, classes, and creeds within it."[2] In saying this they, and all good conservatives, are but following the fine tradition of Bolingbroke, Burke, and Beaconsfield.

CONSTITUTIONAL CONTINUITY

A second and hardly less important corollary to the conservative conception of society as an organism is the idea and ideal of continuity. Such a breach in the

[1] Begbie, H. ("A Gentleman with a Duster"), *The Conservative Mind* (1924), p. 145.
[2] *The Times*, March 14, 1924.

natural and orderly development of the constitution as occurred in seventeenth-century England or eighteenth-century France fills the conservative with repulsion and alarm. He regards it in much the same way as a normal individual would regard the action of a physician or surgeon who, when called in to treat the ailment of a parent beloved, should, by way of experiment in some novel therapy, inflict upon the sufferer an all-but-fatal injury. So prominent in conservatism is this principle of continuity—this conception of the vital connection between past, present, and future; this idea of a communal life ever one and the same, although constantly evolving in order to correspond with a changing environment—that Mr. Walter Elliot regards it as its "major tenet," and says that conservatism is "first of all the creed of continuity."[3] An anonymous but excellent writer in the *Saturday Review* expresses the same opinion more at large in the words: "Conservatism is not a bundle of political expedients, but the very imperfect expression through political action of certain deep-rooted and far-reaching convictions in regard to both the national and the individual life. These convictions are hard, nay impossible, to define. They amount in sum to a passionate belief in the principle of continuity.[4]

OPPOSITION TO REVOLUTION

The principle of continuity, of course, implies instinctive and emphatic antagonism to revolution. For the essence of revolution is complete severance from the past. The revolutionary, as distinct from the reformer, seeks to destroy existing institutions, not to amend them; to slay and not to cure. In place of communal unity he stirs up civil war. Instead of treating society tenderly as an organism liable to injury and death, he smites and blasts it as though it were a mechanism which can be scrapped and made new again. He is, as a rule, obsessed by some abstract (and viciously erroneous) theory, such as the Jacobinical theory of the rights of man, or the bolshevik theory of the wrong of private property. He is commonly a gloomy fanatic, filled with envy, hatred, malice, and all uncharitableness; a raging Philistine wholly devoid of both sweetness and light. The conservative, however, while unalterably opposed to revolution, recognises that the revolutionary is a natural, if horrible, product of ignorance and wretchedness. Hence while resisting revolutionary violence and denouncing subversive dogma, he seeks to find the causes that produce the would-be destroyer of society, and to remove them in so far as the demand for their removal is real and rational.

CAUTIOUS OR EVOLUTIONARY REFORM

Since ignorance and wretchedness are the prime propagators of the revolutionary virus, the conservative policy is one of education and betterment. Nothing could be more contrary to fact than the statement that conservatism is opposed to reform. Reform is of its very essence. Well says Mr. E. J. Payne concerning Burke: "He led the way in reform, while raising his voice against innovation," adding: "The spirit of conservatism and the spirit of reform are the necessary complements of each

[3] Elliot, W., *Toryism and the Twentieth Century* (1927), pp. 18-19.
[4] *Saturday Review*, July 6, 1929.

other: no statesman ever pretends to separate them."[5] And Burke himself remarked with his usual profound wisdom: "A state without the means of some change is without the means of its conservation."[6] No persons are less true to the conservative genius than the reactionaries or "diehards" who resist all alteration whatsoever without ever inquiring into the causes that have led to its demand. Nothing could be more alien from the true spirit of conservatism than the famous saying of the Duke of Cumberland (son of George III.): "Any change, at any time, for any purpose, is highly to be deprecated." If the Cumberland spirit should at any time gain possession of the conservative party, the day of triumphant revolution will have dawned. And the Cumberland spirit has had many embodiments among those who call themselves conservative. Indeed, the very man, Mr. J. W. Croker, who gave currency to the term "conservative," a hundred years ago, was one of them. Mr. Keith Feiling has presented us with an unforgettable picture of the man—able, honest, energetic, but hopelessly obscurantist and out of touch with reality. His dread of novelty, and his worship of the fetish of stability, made him blind to the immense transformations that were going on around him. "Who," says Mr. Keith Feiling, surveying his well-intentioned but disastrous career—"who can measure the damage inflicted on sane conservatism by one reactionary of high character and personal charm?"[7] The true conservative attitude is that of Sir Robert Peel, at one time but not always Croker's friend. Writing about "conservative principles" in 1834, he said: "Those principles I for one consider to be perfectly compatible with cautious and well-digested reforms in every institution which really requires reforms, and with the redress of approved grievances."[8] Mr. Ludovici puts the matter well when he remarks: "Conservatism is not a brake on progress . . . it is a brake on indiscriminate change," adding, "It is the lofty mission of conservatism to prevent national changes from degenerating into a process of general decomposition."[9] But the true key to the whole problem is found in the organic conception of society. For if, on the one hand, the principle of life negatives any breach in the continuity of communal development, on the other hand the principle of healthy and vigorous growth (which is the only alternative to the doom of decadence and death) demands the constant adaptation of the enduring organism to the ever-changing environment. Conservatism accepts and applies the doctrine of organic evolution.

THE RELIGIOUS BASIS OF THE STATE

The conservative doctrine of organic evolution implies the existence of a corporate Being—the Great Society, the Community-as-a-Whole, the State—a Being possessed of a social conscience, a communal intelligence, a public opinion, and a general will; a Being vaster and more permanent than any of the individuals who at any time constitute its members. Devotion to this Being, which Hobbes termed "Leviathan,"

[5] Payne, E. J., *Select Works of Burke,* vol. i., Introduction, p. xxvi.
[6] Burke, E., *Reflections on the French Revolution,* iv., 23. On Burke's attitude generally, see Opzoomer, C. W., *Conservatismus und Reform, eine Abhandlung über Edmund Burke's Politik* (Utrecht, 1852).
[7] Feiling, K., *Sketches in Nineteenth-Century Biography* (1930), p. 55.
[8] Clark, G. K., *Peel and the Conservative Party* (1929), p. 176.
[9] Ludovici, A. M., *A Defence of Conservatism* (1927), pp. 11-13.

and defined as "that Mortal God to which we owe under the Immortal God our peace and defence,"[10] is itself a religion. Devotion to the state was, indeed, the real religion of both Greeks and Romans. Athena was but Athens personified, and in Rome the worship of the emperor's genius was no more than a symbolic reverence for the dominion of which the emperor was the momentary representative.

To the Christian, however, religion means more than it did to his pagan predecessor. He recognises society as existing by the will of God; he regards it as continually directed and guided by a divine Providence; he considers its end to be akin to that of the church itself—namely, righteousness and peace. Hence, as a rule, he holds it to be right and proper that the state should formally and publicly recognise its sacred character by the legal establishment of religion, and by the association of all the most solemn and important acts of government with the august ceremonial of the service of God. "In a Christian commonwealth," said Burke, "the church and the state are one and the same thing, being different parts of the same whole."[11] And this great idea, which was akin to that of the *Respublica Christiana* of the Middle Ages, was the very essence of Coleridge's notable contribution to conservative thought in the early nineteenth century.

THE DIVINE SOURCE OF LEGITIMATE AUTHORITY

The conservative who regards the state as organic in nature, as sacred in character, as founded upon a religious basis, and as akin to a church, naturally tends to accept the ancient Christian view that all legitimate authority is, whether directly or indirectly, divine in its origin. He remembers the cardinal pronouncement of St. Paul: "The powers that be are ordained of God. Whosoever therefore resisteth the power, resisteth the ordinance of God."[12] He traces the influence of this great utterance through the writings of countless thinkers down all the Christian centuries, and in the acts of innumerable ecclesiastical statesmen. He feels, with Disraeli, that "the divine right of kings may have been a plea for feeble tyrants, but the divine right of government is the keystone of human progress, and without it governments sink into police, and a nation is degraded into a mob." Even conservatives who are not able to accept the Christian view—such as Hobbes, and Bolingbroke, and Hume, and Matthew Arnold—hold that authority springs from a source superior to the individual, "a power not ourselves that makes for righteousness," a spirit universal and eternal. Well says Mr. Keith Feiling in his fine study of Newman: "In the permanent essence of a teaching which is successfully to defend authorty, there must be something in the widest sense catholic."[13]

THE PRIORITY OF DUTIES TO RIGHTS

There are few things that more sharply distinguish the conservative from the radical or the socialist than his attitude towards rights and duties. The radical concentrates

[10] Hobbes, T., *Leviathan* (1651), chapter xvii.
[11] Speech, May 11, 1792.
[12] *Romans* xiii. 1-2; *cf.* also 1 *Timothy* ii. 1-3, *Titus* iii. 1, and 1 *Peter* ii. 13-17.
[13] Feiling, K., *Sketches in Nineteenth-Century Biography* (1930), pp. 114-115.

his attention almost wholly on the rights of the individual. He asserts his right to the franchise, even though he use his vote merely to further his own personal interest—*e.g.*, to secure ninepence for fourpence. He maintains his right to freedom of speech, even though his speech be nothing except libel and blasphemy, sedition and nonsense. And so on. Similarly the socialist, with an extreme individualism that accords very ill with the alleged main principle of his creed, proclaims the proletarian's right to work or maintenance (which means the right to compel other people to support him in perennial idleness), or his right to the whole produce of labour (which means the right to deprive the landlord and the capitalist of their just dues). And so on.

As against this one-sided and self-centred assertion of personal rights, the conservative stresses the principle of civic duties. His ideal is public service rather than private gain. He regards the franchise not as a possession which he can claim as his own, but as an obligation which he must exercise in the interests of the body politic. Similarly, in rspect of such matters as freedom of speech and writing, he thinks rather of how they may be employed (and if necessary limited) in the interest of the community-as-a-whole than of how he may assert them on his own behalf in all circumstances. Well says Mr. Harold Begbie of conservatism: "The great word on its lips is the word *duty*. It does not stoop to flatter; it does not wish to deceive; it does not seek to infuriate and excite the passions of the ignorant and the half-educated. It appeals to what is best in man's nature—to his moral strength, to his spiritual self-respect, to his human kindness—and it bids men rise to a level of self-forgetfulness from which they can see the path of their duty stretching to the land of their children's glory." [14]

THE PRIME IMPORTANCE OF CHARACTER

The prime concern of the radical, with his demands for freedom and franchise, is power. The prime preoccupation of the socialist, in spite of all his fine phrases, is pelf. The conservative, if he be true to the genius of his creed, is concerned neither for power nor for pelf, but for character—character both individual and national. He repudiates, in particular, the socialist's gross over-emphasis on the influence of environment as a determinant of a man's condition, and stresses the fact that his condition depends very largely upon what he is himself. Mr. Baldwin put the point excellently in a great speech delivered on March 19, 1924, when he said: "The conservative believes that the only salvation of the country is to concentrate on the individual, and to continue to cherish in him a spirit of character, marked by the virtues of thrift, hard work, and prudence." In saying this, Mr. Baldwin was but echoing the teaching of his revered master, Disraeli, who in his day proclaimed that "the wealth of England is not merely material wealth . . . we have a more precious treasure, and that is the character of the people." If, then, the conservative resists and denounces the socialist's nostrums of doles and subventions and transitional benefits and all the other euphenisms for poor-relief, he does so not merely or mainly because they are economically ruinous and socially disastrous, but because they are hopelessly demoralising and degrading. They tend to debauch and debase the English people. Rarely, indeed, has a more subtle and deadly enemy to

---

[14] Begbie, H. ("A Gentleman with a Duster"), *The Conservative Mind* (1924), p. 147.

character revealed itself than socialism. Under its malign influence the national integrity is gravely menaced. Rightly says Mr. Arthur Bryant: "Our English character is in danger to-day. We all know it. We can all think of ways in which it is being undermined—its jealous, bold independence by an ever-growing pauperisation of our people; its frank, just courage—honouring gallant foe as well as friend—by the false sentimentality which is swamping our education and philosophy; its good nature and humorous tolerance by the alien gospel of class hatred. The overmastering thought of every conservative must be how we can save this precious thing, handed down to us by so many generations of good, honest, clean-living English men and women, from the foes that threaten it."[15]

LOYALTY

Of all the elements of character which the conservative values and cherishes, loyalty stands pre-eminent. He tends to support men rather than measures; he is devoted to institutions rather than to ideas. In so far as he is true to the high standard of his creed, he is loyal—that is, faithful—to his best self, suppressing all inclinations of his baser self towards self-aggrandisement at the expense of his fellows; he is loyal to his family, to his school, to his university, to his party, and to whatever professional group he may be attached. But his larger and supreme loyalties he reserves for his church, his king, his country, and his empire. Piety, fidelity, patriotism, imperialism—these are words that are dear to him, and the noble principles which they connote are among his most treasured spiritual posessions.

A clever and observant French writer, M. Floris Delattre, making a survey of post-war England, perceives loyalty to be one of the outstanding features of its conservative elements. His remarks have been summarised as follows: "Conservatism lies at the very heart of the collective psychology of England. Everything runs into it and converges here—the sense of tradition, the tenacity with which the people hold to what they have received from their forebears, the respect for authority, the social discipline, and even a certain homesickness for the past, which confers on the democratic middle class of to-day a sort of aristrocratic flavour. No word is dearer to an Englishman than *loyalty*, which implies a cordial devotion to his country, his family, his friends, the ideas and even the prejudices of his group."[16]

COMMON SENSE, REALISM, PRACTICALITY

Perhaps in treating of the conservative principle of loyalty—that is, of fidelity to persons, devotion to institutions, and staunch adherence to causes—we have come suspiciously near the visionary region wherein abstract ideas hold sway. We have not, however, as a matter of fact, crossed the line that divided the real from the fantastic. We are still in the midst of actualities, which are none the less real for being spiritual. For the conservative—unlike the jacobite, the non-juror, or other reactionary—recognises the fact that even loyalty can on occasion be carried too

[15] *The Ashridge Journal*, No. 5 (February, 1931), p. 33.
[16] Delattre, F., *L'Angleterre d'Après-Guerre* (Paris, 1930), reviewed in *The Times Literary Supplement*, September 11, 1930.

far. It may be bestowed on persons unworthy, on institutions obsolete, or on causes discredited. Mr. Keith Feiling, indeed, says of toryism that it tends "to drag the chain of lost loyalties, superannuated leaders, and indefensible chivalries."[17] From this excess of an excellent quality conservatism is saved by its balancing common sense, by its instinct for the practical and possible. "The essential strength of the conservative party," it has been well remarked, "lies largely in its claim to be the party of practical compromise and common sense."[18] It is the party of affairs rather than of theories; the party of strong and efficient administration rather than of incessant and ill-digested legislation; the party which adapts policy to circumstances instead of attempting (like the bolsheviks) to fit circumstances into the Procrustean bed of fixed obsessions. The late Lord Younger, one of the ablest organisers that the conservative party ever produced, summed up the whole matter in the sentence: "Were I asked to define the basic principle of the conservative and unionist party, I would reply in a single word—*commonsense.*"[19]

[17] *The Times Literary Supplement*, September 26, 1929.
[18] *Ibid.*, June 19, 1924.
[19] *Sunday Times,* June 12, 1927.

Conservatism as an Ideology
Samuel P. Huntington

Samuel P. Huntington (1927–   ) is a Professor of Government at Harvard University. He is the author of *The Soldier and the State* (1957), *The Common Defense* (1961), and *Political Order in Changing Societies* (1968) and the editor of *Changing Patterns of Military Politics* (1962).

Does conservative political thought have a place in America today? The answer to this question depends upon the general nature of conservatism as an ideology: its distinguishing characteristics, its substance, and the conditions under which it arises. By ideology I mean a system of ideas concerned with the distribution of political and social values and acquiesced in by a significant social group.[1] Interpretations of the role and relevance of conservative thought on the contemporary scene vary greatly. Underlying the debate, however, are three broad

From Samuel P. Huntington, "Conservatism as an Ideology," *American Political Science Review*, 1958, pp. 454-473. Reprinted by permission of The American Political Science Association.

[1] This essay deals only with conservative theory. It is not concerned with conservative instincts, attitudes, political parties, or governmental policies. For contrasting views on the meaning of ideology, see Karl Mannheim, *Ideology and Utopia* (New York, 1949), pp. 49 ff. and Carl J. Friedrich and Zbigniew K. Brzezinski, *Totalitarian Dictatorship and Autocracy* (Cambridge, 1956), pp. 71 ff.

and conflicting conceptions of the nature of conservatism as an ideology. This essay deals with the relative merits of these concepts.

THEORIES OF CONSERVATISM

First, the *aristocratic* theory defines conservatism as the ideology of a single specific and unique historical movement: the reaction of the feudal-aristocratic-agrarian classes to the French Revolution, liberalism, and the rise of the bourgeoisie at the end of the eighteenth century and during the first half of the nineteenth century. In Mannheim's words, modern conservatism is "a function of *one particular* historical and sociological situation."[2] Liberalism is the ideology of the bourgeoisie, socialism and Marxism the ideologies of the proletariat, and conservatism the ideology of the aristocracy. Conservatism thus becomes indissolubly associated with feudalism, status, the *ancien régime,* landed interests, medievalism, and nobility; it becomes irreconcilably opposed to the middle class, labor, commercialism, industrialism, democracy, liberalism, and individualism. This concept of conservatism is popular among critics of the "New Conservatism." For, as Louis Hartz has brilliantly demonstrated, the United States lacks a feudal tradition. Hence, the efforts of intellectuals and publicists to propagate conservative ideas in middle-class America must be doomed to failure.

Second, the *autonomous* definition of conservatism holds that conservatism is not necessarily connected with the interests of any particular group, nor, indeed, is its appearance dependent upon any specific historical configuration of social forces. Conservatism is an autonomous system of ideas which are generally valid. It is defined in terms of universal values such as justice, order, balance, moderation. Whether or not a particular individual holds these values high depends not on his social affiliations but upon his personal capacity to see their inherent truth and desirability. Conservatism, in this sense, is, as Russell Kirk says, simply a matter of "will and intelligence"; the principles of conservatism "are not confined to the interests of a single class"; conservatives may be drawn from "all classes and occupations. . . ."[3] This theory of conservatism is obviously popular among the "New Conservatives." It implies not only that conservatism is relevant and desirable in contemporary America, but that it is the preferable political philosophy under any historical circumstances.

Third, the *situational* definition views conservatism as the ideology arising out of a distinct but recurring type of historical situation in which a fundamental challenge is directed at established institutions and in which the supporters of those institutions employ the conservative ideology in their defense.[4] Thus, conservatism

---

[2] Karl Mannheim, "Conservative Thought," *Essays on Sociology and Social Psychology,* ed. Paul Kecskemeti (New York, 1953), pp. 98-99. For contemporary use of the aristocratic definition with respect to the "New Conservatism," see Arthur M. Schlesinger, Jr., "The New Conservatism in America: A Liberal Comment," *Confluence,* Vol. 2, pp. 61-71 (December, 1953), and "The New Conservatism: Politics of Nostalgia," *Reporter,* Vol. 12, pp. 9-12 (June 16, 1955); Bernard Crick, "The Strange Quest for an American Conservatism," *Review of Politics,* Vol. 17, pp. 361-63 (July, 1955); Gordon K. Lewis, "The Metaphysics of Conservatism," *Western Political Quarterly,* Vol. 6, pp. 731-32 (December, 1953).

[3] Russell Kirk, *A Program for Conservatives* (Chicago, 1954), pp. 22, 38-39; Peter Viereck, *Conservatism Revisited* (New York, 1949), p. 9.

[4] See Clinton Rossiter, *Conservatism in America* (New York, 1955), p. 9; Francis G. Wilson, "A Theory of Conservatism," this Review, Vol. 35, pp. 399-40 (February, 1941); Raymond

is that system of ideas employed to justify any established social order, no matter where or when it exists, against any fundamental challenge to its nature or being, no matter from what quarter. The essence of conservatism is the passionate affirmation of the value of existing institutions. This does not mean that conservatism opposes all change. Indeed, in order to preserve the fundamental elements of society, it may be necessary to acquiesce in change on secondary issues. No person can espouse the conservative ideology, however, unless he is fundamentally happy with the established order and committed to its defense against any serious challenge. Conservatism in this sense is possible in the United States today only if there is a basic challenge to existing American institutions which impels their defenders to articulate conservative values.

Now, the question may be legitimately raised: What is gained by arguing over definitions? Are not all definitions essentially arbitrary? How is it possible to demonstrate the superiority of one to another? This argument is valid if no common assumptions exist among the conflicting theories. Such, however, is not the case with the three definitions of conservatism. They differ only with respect to the relation of conservative ideology to the historical process. The aristocratic definition limits conservatism to a particular social class in a particular society. The autonomous definition permits the appearance of conservatism at any stage in history. The situational definition holds that conservatism appears when challenging and defending social groups stand in a particular relation to each other. Yet all three approaches agree fundamentally as to the content of conservatism as an ideology: the substance of the values and ideas in which conservatives believe. Russell Kirk, for instance, criticizes Arthur Schlesinger, Jr., for identifying conservatism with feudalism, but he agrees substantially with Schlesinger's statement of the essentials of the conservative ideology.[5]

All the analysts of conservatism, moreover, unite in identifying Edmund Burke as the conservative archetype and in assuming that the basic elements of his thought are the basic elements of conservatism. These areas of consensus permit a rational evaluation of the three definitions. The historical function of conservatism must be derived from its substance. That theory of conservatism is to be preferred which most adequately and completely explains the manifestations in history of the Burkeian ideology. The thesis of this article is that the situational theory most closely meets these criteria.

IDEATIONAL AND INSTITUTIONAL IDEOLOGIES: THE ABSENCE OF A CONSERVATIVE IDEAL

Among writers espousing all three definitions of conservatism substantial agreement exists that at least the following are major components of the conservative creed—the essential elements of Burke's theory.

1. Man is basically a religious animal, and religion is the foundation of civil society. A divine sanction infuses the legitimate, existing, social order.

English, "Conservatism: The Forbidden Faith," *American Scholar*, Vol. 21, pp. 399-401 (October, 1952); Arthur M. Schlesinger, Jr., "Conservative vs. Liberal—A Debate," *New York Times Magazine*, March 4, 1956, pp. 11 ff.

    [5] See Kirk, *op. cit.*, p. 37, and compare Schlesinger's summary of conservative concepts *Confluence*, Vol. 2, pp. 64-65, with Kirk's summary, *The Conservative Mind* (Chicago, 1953), pp. 3-10. See also below, note 27.

2. Society is the natural, organic product of slow historical growth. Existing institutions embody the wisdom of previous generations. Right is a function of time. "Prescription," in the words of Burke, "is the most solid of all titles. . . ."

3. Man is a creature of instinct and emotion as well as reason. Prudence, prejudice, experience, and habit are better guides than reason, logic, abstractions, and metaphysics. Truth exists not in universal propositions but in concrete experiences.

4. The community is superior to the individual. The rights of men derive from their duties. Evil is rooted in human nature, not in any particular social institutions.

5. Except in an ultimate moral sense, men are unequal. Social organization is complex and always includes a variety of classes, orders, and groups. Differentiation, hierarchy, and leadership are the inevitable characteristics of any civil society.

6. A presumption exists "in favour of any settled scheme of government against any untried project. . . ." Man's hopes are high, but his vision is short. Efforts to remedy existing evils usually result in even greater ones.

Assuming these propositions to be a fair summary of representative conservative ideas, what do they suggest as to the relative merit of the aristocratic, autonomous, and situational theories? Nothing in these conservative principles limits them exclusively to the feudal-aristocratic reaction. To be sure, the ideology stresses the inevitability of classes and leadership in society, but it does not particularize any specific form of social organization or source of leadership. Nor is there anything in the ideology which presumes a partiality towards an agrarian society, the feudal system of land tenure, monarchy, or a titled aristocracy. Similarly, the autonomous theory is inadequate because the conservative ideology lacks the broad sweep and catholic appeal of an ideology of universal and permanent relevance. Indeed, conservatism itself stresses the particular nature of truth and warns of the danger of overarching principles. Manifestly, the ideology has little appeal to any one discontented with the status quo. In short, the aristocratic definition fails because no necessary connection exists between aristocracy or feudalism, on the one hand, and conservatism on the other: nonaristocrats can expound conservative ideology; aristocrats can expound nonconservative ideologies.

The autonomous definition fails because the appearance of conservatism in history is not a matter of random chance. The aristocratic definition restricts conservatism to too small a segment of the social process. The autonomous definition frees it too completely from any connection with the social process. The characteristic elements of conservative thought—the "divine tactic" in history; prescription and tradition; the dislike of abstraction and metaphysics; the distrust of individual human reason; the organic conception of society; the stress on the evil in man; the acceptance of social differentiation—all serve the overriding purpose of justifying the established order. The essence of conservatism is the rationalization of existing institutions in terms of history, God, nature, and man.

The usefulness of the conservative ideology in justifying any existing order is manifest from the above summary of Burkeian principles. Nowhere in that summary is there any indication of the character of the institutions which these ideas might be used to defend. In this respect conservatism differs from all other ideologies except radicalism: it lacks what might be termed a substantive ideal. Most ideologists posit some vision as to how political society should be organized. The words "liberalism," "democracy," "communism," "fascism," all convey an intimation as to what should be the distribution of power and other values in society, the relative importance of the state and other social institutions, the relations among economic, political, and military structures, the general system of government and representation, the forms of executive and legislative institutions. But what is the political vision of conservatism? Is it possible to describe a conservative society? On the contrary, the essence of conservatism is that it is literally, in Mühlenfeld's phrase, "*Politik ohne Wunschbilder.*"

It may be argued, for instance, that the Portuguese political system is closer to the authoritarian ideal than the British and American Systems, that the British system is closer to the socialist ideal than the Portuguese and American systems, that the American system is closer to the democratic ideal than the British and Portuguese systems, and that all three systems are far from the communist ideal. But which of the three is closest to the conservative ideal? Portugal? Great Britain? The United States? It is impossible to say because no conservative ideal exists to serve as the standard of judgment. No political philosopher has ever described a conservative utopia. In any society, there may be institutions to be conserved, but there are never conservative institutions. The lack of a conservative ideal necessarily vitiates the autonomous definition of conservatism.

The ideal of nonconservative ideologies change from thinker to thinker and generation to generation, but their fundamental characteristic remains the same: the ascription of value to theoretically-defined formulations and the appraisal of existing reality in terms of those formulations. Non-conservative ideologies are thus *ideational* or transcendent in nature, while conservatism is *institutional* or immanent. All the common ideational ideologies of modern western society approach existing institutions with an "ought demand" that the institutions be reshaped to embody the values of the ideology. In this sense all ideational theories involve some degree of radicalism, *i.e.*, criticism of existing institutions. The greater the gap between existing institutional reality and the ideal of the nonconservative ideology, the more radical is the ideology with respect to that reality. Radicalism is thus the opposite of conservatism, and, like conservatism, it denotes an attitude toward institutions rather than a belief in any particular ideals. Conservatism and radicalism derive from orientations toward the process of change rather than toward the purpose and direction of change.

The conservative ideology is the product of intense ideological and social conflict. It appears only when the challengers to the established institutions reject the fundamentals of the ideational theory in terms of which those institutions have been molded and created. If the challengers do not question the basic values of the prevailing philosophy, the controversy between those for and against institutional change is carried on with reference to the commonly accepted ideational philosophy. Each group attempts to show that its policies are more in accord with the common ideals than those of the other group. After the Civil War in America, for instance, the conflict between American Whig and American Democrat was fought, as Hartz has pointed out, within a shared framework of Lockean values. Consensus precluded conservatism.

When the challengers fundamentally disagree with the ideology of the existing society, however, and affirm a basically different set of values, the common framework of discussion is destroyed. The rejection of the prevailing ideology by the challengers compels it to be abandoned by the defenders also. No ideational theory can be used to defend established institutions satisfactorily, even when those institutions in general reflect the values of that ideology. The perfect nature of the ideology's ideal and the imperfect nature and inevitable mutation of the institutions create a gap between the two. The ideal becomes a standard by which to criticize the institutions, much to the embarrassment of those who believe in the ideal and yet still wish to defend the institutions.[6] Eventually the defenders are faced with an unavoidable choice: either they must abandon their ideology in order to defend their institutions and substitute a conservative philosophy for their old ideational theory, or they must adhere to their ideational theory at the risk of further contributing to the downfall of those institutions which largely embody their ideals. The defense of any set of institutions against a fundamental challenge, consequently, must be phrased in terms of the conservative logic, sanctity, and necessity of the institutions *qua* institutions irrespective of the degree to which they correspond to the prescriptions of this or that ideational philosophy.[7]

The challenging social force must present a clear and present danger to the institutions. The mere articulation of a dissident ideology does not produce conservatism until that ideology is embraced by significant social groups. The *philosophes* of the mid-eighteenth century generated no conservative ideology; the events of 1789 and the subsequent years did. Conservatism, in Mannheim's words, "first becomes conscious and reflective when other ways of life and thought appear on the scene, against which it is compelled to take up arms in the ideological struggle."[8] If the defenders of the established order are successful, in due course they gradually cease to articulate their conservative ideology and substitute for it a new version of their old ideational theory. If their defense is unsuccessful, they abandon either their old ideational premises or their new conservative ideology. If they are inclined to be congenital conservatives, they will accept the new order as the inevitable work of destiny. Burke, Bonald, and de Maistre, for instance, all in part believed that the triumph of the French Revolution might be decreed by

[6] Hence any theory of natural law as a set of transcendent and universal moral principles is inherently nonconservative. Mannheim, consequently, is quite right in identifying opposition to natural law as a distinguishing characteristic of conservatism, *op. cit.,* pp. 116-19. On Burke's denial of natural law, see Alfred Cobban, *Edmund Burke and the Revolt against the Eighteenth Century* (London, 1929), pp. 40 ff., 75, and Leo Strauss, *Natural Right and History* (Chicago, 1953), pp. 13-14 and 318-19, who makes the point that Burke differed from previous thinkers precisely in that he did not judge the British constitution by a standard transcending it. The efforts of contemporary publicists such as Russell Kirk to appear conservative and yet at the same time to espouse a universal natural law are manifestly inconsistent.

[7] Since conservatism is the ideological justification of established social and political institutions, a conservative defense of sheer chaos or of a society in a continuing state of rapid revolutionary change would be impossible except for an individual so nimble, so cunning, so strong as to be confident of his talent for flourishing as an outlaw. This raises the question as to the chances of conservatism in a modern totalitarian state. If totalitarian society is, as Franz Neumann described Nazi Germany, "a non-state, a chaos, a rule of lawlessness and anarchy," a conservative defense of such a society is impossible. On the other hand, if a totalitarian regime under attack did articulate a theory characterized by a number of conservative elements, this in itself would be supporting evidence that it had "settled down" and was no longer in a state of permanent revolution. The answer to this general question obviously depends upon the nature of totalitarianism rather than on the nature of conservatism. See Carl J. Friedrich (ed.), *Totalitarianism* (Cambridge, 1954); Hannah Arendt, "Ideology and Terror: A Novel Form of Government," *Review of Politics,* Vol. 15, pp. 303-27 (July 1953); Franz Neumann, *Behemoth: The Structure and Practice of National Socialism* (New York, 1942); Zbigniew K. Brzezinski, "Totalitarianism and Rationality," this Review, Vol. 50, p. 751 (Sept., 1956).

[8] *Op. cit.,* p. 115.

Providence and that once this became obvious, it would "not be resolute and firm, but perverse and obstinate" to oppose it.[9]

On the other hand, the unsuccessful conservative who remains attached to the ideals of his old ideational philosophy becomes a reactionary, *i.e.*, a critic of existing society who wishes to recreate in the future an ideal which he assumes to have existed in the past. He is a radical. No valid distinction exists between "change backward" and "change forward." Change is change; history neither retreats nor repeats; and all change is away from the status quo. As time passes, the ideal of the reactionary becomes less and less related to any actual society of the past. The past is romanticized, and, in the end, the reactionary comes to support a return to an idealized "Golden Age" which never in fact existed. He becomes indistinguishable from other radicals, and he normally displays all the distinctive characteristics of the radical psychology.

The nature of conservatism as an institutional ideology precludes any permanent and inherent affiliation or opposition between it and any particular ideational ideology. No necessary dichotomy exists, therefore, between conservatism and liberalism. The assumption that such an opposition does exist derives, of course, from the aristocratic theory of conservatism and reflects an overconcern with a single phase of western history at the end of the 18th and the beginning of the 19th centuries. The effort to erect this ephemeral relationship into a continuing phenomenon of political history only serves to obscure the fact that in the proper historical circumstances conservatism may well be necessary for the defense of liberal institutions. The true enemy of the conservative is not the liberal but the extreme radical no matter what ideational theory he may espouse. Different radicals advance different panaceas, but they all have the same psychology which conservative thinkers have not been slow to identify. Hooker's sixteenth-century Puritan, Metternich's "presumptuous man," Burke's "metaphysical scribbler," Hawthorne's Hollingsworth, Cortés' "self-worshipping man," Hoffer's twentieth century "true believer," are all one and the same.

The distinction between conservatism and the ideational ideologies has led some nonconservatives to deny any intellectual content to conservatism and has led some conservatives to attack all ideologies. Both the critics and the defenders of conservatism are wrong, however, when they minimize its intellectual significance. Conservatism is the intellectual rationale of the permanent institutional prerequisites of human existence. It has a high and necessary function. It is the rational defense of being against mind, of order against chaos. When the foundations of society are threatened, the conservative ideology reminds men of the necessity of some institutions and the desirability of the existing ones. All ideologies need not be ideational ideologies. The theory of conservatism is of a different order and purpose than other common political theories, but it is still theory. Conservatism is not just the absence of change. It is the articulate, systematic, theoretical resistance to change.

---

[9] See Bonald's famous comment: "Quand Dieu a voulu punir la France, il a fait retirer les Bourbons." "Pensees sur Divers Sujets," *Oeuvres* (Paris, 1817), Vol. 6, 172. Also: Joseph De Maistre, "Considerations sur la France," *Oeuvres* (Bruxelles, 1838), Vol. 7, Ch. 1, 2; and Strauss's discussion of Burke, *op. cit.,* pp. 317-19.

INHERENT AND POSITIONAL IDEOLOGIES: THE ABSENCE OF A CONSERVATIVE TRADITION

Most writers agree, and it is assumed here, that Burke is properly called a conservative. The question, consequently, is: can Burke best be understood as the spokesman for the feudal aristocratic order, the expounder of values and ideals universally valid, or as the defender of established institutions? The aristocratic definition fails to explain Burke because: (1) the English society Burke defended was neither primarily feudal nor exclusively aristocratic; (2) Burke was concerned with the defense of other established societies, notably in India and America; and (3) insofar as Burke had views on the desirable organization of society, he was a liberal, a Whig, and a free trader. The autonomous concept similarly does not offer a complete explanation of Burke because: (1) Burke's political writings and speeches were all directed to immediate problems and needs; (2) he rejected the desirability and the possibility of a moral or political philosophy of universal applicability; and (3) the principal elements of his political thought are relevant chiefly to the limited purpose of justifying established institutions.

On the Continent at the beginning of the nineteenth century Burke's ideas were used to defend aristocracy and feudalism against the rising middle class. The English society and constitution with which Burke was concerned, however, were quite different from those existing across the Channel. The fact that his ideas could be used to justify the established order in both places demonstrates not the similarity of the two orders but the transferability of his philosophy. In a penetrating epigram, Louis Hartz has declared that "In America Burke equalled Locke." This is true enough, but it was equally true in England. Burke defended the English constitution of his day first against the efforts of George III to reassert the influence of the Crown over Parliament and then against the efforts of the democrats to broaden the control of the people over Parliament. He was a conservative because one hundred years after Locke he was still attempting to preserve the institutions of 1689. A devotee of mixed government, he was resolved, he said, "to keep an established church, an established monarchy, an established aristocracy, and an established democracy, each in the degree it exists, and in no greater."[10] Burke recognized that the people had an important, although limited, role to play in the English system.[11] Accepting aristocracy as an inherent and necessary element of the British constitution, he showed, however, little partiality towards it. A commoner himself, he suffered on more than one occasion from the aristocratic disdain of the great lords who tended to view him as an "Irish adventurer." Like Jefferson and Adams, Burke was a supporter of a natural aristocracy, not an artificial aristocracy.[12]

[10] "Reflections on the Revolution in France," *Works* (Boston, 1865), Vol. 3, p. 352 (hereafter cited as *Works*).
[11] See *e.g.*, "Thoughts on the Cause of the Present Discontents," *Works*, Vol. 1, pp. 436, 440-41, 469, 472-74, 491-93, 508.
[12] For Burke's views on aristocracy, see *ibid.*, Vol. 1, p. 458; "An Appeal from the New to the Old Whigs," *ibid.*, Vol. 4, pp. 174-75; "Reflections on the Revolution in France," *ibid.*, Vol. 3, p. 297; "Speech on the Second Reading of a Bill for the Repeal of the Marriage Act," *The Works of Edmund Burke* (London, World's Classics), Vol. 3, p. 385; John MacCunn, *The Political Philosophy of Burke* (London, 1913), pp. 157-60, 173 ff., 258-68. On Burke's difficulties with the aristocracy, see John Viscount Morley, *Burke* (London, 1923), pp. 198-208.

The social order which Burke defended was to a large extent commercial, and it was becoming increasingly industrial. The eighteenth century had seen the rise of the Bank of England, the South Sea Bubble, joint stock companies, expanding shipping and trade, the accumulation of commercial fortunes and industrial capital, a rash of industrial inventions, and the steady growth of manufacturing. Commerce was "the dominant factor" in eighteenth-century England.[13] Voltaire's astonishment that the great gentlemen of England were not ashamed of trade was but one indication of the difference between English and continental society. For thirty years before Burke arrived in London in 1750 the promotion of industry had been a primary objective of the English government. By 1790, when according to the aristocratic theory of conservatism Burke was defending the feudal corporate order, the Industrial Revolution in England was already a generation old. Was Burke repelled by the growth of commerce and industry? Did he seek to return to the feudal agrarian order of a previous age? Far from it. For Burke, as Namier declares, "trade was the soul of empire." As early as 1770 Burke stated his position in no uncertain terms: "There is no such thing as the landed interest separate from the trading interest. . . . *Turn your land into trade.*"[14] Is this the advice of a feudal apologist? Six years later Burke praised to the skies "for sagacity and penetration of mind, extent of views, accurate distinction, just and natural connexion and dependence of parts" a book which accurately reflected his own views on economics: *The Wealth of Nations.*[15] In Parliament Burke was consistently for laisser faire; the state should stay out of economic matters; the laws of commerce were the laws of nature; labor itself was an "article of trade." Is it any wonder that Adam Smith, after discussing political economy with Burke, should declare that Burke "was the only man, who, without communication, thought on these topics exactly as he did"?[16] If Burke is an apologist for the feudal corporate order, what becomes of Adam Smith? The plain fact of the matter is that, insofar as he had views on the desirable organization of society, in politics Burke was a liberal and a Whig, the defender of the Lockean constitution; in economics, he was a liberal free trader, his ideas at one with those of Adam Smith. There was little or nothing that was corporate, or feudal, or aristocratic about him at all.

While Burke preferred a balanced constitution and a commercial economy, his preference derived not so much from their peculiar virtues as from the fact of their existence. Montesquieu and Adam Smith developed the ideational rationale for the

[13] L. B. Namier, *England in the Age of the American Revolution* (London, 1930), pp. 15, 38, 40: "Trade was not despised in eighteenth-century England—it was acknowledged to be the great concern of the nation. . . ." See also W. E. H. Lecky, *A History of England in the Eighteenth Century* (New York, 1878), Vol. 1, p. 433: "In very few periods in English political history was the commercial element more conspicuous in administration. . . . The questions which excited most interest were chiefly financial and commercial ones." And J. L. and Barbara Hammond, *The Rise of Modern Industry* (New York, 1926), pp. 64-65; "In eighteenth-century England, industry seemed the most important thing in the world. All classes put industrial expansion high among the objects of public policy. . . ." On the beginning of the Industrial Revolution in England and the prestige of commerce and industry, see also: W. Cunningham, *The Industrial Revolution* (Cambridge, 1908), p. 494; W. T. Selley, *England in the Eighteenth Century* (London, 1934), pp. 218-19; Witt Bowden, *The Rise of the Great Manufacturers in England, 1760-1790* (Allentown, 1919), *passim.*

[14] *Cavendish Debates*, Vol. 1, p. 476, quoted in Robert H. Murray, *Edmund Burke: A Biography* (Oxford, 1931), p. 192 (italics added).

[15] *Annual Register*, 1776, Vol. 19, p. 241.

[16] Robert Bisset, *The Life of Edmund Burke,* 2 vols. 2d ed. (London, 1800), Vol. 2, p. 429.

institutions which Burke accepted. Burke's contribution was different. He was concerned not with the substance of institutions but with their preservation. Impartially he defended Whig institutions in England, democratic institutions in America, autocratic institutions in France, and Hindu institutions in India. Indian institutions, he warned, for example, must be based "upon their own principles not upon ours," denouncing those Britishers in India who subverted "the most established rights and the most ancient and most revered institutions of ages and nations."[17] "He changed his front," as Morley remarked in a classic phrase, "but he never changed his ground." Since Morley, scholars have united in clearing Burke of charges of inconsistency. But if Burke was consistent, how can he have been an aristocrat? If his primary concern had been the preservation of the feudal corporate order in Europe, why would he have any concern for America or India? Most conservatives adopt conservative ideas in order to defend one particular established order. In this respect their conservatism is instrumental rather than primary. Burke, however, was the conservative archetype because his impulse was to defend all existing institutions wherever located and however challenged.

Supporters of the aristocratic theory of conservatism argue that modern conservatism originated with the reaction to the French Revolution. They are mistaken. It is possible to identify at least four major manifestations of conservatism in western political history. The first was the response in the sixteenth and seventeenth centuries to the challenge of centralized national authority to medieval political institutions and the challenge of the Reformation to established church-state relationships. On the Continent, for instance, Francis Hotman in his *Franco-Gallia* and Juan de Mariana in his *De Rege et Regis Institutione* attempted a conservative defense of the medieval pluralistic order against the growing power of the national monarchs. That Hotman was a Frenchman and a Protestant and Mariana a Spaniard and a Jesuit made little difference. They had similar purposes and similar arguments. Unfortunately for both, however, the historical facts did not entirely support the uses which they made of them, and the trend toward royal power had already undermined most of the significant institutions of the old order. As a result, the argument of the monarchomachs was shifted from a conservative base to an ideational one. It was restated in terms of principle rather than precedent. *Franco-Gallia* was eclipsed by the *Vindiciae*, and Mariana was overshadowed by Suarez.[18]

In England, on the other hand, the existence of a strong national monarchy and of a national church permitted a conservative defense of both. The ideas which on the Continent had been used to defend the estates against royal authority were used in England to defend royal authority against political dissidents and theological radicals. The politcal thinking of the Tudor apologists—Tyndale, Gardiner, Hooper, and numerous others—was suffused with conservative appeals to order and obedience.[19] Rebellion and anarchy were held out as the worst of evils;

[17] Quoted in Morley, *Burke*, pp. 190-91, 245, and George H. Sabine, *A History of Political Theory* (New York, 1950, rev. ed.)., p. 616.

[18] Some conservative elements persisted in the *Vindiciae*, but they were obscured by the appeal to the social contract and natural law. *Cf.* J. N. Figgis, *From Gerson to Grotius* (Cambridge, 1916), pp. 174-79 and Sabine, *A History of Political Theory*, pp. 375-77.

[19] See Charles Nevinson (ed.), *Latter Writings of Bishop Hooper* (Cambridge, 1852), esp. "Annotations on Romans XIII," pp. 93-116; Pierre Janelle (ed.), *Obedience in Church and State: Three Political Tracts by Stephen Gardiner* (Cambridge, 1930); Henry Walter (ed.),

disobedience was an effort to break a divinely ordained chain of being. Restated again and again in Tudor literature was Shakespeare's warning: "Take but degree away, untune that string, And, Hark! what discord follows. . . ."

Toward the end of the sixteenth century as the Puritan attack gathered strength and became more extreme—the episcopacy came under sustained criticism in 1570—the need arose for a more thorough conservative defense of the national civil and religious establishment. This need was met by Richard Hooker in his *Laws of Ecclesiastical Polity* published in 1594. This multivolume work stands as a towering and eloquent statement of the conservative ideology. Here, two hundred years before Burke, was delineated every significant strand of Burkean thought.[20] The substance of their conservatism is virtually identical. Yet the institutions they were defending and the challenges to which they were reacting were dissimilar. The Tudor constitution of 1590 differed from the Whig constitution of 1790. The threat to Hooker's institutions came from Puritan sects advocating the complete separation of Church and State, the supremacy of faith over reason, and the authority of scripture against the authority of the church. The Puritans viewed man as depraved and evil; they were spiritualistic, deterministic, anti-intellectual, fundamentalist and pessimistic. The challenge to Burke's institutions, on the other hand, came from democratic groups assured of the efficacy of reason and possessed of an unbounded confidence in human nature and man's capacity for progress. They were everything which the Puritans were not: materialistic, rationalistic, anti-religious, optimistic, and libertarian. Yet despite the differences, the similar situations in which Hooker and Burke found themselves led them to expound similar political ideas.

The second great manifestation of conservatism was the response to the French Revolution. That social upheaval, the ideologies it advanced, and the classes it propelled towards power were undoubtedly the greatest threat to existing institutions in the history of western civilization up to that time. Consequently, they produced the greatest outpouring of conservative thought in western history. The conservative response to the Revolution was largely but not exclusively a defense of the feudal, agrarian, aristocratic order against a rising, urban, enlightened middle class. Nonetheless, the Revolution endangered not only feudal aristocratic institutions but all established institutions. In England Burke made a conservative defense of a commercial society and a moderate, liberal constitution. In America, the Federalists—from John Adams through Hamilton to Fisher Ames—expounded conservative ideas to defend a liberal constitution against what they thought to

Doctrinal Treatises by William Tyndale (Cambridge, 1848), esp. pp. 173 ff., 195-97, 240 ff.; Christopher Morris, *Political Thought in England, Tyndale to Hooker* (London, 1953), pp. 15, 17, 57, 68-77. One hundred years later Bramhall duplicated those arguments in his controversies with Hobbes. See John Bramhall, *Works* (Oxford, 1844), Vol. 3, "A Fair Warning to take Heed of the Scotch Discipline," and "The Serpent-Salve, or, the Observator's Grounds Discussed," esp. pp. 236, 241, 272, 298, 309, 318; John Bowle, *Hobbes and His Critics* (New York, 1952), pp. 114 ff.; T.S. Eliot, *For Lancelot Andrewes* (Garden City, 1929), pp. 27-46.

[20] For typical conservative expressions in the *Laws of Ecclesiastical Polity*, see: Pref., i, 2, iii, 7, iv, 4, vi, 5-6; I, v, 1, x, 4; IV, i, e, iv, 2, xii, 2, xiv, 1-2; V, vii, 3, lxxi, 4; VII, i, 1-2; VIII, ii, 2, 17. On Hooker's conservatism generally, see Sheldon Wolin, "Richard Hooker and English Conservatism," *Western Political Quarterly*, Vol. VI, pp. 28-47 (March, 1953). On the nature of the Puritan challenge and the origins of Hooker's work, see C. J. Sisson, *The Judicious Marriage of Mr. Hooker and the Birth of the Laws of Ecclesiastical Polity* (Cambridge, 1940), *passim*, and E. T. Davies, *The Political Ideas of Richard Hooker* (London, 1946), Ch. 1, 2.

be the threat of a democratic revolution. On the Continent, too, the initial conservative reaction came not from the feudal aristocrats but from thinkers associated with more liberal, commercial, and bureaucratic elements. In Germany, for instance, Brandes, Rehberg, and Möser, representatives of the north German cities where the middle class was strongest, made the first attacks on the Revolution.[21] A few of the continental conservatives, such as Gentz, were liberal in their economics. Even among the spokesmen for the aristocracy, differences existed in the societies which they defended: the France of Bonald and de Maistre, the Prussia of von der Marwitz and Haller, and the Austria of Gentz, Metternich, and Müller did not have identical social structures. Nevertheless, the common strands of conservatism ran through the political ideas of the Reaction thinkers irrespective of the immediate social order which they desired to preserve.

The conservatism of the feudal-aristocratic thinkers of the Reaction was the product of their temporary defensive position rather than of the permanent and inherent nature of their class interests. The fundamental character of those interests did not change in 1789. Yet prior to that year the aristocracy produced no significant conservative thinking. They had no need for it. On the other hand, after the aristocrats were driven from power, they ceased to be conservative without surrendering their aristocratic ideals. In France, in particular, aristocratic thought, once conservative, rapidly became reactionary and eventually became radical. De Maistre had exalted order and stability. In the bourgeois democracy of the Third Republic *L'Action Française* preached violence and the "coup de force." The revolutionaries were on the Right.[22]

The third manifestation of conservatism was the response of the governing classes to the popular lower class demands for a share in the direction of society in the middle years of the nineteenth century. The single most important symbol of this challenge was the cry for the extension of the suffrage. It was a challenge, however, that involved only a partial divergence from accepted values and, consequently, occasioned a weak conservative response. In France, in particular, where the middle classes had to face in two directions, the typical exponents of their viewpoint—Royer-Collard and Guizot, for instance—expounded liberal ideas against the aristocrats and conservative ideas against the masses. In Germany, where a major upheaval had not destroyed the structure of society, Stahl, Ranke, Savigny, and Ludwig von Gerlach articulated a more broadly conceived conservatism emphasizing the organic growth of society. In England, Coleridge and, subsequently, Newman, Maine, and Lecky warned of the dangers of substituting popular rule for class rule. In the United States, the neo-Federalists, Story, Choate, Kent, made a brief conservative defense of a restricted governing class before they were overwhelmed by the Jacksonian tidal wave.

A fourth manifestation of conservatism was the outpouring of political thought produced in the southern United States by the challenge of industrialism, free

---

[21] See Reinhold Aris, *History of Political Thought in Germany* (London, 1936), pp. 54-58, 256. Brandes and Rehberg wrote their conservative works before reading Burke. Moser was closer to feudalism, but even he, as Mannheim points out, "Conservative Thought," pp. 144-45, had little use for the nobility, and was primarily concerned with the preservation of the medieval social system as a whole.

[22] Joseph C. Murray, "The Political Thought of Joseph de Maistre," *Review of Politics*, Vol. 11, p. 86 (January, 1949); Charles A. Micaud, *The French Right and Nazi Germany, 1933-1939* (Durham, 1943), pp. 1-15.

labor, and abolition in the middle of the nineteenth century. Prior to 1830 southern political thought was shaped largely in the Jeffersonian image. After 1830 southern thinking became increasingly conservative as a result of the increasingly articulate theories of abolition and the rise of northern industry and population. William Lloyd Garrison—the epitome of the radical reformer—founded *The Liberator* in 1831 and in the same year Nat Turner led his slave insurrection. The combination of forces which these events symbolized forced the South on the defensive and led it to abandon its Jeffersonian heritage and develop a conservative apologia in the language of Burke. It was possible to be at once a Jeffersonian and a slaveowner only so long as no one set the Declaration of Independence against slavery. When this happened, the slaveowner had to abandon either his liberalism or his livelihood. Inevitably the ideational philosophy was sacrificed and replaced by a far-reaching conservatism.[23] Just as the rising tide of Puritan radicalism against the Tudor establishment eventually produced Hooker, the rising tide of abolitionist reform eventually produced Calhoun and Fitzhugh. In their writings and in those of the others of the "reactionary enlightenment"—Holmes, Hammond, Hughes, and Harper, in particular—there was "duplicated in every essential aspect the argument of Europe's feudal reaction."[24] All the basic ideas of Burke were reproduced in the treatises and pamphlets with which they came to the defense of their established social order against a threat which was concrete, potent, and eventually successful.

Louis Hartz has suggested that southern conservatism was a "fraud."[25] Starting from the aristocratic conception of conservatism, Hartz argues that there was an inherent conflict in the effort of the southerners to use Burke to defend slavery, on the one hand, and a political tradition containing many elements of liberalism, on the other. Notwithstanding definite inconsistencies in the southern system, however, there was no inconsistency in the South's use of Burke to defend that system. The conservative philosophy was appropriate to the defense of the institutions of Jefferson, the "peculiar institution" of slavery, or any combination of the two. It was no more of a fraud for Calhoun to combine Burke and slavery than it was for Burke himself to combine Burke and laisser faire. Nor does the fact that southern conservative political thought ended with the Civil War prove that the southerners were "false Burkes, halfway Burkes." When the southern social-political system was destroyed, the theory elaborated in its defense necessarily had to die with it. Hartz himself describes southern conservatism as "one of the great and creative episodes in the history of American thought." Could it be this, however, if it were simply a "fraud," an artificial importation without roots in the American situation? Is it not possible to avoid this problem by a more simple explanation of southern conservatism? The southern experience was a clear example of a society shifting from a liberal ideational theory to an uncompromising conservatism as the result of the rise of a fundamental challenge to its existence. Given the change in the southern position, the change in southern thought was both necessary and natural.

The basic inadequacy of the aristocratic theory of conservatism is that it conceives conservatism to be an *inherent* ideology rather than a *positional* ideology.

---

[23] For the change in southern thinking about 1830, see William E. Dodd, *The Cotton Kingdom* (New Haven, 1921), pp. 48 ff., and Arthur Y. Lloyd, *The Slavery Controversy* (Chapel Hill, 1939), pp. 119 ff.

[24] Louis Hartz, *The Liberal Tradition in America* (New York, 1955), p. 146.

[25] *Ibid.*, pp. 147 ff.

An inherent ideology is the theoretical expression of the interests of a continuing social group. It is derived from the fundamental common characteristics which make the group a group. Consequently, an inherent ideology evolves and changes as the interests and needs of the group change, but, at the same time, it maintains certain essential characteristics reflecting the continuing and inherent identity of the group. True to its essential nature as the ideology of the bourgeois middle class, the liberalism of one generation has differed from and yet grown out of the liberalism of a previous generation. An inherent philosophy may also be differently interpreted and expressed by conflicting subschools existing at the same time. American liberalism has been split between a Whig, "property rights," version, on the one hand, and a popular, "human rights," version, on the other. None the less, American Whig and American democrat both share the essentials of Locke. Marxism, too, has existed in a variety of forms and evolved through a number of phases, all of which, however, have retained the same underlying fundamentals which distinguish Marxism as a theory. It is thus possible to relate the various expressions of an inherent theory to each other, to trace patterns of development and influence, and to identify schisms and subvarieties within the common intellectual tradition. In brief: the substance of an inherent theory evolves and proliferates, and the expressions of the theory are interrelated and interdependent. The theory and its exponents all constitute a *school of thought*.

Positional ideologies are quite different. They do not reflect the continuing interests and needs of a particular social group. Rather they depend upon the relations existing among groups. A group may espouse one positional ideology when its relations with other groups assume one form and another positional ideology when those relations assume a different form. Positional ideologies reflect the changing external environment of a group rather than its permanent internal characteristics. Inherent ideologies are functions of groups no matter what their positions; positional ideologies are functions of situations no matter what groups occupy those situations.[26] With positional ideologies, it is a question not of "who" but of "where." Thus, the theory of "states' rights" in the United States has been primarily a positional ideology espoused by a succession of different groups whenever their power in the central government vis-à-vis their opponent groups has been less than their power in the states.

If the situational definition of conservatism is correct, conservatism is a positional ideology. Conservatism develops to meet a specific historical need. When the need disappears, the conservative philosophy subsides. In each case, the articulation of conservatism is a response to a specific social situation. The manifestation of conservatism at any one time and place has little connection with its manifestation at any other time and place. Conservatism thus reflects no permanent group interest. Depending upon the existence of a particular relation among groups rather than upon the existence of the groups themselves, it lasts only so long as the relation lasts, not so long as the groups last. And the relation is necessarily ephemeral, seldom continuing more than one generation. Consequently, the conservative ideology is not developed and transmiteed with alterations, elaboration, and revision from one age to the next. Nor does it have a set of basic

[26] The significance of positional ideologies has been obscured by the assumption, deriving from Mannheim's sociology of knowledge, that every ideology has a "carrier" in the form of a specific group or class. The argument here is that ideologies may also have "carriers" in the form of recurring patterns of relations among groups.

writings to be annotated, interpreted, and argued over by contending sets of disciples. The manifestations of conservatism are simply parallel ideological reactions to similar social situations. The substance of conservatism is essentially static. Conservative thought is repetitive, not evolutionary. Its manifestations are historically isolated and discrete. Thus, paradoxical though it may seem, conservatism, the defender of tradition, is itself without tradition; conservatism, the appeal to history, is without history.

The static and repetitious character of conservative thought is reflected in the extent to which conservatism lends itself to itemization. More so than any other political ideology, conservatism can be condensed into a brief catalog of principles or concepts which constitute the conservative catechism common to all conservative thinkers. Both the proponents and critics of conservatism agree that the essence of conservatism can be summed up in a small number of basic ideas. The number of these ideas may vary in the different formulations, but their content is universally the same. Hearnshaw, for instance, lists "twelve principles of conservatism," Kirk "six canons of conservative thought," and Rossiter " 'twenty-one points' of the Conservative tradition."[27]

In part, these brief and similar catalogs of conservative ideas simply reflect the general consensus on the substance of conservatism as an ideology. But, in addition, they reflect the static and limited nature of that ideology. Other ideologies have basic ideas which recur in various manifestations. But these ideas are the starting point, not the sum and substance of the ideology. Individualism is basic to liberalism but the individualism of Locke is quite different from that of Bentham. Class conflict is basic to Marxism, but the class struggle in Kautsky is different from the class struggle in Lenin. Conservatives, however, do not subdivide into schools, nor do they, like liberals and Marxists, engage in fiery arguments over the meaning of their faith. Individual conservative thinkers, of course, may phrase their ideas in slightly different ways and may modify them in the light of their particular ideational leanings. But in general they simply repeat their catechism, and once they have said their catechism, they have said all there is to be said of the substance of conservative thought. A history of liberal or Marxist thought reveals the transmutation of the ideology through different times and circumstances. A history of conservative thinkers, such as Kirk's *Conservative Mind*, necessarily involves the repetition over and over again of the same ideas.

This peculiar character of conservative thought explains one frequently commented upon aspect of conservatism cited by Mannehim: "The careers of most conservatives and reactionaries show revolutionary periods in their youth."[28] Many of the early nineteenth century conservatives—Görres, Gentz, Müller in Germany; Coleridge, Wordsworth, Southey in England—were initially enthusiasts for the French Revolution. The Federalists began as successful revolutionaries, and America's premier conservative, John C. Calhoun, started his career as a fire-eating Jeffersonian nationalist. Why does this pattern exist? Is it not simply because

---

[27] F. J. C. Hearnshaw, *Conservatism in England* (London, 1933), pp. 22 ff.; Kirk, *Conservative Mind*, pp. 7-8; Rossiter, *Conservatism in America*, pp. 61-62; Mannheim, "Conservative Thought," p. 114; Lord Hugh Cecil, *Conservatism* (London, 1937), p. 48; William O. Shanahan, "The Social Outlook of Prussian Conservatism," *Review of Politics*, Vol. 15, pp. 222-25 (April, 1953); R. J. White (ed.), *The Conservative Tradition* (London, 1950), pp. 1-10.

[28] "Conservative Thought," p. 120.

conservatism is not the permanent ideological expression of the needs of any social group? No one is born to conservatism in the way in which a Mill is born to utilitarianism. The impulse to conservatism comes from the social challenge before the theorist, not the intellectual tradition behind him. Men are driven to conservatism by the shock of events, by the horrible feeling that a society or institution which they have approved or taken for granted and with which they have been intimately connected may suddenly cease to exist. The conservative thinkers of one age, consequently, have little influence on those of the next. There are few second generation conservatives. Hooker, for instance, anticipated Burke in all the essentials of conservative philosophy; but Burke's conservatism was derived not from a study of Hooker but from the impact of events about him. Similarly, in France, "Maistre never had a school, so to speak." In the United States, Fitzhugh, the apologist for the South, gained little inspiration from earlier conservative thinkers.[29] Each individual statement of the conservative position, in itself, moreover, tends to be generated by some immediate intellectual challenge. Christopher Morris describes the *Laws of Ecclesiastical Polity* as a "livre de circonstance." The same phrase could apply equally well to the *Elemente der Staatskunst*, the *Reflections on the Revolution in France*, and *A Disquisition on Government.*[30]

THE RELEVANCE OF CONSERVATISM

In the light of the above analysis, what role has the conservative ideology in America today? Is the "New Conservatism" really conservative? Does room exist for a more profound and far-reaching exposition of conservative ideas?

Much of the New Conservatism is characterized by at least three deficiencies as a conservative movement. First, many New Conservatives appear uncertain as to what they wish to defend. Some simply continue the old identification of conservatism with business liberalism. Others are radical aristocrats, ill at ease in and disgusted with American society as it exists today. Desiring to import European aristocracy to bourgeois America, they dream of an age of less democracy, less equality, less industrialism, an age in which the elite ruled and the mass knew their place. Their rejection of the existing American political and social system makes it impossible

---

[29] Murray, *Review of Politics*, Vol. 11, p. 86; Arnaud B. Leavelle and Thomas I. Cook, "George Fitzhugh and the Theory of American Conservatism," *Journal of Politics*, Vol. 7, pp. 146-47 (May, 1945).

[30] Its lack of both an intellectual tradition and a substantive ideal account for another peculiar aspect of conservatism: the extent to which it has been ignored by political scientists writing on political theory. In the political theory textbooks conservatism rarely, if ever, appears, and when it does it is treated, on the whole, in a very skimpy manner. Similarly, there are no decent histories of conservative thought. The reason for this lies partly in the nature of conservatism and partly in the training of political scientists. The latter learn to analyze historical schools of thoughts, to trace the development of ideas, to identify the influence of one man on another, and to search out the ideological schisms and doctrinal divergencies in a school of thought. They are also taught to dissect the substantive ideals of ideologies in terms of their inherent logic and consistency, the theories of man and nature which they reflect, and the group interests which they rationalize and project. Lacking an intellectual tradition and a substantive ideal, conservatism does not lend itself to fruitful analysis along these lines. Not knowing what questions to ask about conservatism or how to evaluate its significance, political scientists have tended to ignore it.

for them to be truly conservative. Russell Kirk's view of contemporary America, for instance, could hardly be more unflattering: "near to suicide," "cheap," "materialistic," "sterile," "standardized."[31] Is this the language of a conservative? Or is it the language of a maligner of existing society? Instead of a vigorous defense of American constitutional democracy, Kirk's books are filled with a strained, sentimental, nostalgic, antiquarian longing for a society which is past. He and his associates are out of tune and out of step in modern America.

Secondly, many New Conservatives are astonishingly vague as to the nature and source of the threat to what they wish to conserve. Historically, conservatism has always been the response to a direct and immediate challenge. Conservatives have not usually been in doubt as to the identity of their opponents. Among the New Conservatives, however, the enemy is seldom brought clearly into focus. To some, the foe is Liberalism, although little agreement exists as to the meaning of this term. To others, it is modernism, totalitarianism, popularism, secularism, or materialism. For some New Conservatives the enemy is irrationalism and to others it is rationalism. This confusion, of course, merely reflects the fact that the economic prosperity and political consensus of American society make any conservatism oriented towards domestic enemies absurdly superfluous. Hooker, Burke, and Calhoun fought real political battles against real political enemies. Lacking any flesh and blood social-political challenge, however, the New Conservatives fashion imaginary threats out of abstract "isms."

A third deficiency of the New Conservatism is the effort to uncover a conservative intellectual tradition in America. Apparently desiring the security of identification with an intellectual movement, the New Conservatives scurry through America's past, resurrecting political and intellectual figures long since forgotten. Few enterprises could be more futile or irrelevant. In *The Conservative Mind*, for instance, Russell Kirk defines a conservative as one who stands by established institutions. Yet in his efforts to find a conservative tradition in America, Kirk classifies as conservative: James Russell Lowell, who was "frightened" by what he saw about him; Brooks Adams, who was "disgusted with American society"; Henry Adams, who has become the classic symbol of frustrated alienation;[32] Irving Babbitt, who fled from America to Buddhism, and Santayana, who fled from America to his Roman cloister. All these men were malcontents, and in many respects they were much more fundamentally malcontent than Debs, Henry George, de Leon, and LaFolletee, whom presumably Kirk would never dream of classifying as conservatives. The New Conservatives' search for forebears merely reflects their own uncertainty of purpose, role, and identity. They seek to conserve an intellectual tradition which does not exist rather than institutions which do exist. Were they true conservatives, immediately engaged in the defense of an institution or society against a real and imminent threat, they would have little interest in establishing a conservative pedigree.

The dubious side of the New Conservatism, however, does not exhaust the possibilities of conservatism in America today. Some New Conservatives recognize

---

[31] *Conservative Mind*, pp. 10, 428, and *Program for Conservatives, passim.* It is essential to distinguish between those such as Kirk who criticize the institutions *and* the theory of modern liberal democracy and those such as Reinhold Niebuhr who limit their critique to the theory of liberalism while praising the inherent wisdom of its institutions.

[32] But see Henry S. Kariel's reinterpretation of him, "The Limits of Social Science: Henry Adams' Quest for Order," in this Review, Vol. 50, p. 1074 (December, 1956).

the essentially situational character of conservative ideology. They realize the sterility of a conservative defense of one segment of American society against another segment. The only threat extensive and deep enough to elicit a conservative response today is the challenge of communism and the Soviet Union to American society as a whole. In this respect, as Max Beloff has pointed out, a marked parallel exists between the position of the South in the 1850s and the position of the United States in the 1950s: both societies challenged by an expanding external order.[33] Just as the South produced a conservative defense in Fitzhugh and Calhoun, it is not unreasonable to expect that America too will have its conservative apologists. The more profound recent writings in a conservative vein, such as those of Niebuhr, were in many respects a direct response to the challenge of foreign totalitarianism. As an island of plenty and freedom in a straitened world, America has much to defend.

American institutions, however, are liberal, popular, and democratic. They can best be defended by those who believe in liberalism, popular control, and democratic government. Just as aristocrats were the conservatives in Prussia in 1820 and slaveowners were the conservatives in the South in 1850, so the liberals must be the conservatives in America today. Historically, American liberals have been idealists, pressing forward toward the goals of greater freedom, social equality, and more meaningful democracy. The articulate exposition of a liberal ideology was necessary to convert others to liberal ideas and to reform existing institutions continuously along liberal lines. Today, however, the greatest need is not so much the creation of more liberal institutions as the successful defense of those which already exist. This defense requires American liberals to lay aside their liberal ideology and to accept the values of conservativatism for the duration of the threat. Only by surrendering their liberal ideas for the present can liberals successfully defend their liberal institutions for the future. Liberals should not fear this change. Is a liberal any less liberal because he adjusts his thinking so as to defend most effectively the most liberal institutions in the world? To continue to expound the philosophy of liberalism simply gives the enemy a weapon with which to attack the society of liberalism.[34] The defense of American institutions requires a conscious articulate conservatism which can spring only from liberals deeply concerned with the preservation of those institutions. As Boorstin, Niebuhr, and others have pointed out, the American political genius is manifest not in our ideas but in our institutions. The stimulus to conservatism comes not from the outworn creeds of third-rate thinkers but from the successful performance of first-rate institutions. Current conflict rather than ancient dogma will yield a "New Conservatism" which is truly conservative.

Conservatism is not, as the aristocratic interpretation argues, the monopoly of one particular class in history. Nor is it, as the autonomous school contends, appropriate in every age and place. It is, instead, relevant in a particular type of

---

[33] *Foreign Policy and the Democratic Process* (Baltimore, 1955), pp. 5-7.

[34] A good example is the common experience of the American in Europe who extols the United States as the land of freedom, equality, and democracy, and then is asked: "What about the Negro in the South?" In reply, the American inevitably stresses the magnitude of the social problems involved, the inevitability of gradualness, the impossibility of altering habits overnight by legislative fiat, and the tensions caused by too rapid social change. In short, he drops the liberal language of equality and freedom and turns to primarily conservative concepts and arguments.

historical situation. That is the situation in which American liberalism finds itself today. Until the challenge of communism and the Soviet Union is eliminated or neutralized, a major aim of American liberals must be to preserve what they have created. This is a limited goal but a necessary one. Conservatism does not ask ultimate questions and hence does not give final answers. But it does remind men of the institutional prerequisites of social order. And when these prerequisites are threatened, conservatism is not only appropriate, it is essential. In preserving the achievements of American liberalism, American liberals have no recourse but to turn to conservatism. For them especially, conservative ideology has a place in America today.

Capitalism and Freedom
Milton Friedman

Milton Friedman (1912-   ) is a professor at the University of Chicago and the author of *Taxing to Prevent Inflation* (1943) and *Price Theory* (1962).

In the 1920's and the 1930's, intellectuals in the United States were overwhelmingly persuaded that capitalism was a defective system inhibiting economic well-being and thereby freedom, and that the hope for the future lay in a greater measure of deliberate control by political authorities over economic affairs. The conversion of the intellectuals was not achieved by the example of any actual collectivist society, though it undoubtedly was much hastened by the establishment of a communist society in Russia and the glowing hopes placed in it. The conversion of the intellectuals was achieved by a comparison between the existing state of affairs, with all its injustices and defects, and a hypothetical state of affairs as it might be. The actual was compared with the ideal.

At the time, not much else was possible. True, mankind had experienced many epochs of centralized control, of detailed intervention by the state into economic affairs. But there had been a revolution in politics, in science, and in technology. Surely, it was argued, we can do far better with a democratic political structure, modern tools, and modern science than was possible in earlier ages.

The attitudes of that time are still with us. There is still a tendency to regard any existing government intervention as desirable, to attribute all evils to the market, and to evaluate new proposals for government control in their ideal form, as they might work if run by able, disinterested men, free from the pressure of special interest groups. The proponents of limited government and free enterprise are still on the defensive.

Yet, conditions have changed. We now have several decades of experience with

From Milton Friedman, *Capitalism and Freedom* (Chicago: The University of Chicago Press, 1962), pp. 196-202. Reprinted by permission.

governmental intervention. It is no longer necessary to compare the market as it actually operates and government intervention as it ideally might operate. We can compare the actual with the actual.

If we do so, it is clear that the difference between the actual operation of the market and its ideal operation—great though it undoubtedly is—is as nothing compared to the difference between the actual effects of government intervention and their intended effects. Who can now see any great hope for the advancement of men's freedom and dignity in the massive tyranny and depotism that hold sway in Russia? Wrote Marx and Engels in *The Communist Manifesto*: "The proletarians have nothing to lose but their chains. They have a world to win." Who today can regard the chains of the proletarians in the Soviet Union as weaker than the chains of the proletarians in the United States, or Britain or France or Germany or any Western state?

Let us look closer to home. Which if any of the great "reforms" of past decades has achieved its objectives? Have the good intentions of the proponents of these reforms been realized?

Regulation of the railroads to protect the consumer quickly became an instrument whereby the railroads could protect themselves from the competition of newly emerging rivals—at the expense, of course, of the consumer.

An income initially enacted at low rates and later seized upon as a means to redistribute income in favor of the lower classes has become a facade, covering loopholes and special provisions that render rates that are highly graduated on paper largely ineffective. A flat rate of 23½ per cent on presently taxable income would yield as much revenue as the present rates graduated from 20 to 91 per cent. An income tax intended to reduce inequality and promote the diffusion of wealth has in practice fostered reinvestment of corporate earnings, thereby favoring the growth of large corporations, inhibiting the operation of the capital market, and discouraging the establishment of new enterprises.

Monetary reforms, intended to promote stability in economic activity and prices, exacerbated inflation during and after World War I and fostered a higher degree of instability thereafter than had ever been experienced before. The monetary authorities they established bear primary responsibility for converting a serious economic contraction into the catastrophe of the Great Depression from 1929-33. A system established largely to prevent bank panics produced the most severe banking panic in American history.

An agricultural program intended to help impecunious farmers and to remove what were alleged to be basic dislocations in the organization of agriculture has become a national scandal that has wasted public funds, distorted the use of resources, riveted increasingly heavy and detailed controls on farmers, interfered seriously with United States foreign policy, and withal has done little to help the impecunious farmer.

A housing program intended to improve the housing conditions of the poor, to reduce juvenile delinquency, and to contribute to the removal of urban slums, has worsened the housing conditions of the poor, contributed to juvenile delinquency, and spread urban blight.

In the 1930's, "labor" was synonomous with "labor union" to the intellectual community; faith in the purity and virtue of labor unions was on a par with faith in home and motherhood. Extensive legislation was enacted to favor labor unions and to foster "fair" labor relations. Labor unions waxed in strength. By the 1950's, "labor union" was almost a dirty word; it was no longer synonomous with "labor," no longer automatically to be taken for granted as on the side of the angels.

Social security measures were enacted to make receipt of assistance a matter of right, to eliminate the need for direct relief and assistance. Millions now receive social security benefits. Yet the relief rolls grow and the sums spent on direct assistance mount.

The list can easily be lengthened: the silver purchase program of the 1930's, public power projects, foreign aid programs of the post-war years. F.C.C., urban redevelopment programs, the stockpiling program—these and many more have had effects very different and generally quite opposite from those intended.

There have been some exceptions. The expressways crisscrossing the country, magnificent dams spanning great rivers, orbiting satellites are all tributes to the capacity of government to command great resources. The school system, with all its defects and problems, with all the possibility of improvement through bringing into more effective play the forces of the market, has widened the opportunities available to American youth and contributed to the extension of freedom. It is a testament to the public-spirited efforts of the many tens of thousands who have served on local school boards and to the willingness of the public to bear heavy taxes for what they regarded as a public purpose. The Sherman antitrust laws, with all their problems of detailed administration, have by their very existence fostered competition. Public health measures have contributed to the reduction of infectious disease. Assistance measures have relieved suffering and distress. Local authorities have often provided facilities essential to the life of the communities. Law and order have been maintained, though in many a large city the performance of even this elementary function of government has been far from satisfactory. As a citizen of Chicago, I speak feelingly.

If a balance be struck, there can be little doubt that the record is dismal. The greater part of the new ventures undertaken by government in the past few decades have failed to achieve their objectives. The United States has continued to progress; its citizens have become better fed, better clothed, better housed, and better transported; class and social distinctions have narrowed; minority groups have become less disadvantaged; popular culture has advanced by leaps and bounds. All this has been the product of the initiative and drive of individuals co-operating through the free market. Government measures have hampered not helped this development. We have been able to afford and surmount these measures only because of the extraordinary fecundity of the market. The invisible hand has been more potent for progress than the visible hand for retrogression.

Is it an accident that so many of the governmental reforms of recent decades have gone awry, that the bright hopes have turned to ashes? Is it simply because the programs are faulty in detail?

I believe the answer is clearly in the negative. The central defect of these measures is that they seek through government to force people to act against their own immediate interests in order to promote a supposedly general interest. They seek to resolve what is supposedly a conflict of interest, or a difference in view about interests, not by establishing a framework that will eliminate the conflict, or by persuading people to have different interests, but by forcing people to act against their own interest. They substitute the values of outsiders for the values of participants; either some telling others what is good for them, or the government taking from some to benefit others. These measures are therefore countered by one of the strongest and most creative forces known to man—the attempt by millions of individuals to promote their own interests, to live their lives by their own values. This is the major reason why the measures have so often had the opposite of the effects intended. It is also one of the major strengths of a free society and explains why governmental regulation does not strangle it.

The interests of which I speak are not simply narrow self-regarding self-interests. On the contrary, they include the whole range of values that men hold dear and for which they are willing to spend their fortunes and sacrifice their lives. The Germans who lost their lives opposing Adolf Hitler were pursuing their interests as they saw them. So also are the men and women who devote great effort and time to charitable, educational, and religious activities. Naturally, such interests are the major ones for few men. It is the virtue of a free society that it nonetheless permits these interests full scope and does not subordinate them to the narrow materialistic interests that dominate the bulk of mankind. That is why capitalist societies are less materialistic than collectivist societies.

Why is it, in light of the record, that the burden of proof still seems to rest on those of us who oppose new government programs and who seek to reduce the already unduly large role of government? Let Dicey answer: "The beneficial effect of State intervention, especially in the form of legislation, is direct, immediate, and, so to speak, visible, whilst its evil effects are gradual and indirect, and lie out of sight. ... Nor ... do most people keep in mind that State inspectors may be incompenent, careless, or even occasionally corrupt . . .; few are those who realize the undeniable truth that State help kills self-help. Hence the majority of mankind must almost of necessity look with undue favor upon governmental intervention. This natural bias can be counteracted only by the existence, in a given society, . . . of a presumption or prejudice in favor of individual liberty, that is, of laissez-faire. The mere decline, therefore, of faith in self-help—and that such a decline has taken place is certain in—is of itself sufficient to account for the growth of legislation tending towards socialism."

The preservation and expansion of freedom are today threatened from two directions. The one threat is obvious and clear. It is the external threat coming from the evil men in the Kremlin who promise to bury us. The other threat is far more subtle. It is the internal threat coming from men of good intentions and good will who wish to reform us. Impatient with the slowness of persuasion and example to achieve the great social changes they envision, they are anxious to use the power of the state to achieve their ends and confident of their own ability to do so. Yet if they gained the power, they would fail to achieve their immediate aims and, in addition, would produce a collective state from which they would recoil in horror and of which they would be among the first victims. Concentrated power is not rendered harmless by the good intentions of those who create it.

The two threats unfortunately reinforce one another. Even if we avoid a nuclear holocaust, the threat from the Kremlin requires us to devote a sizable fraction of our resources to our military defense. The importance of government as a buyer of so much of our output, and the sole buyer of the output of many firms and industries, already concentrates a dangerous amount of economic power in the hands of the political authorities, changes the environment in which business operates and the criteria relevant for business success, and in these and other ways endangers a free market. This danger we cannot avoid. But we needlessly intensify it by continuing the present widespread governmental intervention in areas unrelated to the military defense of the nation and by undertaking ever new governmental programs—from medical care for the aged to lunar exploration.

As Adam Smith once said, "There is much ruin in a nation." Our basic structure of values and the interwoven network of free institutions will withstand much. I believe that we shall be able to preserve and extend freedom despite the size of the military programs and despite the economic powers already concentrated in Washington. But we shall be able to do so only if we awake to the threat that we face, only if we persuade our fellow men that free institutions offer a surer, if perhaps at times a slower, route to the ends they seek than the coercive power of the state. The glimmerings of change that are already apparent in the intellectual climate are a hopeful augury.

Suggested Readings

Auerbach, Morton, *The Conservative Illusion* (New York: Columbia University Press, 1959).

Hogg, Quintin M. (Lord Hailsham), *The Case for Conservatism* (Baltimore: Penguin Books, Inc., 1947).

Kirk, Russel, *The Conservative Mind: From Burke to Eliot*, 3rd ed. (Chicago: Henry Regnery Co., 1960).

Oakeshott, Michael, *Rationalism in Politics and Other Essays* (New York: Basic Books, Inc., Publishers, 1962).

Rossiter, Clinton, *Conservatism in America: The Thankless Persuasion,* 2nd ed., rev. (New York: Alfred A. Knopf, Inc., 1962).

Strauss, Leo, *Natural Right and History* (Chicago: University of Chicago Press, 1953).

Viereck, Peter, *Conservatism Revisited: Revolt Against Revolt* (New York: Charles Scribner's Sons, 1949).

The Ideology of the Radical Right

INTRODUCTION

It was in the winter of 1961-1962 that the "radical right" emerged with force on the American political scene. The Republican Party, which at the time was out of power, split, and the ultraconservative branch of the party emerged as a separate group. They ultimately became so powerful that they were able in 1964 to nominate Senator Goldwater, who shared many of their beliefs. The most prominent and most publicized group associated with this radical right movement was the John Birch Society, but there were many other people who advocated this ideology.

The ideology of the radical right consists of a strong belief in individualism along with a strong revulsion toward any form of collectivism; a belief in a republican as opposed to a democratic form of government; a fundamentalist interpretation of the Bible; a belief that world events and American politics as presently exist are wholly conspiratorial, hence the consequent need to purify American society; a need to restore the United States to the golden age of its founding fathers; a belief that there are always solutions to both the national and domestic problems; and a strong ultrapatriotism and belief in "direct action" in order to break the net of conspiracy and establish the "right" system. The radical right is different from the moderate right in that the latter includes most of the large corporation world, which has come to accept changes in American society during the past three decades, including trade unions, medical care, and other social reforms which the radical right sees as threats to the American system.

In the following articles Secretary Benson points out the international trends that he believes are harming the American way of life, and Dean Manion argues for republicanism as opposed to democracy.

Conservatism and the Threats to the American Way of Life

Ezra Taft Benson

Ezra Taft Benson (1899-   ), who obtained his B.S. from Brigham Young University in 1926, attended the universities of Utah, California, Maine, and Rutgers. He is a member of the Church of Jesus Christ of Latter-day Saints (ordained apostle, member Council of Twelve). Mr. Benson was the Secretary of Agriculture from 1953 to 1961.

My fellow Americans, we are in the midst of continuing international crisis. The outlook for world peace and security is dark indeed. The gravity of the world situation is increasing almost daily. The United Nations seem unable to settle the troubles of the world. In truth we are faced with the hard fact that the United Nations seems to have largely failed in its purpose. Yes, the days ahead are sobering and challenging.

We live today in an age of peril. It is an age in which we are threatened with the loss not only of wealth and material prospertiy, but of something far more precious—our freedom itself. The very thing that distinguishes man from the beasts—his freedom to act, freedom to choose is threatened as never before by a total and atheistic philosophy of life known as communism.

To the true Communist, nothing is evil if it is expedient. Being without conscience or honor, he feels completely justified in using whatever means are necessary to achieve his goal: force, trickery, lies, broken promises, mayhem, and individual and mass murder.

The Communists bring to the nations they infiltrate a message and a philosophy that affects human life in its entirety. Communism seeks to provide what in too many instances a lukewarm Christianity has not provided—a total interpretation of life. Communists are willing to be revolutionary, to take a stand for this and against that. They challenge what they do not believe in—customs, practices, ideas, traditions. They believe heatedly in their philosophy.

But our civilization and our people are seemingly afraid to be revolutionary. We are too broadminded to challenge what we do not believe in. We are afraid of being thought intolerant, uncouth, ungentlemanly. We have become lukewarm in our beliefs. And for that we perhaps merit the bitter condematnion stated in the Book of Revelation 3:15: "So then because thou art lukewarm, and neither cold or hot, I will spue thee out of my mouth."

This is a sad commentary on a civilization which has given to mankind the greatest achievements and progress ever known. But it is even a sadder commentary on those of us who call themselves Christians, who thus betrary the word given to us by the Son of God Himself. Again I ask, are we going to permit the atheistic Communist masters, fellow travelers and dupes to deceive us any longer?

From the *Congressional Record*, March 7, 1962, pp. 3263-3265.

All of us are anxious to see our country progress, but we want to know by what means. The whole American concept of progress, which has outstripped every other nation on earth, is based on certain fundamental principles which these men now ask us to abandon. Certainly we are entitled to challenge such proposals when they are asking us to give up what has worked so well and substitute something which they merely hope will work.

What are these fundamental principles which have allowed the United States to progress so rapidly and yet remain free?

First, a written Constitution clearly defining the limits of government so that government will not become more powerful than the people.

Second, an economic system which is characterized by:

Free enterprise—the right to venture, the right to choose;

Private property—the right to own, develop and enjoy, and

A market economy—the right to exchange and to profit.

Third, building an open society where each individual enjoys the greatest opportunity to improve himself, to travel, to become educated, to invent, to compete, to build, to speak, to worship, and to pursue happiness in whatever way the individual finds most satisfying and worthwhile.

Fourth, assigning government the role of referee rather than competitor—giving it enough power to provide peace, order, and security but not enough power to rob the people of their liberty or take away their property without due process of law.

Of course, it immediately becomes apparent that if certain people wanted to seize control of private property, if they wanted to nationalize the land, if they wanted to have the government take over all the industries, the schools, the transportation complex, and communications network, the way to do it would be by due process of law. Therefore, certain people have set out to do this very thing.

Is this possible? It is indeed, and every American should know it. As the Marxist-Socialists declared over 70 years ago: "Convert the electorate and capture the county councils."

But notice what happened in Russia. It was the Social Democrats, or the ones who wanted to seize power by due process of law who organized the original soviets, who concentrated the power over the industrial workers into a few hands, who overthrew the czar, and who set up conditions in Russia from March to October 1917, which made it possible for the Communists or Bolsheviks to move in with force and violence and take over Russia in November 1917. Notice that the Social Democrats did their organizing in the name of the welfare of the people. After they had provided the basic concentration of power, the forces of Lenin seized control and the people found themselves under the harsh cruelty of a Communist dictatorship.

This is a most important lesson for all of us to learn, namely, that the Communists use the Socialists to pave the way for them whenever possible. This is why Communists and Socialists are often found supporting each other, collaborating together and fighting for the same goals.

The paramount issue today is freedom against creeping socialism. The well-known British writer, John Strachey, who for many years was an openly avowed Communist and who served as Minister of War in the Socialist Government in 1950, made this very plain in his book, "The Theory and Practice of Socialism." He said:

"It is impossible to establish communism as the immediate successor to capitalism. It is, accordingly, proposed to establish socialism as something which we can put in the place of our present decaying capitalism. Hence, Communists work for the establishment of socialism as a necessary transition stage on the road to communism."

We must ever keep in mind that collectivized socialism is part of the Communist strategy. Communism is fundamentally socialism. We will never win our fight against communism by making concessions to socialism. Communism and socialism must be defeated on principle.

When socialism is understood, we will realize that many of the programs advocated, and some of those already adopted in the United States, fall clearly within the category of socialism. What is socialism? It is simply governmental ownership and management of the essential means for the production and distribution of goods.

We must never forget that nations may sow the seeds of their own destruction while enjoying unprecedented prosperity.

The socialistic Communist conspiracy to weaken the United States involves attacks on many fronts. To weaken the American free-enterprise economy which outproduced both its enemies and allies during World War II is a high priority target of the Communist leaders. Their press and other propoganda media are therefore constantly selling the principles of centralized or federal control of farms, railroads, electric power, schools, steel, maritime shipping, and many other aspects of the economy—but always in the name of public welfare.

I believe J. Edgar Hoover and the investigating committees of Congress know whereof they speak when they warn us of a serious internal threat to the American way of life. I hear that some people and more particulary the Communists and the Social Democrats don't want us to examine this internal threat, but I believe we should. I think we should study communism and study socialism so we can recognize the influence of each. We can leave the spies to the FBI, but learning how our enemies are trying to subvert us is everybody's job. I also recognize that it is not popular in some circles to be called an anti-Communist, but I consider communism a godless political and economic disease. I do not believe an American citizen can be patriotic and loyal to his own country, and its God-inspired Constitution of freedom without being anti-Communist.

My own political and economic creed is a simple one. I commend it to you:

I am for freedom and against slavery.

I am for social progress and against socialism.

I am for a dynamic economy and against waste.

I am for the private competitive market and against unnecessary Government intervention.

I am for private ownership and against governmental ownership and control of the means of production and distribution.

I am for national security and against appeasement and capitulation to an obvious enemy.

This contest in which we are engaged is as old as man and as young as hope. The issue is over the God-given eternal principle of freedom—free agency, the right of choice. In this struggle it is not enough to be right—we must put strength and action back of that which is right.

In the conflict with socialistic communism we must have patience, courage, and wisdom. We must also have friends. Russia has hostages—we have friends—millions of them in temporary slavery back of the Iron Curtain, and millions more to be mobilized throughout the free world. In Russia people are unable to challenge the despotic godless dogmas forced on the people. We must take greater risks for freedom. We must dramatize American might and Soviet myth.

With God's help the light of high resolve in the eyes of the American people must never be dimmed. Our freedom must and will be preserved.

May God give us the wisdom to recognize the threat to our freedom and the strength to meet this danger courageously.

The United States Should Be a Republic

Clarence E. Manion

Clarence E. Manion (1896-   ) was a Professor of History and Government at Notre Dame and Dean of the College of Law. He is the author of *American History* (1926), *What Price Prohibition* (1927), and *The Conservative American* (1964).

The truly significant word symbols of Political Science, like rare pieces of priceless porecelain, should be used only when their use is appropriate. Even on these proper and rare occasions such terms should be handled with great care and consideration. The most meaningful word can be flattened out of all depth of precision by the ceaseless pounding of indiscriminate repetition.

Once upon a time the word "democracy" may have meant the same thing to all who spoke and heard it. Today, however, it is such a limp and vapid expression that the Russian Foreign Minister and the chairman of the Republican National Committee can both praise it highly on the self-same afternoon.

Any word that can be used at one and the same time to suggest the despotic political ideals of Soviet Russia and the treasured principles of Americanism has certainly lost every vestige of usefulness.

The word "democracy" has now become very much like the key to a highly exclusive private club which some waggish member caused to be secretly duplicated and widely distributed. Before the bona-fide "brothers" knew what was up, the plush and cosy clubhouse was swarming with all the questionable characters in the neighborhood. A disillusioned board of managers was finally forced to change the lock.

From Clarence E. Manion, *The Key to Peace* (Chicago: The Heritage Foundation, Inc., 1951), pp. 48-62. Reprinted by permission.

MEANINGLESS TERM

Whatever significance may have been attached to it in the ancient past, the term "democracy" is not now a dependable key to the secret of a free society. Its continued use simply serves to make existing "confusion worse confounded" by giving notoriously tyrannical despotisms a distorted false face which seems to resemble American freedom. The friends and agents of these undeserving pretenders have given every encouragement to the currency of this word which dilutes the priceless and unique quality of Americanism by mixing and confusing it with the crude and forceful "leveling" devices of European politics.

The honest and serious students of American history will recall that our Founding Fathers managed to write both the Declaration of Independence and the Constitution of the United States without using the term "democracy" even once. No part of any one of the existing forty-eight State constitutions contains any reference to the word. Such men as John Adams, Madison, Hamilton, Jefferson and others who were most influential in the institution and formation of our government refer to "democracy" only to distinguish it sharply from the republican form of our American Constitutional System.

EXCLUSIVE FORM

The Founding Fathers were not forgetting that the single official purpose of all American government is to secure and protect the unalienable God-given attributes of the individual human being, majorities to the contrary notwithstanding. Like Madison, Thomas Jefferson was convinced that this object and purpose of American government could best be accomplished through the republican form and he never ceased to praise the republicanism of the new Federal Constitution. On October 31, 1823, less than two years before his death, he wrote to a friend in Greece who had just sent him a new edition of Aristotle:

The equal rights of men and the happiness of every individual are now acknowledged to be the only legitimate objects of government. Modern times have the single advantage too, of having discovered the only device by which these rights can be secured, to wit: government by the people acting not in person but by representatives chosen by themselves.

To underscore the exclusively republican character of all American government the Federal Constitution itself says:

The United States shall guarantee to every State in the Union, a Republican Form of Government, and shall protect each of them against invasion.[1]

Shakespeare has Juliet say truthfully that "a rose by any other name would smell as sweet." Many will therefore ask why the use of such a popular term as "democracy" may not be employed to serve the desirable convenience of putting all ramifications of our Free American society into a single word?

The answer is that the political system of our country is definitely in a class by itself.

[1] Art. IV, Sec. 4.

No descriptive word which suggests or includes any existing political system in addition to our own will adequately describe the political system of the United States. On the contrary, the great majority of such words are fatally misleading, and in this respect the word "democracy" is one of the worst offenders.

DETERMINING DISTINCTION

In both "form" and "substance" our American system is basically different from any politically organized society now or heretofore existing in the world. Thomas Jefferson attests this fact in the foregoing letter when he says that

Modern times have the single advantage too, of having discovered the only device by which these rights can be secured.

The "rights," namely the unalienable rights of each person in the land, constitute the "substance" of American government. The "device" by which these rights can be secured is the American "form" of government. The conjunction of this "form" and this "substance" was unique and new in Jefferson's time and it is completely unique today.

A Republican form of government strictly and constitutionally dedicated to the protection of the God-given unalienable rights of men appeared in the world for the first time with the organization of the United States of America. This "form" was then and there composed and designed to hold and contain its precious substance.

The indissoluble union of this form and this substance equals Americanism and it equals nothing else.

No useful and informative purpose is served by tossing this singular and exclusive American development into all of any of such meaningless generalizations as "freedom-loving-democratic- Anti-Fascist Peoples of the World." This is not to say that we are selfishly and officially allergic to the ideal of the world wide human brotherhood.

On the contrary Americanism offers the only valid formula for the ultimate achievement of that ideal.

The basis of this formula is the indestructible God-given human personality which is the one thing that every American definitely and officially holds in common with each human being on Earth. It is unfortunate that this is also the one thing that every political system in the Un-American world officially and categorically denies.

BY THEIR FRUITS

By their perennial harvest of bitter fruits these foreign governmental systems are shown to be fatally wrong. Since the time that America was discovered the *power* of these systems has shifted from autocratic kings to political or parliamentary ministers. At the moment all the governing politicians, premiers, ministers and magistrates of Europe pretend to be devoted to "popular" government and some of them hold office as the result of popular elections. Nevertheless, from the autocratic kings to the conscienceless commissars, European political science has always held consistently to the proposition that government, once installed,

is unlimited in its power over its subjects.

The continuing and controlling principle of European politics has thus been BIG AND ALL POWERFUL GOVERNMENT which does not recognize and consequently need not respect any such thing as an *unalienable right in the individual citizen.*

More than one hundred years before the French Revolution, the then ruling royal autocrate of France, Louis XIV declared "*I* am the state." His BIG AND ALL POWERFUL GOVERNMENT was thus entirely personal and the individual Frenchman could expect only such "liberty" as King Louis chose to extend to him. Two hundred years later, the European Karl Marx, prophet of the modern Socialist-Communist political and economic dispensation, disposed of the individual citizen in these words:

The democratic concept of man is false, because it is Christian. The democratic concept holds that each man is a sovereign being. This is the illusion, dream *and* postulate *of Christianity.*

One hundred years after Karl Marx thus wrote off the importance of the individual human personality in that derisive condemnation of Christianity, Adolf Hitler made his decisive bid for the control of Europe on what he represented to be a drive *against Communism.* Nevertheless this is what Hitler said about the unalienable rights of the individual man:

To the Christian doctrine of infinite significance of the individual human soul, I oppose with icy clarity the saving doctrine of the nothingness and insignificance of the human being.

LOUIS, MARX AND HITLER

Students of political science would probably be hard pressed to find a recognized modern "authority" who puts Louis XIV, Karl Marx and Adolf Hitler into the same political bed. Nevertheless, on the *vital* principle of BIG AND ALL POWERFUL GOVERNMENT with no inherent responsibility for or duty toward the individual human being, these important European characters were in perfect accord.

The disappearance of Hitler has brought no observable change in European political ideals. Since the end of the war, England has moved *officially* into the orbit of the all-powerful States, while on the European Continent, both East and West of the "Iron Curtain," the "nothingness and insignificance of the human being" is everything that Adolph Hitler could have wished for.

If BIG AND ALL POWERFUL GOVERNMENT was the secret of general popular welfare, Europe would have always been the land of milk and honey, while the history of the United States would be a story of general misery, poverty and destitution. The facts are the other way round. Europe's record proves that BIG AND ALL POWERFUL GOVERNMENT, whether its sanction be royal, "democratic" or revolutionary, produces general warfare instead of general welfare and promotes penury and pestilence rather than progress and prosperity.

COMPROMISE SUICIDAL

The all-time record discloses that wheresoever government gets bigger and bigger and more and more powerful it moves at the same time and at the same speed toward the hellish goal of Adolf Hitler, namely, the "nothingness and insignificance" of the individual human being. Modern English history shows that "democracy" is no inherent and absolute defense against the pernicious increase of governmental strength.

It is not *how* the government gets its power but the amount of power it gets that determines the fate of each and every individual John Doe who lives under its jurisdiction. The God-given nature of the said John Doe lays upon all human government a drastic and vital set of limitations. In the United States these limitations are written into Constitutions which all of our governments must observe. In Europe no such limitations are acknowledged. This is the precise issue between the foreign systems of power politics and the American system of personalized justice. The issue is both sharp and pointed. Efforts to blunt or compromise it by the use of "democracy" to describe both systems are worse than useless. Such attempts discredit Americanism by making its distinctive architecture look like the standard model for European Power Houses.

IRREPARABLE LOSS

We do not serve the cause of international peace and world wide understanding by deliberately obscuring the essential fundamental cleavage between Americanism and Europeanism. On the contrary, when we shade or soften the sharp line which separates our system from theirs, we risk a great loss at home and with no possibility of compensating gain to any of our foreign neighbors. Real and permanent world order must be built upon a system which insures the universal dispensation of personal man to man justice. This means that individual rights, the substance of our system, must be acknowledged and protected by the government of every state in the world. Outside of the United States there is no source from which un-American peoples can learn about such a system. If they are led to believe that there is no essential difference between their governments and ours their political aspirations will continue to center upon

The good old rule, the simple plan, that they should take who have the power and they should keep who can.

There is every reason to believe that Republican forms of government, every branch of which is constitutionally committed to the protection of unalienable individual rights, could and would permanently solve the political aches and pains of the whole world. But there, as here and everywhere, mere form without substance must collapse of its own weight. The obvious and peculiar blessings of American life which so many thoughtlessly attribute to our American "form" of government, would automatically disappear if the "purpose" and "object" of that form were suddenly changed or withdrawn. Regardless of the beauty of its shape and design an empty glass offers no consolation to a desperately thirsty man. In like manner the American form of government when emptied of its substantial element of personal rights and personal justice is tripped of every logical excuse for its continued existence.

INTENTIONAL INEFFICIENCY

Considered merely as a governmental mechanism, separate and apart from its special purpose, singular object and essential substance, the American form of government is the most cumbersome and inefficient system ever put into operation. Its separate and distinct authorities are divided into six mutually exclusive water-tight compartments, namely the legislature, executive and judiciary of both the State and Federal Governments. Regardless of the urgency of public business no one of these authorities may encroach upon the other. From the sum total of these divided powers are subtracted important specifications of two separate bills of personal rights, one prefixed to the Constitution of the State, the other appended to the Constitution of the Federal Government.

The salient feature of this famed form of government is an involved system of so-called "checks and balances." Congress checks the President and vice versa while the Federal Courts check both. On the State side, the legislature checks the governor who in turn checks the legislature while both are checked by the State Courts. In addition to these checks, the whole power of the Federal Government is restrained by the reserved powers of the States. These powers in turn are perpetually balanced against those granted to the Federal Government in the Federal Constitution.

Seen in perspective, this constitutional system, which is our American form of government, is a veritable latticework of barbed wire entanglements thrown around every governmental official in the land. It is a pattern of slow motion and inefficiency which no "expediter" would tolerate for five minutes in any private business organization. Is it any wonder therefore that the eager-beavers of modern jurisprudence chafe under these impediments to prompt and efficient public service? What possible answer can be made to the ever swelling chorus which demands that our *antiquated* form of government be *streamlined* toward centralized authority and sharpened responsibility? There is no answer—except one. That answer is drawn from the *substance* which this complicated *form* was built to hold safe and secure.

PURPOSE CLEAR

The men who fashioned this form of government were thinking of John Doe's life, liberty and pursuit of happiness. Their principal concern was not with the efficiency of government, but with the safety of the God-created human personality. These Founding Fathers knew that the most *efficient* government on earth is that of an absolute and unrestricted despotism. They had learned their political science the hard way. In their own experience they had discovered that the God-given liberty of the individual citizen inevitably withers and disappears under the tender ministrations of an unrestricted government. Between the disorders of anarchy and the inevitable despotic development of the best-intentioned un-limited government they chose the golden mean. The resulting American form is a series of *servant-governments* all charged with the duty of protecting personal rights and enforcing personal duties.

The Founding Fathers loaded these new servant-governments with limitations and restrictions calculated to keep all of their noses to the grindstone of their fundamental purpose and prevent them from using their necessary tools to destroy what the servants were hired to preserve. The Framers made sure that the rights of one man could be maintained against other men but they also made sure that those same rights could be asserted at all times *against the power of government* itself. They knew that it is in the very nature of every government to resent this last assertion as an affront to its sovereign dignity. Hence, they tied the new servant-governments down into their proper place by a system of strong checks and balances. In addition to extended bills of personal rights they limited one government by another government and each of their branches by another branch. They thus protected the citizen by rivalries and divisions within the governmental structure itself.

THE TEST OF THE PUDDING

Within its designated sphere of constitutionally allotted powers and subject always to its guiding purpose as stated in the Declaration of Independence, American government was designed to function through representatives chosen either directly or indirectly by the people, and responsible to the people on regularly recurring election days. This *representative system* is the essence of the *Republican Form* of government to which all of the Founding Fathers were so enthusiastically devoted. In State and Federal constitutions they deliberately withheld from the people the right to directly and "democratically" decide governmental questions for themselves. The Founders would have been appalled at the idea of *rubber stamp* legislators, *office boy* executives or *pressure group* government on the Federal or State level. Thomas Jefferson, whose political ideas were considerably more "democratic" than any of his contemporaries, wrote in 1816

that (the people) being unqualified for the management of affairs requiring intelligence above the common level, yet competent judges of human character, (they) chose for their management representatives, some by themselves immediately, others by electors chosen by themselves. Action by citizens in person, in affairs within their reach and competence, and in all others by representatives chosen immediately and removable by themselves (the people) constitutes the essence of a Republic.

EFFICIENCY vs. FREEDOM

Those who do not share the Founding Fathers' devotion to the unalienable sacredness of the human personality, will regard this form of government as a crazy quilt of cross purposes. Such persons will argue quite plausibly for a new type of government immediately responsible to "the people" in which the administrative and legislative functions are blended for efficiency while the courts are relegated to the simple duty of resolving quarrels between private individuals. These advocates of the "democratic process" maintain that in such a streamlined system society would have the only protection to which it is logically entitled, namely, frequent and free elections. This is the system that prevailed in England at the time of the American Revolution, and it is exactly the kind of government that Socialist England has today. The American form and the English form have thus worked side by side in the same world for more than 150 years. From the separate inventories of their respective accomplishments, you may take your ultimate choice. Meanwhile, Americans are asked to devise new and more generous "Marshall Plans" for the further American relief of England and other so-called "democratic" nations throughout the world.

The Ideology of the Radical Right
Gilbert Abcarian
Sherman M. Stanage

Gilbert Abcarian (1927-   ) has taught political science at Bowling Green University. Among his books are *Social Psychology and Political Behavior* (1971), *American Political Radicalism* (1970), and *Contemporary Political Systems* (1969).

Sherman M. Stanage (1927-   ) is Chairman of the Department of Philosophy at Northern Illinois University.

The task of conducting empirical, and particularly quantitative, inquiry into the characteristics and implications of contemporary rightwing extremism has hardly begun. Of such work that is now available, little reflects systematic attention to the conceptual grounds on the basis of which data accumulated will serve to test interpretive hypotheses.

This paper is a conceptual elaboration of the hypothesis that the ideology and operational style of the contemporary radical rightist "movement"[1] reflect antecedent conditions of political alienation.

From Gilbert Abcarian and Sherman M. Stanage, "Alienation and the Radical Right," *The Journal of Politics*, Vol. 27 (November 1965, pp. 776-796. Reprinted by permission. Presented by Gilbert Abcarian to the Midwest Conference of Political Scientists, May 2, 1964, at Madison, Wisconsin. The authors gratefully acknowledge the assistance of Arthur G. Neal in the preparation of this study.

[1] By "contemporary," reference is made to rightwing extremism since the rise to prominence in the 1960's of the John Birch Society. By "radical right" and "rightwing extremism," reference is made to a political grouping or ideological coalition occupying the political terrain between (but not including) Midwestern Republicanism and American Fascism, populated by organizations such as: The American Coalition of Patriotic Societies; The American Security Council; Americans for Constitutional Action; America's Future, Inc.; The Cardinal Mindszenty Foundation; the Christian Anti-Communism Crusade; The Christian Crusade; The Circuit Riders; The Christian Nationalist Crusade; The Church League of America; The Conservative Society of America; The Conservative Union; The Council of Christian Churches; Defenders of the American Constitution; Facts Forum, Inc.; For America; Freedom in Action; Human Events, Inc.; The John Birch Society; Liberty Lobby; Life Lines, Inc.; The Manion Forum; The Minutemen; The National Education Program; National Indignation Convention; Veritas Foundation; We, The People!; Young Americans for Freedom, to name but a representative and prominent few.

Observations relating to rightwing manifestations of ideology, style and alienation are considered separately, followed by consideration of their interrelations as these in turn help to clarify the major hypothesis.

Development of the hypothesis will necessitate the identification and analysis of several categories. These categories will be central to the conceptual grounds upon which refined quantitative analysis of rightwing extremism may be investigated in separate studies.

The sample of rightist literature selected for thematic identification and analysis was drawn from a large universe of rightist sentiments and treated as typical of trends within that movement.[2] It is hoped that the analysis of that sample below may help to throw light on aspects of the universe of rightwing extremism. That is, through clarification of the conceptual categories presented, it will become possible to develop unidimensional scales for the conduct of investigations into rightist as well as nonrightist populations.

The method employed in arriving at the fundamental characteristics of rightwing

---

[2] The sample analyzed included regular and miscellaneous publications of the organizations listed in footnote #1. In addition to these and others cited in footnotes, the following sources were utilized:

Books and Pamphlets: Anthony Bouscaren, *Guide to Anti-Communist Action*, New York: Regnery, 1959; Kenneth Colegrove, *Democracy Versus Communism*, New York: Van Nostrand, 1957; *The Communist Conspiracy*, pamphlet, no date, Koster-Dana Corp.; M. Stanton Evans, *Americans for Democratic Action: The Enemy Within*, no date; John T. Flynn, *While You Slept*, New York: American Opinion, 1961; Rosalie M. Gorden, *Nine Men Against American*, New York: Devin-Adair, 1958; J. Evatts Haley, *A Texan Looks at Lyndon*, Canyon, Texas: Palo Duro Press, 1964; Frank C. Hanighen, *The Web of Warren*, no date; *How "Progressive" Is your School?*, America's Future, Inc., no date; Robert Hunter, *Brainwashing in Red China*, New York: Vanguard, 1963; *Ideology and Coexistence*, Moral Rearmament, Inc., no date; V. B. Kaub, *Communist-Socialist Propaganda in American Schools*, Madison: American Council of Christian Laymen, 1960; Dean C. Manion, *The New War Against Despotism*, no date; C. P. Oakes (ed.), *Education and Freedom in a World of Conflict*, Chicago: Regnery, 1963; J. Howard Pew, *The Church and Politics*, no date; E. Merrill Root, *Collectivism on the Campus*, New York: Devin-Adair, 1956; *Brainwashing in the High Schools*, New York: Devin-Adair, 1958; Phyllis Schafly, *A Choice Not an Echo*, Alton, Ill.: Pere Marquette Press, 1964; Fred Schwarz, *You Can Trust the Communists*, Englewood Cliffs: Prentice-Hall, 1960; W. C. Skousen, *The Naked Communist*, Salt Lake City: Ensign Publications, 1961; *Speak Up or Else*, Employee Relations, Inc., no date; John Stormer, *None Dare Call it Treason*, Liberty Bell Press, 1964; *The Truth About the American Civil Liberties Union*, Christian Anti-Communism Crusade, no date.

Newspapers, Speeches, Broadsides, Etc.: "What can Students Do?," "Breadbasket Diplomacy," "Modern 'McCarthyism'," Christian Anti-Communism Crusade, no dates; "Dawn" (Portland, Indiana, 1963 issues); "A Declaration of Conservative Principles," *The Conservative Society of America*, (April 15, 1961); Paul Harvey, "Why not Return to the 'Old Country'?," *Human Events*, (Sept. 7, 1963), p. 10; Rev. E. Irving Howard, "What Did Jesus Believe About Wealth?," *Christian Economics*, (June 4, 1955); Edward Hunter, "Edward Hunter on Fulbright Memorandum," *Congressional Record*, (Feb. 6, 1962), pp. A906-7; "Appreciation and Encouragement," no date; "On the Difference Between a Democracy and a Republic," (January, 1961), *The John Birch Society*; A. G. Malinowski, "Our Invisible Government and How it Operates," published by the author, no date; "An Open Letter to the Patrons of the Bolshoi Ballet," *The Organization to Fight Communism, Inc.*, Cleveland, Nov. 27, 1963); "Seven Ways to Overcome Communism," *Christopher News Notes* #119, no date; Gordon H. Scherer, "Key Targets of the Communists," *American Legion Magazine*, (August, 1962); Skepticus, "Why the John Birch Society Is Under Fire," *Human Events*, (July 21, 1961); Statement of Principles and Purposes of *For America*, no date; Strom Thurmond, "Senate Investigation of Military Muzzling," *Congressional Record*, (March 7, 1962), pp. 3263-65; "Keyneism–Marxism at Harvard," *Veritas Foundation*, no date.

ideology and style was that of searching out the recurrent themes encountered in the publications of a large number of organizations and their spokesmen. In addition a variety of interpretive sources was examined to check against personal predilections and to determine the extent to which alienation themes were present.[3]

Analysis of the sample yielded nine recurrent themes. These provided us with presumptive grounds for the clarification of our major hypothesis. What finally emerges in the paper is a conceptual model whose validity is to be ascertained by further empirical studies.

This paper hence represents a preliminary step in the direction of certain empirical investigations of rightwing extremism. As a first step, it is presented as a viable alternative to the few conceptual models now available, viz., status, economic, political, etc., and is meant to serve as a prelude to both quantitative content analysis and as a guide in constructing items to be used in empirical investigations.

While the logical coherency and validity of radical rightist ideology may be challenged, its pervasiveness and potential impact on American society today may not. Each component of that ideology reflects a range of latent emotions and negative responses to selected aspects of contemporary American life. But each component is also encountered in the form of an imperative, or prescription. In short, beyond manifest content, the political style of the radical right will be taken as suggestive of conditions generating rightwing extremism, as well as characteristic of its modes of public expression.

[3] The following references are particularly germane to this study: Lloyd J. Averill, "Political Fundamentalism in Profile," *The Christian Century*, (Aug. 12, 1964); Alan Barth, "Report on the Rampageous Right," *New York Times Magazine*, (Nov. 26, 1961); Daniel Bell (ed.), *The Radical Right*, Garden City: Doubleday, 1963; Harry and Bonaro Overstreet, *The Strange Tactics of Extremism*, New York: Norton, 1964; Sen. Clifford Case, remarks on the radical right to the Anti-Defamation League, New York City, (Jan. 13, 1962), reprinted in the *Congressional Record*, (Jan. 23, 1962), Louis Cassels, "The Rightist Crisis in our Churches," *Saturday Evening Post*, (April 23, 1962); Fred Cook, "The Ultras," *Nation*, (June 30, 1962); Rev. John F. Cronin, "Communism: Threat to Freedom," National Catholic Welfare Conference, 1962; David Danzig, "Conservatism After Goldwater," *Commentary*, (March, 1965); "The Radical Right and the Rise of the Fundamentalist Minority," *Commentary*, (April, 1962); "Rightists, Racists, and Separatists," *Commentary*, (August, 1964); Col. J. E. Dwan, "Why They are Frustrated," *Army*, (April, 1962), reprinted in the *Congressional Record*, (April 11, 1962); Victor C. Ferkiss, "Political and Intellectual Origins of American Radicalsim, Right and Left," *Annals of The American Academy of Political And Social Science*, (November, 1962); Sen. J. W. Fulbright, memorandum on rightwing military activities to Sec. of Defense MacNamara, *New York Times*, (July 21, 1961); Andrew Hacker, "Inquiry into the New Conservatism," *New York Times Magazine*, (Feb. 16, 1964); Richard Hofstadter, "The Paranoid Style in American Politics," *Harper's Magazine*, (November, 1964); D. Janson and B. Eisman, *The Far Right*, New York: McGraw-Hill, 1963; "American Political Extremism in the 1960's," series of studies, *Journal of Social Issues*, (April 1963); Fletcher Knebel, "Who's on the Far Right?," *Look*, (March 13, 1962); Stanley Mosk and Howard H. Jewel, "The Birch Phenomenon Analyzed," *New York Times Magazine*, (Aug. 20, 1961); Arthur Schlesinger, Jr., "No Back-of-the-Book Solutions in Freedom," speech reprinted in the *Congressional Record*, (Jan. 24, 1962); "The 'Threat' of the Radical Right," *New York Times Magazine*, (June 17, 1962); Eugene V. Schneider, "The Radical Right," *Nation*, (Sept. 30, 1961); Robert G. Sherrill, "New Curricula for Bigotry," *Nation*, (Mar. 29, 1965); Cushing Strout, "Fantasy on the Right," *New Republic*, (May 1, 1961); Alan Westin, "The Deadly Parallels, Radical Right and Radical Left," *Harper's Magazine*, (April, 1962); William S. White, "New Irresponsibles: Ultra-Conservatives," *Harper's Magazine*, (November, 1961); Sen. Stephen M. Young, "Danger on the Right," *Saturday Evening Post*, (Jan. 13, 1962), reprinted in the *Congressional Record*, (Jan. 29, 1962).

THE IDEOLOGY OF THE RADICAL RIGHT

The ideology of the radical right consists of the first six of the nine features discussed below. Each element of that ideology will be illustrated briefly.

Individualism.   An imperative and unavoidable "choice" is posited by the Right between a "free" and a "collectivist" political destiny for Americans. Collectivism, in the words of Robert Welch, is a European "cancer" that has spawned governmental centralization that has resulted in massive bureaucracy, erosion of individual freedom and initiative, subversion of the federal system, and violation of the economic "laws of man and nature."[4] Only a determined campaign of anticollectivism holds any promise of rediscovering traditional American individualism.

Republicanism.   "This is a Republic, not a democracy—Let's keep it that way!," says a mail sticker popular in Birch Society circles. This nation is not, cannot be, a democracy, for the central credo of democracy is equality, which is contrary to the laws of nature and which science demonstrates to be a false premise in the light of human experience. The philosophical presuppositions and functional processes of contemporary American democracy have proven bankrupt.[5] In a "true republic," the will of the masses will be represented, but only through the consciences of representatives whose task it is to evaluate and interpret the intent of such will. Only republicanism, or government for the people by a qualified elite, can save us from the ravages of immoral mob-rule.

Fundamentalism.   Americans are implored to return to divine and eternal truths, both biblical and secular. On the religious side, the call is for a return to literal interpretation of the bible; on the political side, the call is for a return to "Americanism" and "Constitutionalism." Everywhere, we are tempted and seduced by ungodly forces.[6] Our young must be protected against the siren calls of moral relativism and youthful idealism.[7]

---

[4] "For thirty years we have aided the cause of atheistic, socialistic communism by permitting communists in high places in Government; by giving away much of our material resources; by recklessly spending ourselves to near bankruptcy; by weakening our free enterprise system through adoption of socialistic policies; by wasteful bungling of our foreign affairs; by ever increasing confiscatory taxation and by permitting the insidious infiltration of communist agents and sympathizers into almost every segment of American life." (From a speech by Ezra Taft Benson: "The Internal Threat to the American Way of Life," reprinted in the *Congressional Record*, Feb. 19, 1962, p. A1204.)

[5] "We are," says ex-General Edwin Walker, "at war. We are infiltrated. We are losing that war every day. Are your hands tied, yours and mine? We need a substitute for defeat. If it is not within the power of this Congress to provide it—then the people of these United States are not truly represented." (From testimony before the subcommittee of the Senate Armed Services Committee, quoted in the *New York Times*, Nov. 3, 1961, p. 22.)

[6] "Long ago the devil was cast out of heaven for seeking to supplant God. Now he dons the seductive attire of the welfare state and makes another attempt to seduce man from his status as potential son of God and degrade him to servile dependence and the uniformly low level of beggary and slavery. If he can teach men that they are dependent upon the state and must pray to it, he will have succeeded in supplanting God in the minds of men." (Howard E. Kershner, ed., *Christian Economics*, Sept. 4, 1962, p. 2.)

[7] "The stressing of both sides of a controversy only confuses the young and encourages them to make snap judgments based on insufficient evidence. Until they are old enough to understand both sides of a question, they should be taught only the American side." (J. Evatts Haley, quoted in Cook, *op. cit.*, p. 601.)

The nation is drifting aimlessly. National purpose has been lost. Worse than that, its very existence is threatened, for "we are at war, and we are losing that war simply because we don't or won't realize that we are in it."[8] Opinion leaders have failed, or in some cases deliberately betrayed, us. Remedial action appears impossible owing to an inability to locate and exert effective influence upon those persons commanding the "real" centers of power—unless, that is, God-fearing, flag-respecting Americans return to the fundamentals. A small body of true believers can lead a return to the pristine fundamentals that once set this nation on a true course.

Purification. Conspiracy and betrayal—in the guise of social change—are felt to have reached ominous proportions. Monumental errors of judgment over the past several decades point to an alarming truth: "How can you explain the mistakes of our leaders for the last 30 years," the head of the Christian Crusade inquires, "if there aren't Communists giving them advice?"[9] Destruction of the conspiracy cannot be separated from halting social and political change, for the primary threat to the nation is "treason right in our government."[10]

The nation must be purified and redeemed. It is urgently necessary to expose the hydra-headed conspiracy that infests government, churches, educational institutions, and the mass media of communication. Purification is an urgent, patriotic duty.

Restoration. The U.S. is presumed to have attained a Golden or Heroic Age, usually, though not invariably, located somewhere in the century preceding "that man" F.D.R. The Golden Age constitutes a universally valid political model to which Americans must return, and one that the rest of the world must respect and emulate. But Americans have become careless with their sacred legacy. "In this land occurred the only true revolution in man's history. . . . It must be fought for, protected, and handed on . . . or one day we will spend our sunset years telling our children and our children's children what it was once like in the United States when men were free."[11]

Domestically, the golden age is sometimes equated with the *status quo*, though more frequently located in the past. Internationally, the golden age is typically regarded as lost by the early twentieth century, owing to seduction into degrading

---

[8] Ronald Reagan, "Encroaching Government Controls, *Human Events*, (July 21, 1961), p. 457.

[9] Rev. Billy James Hargis, quoted in Knebel, *loc. cit.*, p. 27.

[10] Welch, *op. cit.*, p. 32. General Walker stated before the Armed Services Committee: "It is fair to say that in my opinion the fifth column conspiracy and influence in the United States minimize or nullify the effectiveness of my ideals and principles, military mission and objectives, and the necessary American public spirit to support sons and soldiers. I have no further desire for military service at this time with this conspiracy and its influences on the home front." (*New York Times loc. cit.*, p. 22.)

In a much-discussed article, Revilo P. Oliver, Professor of Classics at the University of Illinois and a Board member of the Birch Society, states that ". . . the (communist) conspiracy ordered the assassination as part of a systematic preparation for a domestic take-over . . . . (T)here is not a single indication that the Conspiracy did not plan and carry out the assassination of Kennedy. On the other hand, there is evidence which very strongly suggests that it did." ("Marxmanship in Dallas," part I, *American Opinion*, organ of the Birch Society, February, 1964.)

[11] Reagan, *op. cit.*, p. 460.

and humiliating foreign entanglements. Despite the obstacles, the golden age can and must be restored by achieving victory over the domestic forces that block the return to authenticity by preaching and practicing compromise, coexistence and cooperation with national enemies.

Unilateralism. Because it has presumably failed to protect "vital" and "legitimate" interests and moral values, the complex of assumptions, policies and programs governing American foreign policy during the past several decades must be rejected. The prevailing policy consensus is a failure and has actually accelerated the communist plan for world enslavement. Public officials are guilty of "surrender" and "appeasement" and must be purged. Rep. Bruce Alger of Texas demands, characteristically, to know "If treason be defined as giving aid and comfort to the enemy, why isn't aid to Yugoslavia treason?"[12]

The U.S. must invade Cuba, terminate diplomatic relations with communist states, withdraw from the U.N. and N.A.T.O., halt cultural exchange programs, encourage rebellion behind the iron curtain, etc. In short, the U.S. should act, rather than humbly react, and should do so in the spirit of justified unilateralism, unencumbered by false principles of diplomacy, expedience or multilateralism.

THE POLITICAL STYLE OF THE RADICAL RIGHT

The political style of the radical right is reflected in the three remaining features to be discussed.

Telescoping. Rightwing extremism expresses itself publicly in the form of telescoping—the process of compressing or coalescing levels and categories of political events and analyses which are ordinarily treated as distinct or unique. A characteristic example of telescoping is provided by Senator Thurmond's assertion that "communism is fundamentally socialism. When socialism, in turn, is understood, one cannot help but to realize that many of the domestic programs advocated in the U.S., and many of those adopted, fall clearly within the category of socialism."[13]

In the same manner, former President Eisenhower has been portrayed as an instrument of the communist movement, while recent Supreme Court decisions on religion in the public schools, through compression of facts and reasoning, are regarded as facilitating various plots.[14] Oversimplification is hence the central outcome of telescoping.[15]

---

[12] Quoted in Knebel, *loc. cit.*, p. 28.

[13] Quoted in *Human Events*, (Sept. 29, 1961), p. 640. The same statement appears in the speech by Benson, previously cited.

[14] "The Supreme Court has set the stage for a return to paganism: the ideal condition under which the seeds of Communism flourish. Whether this was intended or not is inconsequential; there is only a fine line between American stupidity and planned Communism." (From a letter to the editor, *Saturday Review*, Aug. 18, 1962, p. 45.)

[15] "Some political writers claim that anti-Communists try to simplify what they (the writers) call complex problems. With this word, "complex," they try to muddy the water with fuzzy thinking so as to make common-sense conclusions virtually impossible. I violently oppose those who try to discourage the American people from studying, understanding and undertaking the task of doing something about the Communist threat, claiming that it is too complex for them. The strength of our Nation lies in the composite judgment of an informed citizenry—common-

Reductionism. In its belief that every major irritation in society has a simple cause, a simple explanation and a simple solution, the radical right reduces such irritations to communism. The list of problems and events treated reductionistically is enormous, ranging from urban renewal (a Marxist scheme to subvert state and local governments), to the cost of funerals (anti-capitalist subversion of the American way of life and death). International problems are similarly viewed in the reductionistic framework in terms of assessing those courses of action that will minimize or maximize the communist threat.

Protest Through Direct Action. Rightwing ideology is clarified and popularized through action programs, usually in the form of public protest. Welch speaks of the need to organize "all kinds of fronts." He insists that "for us to be too civilized is unquestionably to be defeated" and that the Birth Society "means business every step of the way." Direct action takes the form of censorship drives and demands, denunciation of public officials by private citizens, and a broad range of "seminars," "alerts," "schools" and "forums."

ALIENATION AND THE RADICAL RIGHT

In order to develop certain relationships between radical rightist ideology and style, and the condition of alienation[16]—the major burden of this study—it will be helpful to refer in passing to rightist literature for manifestations of specific forms of political alienation. As a prelude to such examination, let us be clear what alienation in general implies as the concept is employed by an increasing number of social and political scientists.

Alienation is experienced in varying forms and degrees of intensity when certain forces block the individual's quest for so-called authentic, or true, existence, when

---

sense mixed with personal study and education. Every man has the capacity to contribute to the fight for survival against the international Communist criminal conspiracy. If this is superpatriotism, I am proud to be called a superpatriot." (From a speech, "Positive Program for Victory over Communism," by then congressman John H. Rouselot, Dec. 4, 1961, cited in the *Congressional Record*, April 18, 1962, p. 6410.)

[16] The following studies of alienation are particularly germane to this paper: Erich Fromm, *Escape From Freedom*, New York: Rinehart and Co., 1946; *The Sane Society*, New York: Rinehart and Co., 1955; by the same author; Robert K. Merton, *Mass Persuasion*, New York: Harper and Bros., 1946; Nathan Glazer, "The Alienation of Modern Man," *Commentary*, 3, (April, 1947); David Riesman, *et al.*, *The Lonely Crowd*, New Haven: Yale University press, 1950; C. Wright Mills, *White Collar*, New York: Oxford University Press, 1953; Robert Nisbet, *The Quest for Community*, New York: Oxford University Press, 1953; Herbert Marcuse, *Reason and Revolution*, New York: The Humanities Press, 1954; Gwynn Nettler, "A Measure of Alienation," *American Sociological Review*, 22 (December, 1957); Herbert Marcuse, *Soviet Marxism: A Critical Analysis*, New York: Columbia University Press, 1958; John P. Clark, "Measuring Alienation Within a Social System," *American Sociological Review*, 24 (December 1959); Maurice R. Stein, et al., (editors), *Identity and Anxiety*, Glencoe: The Free Press, 1960; Dwight G. Dean, ' Alienation: Its Meaning and Measurement," *American Sociological Review*, 26, (October, 1961); Franz Neumann, *The Democratic and the Authoritarian State*, Glencoe: The Free Press, 1957; Jan Hajda, "Alienation and Integration of Student Intellectuals," *American Sociological Review*, 26, (October, 1961); Joseph R. Gusfield, "Mass Society and Extremist Politics," *American Sociological Review*, 27, (February, 1962); Edward A. Tiryakian, *Sociologism and Existentialism*, Englewood Cliffs: Prentice Hall, Inc., 1962.

he feels unable to shake off a sense of cleavage, or an abyss, within himself, and between himself and other men. At bottom, the alienated man is convinced that he is unable to assume what he believes to be his rightful role in society. Or we may say, alternatively, that "The alienated man is acutely aware of the discrepancy between who he is and what he believes he should be."[17]

Behind this bare hint at alienation is a large, impressive, but heterogeneous literature that traces alienation in its philosophical, political, religious, psychiatric, sociological and other aspects. One can hardly avoid encountering references these days to investigations of the "unattached," the "marginal," the "obsessed," the "normless" and the "isolated" man. Release from traditional ties and certitudes, the stresses created by large-scale industry and technology, the bureaucratization of the Western state—these and many other forces have been viewed as instrumentalizing and mechanizing the individual.

In summary, alienation analysis suggests that while the individual has achieved freedom of sorts from traditional restraints, that very freedom converts him into an instrument of purposes outside himself. His new-found freedom makes him apprehensive in the extreme. As Erich Fromm notes: "Freedom has reached a critical point where, driven by the logic of its own dynamism, it threatens to change into its opposite."

Resuming the main line of analysis, the general concept of alienation will be developed by employing four of its major variables—meaninglessness, normlessness, powerlessness and social isolation—as tools of analysis of radical rightist literature.

Meaninglessness. The experiences of the rightwing extremist leave him in great apprehension regarding the "absolutes" of truth, value and meaning. For he senses, often unconsciously, that traditional conceptions of such absolutes have atrophied or disappeared in the life of contemporary man. Robert Welch speaks of a "deep and basic anxiety" which he traces to a "loss of faith . . . in [the individual's] reasons for existence, in his purposes, and his hopes."[18] Referring to the campus scene, William F. Buckley Jr. notes a student turn to the Right as a result of an awakening "to the great nothingness of liberalism" and the realization "that there is nothing in the liberal creed save an intricate methodological structure (Academic Freedom, Dissent, Democracy, the United Nations, Mrs. Roosevelt) on which you build and build and build, as tirelessly as Sisyphus, but which ends up . . . helpless before the barbarians."[19]

As a consequence of the tension brought on by apprehension about the efficacy of traditional absolutes and the compulsion to believe that some version of them is nevertheless operative, the rightwing extremist suffers from a sense of meaninglessness. He is troubled persistently by a realization that he is losing, or has already lost, his feeling of significance, worth, belonging and rootedness of thought and action. In the end, "things don't make sense anymore." Hence meaninglessness is simultaneously experienced and bitterly condemned.

[17] Murray B. Levin, *The Alienated Voter*, New York: Holt, Rinehart & Winston, Inc., 1960, p. 59. Rightwing insistence that the U.S. is massively diseased—apart from the question of validity—is a direct commentary on the Right's own psychological state. Such imputations are treated as expressions of alienation.

[18] *The Blue Book of the John Birch Society*; Belmont: Birch Society, 1961, p. 57.

[19] "Liberal Policies Bring Uncertainty, Emptiness," *Toledo Blade*, (Dec. 10, 1961), section 2, p. 1.

Normlessness. The experienced loss of absolutes, of anchorage in necessary standards, rules and models results in the loss of a personal center of values and standards of certitude. The result is normlessness.

The fabric of morality provided through the centuries by Christianity is now "pierced and torn and weakened beyond needed dependability. . .," says Mr. Welch. The outcome "is the rise of the amoral man" whose hallmark is "pragmatic opportunism with hedonistic aims."[20]

Normlessness is evident in constant appeals of the Right for a "return" to the sacred "heritage" of traditional "Americanism." Return to purity and historical fidelity is presented as the overriding duty of patriots. "A great cleansing and uniting force for the nation" is urgently required, says Moral Re-Armament, Inc. For "Unfaithfulness in the home, perversion in high places and low, decadence in the arts, lawless youth, class war, race war, dishonesty—these are becoming the marks of American life. We are all responsible."[21]

Powerlessness. The feeling that one has lost personal efficacy and the ability to act influentially and significantly within his social universe reflects alienation in the form of powerlessness.

In his remarks to a Senate subcommittee shortly after being relieved of his command in Germany, General Edwin Walker indicated loss of personal efficacy as follows: "We are at war, we are infiltrated. We are losing that war every day. Are our hands tied, yours and mine? We need a substitute for defeat. If it is not within the power of this Congress to provide it—then the people of these United States are not truly represented."[22]

The powerless man feels unable to influence or control opinion and action within his environment. He may feel this way with such intensity that it becomes a serious, intrusive concern in the lives of others, as well as in his own. He does not understand or accept resignation and helplessness either in himself or others. "America is at war, a war we are losing," says Moral Re-Armament. Republicans and Democrats—it is the same. We move heedless and headless without an ideology against an ideological enemy."[23]

Perhaps nowhere is powerlessness expressed more forcefully or unmistakably than in the following statement by a Council member of the Birch Society: "The history and rise of the John Birch Society is the history of the revolted, misinformed, deceived, abused, angry American. . . . The basic fact which explains the creation and rise of the John Birch Society is that the American people are sick and tired of defeatism, humiliation, incompetence, surrender, and treason."[24] The rightist is convinced that he is relatively powerless to exert levers against those who occupy local, state and national politic commandposts.

Social Isolation. Loneliness and solitariness, the hallmarks of social isolation, result from loss of a personal center of values and standards of certitude, and the feeling of functional insufficiency and ineffectiveness.

---

[20] *Op. cit.,* pp. 62-67, *passim.*
[21] Full page advertisement, "To the American People: The Hour is Late, 'Here is the Answer, For God's Sake, Wake Up!," *New York Times*, (Jan. 15, 1961), p. E 7.
[22] *New York Times*, (Nov. 3, 1961), p. 22.
[23] *New York Times, loc. cit.*
[24] S. M. Draskovich, as quoted in *American Opinion*, no date.

The head of the Christian Crusade, Rev. Billy James Hargis, has remarked sadly: "Everything is so impersonal now. The Government takes care of you with a check. ... The government can't do anything about spiritual needs. It just hands out money."[25]

Impersonality, emptiness and distrust come to characterize one's life. "Let us all thank whatever God we severally worship," says Welch, "that there is so large a remnant of the really true believers still left." Welch goes on to note that precisely because the community of true believers is so small, "We desperately need their unshakable confidence in absolutes, in eternal principles and truths, in a world of increasing relativism, and transitoriness in all things."[26]

Social isolation creates an obsessive interest in distinguishing between "friends" and "enemies," until preoccupation with that distinction frequently becomes the central concern of interpersonal relations.

General alienation as previously described manifests itself as *political* alienation when any of four mechanisms are adopted by individuals.

Activism occurs when alienation prompts one to engage both in rational evaluation of the political scene, and a consequent decision to play a role in it. The decision to become an activist may be the direct consequence, for example, of the conviction that opposition must be mounted against public officials who are inefficient, venal, or who otherwise violate norms that are equated with the public interest. *Withdrawal* from any role whatever in political affairs may occur as a rational decision based on realistic assessments of political probabilities, but more often occurs when one is convinced that activism is pointless since desired results are impossible. *Projection* occurs when anger, disgust and estrangement stemming from alienation are transferred to other persons or groups that are perceived as engaged in hostile or subversive conspiracy. *Charismatic identification* takes place through the attempt of an individual to feel powerful and invulnerable by incorporating within himself the magical, extraordinary qualities of a leader he perceives as highly exceptional and unique.

We turn next to analysis of certain interrelationships among radical rightist ideology, style and alienation. At this point, we will want to pay particular attention to two dimensions of alienation—normlessness and powerlessness—for these provide substantial clues to the nature of and vulnerability to rightwing extremism. It will also be helpful to remember that rightist ideology and style are generated by and also reflective of the four alienation dimensions previously discussed.

Meaninglessness within the radical right is manifested through fundamentalism, restoration, unilateralism, telescoping and protest.

Political life in America is regarded as having departed from the path of rectitude and to function in an aimless, rudderless manner. The American way of life must then be restored through spiritual rediscovery of the divine heritage that blesses us domestically and rewards us internationally. The international sphere in particular is seen as an arena of power posturing, self-interest, betrayal and connivance into which the United States has unfortunately been ensnared. The remedy is to govern our conduct by the rules we at least know are valid, and if necessary to do so unilaterally, for our conception of the "game" is in accord with well-recognized

[25] Cited in John K. Adams, "Saving America, Incorporated," *Nation*, (Sept. 30, 1961), p. 192.

[26] *Op. cit.*, p. 57.

principles of truth and justice, and will, if acted upon, restore moral purpose to a political arena which is presently amoral and destructive. Thus it is that as national and international political life appears to lose contextuality and predictability for the rightwing extremist, the compulsion toward compensatory absolutes becomes irresistible. Those, he says, who carp about political complexity and the need to take many factors into consideration before making basic decisions make their own contribution to domestic decline and international chaos and appeasement. These alleged complexities can and must be overcome through the application of simple principles within the grasp of every ordinary, sincere person. Protest through direct action will reinvest political life with meaning if such protest aims at resurrecting the sacred and secular fundamentals to which America was once dedicated.

Normlessness is manifested through all elements of radical rightist ideology and style.

Great apprehension is felt over the alleged shift of authoritative values from the autonomous individual to the bureaucratic State. One's capacity to live within an ethical context appears to have been nullified by the unwarranted intrusion of governmental power. The enshrinement of majority opinion, which makes mere passions and emotions driving political forces, means that America's historical role as a God-centered Republic has been thwarted through the moral relativism and political opportunism that characterize mass democracy. The inefficacy of ethical principles in public and private life will only be overcome, it is held, through a return to traditional standards of certitude and justice. The people must rise up in righteous, organized indignation and cleanse the nation of the amoral, self-centered incomponents and conspirators who do violence to the sacred and secular norms to the consecration of which this nation was once dedicated. The nation must be purified of those public officials and opinion leaders who preside over the sacrifice of principles to expediency. The guide for such purification is to be found through a rediscovery of the Golden Age of "Americanism" and the political and moral authenticity that characterized it.

An important step in the direction of rediscovery is to expunge from our minds and institutions those "alien" practices and ideas that have diseased our way of life. One locus of disease is the international sphere, where we have compromised our principles and appeased our enemies. The latter must be dealt with summarily and unilaterally, if necessary, by an American government that has itself been previously redeemed. We must beware of the constant din regarding the alleged dangers of over-simplification of presumably complex political issues. This, says the rightwinger, is downright obfuscation. In truth, there is no complexity not responsive to the fundamental norms of morality, citizenship and decency, as any loyal American should know. The final proof of moral decay is the inability or unwillingness of so many Americans to confront its most dramatic symptom— communism. The breakdown of the normative order urgently requires patriotic political action lest chaos become a permanent condition of American and international life.

As in the case of normlessness, powerlessness is manifested through all elements of rightist ideology and style.

Rightwing emphasis on individualism reflects anxiety over the individual's apparent inability to make autonomous or free decisions that affect public and private life. Increased collectivism is held to have violated the political, moral, economic and other "laws" of nature, creating a hostile, normless world which the individual faces with a sense of dread and shame. Personal redemption, the antidote to normlessness, is also the necessary prelude to the capacity to exert power for rightful purposes. The rightwing admonition to forsake democracy and return to republicanism is partly generated by hostility to prevailing currents of equalitarianism and social welfare. Such hostility suggests divergence from the national consensus on a wide variety of domestic commitments. The awareness of such divergence sharpens feelings of powerlessness so far as sharing in the shaping and direction of the political system is concerned. Further, the "real" levers of power appear to be in the hands of a conspiracy or establishment that permits no outsider a share in decision-making. In the end, one is powerless to influence the course of political events under present circumstances. Indeed, the insiders are massively entrenched, and have gained control of the mass media, government agencies, public opinion, colleges, churches, etc. While presently inaccessible and unresponsive to the public, ways and means will be found to root the insiders out, and to restore the nation to its true legatees. Overseas, we continue to lose every important struggle because we haven't the courage to do what is "right" and "just" out of misconceived multilateralism or outright surrender and appeasement. As communism advances abroad, however, the rightwing extremist attempts to overcome his sense of powerlessness by convincing himself that knowledge *per se* of the normative keys promises to make him a potent force in political decision-making.

Social isolation is manifested through fundamentalism, purification, telescoping and protest.

The feeling that, alone among his numerous associates, one remains steadfast in commitment to fundamental truths and values generates the sense of social isolation for the rightist. Except for occasional contact with fellow true believers, his interpersonal relationships are almost wholly functional and formal, lacking the ingredients of gratification and esteem. Furthermore, many of his daily associates are regarded as "unwitting dupes" or supporters of the betrayers, the realization of which intensifies the conviction that awareness of the true course of events comes at the price of solitariness and ideological ostracism. But there is comfort in the knowledge that the small band of true believers, however beset, will one day inherit the earth and provide salvation for the faithful. Until that day, calumny, insults and ostracism must be borne in patience. However difficult, one must learn to channel his sense of isolation into effective forms of public protest.

The preceding analysis suggests that normlessness and powerlessness are the distinctive dimensions of alienation that are reflected in rightwing politics. Several further observations about the mechanisms through which alienation is expressed will be seen as corroborating this conclusion.

Studies such as those by Levin indicate that lesser degrees of alienation frequently stimulate rational political activism, but not so intense as to result in gross distortions of reality. The implication is that meaninglessness does not as readily precipitate regressive political mechanisms as do normlessness and powerlessness. Social isolation, on the other hand, frequently expresses itself in the form of withdrawal or retreat from political involvement. The remaining two mechanisms, projection and charismatic identification, are the most regressive and are closely linked with powerlessness and normlessness. It is a major conclusion of this study that alienation in the dominant forms of powerlessness and normlessness provides the most reliable and basic interpretation of radical rightist ideology and style. It is these forms of alienation that are at the basis of the frequently heard charge that rightwing extremism suffers from inaccurate perception of political realities.

CONCLUDING REMARKS

In turning to final remarks, later observations of a speculative and inferential nature will be distinguished from those we believe sustained by the study of the radical right.

The alienation focus is significant in enabling one to complement behavioral description with pre-behavioral explanation of rightwing extremism. Such a focus may be contrasted with the popular explanations of rightwing extremism as in essence "nihilistic," "irrational," or "negative." The view that rightist ideology reflects alienation impels one to take issue with the notion that ideology is wholly lacking, or that it consists purely of "negative" formulations. Indeed, the ideology of the Birch Society and similar organizations is at once diagnostic, or negative, but also perceptive, or positive. (For example, the rightist call for a return to "individualism" contains prescriptive overtones, whatever may be said about the nature or validity of such "individualism.") Hence the basic components of that ideology contain prescriptive recommendations that are inseparable from the diagnostic accounts of what the rightist believes to be wrong with American society.

The study indicates a congruence among ideological, stylistic, and alienational aspects. That congruence must not be exaggerated. All that we are justified in asserting is that alienation is one of a probable complex of causal factors that account for rightwing iedology and style; no evidence emerging from the study sustains the conclusion that there is a necessary correlation between all instances of intense alienation, and commitment to extremism. The evidence does, however, indicate that the alienation dimensions of normlessness and powerlessness are generative conditions of ideology and style. It is a matter to be settled by further empirical inquiry as to whether or not all persons exhibiting high degrees of normlessness and powerlessness are politically predisposed toward sympathy or affiliation with the radical right. The study suggests only that these two dimensions of alienation appear markedly in rightwing extremism as presently understood.

Radical rightist insistence that certain internal forces constitute the sole or primary danger facing the nation is instructive in several ways. It is hardly surprising that many individuals manifesting intense normlessness and powerlessness are prone to trace personal and political problems to the surrounding environment. For unlike the remote international arena in which the average citizen has no direct experiential involvements, the immediate environment serves as a generative center and object of political values and behavior. Since alienation is one type of personal response to that environment, we can understand that internal "dangers" are close to mind. The outcome of such emphasis on internal or domestic factors is by now classic: anger, through the mechanism of displaced animosity or projection, is vented on scapegoats in convenient proximity. Censorship drives, allegations of subversion and disloyalty, demands for investigations and purges, and quasi-religious meetings of various kinds give form and substance to such animosity.

By distinguishing between ideology and style on the one side as a manifest expression, and alienation on the other as a latent expression of rightwing extremism, it will be seen that responses to frustrations growing out of the immediate environment become formalized into political vocabularies and are projected to areas of concern for which they are inappropriate and misleading.

Telescoping, reductionism and protest are to be viewed as mechanisms for the attempted reduction of alienation. Telescoping and reductionism are particularly significant in this connection insofar as they aimed at superimposing order and clarity on political phenomena believed to be chaotic. Where successful, telescoping and reductionism accomplish two important goals: Normlessness is reduced by the desperate insistence that absolute moral standards do truly exist, and meaninglessness is reduced by appearing to "make sense" of the political world. Successful protest through direct action holds similar hope in that any resulting gains in political influence may further reduce feelings of powerlessness and social isolation. As with other aspects of rightwing extremism, protest simultaneously reflects and attempts to reduce alienation.

We end with several speculative and personal observations.

It would be most interesting to learn the extent to which Americans who experience intense normlessness and powerlessness do not attach themselves to or sympathize with rightwing extremist groups. We suspect that if a test of vulnerability to such groups were devised, it should rely at least in part on indices of normlessness and powerlessness. It should not be surprising if individuals feeling highly normless and powerless were found to be strongly attracted to such groups. But there is very little empirical data confirming or disputing this speculation. For such data would presuppose predictive indices of vulnerability to rightwing extremism, a technique only in embryonic stages of development.

Since the causes and consequences of alienation vary greatly from person to person, the radical right has been unable to overcome various schisms and antagonisms in order to achieve a unified, potent voice in national political affairs. While campaigns to spread rightist ideology have had success, that success has been limited since the logic of such campaigns actually is to intensify the very feelings of alienation which organizational unity requires to be reduced. In fact, such campaigns have engendered personal resistance to any further increase in feelings of alienation, despite a certain ideological attractiveness or temptation. In the absence of severe social shock (e.g., war or depression), rightist style will remain most effective on the local and regional levels, and acceptance of rightist ideology will hence be confined to a relatively small body of true believers.

Because it conveys the image of disruptive protest, the radical right is excluded by and large from national political debate. This occurs not merely because its ideology is unwelcome, but perhaps more importantly because its highly alienated members are not ultimately interested in meaningful debate when the preconditions of such participation are self-scrutiny, political compromise and toleration. As we have said, the Right has made a limited national impact. Perhaps that impact has a roughly proportional relationship to the incidence and intensity of alienation within the general population. Once again, empirical research aimed at establishing measures of political vulnerability to rightwing ideology would be most helpful in testing such a hypothesis.

Scapegoating or baiting of the radical right through public derision and scorn accomplishes little. Alienation is not absurd; to treat its manifestations as such is itself to act absurdly.[27] If we insist on regarding rightwing extremism as an aberration, as a corruption or deviation from political "normality," we are compelled to decide whether we are dealing with aberration of the political system or of individuals. On the whole, alienation analysis tends toward the view that while the antecedent conditions of alienation are sociological, response patterns will vary greatly from person to person even under identical conditions.

It is all too obvious that feelings of political alienation expressed through projection and charismatic identification can be a threat to a democratic society. It follows that such consequences of alienation as political cynicism, distrust and violence ought not be underestimated. At a very wide point, it has been suggested that alienation reduction requires that eighteenth-century democratic assumptions be reconsidered and qualified in the direction of a more realistic, less utopian and demanding theory of democracy. One may speculate that rightwing extremism is in part a consequence of the belated realization that political realities do not wholly comport with the Lockian version of democratic theory and rational man which have for so long dominated American political thought. Levin puts it succinctly in observing that "Feelings of alienation will arise in individuals who accept the classic democratic theory because it demands more of the individual citizen than he can realistically fulfill and promises more than can be delivered." The implication here is the obvious one that the substantial gap between democratic rhetoric and political reality requires an adjustment in rhetoric. In the opening words of a thought-provoking essay, Louis Hartz says: "The system of democracy works by virtue of certain processes which its theory never describes, to which, indeed, its theory is actually hostile."[28] Perhaps it is not too extravagant to postulate that one of the costs many Americans pay for the polarity between rhetoric and reality is political alienation.

[27] Studies explicitly employing alienation analysis of the radical right are virtually non-existent. There is an obvious need for case studies on rightwing extremism from this point of view in order to shed light on such as the following questions: why do only some highly alienated individuals associate with or support radical rightist groups? Or conversely, what are the conditions under which alienation does not lead to such association or support? What are the interrelationships among the specific measures of alienation, as applied to political commitments in general? What are the chief sources of alienation, speaking both individualistic-ally and sociologistically? To what extent does rightwing extremism attract the non-alienated?

[28] "Democracy: Image and Reality," in *Democracy in the Mid Twentieth Century*, The Washington University Press, 1960.

Suggested Readings

Bell, Daniel, *Radical Right* (New York: Doubleday & Company, Inc., 1963).

Bouscaren, Anthony, *Guide to Anti-Communist Action* (Chicago: Henry Regnery Co., 1958).

Colegrove, Kenneth, *Democracy Versus Communism* (Princeton N.J.: Van Nostrand, 1961).

Epstein, B., and A. Forster, *Radical Right: Report on the John Birch Society and Allies* (New York: Random House, Inc., 1967).

John Birch Society, *The Blue Book of the John Birch Society* (Belmont: Birch Society, 1961).

Oakes, C. P. *Education and Freedom in a World of Conflict* (Chicago: Henry Regnery Co., 1963).

Schwarz, Fred, *You Can Trust the Communists* (Englewood Cliffs, N.J.: Prentice-Hall, Inc. 1960).

Stormer, John, *None Dare Call It Treason* (Florissant, Mo: Liberty Bell Press, 1964).

Traditional Marxist and Marxist-Leninist Ideology

INTRODUCTION

In his essay on the wages of labor, Karl Marx lays the groundwork upon which the political and programmatic elements of Marxism are later to be erected. The basic premise is quite simple: The capitalist mode of production is fatal for the worker. This is because the capitalist, in order to maximize his profits, will pay in wages only what is necessary. The worker, kept at a subsistence wage, can live only a marginal or impoverished existence. When it is profitable to cut back the work force (because of overproduction, depression, and so on), the capitalist will let the worker starve.

The ideological doctrine of Marxism turns on two points: (1) the inevitable collapse of capitalism under the weight of its inherent contradictions, which lead to the absolute impoverishment of the proletarian class, and (2) the postulate that all value is created by labor and therefore should (morally) be returned to labor (that is, the workers control the instruments of production and the workers consume the whole of what is produced—the abolition of profit).

The political requirements of this doctrine are clear: The working class must combine collectively to overthrow the capitalist system of private ownership of the means of production and then supplant it with a system of social production and public ownership of the means of production. Another significant dimension of Marx's critique of capitalist society is to be found in the selection on estranged labor. Here Marx argues that work has been dehumanized and alienated under capitalism. The worker produces commodities not for himself, not for self-consumption, but for an alien or foreign interest. The profit secured by the owner of the means of production is extracted at the expense of the worker, for the worker receives less in wages than the amount of labor expended in production. Furthermore, the very nature of capitalism forces the worker to sell his labor power on the market, thus robbing labor of an intrinsic satisfying quality. And finally, the more the worker produces, the more he increases the power of his class enemy, the capitalist, who thus gains greater and greater control over his employees. The solution to this state of affairs is a revolutionary transformation of the economic and productive basis of society—the achievement of socialism.

Lenin's first two contributions to this volume advocate a worker's democracy and the conquest of state power by the revolutionary proletariat. He argues that only the proletariat among all historical and social classes can be truly democratic, for it alone among classes comprises the majority of humanity. The victory of the proletariat will assure the triumph of universal democracy because working-class interests, unlike the class interests of the bourgeoisie, the aristocracy, the clergy, the military, and so on, support the extension of equality and democracy to all people. In *The State and Revolution*, Lenin argues that the dictatorship of the proletariat is far from being a dictatorship in the ordinary sense because (1) it supplants the now-existing (then-existing) dictatorship of capital, which is disguised behind the machinations of bourgeois parliamentarians, and (2) the dictatorship of the proletariat and its utilization of state power is a temporary or transitional exercise of political power the final end of which will be the abolition of political institutions and the establishment of democratic management of resources in the achievement of communism.

In a third selection Lenin reformulates the critique of capitalism to show that capitalist development and expansion are not limited to the national, domestic sphere. Capitalism, he argues, has become international in character and scope; it has become imperialism, the highest stage of capitalist development. Only an international working-class movement can combat imperialism. And it may even be the case that oppressed workers in the underdeveloped countries will play a leading role in the international struggle for socialism.

This thesis was to become a significant issue after Lenin's death. Stalin wanted to concentrate on building socialism in one country, the U.S.S.R. In so doing he deemphasized the importance of the Internationale and the international communist movement. Trotsky, his exiled adversary, took up the internationalist banner and tried to combat Stalinism through the formation of a Fourth Internationale. The main point of the Trotsky selection is to defend the international communist movement against the statism of Stalin. The last two selections, by Plekhanov and Schaff, are somewhat more theoretical and less programmatic. Against the assertion that Marxism (historical materialism) is a deterministic system that eliminates the importance of the historical agent, Plekhanov argues that individuals can and do play an important role in shaping history. His essay on the role of the individual in history has become a Marxist classic. Schaff argues that even though Marxism considers human nature to be an ensemble of social relations, this does not diminish the uniqueness of each human individual, for each is a specifically determined individual with unique needs and propensities. Marxism, he says, is not inconsistent with humanism and individualism; it explains both and points the way to greater individual, human, and social realization.

Wages of Labor
Karl Marx

Wages are determined through the antagonistic struggle between capitalist and worker. Victory goes necessarily to the capitalist. The capitalist can live longer without the worker than can the worker without the capitalist. Combination among the capitalists is customary and effective; workers' combination is prohibited and painful in its consequences for them. Besides, the landowner and the capitalist can augment their revenues with the fruits of industry; the worker has neither ground-rent nor interest on capital to supplement his industrial income. Hence the intensity of the competition among the workers. Thus only for the workers is the separation of capital, landed property and labour an inevitable, essential and detrimental separation. Capital and landed property need not remain fixed in this abstraction, as must the labour of the workers.

The separation of capital, ground-rent and labour is thus fatal for the worker.

The lowest and the only necessary wage-rate is that providing for the subsistence of the worker for the duration of his work and as much more as is necessary for him to support a family and for the race of labourers not to die out. The ordinary wage, according to Smith, is the lowest compatible with common humanity (that is a cattle-like existence).[1]

The demand for men necessarily governs the production of men, as of every other commodity. Should supply greatly exceed demand, a section of the workers sinks into beggary or starvation. The worker's existence is thus brought under the same condition as the existence of every other commodity. The worker has become a commodity, and it is a bit of luck for him if he can find a buyer. And the demand on which the life of the worker depends, depends on the whim of the rich and the capitalists. Should the quantity in supply exceed the demand, then one of the constituent parts of the price—profit, ground-rent or wages—is paid below its *rate*[2]; a part of these factors is therefore withdrawn from this application, and thus the market-price gravitates towards the natural price as the centre-point. But (i) where there is considerable division of labour it is most difficult for the worker to direct his labour into other channels; (ii) because of his subordinate relation to the capitalist, he is the first to suffer.

Thus in the gravitation of market-price to natural price it is the worker who loses most of all and necessarily. And it is just the capacity of the capitalist to direct his capital into another channel which renders destitute the worker who is restricted to some particular branch of labour, or forces him to submit to every demand of this capitalist.

From Karl Marx, *Economic and Philosophic Manuscripts of 1844* (Moscow: Foreign Languages Publishing House, 1959).

[1] A. Smith, *Wealth of Nations*, Everyman edition, Vol. I, pp. 60-61.—*Ed.*

[2] Ibid., pp. 71-72, and pp. 50-51.—*Ed.*

The accidental and sudden fluctuations in market-price hit rent less than they do that part of the price which is resolved into profit and wages; but they hit profit less than they do wages. In most cases, for every wage that rises, one remains *stationary* and one *falls*.

The worker need not necessarily gain when the capitalist does, but he necessarily loses when the latter loses. Thus, the worker does not gain if the capitalist keeps the market-price above the natural price by virtue of some manufacturing or trading secret, or by virtue of monopoly or the favourable situation of his property.

Furthermore: *the prices of labour are much more constant than the prices of provisions*, often they stand in inverse proportion. In a dear year wages fall on account of the fall in demand, but rise on account of the rise in the prices of provisions—and thus balance. In any case, a number of workers are left without bread. In cheap years wages rise on account of the rise in demand, but fall on account of the fall in the prices of provisions—and thus balance.[3]

Another respect in which the worker is at a disadvantage: *The labour-prices of the various kinds of workers show much wider differences than the profits in the various branches in which capital is applied.* In labour all the natural, spiritual and social variety of individual activity is manifested and is variously rewarded, whilst dead capital always shows the same face and is indifferent to the *real* individual activity.

In general it has to be observed that in those cases where worker and capitalist equally suffer, the worker suffers in his very existence, the capitalist in the profit on his dead mammon.

The worker has to struggle not only for his physical means of subsistence: he has to struggle to get work, i.e., the possibility, the means, to perform his activity. Take the three chief conditions in which society can find itself and consider the situation of the worker in them:[4]

1. If the wealth of society declines the worker suffers most of all, for: although the working class cannot gain so much as can the class of property-owners in a prosperous state of society, *no one suffers so cruelly from its decline as the working class.*[5]

2. Take now a society in which wealth is increasing. This condition is the only one favourable to the worker. Here competition between the capitalists sets in. The demand for workers exceeds their supply. But:

In the first place, the raising of wages gives rise to *overwork* among the workers. The more they wish to earn, the more must they sacrifice their time and carry out slave-labour, in the service of avarice completely losing all their freedom, thereby they shorten their lives. This shortening of their life-span is a favourable circumstance for the working class as a whole, for as a result of it an ever-fresh supply of labour becomes necessary. This class has always to sacrifice a part of itself in order not to be wholly destroyed.

Furthermore: when does a society find itself in a condition of advancing wealth?

---

[3] Ibid. p. 77.—*Ed.*

[4] Cf. *Wealth of Nations*, Vol. I, p. 230; also pp. 61-65, where Smith illustrates these three possible conditions of society by referring to contemporary conditions in Bengal, China, and North America. (*The Wealth of Nations* was first published in 1776.)—*Ed.*

[5] Cf. Smith, l.c., p. 230; in Marx's manuscript the last clause of this sentence is in French, being taken direct from Garnier's translation, Tome II, p. 162.—*Ed.*

When the capitals and revenues of a country are growing. But this is only possible

(a) as a result of the accumulation of much labour, capital being accumulated labour; as the result, therefore, of the fact that his products are being taken in ever-increasing degree from the hands of the worker, that to an increasing extent his own labour confronts him as another's property and that the means of his existence and his activity are increasingly concentrated in the hands of the capitalist.

(b) The accumulation of capital increases the division of labour, and the division of labour increases the numbers of the workers. Conversely, the workers' numbers increase the division of labour, just as the division of labour increases the accumulation of capitals. With this division of labour on the one hand and the accumulation of capitals on the other, the worker becomes ever more exclusively dependent on labour, and on a particular, very one-sided, machine-like labour. Just as he is thus depressed spiritually and physically to the condition of a machine and from being a man becomes an abstract activity and a stomach, so he also becomes ever more dependent on every fluctuation in market-price, on the application of capitals, and on the mood of the rich. Equally, the increase in the class of people wholly dependent on work intensifies competition among them, thus lowering their price. In the factory-system this situation of the worker reaches its climax.

(c) In an increasingly prosperous society it is only the very richest people who can go on living on money-interest. Everyone else has to carry on a business with his capital, or venture it in trade. As a result, the competition between capitals becomes more intense. The concentration of capitals increases, the big capitalists ruin the small, and a section of the erstwhile capitalists sinks into the working class, which as a result of this supply again suffers to some extent a depression of wages and passes into a still greater dependence on the few big capitalists. The number of capitalists having been diminished, their competition with respect to workers scarcely exists any longer; and the number of workers having been augmented, their competition among themselves has become all the more intense, unnatural and violent. Consequently, a section of the working class falls into the ranks of beggary or starvation just as necessarily as a section of the middle capitalists falls into the working class.

Hence even in the condition of society most favourable to the worker, the inevitable result for the worker is overwork and premature death, decline to a mere machine, a bond servant of capital, which piles up dangerously over against him, more competition, and for a section of the workers starvation or beggary.

The raising of wages excites in the worker the capitalist's mania to get rich, which he, however, can only satisfy by the sacrifice of his mind and body. The raising of wages presupposes and entails the accumulation of capital, and thus sets the product of labour against the worker as something ever more alien to him. Similarly, the division of labour renders him ever more one-sided and dependent, bringing with it the competition not only of men but of machines. Since the worker has sunk to the level of a machine, he can be confronted by the machine as a competitor. Finally, as the amassing of capital increases the amount of industry and therefore the number of workers, it causes the same amount of industry to manufacture a *greater amount of product*, which leads to over-production and thus either ends by throwing a large section of workers out of work or by reducing their wages to the most miserable minimum. Such are the consequences of a condition of society most favourable to the worker—namely, of a condition of *growing, advancing wealth*.

Eventually, however, this state of growth must sooner or later reach its peak. What is the worker's position now?

3. "In a country which had attained the utmost degree of its wealth, both wages of labour and interest of stock would be very low. The competition among the workers to obtain employment would be so great that wages would be reduced to a point sufficient for the maintenance of the given number of workers; and as the country would already be sufficiently populated, this number could not be increased."[6]

The surplus would have to die.

Thus in a declining state of society—increasing misery of the worker; in an advancing state—misery with complications; and in a fully developed state of society—static misery.

Since, however, according to Smith, a society is not happy, of which the greater part suffers[7]—yet even the wealthiest state of society leads to this suffering of the majority—and since the *economic system*[8] (and in general a society based on private interest) leads to this wealthiest condition, it follows that the goal of the economic system is the *unhappiness* of society.

Concerning the relationship between worker and capitalist one should add that the capitalist is more than compensated for the raising of wages by the reduction in the amount of labour-time, and that the raising of wages and the raising of interest on capital operate on the price of commodities like simple and compound interest respectively.

Let us put ourselves now wholly at the standpoint of the political economist, and follow him in comparing the theoretical and practical claims of the workers.

He tells us that originally and in theory the *whole produce* of labour[9] belongs to the worker. But at the same time he tells us that in actual fact what the worker gets is the smallest and utterly indispensable part of the product—as much, only, as is necessary for his existence, not as a man but as a worker, and for the propagation, not of humanity but of the slave-class of workers.

The political economist tells us that everything is bought with labour and that capital is nothing but accumulated labour; but at the same time he tells us that the worker, far from being able to buy everything, must sell himself and his human identity.

Whilst the rent of the lazy landowner usually amounts to a third of the product of the soil, and the profit of the busy capitalist to as much as twice the interest on money, the "something more" which the worker himself earns at the best of times amounts to so little that of four children of his, two must starve and die. Whilst according to the political economists it is solely through labour that man enhances

---

[6] Cf. A. Smith, *Wealth of Nations*, Vol. I, p. 84 (Garnier, T. I., p. 193). Despite Marx's quotation marks, this is not in fact an exact quotation from Smith but a condensed version of some sentences of his.—*Ed.*

[7] Cf. A. Smith, *Wealth of Nations*, Vol. I, p. 70.—*Ed.*

[8] In this sentence the phrase "economic system" has been used to render the German term *Nationalökonomie*—the term used by Marx in these manuscripts for "Political Economy." Here, and occasionally elsewhere, Marx seems to use *Nationalökonomie* to stand not simply for Political Economy as a body of theory, but for the economic system, the developing industrial capitalist system, portrayed and championed by the classical political economists.—*Ed.*

[9] Cf. A. Smith, *Wealth of Nations*, Vol. I, p. 57.—*Ed.*

the value of the products of nature, whilst labour is man's active property,[10] according to this same political economy the landowner and the capitalist, who *qua* landowner and capitalist are merely privileged and idle gods, are everywhere superior to the worker and lay down the law to him.

Whilst according to the political economists labour is the sole constant price of things, there is nothing more contingent than the price of labour, nothing exposed to greater fluctuations.

Whilst the division of labour raises the productive power of labour and increases the wealth and refinement of society, it impoverishes the worker and reduces him to a machine. Whilst labour brings about the accumulation of capitals and with this the increasing prosperity of society, it renders the worker ever more dependent on the capitalist, leads him into competition of a new intensity, and drives him into the headlong rush of over-production, with its subsequent corresponding slump.

Whilst the interest of the worker, according to the political economists, never stands opposed to the interest of society, society always and necessarily stands opposed to the interest of the worker.

According to the political economists, the interest of the worker is never opposed to that of society: (1) because the raising of wages is more than made up for by the reduction in the amount of labour-time, together with the other consequences set forth above; and (2) because in relation to society the whole gross product is the net product, and only in relation to the private individual has the "net product" any significance.

But that labour itself, not merely in present conditions but in general in so far as its purpose is the mere increase of wealth—that labour itself, I say, is harmful and pernicious—follows, without his being aware of it, from the political economist's line of argument.

In theory, ground-rent and profit on capital are *deductions* suffered by wages. In actual fact, however, wages are a deduction which land and capital allow to go to the worker, a concession from the product of labour to the workers, to labour.

When society is in a state of decline, the worker suffers most severely. The specific severity of his burden he owes to his position as a worker, but the burden as such to the position of society.

But when society is in a state of progress, the ruin and impoverishment of the worker is the product of his labour and of the wealth produced by him. The misery results, therefore, from the *essence* of present-day labour itself.

Society in a state of maximum wealth, an ideal, but one which is more or less attained, and which at least is the aim of political economy as of civil society, means for the workers *static misery*.

It goes without saying that the *proletarian*, i.e., the man who, being without capital and rent, lives purely by labour, and by a one-sided, abstract labour, is considered by political economy only as a *worker*. Political economy can therefore advance the proposition that the proletarian, the same as any horse, must get as much as will enable him to work. It does not consider him when he is not working, as a human being; but leaves such consideration to criminal law, to doctors, to religion, to the statistical tables, to politics and to the workhouse beadle.

---

[10] Property, that is, in the sense of "a possession," not "an attribute." The German term is *Eigentum*, not *Eigenschaft.* —Ed.

Let us now rise above the level of political economy and try to answer two questions on the basis of the above exposition, which has been presented almost in the words of the political economists:

1. What in the evolution of mankind is the meaning of this reduction of the greater part of mankind to abstract labour?

2. What are the mistakes committed by the piecemeal reformers, who either want to *raise* wages and in this way to improve the situation of the working class, or regard *equality* of wages (as Proudhon does) the goal of social revolution?

In political economy *labour* occurs only in the form of *wage-earning activity*.

Estranged Labor

The worker becomes all the poorer the more wealth he produces, the more his production increases in power and range. The worker becomes an ever cheaper commodity the more commodities he creates. With the *increasing value* of the world of things proceeds in direct proportion the *devaluation* of the world of men. Labour produces not only commodities; it produces itself and the worker as a *commodity*—and does so in the proportion in which it produces commodities generally.

This fact expresses merely that the object which labour produces—labour's product—confronts it as *something alien*, as a *power independent* of the producer. The product of labour is labour which has been congealed in an object, which has become material: it is the *objectification* of labour. Labour's realization is its objectification. In the conditions dealt with by political economy this realization of labour appears as *loss of reality* for the workers; objectification as *loss of the object* and *object-bondage*; appropriation as *estrangement*, as *alienation*.

So much does labour's realization appear as loss of reality that the worker loses reality to the point of starving to death. So much does objectification appear as loss of the object that the worker is robbed of the objects most necessary not only for his life but for his work. Indeed, labour itself becomes an object which he can get hold of only with the greatest effort and with the most irregular interruptions. So much does the appropriation of the object appear as estrangement that the more objects the worker produces the fewer can he possess and the more he falls under the dominion of his product, capital.

All these consequences are contained in the definition that the worker is related to the *product of his labour* as to an *alien* object. For on this premise it is clear that the more the worker spends himself, the more powerful the alien objective world becomes which he creates over-against himself, the poorer he himself—his inner world—becomes, the less belongs to him as his own. It is the same in religion. The more man puts into God, the less he retains in himself. The worker puts his life into the object; but now his life no longer belongs to him but to the object. Hence, the greater this activity, the greater is the worker's lack of objects. Whatever the product of his labour is, he is not. Therefore the greater this product, the less is he himself. The *alienation* of the worker in his product means not only that his labour becomes an object, an *external* existence, but that it exists *outside him*, independently, as something alien to him, and that it becomes a power of its own confronting him; it means that the life which he has conferred on the object confronts him as something hostile and alien.

Let us now look more closely at the *objectification*, at the production of the worker; and therein at the *estrangement*, the *loss* of the object, his product.

The worker can create nothing without *nature*, without the *sensuous external world*. It is the material on which his labour is manifested, in which it is active, from which and by means of which it produces.

But just as nature provides labour with the *means of life* in the sense that labour cannot *live* without objects on which to operate, on the other hand, it also provides the *means of life* in the more restricted sense—i.e., the means for the physical subsistence of the *worker* himself.

Thus the more the worker by his labour *appropriates* the external world, sensuous nature, the more he deprives himself of *means of life* in the double respect: first, that the sensuous external world more and more cases to be an object belonging to his labour—to be his labour's *means of life*; and secondly, that it more and more ceases to be *means of life* in the immediate sense, means for the physical subsistence of the worker.

Thus in this double respect the worker becomes a slave of his object, first, in that he receives an *object of labour*, i.e., in that he receives *work*; and secondly, in that he receives *means of subsistence*. Therefore, it enables him to exist, first, as a *worker*; and, second, as a *physical subject*. The extremity of this bondage is that it is only as a *worker* that he continues to maintain himself as a *physical subject*, and that it is only as a *physical subject* that he is a *worker*.

(The laws of political economy express the estrangement of the worker in his object thus: the more the worker produces, the less he has to consume, the more values he creates, the more valueless, the more unworthy he becomes; the better formed his product, the more deformed becomes the worker; the more civilized his object, the more barbarous becomes the worker; the mightier labour becomes, the more powerless becomes the worker; the more ingenious labour becomes, the duller becomes the worker and the more he becomes nature's bondsman.)

Political economy conceals the estrangement inherent in the nature of labour by not considering the direct relationship between the worker (labour) *and production*. It is true that labour produces for the rich wonderful things—but for the worker it produces privation. It produces palaces—but for the worker, hovels. It produces beauty—but for the worker, deformity. It replaces labour by machines—but some of the workers it throws back to a barbarous type of labour and the other workers it turns into machines. It produces intelligence—but for the worker idiocy, cretinism.

The direct relationship of labour to its produce is the relationship of the worker to the objects of his production. The relationship of the man of means to the objects of production and to production itself is only a *consequence* of this first relationship—and confirms it. We shall consider this other aspect later.

When we ask, then, what is the essential relationship of labour we are asking about the relationship of the *worker* to production.

Till now we have been considering the estrangement, the alienation of the worker only in one of its aspects, i.e., the worker's *relationship to the products of his labour.* But the estrangement is manifested not only in the result but in the *act of production*—within the *producing activity* itself. How would the worker come to face the product of his activity as a stranger, were it not that in the very act of production he was estranging himself from himself? The product is after all but the summary of the activity of production. If then the product of labour is alienation, production itself must be active alienation, the alienation of activity, the activity of alienation. In the estrangement of the object of labour is merely summarized the estrangement, the alienation, in the activity of labour itself.

What, then, constitutes the alienation of labour?

First, the fact that labour is *external* to the worker, i.e., it does not belong to his essential being; that in his work, therefore, he does not affirm himself but denies himself, does not feel content but unhappy, does not develop freely his physical and mental energy but mortifies his body and ruins his mind. The worker therefore only feels himself outside his work, and in his work feels outside himself. He is at home when he is not working, and when he is working he is not at home. His labour is therefore not voluntary, but coerced; it is *forced labour.* It is therefore not the satisfaction of a need; it is merely a *means* to satisfy needs external to it. Its alien character emerges clearly in the fact that as soon as no physical or other compulsion exists, labour is shunned like the plague. External labour, labour in which man alienates himself, is a labour of self-sacrifice, of mortification. Lastly, the external character of labour for the worker appears in the fact that it is not his own, but someone else's, that it does not belong to him, that in it he belongs, not to himself, but to another. Just as in religion the spontaneous activity of the human imagination, of the human brain and the human heart, operates independently of the individual—that is, operates on him as an alien, divine or diabolical activity—in the same way the worker's activity is not his spontaneous activity. It belongs to another; it is the loss of his self.

As a result, therefore, man (the worker) no longer feels himself to be freely active in any but his animal functions—eating, drinking, procreating, or at most in his dwelling and in dressing-up, etc.; and in his human functions he no longer feels himself to be anything but an animal. What is animal becomes human and what is human becomes animal.

Certainly eating, drinking, procreating, etc., are also genuinely human functions. But in the abstraction which separates them from the sphere of all other human activity and turns them into sole and ultimate ends, they are animal.

The Working Class as Vanguard Fighter for Democracy

V. I. Lenin

V. I. Lenin (1870-1924) led the Communist Revolution in Russia in 1917 and then founded the Soviet government. His analyses of Marxism and capitalism have played a very important role in the spreading of communism in various parts of the world.

. . . Let us return, however, to our thesis. We said that a Social-Democrat,[1] if he really believes it necessary to develop comprehensively the political consciousness of the proletariat, must "go among all classes of the population". This gives rise to the questions: how is this to be done? have we enough forces to do this? is there a basis for such work among all the other classes? will this not mean a retreat, or lead to a retreat, from the class point of view? Let us deal with these questions.

We must "go among all classes of the population" as theoreticians, as propagandists, as agitators, and as organisers. No one doubts that the theoretical work of Social-Democrats should aim at studying all the specific features of the social and political condition of the various classes. But extremely little is done in this direction, as compared with the work that is done in studying the specific features of factory life. In the committees and study circles, one can meet people who are immersed in the study even of some special branch of the metal industry; but one can hardly ever find members of organisations (obliged, as often happens, for some reason or other to give up practical work) who are especially engaged in gathering material on some pressing question of social and political life in our country which could serve as a means for conducting Social-Democratic work among other strata of the population. In dwelling upon the fact that the majority of the present-day leaders of the working-class movement lack training, we cannot refrain from mentioning training in this respect also, for it too is bound up with the "Economist" conception of "close organic connection with the proletarian struggle." The principal thing, of course, is *propaganda* and *agitation* among all strata of the people. The work of the West-European Social-Democrat is in this respect facilitated by the public meetings and rallies which *all* are free to attend, and by the fact that in parliament he addresses the representatives of *all* classes. We have neither a parliament nor freedom of assembly; nevertheless, we are able to arrange meetings of workers who desire to listen to *a Social-Democrat*. We must also find ways and means of calling meetings of representatives of all social classes that desire to listen to *a democrat*; for he is no Social-Democrat who forgets in practice that "the Communists support every revolutionary movement," that we

From V. I. Lenin, *Collected Works*, Vol. 5 (Moscow: Foreign Languages Publishing House, 1961).

[1] The Social Democratic Party referred to here was the Marxist revolutionary party, not to be confused with later nonrevolutionary Social Democratic parties in Western Europe.—*Ed.*

are obliged for that reason to expound and emphasise *general democratic tasks before the whole people*, without for a moment concealing our socialist convictions. He is no Social-Democrat who forgets in practice his obligation to be *ahead of all* in raising, accentuating, and solving *every* general democratic question.

"But everyone agrees with this!" the impatient reader will exclaim, and the new instructions adopted by the last conference of the Union Abroad for the Editorial Board of *Rabocheye Dyelo* definitely say: "All events of social and political life that affect the proletariat either directly as a special class or as *the vanguard of all the revolutionary forces in the struggle for freedom* should serve as subjects for political propaganda and agitation" (*Two Conferences*, p. 17, our italics). Yes, these are very true and very good words, and we would be fully satisfied if *Rabocheye Dyelo understood* them *and if it refrained from saying in the next breath things that contradict them.* For it is not enough to call ourselves the "vanguard", the advanced contingent; we must act in such a way that *all* the other contingents recognise and are obliged to admit that we are marching in the vanguard. And we ask the reader: Are the representatives of the other "contingents" such fools as to take our word for it when we say that we are the "vanguard"? Just picture to yourselves the following: a Social-Democrat comes to the "contingent" of Russian educated radicals, or liberal constitutionalists, and says, We are the vanguard; "the task confronting us now is, as far as possible, to lend the economic struggle itself a political character." The radical, or constitutionalist, if he is at all intelligent (and there are many intelligent men among Russian radicals and constitutionalists), would only smile at such a speech and would say (to himself, of course, for in the majority of cases he is an experienced diplomat): "Your 'vanguard' must be made up of simpletons. They do not even understand that it is our task, the task of the progressive representatives of bourgeois democracy to lend the workers' economic struggle *itself* a political character. Why, we too, like the West-European bourgeois, want to draw the workers into politics, *but only into trade-unionist, not into Social-Democratic politics.* Trade-unionist politics of the working class is precisely *bourgeois politics* of the working class, and this 'vanguard's' formulation of its task is the formulation of trade-unionist politics! Let them call themselves Social-Democrats to their heart's content, I am not a child to get excited over a label. But they must not fall under the influence of those pernicious orthodox doctrinaires, let them allow 'freedom of criticism' to those who unconsciously are driving Social-Democracy into trade-unionist channels."

And the faint smile of our constitutionalist will turn into Homeric laughter when he learns that the Social-Democrats who talk of Social-Democracy as the vanguard, today, when spontaneity almost completely dominates our movement, fear nothing so much as "belittling the spontaneous element," as "underestimating the significance of the forward movement of the drab everyday struggle, as compared with the propaganda of brilliant and completed ideas," etc., etc.! A "vanguard" which fears that consciousness will outstrip spontaneity, which fears to put forward a bold "plan" that would compel general recognition even among those who differ with us. Are they not confusing "vanguard" with "rearguard"? . . .

. . . In our time only a party that will *organise* really *nationwide* exposures can become the vanguard of the revolutionary forces. The word "nation-wide" has a very profound meaning. The overwhelming majority of the non-working-class exposers (be it remembered that in order to become the vanguard, we must attract other classes) are sober politicians and level-headed men of affairs. They know perfectly well how dangerous it is to "complain" even against a minor official, let alone against the "omnipotent" Russian Government. And they will come *to us* with their complaints only when they see that these complaints can really have effect, and that we represent *a political force*. In order to become such a force in the eyes of outsiders, much persistent and stubborn work is required *to raise* our own consciousness, initiative, and energy. To accomplish this it is not enough to attach a "vanguard" label to rearguard theory and practice.

But if we have to undertake the organisation of a really nation-wide exposure of the government, in what way will then the class character of our movement be expressed?—the overzealous advocate of "close organic contact with the proletarian struggle" will ask us, as indeed he does. The reply is manifold: we Social-Democrats will organise these nation-wide exposures; all questions raised by the agitation will be explained in a consistently Social-Democratic spirit, without any concessions to deliberate or undeliberate distortions of Marxism; the all-round political agitation will be conducted by a party which unites into one inseparable whole the assault on the government in the name of the entire people, the revolutionary training of the proletariat, and the safeguarding of its political independence, the guidance of the economic struggle of the working class, and the utilisation of all its spontaneous conflicts with its exploiters which rouse and bring into our camp increasing numbers of the proletariat.

But a most characteristic feature of Economism is its failure to understand this connection, more, this identity of the most pressing need of the proletariat (a comprehensive political education through the medium of political agitation and political exposures) with the need of the general democratic movement. This lack of understanding is expressed, not only in "Martynovite" phrases, but in the references to a supposedly class point of view identical in meaning with these phrases. Thus, the authors of the "Economist" letter in *Iskra*, No. 12, state[2]: "This basic drawback of *Iskra* [overestimation of ideology] is also the cause of its inconsistency on the question of the attitude of Social-Democracy to the various social classes and tendencies. By theoretical reasoning [not by "the growth of Party tasks, which grow together with the Party"], *Iskra* solved the problem of the immediate transition to the struggle against absolutism. In all probability it senses the difficulty of such a task for the workers under the present state of affairs [not only senses, but knows fully well that this task appears less difficult to the workers than to the "Economist" intellectuals with their nursemaid concern, for the workers are prepared to fight even for demands which, to use the language of the never-to-be-forgotten Martynov, do not "promise palpable results"] but lacking the patience to wait until the workers will have gathered sufficient forces for this struggle, *Iskra* begins to seek allies in the ranks of the liberals and intellectuals." . . .

Yes, we have indeed lost all "patience" "waiting" for the blessed time, long promised us by divers "conciliators," when the Economists will have stopped charging the workers with *their own* backwardness and justifying their own lack of energy with allegations that the workers lack strength. We ask our Economists:

---

[2] Lack of space has prevented us from replying in detail, in *Iskra*, to this letter, which is highly characteristic of the Economists. We were very glad at its appearance, for the allegations that *Iskra* did not maintain a consistent class point of view had reached us long before that from various sources, and we were waiting for an appropriate occasion, or for a formulated expression of this fashionable charge, to give our reply. Moreover, it is our habit to reply to attacks, not by defence, but by counter-attack.

What do they mean by "the gathering of working-class strength for the struggle"? Is it not evident that this means the political training of the workers, so that *all* the aspects of our vile autocracy are revealed to them? And is it not clear that *precisely for this work* we need "allies in the ranks of the liberals and intellectuals," who are prepared to join us in the exposure of the political attack on the Zemstvos, on the teachers, on the statisticians, on the students, etc.? Is this surprisingly "intricate mechanism" really so difficult to understand? Has not P. B. Axelrod constantly repeated since 1897 that "the task before the Russian Social-Democrats of acquiring adherents and direct and indirect allies among the non-proletarian classes will be solved principally and primarily by the character of the propagandist activities conducted among the proletariat itself"? But the Martynovs and the other Economists continue to imagine that "by economic struggle against the employers and the government" the workers must *first* gather strength (for trade-unionist politics) and *then* "go over"—we presume from trade-unionist "training for activity"—to Social-Democratic activity!

". . . In this quest," continue the Economists, "*Iskra* not infrequently departs from the class point of view, obscures class antagonisms, and puts into the forefront the common nature of the discontent with the government, although the causes and the degree of the discontent vary considerably among the 'allies.' Such, for example, is *Iskra*'s attitude towards the Zemstvo. . . ." *Iskra*, it is alleged, "promises the nobles that are dissatisfied with the government's sops the assistance of the working class, but it does not say a word about the class antagonism that exists between these social strata." If the reader will turn to the article "The Autocracy and the Zemstvo" (*Iskra*, Nos. 2 and 4), to which, *in all probability*, the authors of the letter refer, he will find that they[3] deal with the attitude of the *government* towards the "mild agitation of the bureaucratic Zemstvo, which is based on the social-estates," and towards the "independent activity of even the propertied classes." The article states that the workers cannot look on indifferently while the government is waging a struggle against the Zemstvo, and the Zemstvos are called upon to stop making mild speeches and to speak firmly and resolutely when revolutionary Social-Democracy confronts the government in all its strength. What the authors of the letter do not agree with here is not clear. Do they think that the workers will "not understand" the phrases "propertied classes" and "bureaucratic Zemstvo based on the social-estates"? Do they think that *urging* the Zemstvo to abandon mild speeches and to speak firmly is "overestimating ideology"? Do they imagine the workers can "gather strength" for the struggle against the autocracy if they know nothing about the attitude of the autocracy towards the Zemstvo *as well*? All this too remains unknown. One thing alone is clear and that is that the authors of the letter have a very vague idea of what the political tasks of Social-Democracy are. This is revealed still more clearly by their remark: "Such, too, is *Iskra*'s attitude towards the student movement" (i.e., it also "obscures the class antagonisms"). Instead of calling on the workers to declare by means of public demonstrations that the real breeding-place of unbridled violence, disorder, and outrage is not the university youth but the Russian Government (*Iskra*, No. 2*), we ought probably to have inserted arguments in the spirit of *Rabochaya Mysl*! Such ideas were expressed by Social-Democrats in the autumn of 1901, after the events

---

[3] In the interval *between* these articles there was one (*Iskra*, No. 3), which dealt especially with class antagonisms in the countryside.

of February and March, on the eve of a fresh upsurge of the student movement, which reveals that even in this sphere the "spontaneous" protest against the autocracy is *outstripping* the conscious Social-Democratic leadership of the movement. The spontaneous striving of the workers to defend the students who are being assaulted by the police and the Cossacks surpasses the conscious activity of the Social-Democratic organisation!

"And yet in other articles," continue the authors of the letter, "*Iskra* sharply condemns all compromise and defends, for instance, the intolerant conduct of the Guesdists." We would advise those who are wont so conceitedly and frivolously to declare that the present disagreements among the Social-Democrats are unessential and do not justify a split, to ponder these words. Is it possible for people to work together in the same organisation, when some among them contend that we have done extremely little to explain the hostility of the autocracy to the various classes and to inform the workers of the opposition displayed by the various social strata to the autocracy, while others among them see in this clarification a "compromise"—evidently a compromise with the theory of "economic struggle against the employers and the government"?

We urged the necessity of carrying the class struggle into the rural districts in connection with the fortieth anniversary of the emancipation of the peasantry (issue No. 3**), and spoke of the irreconcilability of the local government bodies and the autocracy in relation to Witte's secret Memorandum (No. 4). In connection with the new law we attacked the feudal landlords and the government which serves them (No. 8***) and we welcomed the illegal Zemstvo congress. We urged the Zemstvo to pass over from abject petitions (No. 8*) to struggle. We encouraged the students, who had begun to understand the need for the political struggle, and to undertake this struggle (No. 3), while, at the same time, we lashed out at the "outrageous incomprehension" revealed by the adherents of the "purely student" movement, who called upon the students to abstain from participating in the street demonstrations (No. 3, in connection with the manifesto issued by the Executive Committee of the Moscow students on February 25). We exposed the "senseless dreams" and the "lying hypocrisy" of the cunning liberals of *Rossiya*[173] (No. 5), while pointing to the violent fury with which the government-gaoler persecuted "peaceful writers, aged professors, scientists, and well-known liberal Zemstvo members" (No. 5, "Police Raid on Literature"). We exposed the real significance of the programme of "state protection for the welfare of the workers" and welcomed the "valuable admission" that "it is better, by granting reforms from above, to forestall the demands for such reforms from below than to wait for those demands to be put forward" (No. 6**). We encouraged the protesting statisticians (No. 7) and censured the strike-breaking statisticans (No. 9). He who sees in these tactics an obscuring of the class-consciousness of the proletariat and *a compromise with liberalism* reveals his utter failure to understand the true significance of the programme of the *Credo* and *carries out that programme de facto*, however much he may repudiate it. For by *such an approach* he drags Social-Democracy towards the "economic struggle against the employers and the government" and *yields to liberalism*, abandons the task of actively intervening in *every* "liberal" issue and of determining *his own*, Social-Democratic, attitude towards this question. . . .

Class Society and the State

THE STATE—A PRODUCT OF THE IRRECONCILABILITY OF CLASS ANTAGONISMS

What is now happening to Marx's theory has, in the course of history, happened repeatedly to the theories of revolutionary thinkers and leaders of oppressed classes fighting for emancipation. During the lifetime of great revolutionaries, the oppressing classes constantly hounded them, received their theories with the most savage malice, the most furious hatred and the most unscrupulous campaigns of lies and slander. After their death, attempts are made to convert them into harmless icons, to canonise them, so to say, and to hallow their *names* to a certain extent for the "consolation" of the oppressed classes and with the object of duping the latter, while at the same time robbing the revolutionary theory of its *substance*, blunting its revolutionary edge and vulgarising it. Today, the bourgeoisie and the opportunists within the labour movement concur in this doctoring of Marxism. They omit, obscure or distort the revolutionary side of this theory, its revolutionary soul. They push to the foreground and extol what is or seems acceptable to the bourgeoisie. All the social-chauvinists are now "Marxists" (don't laugh!). And more and more frequently German bourgeois scholars, only yesterday specialists in the annihilation of Marxism, are speaking of the "national-German" Marx, who, they claim, educated the labour unions which are so splendidly organised for the purpose of waging a predatory war!

In these circumstances, in view of the unprecedentedly widespread distortion of Marxism, our prime task is to *re-establish* what Marx, really taught on the subject of the state. This will necessitate a number of long quotations from the works of Marx and Engels themselves. Of course, long quotations will render the text cumbersome and not help at all to make it popular reading, but we cannot possibly dispense with them. All, or at any rate all the most essential passages in the works of Marx and Engels on the subject of the state must by all means be quoted as fully as possible so that the reader may form an independent opinion of the totality of the views of the founders of scientific socialism, and of the evolution of those views, and so that their distortion by the "Kautskyism" now prevailing may be documentarily proved and clearly demonstrated.

Let us begin with the most popular of Engels's works, *The Origin of the Family, Private Property, and the State*, the sixth edition of which was published in Stuttgart as far back as 1894. We shall have to translate the quotations from the German originals, as the Russian translations, while very numerous, are for the most part either incomplete or very unsatisfactory.

Summing up his historical analysis, Engels says:

The state is, therefore, by no means a power forced on society from without; just as little is it "the reality of the ethical idea," "the image and reality of reason," as Hegel maintains. Rather,

From V. I. Lenin, *Collected Works*, Vol. 25 (Moscow: Foreign Languages Publishing House, 1964).

it is a product of society at a certain stage of development; it is the admission that this society has become entangled in an insoluble contradiction with itself, that it has split into irreconcilable antagonisms which it is powerless to dispel. But in order that these antagonisms, these classes with conflicting economic interests might not consume themselves and society in fruitless struggle, it became necessary to have a power, seemingly standing above society, that would alleviate the conflict and keep it within the bounds of "order"; and this power, arisen out of society but placing itself above it, and alienating itself more and more from it, is the state. (Pp. 177-78, sixth German edition.)

This expresses with perfect clarity the basic idea of Marxism with regard to the historical role and the meaning of the state. The state is a product and a manifestation of the *irreconcilability* of class antagonisms. The state arises where, when and insofar as class antagonisms objectively *cannot* be reconciled. And, conversely, the existence of the state proves that the class antagonisms are irreconcilable.

It is on this most important and fundamental point that the distortion of Marxism, proceeding along two main lines, begins.

On the one hand, the bourgeois, and particularly the petty-bourgeois, ideologists, compelled under the weight of indisputable historical facts to admit that the state only exists where there are class antagonisms and a class struggle, "correct" Marx in such a way as to make it appear that the state is an organ for the *reconciliation* of classes. According to Marx, the state could neither have arisen nor maintained itself had it been possible to reconcile classes. From what the petty-bourgeois and philistine professors and publicists say, with quite frequent and benevolent references to Marx, it appears that the state does reconcile classes. According to Marx, the state is an organ of class *rule*, an organ for the *oppression* of one class by another; it is the creation of "order," which legalises and perpetuates this oppression by moderating the conflict between the classes. In the opinion of the petty-bourgeois politicians, however, order means the reconciliation of classes, and not the oppression of one class by another; to alleviate the conflict means reconciling classes and not depriving the oppressed classes of definite means and methods of struggle to overthrow the oppressors.

For instance, when, in the revolution of 1917, the question of the significance and role of the state arose in all its magnitude as a practical question demanding immediate action, and, moreover, action on a mass scale, all the Socialist-Revolutionaries and Mensheviks descended at once to the petty-bourgeois theory that the "state" "reconciles" classes. Innumerable resolutions and articles by politicians of both these parties are thoroughly saturated with this petty-bourgeois and philistine "reconciliation" theory. That the state is an organ of the rule of a definite class which *cannot* be reconciled with its antipode (the class opposite to it) is something the petty-bourgeois democrats will never be able to understand. Their attitude to the state is one of the most striking manifestations of the fact that our Socialist-Revolutionaries and Mensheviks are not socialists at all (a point that we Bolsheviks have always maintained), but petty-bourgeois democrats using near-socialist phraseology.

On the other hand, the "Kautskyite" distortion of Marxism is far more subtle. "Theoretically," it is not denied that the state is an organ of class rule, or that class antagonisms are irreconcilable. But what is overlooked or glossed over is this: if the state is the product of the irreconcilability of class antagonisms, if it is a power standing *above* society and "*alienating* itself *more and more* from it," it is obvious that the liberation of the oppressed class is impossible not only without a violent revolution, *but also without the destruction* of the apparatus of state power which was created by the ruling class and which is the embodiment of this "alienation." As we shall see later, Marx very explicitly drew this theoretically self-evident conclusion on the strength of a concrete historical analysis of the tasks of the revolution. And—as we shall show in detail further on—it is this conclusion which Kautsky has "forgotten" and distorted.

Engels gives a general summary of his views in the most popular of his works in the following words:

The state, then, has not existed from all eternity. There have been societies that did without it, that had no idea of the state and state power. At a certain stage of economic development, which was necessarily bound up with the split of society into classes, the state became a necessity owing to this split. We are now rapidly approaching a stage in the development of production at which the existence of these classes not only will have ceased to be a necessity, but will become a positive hindrance to production. They will fall as inevitably as they arose at an earlier stage. Along with them the state will inevitably fall. Society, which will reorganise production on the basis of a free and equal association of the producers, will put the whole machinery of state where it will then belong: into a museum of antiquities, by the side of the spinning-wheel and the bronze axe.

We do not often come across this passage in the propaganda and agitation literature of the present-day Social-Democrats. Even when we do come across it, it is mostly quoted in the same manner as one bows before an icon, i.e., it is done to show official respect for Engels, and no attempt is made to gauge the breadth and depth of the revolution that this relegating of "the whole machinery of state to a museum of antiquities" implies. In most cases we do not even find an understanding of what Engels calls the state machine.

THE "WITHERING AWAY" OF THE STATE, AND VIOLENT REVOLUTION

Engels's words regarding the "withering away" of the state are so widely known, they are so often quoted, and so clearly reveal the essence of the customary adaptation of Marxism to opportunism that we must deal with them in detail. We shall quote the whole argument from which they are taken.

The proletariat siezes state power and turns the means of production into state property to begin with. But thereby it abolishes itself as the proletariat, abolishes all class distinctions and class antagonisms, and abolishes also the state as state. Society thus far, operating amid class antagonisms, needed the state, that is, an organisation of the particular exploiting class, for the maintenance of its external conditions of production, and, therefore, especially, for the purpose of forcibly keeping the exploited class in the conditions of oppression determined by the given mode of production (slavery, serfdom or bondage, wage-labour). The state was the official representative of society as a whole, its concentration in a visible corporation. But it was this only insofar as it was the state of that class which itself represented, for its own time, society as a whole: in ancient times, the state of slave-owning citizens; in the Middle Ages, of the feudal nobility; in our own time, of the bourgeoisie. When at last it becomes the real representative of the whole of society, it renders itself unnecessary. As soon as there is no longer any social class to be held in subjection, as soon as class rule, and the individual struggle for existence based upon the present anarchy in production, with the collisions and excesses arising from this struggle, are removed, nothing more remains to be held in subjection—nothing necessitating a special coercive force, a state. The first act by which the state really comes forward as the representative of the whole of society—the taking possession of the means of production in the name of society—is also its last independent act as a state. State interference in social relations becomes, in one domain after another, superfluous, and then dies down of itself. The government of persons is replaced by the administration of things, and by the conduct of processes of production. The state is not "abolished." It withers away. This gives the measure of the value of the phrase "a free people's state," both as to its justifiable use for a time from an agitational point of view, and as to its ultimate scientific insufficiency; and also of the so-called anarchists' demand that the state be abolished overnight. (Herr Eugen Dühring's Revolution in Science [Anti-Dühring], *pp. 301-03, third German edition.*)

It is safe to say that of this argument of Engels's, which is so remarkably rich in ideas, only one point has become an integral part of socialist thought among modern socialist parties, namely, that according to Marx the state "withers away"—as distinct from the anarchist doctrine of the "abolition" of the state. To prune Marxism to such an extent means reducing it to opportunism, for this "interpretation" only leaves a vague notion of a slow, even, gradual change, of absence of leaps and storms, of absence of revolution. The current, widespread, popular, if one may say so, conception of the "withering away" of the state undoubtedly means obscuring, if not repudiating, revolution.

Such an "interpretation," however, is the crudest distortion of Marxism, advantageous only to the bourgeoisie. In point of theory, it is based on disregard for the most important circumstances and considerations indicated in, say, Engels's "summary" argument we have just quoted in full.

In the first place, at the very outset of his argument, Engels says that, in seizing state power, the proletariat thereby "abolishes the state as state." It is not done to ponder over the meaning of this. Generally, it is either ignored altogether, or is considered to be something in the nature of "Hegelian weakness" on Engels's part. As a matter of fact, however, these words briefly express the experience of one of the greatest proletarian revolutions, the Paris Commune of 1871, of which we shall speak in greater detail in its proper place. As a matter of fact, Engels speaks here of the proletarian revolution "abolishing" the *bourgeois* state, while the words about the state withering away refer to the remnants of the *proletarian* state *after* the socialist revolution. According to Engels, the bourgeois state does not "wither away," but is "*abolished*" by the proletariat in the course of the revolution. What withers away after this revolution is the proletarian state or semi-state.

Secondly, the state is a "special coercive force." Engels gives this splendid and extremely profound definition here with the utmost lucidity. And from it follows that the "special coercive force" for the suppression of the proletariat by the bourgeoisie, of millions of working people by handfuls of the rich, must be replaced by a "special coercive force" for the suppression of the bourgeoisie by the proletariat (the dictatorship of the proletariat). This is precisely what is meant by "abolition of the state as state." This is precisely the "act" of taking possession of the means of production in the name of society. And it is self-evident that *such* a replacement of one (bourgeois) "special force" by another (proletarian) "special force" cannot possibly take place in the form of "withering away."

Thirdly, in speaking of the state "withering away," and the even more graphic and colourful "dying down of itself," Engels refers quite clearly and definitely to the period *after* "the state has taken possession of the means of production in the name of the whole of society," that is, *after* the socialist revolution. We all know that the political form of the "state" at that time is the most complete democracy. But it never enters the head of any of the opportunists, who shamelessly distort Marxism, that Engels is consequently speaking here of *democracy* "dying down of itself," or "withering away." This seems very strange at first sight. But it is "incomprehensible" only to those who have not thought about democracy *also* being a state and, consequently, also disappearing when the state disappears. Revolution alone can "abolish" the bourgeois state. The state in general, i.e., the most complete democracy, can only "wither away."

Fourthly, after formulating his famous proposition that "the state withers away", Engels at once explains specifically that this proposition is directed against both the opportunists and the anarchists. In doing this, Engels puts in the forefront that conclusion, drawn from the proposition that "the state withers away", which is directed against the opportunists.

One can wager that out of every 10,000 persons who have read or heard about the "withering away" of the state, 9,990 are completely unaware, or do not remember, that Engels directed his conclusions from that proposition *not* against the anarchists *alone*. And of the remaining ten, probably nine do not know the meaning of a "free people's state" or why an attack on this slogan means an attack on the opportunists. This is how history was written! This is how a great revolutionary teaching is imperceptibly falsified and adapted to prevailing philistinism. The conclusion directed against the anarchists has been repeated thousands of times; it has been vulgarised, and rammed into people's heads in the shallowest form, and has acquired the strength of a prejudice, whereas the conclusion directed against the opportunists has been obscured and "forgotten"!

The "free people's state" was a programme demand and a catchword current among the German Social-Democrats in the seventies. This catchword is devoid of all political content except that it describes the concept of a democracy in a pompous philistine fashion. Insofar as it hinted in a legally permissible manner at a democratic republic, Engels was prepared to "justify" its use "for a time" from an agitational point of view. But it was an opportunist catchword, for it amounted to something more than prettifying bourgeois democracy, and was also failure to understand the socialist criticism of the state in general. We are in favour of a democratic republic as the best form of state for the proletariat under capitalism. But we have no right to forget that wage slavery is the lot of the people even in the most democratic bourgeois republic. Furthermore, every state is a "special force" for the suppression of the oppressed class. Consequently, *every* state is *not* "free" and *not* a "people's state". Marx and Engels explained this repeatedly to their party comrades in the seventies.

Fifthly, the same work of Engels's, whose argument about the withering away of the state everyone remembers, also contains an argument of the signficance of violent revolution. Engels's historical analysis of its role becomes a veritable panegyric on violent revolution. This "no one remembers". It is not done in modern socialist parties to talk or even think about the significance of this idea, and it plays no part whatever in their daily propaganda and agitation among the people. And yet it is inseparably bound up with the "withering away" of the state into one harmonious whole.

Here is Engels's argument:

... That force, however, plays yet another role [other than that of a diabolical power] in history, a revolutionary role; that, in the words of Marx, it is the midwife of every old society which is pregnant with a new one, that it is the instrument with which social movement forces its way through and shatters the dead, fossilised political forms—of this there is not a word in Herr Dühring. It is only with sighs and groans that he admits the possibility that force will perhaps be necessary for the otherthrow of an economy based on exploitation—unfortuantely, because all use of force demoralises, he says, the person who uses it. And this in spite of the immense moral and spiritual impetus which has been given by every victorious revolution! And this in Germany, where a violent collision—which may, after all, be forced on the people—would at least have the advantage of wiping out the servility which has penetrated the nation's mentality following the humiliation of the Thirty Years' War. And this parson's mode of thought—dull, insipid and impotent—presumes to impose itself on the most revolutionary party that history has known! (P. 193, third German edition, Part II, end of Chap. IV.)

How can this panegyric on violent revolution, which Engels insistently brought to the attention of the German Social-Democrats between 1878 and 1894, i.e., right up to the time of his death, be combined with the theory of the "withering away" of the state to form a single theory?

Usually the two are combined by means of eclecticism, by an unprincipled or sophistic selection made arbitrarily (or to please the powers that be) of first one, then another argument, and in ninety-nine cases out of a hundred, if not more, it is the idea of the "withering away" that is placed in the forefront. Dialectics are replaced by eclecticism—this is the most usual, the most widespread practice to be met with in present-day official Social-Democratic literature in relation to Marxism. This sort of substitution is, of course, nothing new; it was observed even in the history of classical Greek philosophy. In falsifying Marxism in opportunist fashion, the substitution of eclecticism for dialectics is the easiest way of deceiving the people. It gives an illusory satisfaction; it seems to take into account all sides of the process, all trends of development, all the conflicting influences, and so forth, whereas in reality it provides no integral and revolutionary conception of the process of social development at all.

We have already said above, and shall show more fully later, that the theory of Marx and Engels of the inevitability of a violent revolution refers to the bourgeois state. The latter *cannot* be superseded by the proletarian state (the dictatorship of the proletariat) through the process of "withering away," but, as a general rule, only through a violent revolution. The panegyric Engels sang in its honour, and which fully corresponds to Marx's repeated statements (see the concluding passages of *The Poverty of Philosophy* and the *Communist Manifesto*, with their proud and open proclamation of the inevitability of a violent revolution; see what Marx wrote nearly thirty years later, in criticising the Gotha Programme of 1875, when he mercilessly castigated the opportunist character of that programme)—this panegyric is by no means a mere "impulse", a mere declamation or a polemical sally. The necessity of systematically imbuing the masses with *this* and precisely this view of violent revolution lies at the root of the *entire* theory of Marx and Engels. The betrayal of their theory by the now prevailing social-chauvinist and Kautskyite trends expresses itself strikingly in both these trends ignoring *such* propaganda and agitation.

The supersession of the bourgeois state by the proletarian state is impossible without a violent revolution. The abolition of the proletarian state, i.e., of the state in general, is impossible except through the process of "withering away."

A detailed and concrete elaboration of these views was given by Marx and Engels when they studied each particular revolutionary situation, when they analysed the lessons of the experience of each particular revolution. We shall now pass to this, undoubtedly the most important, part of their theory. . . .

On Imperialism

Half a century ago, when Marx was writing *Capital*, free competition appeared to the overwhelming majority of economists to be a "natural law." Official science tried, by a conspiracy of silence, to kill the works of Marx, who by a theoretical and historical analysis of capitalism had proved that free competition gives rise to the concentration of production, which, in turn, at a certain stage of development, leads to monopoly. Today, monopoly has become a fact. Economists are writing mountains of books in which they describe the diverse manifestations of monopoly, and continue to declare in chorus that "Marxism is refuted." But facts are stubborn things, as the English proverb says, and they have to be reckoned with, whether we like it or not. The facts show that differences between capitalist countries, e.g., in the matter of protection or free trade, only give rise to insignificant variations in the form of monopolies or in the moment of their appearance; and that the rise of monopolies, as the result of the concentration of production, is a general and fundamental law of the present stage of development of capitalism.

For Europe, the time when the new capitalism *definitely* superseded the old can be established with fair precision; it was the beginning of the twentieth century. In one of the latest compilations on the history of the "formation of monopolies," we read:

"Isolated examples of capitalist monopoly could be cited from the period preceding 1860; in these could be discerned the embryo of the forms that are so common today; but all this undoubtedly represents the prehistory of the cartels. The real beginning of modern monopoly goes back, at the earliest, to the sixties. The first important period of development of monopoly commenced with the international industrial depression of the seventies and lasted until the beginning of the nineties." "If we examine the question on a European scale, we will find that the development of free competition reached its apex in the sixties and seventies. It was then that Britain completed the construction of her old-style capitalist organisation. In Germany, this organisation had entered into a fierce struggle with handicraft and domestic industry, and had begun to create for itself its own forms of existence". . . .

This is something quite different from the old free competition between

From V. I. Lenin, *Collected Works*, Vol. 22 (Moscow: Foreign Languages Publishing House, 1964).

manufacturers, scattered and out of touch with one another, and producing for an unknown market. Concentration has reached the point at which it is possible to make an approximate estimate of all sources of raw materials (for example, the iron ore deposits) of a country and even, as we shall see, of several countries, or of the whole world. Not only are such estimates made, but these sources are captured by gigantic monopolist associations. An approximate estimate of the capacity of markets is also made, and the associations "divide" them up amongst themselves by agreement. Skilled labour is monopolised, the best engineers are engaged; the means of transport are captured—railways in America, shipping companies in Europe and America. Capitalism in its imperialist stage leads directly to the most comprehensive socialisation of production; it, so to speak, drags the capitalists, against their will and consciousness, into some sort of a new social order, a transitional one from complete free competition to complete socialisation.

Production becomes social, but appropriation remains private. The social means of production remain the private property of a few. The general framework of formally recognised free competition remains, and the yoke of a few monopolists on the rest of the population becomes a hundred times heavier, more burdensome and intolerable. . . .

The old capitalism has had its day. The new capitalism represents a transition towards something. It is hopeless, of course, to seek for "firm principles and a concrete aim" for the purpose of "reconciling" monopoly with free competition. The admission of the practical men has quite a different ring from the official praises of the charms of "organised" capitalism sung by its apologists, Schulze-Gaevernitz, Liefmann and similar "theoreticians."

At precisely what period were the "new activities" of the big banks finally established? Jeidels gives us a fairly exact answer to this important question:

"The connections between the banks and industrial enterprises, with their new content, their new forms and their new organs, namely, the big banks which are organised on both a centralised and a decentralised basis, were scarcely a characteristic economic phenomenon before the nineties; in one sense, indeed, this initial date may be advanced to the year 1897, when the important 'mergers' took place and when, for the first time, the new form of decentralised organisation was introduced to suit the industrial policy of the banks. This starting-point could perhaps be placed at an even later date, for it was the crisis of 1900 that enormously accelerated and intensified the process of concentration of industry and of banking, consolidated that process, for the first time transformed the connection with industry into the actual monopoly of the big banks, and made this connection much closer and more active."

Thus, the twentieth century marks the turning-point from the old capitalism to the new, from the domination of capital in general to the domination of finance capital. . . .

DIVISION OF THE WORLD AMONG CAPITALIST ASSOCIATIONS

Monopolist capitalist associations, cartels, syndicates and trusts first divided the home market among themselves and obtained more or less complete possession of the industry of their own country. But under capitalism the home market is inevitably bound up with the foreign market. Capitalism long ago created a world market. As the export of capital increased, and as the foreign and colonial connections and "spheres of influence" of the big monopolist associations expanded in all ways, things "naturally" gravitated towards an international agreement among these associations, and towards the formation of international cartels.

.   .   .

Colonial policy and imperialism existed before the latest stage of capitalism, and even before capitalism. Rome, founded on slavery, pursued a colonial policy and practised imperialism. But "general" disquisitions on imperialism, which ignore, or put into the background, the fundamental difference between socio-economic formations, inevitably turn into the most vapid banality or bragging, like the comparison: "Greater Rome and Greater Britain." Even the capitalist colonial policy of *previous* stages of capitalism is essentially different from the colonial policy of finance capital.

The principal feature of the latest stage of capitalism is the domination of monopolist associations of big employers. These monopolies are most firmly established when *all* the sources of raw materials are captured by one group, and we have seen with what zeal the international capitalist associations exert every effort to deprive their rivals of all opportunity of competing, to buy up, for example, ironfields, oilfields, etc. Colonial possession alone gives the monopolies complete guarantee against all contingencies in the struggle against competitors, including the case of the adversary wanting to be protected by a law establishing a state monopoly. The more capitalism is developed, the more strongly the shortage of raw materials is felt, the more intense the competition and the hunt for sources of raw materials throughout the whole world, the more desperate the struggle for the acquisition of colonies.

"It may be asserted," writes Schilder, "although it may sound paradoxical to some, that in the more or less foreseeable future the growth of the urban and industrial population is more likely to be hindered by a shortage of raw materials for industry than by a shortage of food." For example, there is a growing shortage of timber—the price of which is steadily rising—of leather, and of raw materials for the textile industry. "Associations of manufacturers are making efforts to create an equilibrium between agriculture and industry in the whole of world economy; as an example of this we might mention the International Federation of Cotton Spinners' Associations in several of the most important industrial countries, founded in 1904, and the European Federation of Flax Spinners' Associations, founded on the same model in 1910."

Of course, the bourgeois reformists, and among them particularly the present-day adherents of Kautsky, try to belittle the importance of facts of this kind by arguing that raw materials "could be" obtained in the open market without a "costly and dangerous" colonial policy; and that the supply of raw materials "could be" increased enormously by "simply" improving conditions in agriculture in general. But such arguments become an apology for imperialism, an attempt to paint it in bright colours, because they ignore the principal feature of the latest stage of capitalism: monopolies. The free market is becoming more and more a thing of the past; monopolist syndicates and trusts are restricting it with every passing day, and "simply" improving conditions in agriculture means improving the conditions of the masses, raising wages and reducing profits. Where, except in the imagination of sentimental reformists, are there any trusts capable of concerning themselves with the condition of the masses instead of the conquest of colonies?

Finance capital is interested not only in the already discovered sources of raw materials but also in potential sources, because present-day technical development is extremely rapid, and land which is useless today may be improved tomorrow if new methods are devised (to this end a big bank can equip a special expedition of engineers, agricultural experts, etc.), and if large amounts of capital are invested. This also applies to prospecting for minerals, to new methods of processing up and utilising raw materials, etc., etc. Hence, the inevitable striving of finance capital to enlarge its spheres of influence and even its actual territory. In the same way that the trusts capitalise their property at two or three times its value, taking into account its "potential" (and not actual) profits and the further results of monopoly, so finance capital in general strives to seize the largest possible amount of land of all kinds in all places, and by every means, taking into account potential sources of raw materials and fearing to be left behind in the fierce struggle for the last remnants of independent territory, or for the repartition of those territories that have been already divided. . . .

. . . If it were necessary to give the briefest possible definition of imperialism we should have to say that imperialism is the monopoly stage of capitalism. Such a definition would include what is most important, for, on the one hand, finance capital is the bank capital of a few very big monopolist banks, merged with the capital of the monopolist associations of industrialists; and, on the other hand, the division of the world is the transition from a colonial policy which has extended without hindrance to territories unseized by any capitalist power, to a colonial policy of monopolist possession of the territory of the world, which has been completely divided up.

By the critique of imperialism, in the broad sense of the term, we mean the attitude of the different classes of society towards imperialist policy in connection with their general ideology.

The enormous dimensions of finance capital concentrated in a few hands and creating an extraordinarily dense and widespread network of relationships and connections which subordinates not only the small and medium, but also the very small capitalists and small masters, on the one hand, and the increasingly intense struggle waged against other national state groups of financiers for the division of the world and domination over other countries, on the other hand, cause the propertied classes to go over entirely to the side of imperialism. "General" enthusiasm over the prospects of imperialism, furious defence of it and painting it in the brightest colours—such are the signs of the times. Imperialist ideology also penetrates the working class. No Chinese Wall separates it from the other classes. The leaders of the present-day, so-called, "Social-Democratic" Party of Germany are justly called "social-imperialists," that is, socialists in words and imperialists in deeds; that as early as 1902, Hobson noted the existence in Britain of "Fabian imperialists" who belonged to the opportunist Fabian Society.

Bourgeois scholars and publicists usually come out in defence of imperialism in a somewhat veiled form; they obscure its complete domination and its deep-going roots, strive to push specific and secondary details into the forefront and do their very best to distract attention from essentials by means of absolutely ridiculous schemes for "reform," such as police supervision of the trusts or banks, etc. Cynical and frank imperialists who are bold enough to admit the absurdity of the idea of reforming the fundamental characteristics of imperialism are a rarer phenomenon. . . .

.   .   .

The questions as to whether it is possible to reform the basis of imperialism, whether to go forward to the further intensification and deepening of the antagonisms which it engenders, or backward, towards allaying these antagonisms, are fundamental questions in the critique of imperialism. Since the specific political features of imperialism are reaction everywhere and increased national oppression due to the oppression of the financial oligarchy and the elimination of free competition, a petty-bourgeois-democratic opposition to imperialism arose at the beginning of the twentieth century in nearly all imperialist countries. Kautsky not only did not trouble to oppose, was not only unable to oppose this petty-bourgeois reformist opposition, which is really reactionary in its economic basis, but became merged with it in practice, and this is precisely where Kautsky and the broad international Kautskian trend deserted Marxism.

In the United States, the imperialist war waged against Spain in 1898 stirred up the opposition of the "anti-imperialists," the last of the Mohicans of bourgeois democracy who declared this war to be "criminal," regarded the annexation of foreign territories as a violation of the Constitution, declared that the treatment of Aguinaldo, leader of the Filipinos (the Americans promised him the independence of his country, but later landed troops and annexed it), was "Jingo treachery," and quoted the words of Lincoln: "When the white man governs himself, that is self-government; but when he governs himself and also governs others, it is no longer self-government; it is despotism."* But as long as all this criticism shrank from recognising the inseverable bond between imperialism and the trusts, and, therefore, between imperialism and the foundations of capitalism, while it shrank from joining the forces engendered by large-scale capitalism and its development—it remained a "pious wish". . . .

Socialism: National or International?

Leon Trotsky

Leon Trotsky (1879-1940) was one of the key figures of the Russian Revolution and a masterful chronicler of that event. Author of *History of the Russian Revolution*, (1930), he was murdered by unknown assassins in Mexico.

The resolution on Dimitroff's report on Fascism is finally here. It is just as longwinded and diffuse as the report itself. Here we will deal only with the first sentence of the first paragraph of the resolution which takes up a bare dozen newspaper lines of *l'Humanité*, but at the same time constitutes the cornerstone of

From Leon Trotsky, "Karl Kiebknecht and Rosa Luxemburg: Martyrs of the Third International," *International Socialist Review*, January 1971, pp. 32-37. Translated from the Russian by John Fairlie and Tom Scott. Copyright 1971, *International Socialist Review*, by permission.

the whole theoretical and strategical structure of the so-called Communist International. Let us examine a little closer what this cornerstone is like. We quote this first sentence literally: *"The final, irrevocable victory of socialism in the land of the Soviets*, a victory of world-historical significance which has enormously enhanced the power and the importance of the Soviet Union as the rampart of the exploited and oppressed of the entire world and has inspired the toilers to the struggle against capitalist exploitation, bourgeois reaction and Fascism, and for peace, freedom and the independence of the peoples." The assertions contained in this sentence, however categorical they may sound, are false to the core. What is the "final, irrevocable victory of socialism in the land of the Soviets" supposed to mean? No official theoretician has tried to explain it to us. The resolution too spares itself the slightest hint of the criteria upon which this assertion is based. We must therefore call to mind all over again the A B C of Marxism. The victory of socialism, especially the "final, irrevocable" one, can only consist in this, that the average productivity of every member of the socialist society is higher, even substantially higher, than that of a capitalist worker. Even the most daring Comintern theoretician will not venture such an assertion with regard to the U.S.S.R. We hope to establish statistically in the near future the still very great backwardness of the Soviet Union with respect to both the national and individual incomes. Our present task requires no such proof. The fact that the Soviet government must needs hold fast to the monopoly of foreign trade, represents a sufficient confirmation of the existing backwardness—despite all the successes—of Soviet economy. For, if the costs of production in the country were lower than the capitalist costs, the monopoly of foreign trade would be superfluous. The latest reform of foreign trade, interpreted by many all-too-superficial observers as a surrender of the foreign trade monopoly, is in reality only a technico-bureaucratic reform, which does not in the least infringe upon the basic pillars of the monopoly. Since, on the other hand, the Soviet bureaucracy bases itself upon the nationalized means of production since the introduction of the Five Year Plan and the collectivization, and on the other hand, the Soviet product is still much dearer than the capitalistic, the Soviet bureaucracy, for the sake of its own preservation, cannot abandon the foreign trade monopoly. This decisive fact—the low productivity of labor power in the Soviet Union—gives the key which puts us in a position to open up all the other secrets.

If the per capita national income were calculated in the U.S.S.R. approximately as high as in the United States of America, and if the bureaucracy were not to squander unproductively and consume parasitically a much too large part of it, then the standard of living of the population would have to be incomparably higher than in the capitalist countries, the United States included. But that is not the case in the slightest degree. The Russian peasant, that is, the overwhelming mass of the population, still lives in deep poverty. Even the position of the majority of the industrial proletariat has not yet attained the American, nor even the European level. The honest establishment of this fact naturally says nothing, in any respect, against the socialist mode of production, for in the case of capitalism we are dealing with a decomposing system and in the case of socialism with one which is just in its incipiency. We ought not, however, content ourself with the general tendencies of development, but must characterize quite accurately the stage attained, else we lose ourselves in meaningless commonplaces.

If the socialist society gave its members a half-way assured well-being with the perspective of an uninterrupted improvement of the position of everyone, then the burning worries about individual existence would begin to vanish, covetousness, anxiety and envy would make their appearance merely as increasingly rare remnants of the old state of affairs, economic solidarity would pass from a principle into the daily customs. That this is not the case in the least, hardly needs to be proved: the creation of a semi-privileged labor aristocracy under the fully-privileged Soviet bureaucracy; the endeavors to translate all relationships of man to man into the language of money; the draconic laws for the protection of state property; finally the truly barbaric law against "criminal" children, all these prove in the most striking, the most irrefutable manner that socialism has yet been far from "irrevocably" assured in that field which is decisive precisely for socialism: *in the consciousness of the people*.

If socialism has "finally, irrevocably" triumphed, as the resolution dares to assert, then why does the political dictatorship continue to exist? Still more, why does it congeal with every passing day into a bureaucratic-Bonapartist régime of insufferable harshness, arbitrariness and rottenness? A guaranteed, an "irrevocably" rooted socialism cannot possibly require an omnipotent bureaucracy, with an absolute ruler on top of it, for the dictatorship in general is after nothing but a state means of preserving and protecting the *menaced* and not the *assured* foundations of the socialist state. The intrepid attempt of many "theoreticians" to refer to *external* dangers, is much too absurd to be taken seriously. A society whose socialist structure is assured, whose internal relations thus repose upon the solidarity of the overwhelming mass, does not require an internal dictatorship for protection from external foes but only a technico-military apparatus, just as it requires a technico-economic apparatus for its welfare.

Also the fear of war in which the Soviet bureaucracy lives and which determines its whole international policy, can only be explained by the fact that the socialist construction, upon which the Soviet bureaucracy bases itself, is, historically speaking, not yet assured. The struggle of the workers' state against an imperilling capitalism is—at least it should be—a component part of the class struggle of the international working class. *War* thus has—at least it should have—the same significance for the workers' state as *revolution* has for the proletariat of the capitalist countries. We are of course against any "premature", artificially evoked revolution, because, given an unfavorable relation of forces, it can lead only to defeat. The same holds true of war. A workers' state should avert it only if it is "premature," that is, if socialism is not yet finally and irrevocably assured. The current view that, internally, socialism is assured but that it may be crushed by military force, is senseless: an economic system which effects a higher productivity of human labor, cannot be overthrown by military measures. The victory of the semi-feudal European coalition over Napoleon did not lead to the destruction of the capitalist development of France but to its acceleration in the rest of Europe. History teaches that the victors—should they be situated on a lower economic and cultural plan than the vanquished—take over the latter's technique, social relationships and culture. It is not military force as such that menaces Soviet socialism, but *cheap commodities* which would follow on the heels of the victorious capitalist armies. Moreover, if socialism were really assured in the Soviet Union in the above-described manner, that is, higher technique, higher productivity, higher well-being of the whole population, higher solidarity, there could be no possible talk of a military victory of the internally torn capitalist states over the Soviet Union.

We thus see how thoroughly false is the most important, the really decisive contention of the Seventh World Congress. Revolutionary Marxists should have said: the technical successes in the U.S.S.R. are very significant; the economic successes lag behind. To guarantee even that "well-being" which obtains in the advanced capitalist countries and to reëducate the population, many years are still required, even if one disregards the internal contradictions and the increasingly destructive role of the Soviet bureaucracy, that is, two factors which are, by themselves, capable of exploding into the air the not yet assured social achievements. The decomposition of capitalism, the thrust of Fascism, the growing war danger, all these processes stride forward much more rapidly than the construction of socialism in the U.S.S.R. Only narrowminded fakers and bureaucratic pietists can think that this candid and honest putting of the question will dampen the "enthusiasm" of the international working class. Revolutionary enthusiasm cannot be permanently nurtured on lies. But lies form the basic pillar of the strategical system of the Comintern. Socialism is irrevocably assured in the U.S.S.R., on one-sixth of the world's surface, if only the world proletariat will help along to leave the Soviet state in peace. Thus the slogan is, not preparation for the international revolution, but the *assurance of peace*. Thence the alliance with the "friends of peace," the substitution of class collaboration for class struggle, the creation of the People's Front with the Radical parties of finance capital, etc., etc. All these means are, already in themselves, incapable of prolonging the peace, to say nothing of assuring it. Yet the whole peace program of the Comintern is strategically built upon the premise of an internally "assured" socialism. With this premise, the Seventh World Congress stands and falls, and it is, as indicated above, irrevocably false.

The Role of the Individual in History

George V. Plekhanov

George V. Plekhanov (1856-1918) was a leading figure in the Russian Marxist movement. He collaborated with Lenin in the publication of the revolutionary newspaper *Iskra*. Later he broke with the Bolsheviks on tactical issues. His main books include *Art and Social Life* (1953), *Anarchism and Socialism* (1895), *Essays in the History of Materialism* (1934), and *The Materialist Conception of History* (1940).

Let us, however, examine more closely the case when a man's own—past, present or future—actions seem to him to be entirely colored by necessity. We know already that such a man, regarding himself as a messenger of God, like Mohammed, as one chosen by ineluctable destiny, like Napoleon, or as the expression of the irresistible force of historical progress, like some of the public men in the nineteenth century, displays almost elemental strength of will, and sweeps from his path like a house of cards all the obstacles set up by the small-town Hamlets and Hamletkins.[1] But this case interests us now from another angle, namely, as follows: When the consciousness of my lack of free will presents itself to me only in the form of the complete subjective and objective impossibility of acting differently from the way I am acting, and when, at the same time, my actions are to me the most desirable of all other possible actions, then, in my mind, necessity becomes identified with freedom and freedom with necessity; and then, I am unfree only in the sense *that I cannot disturb this identity between freedom and necessity, I cannot oppose one to the other, I cannot feel the restraint of necessity. But such a lack of freedom* is at the same time its *fullest manifestation.*

Zimmel says that freedom is always freedom from something, and, where freedom is not conceived as the opposite of restraint, it is meaningless. That is so, of course. But this slight, elementary truth cannot serve as a ground for refuting the thesis, which constitutes one of the most brilliant discoveries ever made by philosophic thought, that freedom means being conscious of necessity. Zimmel's definition is too narrow; it applies only to freedom from external restraint. As long

From George V. Plekhanov, "The Role of the Individual in History," an appendix in *Fundamental Problems of Marxism* (New York: International Publishers Co., Inc., 1929). Reprinted by permission of International Publishers Co., Inc.

[1] We will quote another example, which vividly illustrates how strongly people of this category feel. In a letter to her teacher, Calvin Renée, Duchess of Ferrara (of the house of Louis XII) wrote as follows: "No, I have not forgotten what you wrote to me: that David bore mortal hatred towards the enemies of God. And I will never act differently, for if I knew that the King, my father, the Queen, my mother, the late lord, my husband (*feu monsieur mon mari*) and all my children had been cast out by God, I would hate them with a mortal hatred and would wish them in Hell," etc. What terrible, all-destroying energy the people who felt like this could display! And yet these people denied that there was such a thing as free will.

as we are discussing only such restraints it would be extremely ridiculous to identify freedom with necessity: a pick-pocket is not free to steal your pocket-handkerchief while you are preventing him from doing so and until he has overcome your resistance in one way or another. In addition to this elementary and superficial conception of freedom, however, there is another, incomparably more profound. For those who are incapable of thinking philosophically this concept does not exist at all; and those who are capable of thinking philosophically grasp it only when they have cast off dualism and realize that, contrary to the assumption of the dualists, there is no gulf between the subject and the object.

The Russian subjectivist opposes his utopian ideals to our capitalist reality and goes no further. The subjectivists have stuck in the bog of *dualism*. The ideals of the so-called Russian "disciples"[2] resemble capitalist reality far less than the ideals of the subjectivists. Notwithstanding this, however, the "disciples" have found a bridge which unites ideals with reality. The "disciples" have elevated themselves to *monism*. In their opinion, capitalism, in the course of its development, will lead to its own negation and to the realization of their, the Russian "disciples' "—and not only the Russian—ideals. This is historical *necessity*. *The "disciple" serves as an instrument of this necessity and cannot help doing so,* owing to his social status and to his mentality and temperament, which were created by his status. This, too, is an *aspect of necessity*. Since his social status has imbued him with this character and no other, he not only serves as an instrument of necessity and cannot help doing so, but he *passionately desires, and cannot help desiring*, to do so. This is *an aspect of freedom*, and, moreover, of freedom that has grown out of necessity, *i.e.,* to put it more correctly, it is freedom that is identical with necessity—it is necessity transformed into freedom.[3] *This* freedom is also freedom from a certain amount of restraint; it is also the antithesis of a certain amount of restriction. Profound definitions do not refute superficial ones, but, supplementing them, include them in themselves. But what sort of restraint, what sort of restriction, is in question in this case? This is clear: the moral restraint which curbs the energy of those who have not cast off dualism, the restriction suffered by those who are unable to bridge the gulf between ideals and reality. Until the individual has won *this* freedom by heroic effort in philosophical thinking he does not fully belong to himself, and his mental tortures are the shameful tribute he pays to external necessity that stands opposed to him. But as soon as this individual throws off the yoke of this painful and shameful restriction he is born for a new, full and hitherto never experienced life; and his *free* actions become the *conscious and free* expression of necessity. Then he will become a great social force; and then nothing can, and nothing will, prevent him from

> Bursting on cunning falsehood
> Like a storm of wrath divine. . . .

Again, being conscious of the absolute inevitability of a given phenomenon can only increase the energy of a man who sympathizes with it and who regards himself as one of the forces which called it into being. If such a man, conscious of the inevitability of this phenomenon, folded his arms and did nothing, he would show

---

[2] The Marxists. (Translator's note)

[3] "Necessity becomes freedom, not by disappearing, but only by the external expression of their inner identity." Hegel, *Wissenschaft der Logik*, Nurnberg, 1816.

that he was ignorant of arithmetic. Indeed, let us suppose that phenomenon A must necessarily take place under a given sum of circumstances. You have proved to me that a part of this sum of circumstances already exists and that the other part will exist in a given time, T. Being convinced of this, I, the man who sympathizes with phenomenon A, exclaim: "Good!" and then go to sleep until the happy day when the event you have foretold takes place. What will be the result? The following. In your calculations, the sum of circumstances, necessary to bring about phenomenon A, included *my activities*, equal, let us say to *a*. As, however, I am immersed in deep slumber, the sum of circumstances favorable for the given phenomenon at time T will be, not S, but S − *a* which changes the situation. Perhaps my place will be taken by another man, who was also on the point of inaction, but was saved by the sight of my apathy, which to him appeared to be pernicious. In that case, force *a* will be replaced by force *b*, and if *a* equals *b* ($a = b$), the sum of circumstances favorable for A will remain equal to S, and phenomenon A will take place, after all, at time T.

But if my force cannot be regarded as being equal to zero, if I am a skilful and capable worker, and nobody has replaced me, then we will not have the full sum S, and phenomenon A will take place later than we assumed, or not as fully as we expected, or it may not take place at all. This is as clear as daylight; and if I do not understand it, if I think that S remains S even after I am replaced, it is only because I am unable to count. But am I the only one who is unable to count? You, who prophesied that the sum S would certainly be available at time T, did not foresee that I would go to sleep immediately after my conversation with you; you were convinced that I would remain a good worker to the end; the force was less reliable than you thought. Hence, you, too, counted badly. But let us suppose that you had made no mistake, that you had made allowance for everything. In that case, your calculations will assume the following form: you say that at time T the sum S will be available. This sum of circumstances will include my replacement as a *negative magnitude*; and it will also include, as a *positive magnitude*, the stimulating effect on strong-minded men of the conviction that their strivings and ideals are the subjective expression of objective necessity. In that case, the sum S will indeed be available at the time you appointed, and phenomenon A will take place. I think this is clear. But if this is clear, why was I confused by the idea that phenomenon A was inevitable? Why did it seem to me that it condemned me to inaction? Why, in discussing it, did I forget the simplest rules of arithmetic? Probably because, owing to the circumstances of my upbringing, I already had a very strong leaning towards inaction and my conversation with you served as the drop which filled the cup of this laudable inclination to overflowing. That is all. *Only in this sense—as the cause that revealed my moral flabbiness and uselessness—did the consciousness of necessity figure here.* It cannot possibly be regarded as the *cause* of this flabbiness: the causes of it are the circumstances of my upbringing. And so ... and so—arithmetic is a very respectable and useful science, the rules of which should not be forgotten even by—I would say, particularly by—philosophers.

But what effect will the consciousness of the necessity of a given phenomenon have upon a strong man who does *not sympathize* with it and *resists* its taking place? Here the situation is somewhat different. It is very possible that it will cause the vigor of his resistance to *relax*. But when do the opponents of a given phenomenon become convinced that it is inevitable? When the circumstances favorable to it are very numerous and very strong. The fact that its opponents realize that the phenomenon is inevitable, and the relaxation of their energy are merely manifestations of the force of circumstances favorable to it. These manifestations, in their turn, are a part of the favorable circumstances.

But the vigor of resistance will not be relaxed among all the opponents; among some of them the consciousness that the phenomenon is inevitable will cause it to grow and become transformed into the vigor of *despair*. History in general, and the history of Russia in particular, provides not a few instructive examples of this sort of vigor. We hope the reader will be able to recall these without our assistance.

Here we are interrupted by Mr. Kareyev,[4] who, while, of course, disagreeing with our views on freedom and necessity, and, moreover disapproving of our partiality for the "extremes" to which strong men go, nevertheless, is pleased to meet in the pages of our journal the idea that the individual may be a great social force. The worthy professor joyfully exclaims: "I have always said that!" And this is true. Mr. Kareyev, and all the subjectivists, have always ascribed a very important role to the individual in history. And there was a time when they enjoyed considerable sympathy among advanced young people who were imbued with noble strivings to work for the common weal and were, therefore, naturally inclined to attach great importance to individual initiative. In essence, however, the subjectivists have never been able to solve, or even to present properly, the problem of the role of the individual in history. As against the influence of the *laws* of social-historical progress, they advanced the "activities of critically thinking individuals," and thus created, as it were, a new species of the factors theory; critically thinking individuals were *one factor* of this progress; its own laws were the *other* factor. This resulted in an extreme incongruity, which one could put up with as long as the attention of the active "individuals" was concentrated on the practical problems of the day and they had no time to devote to philosophical problems. But the calm which ensued in the 'eighties gave those who were capable of thinking enforced leisure for philosophical reflection, and since then the subjectivist doctrine has been bursting at all its seams, and even falling to pieces, like the celebrated overcoat of Akakii Akakievich. No amount of patching was any use, and one after another thinking people began to reject subjectivism as an obviously and utterly unsound doctrine. As always happens in such cases, however, the reaction against this doctrine caused some of its opponents to go to the opposite extreme. While some subjectivists, striving to ascribe the widest possible role to the "individual" in history, refused to recognize the historical progress of mankind as a process expressing laws, some of their later opponents, striving to bring out more sharply the coherent character of this progress, were evidently prepared to forget that *men make history, and, therefore, the activities of individuals cannot help being important in history*. They have declared the individual to be a *quantité négligeable*. In theory, this extreme is as impermissible as the one reached by the more ardent subjectivists. It is as unsound to sacrifice the *thesis to the antithesis* as to forget the *antithesis* for the sake of the *thesis*. The correct point of view will be found only when we succeed in uniting the points of truth contained in them into a *synthesis.*[5]

This problem has been interesting us for a long time, and we have long wanted to

---

[4] N. I. Kareyev, born 1850, formerly professor of history at St. Petersburg University.

[5] In our striving for a synthesis, we were forestalled by the same Mr. Kareyev. Unfortunately, however, he went no farther than to admit the truism that man consists of a soul and a body.

invite our readers to join us in tackling it. We were restrained, however, by certain fears: we thought that perhaps our readers had already solved it for themselves and that our proposal would be belated. These fears have now been dispelled. The German historians have dispelled them for us. We are quite serious in saying this. The fact of the matter is that lately a rather heated controversy has been going on among the German historians over great men in history. Some have been inclined to regard the political activities of these men as the main and almost the *only* spring of historical development, while others have been asserting that such a view is one-sided and that the science of history must have in view, not only the activities of great men, and not only political history, but historical life as a whole (*das Ganze des geschichtilichen Lebens*). One of the representatives of the latter trend is Karl Lamprecht, author of *The History of the German People*. Lamprecht's opponents accused him of being a *"collectivist"* and a materialist; he was even placed on a par with—*horrible dictu*—the "Social-Democratic atheists," as he expressed it in winding up the debate. When we became acquainted with his views we found that the accusations hurled against this poor savant were utterly groundless. At the same time we were convinced that the present-day German historians were incapable of solving the problem of the role of the individual in history. We then decided that we had a right to assume that the problem was still unsolved even for a number of Russian readers, and that something could still be said about it that would not be altogether lacking in theoretical and practical interest.

Lamprecht gathered a whole collection (*eine artige Sammlung*, as he expresses it) of the views of prominent statesmen on their own activities in the historical milieu in which they pursued them; in his polemics, however, he confined himself for the time being to references to some of the speeches and opinions of *Bismarck*. He quoted the following words, uttered by the Iron Chancellor in the North German Reichstag on April 16, 1869:

Gentlemen, we can neither ignore the history of the past nor create the future. I would like to warn you against the mistake that causes people to advance the hands of their clocks, thinking that thereby they are hastening the passage of time. My influence on the events I took advantage of is usually exaggerated; but it would never occur to anyone to demand that I should make history. I could not do that even in conjunction with you, although together, we could resist the whole world. We cannot make history: we must wait while it is being made. We will not make fruit ripen more quickly by subjecting it to the heat of a lamp; and if we pluck the fruit before it is ripe we will only prevent its growth and spoil it.

Referring to the evidence of Joly, Lamprecht also quotes the opinions which Bismarck expressed more than once during the Franco-Prussian war. Again, the idea that runs through these opinions is that "we cannot make great historical events, but must adapt ourselves to the natural course of things and limit ourselves to securing what is already ripe." Lamprecht regards this as the profound and whole truth. In his opinion, a modern historian cannot think otherwise, provided he is able to peer into the depths of events and not restrict his field of vision to too short an interval of time. Could Bismarck have caused Germany to revert to natural economy? He would have been unable to do this even when he was at the height of his power. General historical circumstances are stronger than the strongest individuals. For a great man, the general character of his epoch is *"empirically given necessity."*

This is how Lamprecht reasons, calling his view a *universal* one. It is not difficult to see the weak side of this "universal" view. The above-quoted opinions of Bismarck are very interesting as a psychological document. One may not sympathize with the activities of the late German Chancellor, but one cannot say that they were insignificant, that Bismarck was distinguished for "quietism." It was about him that Lasalle said: "The servants of reaction are no orators; but God grant that progress has servants like them." And yet this man, who at times displayed truly iron energy, considered himself absolutely impotent in face of the natural course of things, evidently regarding himself as a simple instrument of historical development; this proves once again that one can see phenomena in the light of necessity and at the same time be a very energetic statesman. But it is only in this respect that Bismarck's opinions are interesting; they cannot be regarded as a solution of the problems of the role of the individual in history. According to Bismarck, events occur of themselves, and we can secure what they prepare for us. But every act of "securing" is also an historical event; what is the difference between such events and those that occur of themselves? Actually, nearly every historical event is simultaneously an act of "securing" by somebody of the already ripened fruit of preceding development and a link in the chain of events which are preparing the fruits of the future. How can acts of "securing" be opposed to the natural course of things? Evidently, Bismarck wanted to say that individuals and groups of individuals operating history never were and never will be all-powerful. This, of course, is beyond all doubt. Nevertheless, we would like to know what their power, far from omnipotence, of course, depends on; under what circumstances it grows and under what circumstances it diminishes. Neither Bismarck nor the learned advocate of the "universal" conception of history who quotes him answers these questions.

It is true that Lamprecht gives us more reasonable quotations.[6] For example, he quotes the following words of Monod, one of the most prominent representatives of contemporary historical science in France:

Historians are too much in the habit of paying attention only to the brilliant, clamorous and ephemeral manifestations of human activity, to great events and great men, (instead of depicting the great and slow changes of economic conditions and social institutions, which constitute the really interesting and intransient part of human development)—the part which, to a certain extent, may be reduced to laws and subjected, to a certain extent, to exact analysis. Indeed, important events and individuals are important precisely as signs and symbols of different moments of the aforesaid development. But most of the events that are called historical have the same relation to real history as the waves which rise up from the surface of the sea, gleam in the light for a moment and break on the sandy shore, leaving no trace behind them, have to the deep and constant motion of the tides.

Lamprecht declares that he is prepared to put his signature to every one of these words. It is well known that German savants are reluctant to agree with French savants and the French are reluctant to agree with the German. That is why the Belgian historian Pirenne was particularly pleased to emphasize in *Revue Historique* the fact that Monod's conception of history coincides with that of Lamprecht. "This harmony is extremely significant," he observed. "Evidently, it shows that the future belongs to the new conception of history."

[6] Leaving aside Lamprecht's other philosophical and historical essays, we refer to his essay, "Der Ausgang des geschichtswissenschaftlichen Kampfes," *Die Zukunft*, 1897, No. 41.

We do not share Pirenne's pleasant expectations. The future cannot belong to vague and indefinite views, and such, precisely, are the views of Monod and particularly of Lamprecht. Of course, one cannot but welcome a trend which declares that the most important task of the science of history is to study social institutions and economic conditions. This science will make great progress when such a trend becomes definitely consolidated. In the first place, however, Pirenne is wrong in thinking that this is a new trend. It arose in the science of history as far back as the twenties of the nineteenth century: Guizot, Mignet, Augustin Thierry and, subsequently, Tocqueville and others, were its brilliant and consistent representatives. The views of Monod and Lamprecht are but a faint copy of an old but excellent original. Secondly, profound as the views of Guizot, Mignet and the other French historians may have been for their time, much in them has remained unelucidated. They do not provide a full and definite solution of the problem of the role of the individual in history. And the science of history must provide this solution if its representatives are destined to rid themselves of their one-sided conception of their subject. The future belongs to the school that finds the best solution of this problem, among others.

The views of Guizot, Mignet and the other historians who belonged to this trend were a reaction against the views on history that prevailed in the eighteenth century and constituted their *antithesis*. In the eighteenth century the students of the philosophy of history reduced everything to the *conscious activities of individuals*. True, there were exceptions to the rule even at that time: the philosophical-historical field of vision of Vico, Montesquieu and Herder, for example, was much wider. But we are not speaking of exceptions; the great majority of the thinkers of the eighteenth century regarded history exactly in the way we have described. In this connection it is very interesting to peruse once again the historical works of Mably, for example. According to Mably, Minos created the whole of the social and political life and ethics of the Cretes, while Lycurgus performed the same service for Sparta. If the Spartans "spurned" material wealth, it was due entirely to Lycurgus, who "descended, so to speak, into the depths of the hearts of his fellow-citizens and there crushed the germ of love for wealth" (*descendit pour ainsi dire jusque dans le fond du cœur des citoyens*, etc.).[7] And if, subsequently, the Spartans strayed from the path the wise Lycurgus had pointed out to them, the blame for this rests on Lysander, who persuaded them that "new times and new conditions called for new rules and a new policy."[8] Researches written from the point of view of such conceptions have very little affinity with science, and were written as sermons solely for the sake of the moral "lessons" that could be drawn from them. It was against such conceptions that the French historians of the period of the Restoration revolted. After the stupendous events of the end of the eighteenth century it was absolutely impossible to think any longer that history was made by more or less prominent and more or less noble and enlightened individuals who, at their own discretion, imbued the unenlightened but obedient masses with certain sentiments and ideas. Moreover, this philosophy of history offended the plebeian pride of the bourgeois theoreticians. They were prompted by the same feelings that revealed themselves in the eighteenth century in the rise of bourgeois drama. In combating the old conceptions of history, Thierry used the same

[7] *Oeuvres Complètes de l'abbé de Mably*, London 1783 (Vol. IV), pp. 3, 14-22, 24, 192.
[8] *Ibid.*, p. 10.

arguments that were advanced by Beaumarchais and others against the old aesthetics.[9] Lastly, the storms which France had just experienced very clearly revealed that the course of historical events was by no means determined solely by the conscious actions of men; this circumstance alone was enough to suggest the idea that these events were due to the influence of some hidden necessity, operating blindly, like the elemental forces of nature, but in accordance with certain immutable laws. It is an extremely remarkable fact, which nobody, as far as we know, has pointed to before, that the French historians of the period of the Restoration applied the new conception of history as a process conforming to laws most consistently in their works on the French Revolution. This was the case, for example, in the works of Mignet. Chateaubriand called the new school of history *fatalistic*. Formulating the tasks which it set the investigator, he said:

This system demands that the historian shall describe without indignation the most brutal atrocities, speak without love about the highest virtues and with his glacial eye see in social life only the manifestation of irresistible laws due to which every phenomenon occurs exactly as it inevitably had to occur.[10]

This is wrong, of course. The new school did not demand that the historian should be impassive. Augustin Thierry even said quite openly that political passion, by sharpening the mind of the investigator, may serve as a powerful means of discovering the truth.[11] It is sufficient to make oneself only slightly familiar with the historical works of Guizot, Thierry or Mignet to see that they strongly sympathized with the bourgeoisie in its struggle against the lords temporal and spiritual, as well as with its efforts to suppress the demands of the rising proletariat. What is incontrovertible is the following: the new school of history arose in the twenties of the nineteenth century, at a time when the bourgeoisie had already vanquished the aristocracy, although the latter was still striving to restore some of its old privileges. The proud consciousness of the victory of their class was reflected in all the arguments of the historians of the new school. And as the bourgeoisie was never distinguished for knightly chivalry, one can sometimes discern a note of harshness to the vanquished in the arguments of its scientific representatives. "*Le plus fort absorbe le plus faible*," says Guizot, in one of his polemical pamphlets, "*et il est de droit.*" (The strongest absorbs the weakest, and he has a right to do so.) His attitude towards the working class is no less harsh. It was this harshness, which at times assumed the form of calm detachment, that misled Chateaubriand. Moreover, at that time it was not yet quite clear what was meant when it was said that history conformed to certain laws. Lastly, the new school may have appeared to be fatalistic because, striving firmly to adopt this point of view, it paid little attention to the great individuals in history.[12] Those who had been brought up on the

[9] Compare his first letter on *l'Histoire de France* with *l'Essai sur le genre dramatique sérieux* in the first volume of *Oeuvres complètes de Beaumarchais.*

[10] *Oeuvres complètes de Chateaubriand*, Paris, 1804, VII, p. 58. We also recommend the next page to the reader; one might think that it was written by Mr. N. Mikhailovsky. (Populist publicist against whom Plekhanov and Lenin wrote a great deal in defense of Marxism [Translator's note]).

[11] Cf. "Considerations sur l'histoire de France," appendix to *Récits des temps Mérovingiens*, Paris, 1840, p. 72.

[12] In a review of the third edition of Mignet's *History of the French Revolution*, Sainte-Beuve characterized that historian's attitude towards great men as follows: "In face of

historical ideas of the eighteenth century found it difficult to accept this. Objections to the views of the new historians poured in from all sides, and then the controversy flared up, which, as we have seen, has not ended to this day.

In January, 1826, Sainte-Beuve, in a review, in the *Globe*, of the fifth and sixth volumes of Mignet's *History of the French Revolution*, wrote as follows:

At any given moment a man may, by the sudden decision of his will, introduce into the course of events a new, unexpected and changeable force, which may alter that course, but which cannot be measured itself owing to its changeability.

It must not be thought that Sainte-Beuve assumed that "sudden decisions" of human will occur without cause. No, that would have been too naïve. He merely asserted that the mental and moral qualities of a man who is playing a more or less important role in public life, his talent, knowledge, resoluteness or irresoluteness, courage or cowardice, etc., cannot help having a marked influence on the course and outcome of events; and yet these qualities cannot be explained solely by the general laws of development of a nation; they are always, and to a considerable degree, acquired as a result of the action of what may be called the accidents of private life. We will quote a few examples to explain this idea, which, incidentally, seems to me clear enough as it is.

During the War of the Austrian Succession the French army achieved several brilliant victories and it seemed that France was in a position to compel Austria to cede fairly extensive territory in what is now Belgium; but Louis XV did not claim this territory because, as he said, he was fighting as a king and not as a merchant, and France got nothing out of the Peace of Aix-la-Chapelle. If, however, Louis XV had been a man of a different character, the territory of France would have been enlarged and as a result her economic and political development would have taken a somewhat different course.

As is well known, France waged the Seven Years' War in alliance with Austria. It is said that this alliance was concluded as a result of the strong pressure of Madame Pompadour, who had been extremely flattered by the fact that, in a letter to her, proud Maria-Theresa had called her "cousin" or "dear friend" (*bien bonne amie*). Hence, one can say that had Louis XV been a man of stricter morals, or had he submitted less to his favorite's influence, Madame Pompadour would not have been able to influence the course of events to the extent that she did, and they would have taken a different turn.

Further, France was unsuccessful in the Seven Years' War: her generals suffered several very shameful defeats. Speaking generally, their conduct was very strange, to say the least. Richelieu engaged in plunder, and Soubise and Broglie were constantly hindering each other. For example, when Broglie was attacking the enemy at Villinghausen, Soubise heard the gunfire, but did not go to his comrade's assistance, as had been arranged, and as he undoubtedly should have done, and Broglie was obliged to retreat.[13] The extremely incompetent Soubise enjoyed the

the vast and profound popular emotions which he had to describe, and of the impotence and nullity to which the sublimest genius and the saintliest virtue are reduce; when the masses arise, he was seized with pity for men as individuals, could see in them, taken in isolation, only their weakness, and would not allow them to be capable of effective action, except through union with the multitude."

[13] Incidentally, others say that Broglie was to blame for not waiting for his comrade, as he did not want to share the laurels of victory with him. This makes no difference to us, as it does not alter the case in the least.

protection of the aforesaid Madame Pompadour. We can say again that had Louis XV been less lascivious, or had his favorite refrained from interfering in politics, events would not have turned out so unfavorably for France.

French historians say that there was no need at all for France to wage war on the European continent, and that she should have concentrated all her efforts on the sea in order to resist England's encroachments on her colonies. The fact that she acted differently was again due to the inevitable Madame Pompadour, who wanted to please "her dear friend," Maria-Theresa. As a result of the Seven Years' War, France lost her best colonies, which undoubtedly greatly influenced the development of her economic relations. In this case feminine vanity appears in the role of the influential "factor" of economic development.

Do we need any other examples? We will quote one more, perhaps the most astonishing one. During the aforesaid Seven Years' War, in August, 1761, the Austrian troops, having united with the Russian troops in Silesia, surrounded Frederick near Striegau. Frederick's position was desperate, but the Allies were tardy in attacking, and General Buturlin, after facing the enemy for twenty days, withdrew his troops from Silesia, leaving only a part of his forces as reinforcements for the Austrian General Laudon. Laudon captured Schweidnitz, near which Frederick was encamped, but this victory was of little importance. Suppose, however, Buturlin had been a man of firmer character? Suppose the Allies had attacked Frederick before he had time to entrench himself? They might have routed him, and he would have been compelled to yield to all the victors' demands. And this occurred barely a few months before a new accidental circumstance, the death of Empress Elizabeth, immediately changed the situation greatly in Frederick's favor. We would like to ask: What would have happened had Buturlin been a man of more resolute character, or had a man like Suvorov been in his place?

In examining the views of the "fatalist" historians, Sainte-Beuve gave expression to another opinion which is also worthy of attention. In the aforementioned review of Mignet's *History of the French Revolution*, he argued that the course and outcome of the French Revolution were determined, not only by the general causes which had given rise to the Revolution, and not only by the passions which in its turn the Revolution had roused, but also by numerous minor phenomena, which had escaped the attention of the investigator, and which were not even a part of social phenomena, properly so called. He wrote:

While these passions [roused by social phenomena] were operating, the physical and physiological forces of nature were not inactive: stones continued to obey the law of gravity; the blood did not cease to circulate in the veins. Would not the course of events have changed had Mirabeau, say, not died of fever, had Robespierre been killed by the accidental fall of a brick or by a stroke of apoplexy, or if Bonaparte had been struck down by a bullet? And will you dare to assert that the outcome would have been the same? Given a sufficient number of accidents, similar to those I have assumed, the outcome might have been the very opposite of what, in your opinion, was inevitable. I have a right to assume the possibility of such accidents because they are precluded neither by the general causes of the Revolution nor by the passions roused by these general causes.

Then he goes on to quote the well-known observation that history would have taken an entirely different course had Cleopatra's nose been somewhat shorter; and, in conclusion, admitting that very much more could be said in defense of Mignet's view, he again shows where this author goes wrong. Mignet ascribes solely to the action of general causes those results which many other, minor, dark and elusive causes had helped to bring about; his stern logic, as it were, refuses to recognize the existence of anything that seems to him to be lacking in order and law.

Are Sainte-Beuve's objections sound? I think they contain a certain amount of truth. But what amount? To determine this we will first examine the idea that a man can "by the sudden decision of his will" introduce a new force into the course of events which is capable of changing their course considerably. We have quoted a number of examples, which, we think, very well explain this. Let us ponder over these examples.

Everybody knows that, during the reign of Louis XV, military affairs went steadily from bad to worse in France. As Henri Martin has observed, during the Seven Years' War, the French army, which always had numerous prostitutes, tradesmen and servants in its train, and which had three times as many pack horses as saddle horses, had more resemblance to the hordes of Darius and Xerxes than to the armies of Turenne and Gustavus-Adolphus.[14] Archenholtz says in his history of this war that the French officers, when appointed for guard duty, often deserted their posts to go dancing somewhere in the vicinity, and obeyed the orders of their superiors only when they thought fit. This deplorable state of military affairs was due to the deterioration of the aristocracy, which nevertheless, continued to occupy all the high posts in the army, and to the general dislocation of the "old order," which was rapidly drifting to its doom. These *general* causes alone would have been quite sufficient to make the outcome of the Seven Years' War unfavorable to France. But undoubtedly the incompetence of generals like Soubise greatly increased the chances of failure for the French army which these general causes already provided. Soubise retained his post, thanks to Madame Pompadour; and so we must count the proud Marquise as one of the "factors" significantly reinforcing the unfavorable influence of these general causes on the position of French affairs.

The Marquise de Pompadour was strong not by her own strength, but by the power of the king who was subject to her will. Can we say that the character of Louis XV was exactly what it was inevitably bound to be, in view of the general course of development of social relations in France? No, given the same course of development a king might have appeared in his place with a different attitude towards women. Sainte-Beuve would say that the action of obscure and intangible physiological causes was sufficient to account for this. And he would be right. But, if that is so, the conclusion emerges, that these obscure physiological causes, by affecting the progress and results of the Seven Years' War, also in consequence affected the subsequent development of France, which would have proceeded differently if the Seven Years' War had not deprived her of a great part of her colonies. Does not this conclusion, we then ask, contradict the conception of a social development conforming to laws?

No, not in the least. The effect of personal peculiarities in the instances we have discussed is undeniable; but no less undeniable is the fact that it could occur only *in the given social conditions*. After the battle of Rosbach, the French became fiercely indignant with Soubise's protectress. Every day she received numbers of anonymous letters, full of threats and abuse. This very seriously disturbed Madame Pompadour; she began to suffer from insomnia.[15] Nevertheless, she continued to

[14] *Histoire de France*, 4th edition, Vol. XV, pp. 520-21.
[15] Cf. *Mémoires de madame du Haliffet*, Paris, 1824, p. 181.

protect Soubise. In 1762, she remarked in one of her letters to him that he was not justifying the hopes that had been placed in him, but she added: "Have no fear, however, I will take care of your interests and try to reconcile you with the king."[16] As you see, she did not yield to public opinion. Why did she not yield? Probably because French society of that day *had no means of compelling* her to do so. But why was French society of that day unable to do so? It was prevented from doing so by its form of organization, which in turn, was determined by the relation of social forces in France at that time. Hence, it is the relation of social forces which, in the last analysis, explains the fact that Louis XV's character, and the caprices of his favorite, could have such a deplorable influence on the fate of France. Had it not been the king who had a weakness for the fair sex, but the king's cook or groom, it would not have had any historical significance. Clearly, it is not the weakness that is important here, but the social position of the person afflicted with it. The reader will understand that these arguments can be applied to all the above-quoted examples. In these arguments it is necessary to change only what needs changing, for example, to put Russia in the place of France, Buturlin in place of Soubise, etc. That is why we will not repeat them.

It follows, then, that by virtue of particular traits of their character, individuals can influence the fate of society. Sometimes this influence is very considerable; but the possibility of exercising this influence, and its extent, are determined by the form of organization of society, by the relation of forces within it. The character of an individual is a "factor" in social development only where, when, and to the extent that social relations permit it to be such.

We may be told that the extent of personal influence may also be determined by the talents of the individual. We agree. But the individual can display his talents only when he occupies the position in society necessary for this. Why was the fate of France in the hands of a man who totally lacked the ability and desire to serve society? Because such was the form of organization of that society. It is the form of organization that in any given period determines the role and, consequently, the social significance that may fall to the lot of talented or incompetent individuals.

But if the role of individuals is determined by the form of organization of society, how can their social influence, which is determined by the role they play, contradict the conception of social development as a process expressing laws? It does not contradict it; on the contrary, it serves as one of its most vivid illustrations.

But here we must observe the following. The possibility—determined by the form of organization of society—that individuals may exercise social influence opens the door to the influence of so-called *accident* upon the historical destiny of nations. Louis XV's lasciviousness was an inevitable consequence of the state of his physical constitution, but in relation to the general course of France's development the state of his constitution was *accidental*. Nevertheless, as we have said, it did influence the fate of France and served as one of the causes which determined this fate. The death of Mirabeau, of course, was due to pathological processes which obeyed definite laws. The inevitability of these processes, however, did not arise out of the general course of France's development, but out of certain particular features of the celebrated orator's constitution, and out of the physical conditions under which he had contracted his disease. In relation to the general course of France's development these features and conditions were *accidental*. And yet,

[16] Cf. *Lettres de la marquise de Pompadour*, London, 1772, Vol. I.

Mirabeau's death influenced the further course of the Revolution and served as one of the causes which determined it.

Still more astonishing was the effect of accidental causes in the above-mentioned example of Frederick II, who succeeded in extricating himself from an extremely difficult situation only because of Buturlin's irresolution. Even in relation to the general course of Russia's development Buturlin's appointment may have been accidental, in the sense that we have defined that term, and, of course, it had no relation whatever to the general course of Prussia's development. Yet it is not improbable that Buturlin's irresolution saved Frederick from a desperate situation. Had Suvorov been in Buturlin's place, the history of Prussia might have taken a different course. It follows, then, that sometimes the fate of nations depends on accidents, which may be called *accidents of the second degree.* *"In allem Endlichen ist ein Element des Zufälligen,"* said Hegel. (In everything finite there are accidental elements.) In science we deal only with the "finite"; hence we can say that all the processes studied by science contain some accidental elements. Does not this preclude the scientific cognition of phenomena? No. *Accident is something relative.* It appears only at the point of intersection of *inevitable* processes. For the inhabitants of Mexico and Peru, the appearance of Europeans in America was *accidental* in the sense that it did not follow from the social development of these countries. But the passion for navigation which possessed West Europeans at the end of the Middle Ages was not accidental; nor was the fact that the European forces easily overcame the resistance of the natives. The consequences of the conquest of Mexico and Peru by Europeans were also not accidental, in the last analysis, these consequences were determined by the resultant of two forces: the economic position of the conquered countries on the one hand, and the economic position of the conquerors on the other. And these forces, like their resultant, can fully serve as objects of scientific investigation.

The accidents of the Seven Years' War exercised considerable influence upon the subsequent history of Prussia. But their influence would have been entirely different at a different stage of Prussia's development. Here, too, the accidental consequences were determined by the resultant of two forces: the social-political conditions of Prussia on the one hand, and the social-political condition of the European countries that influenced her, on the other. Hence, here, too, accidents do not in the least hinder the scientific investigation of phenomena.

We know now that individuals often exercise considerable influence upon the fate of society, but this influence is determined by the internal structure of that society and by its relation to other societies. But this is not all that has to be said about the role of the individual in history. We must approach this question from still another side.

Sainte-Beuve thought that had there been a sufficient number of petty and dark causes of the kind that he had mentioned, the outcome of the French Revolution would have been the *opposite* of what we know it to have been. This is a great mistake. No matter how intricately the petty, psychological and physiological causes may have been interwoven, they would not under any circumstances have eliminated the great social needs that gave rise to the French Revolution; and as long as these needs remained unsatisfied the revolutionary movement in France would have continued. To make the outcome of this movement the opposite of what it was, the needs that gave rise to it would have had to be the opposite of what they were; and this, of course, no combination of petty causes would ever be able to bring about.

The causes of the French Revolution lay in the character of *social relations*; and the petty causes assumed by Sainte-Beuve could lie only in the *personal qualities of individuals*. The final cause of social relationships lies in the state of the productive forces. This depends on the qualities of individuals only in the sense, perhaps, that these individuals possess more or less talent for making technical improvements, discoveries and inventions. Sainte-Beuve did not have these qualities in mind. No other qualities, however, enable individuals directly to influence the state of productive forces, and, hence, the social relations which they determine, *i.e.*, *economic relations*. No matter what the qualities of the given individual may be, they cannot eliminate the given economic relations if the latter conform to the given state of productive forces.

The Individual and Society
Adam Schaff

Adam Schaff (1913-   ) is a Polish sociologist and philosopher who is now President of the European Coordination Center for Research and Documentation in Social Services in Vienna. He is the author of many books, including *Philosophy of Man* (1962) and *Marxism and the Human Individual* (1965).

Man is part of nature as the species *Homo sapiens*, of which human individuals are the specimens. But if the *ontological status* of the individual were confined to this problem only (although this is the most important issue in the struggle against an idealistic, God-centered or, more generally, heteronomous conception), it would be reduced to the existence in every individual of a number of specific species characteristics that are here promoted to the rank of man's "essence"—if the term is taken to express those characteristics that distinguish man from the animal world, that is, are attributes of man, but not of other parts of living nature. In that way, "being human" is reduced to a set of abstract features that are supposed to be "inherent" in every individual, peculiar to him as an element of a class.

Marx protests—and rightly—against this conception of the human individual, for its naturalism is limited and one-sided: it only takes note of the biological aspect as the constituent element of man and ignores the social aspect. Yet the species *Homo sapiens* is distinguished not merely by its biological features but also—and, in a sense, primarily—by its socio-historical characteristics.

In his criticism of Feuerbach, however, Marx uses an inappropriate line of argument (both in *The German Ideology* and the *Theses on Feuerbach*). The point is not that, as Marx expressly states in the sixth "Thesis" by conceiving of the human essence as a species, as a purely natural entity, Feuerbach reduces it to an abstraction inherent in each individual. This would mean that when social bonds appear the situation would change in this respect. But this situation will only change insofar as the constituent features of the individual include not only those arising from the *biological* bond but also those due to the social bond. The sum total of the constituent features will grow and there will be a qualitative change, but the logical status of the conception of the individual will remain the same: each individual will still have a certain set of abstract features which constitute the species, but now these will be not only biological but also social in character.

But this is not what matters most in this context. For, in effect, when the social factor is introduced, the conception of the individual acquires a different *quality*; it becomes *concrete* as compared with the abstract character of the purely biological view that ignores the social involvement of man. Yet man is not only a product of biological evolution, but as a result of this evolution, he is a historical-social product, varying in certain respects which depend on the developmental stage of each society and on the different classes and strata of society. When construed only on the basis of the general biological features common to all human beings, as distinct, for example, from other mammals, man is only an "abstract man," a "man in general"; this is opposed to the concrete interpretation of man on the basis of his social involvement, as a member of a society that has reached a certain stage of historical development, and as a member of a class with a place in the social division of labor, in culture, etc.

Feuerbach's discovery that the human individual is above all a part of nature, a specimen of a biological species, was, in its simplicity, a stroke of genius, banal as it may sound today. No less inspired though its impact still remains fresh was Marx's simple discovery, so closely connected with the further development of historical materialism, that the individual is part of society, enmeshed in concrete human relations—particularly in the field of production—and created by these conditions.

This Marx saw as early as *A Contribution to the Critique of the Hegelian Philosophy of Right*, and expressed it quite clearly in the *Manuscripts* of 1844. Man is both a *product* of society and its *maker*, he says, and because of this he is a social individual:

The individual is the social being. *The manifestation of his life—even when it does not appear directly in the form of a* communal *manifestation, accomplished in association with other men—is therefore a manifestation and affirmation of* social life. *Individual human life and species-life are not* different, *even though the mode of existence of individual life is necessarily a more specific or a more* general *mode of species-life or that of species-life a more* specific *or more* general *mode of individual life. . . .*

Though man is a unique *individual—and it is just has particularity which makes him an individual, a really* individual communal being—he is equally the whole, *the ideal whole, the subjective existence of society as thought and experienced.*

Later, in *A Contribution to the Critique of Political Economy*, Marx gave an excellent commentary of the above exposition. Explaining that the starting point for analysis of production is always the producing individual (in stressing this Marx dissociated himself from every form of what he described as fetishism—a situation in which relations between men are externalized, particularly in the economic market, into relations between the things they produce), he emphasized the point that it is always a *social individual*; and that all the Robinson Crusoes, so fashionable in his day were pure fiction. He did not, however, simply reject these desert island tales, but gave a sociological explanation of their origin. The vision of an *isolated individual* could only have come into being in an atomized free-competition society, but once it did come into being it was easily accepted that this had been the natural state of the individual man. The idea was then read back into the "golden age" of the past. Thus what was a product of history was presented as its point of departure. In reality, however, the individual is always a social individual and all these illusions about him first appeared in the eighteenth century, in the newly emerging bourgeois society.

But the period in which this view of the isolated individual becomes prevalent is the very one in which the interrelations of society (general from this point of view) have reached the highest state of development. Man is in the most literal sense of the word . . . not only a social animal, but an animal which can develop into an individual only in society.

But the conclusions to be drawn from this as far as the concept of the individual is concerned are not restricted to the general statement that man is a part of nature and a part of society; they also require specification of the socio-psychological structure of the individual. "But the human essence," Marx says in the sixth *Thesis on Feurerbach*, "is no abstraction inherent in each single individual. *In its reality it is the ensemble of social relations.*" This statement—often quoted but seldom appreciated, and I fear, seldom understood—I regard as one of the most momentous achievements of Marx's youth, one that paved the way for the further evolution of historical materialism.

Before we deal in more detail with Marx's description of the individual as the totality of social relations, it seems essential to make two points concerning method that should make for a better understanding of the implications and meaning of his statement.

In *The Holy Family*, in a section entitled "The secret of speculative construction," there is an arresting methodological argument about the relationship between the abstract and the concrete, which is of immediate relevance to our subject.

The essence of Hegel's method is to create abstract notions which we absolutize—that is, we imagine them to possess an existence which is independent of us. Then, standing the problem on its head, we try to construct the concrete from this abstraction.

Marx analyzed the predicament of the speculative philosopher, who tried to find a way from the abstraction he has himself created to the concrete and who confuses the normal products of perception with spontaneous mystical processes of abstract ideas. Thus he in effect undertakes the defense of a method whereby the concrete particular is made the basis of analysis. This premise is also valid in the case of anthropology—here it is concrete human individuals that should be the starting point of analysis.

But it is here that we come across a crucial problem in the critique of naturalism: it is not the abstract "man," but living, particular men who should be the point of departure. And yet what does "particular" mean in this context?

Marx gave an explicit answer much later in *A Contribution to the Critique of Political Economy*. But his methodological statement sheds interesting light on the important question of how the notion of the individual should be theoretically constructed in order to achieve a maximum degree of concreteness.

In *A Contribution*, Marx's problem was the specific starting point for an analysis of production. It might seem that the population was a concrete enough basis. But on second thought it becomes clear that this is only apparently so, since the population turns out to be an abstraction if we do not know the classes of which it is composed. In its turn, a social class is an abstraction when we ignore the elements on which it is based—such as hired labor, capital, etc. In a word, if we began our analysis with the notion of population, its more detailed definition would lead us to ever simpler concepts, and so to abstraction. We would then have to reverse our tracks, going back from the abstract to the particular, and this time the latter would no longer be a chaotic mosaic of many terms, but their rich comprehensive whole. Marx thinks that the latter method is correct, and says in conclusion:

The concrete is concrete, because it is a combination of many objects with different destinations, i.e., a unity of diverse elements. In our thought, it therefore appears as a process of synthesis, as a result, and not as a starting point and, therefore, also the starting point of observation and conception . . . the method of advancing from the abstract to the concrete is but a way of thinking by which the concrete is grasped and is reproduced in our mind as a concrete. It is by no means, however, the process which itself generates the concrete.

This methodological postulate of the intellectual reconstruction of the concrete is reconstructed through the abstract and can also be applied to the concept of the human individual. Here the starting point of observation is, naturally, the real human individual. Thus, when defining the ontological status of the indivdual, it is necessary to start from the existence of individuals as specimens of a biological species and parts of nature, just as was done by naturalism. When, however, we have the task of further particularization of the concept of the individual, we have to ascend from what is abstract, and therefore simple, to what is concrete, and therefore complicated. According to Marx, it is only by this method that we can obtain a picture of a complex concrete individual not as a hodgepodge of speculation but a coherent whole. Consequently, observation begins with the real individual whose social analysis should reveal the whole of the relationships that are our frame of reference in intellectual reconstruction of this concrete individual. By his condensed description of human essence as the ensemble of social relations, Marx wanted to explain why a given man, formed as he is by specific social conditions, is characterized by specific attitudes and views.

The above remarks were intended to introduce the climate of methodological presuppositions of Marxian analysis—since this may contribute to a better understanding of the problem. Now let us revert to the main theme of our discussion.

The logical point of departure for Marx's analysis is the conviction that man, both as a species and as an individual specimen of this species, is a result of historical development, that is, a social product. In stating this conviction, Marx does not simply echo Aristotle's truism (for such at bottom it is) that man is a *zoon politikon*—in other words, that he always lives and produces in conjunction with others and is, from his infancy, dependent on society, without which he could not survive. He says much more—that man is a *product* of society, that it is society that makes him what he is. This Marx saw and understood at a very early date; at any rate he was already writing to this effect in *A Contribution to the Critique of Hegel's Philosophy of Right*, and in a more profound and developed form in the *Manuscripts.* But having decided that man is not just a product of nature, that his is not some immutable "human nature" that was given him at birth, that under the impact of historical conditions he changes his attitudes, opinions, evaluations, etc.—in a word, that he is a product of society, he had to explain precisely what all this means.

In the Preface to *A Contribution to the Critique of Hegel's Philosophy of Right*, Marx points out that the critique of religion has posed the problem of man more sharply and writes:

"But *man* is not an abstract being, squatting outside the world. Man is *the world of men*, the State, and society."

The point is not only that man is *linked* with the world and society but—and this is to go much further—that he is also constituted, *created* by this world.

The *Theses on Feuerbach* are another step forward in the deciphering of this proposition: the essence of man = the entirety of social conditions.

From this point of view of historical materialism, the idea is relatively simple and clear. If consciousness does not determine being, but being determines consciousness and if human attitudes, opinions, evaluations, etc., are a historical product and result of mutual interaction between base and superstructure—except however, that over longer periods the movement of the whole is ultimately regulated by the movement of the base—then the general psychological structure of men under given conditions depends on the pattern of social relations, particularly in the sphere of production. These relations are the basis of his consciousness—they *create* it—although this creative process is an extremely complicated one. What philosophers call "human nature" or the "essence of man" is thus reduced to the status of a product—or a function—of social relations.

What is, however, so clear and simple when the existence of a developed theory of historical materialism is taken for granted seems much more complicated at a time it does not yet exist. It is a historical fact that the concept of the human individual in the Marxist theory was not deduced from the premises of historical materialism, but on the contrary, Marx's sociology was developed from the problem of the individual. But this only concerns the ways of reaching the final formulations and not the substance of the case. This was expounded clearly enough in the passage from *The German Ideology* quoted above.

Man is born into a definite society under definite social conditions and human relations; he does not choose them: rather, they exist as a result of the activity of earlier generations. And it is on the foundation of these and no other social conditions—which are based on relations of production—that the entire involved structure of views, systems of values, and their concomitant institutions is erected. Views of what is good or bad, worthy or unworthy, that is, a defined system of values, are socially *given*—and so is knowledge of the world which is determined by the historical development of society. Through the prevailing social consciousness, social relations give shape to the individual who is born and educated in a specific society. In this sense, social relations *create* the individual. This can only be denied by asserting nativism—something that nobody but a racist would publicly risk saying today as of any scientific value. This is a result of the advance of psychological knowledge, but also of Marxist-influenced sociology.

Man is not born with any innate ideas about the world and certainly not with inborn moral ideas—as is proved, at the very least, by the tremendous variability of such views not only over the course of history, but even in the same period among different societies, evolving under different conditions. On the other hand, men are born with certain possibilities of development and these depend on their historically formed psycho-physical structure. This is a result of phylogenesis, which in its turn is also historically determined. But at a certain level of biological evolution, which changes very slowly, man—in the sense of his attitudes, opinions, value-judgments, etc.—is a product of ontogenesis, a wholly social product. For what he becomes in ontogenesis is fully determined socially; and this in a way that is quite beyond his control—through language, which embodies a certain type of thinking, and education, which imparts certain customs, modes of behavior and of ethics, etc. Education does it so thoroughly that even after we realize their origins and their relative nature, we usually remain unable to free ourselves of them. Indeed, even our ways of hearing and seeing—our response to music and art, our literary tastes, and so on—are formed in the same way, in most cases independent of our more mature and conscious reflection on these matters.

Thus man's mental outlook, his consciousness, is formed as a result and expression of certain social conditions. His ontogenesis, which is a function of the whole of social conditions in a given period, can indirectly be described as a whole. This is, naturally, a figurative way of speaking, but the meaning of what we want to convey by this metaphor is obvious.

This description of the individual does not conflict with the statement that the individual is a specimen of a biological species, since neither claims the role of a definition. When dealing with such a complicated entity as man, an analysis only of some of his many aspects or elements is attempted. Now if the statement that the individual man, as a specimen of a biological species, is part of nature settles one aspect of the problem by separating it from the theocentric or heteronomous, then the statement that man's consciousness is in its many forms a function of social relations as a whole takes care of another sphere of problems and queries. There is no competition, no mutual exclusion here. On the contrary, both spheres of investigation are complementary, although even when taken together they do not exhaust the whole of the problem. Some essential questions remain unanswered— and we shall try to take up at least a few of them in our further considerations. These too will be directed toward completing the concept of the human individual, as here set forth, rather than putting forward any competitive formulations.

It may be useful at this point to consider the heuristic value of the description of the individual (in the sense of his attitudes and his consciousness) as a function of the dominant social conditions.

In at least two senses this allows the notion of the individual to become concrete.

First, in the sense of the methodological requirement that the concrete should be arrived at through what is abstract and simpler. There is no doubt that the concrete human individual, from whom any social analysis must start, is structurally a most difficult entity. If the material and spiritual components of this involved structure were to be left aside, then the designations "man" or the "human individual" would be too abstract, and of such generality as to be of little use. But if we begin with the component elements, and an analysis of them can be carried out by their reduction to certain social conditions, then we may arrive at an incomparably richer reconstruction of the concrete individual. Moreover, this brings clarity to such cryptic, often mystified spheres of human life as systems of values and patterns of evaluations and behaviors based on these systems. We shall return to this when we discuss alienation and fetishism.

Second, when problems of the individual man are interpreted as a function of social conditions, then the conception of the individual can be particularized by clarifying his relationships with groups and with society. This is undoubtedly one of the key issues of any philosophical anthropology—and in Marxism it finds an unambiguous solution on the basis of the interaction between the individual and society (or social group).

The individual is in a quite specific sense a function of social relations and social conditions; that is, he is a product of society in the concrete form in which a given society exists. If social relations are class relations, as determined by the mode of production, then the individual is a product of these relations, conditioned by his class membership. But the problem cannot be reduced to broad social classes; it also involves social strata, occupational groups, etc., which depend upon the structure of a society and the role this specific arrangement plays at a given time and in given conditions. The concept of the individual thus acquires a much more concrete shape and becomes more firmly rooted in society, in its separate parts which are the results of the existing conditions.

When this aspect of the question is brought into focus, the heuristic significance of the Marxist conception becomes obvious; it is shown by the fact that it has been ever more widely accepted by modern anthropology.

Suggested Readings

Burns, Emile, *Handbook of Marxism* (New York: Random House, Inc., 1936).

Cole, G. D. H., *The Meaning of Marxism* (Ann Arbor, Mich: University of Michigan Press, 1964).

Dux, Dieter, *Ideology In Conflict: Communist Political Theory* (New York: Van Nostrand Reinhold Company, 1963).

Feuer, Lewis, *Marx and the Intellectuals* (Garden City, N.Y.: Doubleday & Company, Inc., 1969).

Hook, Sidney, *Marx and the Marxists* (New York: Van Nostrand Reinhold Company, 1955).

Lichtheim, George, *Marxism* (New York: Praeger Publishers, Inc., 1961).

Marcuse, Herbert, *Soviet Marxism* (New York: Columbia University Press, 1958).

Petrovic, G., *Marx in the Mid-Twentieth Century* (Garden City, N.Y.: Doubleday & Company, Inc., 1967).

Tucker, Robert, *Philosophy and Myth in Karl Marx* (New York: Cambridge University Press, 1967).

Wolfe, Bertram, *Marxism* (New York: The Dial Press, 1965).

The Ideology of Democratic Socialism

INTRODUCTION

The word *socialism* first appeared about 1830 in both French and English political writings and referred to such socialist groups as the Owenites and the followers of Saint-Simon. By 1840 the term meant the doctrine which contended that the ownership and control of the means of production—land and capital—should be held by the community as a whole. Since that time, countless countries have come to describe themselves as socialist, and their variety is such that it is difficult to give it a definite description. It is in this idea of community that the heart of socialism is to be found. For it is in the community that men can realize their full potential and achieve their human emancipation. In his article in the *Encyclopedia of Social Science* (New York: The Macmillan Company, 1937), Oscar Jaszi listed the following common characteristics:

. . . first, a condemnation of existing political and social order as unjust; second, an advocacy of a new order consistent with moral values; third, a belief that this ideal is realizable; fourth, a conviction that the immorality of the established order is traceable not to a fixed world order or to the unchanging nature of man but to corrupt institutions; fifth, a program of action leading to the ideal through a fundamental remolding of human nature or of institutions or both; and, sixth, a revolutionary will to carry out this program.

This revolutionary attitude prevailed in much of Marxian socialism. It must be seen that state socialism or communism is one kind of Marxism rather than a separate development. Also, there are many kinds of state socialisms just as there are many kinds of Marxist political philosophies. Communism has as its goal the extension of the ideal of the family to the state, that is, a group working together with common interests. Beyond differences in belief as to the necessity of revolution, the contrast between communism and socialism can also be seen in their two maxims: "From each according to his capacity, to each according to his needs" (communism) and "From each according to his capacity, to each according to his merit" (Saint-Simon's socialism).

After the writings of Marx appeared, his thoughts came to dominate most of the socialist movement. A few, such as the Fabians (1890) in England, ignored him. Other socialists, such as Eduard Bernstein (1899), reacted against Marx, claiming that his conception of history was incorrect. They argued that the crises in capitalism had become less rather than more severe; the standard of living of every class had risen; the middle class was increasing in size; and finally, that in democratic states the government was responding significantly to the will of the people. On the basis of these changes, Bernstein argued that reform, not revolution, was the way to a good society. The latter point is one of the major features of contemporary Western European socialism. Wherever socialism exists today in Western Europe, and it exists in most countries, socialist parties accept parliamentary means and reject revolutionary methods. Furthermore, there has been a transformation of socialist parties from *class* parties to *people's* parties, which seek the general welfare. The idea of complete state ownership has been given up. The socialists have substituted the belief in public control of enterprise and planning, which assumes public ownership of some of the key aspects of economic life. Finally, contemporary socialists are strongly opposed to dictatorship and embrace the democratic ideals of political rights. These features can be seen in the writings of both the contemporary English socialists and those of the American socialist Norman Thomas.

The History and Tenets of Democratic Socialism

C. A. R. Crosland

C. A. R. Crosland (1918-   ) is a member of the British Parliament. Among his books are *The Conservative Enemy* (1962), *The Future of Socialism* (1956), and *Britain's Economic Problem* (1953).

A SUMMARY OF SOCIALIST DOCTRINES

The Philosophy of Natural Law. This had its immediate inspiration in Locke, though of course it can be traced much earlier in philosophical history. But it was Locke (suitably interpreted) whose ideas provided a theoretical basis both for the English radicals who rejoiced at the French Revolution, and the early anti-capitalist writers of the Industrial Revolution. He was called in aid to prove that land was originally held in common, and that labour was the only true title to property. These two principles were used to support the revolutionary thesis that common possession, because natural, was therefore also just, and that private property must

Reprinted with permission of The Macmillan Company from *The Future of Socialism* by C. A. R. Crosland. © C. A. R. Crosland 1956, 1957; and Jonathan Cape Ltd.

be abolished: and that all deductions from the produce of labour in the shape of rent, interest or profit were indefensible, and should be reclaimed by the community.

Owenism Robert Owen, believing that character and states of mind depended on economic environment, maintained that so long as the economic system was competitive, it would breed neither good character nor general contentment. Competition must therefore be replaced by a co-operative organisation of industry, with property held in common, and all labour treated as of equal status. This transition does not require class-war, industrial strikes, or even political action. It requires only that the upper classes should be converted, as they must be as soon as they perceive the reality of the situation, to the need for a new social order, which can then be built by a cumulative series of local co-operative experiments, with all classes gladly participating.

The Labour Theory of Value. Derived from Ricardo, this was forged into a weapon of socialist propaganda by the English pre-Marxist socialists (Hodgskin, Bray, etc.), and became the predominant intellectual inspiration of the working-class anti-capitalist movement, and in particular of Chartism. Labour is the source of all exchange-value, yet receives only subsistence-wages. It therefore derives no benefit from the continuous rise in production, wages being held down by what Lassalle later called "the iron law of wages," and the whole increase in wealth accruing to the capitalist and landlord in profit or rent. There is consequently an irreconcilable conflict between capital and labour over the distribution of the product; and this can only ultimately be resolved by labour's securing the whole value of what it produces. The struggle must be waged by a working class organised on militant class lines, and prepared to use either industrial or political action as circumstances dictate. (This is in marked contrast to Owen's reformist, Utopian belief in class co-operation.)

Christian Socialism. The aims of the Christian Socialists bore a close resemblance to those of Owenism, though of course the inspiration was different—in the one case a Benthamite belief in universal happiness, in the other a concern with Christian ethics. But for both the essential evil was the competitive pursuit of private gain, and the objective a co-operative society of communal ownership, in which mutual love and brotherhood would replace the selfish antagonisms inevitably bred by competitive capitalism.

Marxism. Like some earlier socialist doctrines. Marxist economics were based on a Ricardian labour theory of value, and a somewhat more refined theory of surplus value and exploitation. The worker, who could support himself by working only x hours a day, is in fact compelled to work x plus y hours; and the entire fruits of y accrue to the capitalist as surplus product. There is therefore a basic conflict between workers and bourgeoisie, which must be fought out with all the weapons of class-war. The root of capitalist power lies in the ownership of the instruments of production; and the vital condition of success for the working class is therefore the expropriation of these instruments. The struggle over their ownership will grow continuously more bitter, for capitalism suffers from certain insoluble inner contradictions which must lead to growing pauperisation, and eventually to collapse and revolution.

The most novel and, as it has proved, most influential element in this doctrine was the central role ascribed to the capitalist monopoly of the means of production, and the insistence that this must be replaced by state ownership as soon as the workers have created a proletarian state. Marx was in truth the founder of the State or collectivist tradition in socialism, as opposed to earlier notions of communal or co-operative ownership.

The Theory of Rent as Unearned Increment. This was developed from the Ricardian theory of rent by John Stuart Mill, and was later popularised, with for a time enormous success, by Henry George. It was a doctrine directed primarily against landlords. Economic progress causes a constant increase in land-values. This goes to enrich the owners, although they have in no sense 'earned' the increment, which would accrue to them though they were totally passive and idle. It is the product solely of the fact that land is in limited supply, and effectively monopolised by its existing owners. Since it is clearly inequitable that the additional wealth created by society should be sequestered by the landlords, and since this deprives labour of its just reward, the land should be nationalised, or at least land-values heavily taxed, so that the increment may in future be enjoyed by the whole community.

William Morris and Anti-commercialism. Competitive commerce degrades the worker as producer. It drains the craft and satisfaction out of labour; it destroys art and good design; and it creates a vulgarised upper class, and an intolerable gap between rich and poor. There is no help to be looked for from the state, nor from Parliament, nor from the collectivist socialists, who are likely merely to fasten a new bureaucracy and tyranny on the worker. Competition must be replaced by small co-operative units, and economic activity decentralised down to local communes. The need for a central state will then disappear, and even the nation will lose its function. Once the twin evils of central state authority and commercialism have been eliminated, all wealth will be held in common, competitive antagonisms will fade away, and labour, performed for pleasure and not for profit, will again assume the dignity of a craft occupation.

Fabianism. The early Fabians owed little to previous socialist thinkers, and in particular nothing to either Owen or Marx.[1] Their intellectual derivation was wholly non-socialist—from Ricardo, Mill, Jevons, and Henry George.

Specifically, they extended the Mill-George theory of rent as an unearned increment to other factors of production besides land. The owners of any factor which possessed a differential advantage would, with increasing prosperity, become possessed of large economic rents, measuring the natural superiority of the more favoured over the marginal establishments. But since these special advantages are normally inherent qualities of the factors of production concerned, the differential rents are a pure unearned increment: not the product of any efforts on the part of the capitalists themselves, but the automatic consequence of social labour and development. Land and industrial capital must therefore be emancipated from individual or class ownership, and vested in the community by nationalisation.

---

[1] Their contempt for Marx was reciprocated on his behalf by Lenin, who called them 'filthy froth on the surface of the world labour movement'. (Quoted by Gray, op, cit., p. 485n.)

Rent and interest will then accrue to the state, and can be equitably shared amongst the whole population (though not necessarily equally—if labour were to be granted its "whole product," efficiency might suffer).

The Fabians stressed the virtues of collective (state or municipal) action not only in respect of ownership, but in every sphere. Any extention of collective at the expense of individual activity constitutes an advance towards socialism, including the registration by the state of playing-card makers, hawkers, dogs, cabs, places of worship and dancing-rooms.[2] This implies, of course, a view of the state diametrically opposed to that of Marx, who thought that nothing good could come out of the capitalist state, which must be overthrown and replaced by a workers' state *before* collectivisim could be established. The Fabians, instinctive gradualists and permeators, believed on the contrary that reform could come through the existing capitalist media.

The I.L.P. Tradition. This has been extremely influential, but is not easy to define. It was the early Independent Labour Party that Professor Cole had in mind when he wrote of "a Socialism almost without doctrines . . . a broad movement on behalf of the bottom dog;"[3] and what there was of doctrine was a simple amalgam of previous doctrines. Yet there is still something distinctive about the I.L.P. tradition. This unique element is neither doctrinal nor intellectual, but rather a particularly strong insistence, largely Nonconformist in origin, on the brotherhood of man, on fellowship, service, and altruism. This is stressed not only in a domestic context, but equally in relation to other countries. The internationalist tradition of the Labour Party stems far more from the "international brotherhood of man" appeal of the I.L.P., than from the "workers of the world unite!" slogan of the Marxists. It is this generous, idealistic, deeply religious emphasis on brotherhood and altruism which justifies us in identifying the I.L.P. as a separate influence—and one very different in spirit from the Fabian, as may be seen from the contrasted reactions of the two bodies to the Boer War.

The Welfare State or Paternalist Tradition: the rejection of the *laisser-faire* doctrine that the state has no obligation to its citizens (save for the protection of property), and indeed a positive obligation to remain inactive: and the affirmation of the opposite view that the state must accept responsibility for preventing poverty and distress, and for providing at least a subsistence minimum of aid to such citizens as need it.

This has not always been a distinctively socialist doctrine—indeed, it was only in the era of classical competitive capitalism that the "night-watchman" view of the state (to use Lassalle's phrase) was prevalent. The opposite view was normal up to the time of the Industrial Revolution, and of course is now once more widely accepted outside the socialist parties. But the *laisser-faire* view prevailed for the whole of the nineteenth century; and since during that period the socialist movements were the only serious anti-capitalist force, the paternalist view of the state came to be associated with them. It runs through many of the doctrines mentioned above, and others not mentioned here. It can perhaps be traced back first, amongst socialist thinkers, to Louis Blanc, but more reliably to Lassalle and

---

[2] Sidney Webb, *Fabian Essays* (1931 edition), pp. 44-7.
[3] Op. cit., p. 22.

the German Social-Democratic Party. In Britain, it may be said to be implicit in much of the Chartist propaganda for universal suffrage, and traces of it can be found in S.D.F. and early I.L.P. writings. But it was the Fabians who first gave it strong overt expression. Since then it has become, in the shape of demands for social security and a guaranteed national minimum, perhaps the most deeply-felt item in Labour policy.

Syndicalism and Guild Socialism. On the continent, Syndicalism constituted a separate tradition in its own right (especially in the Latin countries), with deep roots in anarchism, a long literature, and many famous exponents. But in Britain continental syndicalism held only a brief sway in the immediate pre-1914 years, and British Guild Socialism owed as much to Ruskin and Morris as to the C.G.T. or the I.W.W.

Guild Socialism was a violent reaction against collectivist state socialism. The state socialist mistook the problem by failing to see that the central evil of the capitalist system was not private property-income, but the wage system, or "wagery." This evil would not be eliminated by collectivisation, which would merely throw up a new industrial bureaucracy, as unpleasant as the old. It could be eliminated only by establishing workers' control in industry by means of syndicalist industrial guilds. This alone would guarantee justice to the worker as producer. It is of no use to look to Parliament or the state to create this transformation; it requires revolutionary strike action by the Trade Unions. The whole emphasis is on the worker as producer, not as consumer: on workers' control, not the division of income: and on the Trade Unions, and not the state, as the spearhead of advance.

The Doctrine of Planning. This was a late development in socialist thought, and attracted scarcely any attention before 1914.[4] It was largely a response to the increasingly severe incidence of unemployment in the inter-war period, combined with the apparent success of the Soviet Five-Year Plans; and it later became caught up in the Keynesian Revolution (though Hobson still deserves credit as an early prophet). By the late 1930s a variety of arguments were being used to support the case for planning—academic theories of "imperfect competition," Pigovian welfare economics, the maldistribution of incomes, the distinction between "production for use" and "production for profit," and so on. But the essential argument was based on unemployment; and from 1931 onwards planning for full employment became the first objective of Labour policy.

THE PREDOMINANT THEMES

What emerges from this brief catalogue? Above all the variety and heterogeneity. It is this which makes it impossible to isolate any one orthodoxy to be consulted now for guidance about the future.

It is obvious enough that socialist thought varies through time, and that different doctrines prevail at different periods. This is as it should be. It is not even surprising

---

[4] Shaw's preface to the 1931 edition of *Fabian Essays*, for example, is wholly concerned with unemployment and the need for socialist planning (plus an end to the Parliamentary Party system) to cure it. But his original essay, and his preface to the 1908 edition, were exclusively concerned with unearned surplus value, and made no mention of planning.

that different doctrines should be supported at the same time—Owenism and Chartism, Marxism and Christian Socialism, Fabianism and Guild Socialism; there must always be divergent views on the right emphasis and order of priorities, and these will prevent a uniformity of thought. The trouble is that some of the divergences are not a matter simply of emphasis or the right priorities. They are fundamental, and the doctrines mutually inconsistent.

Thus Fabian collectivism and Welfare Statism require a view of the State diametrically opposed to the Marxist view. The syndicalist tradition is anti-collectivist. The Marxist tradition is anti-reformist. Owenism differs fundamentally from Marxism and syndicalism on the class-war. Morrisite communes and Socialist Guilds are incompatible with nationalisation: and so on.[5]

How then to decide which is the correct scripture? It is, of course, impossible. All we can do is to pick out certain recurrent themes (whether mutually consistent or not) which have exercised a predominant influence, and which are common to more than one school of thought: and ask whether they are applicable in Britain to-day. In so doing, we need to distinguish in each case between the objective, the means and policies chosen to carry out the objective, and the ideologies or theories by which the objectives and the choice of means are justified.

Five predominant themes can be distinguished (though they often overlap): the appropriation of property incomes, co-operation, workers' control, social welfare, and full employment.

1. The objective of the appropriation by society of the rewards of capital (rent, interest, profits) by means of the abolition of private property, and the substitution for it either of communal co-operative state ownership (the land reformers, Owen, Morris) or collectivist state ownership (Marx, the Fabians, the modern Labour Party), the collectivist view naturally gaining ground with the growth of large-scale units.

The theoretical justification has varied through time, but the constant element has been the theory of a surplus product, due to the effort of labour, but impounded by the owners of property. This theme, of the exploitation of the worker, runs through all the natural law doctrines, the deductions from Ricardo's theory of value, the Marxist theory of surplus value, the Mill-George theory of rent, and the generalised Fabian theory of unearned increment.

Few of these justifications have stood the test of time. Not many people to-day accept the doctrine of *ius naturale*, or the Ricardo-Marx labour theory of value,[6] or the theories of Henry George.[7] This, however, is of no great importance, since a

---

[5] And if anyone doubts the mutual hostility of these various schools of thought, he has only to read any passage in Marx on any other socialist thinker (save naturally for Engels); or he can refer, to take a later English example, to the early literature of the Guild Socialists—'Collectivists may take their choice:' wrote Mr. Cole, they are knaves, who hate freedom, or they are fools, who do not know what freedom means, or they are a bit of both.' (*Self-Government in Industry*, p. 231.) After this outburst, references to 'the dotards of the *New Statesman*', or 'the Sir and Lady Oracle of the Labour Movement', seem positively courteous.

[6] Even Mrs. Robinson, in her gallant endeavour to rehabilitate Marx as an economist, is forced in this connection to quote Voltaire's *mot* that you can kill a flock of sheep by witchcraft if you give them plenty of arsenic at the same time, and to admit that the labour theory of value serves mainly to provide the incantations. (*An Essay on Marxian Economics*, p. 27.)

[7] I am assuming in particular that no socialist now thinks the worker should be paid the whole value of his product—some surplus value must be extracted for capital accumulation (*v.* Chapter XX). The objection is to large property *incomes*.

desire to diminish extravagant property incomes can be quite soundly based on a normative judgment about equality, such as Robert Owen made when he argued that inequality created social discontent, or on a moral objection to large unearned incomes.

But, more serious, the means chosen to carry out the objective are not, in contemporary Britain, necessarily the most appropriate ones. The Labour Party having decided, rightly, to pay full compensation, the transfer of industries to state ownership does not have any large or immediate effect on the distribution of income.[8] Over the long run there is, of course, a connection; but even in the long run other methods of redistribution are now seen to be simpler and more effective. As a determinant of relative shares in total income, the ownership of industrial property is less important than the level of employment, the behaviour of prices, government controls (e.g. over rent or dividends), and above all taxation policy; and a determined government can restrict property incomes more easily than by the collectivisation of industry with full compensation. In addition, nationalisation has thrown up certain stubborn and largely unexpected problems which, so long as they remain unsolved, in any case make it impracticable to rely on public ownership as the main method of raising wages at the expense of property incomes.

In fact the other methods have already gone some way to fulfilling the desired objective. There has been an important transfer from property-incomes to wages since 1939; and that distribution of wealth is now much more egalitarian. Certainly much remains to be done; but fiscal policies offer a simpler and quicker way of doing it than wholesale collectivisation.[9]

This does not mean that nationalisation may not be justified on other grounds, nor that over the long period it has no influence of any kind on income-distribution, nor that the egalitarian objective to which it was directed has lost its relevance. It simply means that the ownership of the means of production, as the last chapter has already shown, is no longer the *essential* determinant of the distribution of incomes; private ownership is compatible with a high degree of equality, while state ownership, as the Russian experience has demonstrated, may be used to support a high degree of inequality.

2. The objective of substituting for unrestricted competition and the motive of personal profit some more social organisation and set of motives, by means either of co-operative undertakings or state ownership. (R. H. Tawney, a magisterial authority in these matters, considers this objective to be the basic element in socialism.)[10] It has two sources of inspiration.

(*a*) The first is ethical, and springs from a desire to replace competitive social relations by fellowship and social solidarity, and the motive of personal profit by a more altruistic and other-regarding motive. The combination of competition and the profit motive was equally offensive to Robert Owen (because it militated against human happiness), the Christian Socialists (because it ran counter to Christian ethics), Ruskin and Morris (because it bred ugliness and commercialism, and debased the quality of labour), and the pioneers of the I.L.P. (because it denied the brotherhood of man).

Few will quarrel with this ethical aspiration towards a more fraternal and

[8] For a detailed discussion of this point, *v.* Chapter XXIII, Section I.

[9] *v.* Chapter II for the change in income-distribution, and Chapters XIV and XV for a discussion of further egalitarian fiscal policies.

[10] In his Introduction to Beer, op. cit., p. vii.

co-operative society—indeed, it is remarkable how it anticipates the writings of many contemporary sociologists. The difficulty is to find the framework within which it can be fulfilled. So far as social organisation is concerned, it will clearly not be fulfilled simply by eliminating industrial competition, since this constitutes only a small (and diminishing) part of the sum total of competition in modern society. We are now more vividly aware of the wide extent, in any country having pretensions to equal opportunity, of feelings of emulation, rivalry, and competitive envy; indeed, the more successful the Left is in equalising opportunities, the more all-pervasive must competition (for jobs, promotion, social prestige) become— whether or not the organisation of industry is formally competitive.

Industry itself, moreover, has become a great deal less competitive since these doctrines were in their prime, so much so that it is now an applauded object of government policy to make the private sector rather *more* competitive. There is little risk, in view of the mild and refined character of the British businessman's competitive instinct, that this will set citizens too violently at one another's throats; and this reinforces the point that there are now more pressing causes of antagonism to be attended to than competition between capitalists.

In addition, most people would now feel doubts about Robert Owen's view of the relation between social organisation and individual character. On the one hand, we know enough to perceive that the simple act of replacing individual group or collective relationships does not necessarily make people more contented, or fraternal, or amiable; while on the other hand, we know too little to dogmatise about how groups can or should be organised in such a way as to achieve these desired results. And the traditional means are either wholly inappropriate, or not sufficient in themselves: small-scale co-operative units are not practicable under modern conditions, while state ownership, as at present conceived in terms of nationalised public boards, does not self-evidently induce a co-operative spirit or sense of social solidarity. At the very least the point remains unproven.

When we turn to the question of personal motives, we find again that developments over the last century have served to complicate the issue. Those socialists who think it immoral and degrading that men should work for money, and not for loving-kindness or social duty, cannot now fasten on profit as the only object of their obloquy; for profits are no different in kind as an incentive from piecework earnings, bonus systems, or even the incentive of a rise in salary. And the steady spread of incentive payments has extended the system of differential rewards for differential effort over so large a part of the population that merely to abolish industrial competition or private ownership would do little to alter matters—the money incentive is just as pervasive under monopoly or public ownership. Even assuming, moreover, that people would work better and be happier, or that the moral tone of society would be improved, if they no longer worked for personal gain, it is increasingly hard, in view of the growth of large-scale production, to see the institutional framework within which a change in motives could be effected. Again the traditional means do not provide a sufficient answer; guilds and communes are ruled out on technical grounds, and state ownership has not produced the hoped-for change. Although, therefore, the aspiration has clearly not been fulfilled, the method of attaining a more co-operative society must be re-appraised in the light of technical changes and greater knowledge.

(*b*) The second objection to private profit and competition was economic, and related to the actual material results of classical capitalism. Poverty, slums, malnutrition—these were ascribed to the fact that production was carried on for profit and not for use, and was directed to satisfying the demands of the rich before the needs of the poor. Only public ownership would ensure a more equitable and socially desirable allocation of resources.

Now it is quite true that production for profit, conducted within a framework of very unequal incomes, must give a distribution of resources highly distasteful to socialists, because it takes no account of needs, however urgent, but only of monetary demand. It is further true that the means chosen (state ownership) could in principle fulfil the objective of a different and more equitable distribution of resources.[11]

But the objective can also be achieved by other means, and has been largely so achieved to-day. The statement that production for profit gives a bad distribution of resources (caviar for the rich before milk for the poor) is only a shorthand. What is meant is that production is undertaken for profit: that the distribution of purchasing power determines what is profitable: and that if this is very unequal, then the wants of the rich will be met before the needs of the poor. But if purchasing power is distributed more equally, it becomes more profitable to produce necessities, and less profitable to produce luxuries. The objection is thus fundamentally not to the role of profit, which is merely to reflect and communicate the distribution of demand, but to the distribution of demand itself—to the fact that the rich had so much money to spend on caviar, and the poor so little to spend on milk.

But to-day the redistribution of incomes, and the rise in working-class purchasing power, have banished the worst effects of production for profit by calling forth a quite different pattern of output. It is now highly profitable to produce articles, whether necessities or luxuries, for mass working-class consumption; indeed, by far the greater part of production for the home market takes this form. Moreover, a further weapon is at hand—fiscal and physical controls—which can also be used, and was widely used by the Labour Government, to enforce a pattern of output even on privately-owned industry different from that which the price-system, left to itself, would call forth. These influences now give an allocation of resources much nearer to what most people would consider desirable; that is, far more resources than previously are devoted to satisfying the wants of 90% of the population, and far fewer to satisfying those of the richest 10%. And if a further move towards an "ideal" distribution is desired, this can be easily accomplished without an extension of state ownership.

Thus the historic anti-competitive theme, in both its aspects, provides a second case where so much has changed that the traditional doctrine now seems over-simplified, and new ways of fulfilling the aspiration either have been, or can be, or must be found.

3. The objective of workers' control. Syndicalists, Morrisites and Guild Socialists, all starting from the belief that the central feature of capitalism was the exploitation of the worker, had as their common objective the control of industry by the actual producers. The means chosen were various—control by the Trade Unions, or Socialist Guilds, or Morrisite communes. But the ideological justification was always a syndicalist version of Marxism, based essentially on the twin notions

[11] I say 'in principle', because in practice the nationalised industries have not always proved either amenable to government planning, or themselves capable of contributing to a more intelligent allocation of resources (v. Chapter XXII, Section II).

of "wagery" (that labour is bought and sold like any other commodity, that its status is thus, as one prominent Guild Socialist put it, "exactly that of manure," and that the wage-bargain is consequently of the essence of slavery), and the uselessness of political action as a method of reform. Only industrial action can liberate the worker from his capitalist chains, and once freed he must reorganise production (having fought off the efforts of the collectivists to re-enslave him) in self-governing guilds.

Now this theoretical analysis clearly makes no sense to-day, whatever truth it may have had fifty years ago. The idea that the worker is an impotent wage-slave, contemptuously and ruthlessly exploited, bears no relation to modern conditions; nor does the belief that no help can ever come from the state. Steadily over recent decades, the individual worker has gained in strength vis-à-vis his employer, and the Trade Unions in relation to society as a whole. The best evidence for this gain lies on the one hand in the constant complaints of individual employers that they can no longer "discipline" their workers, and on the other hand in the widespread admission that even under a Conservative Government the Trade Unions remain effective masters of the industrial scene.[12] A generation ago, victimisation or arbitrary dismissal came as naturally to individual employers, as collective campaigns for wage-cuts to the employing class as a whole; to-day the first is a rarity, the second a complete impossibility. It is clear that a revolutionary change in the balance of power has occurred, which both makes nonsense of the original syndicalist case and constitutes at the same time a partial fulfilment of the objective.

Of course the particular forms of workers' control proposed would in any event have been impracticable, having been outmoded by the mass-production revolution and the trend towards large scale and technical complexity. These make any craft or guild organisation, based on analogies with the Middle Ages, quite inappropriate to-day. Their cost in terms of efficiency and the standard of living would be enormous—like all Utopian schemes, Guild Socialism had a purely static quality, and took no account of the dynamic problems of economic growth and technical innovation.

An important advance has been made, and the desire to improve the worker's status has been partially fulfilled by other than the traditional means. Nevertheless, the objective is not yet fully realised, and is rightly engaging attention to-day. But it must, if confusion is to be avoided, be divorced from the theories and policies with which it was historically linked in socialist doctrine. We now need, for obvious reasons, a form of organisation which is consistent with efficiency and innovation, as well as with democracy; and this the traditional ideas do not provide.

4. The welfare objective: the abolition of primary poverty, and the guarantee of a general subsistence minimum by means of universal social services. To the great

---

[12] v. Chapter I. This is increasingly true in the U.S. also. Even in those industries traditionally considered the citadels of capitalist power, Trade Union strength is now overwhelming. In steel, a trial of strength between Unions and employers has twice recently (1952 and 1955) resulted in the almost complete victory of the former. In coal, John L. Lewis can call a 10-day 'memorial holiday' to give the mine-owners an 'opportunity' of examining their safety precautions; and they can do nothing to stop him. In the auto industry, the U.A.W. not merely forces the employers to accept the principle of the guaranteed annual wage, but compels the smaller firms almost to plead for mercy—American Motors argued publicly last year that it was U.A.W.'s 'responsibility' to take the company's marginal position into account.

majority of British socialists, who never embraced any particular theoretical creed, this practical, non-doctrinal, humanitarian attack on poverty was much the most powerful inspiration from the earliest days of the Labour Party. It appealed equally to the ethical or religious desire to help one's fellow-men, and to the Fabian instinct for social improvement along efficient collectivist lines.

Just as it was the most deep-seated instinct, so it was, in its historic form, the first objective to be substantially fulfilled when Labour came to power. Primary poverty has been largely eliminated; the "Beveridge revolution" has been carried through; and Britain now boasts the widest range of social services in the world, and, as a result, the appellation "Welfare State." It is true that considerable areas of social distress, not mainly due to primary poverty and of a character not always foreseen by pre-war socialists, still remain. But that is a new and different question. The historic objective has, in Britain, largely been attained; and the traditional means of universal, indiscriminate social services are in any case not always the most appropriate to the more subtle social problems which remain.

5. The objective of full employment, to be achieved by government planning, and notably by fiscal and monetary policies. This cannot continue to be a major item in a distinctively socialist programme, so long as it is carried out by the Conservative Government. Of course, if unemployment due to deficient home demand were to reappear, then the full employment theme would provide all the dynamic needed to sweep Labour back into power with an unambiguous programme. But while the Conservatives decline to be so incompetent, the objective must be considered as achieved; and I personally believe . . . that the deflationary tendencies of the inter-war period were exceptional, and that the years ahead are more likely to be characterised by inflation than unemployment.

Evolutionary Socialism
Eduard Bernstein

Eduard Bernstein (1850-1932) was a journalist born in Berlin. He became important in the Socialist Party but had to flee Germany when antisocialist laws were promulgated in 1881. He lived most of the rest of his life in London, where he developed his revisionistic Marxist socialism. He believed that socialism would come about through pragmatic reform rather than revolution. These ideas were expressed in 1899 in his book *Evolutionary Socialism.*

. . . No one has questioned the necessity for the working classes to gain the control of government. The point at issue is between the theory of a social cataclysm and the question whether with the given social development in Germany and the present advanced state of its working classes in the towns and the country, a sudden catastrophe would be desirable in the interest of the social democracy. I have

From *Evolutionary Socialism,* 1899.

denied it and deny it again, because in my judgment a greater security for lasting success lies in a steady advance than in the possibilities offered by a catastrophic crash.

And as I am firmly convinced that important periods in the development of nations cannot be leapt over I lay the greatest value on the next tasks of social democracy, on the struggle for the political rights of the working man, on the political activity of working men in town and country for the interests of their class, as well as on the work of the industrial organisation of the workers.

In this sense I wrote the sentence that the movement means everything for me and that what is *usually* called "the final aim of socialism" is nothing; and in this sense I write it down again to-day. Even if the word "usually" had not shown that the proposition was only to be understood conditionally, it was obvious that it *could* not express indifference concerning the final carrying out of socialist principles, but only indifference—or, as it would be better expressed, carelessness as to the form of the final arrangement of things. I have at no time had an excessive interest in the future, beyond general principles I have not been able to read to the end any picture of the future. My thoughts and efforts are concerned with the duties of the present and the nearest future, and I only busy myself with the perspectives beyond so far as they give me a line of conduct for suitable action now.

The conquest of political power by the working classes, the expropriation of capitalists, are no ends in themselves but only means for the accomplishment of certain aims and endeavours. As such they are demands in the program of social democracy and are not attacked by me. Nothing can be said beforehand as to the circumstances of their accomplishment; we can only fight for their realisation. But the conquest of political power necessitates the possession of political *rights*; and the most important problem of tactics which German social democracy has at the present time to solve, appears to me to be to devise the best ways for the extension of the political and economic rights of the German working classes.

The following work has been composed in the sense of these conclusions.

I am fully conscious that it differs in several important points from the ideas to be found in the theory of Karl Marx and Engels—men whose writings have exercised the greatest influence on my socialist line of thought, and one of whom—Engels—honored me with his personal friendship not only till his death but who showed beyond the grave, in his testamentary arrangements, a proof of his confidence in me.

This deviation in the manner of looking at things certainly is not of recent date; it is the product of an inner struggle of years and I hold in my hand a proof that this was no secret to Friedrich Engels, and moreover I must guard Engels from the suspicion that he was so narrow-minded as to exact from his friends an unconditional adherence to his views. Nevertheless, it will be understood from the foregoing why I have till now avoided as much as possible giving to my deviating points of view the form of a systematic and detailed criticism of the Marx-Engels doctrine. This could the more easily be avoided up till now because as regards the practical questions with which we were concerned Marx and Engels in the course of time considerably modified their views.

All that is now altered. I have now a controversy with socialists who, like me, have sprung from the Marx-Engels school; and I am obliged, if I am to maintain my opinions, to show them the points where the Marx-Engels theory appears to me especially mistaken or to be self-contradictory. . . .

CONCLUSION

. . . The return to the *Communist Manifesto* points here to a real residue of utopianism in the Marxist system. Marx had accepted the solution of the utopians in essentials, but had recognised their means and proofs as inadequate. He therefore undertook a revision of them, and this with the zeal, the critical acuteness, and love of truth of a scientific genius. He suppressed no important fact, he also forebore belittling artificially the importance of these facts as long as the object of the inquiry had no immediate reference to the final aim of the formula to be proved. To that point his work is free of every tendency necessarily interfering with the scientific method.

For the general sympathy with the strivings for emancipation of the working classes does not in itself stand in the way of the scientific method. But, as Marx approaches a point when that final aim enters seriously into the question, he becomes uncertain and unreliable. Such contradictions then appear as were shown in the book under consideration, for instance, in the section on the movement of incomes in modern society. It thus appears that this great scientific spirit was, in the end, a slave to a doctrine. To express it figuratively, he has raised a mighty building within the framework of a scaffolding he found existing, and in its erection he kept strictly to the laws of scientific architecture as long as they did not collide with the conditions which the construction of the scaffolding prescribed, but he neglected or evaded them when the scaffolding did not allow of their observance. Where the scaffolding put limits in the way of the building, instead of destroying the scaffolding, he changed the building itself at the cost of its right proportions and so made it all the more dependent on the scaffolding. Was it the consciousness of this irrational relation which caused him continually to pass from completing his work to amending special parts of it? However that may be, my conviction is that wherever that dualism shows itself the scaffolding must fall if the building is to grow in its right proportions. In the latter, and not in the former, is found what is worthy to live in Marx.

Nothing confirms me more in this conception than the anxiety with which some persons seek to maintain certain statements in *Capital*, which are falsified by facts. It is just some of the more deeply devoted followers of Marx who have not been able to separate themselves from the dialectical form of the work—that is the scaffolding alluded to—who do this. At least, that is only how I can explain the words of a man, otherwise so amenable to facts as Kautsky, who, when I observed in Stuttgart that the number wealthy people for many years had increased, not decreased, answered: "If that were true then the date of our victory would not only be very long postponed, but we should never attain our goal. If it be capitalists who increase and not those with no possessions, then we are going ever further from our goal the more evolution progresses, then capitalism grows stronger, not socialism."

That the number of the wealthy increases and does not diminish is not an invention of bourgeois "harmony economists," but a fact established by the boards of assessment for taxes, often to the chagrin of those concerned, a fact which can no longer be disputed. But what is the significance of this fact as regards the victory of socialism? Why should the realisation of socialism depend on its refutation? Well, simply for this reason: because the dialectical scheme seems so to prescribe it; because a post threatens to fall out of the scaffolding if one admits that the social surplus product is appropriated by an increasing instead of a decreasing number of possessors. But it is only the speculative theory that is affected by this matter; it does not at all affect the actual movement. Neither the struggle of the workers for democracy in politics nor their struggle for democracy in industry is touched by it. The prospects of this struggle do not depend on the theory of concentration of capital in the hands of a diminishing number of magnates, nor on the whole dialectical scaffolding of which this is a plank, but on the growth of social wealth and of the social productive forces, in conjunction with general social progress, and, particularly, in conjunction with the intellectual and moral advance of the working classes themselves.

Suppose the victory of socialism depended on the constant shrinkage in the number of capitalist magnates, social democracy, if it wanted to act logically, either would have to support the heaping up of capital in ever fewer hands, or at least to give no support to anything that would stop this shrinkage. As a matter of fact it often enough does neither the one nor the other. These considerations, for instance, do not govern its votes on questions of taxation. From the standpoint of the catastrophic theory a great part of this practical activity of the working classes is an undoing of work that ought to be allowed to be done. It is not social democracy which is wrong in this respect. The fault lies in the doctrine which assumes that progress depends on the deterioration of social conditions. . . .

Similar conflicts exist with regard to the estimate of the relation of economics and force in history, and they find their counterpart in the criticism on the practical tasks and possibilities of the working class movement which has already been discussed in another place. This is, however, a point to which it is necessary to recur. But the question to be investigated is not how far originally, and in the further course of history, force determined economy and *vice versa*, but what is the creative power of force in a given society.

Now it would be absurd to go back to the prejudices of former generations with regard to the capabilities of political power, for such a thing would mean that we would have to go still further back to explain those prejudices. The prejudices which the utopians, for example, cherished rested on good grounds; indeed, one can scarcely say that they were prejudices, for they rested on the real immaturity of the working classes of the period as a result of which, only a transitory mob rule on the one side or a return to the class oligarchy on the other was the only possible outcome of the political power of the masses. Under these circumstances a reference to politics could appear only to be a turning aside from more pressing duties. To-day these conditions have been to some extent removed, and therefore no person capable of reflecting will think of criticising political action with the arguments of that period.

Marxism first turned the thing round, as we have seen, and preached (in view of the potential capacity of the industrial proletariat) political action as the most important duty of the movement. But it was thereby involved in great contradictions. It also recognised, and separated itself thereby from the demagogic parties, that the working classes had not yet attained the required maturity for their emancipation, and also that the economic preliminary conditions for such were not present. But it spite of that it turned again and again to tactics which supposed both preliminary conditions as almost fulfilled. We come across passages in its publications where the immaturity of the workers is emphasised with an acuteness which differs very little from the doctrinairism of the early utopian socialists, and soon afterwards we come across passages according to which we should assume that all culture, all intelligence, all virtue, is only to be found among the working classes—passages which make it incomprehensible why the most extreme social revolutionaries and physical force anarchists should not be right. Corresponding with that, political action is ever directed towards a revolutionary convulsion expected in an imminent future, in the face of which legislative work for a long time appears only as a *pis aller*—a merely temporary device. And we look in vain for any systematic investigation of the question of what can be expected from legal, and what from revolutionary action.

It is evident at the first glance that great differences exist in the latter respect. But they are usually found to be this: that law, or the path of legislative reform, is the slower way, and revolutionary force the quicker and more radical. But that only is true in a restricted sense. Whether the legislative or the revolutionary method is the more promising depends entirely on the nature of the measures and on their relation to different classes and customs of the people.

In general, one may say here that the revolutionary way (always in the sense of revolution by violence) does quicker work as far as it deals with removal of obstacles which a privileged minority places in the path of social progress: that its strength lies on its negative side.

Constitutional legislation works more slowly in this respect as a rule. Its path is usually that of compromise, not the prohibition, but the buying out of acquired rights. But it is stronger than the revolution scheme where prejudice and the limited horizon of the great mass of the people appear as hindrances to social progress, and it offers greater advantages where it is a question of the creation of permanent economic arrangements capable of lasting; in other words, it is best adapted to positive social-political work.

In legislation, intellect dominates over emotion in quiet times, during a revolution emotion dominates over intellect. But if emotion is often an imperfect leader, the intellect is a slow motive force. Where a revolution sins by over haste, the every-day legislator sins by procrastination. Legislation works as a systematic force, revolution as an elementary force.

As soon as a nation has attained a position where the rights of the propertied minority have ceased to be a serious obstacle to social progress, where the negative tasks of political action are less pressing than the positive, then the appeal to a revolution by force becomes a meaningless phrase. One can overturn a government or a privileged minority, but not a nation. When the working classes do not possess very strong economic organisations of their own, and have not attained, by means of education on self-governing bodies, a high degree of mental independence, the dictatorship of the proletariat means the dictatorship of club orators and writers. I would not wish that those who see in the oppression and tricking of the working men's organisations and in the exclusion of working men from the legislature and government the highest point of the art of political policy should experience their error in practice. Just as little would I desire it for the working class movement itself.

One has not overcome utopianism if one assumes that there is in the present, or ascribes to the present, what is to be in the future. We have to take working men as they are. And they are neither so universally pauperised as was set out in the *Communist Manifesto*, nor so free from prejudices and weaknesses as their courtiers wish to make us believe. They have the virtues and failings of the economic and social conditions under which they live. And neither these conditions nor their effects can be put on one side from one day to another.

Have we attained the required degree of development of the productive forces for the abolition of classes? In face of the fantastic figures which were formerly set up in proof of this and which rested on generalisations based on the development of particularly favoured industries, socialist writers in modern times have endeavoured to reach by carefully detailed calculations, appropriate estimates of the possibilities of production of a socialist society, and their results are very different from those figures. Of a general reduction of hours of labor to five, four, or even three or two hours, such as was formerly accepted, there can be no hope at any time within sight, unless the general standard of life is much reduced. Even under a collective organisation of work, labor must begin very young and only cease at a rather advanced age, it is to be reduced considerably below an eight-hours' day. Those persons ought to understand this first of all who indulge in the most extreme exaggerations regarding the ratio of the number of the nonpropertied classes to that of the propertied. But he who thinks irrationally on one point does so usually on another. And, therefore, I am not surprised if the same Plekhanov, who is angered to see the position of working men represented as not hopeless, has only the annihilating verdict, "Philistine," for my conclusions on the impossibility at any period within sight of abandoning the principle of the economic self-responsibility of those capable of working. It is not for nothing that one is the philosopher of irresponsibility.

But he who surveys the actual workers' movement will also find that the freedom from those qualities which appeared Philistine to a person born in the bourgeoisie, is very little valued by the workers, that they in no way support the morale of proletarianism, but, on the contrary, tend to make a "Philistine" out of a proletarian. With the roving proletarian without a family and home, no lasting, firm trade union movement would be possible. It is no bourgeois prejudice, but a conviction gained through decades of labor organisation, which has made so many of the English labor leaders—socialists and non-socialists—into zealous adherents of the temperance movement. The working class socialists know the faults of their class, and the most conscientious among them, far from glorifying these faults, seek to overcome them with all their power.

We cannot demand from a class, the great majority of whose members live under crowded conditions, are badly educated, and have an uncertain and insufficient income, the high intellectual and moral standard which the organisation and existence of a socialist community presupposes. We will, therefore, not ascribe it to them by way of fiction. Let us rejoice at the great stock of intelligence, renunciation, and energy which the modern working class movement has partly revealed, partly produced; but we must not assign, without discrimination to the masses, the millions, what holds good, say, of hundreds of thousands. I will not repeat the declarations which have been made to me on this point by working men verbally and in writing; I do not need to defend myself before reasonable persons against the suspicion of Pharisaism and the conceit of pedantry. But I confess willingly that I measure here with two kinds of measures. Just because I expect much of the working classes I censure much more everything that tends to corrupt their moral judgment than I do similar habits of the higher classes, and I see with the greatest regret that a tone of literary decadence is spreading here and there in the working class press which can only have a confusing and corrupting effect. A class which is aspiring needs a sound morale and must suffer no deterioration. Whether it sets out for itself an ideal ultimate aim is of secondary importance if it pursues with energy its proximate aims. The important point is that these aims are inspired by a definite principle which expresses a higher degree of economy and of social life, that they are an embodiment of a social conception which means in the evolution of civilisation a higher view of morals and of legal rights.

From this point of view I cannot subscribe to the proposition: "The working class has no ideas to realise." I see in it rather a self-deception, if it is not a mere play upon words on the part of its author.

And in this mind, I, at the time, resorted to the spirit of the great Königsberg philosopher, the critic of pure reason, against the cant which sought to get a hold on the working-class movement and to which the Hegelian dialectic offers a comfortable refuge. I did this in the conviction that social democracy required a Kant who should judge the received opinion and examine it critically with deep acuteness, who should show where its apparent materialism is the highest—and is therefore the most easily misleading—ideology, and warn it that the contempt of the ideal, the magnifying of material factors until they become omnipotent forces of evolution, is a self-deception, which has been and will be exposed as such at every opportunity by the action of those who proclaim it. Such a thinker, who with convincing exactness could show what is worthy and destined to live in the work of our great champions, and what must and can perish, would also make it possible for us to hold a more unbiassed judgment on those works which, although not starting from premises which today appear to us as decisive, yet are devoted to the ends for which social democracy is fighting. No impartial thinker will deny that socialist criticism often fails in this and discloses all the dark sides of epigonism. I have myself done my share in this, and therefore cast a stone at no one. But just because I belong to the school, I believe I am justified in giving expression to the need for reform. . . .

Principles of British Socialism
The Labor Party

The Socialist Union was a group of members of the British Labour Party, whose activities were later merged into the monthly journal *Socialist Commentary*.

THE DISTINCTIVE FEATURES OF SOCIALISM

These ideals, so dear to socialists, are by no means confined to socialists alone. They have a long and venerable history and have commanded the devotion of many different schools of thought. In every age they have inspired movements for social progress; they are no one's monopoly. What then, has distinguished socialists from other strivers for a better world?

In seeking the answer let us turn for a moment to history. The industrial countries of the nineteenth century were the cradle of socialism. The class structure of society, as it took shape in that particular environment, was seen as the fount of evil, the daily violator of every noble ideal. Not the improvidence of workers, nor the cupidity of employers, nor even some divine dispensation had brought this misery to man, but the class system. The first thing to be done, then, was to abolish it. The recognition that social injustice could be removed only by transforming the economic structure gave the socialist movement its special character.

This great task could only be accomplished by the independent organisation of the workers, and circumstances gave the workers their opportunity to organise. Herded together as they were in towns and factories, the very conditions of their existence helped to make them aware of their common suffering and their common need for organisation if they were to improve their lot. They formed trade unions for defence and joined in political agitation to extend their social influence; step by step organised labour became the main vehicle for radical reform. On this practical foundation the modern socialist movement was built.

But these conditions in Western Europe a century ago were neither permanent nor universal. In Britain itself the class structure has been transformed. Our society is no longer split into two distinct classes with a chasm between them. Today power is based on function as well as on ownership of wealth. Managers, administrators, even trade union officials, hold key positions, and privilege has clothed itself in new forms. The composition of the labour movement has also shifted. The organised manual workers are still the hard core, but other underprivileged groups are now embraced as well, and there are many middle-class adherents. The very nature of the Labour Party has changed to reflect these new circumstances. It is no longer a "class" party in the old sense, representing manual workers only; it is a national party in which many diverse interests find a home.

Other countries have other settings. The cleavages may not be between "capital"

From *Socialism: A New Statement of Principles*, 1958. Reprinted by permission of Socialist Commentary Publications, London.

and "labour," and there may not be the conditions for nation-wide working-class organisation. In less developed lands the class structure may rest on slavery, or feudalism or landlordism. The United States, with its large farming community and dominant "middle-class," has a structure all its own. Does this mean that socialism has no place in these different environments?

If we think of socialism in its particular nineteenth century European form, then it can of course have no universal application. But these special features are not its essentials. Some kind of socialist movement has its place in every class society. In most countries there are three main reform movements in democratic political life. The first wishes to conserve the existing order; reforms are necessary but only as grudging concessions to maintain the political influence of the privileged. The second is composed of those genuine reformers, who, while their consciences are outraged by social evils, believe that these can be cured without endangering the class structure. The third are the socialists, who, in view of their analysis of society, take their stand on the need to change the "system"—in the famous phrase of the Irish socialist, James Connolly, to bring "the axe to the root." For them, political action based on the organisation of the underprivileged classes—whether industrial workers, or peasants, or serfs—is necessary, because ideals do not realise themselves; power must be met by power.

Nearly every country has a movement for social reform of this third kind. It may not call itself socialist; conditions may require of it a programme only distantly related to our own. But all these movements are our allies as long as they have the same broad identity of purpose. So in Britain, as long as a class structure persists and is challenged by political action, we as socialists will have our distinctive character, however our detailed policies may change with changing circumstances.

TWO MISLEADING DOGMAS

Just because we have not always recognised that socialist programmes may vary in time and place, and even in name, the belief took root that there is somewhere, even if only in our imaginations, a "socialist system" with its own unique set of institutions. For European socialists in the nineteenth century the position seemed simple. Capitalism was to be overthrown; something known as socialism would naturally replace it. A straight choice was proclaimed between two clear-cut antithetical systems—destroy the one and the other would supersede it.

Today we know that this is a myth. There are no two distinct and opposing systems, only an infinite series of gradations. No one defines British society today as "socialism," yet it is also not nineteenth century capitalism. All the changes we have seen in our lifetime—full employment, planning, controls, housing programmes, social security, the national health service, progressive taxation—have produced a structure to which no ready-made label can be tagged. It may be said that these changes are a part of the transition to socialism. But have any of us knowledge of a system of institutions which would mark the end of the transition? And if we had, would there be any agreement on their nature?

Obviously no such knowledge and no such agreement exists. Our agreement lies deeper—in our ideals, and in a readiness to take the axe to the root causes of social injustice. The essence of socialism is the perpetual struggle to realise its ideals, whenever and wherever possible. From this one statement a number of vital truths flow. Ideals, by their very nature, are never fully realised, but we can strive all the time for their fuller realisation. What is more, just because they are ideals involving the human spirit, their fulfilment cannot depend only upon changes in the social structure; there must be changes in human attitudes and relationships as well. Further, since institutions are means to an end, their exact form will certainly vary in time and place. No one pattern is sacrosanct. Nor can we ever assert the inevitable success of any new institution; it must always be subject to trial and error. In other words, we must come to the making of institutions with an empirical and not a doctrinaire attitude, for there is no accepted institutional blueprint called "socialism."

Are these statements mere platitudes? Although no one of them is original, yet taken together they may dispel some of the anxieties which cloud socialist thinking today. They deny the dogmas of the past, the failure of which has sapped our confidence. They glorify no particular institution which is bound, like all human creations, to be imperfect. They save us from the disillusionment which is the price of a faith in panaceas. And they show us, with an unflinching certainty, where our own tasks lie. Our first responsibility is to be aware of the implications of our own ideals, and to try to shape society and human attitudes accordingly. After all, society is always in a state of transition. Socialists should strive, unremittingly, for its betterment and not shirk current problems by waiting for the miraculous arrival of a Utopia.

Just as the myth of a "socialist system" took hold of men's minds, so did the illusion that to achieve it the "class struggle" must be intensified. Class struggle is an inevitable feature of class society, but its elevation into the supreme rule of socialist action is another of those doctrines which have not stood the test of events. It served, at one time, to drive home to the workers the important lesson that "no saviour from on high delivers," and so was a dynamic idea helping to bring the organised labour movement into being. But Marxism turned it into a dogma, decreeing that growing class conflict would hasten the great day of the successful, creative revolution. The proletariat was sanctified; it could do no wrong except when misled by its class enemies. The emancipation of the working class was the task of workers alone.

The class struggle is no more a fixed pattern of action for the achievement of socialism than socialism itself is a fixed set of institutions. It is true that those who suffer from the class structure are more likely to fight against it than those to whom it brings advantages. But members of the privileged classes have also played an important part in the struggle for a better society; and some of the underprivileged have, at times, rebelled only in order to gain new privileges for themselves. Classes cannot be divided off into sheep and goats. Even if they could, to pit class against class in the end leads to a naked struggle for power and advantage, destroying the very values which socialists wish most to uphold.

Do we even wish, in a democratic country, deliberately to foster class hatred? There are dangers enough in this sort of hostility, as socialists have experienced in office. Democracy demands a willingness to compromise, an attempt to reconcile conflicting interests. Some common standards of behaviour must be accepted. In any community, interests conflict and power may determine the outcome. But what socialists want are civilised methods for resolving conflicts; power alone must not be the arbiter. Strike action was used to gain recognition and respect for the trade unions, but industrial conflict is not an end in itself. On the contrary, the unions have consistently tried to avoid it through agreed and peaceful methods of settling disputes. The concept of advancing towards our ideal society through hatred and schism has already, at least in this country, been largely discarded in practice.

THE DUALITY OF THE LABOUR MOVEMENT

With all the comforting myths destroyed, we turn back on our own resources. We are not provided, as many socialists have believed, with a ready-made guidebook in our struggles. All we have is the compass of our ideals. Each new set of circumstances is unmapped terrain; each situation demands special treatment. Constant thought and adaptation, and an undogmatic flexibility in solving problems as they arise, are asked of us. We have not the support of a guarantee of success; everything depends wholly on us; there is no escape from our responsibilities. But this does not mean that the individual must bear his responsibility alone. Society cannot be changed without the effort of an organised movement. Power must be won, and the labour movement remains the main vehicle in the battle.

In twentieth century Britain little distinction is made between the labour and socialist movements. The Labour Party was first called the Socialist Party by its opponents who thought that the name would lose its votes, and socialists were happy enough to carry this burden. Yet it creates confusion, for there is a real difference between the labour movement as a whole and its socialist part.

The labour movement has grown through its ability to meet the natural desire of workers to better their conditions. Immediate, tangible results have increased the membership of the trade unions and the Labour Party, and many workers have supported particular socialist measures for the sake of the advantages they would bring to them. But this is only one side of the medal. Behind the daily struggle for "more and more, here and now" there has been a bigger purpose—the desire for just treatment and for self-determination. As producers in trade unions the workers have not only bargained for better wages, they have wanted control over their working conditions and a share in the direction of industry. As consumers in co-operative societies they have been attracted by the "divi" but also by the idea of independence from capitalist monopolies. As citizens in their local parties they have been concerned not only with class measures, such as taxing the rich, but with the broadening of democracy through education and the vote. These deeper purposes in the labour movement have made it receptive to socialist ideas, and brought about the present identification of labour with socialism, even though there may be many trade unionists, co-operators and members of the Party whose interest in socialist goals is slight, if there at all.

Socialists as such—and this is the key difference—cannot be guided by the immediate interests on one class alone. They identify themselves with the manual workers as the underprivileged of our society, but the main dynamic has not been and could not be a drive for material gain. How else could we explain the struggles of the pioneers, the solidarity, loyalty and sacrifice on which the movement still depends, or the sense of common purpose with which it is permeated? The driving-force has come from convictions, ethical convictions as to what is right and good, and should prevail.

The labour movement, in other words, has its materialist and its idealist aspects, its body and its spirit, and sometimes they conflict. A trade union may, for instance, be able to do better for its own members if it rides roughshod over the interests of other workers. Whether it yields to this temptation depends on the spirit of solidarity within its ranks. On the whole the British labour movement, because of its origins, its structure and its leadership, has maintained its larger, social aspirations. But its very success, the power and influence it has achieved, increase the danger that the ideals, which played so great a part in the early stages, may be submerged in a growing materialism. Trade unions may, as experience elsewhere has shown, become nothing more than sectional pressure groups, bodies without a spirit, "business unions" to use the apt term familiar in the United States.

There is no inevitability about the link between the labour movement and socialism, any more than there is that socialism will one day be achieved. All that we can say with certainty is that socialists must uphold their ideals persistently, day by day, within the movement—not as abstractions, not as the decorative dressing to occasional flights of oratory, but in application to policy and in daily life.

IDEALS AND REALITIES

The principles of socialism will not of themselves give us a programme for the next General Election, nor map out our path for the next fifty years. This would require, in addition, a thorough analysis of all the facets of social life, which it is not our intention to attempt here. But principles are something more than pious abstractions. They can be given life and meaning by proving their immediate relevance. Our purpose now is to show that they alone can offer a sure guide through the complexity of the world we live in; in the confusing decisions which press on us daily, they are the only trustworthy criterion for determining our choice.

Let us, then, summarise these principles and their implications:

1. The socialist goal is a society so organised as to provide each one of its members with an equal opportunity for the development and expression of his personality. This is the right of everyone, and institutions should be shaped accordingly. But the human personality will not find its full expression unless men are able to live in freedom and fellowship, that is in the exercise of responsibility and in the spirit of service. These are ideals which give value to human existence and the degree to which they are expressed will determine the quality of the society we hope to build.

2. This conception of society has from the start been the ethical inspiration of the socialist movement, the deeper reason for its opposition to the exploitation of man by man. It is, of course, a conception of an ideal society which will never be wholly attained. But providing we make it our conscious goal and are not content to regard its coming as inevitable, we can advance towards it. To achieve this advance is the essence of socialist action.

3. Socialism, in this sense, cannot be expressed in any single pattern of institutions; nor does its realisation depend on any one line of political strategy. It does, however, involve a continuous struggle in various ways to change the class structure of society and the power relationships on which the

class structure rests. In this struggle the labour movement, composed mainly of the organisations of the under-privileged classes, is the natural vehicle.

These are the fundamentals of our approach. But today two problems command our immediate attention—peace and economic survival. What point is there, it may be asked, in thinking of an ideal society, when we live under the threat of bankruptcy in a divided and insecure world? War is with us in all but name and what we do at home will hardly survive a new cataclysm. The two world wars we have endured in half a century have already seriously shaken our economic stability. Surely the only realistic aim for this island at the present time is to secure peace and increase productivity?

Socialists cannot formulate their tasks so simply. The immediate threats must of course be overcome, but is it to be at the cost of everything else we care for? We may be carried even further from our real goal if we concentrate only on avoiding war and achieving an economic equilibirum. We have to find a way of meeting these dangers which is in accord with socialist principles, so that in the very act of countering them our values will be yet more firmly established.

THE PRICE OF PEACE

As soon as one considers the problem of peace or war, these thoughts become pertinent. Anyone who prizes human well-being must look upon war with horror. War destroys life and more than life; it reduces justice to a mockery, and the very things we fight to save may be lost in the battle. At bottom we all know that war will not be abolished as long as world anarchy prevails, with separate nations clinging to their sovereignty and maintaining independent armed forces. Our objective must always be to extend the rule of law beyond national frontiers, through every method that holds out hope. So great an ideal is worthy of the heaviest sacrifice. Yet in the state of things today, world government and all its institutions lie beyond our horizon, and in the meanwhile what price are we prepared to pay for peace? There are times when people prefer the tragic suffering and risks of war to the certain loss of freedom; they may rate their ideals higher than their lives.

Today, once again, there is the possibility that democratic society may be destroyed by totalitarianism. Are we as a people prepared to take a negative pacifist or neutralist line seeing nation after nation succumbing, and in the end going down in darkness ourselves, for the sake of peace? All we will have attained will be the peace of the graveyard where our ideals lie buried. This course was rejected in 1939, and we cannot endorse it now. Whatever may be the merits of a personal pacifist conviction, the vast majority of us do not accept pacifism as a practical political policy and disagree with its assumptions.

But even the most aggressive state will not lightly provoke a world-wide conflict today, for modern war brings terrible destruction to both sides and its outcome can never be certain. The best insurance in existing circumstances lies, then, in bringing home the certain knowledge that aggressive acts will be met with the whole strength of the free world. For this reason we are compelled, however reluctantly, to rearm.

Our natural reluctance, as socialists, to divert resources into instruments of destruction can only be overcome if there is a clear understanding of what is at stake. Totalitarianism reduces life to the negation of everything we consider good. It is no answer to say that dictatorship is only a "transition stage" in the communist countries, or that they are after all "socialist" states because they have adopted the economic institutions of state ownership. It is not only the economic institutions which make a country "socialist" but also the values which these express. The values we cherish most are now suppressed in communist countries, and there is not the slightest sign of their being revived. They will be destroyed with the same relentlessness in our own or any other land which falls under totalitarian sway.

But is understanding the issues involved and advocating military preparedness to counter aggression the limit of what socialists in this country can do? The forces which will decide for peace or war are not wholly under British control. Yet something more than resignation and readiness for the worst is left us. The cold war is as much a conflict of ideas as a conflict between states. If we have something convincing to offer the world—and can offer it sincerely and effectively—we may yet turn the scales. A resolute stand on behalf of our ideals may yet influence world opinion.

This stand can be taken in many fields of international policy. Our attitude must, in the first place, always distinguish between countries in the grip of suppression and countries all of whose citizens are free to decide their own destiny. Our international socialist ideals would be betrayed if we ignored the submerged cravings for freedom which undoubtedly continue to exist everywhere. We can show, on every possible occasion, our complete opposition to oppressive regimes, be they communist, fascist or racialist.

It is perhaps in the undeveloped areas of the world that our socialist principles have the more direct application; it is there that the conflict of ideologies is most open. With some exceptions, the democratic powers have been unimaginative in helping forward the great changes which are revolutionising these regions. We are still tainted by imperialist traditions, and are niggardly in extending economic assistance. Great schemes of World Mutual Aid are planned, but little emerges because we fight shy of sacrifices. Even socialists are unready to project the ideal of equality on to a world-wide scale. When help is offered the personal approach is crude and inept, just because we have not learnt to respect fully the dignity of individuals of other races. To approach them in the spirit of fellowship requires that we should identify ourselves with their feelings, and the secret of such an attitude too often eludes us. The result is that even our best actions are greeted with cool suspicion. We have not yet explored—with some rare exceptions—how to apply socialist ideals in international relations. India has been one of the exceptions, and no one can deny the success with which the new policy there was crowned, nor the influence which this one act of liberation has had on the attitude of the East towards the West.

One fallacy must be shed—that by helping the backward countries to raise their standards of living they will automatically create democratic societies, which will turn to us in friendship. Something more is required; we need to extend our help and intimate association to all the progressive forces in these lands, particularly to the socialists there, so as to bring them into our common effort for enlarging the free area of the world.

In general we should insist that Britain gives a more forceful moral leadership in international councils. There are more opportunities than is often assumed. At the one extreme we could associate ourselves wholeheartedly with the constructive work that the United Nations is doing in many fields and, as a country, contribute generously to the needed funds. At the other, we could display a greater readiness to welcome foreign workers on our soil. Above all, we could offer to renounce something of our national sovereignty and of our standard of living, not only to help Western Europe out of her present difficulties, but to advance to that world order which is the condition of a lasting peace. . . .

SOCIALIST ACTION

The difficulty with which socialists contend today is that their programmes, their ways of thought, their very language, have all grown out of the discontents of the past, and were designed to meet the injustices of a past age. They were directly concerned with economic exploitation and the resulting inequalities. Today capitalist exploitation is no longer the burning question that it was. The class struggle has, it is true, not disappeared—its prosecution may sometimes still be necessary in face of the selfish action of the privileged—but it is clearly no longer the main path of progress.

To have the inspiration of the good society on the one hand, and the knowledge of what is wrong on the other, is still not enough. Out of the marriage of inspiration and knowledge must come a clear line of action. The leading task of the movement today and the duty of each individual socialist must be clearly and freshly defined. The historical significance of the *Communist Manifesto* was not the theory on which it was based, but the fact that it reduced the bewildering complex of social problems to a straight-forward, categorical imperative: Workers of the world, unite! It called upon the workers in all countries to recognise their common cause, to take up the struggle against capitalism and to establish their own independent organisations and political parties. Whatever may have been the errors of Marxism, in 1848 Marx and Engels influenced the course of history.

What emerges now as the leading task for socialists? The old struggle for political power to eradicate the remaining evils of a class society must go on. The ground that has been won is again being threatened and large areas still stand unconquered. But more and more must this attack on the bad be matched by a new, and in some ways more difficult struggle to establish the good. What does this involve? The answer, if it is to be brief, can be summed up in a phrase—to arouse *responsible participation*. All that we have said of the pressing problems of our time, the world conflict and the need to raise productivity, all our analysis of the dangers and discontents in our society, point to this conclusion.

In international affairs, for example, the whole of the people are involved to an unprecedented extent: grave decisions have to be faced which transcend more than ever the details of diplomacy. These great decisions of peace or war, of sacrifice to help others, cannot be taken by statesmen and politicians alone, they are to some extent in the hands of every individual citizen. The strongest sense of responsibility is asked for in taking them. In the same way, every citizen is involved when it comes to building up the material basis for international action and for the further unfolding of social policies at home. How are we to succeed unless workers and management alike accept their new responsibilities?

The dangers of the managerial society flow out of apathy and the lack of responsible participation from below. There is a deplorable tendency to leave the choice of aims to the "experts," whose only qualification is the technical knowledge which enables them to advise on the means. The counterpart of this acquiescent attitude are those discontents to which we have referred. They will only be overcome when men are themselves able to give shape to the creative tasks of citizenship. Then, only, will they know the joy which comes from making a contribution to the lives of others, and from the development of their own potentialities.

Thus, every citizen must be encouraged to play a more responsible part in shaping his own and his neighbour's environment, through all the institutions that link them together—in their locality, their job, their political action or their leisure activities. Mere participation is not sufficient. One may participate in the consultative committee at work without mastering the problems or caring greatly about the results. One may be an active member of a trade union without thinking much about the policy one advocates. One may vote in an election without trying to understand the issues at stake, and then grumble when things go wrong. Responsible participation is something quite different. It demands knowledge and effort, an awareness of the interests of others and a readiness to accept the consequences of one's actions, which is the real meaning of freedom of choice.

But the will to participate does not grow of its own accord; it must be developed. It depends on the opportunities which open up for the individual, and this depends in turn on the structure of institutions. In a totalitarian society the opportunities to play a responsible part in social affairs are either trivial or non-existent. In a democracy they can exist in varying degrees, and the right to vote is only one small expression. A socialist programme should now aim at deliberately shaping all the institutions of our society in the light of their effects on the individual.

If this had been the criterion in the past, the institutions which socialists have laboured and struggled so hard to create would now have a very different appearance. The aim in the nationalised industries, for example, would have been to make them a model, not merely of economic efficiency, but of wholesome human relations of a kind to cause the workers in them to point to them with pride, as examples of happiness, dignity and good fellowship in work. The social services, again, would have been regarded not as mere palliatives mitigating the evils of poverty and insecurity, but as the expression in institutions of a spirit of social solidarity bent on creating a nobler life for all. In planning education, we would have put less stress on the competitive struggle at the foot of the ladder of opportunity, and more on the introduction of the whole of the rising generation to a common enjoyment of man's achievements in letters, art and science. Every institution should be seen as a means of broadening the opportunities for each participant to make his contribution.

But the effects of institutional change have their limits, and socialists have sometimes erred in ignoring them. Too much emphasis has been placed on forms of organisation and too little on changing, directly, the attitudes of people. "Men's characters," wrote Robert Owen in 1814, "are made for them and not by them." At that time it was necessary to cry out against the degradation of man into the helpless product of his environment. But in fighting for the recognition of this truth, the socialist movement has tended to the other extreme. There is still a deep-rooted belief that, given only the right sort of machinery—in government, in industrial organisation and in social life generally—the good society would come into being.

We can no longer afford to act on that assumption. However excellently conceived a piece of legislation, however perfectly shaped an institution, much still depends on the response which can be drawn from the men and women whose lives are caught up in the various forms of social organisation, whether they are factories, or schools, or local government or welfare services. The state can achieve no more than establish minimum standards of behaviour, unless it indulges in intolerable coercion. And even if, through an unlimited use of power, it could compel people to refrain from harming others, they cannot—no matter what powers are used—be coerced into acting out of respect and consideration, let alone love for each other.

To work for this change in attitude is the special task of education in general, and of socialist leadership in particular. What is needed most of all is education designed deliberately in order to foster the will for responsible participation. In part this depends on the spirit in our schools, on the values which are held before children, and the opportunities given every child to contribute according to his capacities. But the labour movement, if it is in earnest about this aspect of its work, must lead the way. In its own organisations, in the Labour Party, in the trade unions and in the co-operative societies, it must pursue the type of education which will help members to be responsible participants, both in the organisations themselves and on the outside bodies where they are represented. We have used the term "education" very broadly to include any deliberate effort to change the minds and hearts of men. In this sense it includes propaganda and training; it includes also the force of personal example, which is the essence of leadership.

This brings us to our final word. In all these efforts socialists have to give resolute leadership. To exert such leadership and to believe that people are prepared to respond demands, it is true, a certain conviction. It has often been said that most people do not wish to exercise responsibility. In the nineteenth century, socialists were told that the common man was not interested in politics, economics and education; that, given food and shelter, he was at bottom content with his lot. This they steadfastly refused to accept; they held their fellow-men in greater esteem.

We will not abandon that conviction now. We continue to believe that all men are able to recognise and act upon the ultimate values which give life meaning. There would otherwise be no basis left for further struggle. We could content ourselves with full employment, social security and a minimum standard for all, supplemented by more refrigerators and television sets. The very fact that men are not content with this alone points to the pent-up idealism within them. Socialism has in its trust the key which will release the great creative energies still so often dominant in humanity.

American Socialism
Norman Thomas

Norman Thomas (1884-1968) was six times between 1928 and 1948 the unsuccessful Socialist Party candidate for the U.S. Presidency. Among his books are *Great Dissenters* (1961), *A Socialist's Faith* (1951), *The Prerequisites for Peace* (1959), and *The Test of Freedom* (1954).

In restating its philosophy and formulating its program, democratic socialism in the Western nations, and most certainly in the United States, must recognize and explore certain challenges and difficulties:

1. The constant cry that democratic socialism denies liberty. This we can dispose of rather promptly. The liberty that it denies is the liberty of exploitation and the personal enjoyment of special privilege at others' expense. If, by liberty, one refers to Milton's right "to know, to utter and to argue freely, according to conscience," or to our constitutional right of freedom of speech, press, religion and association irrespective of race, creed or color, or to the abolition of such discriminations against Negroes as have disgraced us Americans and our pretensions to equality of right in our culture, then democratic socialists have a good record. We have stood for such freedom in behalf of communists who would deny it to us. We have repeatedly argued the case against such legislation as the Smith and McCarran Acts.

I remember with joy the cooperation of socialists in the struggle for civil liberty in our country, but I can't recall that we fighters for civil liberty ever received much help from the self-proclaimed champions of freedom to whom socialism is the bogy. Our economic conservatives, far short of John Birch Society extremism, have not done conspicuously well for civil liberty. Governments of the Scandinavian and the British nations, which have been under socialist party rule, have by no means emulated communists or fascists in restricting democratic freedoms.

There is, it must be admitted, a deeper problem of the individual and his freedom of choice and action in a modern interdependent society. Such a society has its own pressures for uniformity. They should be less, I think, in a democratic socialist society than in a society whose economy is dominated so largely by great corporations concerned with profit, power, and the cultivation of safe conformity. But it is true that, as we men are made, liberty and equality often seem incompatible. One of the constant tasks of socialism is to wrestle successfully with this aspect of the problem of the one and the many. It has been constantly in the back of my mind as I have thought about socialist programs. One should remember that it is the equality of legal right and opportunity which should be cherished. It is not an impossible equality of ability or of position earned by ability. Socialist economy by no means should exclude all competition or emulation.

2. The general progress of the welfare state has gradually blurred the once sharp distinctions between the socialist immediate demands and the programs of

increased welfare which non-socialist parties, under various pressures, are willing to grant through democratic and constitutional procedures. In our complex society, sudden and drastic revolution against a still deep-seated social injustice within our institutions would almost certainly be attended by violence and most certainly by terribly costly confusion. Why, then, socialism, at least in these welfare states?

3. Certain of the most serious problems of democratic socialism, or of democracy itself, do not lend themselves to easy solution by socialist formulas thus far proposed, and sometimes tested in action. Thus, it is clear that ownership of basic industries by the state as agent for society would leave us with questions of relations between management and men; an undemocratic bureaucracy of control in many unions; the exceedingly rapid displacement of workers by automation, much of it in the once better organized occupations; the domination of our economy and our politics by a military-industrial complex, virtually inevitable while the cold war lasts, and while the overriding concern is for national military security.

4. While labor unions are vitally important to the economy and politics of Western nations, their very success has reduced their dynamic propensities for comprehensive socialist change. In general, notably in the United States, organized labor in itself cannot completely represent mankind in a struggle for the kind of justice socialists envision.

5. Finally, and most important of all, is the fact that socialism, as we have known it, does not automatically solve the greatest challenge of our time: the winning of peace. The economics of capitalism is not the sole cause of war, and to supplant it by socialism, nation by nation, would not necessarily guarantee peace. To quote Paul Henri Spaak, the thing socialists have learned to nationalize best is socialism.

This chapter will be devoted principally to socialism and the welfare state. Has the welfare state made socialism reformist? Should socialism, then, be revolutionary? If so, how? The welfare state has indeed appropriated many measures originally considered socialist. It has acknowledged a national responsibility for unemployment, decent housing, and general health, education and welfare.

But it has been using welfare legislation to cover the inadequacies of a reformed capitalism which failed to conquer poverty because it failed to end essential injustices incorporated in the system. Even as welfare it is inadequate; those who need help most get it least.

It is worth noting that we try to moralize about our system by describing it as a system of free enterprise. Compared to totalitarian system, it is. I repeat one successful economist's observation that the only practitioners of free enterprise in the classic sense are small boys playing marbles for keeps. What free enterprise mostly means to our enterprisers is the right to make a profit. A college student spoke for a great many Americans. When asked what he meant by the noble word, freedom, he said, "My right to try to make as much money as Paul Getty" (the manipulator of oil stocks).

In 1962, the Kennedy Administration, and a Democratic Congress—even more than the Administration—gave interesting proof of this adoration of profit. Our rulers put themselves to much trouble to create a corporation that would help the American Telephone and Telegraph Company, and others, realize an undeserved profit out of world-wide communication-satellites; all the preliminary scientific and technical work was done by scientists in government employ. A.T.&T. could have been paid to build the Telstar as other organizations were paid for building more complicated satellites. In addition, the government must maintain elaborate controls over this newly created corporation because its work so inevitably involves relations with other nations. All logic of economy and politics called for this international communication to be placed under a public, non-profit-making corporation—somewhat like the very successful T.V.A. But no, in this case, "free enterprise" meant the creation at public expense of a private monopolist corporation that limits the right to make profit to a few only of America's millions. So firmly entrenched is this worship of profit that only nine members of the House voted against it, and public response to an attack on it in the Senate was torpid.

Or take the case of "medicare." The bill pushed by the Administration failed to get the support of Congress. It wasn't a very good bill. It applied only to hospital care for the aged. But it failed, not because of its inadequacies, but because powerful lobbies of private insurance companies and the American Medical Association feared that it would grow into a genuine system of socialized medicine of the sort that has worked so well and proved so popular in Great Britain, the Scandinavian countries and elsewhere. In this day and age, public access to medical help should be much the same as public access to education—not on the basis of a fee-to-doctors system. Britain proves that it need violate no valuable freedom to doctors or patients except the freedom of doctors and private insurance companies to grow rich. (British doctors are, as they should be, very well paid in the context of British incomes.)

The usual cry of A.M.A. lobbyists was that even government hospital aid to the aged portended the end of personal freedom and the beginning of the horrors of George Orwell's *1984*. (You should have heard the young physician with whom I debated this issue before a high school class!) John Herling, in his *Labor Letter*, after deploring the image of the doctor which the A.M.A. is creating, writes:

In fact, the AMA seeks to equate the functioning of the medical profession with that of the commercial market place. The journal, Medical Economics, quotes with approval the position taken by Senator Bennett of Utah in defending the AMA: "The American system of private enterprise has resulted in the highest standards of medical care known anywhere. Competition and incentive are factors in producing quality, whether in business or in medicine. The voluntary American system, although far from perfect, shouldn't be sacked because the United States stands alone as a bulwark of successful capitalism. In no field—railroads, farming, communications, electrical power—has Federal control demonstrated superiority over competitive private enterprise in the U.S."

This, as Nelson H. Cruikshank, director of the AFL-CIO's Department of Social Security points out, is the "bland, unconscious surrender of the standards of a great profession to the code of the market place." Of course, historically, also, Bennett's analysis runs wide of the truth.

This sanctification of profit in our welfare state interferes with proper social planning necessary to any economic system in our modern, highly specialized, but interdependent society. The common good cannot be a social byproduct of the desperate struggle for private profit under free competition, out of which, inevitably, have grown overreaching monopolies and oligarchies. Socialist economists have shown how under the general socialist idea of production for common use there is room for something like our present price system for exchange of goods and for private enterprises operated for private profit subject to control by taxation and enlightened labor legislation. American socialists nowadays generally accept, as they should, a mixed economy, controlled by the overall concept that production should be for the good of all. For the state, under any system, to try to own and operate everything, would deprive us of some of the important values of private initiative and responsibility. It would put too heavy a strain on the state. Cooperatives, both of producers and consumers, as alternative forms of social ownership, have their very valuable place.

What, then, about public ownership? I have always said that what the government ought to own depends upon who owns the government. Moreover, priority in extending public ownership depends in part upon special conditions, including the state of public opinion and particular plans for extension. I believe in acquisition by purchase. Obviously, it would be unfair arbitrarily to expropriate some owners without compensation, leaving others to exist as before. Moreover, expropriation invites violence and strife far more costly than compensation. Socialists, however, oppose the business of unloading on the government bankrupt or nearly bankrupt public utilities, and the like at a very high price. (New York City paid an astronomical price for the wobbly corporations which operated its subways.) It is grimly amusing that the state, the target for the arrows of conservative critics, is accepted by many of them as the essential savior of ill-run or ill-fated enterprises, such as the British coal mines and railroads.

What, then, should be owned socially?

The Federal government is, by far, in the best position to organize a socially owned coal, iron, copper, or oil industry. It should be the principal agent of society. But state governments must participate in working out plans because they own much of the land where minerals exist, and because they depend on land taxes to provide funds for education and other functions of local government.

Large forests and acreages of reforested land should be socially owned and socially used, not only for lumber and wood products, but for protection against floods. Woodlots of any considerable size on private farms should be subject to regulation as to use and replanting. Some public ownership of land is necessary for urban planning and slum removal.

The coal mining industry vividly illustrates the practical value of socialization, apart from the ethical objection to private ownership of a natural resource. Some time ago, *Fortune* magazine developed a marvelous, detailed formula for coal mining. Under its formula, coal would be turned into power and heat near the mine mouth; by special process all its by-products would be utilized, thus greatly minimizing waste; mining methods would be safer, and cities and towns would be rid of the smoke nuisance. It would be fantastic to expect so good a plan to be carried out by competing managers of mines of various sizes, whose primary concern is to produce profits for private owners.

Coal and all mineral wealth should be public property, and equally available to all the people. Men may be rewarded for discovering or extracting oil, iron, lead, etc., but they should not own what they did not make. This ownership, ideally, especially in the case of petroleum, should not be so exclusively national as to prevent other nations from benefiting from these resources, except on terms fixed by either national or private owners. Here lies a task for the makers of lasting peace.

As for the surface of the earth, man's desire for a piece of land he can call his own is deeply rooted and widespread. Private ownership of land, with exceptions I have mentioned, should therefore be permitted, but on the basis of occupancy and use. It is axiomatic that the rental value of land is a social creation. I may let my lot go to ragweed, but I can get far more for it than my friend who has cultivated his garden if my lot is located near a town or city. I think socialists might well adopt Henry George's principle that the rental value of land, apart from improvement, belongs to society and should be taxed accordingly. The tax, however, should not be a single tax. This land tax should be supplemented by income and heavy inheritance taxes as the major basis for the support of government and government activities at all levels. Incentive will not be threatened so much by proper tax on land values, as it may be eventually by heavy income taxation. Very heavy inheritance taxes, properly adjusted to care of widows and minor children, would be an expression of justice that would not paralyze incentives.

Wherever efficient production of farm lands requires a plantation or a factory system, there is a strong case for collective ownership and cooperative management.

A remarkable article on the way we have been exploited under our present system and the current real estate boom appeared in *Harper's* magazine, June, 1961. Daniel M. Friedenburg, a successful real estate operator, tells how tax loopholes and our basic doctrine of private ownership are blighting our cities. He quotes with approval a statement in *House and Home* that land speculations have created more millionaires since World War II than any other form of business investment. He tells a story of land bought by his father as a speculation by the *acre* in the 1930's, and sold by him ten years later by the *yard*. "Around 1949, the late Sam Minkoff, a well known builder, bought the same property by the *yard* and after five years was able to sell it by the *foot* making far more money in half the time. And this transaction occurred before the last decade, when over two million people fled the city for the suburbs—making millionaires out of dozens of Long Island potato growers in the process."

The proper management of money or, more accurately, of money, banking and credit ranks in importance with the proper use of land and its mineral wealth. To a great extent, this is already a government function. When Franklin D. Roosevelt first took office, he took over, temporarily, the whole private banking system, which had collapsed. There may be room for some privately owned banks, and more certainly for credit unions or cooperative banks, but the whole Federal Reserve system, or more specifically, all banks of issue, should be owned completely by government, as the agent of society. In a real sense, major decisions on fiscal policy must be political. But the Federal Reserve Board, under socialism, should not be captive to any cabinet minister. It should be free from narrowly partisan political control. I still believe, as I wrote at more length in *A Socialist's Faith*, that we can and should end the system under which generation after generation pays interest to private banks for the social function of creating money in the form of credit.

To this list I should add public utilities, certainly those which serve us best as monopolies. The system of ownership should be flexible, allowing both for extension of T.V.A.-type enterprises, and of the existing successful rural electrification plans.

Steel is the kind of industry which I think should be taken over by government. It is basic to our modern industry; it currently is in the hands of an oligopoly which manages to administer prices with little or no regard for competition. In 1962 President Kennedy felt compelled to crack down on U.S. Steel for its attempt to raise prices after a settlement on wages with the union. Most conservatives and businessmen resented his action as government interference. Would it not be better if the whole steel industry were operated for general use under a public authority similar to T.V.A.? In 1962, labor would probably have said no, chiefly because it would fear that public ownership of the steel industry would deprive it of the right to strike, a matter which will be discussed later.

Extension of public ownership is good, but will not cure all our economic ills. Other steps are necessary. Socialism, far more openly and directly than the welfare state, must challenge the way in which the national income is divided among the people. The noblest ideal would be the Marxist theory "from every man according to his ability, to every man according to his need." For that I am afraid we are not yet ready. And I'm not sure we ever will be. I doubt also whether we are ready for equality of monetary pay. We are, or ought to be, ready to overhaul our present system of apportionment of what the nation produces.

We like to think that now we are rewarded fairly generally according to the value of our work. This is to ignore the large sums paid out to inheritors of wealth, who did nothing to earn it, and to stockmarket speculators who are scarcely better than glorified gamblers. It is also to ignore the capricious way in which value is estimated in terms of monetary reward.

To some extent, pay differentials may reflect differentials in the social values of the work done; far more usually they reflect differences in the uniqueness of the ability a man or woman brings into the market place. He who is endowed by a unique ability to provide what the public needs or wants, will usually be better rewarded for his efforts than if he possessed a similar ability in an even more necessary line of work in which, however, such ability is more common.

Justice in this area is not easily applied. More is necessary, as the Soviet Union abundantly proves, than the dethronement of private profit as economic master. Differentials in salary and wage scales were—and still are—proportionately greater than in the U.S. The communist state knows how to take care of its own. Under any system, it is better to use pay differentials to attract men than to conscript them for jobs.

We in the West are making some progress in the advancement of justice. There is now a floor under wages and salaries prescribed by law, and a ceiling on top of them maintained by taxes. Excessive monetary reward for individual excellence among workers is hindered, if not prevented, by uniformity of wage scales for the same job in factories, offices and schools. Spurs to special individual competence or rewards for it are already mostly other than monetary. It is the over-reward of certain abilities which is rationally ridiculous. Creative work in science and invention has furnished few of our millionaires; the latter are usually administrators or manipulators of stocks or heirs to millionaires. We socialists should give far more attention to progressive, non-violent changes in distribution of the total national— yes—and the world income. The contrast between luxury and poverty, even in affluent America, is a soul-destroying thing. More so, in a world where two-thirds of mankind live on a narrow margin between hunger and starvation.

About the best we democratic socialists can do now is to insist on improvements in the right of collective bargaining, progressive minimum wage laws, and proper income tax legislation. General sales taxes are regressive and fall unfairly on those whose entire income, for the most part, is needed for necessities. Sales taxes on luxury goods are another matter. (When I recommend John Kenneth Galbraith's *Folklore of Capitalism*, and *The Affluent Society*, I try to remember to exempt his support of sales taxes from my praise.)

There is a strong tendency in the U.S. to brush aside theoretical arguments on social justice in our economic system by saying, "Well, don't we live in an affluent society wherein the welfare state, at our expense, keeps everybody from starving?" To such astigmatic viewers of the modern scene, let me recommend an excellent, very readable, little book, *The Other America*, by that good socialist, Michael Harrington.

We boast of progress in fairer distribution of income, but Gabriel Kolko, in his careful, statistical study, *Wealth and Power in America*, gives figures which show that the lowest three-tenths of our working population receive proportionately less personal income before taxes than in 1910. Harrington says that the poor, those below any proper standard of subsistence, now number between 40 and 50 million. Millions of young people start life in a condition of "inherited poverty" and lack of proper health and educational opportunity.

Unemployment among youths is running to 18 per cent; it is a factor in juvenile delinquency and justifies the revival of Civilian Conservation Corps camps—an alleviation, but not a cure.

We are faced with the fact that, because of automation and general technological progress, it is precisely those who drop out of school without special skills who face, under present conditions, something like permanent unemployment. That is an evil whatever the rate of relief.

Reviewing the whole situation in the *New Yorker*, Dwight Macdonald concludes:

"Nobody starves" in this country any more, but, like every social statistic, this is a tricky business. Nobody starves, but who can measure the starvation, not to be calculated by daily intake of proteins and calories, that reduces life for many of our poor to a long vestibule to death? Nobody starves, but every fourth citizen rubs along on a standard of living that is below what Mr. Harrington defines as "the minimal levels of health, housing, food, and education that our present stage of scientific knowledge specifies as necessary for life as it is now lived in the United States." Nobody starves, but a fourth of us are excluded from the common social existence. Not to be able to afford a movie or a glass of beer is a kind of starvation—if everybody else can. (Dwight Macdonald, The New Yorker, Jan. 19, 1963.)

This whole situation in affluent America, with its flaunting luxury of the rich, requires a more fundamental approach than the capitalist welfare state will give. It requires not only a far more substantial relief program, but also a cure going beyond relief. Technical progress does not necessarily mean social progress. Automation in many lines will aggravate the problem of unemployment, not merely of untrained youths, and at least temporarily add to the population of Mr. Harrington's other America. Automation brings great gains in man's mastery over work, and will doubtless open new lines of employment. But planning inspired by the socialist ideal is especially necessary in times of rapid dislocation of workers.

There will be, indeed there should be, further progressive shortenings of the working week, but that alone will not solve the problem. Our times put heavy emphasis on the necessity of controlling the introduction of automation, of retraining workers, and of increasing consumption. Such planning will not be infallible. It cannot be entrusted wholly to government or corporation experts drawn from bureaucracy and management. Labour must be drawn into the picture. Socialism's role should be to insist that such planning be on the principle of a general increase of goods and services for all, to be equitably shared by all. This principle can guide us to a use of the wonders of automation for the common good; the dominance of the profit motive cannot.

But socialism has much work to do in facing the problem. There is no conceivable apocalyptic revolution that will suddenly do the job. Great violence would be an ugly and clumsy tool. Here I doubtless shall be told by some of my friends that I am only talking reformism while socialism is, or should be, revolutionary and that revolution requires some acceptance of violence.

To which I reply that many of the problems I have discussed will not automatically disappear, however total the revolution. They—for instance the problem of management and man and automation—are rooted in what we call human nature, the complexities of modern production, and the changes in it. As Russian experience proves, problems of society do not disappear with the exchange of one dominant elite for another. To transform a social order resting on gross injustice and inequity is our task, but such a transformation does not automatically constitute perfection in a revolutionary successor. Ours is a continuing task.

Certainly in 1963 we need not be told that violence, in the best cause, is no cleansing bath for the souls of men. Indeed to end the gross violence which has cursed our race is a socialist goal. There have been men (like Sorel) with sick, if brilliant minds, who have extolled violence per se as glorious. The great revolutionists have not agreed with their theory of violence except as a necessity for the end in view. Through its purgatory, the road led to an earthly paradise. Today we have reason to be surer of the purgatory than of the paradise.

I do not write as an absolute pacifist. In the light of history and the record of the years I have lived, pacifism seems to me sadly impossible. There have been wars and revolutions which have advanced mankind, and for which no better alternative seemed available. However legitimately one should distinguish police action from war or private violence, and police action cannot always be non-violent. Yet we have no scientific right to make that statement so dogmatically as to preclude the possibility of finding alternatives to violence. History is an invaluable teacher, but her lessons are by no means crystal clear, nor are her precedents rigidly mandatory on the present or the future.

Even the physical sciences today deal with high probability or with a limited working certainty. Scientists today doubt that our knowledge about natural forces and their operation enables us infallibly to read the future from the present. How much more true is this in the field of social science. We cannot do laboratory tests in history, or repeat experiments to be certain of the role of each operative cause. We might endlessly debate how freedom would have fared without the French Revolution. Its violence was bred by the oppressions of the old regime. Great Britain, mother of modern capitalism and capitalist imperialism, had no equivalent in violence, nor did the Scandinavian countries. Yet in their democracy, freedom fares at least as well as it does in France. Change came by way of reforms under an expanding democracy. Marx, and more specifically, Engels, admitted the possibility of peaceful revolution in some countries, even if generally violence was to be the midwife of revolution. (More frequently, it has been simply the mother of more violence.)

Within this century, revolutions have indeed risen out of wars between nations and have prolonged suffering. Lenin would probably have died in exile but for World War I and Russia's catastrophic defeat. It was followed by one type of nondemocratic socialist revolution. But total defeat in Germany and costly victory in Italy—without great glory to her arms—led to no democratic or communist version of socialism, but to horrible Nazi and Fascist revolutions.

The second world war in Western Europe, including Germany, was followed by a revival of modified capitalism, not by socialist revolution, violent or peaceful. I had hoped for a peaceful, socialist revolution. Far more violent social revolution than Cuba's may well occur in many of the poorer, badly exploited nations—without the background of a foreign war. But in the stronger, richer nations, especially the U.S., it would take catastrophe or near-catastrophe, destruction in war, or a worse depression than in the thirties, to make the people willing to risk the pains of violent revolution in order to change its own dominant elite for a revolutionary governing class or group. If history has proved anything, it has proved that sudden, violent revolutions require—or produce—a sterner, crueler, more dictatorial elite than exists in our welfare state, or even under our military-industrial complex. History is written, and public opinion is made, not by the fallen, but by the survivors of great crises. I have acknowledged my surprise at Russian elan after the tyranny of Stalin, but I doubt if survivors of it would have supported the communist revolution in Russia had they had any choice and any foreknowledge of its cost. Only the breakdown in war of Tsarist tyranny made communism's victory possible.

American socialists, charged with advocating revolutionary violence, have long insisted that violence would be introduced only—if at all—by opponents of a socialist government victorious at the polls. The victory we want is genuinely revolutionary in its economic and political requirements. This we must not lose from sight. Our own inspiration, our reason for existence, is a desire for a change in our way of life which will be more than the sum of successive reforms. Indeed it requires more than can ever be brought about simply by ballots or bullets. It requires a victory within ourselves of the desire and capacity for peace, freedom, cooperation; a desire for economic order geared to production for use and an equable sharing of what is produced.

It is not enough to blame our slow progress toward these goals on the owning class or the dominant elite and their self-interest. It is true that they have a degree of control over communication, education and public opinion that must be fought. The struggle is made more difficult and more acute by the power of the military-industrial complex, which has accurately been described by a recent journalist as a juggernaut.

But the effort to overcome those dominant forces, and the system through which they hold such power, will not be furthered by such loud talk of social *revolution*, as would conjure up in the mind of the listener visions of a coming Armageddon. There is a practical reason why the effort of many groups to use Gandhian tactics of nonviolent resistance is so valuable. We have especial reason to rejoice that our Negro fellow citizens under leadership of men like Martin Luther King are using these methods.

Suggested Readings

Buber, Martin, *Paths in Utopia* (New York: The Macmillan Company, 1947).

Chalmers, Douglas A., *The Social Democratic Party of Germany: From Working Class Movement to Modern Political Party*, Yale Studies in Political Science, No. 10 (New Haven: Yale University Press, 1964).

Cole, G. D. H. *A History of Socialist Thought*, 5 vols. (New York: St. Martin's Press, Inc., 1953-1960).

Crosland, C. A. R., *The Future of Socialism* (New York: The Macmillan Company, 1956).

Durbin, Evan F. M., *The Politics of Democratic Socialism: An Essay on Social Policy* (London: Routledge & Kegan Paul, Ltd., 1940).

Fried, A., and R. Saunders, *Socialist Thought* (New York: Doubleday & Company, Inc., 1964).

Friedland, William H., and Carl G. Roseberg, Jr., Eds. *African Socialism* (Stanford, Calif.: Stanford University Press, 1964).

Gay, Peter, *The Dilemma of Democratic Socialism: Eduard Bernstein's Challenge to Marx* (New York: Columbia University Press, 1952).

Gray, Alexander, *The Socialist Tradition: Moses to Lenin* (London: Longmans Group Ltd., 1946).

Halévy, Elie, *The Era of Tyrannies: Essays on Socialism and War*, translated by R. K. Webb. (Garden City, N.Y.: Doubleday & Company, Inc., 1965).

Landauer, Carl, *European Socialism: A History of Ideas and Movements from the Industrial Revolution to Hitler's Seizure of Power*, 2 vols. (Berkeley: University of California Press, 1959).

Mehta, Asoka, *Studies in Asian Socialism* (Bombay: Bharatiya Vidya Bhavan, 1959).

Pelling, Henry, *The Origins of the Labour Party 1880-1900* (New York: St. Martin's Press, Inc., 1954).

Rose, Saul, *Socialism in Southern Asia* (New York: Oxford University Press, Inc., 1959).

Rosenberg, Arthur, *Democracy and Socialism: A Contribution to the Political History of the Past 150 Years* (New York: Alfred A. Knopf, Inc., 1939).

Schorske, Carl E., *German Social Democracy, 1905-1917: The Development of the Great Schism* (Cambridge, Mass.: Harvard University Press, 1955).

New Left Ideologies

INTRODUCTION

It is not surprising that the "new left" first emerges in the form of student movements in West Germany and the United States. It emerges as a new left mainly because the old left in these countries had been relentlessly destroyed, first in Germany by the Nazis and later in the United States by a convergence and combination of ideological forces the chief spokeman of which was Joseph McCarthy in the early 1950s.

The absence of an older, entrenched, Marxist movement enabled the new left to seek new answers to the acute problems of the day. Foremost among these in the beginning were the problems of the individual in an administered mass society, the nuclear armaments industry and the threat of nuclear war, civil rights issues relating to the repression of black people, the Cold War, and the dehumanization of many social institutions, including the university. The war in Indo-China greatly stimulated the movement as it and the military industrial complex became the foci of criticism. These developments are reviewed by Oglesby and Lichtman.

From the early manuscripts of Marx, from the writings of Freud and Marcuse, from varied existentialist sources, there came rich new materials that were used to form a new critical ideology. The Polish philosopher Kolakowski examines the concept of left in a new way, which is characterized as negation and the dialectical tension between revolution and utopia. In this way he achieves a new synthesis, which can be called Marxist humanism. He concludes that the essential core of the left concept is the negative stand that it takes on specific issues, for example, the condemnation of war and racism. This concept of the left is implicit in Marx's early writings, and it transcends political expediencies, such as the dictatorship of the proletariat and Stalinism, that were adapted under specific historical circumstances to secure specific ends.

Ernest Mandel, in his article on the economics of advanced monopoly capitalism, has formulated an economic doctrine which is widely accepted by the New Left and which in part explains its emergence and class composition. Mandel analyzes the material factors that radicalize and unite student leftists with oppressed ethnic minorities. He also projects an economic crisis in which American capital will no longer be in a position to compete with European and Japanese capital. This will result ultimately in the decline of American capitalism and consequently in the weakening of international capitalism. A gradual victory of socialist countries and movements in the economic sphere will follow.

Marcuse examines the dialectics of liberation within affluence. At first sight such a proposition may appear preposterous to many. However, it is Marcuse's contention that the brutal instrumentalities of force which were employed in earlier stages of capitalism to contain and destroy the labor movement and other forms of dissent have given way to more pleasant but insidious instruments of coercion which are not recognized for what they are. Thus masses of people are indoctrinated and manipulated not only in their employment but also in their "free" time by schools, mass media, and other sources of information control. People are sated with commodities that are worthless but for which a market has been created in advance by advertising and through the inculcation of false needs. All of this is bought at a price: the systematic subjugation of vast areas of the globe to exploitation and the maintenance in the domestic economy of pocket and peripheral areas of utter deprivation. The irreconcilability of productive potential and real-life experience for many people, particularly ethnic minorities and students, has led to an explosive dialectical situation.

In a concluding selection Christopher Lasch suggests that the New Left is in a state of decline. This he attributes to several factors: the academic origin of the movement, which segregated it from the masses of workers and dissenting ethnic minorities; the antitheoretical tendencies of the movement, which reinforced its segregation from the traditional left; the uncritical acceptance of the crudest elements of Marxist ideology when the absence of theory was recognized (in a sense the substitution of slogans for adequate theory), and the isolationist-withdrawal tendencies of many New Left communitarian factions. Lasch, nonetheless, foresees in this deterioration the potential for a new movement more solidly rooted in Marxist theory and more thoroughly acquainted with the needs and aspirations of working people. Though much of Lasch's criticism of the New Left does not appear to be directed at the ideas of the spokesmen represented in this section, perhaps the presence of such a discrepancy underscores the separation of theory and practice that is the principal focus of his critique.

There are three general perspectives on women's liberation represented in this section. The first of these is formulated by Millet. Although not a New Leftist or a Marxist, her contribution is crucial, for it articulates the original concerns of the women's movement with male domination. The selection included here stresses the transcultural nature of patriarchy and sexism. The cultural institution of male domination, it is argued, is not primarily a class problem and cannot be adequately articulated in terms of class struggle. Patriarchy and sexism are perpetuated by most, if not all, forms of Western political organization. Sexist institutions, including economic discrimination, are sustained and rationalized in turn by means of pseudo-biological and pseudo-anthropoligical mythology and through the exclusion of women from the political process.

The New Left-Marxist position on women's liberation is set out in the essay by Mitchell. This position relies heavily on Engel's study of the evolution of the family. Here it is claimed that the subservence of women is reinforced by the institutions of capitalism and that the radical democracy of the classless society is essential in securing equality for women. Therefore, a transformation in the sphere of political economy is the precondition to psychological and social equality. Lenin had favored a similar approach to the women's question in his correspondence with Clara Zetkin. He felt that if women were equally represented in the work force (including, of course, the professions) with equal pay, their liberation in other spheres would quickly follow. Mitchell demands more than this, for a cultural revolution must necessarily accompany the economic revolution if women are to be fully liberated.

The Idea of the New Left
Carl Oglesby

Carl Oglesby (1940-) is a New Left leader and author of *Containment and Change: Two Dissenting Views of American Society and Foreign Policy in the New Revolutionary Age* (1970).

Why not simply the *current* Left? What makes it new?

The themes of last century's radicals remain vivid in this half of the twentieth century. The Left has always wanted something called progress, aspired to something called human mastery over something called social destiny, seen itself as the winner in the long distance, viewed its general program as being the same thing as humanity's proper historical agenda.

A new pattern of stresses has emerged in the post-World War II world. They may imply the larger point that this same world had changed structurally since the fixing of the basic radical definitions, that it needed to be understood again, conceptualized and acted upon from a standpoint uncommon to classical Marxism and through political modes suggested no more by the experience of the Bolsheviks than by that of the parliamentary socialists or the Stalinists.

No one was thinking of anything like this when the name New Left began to acquire small currency in the America of the early Sixties, where politics had grown so used to having no Left at all that any Left at all would already be a novelty. Leftwards of Congress's famous Class of '48 lay the ruins of Henry Wallace; beyond, a few small magazines and some fugitives.

This has all been explained, of course: the purge of communists from the trade-union movement, the explicit national resumption of domestic and foreign anti-Bolshevism, McCarthyism, etc.

But why did the workers permit the purge, the people authorize the anti-Bolshevism, their leaders allow the top-down liquidation of McCarthy to provide, above all, for the continuation of McCarthyism by more subtle means, etc.? The explanations do not explain themselves.

From *The New Left Reader*, Carl Oglesby, ed. (New York: Grove Press, Inc., 1969), pp. 1-20.

Everywhere in Europe at the end of World War II the heroes of the anti-Fascist resistance movements were the Reds. Allied war propaganda had stressed the progressive nature of the Alliance, the reactionary nature of the Axis Powers. The Soviet army had won the West's respect, the Soviet people its admiration, the Soviet government its acceptance as the voice of a Great Power. The economic ruination of the Continent, the urgency and magnitude of the forthcoming reconstruction effort seemed a self-evident case for precisely that sort of state planning for which an important strain of socialism had made itself famous.

How could the Left have been destroyed?

The centerpiece of radical politics was in that period what it had been for a century, namely, the conception of capitalism as an inherently contradictory system which was fated to destroy itself. With businesses required steadily to lower their rate of profit in order to compete, but, on the other hand, required to maximize profits in order to grow, capitalism could not protect itself from chronic social disaster—warehouses bulging with inventories everyone needed but no one could buy, machines standing idle, and unemployed workers everywhere. The maturing of the fateful economic crisis would destroy the false consciousness that had depoliticized the proletariat and deflected it from its historical mission, the making of the socialist revolution.

It is almost a carrion-bird politics. Distant and above it all for the moment, the revolutionary cadre circles, awaiting the hour of his predestinated dinner. Capitalism weakens, lay-offs and inflation converge, a rash of strikes—the bird moves in. But not so fast: the government also moves. A different money policy, stepped-up federal spending, a public-works project, selective repression of the militants—the bird resumes his higher orbit.

How could there be a practical politics for a radicalism whose most honest slogan must have been "This is a bubble which must burst?"

The Left was liquidated in the fifties because it was defenseless. It was defenseless because its most essential claims amounted to so many dire conjectures or predictions or prophecies, whether sound or not is beside the point. A politically practical Left must be able convincingly to say, "This is not even a good bubble." But how could the American Left have said that, since it had traditionally endorsed a program whose simplest driving objective was for the same economic security "for the masses" which the "masses" in question believed themselves already to possess? If the argument for socialism is reduced in practice to the argument that capitalism cannot deliver the goods, then there is no practical argument for socialism when the goods are being delivered. Radicals tirelessly explained, first, that the general level of national prosperity was not so incredible as all that (the South, the inner cities, the blacks), and second, that this prosperity was, in any case, much less the flower of an organically healthy system than of the Cold War politics which allowed an irrational system to subsidize its incapacities through the Pentagon. Take away this annually swelling defense budget, and what will happen then to this vaunted "neocapitalism"? The first point, however, could not meet the rejoinder that things were better here than anyplace else and getting better, and the second point could hardly have been defended for long unless the American radicals had been willing to attack the main assumptions of the Cold War, something which was scarcely a task for men whose highest hopes had so recently been abused by the Stalinist consummation in Russia, and something which would would scarcely have mobilized the revolution anyway.

Even during the Eisenhower Fifties, when a flagging growth rate and occasional recessions gave some substance to a conventional left-wing critique the intellectual initiative lay with those whose chief point was that, within the West, there were no more fundamental economic problems to be solved. Granting sometimes, in parenthetical asides, that the situation elsewhere might be different, political critics like Daniel Bell argued that we had come upon "the end of ideology," meaning simply that an achieved welfare-state capitalism, equipped with Keynesian control devices, had met all the objections of the nineteenth century and the Thirties, and there being apparently no new objections, the matter was closed. Herbert Hoover's concept of a corporate society, a working national coalition of business, labor, and government meritocracies, had so nearly materialized that ideological thought in the grand manner, not even to mention revolutionary politics, was henceforth required to yield to another kind of task, the extension of administrative and technical expertise. The only practical question still left on the agenda was no longer "How must we restructure our relations of production?" but rather "How can we most efficiently maintain the present course, steadily extending to now-excluded groups the self-evidently adequate system we have already contrived, tested, proved, and installed?" On this base of domestic tranquility. American foreign policy could return with confidence to a modernized Wilsonian line: anti-Bolshevism with the loophole of detente, commercial and political integration of the world's Great Powers, and continued extension of the Atlantic world's mastery (*noblesse oblige*, of course, the mastery must be technologically generous and financially paternal) over the whole of the earth.

But no one can now say there was anything placid about the consciousness, the spirit, of the American Fifties, a decade which belonged also, though we tried hard to ignore the fact, to such other peoples as the Chinese, the Vietnamese, the Cubans, the Algerians, the decolonizing African states.

On the contrary. It was in that period, for example, that the phenomenon of middle-class juvenile crime emerged, posing a great mystery to liberalism's conviction that crime came from material want. Young white gangs in the best of the suburbs? What sense did that make? Crime was for the poor, for it was only the gall of poverty that could motivate the risks of crime. And the same generation which authored this mystery seemed almost purposively quiet as to its motives. The Silent Generation—queried, analyzed, and rebuked in a thousand commencement-day addresses—stood mute, unexplained, and innocent before its accusers; and choosing neither to know itself nor to be condemned, it made its uniform not only the gray flannel suit but also the beard and the fatigue jacket. The Silent Generation: Perhaps there was not so much silence after all. At least, this was also the Beat Generation—owners of that supremely ambiguous title which said: We are beaten and shall endure.

Of course it could not have been clearer to their interpreters that these Beaten and Beatified renegades—Kerouac, Ginsberg, Ferlinghetti—had precisely no political ambitions. The question hardly occurred. Who imagined that Normal Mailer would become—a Candidate? What the Beat Generation wanted was a bit of free social space for a few spiritual and literary experiments. Like any subcult, it was a nuisance, an insult, a circus, and a kind of pantomimed moral criticism: Culture Gypsies, not Candidates. So it seemed.

Elsewhere in the same period, still another demurrer from happy consciousness was being entered: "If We're So Rich, What's Eating Us?"—very typical title of a very typical mid-Fifties middlebrow essay (this one, for *Harper's,* by economist Robert Lekachman). Vance Packard assembles three politically absent-minded indictments against an unspecified suspect: *The Waste Makers, The Status Seekers, The Hidden Persuaders* ache with unliberated conclusions about a certain form of civilization. Much more insightfully but still without a sharp conception of the political imperatives he had encountered, David Riesman reconsidered individualism and probed the loneliness of the American crowd. By the end of the decade, these themes were so commonplace as to have become the property of all points of view—Left, Right, and Center.

Everybody knew it: something was wrong.

But how could that be, since everybody also knew that there was no more need for ideology? A soft, deft pessimism became the main philosophical stance of the best of the non-Beat novelists and poets. Salinger, Roth, Updike, Bellow, Lowell, and Roethke—variously schooled on Freud but not Riech, Eliot but not Neruda, and Dewey but not Marx—developed remarkably cognate points of view, a set of implicit judgments amounting to an informal canon of the modern sensibility. The inner experience is paramount. Neurosis is man's ordinary condition and can even be husbanded to a certain eerie grace. History has been preempted by science and magic, which have fused into psycho-analysis.

Through such moves, the gap between what the world looked like and what it felt like was not so much bridged as converted into a national park for the exploratory cultivation of ambiguity, the characteristically modern adventure. There was a fey sort of loveliness, it seemed, which survived even economic perfection. One could even grow enamoured of all this melancholy. Had it remained for modern man to discover the allures of *angst*, of defeat? The famous antihero whom the Fifties had created in its image: was he the central figure in a circus? Or in a trial?

We were not to be very long in doubt.

The political imagination, necessarily banished from even so chilly an Eden, had therefore disguised itself as nostalgia, to reinfiltrate first consciousness and then discourse with a happy orgasm in its pocket like a concealed weapon—a threat and a promise, this orgasm, and in both aspects revolutionary.

There had been no end of ideology at all. Rather, ideological thought—*critical thought with historical structure*—had merely gone out of its conventional metier to prepare its negation of contemporary Western life. The advent of what we have lately been asked to call the "post-scarcity" or "post-industrial" state had confronted critical analysis with a subject matter before which the conventional methods of political economics and sociology were insufficiently descriptive. A subject matter, moreover, whose features ran so far beyond the conceptual power of ordinary politics that it required a wild leap of the imagination to see that it was precisely politics that was being put into question. Salinger's Holden Caulfield. Mailer's White Negro, Kerouac's Dean Moriarty, Bellow's Augie March or Herzog: Do they *enjoy* capitalism?

No misunderstanding: The informal pattern of negations which such figures constituted was almost never explicitly political, nor was there much of even an underlying reprieve for the period's conception of a "radical" politics. No doubt there is some reserve of special compassion for the man who does not yet have enough, but no one supposed that his suffering was beyond the available remedies or that curing it might need structural changes in our mode of economic organization. The fear, rather, was that curing it might not even help very much. Indeed, the white writer in his white ambience would more than once see something enviable in the situation of the affluent society's outsiders. Apparently these outsiders had more soul than those who had made it—passion instead of bitchiness, a vivifying community of social pain instead of the naggingly selfish itch of a $100-a-week neurosis. To be materially secure was evidently to be spiritually bland. How unsatisfying. The point is that the assumptions of the then-current radical viewpoint could catch the political drift of this ennui scarcely any better than the assumptions of the more familiar liberal viewpoint could dissipate it. Revolution? Something the workers were supposed to make in order that they never again be wiped out by economic (but not spiritual) depression. The radical? Either a Dostoyevskian fanatic or someone who believed that capitalism would fail to rationalize the industrial society—either a freak or a bore. Socialism? What happens to imperial states shorn of their empires. Communism? An extravagant horror produced by killer utopians.

The deepening American malady seemed beyond all known therapies. It did not even seem to have a political name.

But when a lonely and doubtless very brave American radical, C. Wright Mills, began to put political pieces together in a political way, he could hardly have guessed how quickly—a matter of half a decade?—a rising generation would move to refute one of his cardinal political observations. Refute: for even through the remarkable moral and physical energy which sustained him, one could not fail to understand that Mills saw himself as a political desperado whose most difficult struggle was against a very persuasive despair. The first and continuing need of those whom his polemic would bring to activism would be to prove the possibility of what he considered next to impossible, a radical movement with some serious power behind it.

How could there be a radical politics without mass support? Then where were America's potentially radical masses? The poor? They have been chronically hard to organize, and even granting their possible mobility, Mills could see no barrier to their being geared into the same mass-consumer society which had emasculated everyone else. The blacks? The odds again seemed to be with the system: over and over it had shown its skills at legalistic maneuver and cooptation; and what could the blacks demand except inclusion, access to the general beehive? Labor? Bureaucratized and politically docile, the trade-unionist seemed happy to forget his prewar militancy; socialism could find no more indifference and the Cold War no more ardent a partisan.

There remained, thought Mills, only the academic intellectuals. But what good were they? They did not even begin to constitue a class in the political sense, and as one career group among others, their postwar record had been dreary. They had professionally supported the official American equation of revolution with Stalinism; they had learned, moreover, how to fatten off the Cold War, and at their radical best, they drew the line at an unexhilirating social democracy whose most lively pursuit seemed to be the sycophantic care and feeding of welfare-state capitalism. Still, their training—and their vanities—made them on some terms prepared to answer for their view of the world. Considering themselves to be responsible to the humane criteria of classical liberalism, maybe they could be made to think some second and third thoughts. And then perhaps to make a few small waves.

Mills described from his sociological orientation essentially the same world which Herbert Marcuse faced from his philosophical one, namely, the internal rationalization of an externally irrational culture. How to make bigger bombs, crazier cars, greedier consumers: the impressive capacities of science and technology were routinely brought to bear on such projects, but the culture lacked entirely the methodological and institutional means for posing practical questions about these pursuits in themselves. One could grumble about the Bomb and Madison Avenue manipulation; people grumbled about such things all the time. But what could be done? A letter? A petition? A committee?

Reason itself seemed arrogantly to have forgotten mere man in its sublime quest for pure knowledge. To every frail challenge which an addled humanism could muster, pure knowledge answered: sentimentality. The imperious "value-free" positivism, which still gives Western science its apologies, explained that the *idea* of "man's destiny" is an unworkable abstraction about which proper science has nothing to say. Wholly permeated with the bourgeois ideology which it therefore refused to recognize as such, science's chief assumptions, already laid out by Galileo in the seventeenth century, remained that the physical world was given and that the scientist merely interrogated it by means of hypothesis and test to discover its nature, the end objective being an integrated, global system of verified propositions. Not, for example, a better world. No doubt a provisionally successful treasure hunt, however disinterested, would make the world better. But however interesting an incidental that might be, it remained an incidental; and it could not occur to science in any practical, operational way that it remained continuously a human instrument—merely human—created and developed precisely by that same social man whom it refused to recognize as having any principled claims upon it, and that, as such, its definitive purpose might be (of all things) a *moral* one: less to discover than to *create* the "truth" of nature, the meaning of the cosmos—of human history.

That far had the spirit of the Enlightenment declined. The method of thought which the eighteenth century had imagined would liberate mankind turned out in the twentieth—we allow for ivy-day ceremonializing about miracles—not even to understand the idea of such a project. Challenge the Manhattan Project and CBW research? But not as a scientist, for between scientific thought and moral thought there is and can be no structural link. Was it not the final divorce of the two domains which defined the platform of science at the onset of the modern era? To put science again at the mercy of a moral system, whether profane or sacred, is to restore the politics of Inquisition and the need for martyrs.

Precisely. It is science's old and current servitudes which continue to demand its special war of liberation: liberation from an imperial system of social classes, from the subordination of its work to the conflict-based imperatives which class societies produce.

A humdrum example from technology: The effect of America's overland transportation system—fast cars, fast roads—is to create a worsening array of problems at the urban ganglia upon which the impeccable ribbons all converge. Neighborhoods are first lacerated, then buried under the thickening whirls of concrete and steel; the air is casually poisoned; fatalities are perpetually of epidemic scale; nevertheless, transportation is bad and gets worse. This is the objective result of our having spent the transporation share of the national budget in a certain way. There were other ways we might have spent our money—on a fast-train system, for example—if the purpose had really been to get the best transportation system, and if such decisions were really made the disinterested science and rational technology to which we pretend we have ceded our collective social fate. That we never even had a chance to pose the alternatives is above all a *political* fact whose simple meaning is that the combined political power of the auto makers, the road builders, and the oil refiners is peerless. This combine tells us that we really *want* to ride around in mustangs, cougars, and other untamed animals (our totemistic animal cultism surpasses, even in its rituals, the known primitive atavisms)—and being civilized, we gracefully swoon. Take the auto industry as a paradigm: "What's good for General Motors is good for America," said Charles Wilson, making up in clarity what he may have lacked in finesse. The Inquisitor did not disappear at all. He was merely victorious. This "value freedom" claimed by science is nothing but a churchy dogma whose function is to disguise the difference between the special interests of a dominant class and the general interests of mankind.

Nothing new, of course, not even the magnificence of the disguise, which as usual is least understood by those who are most victimized by it. Thus, the pessimism of Mills and Marcuse, Contemporary Western culture appears to be distinguished by its failure to produce a class whose essential objectives transcend the capacities of the given order and whose presence would therefore force a structural transformation of the relations of production. Dismal surprise: a political situation which was supposed to materialize only under the auspices of the revolution has arrived prematurely, making the prospects of the revolution dimmest exactly within the culture which stands in greatest apparent need of the revolution. If Mills saw some chance that the academic intellectuals might successfully challenge, if not the System, then at least its policy, Marcuse could scarcely venture so far from despair: "[The] absolute need for breaking out of this whole does not prevail where it could become the driving force of a historical practice, the effective cause of qualitative change. Without this material force, even the most acute consciousness remains powerless."[1]

So. Does this amount to the concrete actualization of that famous whimper? Or are the disciples of an exhausted critical tradition chewing sour grapes?

But there is a third possibility. What if a changing world configuration of forces has been creating new social needs—and the political possibility of pursuing them—which remain invisible only to the old system of anticipations?

Isaac Deutscher closed a 1965 commentary on the Vietnam War with the following observation:

We may not be able to get away from the severe conflicts of our age and we need not get away from them. But we may perhaps lift those conflicts above the morass into which they have been forced. The divisions may once again run within nations, rather than between nations. We may give back to class struggle its old dignity. We may and we must restore meaning to the great ideas by which mankind is still living, the ideas of liberalism, democracy, and communism.[2]

Peculiar: Before class struggle can recapture an old dignity which it has

[1] Herbert Marcuse, *One-Dimensional Man* (Boston: Beacon Press, 1964), p. 253.
[2] Isaac Deutscher, *The Ironies of History* (New York: Oxford University Press, 1966), p. 163.

apparently lost, and before the vivifying ideas can recover their meaning, also lost, we will (somehow) have to return class conflict to that national framework which it has apparently burst through. We find Deutscher here in the grips of nostalgia for a world which was at once industrialized *and* politically convulsed—Europe before and between the great wars. Elsewhere in the same collection of essays, he is no less disturbed by the current form of class struggle but more lucid as to its reversibility:

The impossibility of disentangling progress from backwardness is the price that not only Russia and China but mankind as a whole is paying for the confinement of the revolution to the underdeveloped countries. But this is the way history has turned; and now nothing can force its pace. [3]

No doubt. The problem is to try to deal somehow with this development; and it may be that the conceptual apparatus of Marxism as practiced up to the advent of the Cold War, when not only the whole of Europe but the entire world found itself fixed helplessly by the politics of class, cannot meet such a need.

The practical core of classical Marxism is the presumption of an irreconcilable conflict between capital and labor. The two must fight. If they are not fighting at some moment, that must only be owing to capital's skills at momentarily obscuring the fateful class opposition. That opposition nevertheless remains basic until the revolution liquidates it by liquidating the forms and instruments of class domination, and it is therefore present even when it seems to be absent. To explain the absence of this fight, Marxism resorted to a conceptual distinction between objective and subjective conditions, corresponding to true (or class) consciousness versus false consciousness at the level of politics and infrastructural (economic) reality versus superstructural (social) reality at the level of culture. That distinction carried with it the belief that subjective awareness must at some point encompass objective fact, that class consciousness must finally overcome false consciousness, that the pivotal realities of class relations in the system of production must at some juncture be fully and openly expressed in the politics of class conflict. The revolution will thereupon have been prepared.

Regardless of the validity of this conceptualization, the fact is that it had lost, at both the theoretical and practical levels, the power to criticize itself. It amounted to an hypothesis which could not be negated, therefore a false hypothesis. There was simply no way to put a time scale underneath the test of history. The workers will move to take control of the means of production? When, ultimately? But what can "ultimately" mean? Predictions and excuses multiplied, each more "rigorous," more "scientific" than the last. Since the situation was always in turmoil, since the air was always filled with rumors of crisis and speculations of disaster, the anticipatory stance into which the Western revolutionary had frozen himself never became embarrassing. Like Vladimir and Estragon waiting for Godot, he could never be sure that the very next moment might not divulge the practical means to that victory which his "final analysis" always guaranteed. Meanwhile, tactical battles of all sorts needed to be waged; one could keep busy. And beyond the furies of the moment, giving them scale and a meaning to which he and his comrades alone were privy, a horizon about which everything but its distance was known held the revolutionary cosmos firmly in place.

But the waiting game to which the Western communist parties had committed

[3] *Ibid.*, p. 120.

themselves in the aftermath of the Truman Doctrine and the Marshall Plan was, of course, by no means theoretically derived, nor was it merely a response to the success of American reconstruction of West European capitalism. The motive was simpler.

The communist parties of the Continent had matured in a period when all socialist hopes were pinned to the survival of the Soviet Union. Even for a long time after the advent of Stalin, a living strain of European Bolshevism still held that protecting the world's solitary socialist state required prompt revolutions in Europe's industrial heartland. But by the end of World War II and the emergence of the U.S.S.R. as a troubled but evidently stable Great Power, an unchanged aim was being served by a wholly reversed strategy. The security of the U.S.S.R., as central an aim as ever, was now held to require the *passivity* of European (and Asian) revolutionaries. "Socialism in one country," as Deutscher points out, was the slogan by means of which Stalin announced socialism's intention to cooperate with capitalism's intention to contain the revolution. The U.S.S.R.'s self-containment, expressed finally as the doctrine of coexistence, could hardly have been a more explicit directive to revolutionaries elsewhere *also* to coexist. A hard-fisted irony had closed: revolution needs the security of the U.S.S.R., but the security of the U.S.S.R. outlaws revolution.

Thus, the European communist parties, confronting a massive array of problems—theoretical, organizational, practical, ethical—found themselves both tempted and driven to a politics without a future. With no clear goals beyond those of more rational industrialization which Cold War capitalism seemed to have subverted, with few methods of political struggle beyond those of more rational industrialization which Cold War capitalism seemed to have subverted, with few methods of political struggle beyond the parliamentary ones which were capitalism's proudest legal achievement, with no concrete response to the internationalizing of the class struggle which would not immediately contradict the U.S.S.R.—first dogma (standard until the Twentieth Party Congress and "polycentrism"), the communist parties of Europe (and Latin America) came upon an impasse which they could not surmount or even very honestly survey.

But it seemed they could make camp before this impasse—even build a rather comfortable suburb in the outskirts of this Cold War capitalism. Coexistence, initially a concession to a passing strategic necessity, had finally become an unconditional demand. Struggle had been supplanted by dialogue. According to Alain Geismar, an activist in the French uprising of spring, 1968, "Under its present organization, the French Communist Party has emerged as the anti-communist structure *par excellence.*"

In essence, the institutionalized European Left of the post-war period could not relate to the internationalizing of the class war because it had itself become objectively counterrevolutionary.

The fury of events, of course, did not therefore subside. Outside the West, other peoples would understand themselves to be the only liberators of their destiny; and within the West, another generation would be unable to see why the U.S.S.R. deserved so much protection—or why their own sharpening needs for a changed world should remain locked in the hands of those who no longer seemed so interested in changing it.

The New Left is properly so called because in order to exist it had to overcome the memories, the certitudes, and the promises of the Old Left. Russia-firstism had been made insupportable by Hungary and then unintelligible by the Sino-Soviet split, well before Czechoslovakia was to make it grotesque. The doctrine of coexistence had therefore lost such binding practical authority as it had formerly possessed. The internationalizing of the class war, momentous event, along with the directly connected triumph of international monopoly as the prime mode of Western economic organization, called implicitly for a new conception of the participants in the ongoing conflict of classes. "You are nothing without the workers," advises a grand old revolutionary warhorse who won in colors in the anti-Fascist resistance, and who cannot fathom why his sons should now say, "Who precisely are they?"

The confidence needed to pose such a question could not come overnight, not even in Europe, where the methods of critical philosophy were much more available than in the United States. An American generation with obscure new projects rolling in the back of its mind, not finding itself suitably identified within the class typologies of a barely audible domestic radicalism, would initially misunderstand its political motivation as bad conscience about the blacks.

The high tide of the civil-rights movement began in February 1960 with the Greensboro sit-ins which led to the formation of the Student Nonviolent Coordinating Committee (SNCC). It ended with the Democratic Party's Atlantic City convention in August 1964, when the Mississippi Freedom Democratic Party's solid case for the unseating of the regular delegation was overridden in a well-televised exhibition of backroom politics. The main political event of the following summer was the Watts rebellion.

SNCC and SDS (Students for a Democratic Society) were answering to the name New Left early in the Sixties, but this needs two cautions. Both groups shared a pathological distrust for what they sneeringly called ideology. This was often noted by the early commentators, who understood it no better than did the New Left itself. It was accounted to be anti-intellectualism and the activist cheerfully accepted that account. In fact, it was a necessary defense against the power of an exhausted but nonetheless practiced ideology, the net effect of whose truths might easily have been to send the activists packing to the socialist clubs, where they would have been made either skillful at writing themselves off as change agents, or bored. They wanted neither. They wanted instead to go south and get their hands and their heads—their lives—into the dangerous, the moral, and therefore the authentic. The instinct from the beginning was to discover the streets, and there was nothing at all anti-intellectual about this. It embodied rather a refusal to tolerate the further separation of thought from its consequences: books argued with each other and lied and in any case did not make much of a difference; only direct experience was incontrovertible.

The second caution: there was simply nothing very radical or in need of ideology about the Movement's civil rights, Heroic Period, 1960-1964. What was so leftist about SNCC's "one man, one vote" demand? Or the abiding SDS principle of participatory democracy, the view that people should make the decisions that affect their lives? No one bothered to notice in those days that such a principle, fully understood, would lead through draft-card burning toward a demand for workers' control of the means of production.

From the beginning, the Movement gave the System the benefit of every doubt. An SDS slogan in 1964: "Part of the way with LBJ." There were always Movement people who understood that the seemingly innocuous demands were saturated with deeply radical implications, but it was not before 1965 or 1966 that this consciousness began to be widely shared. "Take the bourgeoisie at its word," Marx says somewhere, and this is precisely what the movement did, in its nearly spotless ignorance of Marx. Did it matter—as the schooled and knowing leftists insisted it did—that the early integrationist or student-power demands were only reformist or corporative? English New Leftist Tom Fawthrop, commenting on the June 1968 student rising at the University of Hull, wrote, "We chose the real politics of revolutionary democracy as opposed to the sham politics of revolutionary semantics. Every real struggle, every engagement with the power structure is worth a hundred revolutionary slogans."

German New Leftist Rudi Dutschke makes a point about this process which applies at least as forcibly to the American experience, and probably just as well to the French, English, Spanish, Mexican—and Czechoslovak. The new activists acquired their radical anti-authoritarianism at the end of police sticks that are swinging from one end of the earth to the other in behalf of everything dead and dry, in defense of social orders that prosper by denying life its possibilities and that greet every new aspiration with increasing indifference, derision, and violence. The policeman's riot club functions like a magic wand under whose hard caress the banal soul grows vivid and the nameless recover their authenticity—a bestower, this wand, of the lost charisma of the modern self: I bleed, therefore I am.

This is a ferocious but effective way to be a student—to be *educated*. By the end of the Chicago Democratic Party convention in August 1968, such young white activists as may still have supposed they were making this curiously unexamined revolution in the name of the blacks or the Vietnamese—or even the workers who (out of "false consciousness" no doubt) were cheering on the police—had had second thoughts pounded into their heads. The bad conscience which had seemed motive enough in the earlier period had been supplanted by a weightier sense of their own cultural need and hence of their own political mission. It was for themselves, these sons and daughters of the well-appointed classes, that the revolution would have to be made; for short of surrender—spiritual suicide—they seemed to have no other way to survive.

Whereupon the *need* for ideological thought, growing bit by bit as the Movement cantilevered itself steadily further from the liberal value system which had given it its first platform, had finally restored the *possibility* of ideological thought. The essentially personalistic apology for action which had satisfied all earlier engagements had become—one could *feel* this—insufficient. Its power to motivate and defend had dwindled with respect to the changing character of Movement actions and mood. An undistinguished idealism, really a fetish of innocence, could support Selma but not Watts, the campus teach-ins but not the Columbia insurrection. An existential morality had precipitated a chain of collisions which could finally be explained only in terms of historical politics. It had become necessary for a "youth movement" to discover—or create—a class identity.

Thus, having begun with a misreading of Camus, the American New Left at last begins to take up Marx, more than a little fearful that yet another misreading will be required, but hoping to sustain an additive revision. Can such a project succeed? Will a habituation to old certitudes even disallow the attempt? In any case, the clubs and committees have convinced the Movement that dialogue has certain limits and that a politics rooted in class imperatives is more likely to prosper than a politics rooted in that sort of moral fineness which is one product of the idleness of the few.

What is at stake is the political self-confidence of the Movement. Does the white "middle-class" New Left constitute the embryonic beginnings of a class-for-itself? Does it embody the beginnings of an identifiable historical practice which can neither be transferred to another class nor abandoned nor permanently defeated? Or, on the contrary, is this Movement merely the suds, the effervescing, of a globalized class war in which the entire West plays the role of capital and the entire neocolonial South that of labor, and whose basic features therefore differ only in scale from the class conflict of the nineteenth century?

The sharpest form of the question: in view of modern radicalism's unchallenged doctrine that the revolution is to be made by the army of industrial labor, how does the new radical dare to proceed (putting it mildly) in conspicous absence of that army?

First things first. *He does proceed.* Perhaps he has no choice and he is pure fatality; perhaps there is no fatality and he is pure will. His self-estimate may be sophisticated and in error or primitive and correct. His position may be invincible, absurd, both, or neither. It does not matter. He is on the scene, caught in events and definitively beyond silence, no longer awaiting some advance demonstration of the prudence or the consequences of engagement. It is not as if he is about to decide something as a precondition of doing something. The hands are out, the chips are down, the New Left is at the table with all the other gamblers.

So much for history.

For the New Left's future, its destiny, it must serve here to say that the debate intensifies at the same tempo as the confrontation, and that the confrontation is by this time clearly general in the West. Barring, by this time, not even England, which made its impressive debut in the spring of 1968, there is no advanced capitalist country which has not given rise to an increasingly self-aware and militant postwar movement centered physically in the universities and politically in anti-authoritarianism. At the same time, none of these countries (*not* excluding France!) has produced a living socialist movement centered in the factories. Further, each of the youth movements coalesced initially around some variation of an anti-imperialist issue (the May demonstrations at Essex, for example, began in protest against a talk given by a government germ-warfare expert). That is, the igniting spark has always jumped to the interior, to the imperial metropolis, from friction points at the frontier, and it has been only in the aftermath of anti-imperialists beginnings that these movements began to develop a more clearly self-interested political stance. This is doubly true of the American New Left. Reacting first against the oppression of the blacks, whose ghettos are like so many colonial native quarters, and then against the attempted suppression of the Vietnamese independence struggle, white activists have only recently discovered in practice the ubiquity of oppressive authoritarianism—discovered that for all the obvious modal differences, they share the victimization of the most humiliated slave.

There are four basic positions on the identity of the New Left.

The first is held by a variety of left-wing liberals and Millsian radicals who believe either that the System can produce a worthwhile self-reform, or (the case with the Millsians) that the absence of radical alternatives forces one to hope that it can. The New Left is understood then as à generator of challenges, of critical energy and ideas which may bear some fruit within the evolving structure of enlightened capitalism.

Second, the most familiarly radical position, is that the industrial workers remain the essential driving force of an inevitable socialist revolution. The student movement's main current purposes must be the building of a radical base among intellectuals and the making of such ties with the factories and the black groups as may be possible.

Third, an exclusively New Left position, is that the composition of the work force has been significantly altered by the massive assimilation of industry and technology. Students and workers are from now on one and the same. "There are no student problems," begins *The Appeal from the Sorbonne*. The factory of the post-industrial state is the multiversity. Students are the new working class.

Fourth is a position which has not yet been argued in a sustained way, although it is perhaps suggested in some of the writings by André Gorz, Louis Althusser, and Martin Nicolaus. Diverging from the conclusions but not the methods of Marx, this view would share with the new-working-class theory the notion that students can no longer be understood as if the modern university retained all the key features of the medieval university. Students constitute the beginnings of a new historical class, produced by a workers' revolution which (within the West) is not still to come but which has already taken place. Such a view implies several departures from classical Marxism. First, it denies that bourgeois society in anything like the original model still exists: bourgeois society was above all a scarcity society, a fact which determined its chief legal, political, and economic features. What we have now, inadequately termed post-scarcity and post-industrial, is, in fact, merely the fulfilled industrial society. Second, it denies that bourgeois society (or any other) is the last of the contradictory social system. On the contrary, there is more reason to believe that each historically successful revolution will produce a new class with a new conception of need and possibility, new objectives which will motivate new historical practices. Third, it denies that the mission of the proletariat was to make the socialist revolution. The objective evidence indicates, rather, that its mission was to industrialize society—a mission which brought it into sharp conflict with the bourgeoisie. Fourth, it denies that current world politics can be understood as a clash of rival socio-ethical systems. Capitalism and socialism, as defined by their practice, are different means, corresponding to different material and political situations, for pursuing the common and general aim of industrialization. Fifth, far from hero-worshipping the proletariat, the new class (unnamed and no doubt at this point unnameable) repudiates in part and in part carries forward the proletarian culture in much the same way that the proletariat both absorbed and transcended bourgeois culture. That an embryonic new class will seek alliance with the proletariat in its struggle with the bourgeoisie—this has the same kind of meaning as the fact that the embryonic proletariat made alliance with the bourgeoisie in the latter's struggle against Versailles.

So much—at the moment—for speculation.

Whether as de-classed provocateur, as an attendant upon another class's temporarily stalled revolution, as a new version of that other class, or as something new, the New Left will create itself through its actions in an arena defined as well as occupied by other forces. Even as this is written—mid-fall of 1968—George Wallace's Presidential campaign has conclusively established the presence of a serious fascist movement: militarism, chauvinism, racism—all bound together by a deformed populist nostalgia which gives this movement both its menace and its irony. At the same moment, Establishment liberalism has altogether lost its former poise, as well as its control of the nation's primary political media. Overnight, the nation's majority coalition, the Democratic Party, has become all but an also-ran. The next four years no doubt will be filled with a continuing crisis within the Atlantic economy and either the agonies of disengagement from Vietnam or the extension of the war to China, thence quickly to the world as a whole. Against this backdrop, domestic politics will be dominated by the continuing rise of the Right and a bewildered Establishment's attempts both to appease populist reaction and New Left militancy and to reassemble a functioning Center coalition, one shade to the left of Nixon. In terms of the day-to-day necessities implied by this over-all conjuncture, the New Left will have to discover or create its historical identity. What we already know is simply that it has one—that through the appropriately discoherent New Left movement, the postwar generations have implicated themselves in history's permanent showdown between fatality and will.

The Concept of the Left
Leszek Kolakowski

Leszek Kolakowski (1927-   ), a Polish philosopher, first received international recognition in the early days of the "thaw" just after Stalin's death. Since then his reputation as a provocative, unsparing thinker has been established on both sides of the Atlantic. Author of *The Alienation of Reason: A History of Positivist Thought* (1968), *Toward a Marxist Humanism: Essays on the Left Today* (1968), and *Marxism and Beyond* (1969).

Every work of man is a compromise between the material and the tool. Tools are never quite equal to their tasks, and none is beyond improvement. Aside from differences in human skill, the tool's imperfection and the material's resistance together set the limits that determine the end product. But the tool must fit the material, no matter how remotely, if it isn't to produce a monstrosity. You cannot properly clean teeth with an oil drill or perform brain operations with a pencil. Whenever such attempts have been made the results have always been less than satisfactory.

THE LEFT AS NEGATION

Social revolutions are a compromise between utopia and historical reality. The tool of the revolution is utopia, and the material is the social reality on which one wants to impose a new form. And the tool must to some degree fit the substance if the results are not to become ludicrous.

There is, however, an essential difference between work on physical objects and work on history; for the latter, which is the substance, also creates the tools used to give this substance shape. Utopias which try to give history a new form are themselves a product of history, while history itself remains anonymous. That is why even when the tools turn out to be grossly unsuited to the material, no one is to blame, and it would be senseless to hold anyone responsible.

On the other hand, history is a human product. Although no individual is responsible for the result of the historical process, still each is responsible for his personal involvement in it. Therefore each is also responsible for his role in fashioning the intellectual tools used upon reality in order to change it—for accepting or rejecting a given utopia and the means employed to realize it.

To construct a utopia is always an act of negation toward an existing reality, a desire to transform it. But *negation is not the opposite of construction—it is only the opposite of affirming existing conditions.* That is why is makes little sense to reproach someone for committing a destructive rather than a constructive act because every act of construction is necessarily a negation of the existing order. At most, you may reproach him for not supporting the reality that exists and for wanting to change it; or, on the other hand, for accepting it without qualification, without seeking change; or, finally, for seeking harmful changes. But a negative position is only the opposite of a conservative attitude toward the world, negation in itself being merely a desire for change. The difference between destructive and constructive work lies in a verbal mystification stemming from the adjectives used to describe the changes, which are considered either good or bad. Every change is, in fact, an act both negative and positive at one and the same time, and the opposite only of an affirmation of things as they are. To blow up a house is just as constructive as to build one—and at the same time just as negative. Of course, this does not mean that it is all the same whether one destroys or builds a house. The difference between the two acts is that the first, in most instances, works to the detriment of the people involved, and the second is almost always to their benefit. The opposite of blowing up a house is not to build a new house but to retain the existing one.

This observation will serve to lead to conclusions whose aim is to define more closely the meaning we give to the concept of the social Left.

The Left—and this is its unchangeable and indispensable quality, though by no means its only one—is a movement of negation toward the existent world. For this very reason it is, as we have seen, a constructive force. It is, simply, a quest for change.

That is why *the Left rejects the objection that its program is only a negative and not a constructive one.*

The Left can cope with reproaches directed at the potential harm or utility that may arise from its negations. It can also contend with the conservative attitude that wants to perpetuate things as they are. It will not defend itself, however, against the accusation of being purely negative, because every constructive program is negative, and vice versa. A Left without a constructive program cannot, by that token, have a negative one, since these two terms are synonymous. If there is no program, there is at the same time no negation, that is, no opposite of the Left—in other words, conservativism.

UTOPIA AND THE LEFT

But the act of negation does not in itself define the Left, for there are movements with retrogressive goals. Hitlerism was the negation of the Weimar Republic, but this does not make it leftist. In countries not controlled by the Right, an extreme counterrevolutionary movement is always a negation of the existing order. Thus the Left is defined by its negation, *but not only by this*; it is also defined by the direction of this negation, in fact, by the nature of its utopia.

I use the word "utopia" deliberately and not in the derogatory sense that expresses the absurd notion that all social changes are pipe dreams. By utopia I mean a state of social consciousness, a mental counterpart to the social movement striving for radical change in the world—a counterpart itself inadequate to these changes and merely reflecting them in an idealized and obscure form. It endows the real movement with the sense of realizing an ideal born in the realm of pure spirit and not in *current* historical experience. Utopia is, therefore, a mysterious consciousness of an actual historical tendency. As long as this tendency lives only a clandestine existence, without finding expression in mass social movements, it gives birth to utopias in the narrower sense, that is, to individually constructed models of the world, as it *should* be. But in time utopia becomes actual social consciousness; it invades the consciousness of a mass movement and becomes one of its essential driving forces. Utopia, then, crosses over from the domain of theoretical and moral thought into the field of practical thinking, and itself begins to govern human action.

Still, this does not make it realizable. Utopia always remains a phenomenon of the world of thought; even when backed by the power of a social movement and, more importantly, even when it enters its consciousness, it is inadequate, going far beyond the movement's potentials. It is, in a way, "pathological" (in a loose sense of the word, for utopian consciousness is in fact a natural social phenomenon). It is a warped attempt to impose upon a historically realistic movement goals that are beyond history.

However—and this is fundamental to an understanding of the internal contradictions of left-wing movements—the Left cannot do without a utopia. The Left gives forth utopias just as the pancreas discharges insulin—by virtue of an innate law. Utopia is the striving for changes which "realistically" cannot be brought about by immediate action, which lie beyond the foreseeable future and defy planning. Still, utopia is a tool of action upon reality and of planning social activity.

A utopia, if it proves so remote from reality that the wish to enforce it would be grotesque, would lead to a monstrous deformation, to socially harmful changes threatening the freedom of man. The Left, if it succeeds, would then turn into its opposite—the Right. But then, too, the utopia would cease to be a utopia and become a slogan justifying every current practice.

On the other hand, the Left cannot renounce utopia; it cannot give up goals that are, for the time being, unattainable, but that impart meaning to social changes. I am speaking of the social Left as a whole, for though the concept of the Left is relative—one is a leftist only in comparison with something, and not in absolute terms—still the extreme element of every Left is a revolutionary movement. The revolutionary movement is a catch-all for all the ultimate demands made upon existing society. It is a total negation of the existing system and, therefore, also a total program. A total program is, in fact, a utopia. A utopia is a necessary component of the revolutionary Left, and the latter is a necessary product of the social Left as a whole.

Yet why is a utopia a condition of all revolutionary movements? Because much historical experience, more or less buried in the social consciousness, tells us that goals unattainable now will never be reached unless they are articulated when they are still unattainable. It may well be that the impossible at a given moment can become possible only by being stated at a time when it is impossible. To cite an example, a series of reforms will never attain the goals of revolution, a consistent reform party will never imperceptibly be transformed into the fulfillment of a revolution. *The existence of a utopia as a utopia is the necessary prerequisite for its eventually ceasing to be a utopia.*

A revolutionary movement cannot be born simultaneously with the act of revolution, for without a revolutionary movement to precede it the revolution could never come about. As long as the revolutionary act has not been accomplished, or is not indisputably and clearly evident, it is a utopia. For today's Spanish proletariat a social revolution is a utopia; but the Spanish proletariat will never achieve a revolution if it does not proclaim it when it is impossible. This is why tradition plays such an important role in the revolutionary movement: the movement would never know any victories if it had not in previous phases suffered inevitable defeats—if it had not initiated revolutionary activity when the historical situation precluded success.

The desire for revolution cannot be born only when the situation is ripe, because among the conditions for this ripeness are the revolutionary demands made of an unripe reality. The continuous influence of social consciousness is one of the necessary conditions for the maturation of history to the point of radical change; utopia is a prerequisite of social upheavals, just as unrealistic efforts are the precondition of realistic ones. That is the reason why revolutionary consciousness cannot be satisfied with mere participation in changes already taking place; it cannot merely follow events, but must precede them at a time when they are neither planned nor anticipated.

Therefore—and this is an elementary practical conclusion—*the Left doesn't mind being reproached for striving for a utopia.* It may have to defend itself against the accusation that the content of its utopia is damaging to society, but it need not defend itself against the charge of being utopian.

The Right, as a conservative force, needs no utopia; its essence is the affirmation of existing conditions—a fact and not a utopia—or else the desire to revert to a state which was once an accomplished fact. The Right strives to idealize actual conditions not to change them. What it needs is fraud, not utopia.

The Left cannot give up utopia because it is a real force even when it is merely a utopia. The sixteenth-century revolt of the German peasants, the Babouvist movement, and the Paris Commune were all utopian. As it turned out, without such utopian activities no nonutopian, progressive social changes would have taken place. Obviously, it does not follow that the task of the Left is to undertake extreme actions in every historical situation. All we are saying is that to condemn utopia for the mere fact that it is a utopia is rightist, conservative, and hampers the prospects of ever creating a utopia. In any event, we are not at the moment formulating social tasks. We are considering the concept of the Left completely in the abstract, trying to ascertain and not to postulate. Since the Left is as "normal" a social phenomenon as the Right, and progressive social movements are as normal as reactionary ones, it is equally normal for the Left, which is a minority, to be persecuted by the Right.

THE LEFT AND SOCIAL CLASSES

The concept of the Left remains unclear to this day. Although only about a hundred and fifty years old, it has acquired universal historical dimensions and is applied to ancient history by virtue of a diffusion of meaning common to all languages. Broadly used, the term has a practical function, but its meaning becomes very obscure, more sensed than understood. One thing is certain: It is easier to say which movements, programs, and attitudes are Left in relation to others than to determine where the Left ends and the Right begins in the political power relationship within society's total structure. We speak of a Left within Hitler's party, but that does not, of course, mean that the German Right was restricted to the party Right and that everything else, including the left wing of that party, was the Left in an absolute sense. Society cannot be divided into a Right and a Left. A leftist attitude toward one movement can be linked with a rightist attitude toward another. It is only in their relative meanings that these words make sense.

But what do we mean when we say a movement or an attitude is Left in relation to another? More specifically, which aspect of the concept of the Left is valid in all social situations? For example, what do we mean when we speak of the Left in the Radical Party of France, or of the social-democratic, Catholic, or communist Left? Is there some common element in the word used in such varied contexts? Or are we simply stating that every political situation reveals some human activity we either approve or find to be the less repugnant, and which we therefore call "the Left"? (I say "we call" because the Left draws the dividing line between the Left and the Right, while the Right fights this division systematically—and in vain, for the Left's self-definition is strong enough to define the Right and, in any event, to establish the existence of the demarcation line.)

No doubt because it has taken on a positive aura, the term "Left" is often appropriated by reactionary groups. For example, there is the "European Left,' a political annex of the European Coal and Steel Community. So the mere use of the word does not define the Left. We must look for other signposts to help us fix our position in this murky area. Slogans like "freedom" and "equality" belong, of course, to the tradition of the Left; but they lost their meaning once they became universal catchwords to which everyone attached his own arbitrary interpretation. As time passes, the Left must define itself ever more precisely. For the more it influences social consciousness, the more its slogans take on a positive aura, the more they are appropriated by the Right and lose their defined meaning. Nobody today opposes such concepts as "freedom" and "equality"; that is why they can become implements of fraud, suspect unless they are explained. What is worse, the word "socialism" has also acquired many meanings.

Naturally, it is quite easy to define the Left in general terms, as we can define "progress." But general definitions are necessarily misleading and difficult to apply in concrete discussions. For example, we can say that "Leftness" is the degree of participation in the process of social development that strives to eliminate all conditions in which the possibility of satisfying human needs is obstructed by social relations. From such a definition we derive a certain number of equally general slogans that are too universally accepted to be useful in fixing political demarcations. The concepts of the Left, of progress, and of freedom are full of internal contradictions; political disputes do not arise from the mere acceptance or rejection of the concepts.

Therefore, rather than construct an easy though ineffective general concept of the Left applicable to all eras, let us accept existing social reality as a fact and look for the basic conflicts and, secondarily, political ones. However, the political battle is not completely identical with the pattern of class relations; it is not a carbon copy of them transposed to relations between political parties. This is so because class divisions are not the only kind, and classes themselves are becoming more, rather than less, complicated because they are split from within by nationality or ideology. Finally, there are political divisions, in so far as they assume diverse forms of autonomy. Under these conditions political life cannot reflect class conflicts purely and directly but, on the contrary, ever more indirectly and confusedly. As a matter of fact, it was never otherwise—if it had been, all historical conflicts would have been resolved centuries ago. That is why the statement that it must be in the interest of the working class to belong to the Left does not always hold true. On the one hand, it is characteristic of the Left to try not to realize men's wishes against their will, nor to force them to accept benefits they do not desire. On the other hand, the working class of a given country may be greatly influenced by nationalism, yet the Left will not support nationalistic demands; elsewhere, the working class may have deep roots in a religious tradition, yet the Left is a secular movement. Even real immediate interests of the working class can be in opposition to the demands of the Left. For example, for a long time the English workers benefited from colonial exploitation—and yet the Left is an enemy of colonialism.

That is why the Left cannot be defined by saying it will always, in every case, support every demand of the working class, or that it is always on the side of the majority. The Left must define itself on the level of ideas, conceding that in many instances it will find itself in the minority. Even though in today's world there is no leftist attitude independent of the struggle for the rights of the working class, though no leftist position can be realized outside the class structure, and though only the struggle of the oppressed can make the Left a material force, nevertheless the Left must be defined in intellectual, and not class, terms. This presupposes that concrete intellectual life is not and cannot be an exact replica of class interests.

On this basis, we can set forth certain characteristics of the position of the Left in various social orders:

In capitalist countries the fight of the Left is to abolish all social privilege. In noncapitalist countries, it is to remove privileges that have grown out of noncapitalist conditions.

In capitalist countries the Left fights all forms of colonial oppression. In noncapitalist ones, it demands the abolition of inequalities, discrimination, and the exploitation of certain countries by others.

In capitalist countries the Left struggles against limitations on freedom of speech and expression. It does so also in noncapitalist lands. In one and the other the Left fights all the contradictions of freedom that arise in *both kinds* of social conditions: How far can one push the demand for tolerance without turning against the idea of tolerance itself? How can one guarantee that tolerance will not lead to the victory of forces that will strangle the principle of tolerance? This is the great problem of all leftist movements. It is also true, obviously, that the Left can make mistakes and act ineffectively, and thus engender a situation that is inimical to itself. However, it is not faulty tactics that are the distinguishing feature of the Left, for, as we have said, its criteria are established on an ideological plane.

In capitalist countries the Left strives to secularize social life. This is also true in noncapitalist countries.

In capitalist countries the destruction of all racism is an essential part of the Left's position. This is so in noncapitalist lands as well.

Everywhere the Left fights against the encroachment of any type of obscurantism in social life; it fights for the victory of rational thought, which is by no means a luxury reserved for the intellectuals, but an integral component of social progress in this century. Without it any form of progress becomes a parody of its own premises.

Finally, under both systems, the Left does not exclude the use of force when necessary, though the use of force is not an invention of the Left, but rather an unavoidable form of social existence. The Left accepts the antinomy of force, but only as an antinomy and not as a gift of fate. Everywhere the Left is ready to compromise with historical facts, but it rejects ideological compromises; that is, it does not abdicate the right to proclaim the basic tenets of its existence regardless of its political tactics.

The Left is free of sacred feelings; it has no sense of sanctity toward any existing historical situation. It takes a position of permanent revisionism toward reality, just as the Right assumes an attitude of opportunism in respect to the world as it is. The Right is the embodiment of the inertia of historical reality—that is why it is as eternal as the Left.

In both systems the Left strives to base its prospects on the experience and evolutionary tendencies of history; whereas the Right is the expression of capitulation to the situation of the moment. For this reason the Left can have a political ideology, while the Right has nothing but tactics.

Within the context of both systems, the Left knows that every human freedom satisfies a specific need, but that there is also a need for freedom as such.

The Left does not fear history. It believes in the flexibility of social relations and of human nature—in the possibility of changing them. Within both camps it rejects all humility vis-à-vis existing situations, authorities, doctrines, the majority, prejudgments, or material pressures.

In both, the Left—not excluding the use of force, not ashamed of it, and not calling it "upbringing" or "benevolence" or "care for children," etc.—nevertheless rejects any means of political warfare that leads to moral consequences which contradict its premises.

All this time I have been describing the Left as a certain ideological and moral attitude. For the Left is not a single, defined political movement, or party, or group of parties. The Left is a characteristic which to a greater or lesser degree can serve particular movements or parties, as well as given individuals or human activities, attitudes, and ideologies. One can be leftist from one point of view and not from another. There rarely occur political movements that are totally leftist in every aspect throughout the entire course of their existence. A man of the Left can participate in the political struggle and be a politician in a leftist party, but refuse to approve actions and opinions that are clearly inimical to a leftist attitude. Which does not mean, obviously, that the leftist position does not lead to internal conflicts and contradictions.

For these reasons the Left, as such and as a whole, cannot be an organized political movement. The Left is always to the left in certain respects with relation to some political movements. Every party has its left wing, a current which is farther to the left than the rest of the party in regard to some trait that can be cited as an example. Still, this does not mean that all the leftist elements of all parties taken together form a single movement, or that they are more closely allied to each other than they are to the party that gave birth to them. This would be so if they fulfilled all the requirements of being left in every aspect; but in that case they would not have been segments of so many diverse parties with such varied programs to begin with. The left wing of the Christian-democratic parties has, as a rule, infinitely more in common with them than with the socialist Left, yet it is the Christian-democratic Left on this very basis. Its "Leftness" may be shown by a stand on one or another actual political problem that, in the particular instance, brings it nearer the left of other parties—for example, a condemnation of colonialism or racialism. On the other hand, the demands of the Left are met to varying degrees by different parties, which for this reason are called more or less leftist.

The Ideology of the University
Richard Lichtman

Richard Lichtman (1930-   ) is a Fellow of the Center for the Study of Democratic Institutions and a founder of the Bay Area School in San Francisco. He is the editor of *Socialist Revolution*.

THE UNIVERSITY: MASK FOR PRIVILEGE?

Nothing can better illustrate the collapse of reason as an independent, critical agent in our society than a comparison of the remarks of two observers, separated by one hundred years, on the nature of a university education. In the middle of the nineteenth century one of its astutest critics noted:

The proper function of a University in national education is tolerably well understood. At least there is a tolerably general agreement about what a University is not.

It is not a place of professional education. Universities are not intended to teach the knowledge required to fit men for some special mode of gaining their livelihood. Their object is not to make skillful lawyers, or physicians, or engineers, but capable and cultivated human beings. It is very right that there should be public facilities for the study of professions. . . . But

Reprinted, with permission, from the January 1968 issue of *The Center Magazine*, a publication of the Center for the Study of Democratic Institutions in Santa Barbara, California.

these things are no part of what every generation owes to the next, as that on which its civilization and worth will principally depend. They are needed only by a comparative few . . . and even those few do not require them until after their education . . . has been completed. . . . Men are men before they are lawyers, or physicians, or merchants, or manufacturers; and if you will make them capable and sensible men, they will make themselves capable and sensible lawyers or physicians.

What professional men should carry away with them from a University, is not professional knowledge, but that which should direct the use of their professional knowledge, and bring the light of general culture to illuminate the technicalities of a special pursuit. . . . And doubtless . . . the crown and consummation of a liberal education . . . [is that the pupil be taught] to methodize his knowledge; to look at every separate part of it in its relation to other parts, and to the whole . . . observing how all knowledge is connected, how we ascend to one branch by means of another, how the higher modifies the lower and the lower helps us to understand the higher . . . combining the partial glimpses which he has obtained of the field of human knowledge at different points, into a general map . . . of the entire region.

This view has given way in our time to a very different conception:

The University . . . once was an integrated community. . . . It had a single purpose. . . . The conversation was in common.

This community chose to destroy itself. It became larger. It became heterogeneous. It came to talk in many tongues. . . . With the rise of science over the past century, more and bigger laboratories have been required. . . . The pressure of population, the explosion of books, the scientific revolution . . . all press for size beyond the limits of the face-to-face and mouth-to-ear community.

Knowledge has expanded and expanded, from theology and philosophy and law and medicine and accounting to the whole range of humanities, the social sciences and the sciences and the professions. More knowledge has resulted from and led to more and more research on a larger and larger scale. Research has led to service for government and industry and agriculture . . . all of this is natural. None of it can be reversed. . . . Small intellectual communities can exist and serve a purpose, but they run against the logic of their times.

The campus has evolved consistently with society. It has been pulled outward to society and pulled to pieces internally. The campus consistent with society has served as a good introduction to society—to bigness, to specialization, to diffusion of interests.

The welfare-state university, or multi-university, developed particularly in the United States to provide something for nearly everybody—for farmers, for the minor and newer professions, for the general citizen who wanted to satisfy his curiosity. . . . It made the welfare of society in nearly all its aspects a part of its concern . . . the University has served many masters in many ways.

The University and segments of industry are becoming more and more alike. As the University becomes tied to the world of work, the professor—at least in the natural and some of the social sciences—takes on the characteristics of an entrepreneur. . . . The two worlds are merging physically. . . . [The University is] a mechanism held together by administrative rules and powered by money.

The first of these comments is from John Stuart Mill; the second, from Clark Kerr, until recently President of the University of California.

I have quoted them at length because they illuminate one of the great transitions of the modern age—the decline of autonomous, rational criticism, and the rise of what Professor Herbert Marcuse entitled "one-dimensional man."

They represent the early and terminal stages in the development of centralized, bureaucratic economic power—extended now to such a point that it is able to absorb what was once proclaimed to be a transcendent center of analysis and judgment.

We need not romanticize Mill's age, nor pretend that the university students of whom he spoke acted in radical concert to revise the foundations of their time. They were, in their own way, as readily absorbed into the hierarchy of domestic civil service and foreign imperialism as students of our own society are absorbed into comparable institutions. Of crucial significance is that the very ideal of autonomy has been denied and that those who speak for higher education in this country come increasingly to derive their definition of purpose from the existing agencies of established power.

The pronouncements of Mill and Clark Kerr differ in several significant ways. The first stresses coherence, the second fragmentation; the first is exclusionary, the second is ready to incorporate any interest that society urges upon it; the first distinguishes between higher and lower knowledge, while the second distributes its emphasis in accordance with available financial support. Of greatest importance, perhaps, is that the older view regards itself as bound by intrinsic canons of culture, while the current conception accommodates and molds itself to prevailing trends.

The first view holds to an ideal of transcendence while the second is grossly imminent in its time. For contemporary doctrine, the ancient tension between what the world is and what it might become has all but vanished. The current perspective is an an apologia, a celebration, an ideological consecration of this most lovely of all possible worlds—in short, a consenting academy.

This conclusion follows directly from Mr. Kerr's own analysis, for if the University performs all the functions that society imposes upon it, it will in due course most ably fulfill the predominant function every social system requires for its very existence—the justification of its established structure of power and privilege, the masking or idealization of its deficiencies, and the discrediting of dissent.

The history of all previous societies reveals to us a group of men whose primary function was to legitimate established authority. Our own time is only notable for the special urgency it imposed on the task. There are various domestic and international reasons for this development.

The first concerns the growing complexity of our technological order and its encompassing social organizations. The requirements of intelligence become more exact and the skills needed for managerial and bureaucratic roles more demanding. Accompanying these economic developments is the parallel transformation of the society from one concerned primarily with the manipulation of material things to one concerned with manipulation of individuals. The role of physical labor declines and the role of intellectual skills and personal services is augmented in a growing white-collar stratum.

There is a change in emphasis in the industrial system from force to persuasion, a growth of public relations, managerial counseling, and mass advertising; in short, an extensive shift from production to consumption and from overt authority to covert ideological inducement.

Second, the development of a mass society tied less to specific locations and cultural traditions than to the common mass media for the formation of their life styles produces a populace eager to be formed and potentially dangerous to the status quo if it is not adequately standardized.

Again, the growing education level and sophistication of some sectors of the population make it necessary to mollify the possible dissent of those who might discover flaws in the social facade. But, paradoxically, the development of education facilitates this enterprise, for there are some deceptions which only a semi-educated man could be expected to believe or sacrifice his life for.

But the most important internal need for ideology grows from the slowly developing awareness of the discrepancy between what this social system has the power to provide its members and what it actually makes available to them. Technological resources are adequate to provide a very high level of material welfare to the entire population if the control over these facilities can be made to pass progressively from the hands of a self-authenticating business autocracy to the authority of the people as a whole.

Venerable arguments for the necessity of social injustice, class privilege, physical and cultural deprivation, and the dehumanization of labor are being corroded by the potentialities of abundance. Those who hold power in this sytem, then, are forced to construct elaborate theories to justify persisting misery. Here, the aid of the University can prove extremely valuable.

But there are two additional motives of illusion which derive from the international position of the United States today. Both stem from the fact of America's predominant economic power and expansiveness in the world, from its dominance over foreign economies on a global scale, and from the need generated by its productive system for subservient foreign nations to act as the suppliers of its resources and the outlets for its dislocations.

The two challenges come from the Soviet Union and China on the one hand, and from the underdeveloped third of the world on the other. The first are threats because they reject capitalistic values and compete with us in the world for economic power. The second set of nations is even more disquieting, however, for they are seeking their self-liberation at the precise moment at which the United States has emerged unmistakably as the world's dominant imperialist power. But we are not prepared to grant them control of their industrial development, and our counter-effort is an attempt to destroy their movement toward economic autonomy through financial pressure when possible, and military intervention when necessary.

The national attempt at defense against these threats to the United States world hegemony produced the hysteria of the last twenty years of rabid anti-communism and cold-war containment—the euphemism for America's self-righteousness in domination. Intellectuals have played a significant role in producing the obsfuscations of the time, and the educational system has been one of the leading contributors to the pathology of awareness.

Vigorous rebellion or revolution may fail to occur for two very different reasons: either because men are so equal to each other in their relations that it is unnecessary, or because, while radically unequal, they perceive no way of altering their situation. But the development of technology in this country is making it progressively clearer to the impoverished in this country and to the underdeveloped countries that the suffering and injustice they are forced to undergo is not inevitable. Therefore, the more technology develops, and the more its benefits are expropriated by the privileged of the world, the greater becomes the need of the dominant class to cloak its injustice and to pretend that its actions are in the common interest or beyond the powers of men to change.

The growing division between what the world is and what it might become is the primary force behind the intensification of ancient ideological functions.

The consequences of these various internal and external pressures is that the

United States is urgently compelled to disarm radical dissent and insure the performance of roles necessary to continued international hostility.

Those in power recognize the importance of domestic consensus to achieve these ends. The educational views of men like Mr. Kerr, which stress the need for molding reason to the pattern of contemporary power, appear conveniently to facilitate economic and military service and the soothing of discontent.

A University patterned after Mill's ideal could not possibly perform this task, but the contemporary University performs it masterfully. Approximately 75 per cent of the research budget of the University derives from Federal contracts, and, as Mr. Kerr notes: "Expenditures have been largely restricted to the physical and bio-medical sciences, and to engineering, with only 3 per cent for the social sciences and hardly any support for the humanities."

This distribution is defended on the grounds that it represents the national interest and the flow of money after "the most exciting new ideas." What we are being offered here is a new version of the invisible hand in which Gresham's Law is inverted to the effect that good money always drives out bad money and produces just that balance which promotes the public good.

The Federal funding of the University is only one of the media through which the pattern of society is impressed on higher education, but it exemplifies the defects transmitted through all the available media. The most crucial of these corruptions is the destruction of the internal community of the University and its replacement by a series of fragmented and isolated departmental structures without common speech, common imagination, or common purpose.

Mill's conception of a university as a place in which the student was taught to "methodize his knowledge; to look at every separate part of it in its relation to the other parts, and to the whole," is not only all but nonexistent in the current academic world, it is increasingly difficult for a growing number of educators to understand. Mr. James A. Perkins, President of Cornell, for example, has suggested that the conflict between research and scholarship might be reconciled by simply abandoning liberal education and beginning the process of specialization at matriculation. (*The University in Transition*. Princeton University Press: 1966.)

The causes of the diffusion of the University need be noted solely for the light they throw on the nature of the disintegration involved. The reason most intrinsic to the University is the fact that knowledge has been growing at a very rapid rate, making it continually more difficult for any one thinker to grasp the whole domain. But this in itself would not produce the fragmentation which occurs (since it is not the case that everything known must be taught by a university) except for the presence of other factors.

First, there is a tendency to refinement in specialized roles which seems to occur in all advanced technological societies. Next, there are the distinctly American elaborations of this theme. One derives from the anti-intellectualism of our life with its distrust of achievement for its own sake and consequent insistence that thought subserve specific ends and redeem itself through the practical results of concrete actions. To this must be added the sense of many intellectuals that if they cannot alter the shape of massive, unresponsive social power they can at least derive some satisfaction by serving it.

In this mood reason gives up the claim to direct social change. It settles instead for the immediate rewards of technical manipulation and becomes an efficient means to ends beyond its power or judgment.

The tendency is strengthened by a widespread assumption that in America the good life has already been achieved in a system of democratic, corporate pluralism. The quest of the ages having been completed, there is nothing more for reason to do but maintain the current structure and make the necessary minor corrections. This tendency is supported by the loose, casual patterning of American life, the laissez-faire climate of American political and economic history, and the general conviction that the pursuit of private, local ends will miraculously produce a public good.

It is not that public life is devoid of integration and rational planning. Industrial firms plan to the limits of their ability, and the foresight of some oligopolies and international cartels is undoubtedly extensive. But these plans are made and the activities coordinated for the sake of individual corporate ends, not for the sake of the policy as a whole. Nothing displays such technical intelligence and ingenuity as an automated factory and produces such irrational dislocation in the lives of men who are unemployed through this human achievement. The sense of the whole system is of rationality defeating its own human requirements.

As Mr. Kerr has led us to expect, this pattern of sporadic rationality in conflict with its own potential achievement is found within the structure of the University. There, education is defined mechanically as the piling up of specific skills and bits of information, as a mound is constructed out of the piling up of individual grains of sand. The student is never required to state the relevance of one area of understanding for another, nor relate their distinctive methodologies and insights in coherent, synthetic connection. It is assumed that the summation of individually correct answers will produce something more than fragmented understanding.

The center of this disruptive environment is the individual department, where men competing for recognition establish small empires under a mutual security agreement that insures each the safety of his own domain. This safety is further enhanced against the forays of others by increasingly narrowing the limits of one's investigation until the subject is so esoteric that each individual can rightly claim to be the only living authority in the field.

Such a systematic fragmenting of knowledge cannot be corrected by the simple insertion into the curriculum of a few inter-disciplinary courses. If the teachers of these courses have to win departmental approval, they are likely to come under the wrath of specialists who rightly see in the man of vision a threat to their insular success. Furthermore, as the current system prevails, the continued existence of comprehensive teachers is more and more problematical.

The immediate result is that the University is more and more populated by scholar-researchers who more closely resemble idiot-savants than men of wisdom; students find it more and more difficult to gain some comprehensive vision of themselves as world-historical beings.

In the social sciences it is very close to the truth to maintain that any problem which appears open to solution within a specific discipline is either misunderstood or of secondary importance. But the most important, over-all effect of this continued division of incommunicable skill is its ideological consequence—the tendency to stifle consciousness and the need for radical social change.

A large social vision need not be radical, but a fragmented vision cannot be radical. The piecemeal, technical thinker can see a small advantage here and a corresponding defect there. His vision is additive; he sums up the merits and defects of a system and makes his judgment in the face of the total balance. What he lacks is dialectical understanding, the capacity to see how a specific social defect is rooted in a large structural pattern—for example, how the abuses revealed in the drug industry stem from the irresponsible power and social avarice of corporate liberalism as a system, and indicate the hopelessness of conventional attempts at regulation. Or the technical thinker sees a particular social benefit, such as the increase in average working class wages and gross national product, but he lacks any capacity to place this fact in the context of fixed maldistribution of income, or in the larger system of exploitative relations which America bears to the under-developed nations of the world.

That ideology is generally an inversion of reality is borne out by the current educational situation, for the University is in the process of intellectual dissolution at that precise moment of history in which the development of centralized, bureaucratic corporate power has been dominating progressively larger areas of national and international life and drawing the world's economy and destiny into an increasingly seamless whole.

The period of American domination over the world economy coincides with the period in which global concepts have been increasingly abandoned by large numbers of social scientists, whose range of interest has contracted; in specific areas of inquiry the problems they confront are of very limited relevance to the emerging world reality.

This confinement of understanding disrupts the foundations of intellectual life. The man of reason is being dismembered before our eyes. In his place appear pairs of adversaries—the teacher stands against the researching scholar, the man of thought against the man of action, the neutral analyst against the man of passionate commitment.

In the University the teacher retreats before the onslaught of the research technologists and knowledge diffusers. Every university maintains a house Negro or two—a professor whose advancement has been based predominantly upon his power as a teacher and who is dragged out on ceremonial occasions to silence the critic. But for every such anachronism there are one hundred practitioners of the conventions who have scrambled to respectability over a mass of journals and anthologies. The teacher who embodies a vision, whose life manifests in its own activity the content of his teaching art, is vanishing from sight.

What the current generation of students discovers immediately in those who profess to teach them is an almost impassable chasm between the nature of their intellectual pronouncements and the content of their lives. This is one of the grounds of the charge of irrelevance in education and one of the main reasons for student disaffection. Nor is it a defect that can be remedied without transforming the University, and that would in turn require the radical reconstruction of the society in which the University exists.

As William Arrowsmith has commented,

At present the universities are as uncongenial to teaching as the Mojave Desert to a clutch of Druid priests. If you want to restore a Druid priesthood, you cannot do it by offering prizes for Druid-of-the-year. If you want Druids, you must grow forests. There is no other way of setting about it.

If it is in fact true that the University has become a service adjunct to prevailing social powers it should not be surprising that so much of its activity is taken up in the intense cultivation of disinterested intelligence. There is a clue to this process in one of the works of the German aesthetician Wilhelm Worringer. In his book, *Abstraction and Empathy* (International Universities Press: 1963), he identifies naturalism with a feeling of confidence in the external world, and particularly the organic, living world. The experience of naturalistic art is held to depend on the subject's identification with organic forms as exemplified in his own existence. Abstract art, on the contrary, is traced to a feeling of anguish and confusion in face of the complexity and instability of living beings; it is viewed as an attempt to flee this realm of dissolution for the sanctity of abstract order.

A great deal of contemporary research appears to be similarly motivated. If it is not immediately useful to established power it tends to withdraw and place between itself and the anxieties and responsibilities of the world what Bullough called "aesthetic distance" and what W. H. Auden referred to as "lecturing on Navigation while the ship is going down."

The University can accommodate itself to national power in one of two ways—overtly or covertly, through subservience or indifference, through the performance of assigned tasks, or the distraction and trivialization of potentially critical thought.

For subservience we can do no better than the introduction to Seymour Martin Lipset's *Political Man* (Doubleday: 1959). We discover there a number of astounding things: "that the United States [is] a nation in which leftist values predominate"; that "the values of liberty and equality become institutionalized within America to a greater extent than in other nations"; that "the values of socialism and Americanism are similar"; that, economic systems apart, Herbert Hoover, Andrew Carnegie, and John D. Rockefeller "advocated the same set of social relations among men" as Marx, Engels, and Lenin; that democratic regimes are characterized by an underlying desire to avoid war.

The key to this innovative reconstruction of history is provided in the last chapter of the volume, wherein we are informed that

> ... the fundamental political problems of the industrial revolution have been solved: the workers have achieved industrial and political citizenship; the conservatives have accepted the welfare state; and the democratic left has recognized that an increase in over-all state power carries with it more dangers to freedom than solutions for economic problems.

How good it must be to see the world as sociologists see it—devoid of economic exploitation, of Iran, Guatemala, the Dominican Republic, and Vietnam; devoid of poverty, injustice, and brutalized technology. History may yet record these sweet reflections less as a hymn to quietude than as the last muffled cry of the ostrich as its mouth fills up with sand. . . .

The fragmented intellect lives in comparative safety and quiet in the security of its own conceptual enclave. Here, it sets barriers against reason and the world. One social scientist tells us:

> ... science achieves its unparalleled powers by the continuous breakdown of its problem into smaller units and refinements of methods made possible by this division. On the other hand, so deeply entrenched is the humanistic supposition that "to see a man at all one must see him whole" that not even the continuous work on the dikes of their separate disciplines by academicians can keep social thought flowing in its prescribed channels without continuous leakage into and from others. (*Don Martindale,* Functionalism in the Social Sciences. *American Academy of Political and Social Sciences: 1960.*)

One can almost feel the shudder along the author's pen as he notes the "leakage" which tends to confuse the comfortable precision of his categories. Nor are we surprised when he proceeds to inform us that the social sciences must analyze their "problems dispassionately in a value-neutral manner," and that the aim of "turning these disciplines into genuine sciences"—that is, of breaking them down into smaller conceptual units—"is only possible through dredging operations to remove moral commitments that block the development of scientific objectivity." In these few lines, fragmentation, neutralism, the assimilation of the social to the physical sciences, and the confinement of thought to disinterested contemplation, the entire mythos of contemporary social science is concentrated and made apparent.

The connection among these factors is no mere accident. There are some perceptive comments on this matter in E. P. Thompson's *The Making of the English Working Class* (Pantheon: 1964). At one point the author comments on the contemporary discussion among historians on what has come to be known as "the standards of living controversy." He maintains:

The objection to the reigning academic orthodoxy is not to empirical studies, per se, but to the fragmentation of our comprehension of the full historical process. First, the empiricist segregates certain events from this process and examines them in isolation. Since the conditions which gave rise to these events are assumed, they appear not only as explicable in their own terms but as inevitable. ... But there is a second stage, where the empiricist may put these fragmentary studies back together from a multiplicity of interlocking inevitabilities, a piecemeal processional ... we arrive at a post facto [sic] determinism. The dimension of human agency is lost.

We have come across the language of inevitability before. It was Mr. Kerr who informed us that the "community of scholars disappeared gradually and inevitably over the centuries ... [that the University] must adapt sufficiently to its culture if it is to survive. All of this is natural. None of it can be reversed." One is inclined to reply that the inevitability of history could only have proceeded through the choice of human beings like Mr. Kerr and others who played a significant role in forming education in our time. In Mr. Kerr's analysis, however, human agency is made to dissolve, and a new rational man appears who is simply the vessel of necessity.

The crux of this conception is Mr. Kerr's judgment that the process is *natural*, a view which assimilates human history to the processes of nature and the physical sciences, in which the observer contemplates the behavior of material which possesses no responsibility for the direction of its process.

No reading of the future could have prescribed to American educators the choice they should have made for the American University—this choice was dependent upon the values, principles, and limited wisdom they brought to their understanding of history. What we are really being told in these fragments is that the American educator chose to capitulate to one of the tendencies of his time, that he agreed to relinquish his rational autonomy, and that, having made this specific decision, he is now incapable of regarding himself as anything more than the medium through which the course of the future blindly passes. But this logic unmasks the myth of neutrality, for the choice of passivity, the commitment to subservience, produced the observer's sense that he is the mere conductor of an irreversible process.

The same loss of rational autonomy and moral responsibility which underlies the division between thought and action is the source, too, of the dichotomies of fact and value, means and ends.

The prevailing credo of contemporary social inquiry limits reason to an analysis of those means which will lead most efficiently to given ends; reason is strictly precluded from passing judgment on the ends themselves. The value of the exercise is said to lie in the accumulation of stores of neutral knowledge, useful for whatever ends we intend to employ them.

The significance of this position is that it places reason and technological expertise at the disposal of prevailing power. The thinker who has abdicated responsibility for the purpose of his life by placing control over his actions in powers beyond his authority has made himself a hostage to the times. Having relinquished his claim to normative reason, he is without mooring in the world. The tides of current times, degenerate as they may be, will sweep the uncommitted in their course.

We are witness to the spectacle of men of small imagination, limited in comprehension to diminishing areas of inquiry, lacking the capacity to note the import of their activity for the more pervasive aspects of human enterprise, subservient to an establishment that does not hesitate to use them for the most inhuman and obnoxious ends—men of technical reason, as skilled at killing as at healing, progressively unconcerned with the distinction, and unaware that value resides anywhere but in technique itself. So, crippled reason pays obeisance to power and the faculty in man most apt to nurture life becomes the instrument of violence and death.

The consequence of fragmentation and of a division in the life of reason is the destruction of human autonomy. The University is thickly populated by cynical or silent men. In response to the compartmentalization of intelligence, pseudo-syntheses appear—unified visions of social man, built on the crudest model of physics or animal psychology. A widespread behaviorism appears in social thought, grounded in a methodology derived third-hand from a defunct philosophy. Quality, uniqueness, creativity, and the moral dimension of existence fall before a reductive insistence upon measurement, quantification, and restrictive processes of infinitely tedious and irrelevant observation. The view of man which emerges is ahistorical, atomistic, mechanical, disjunctive, and, again, ostensibly neutral.

We come at last to the scholarship of civility: devoid of passion, lacking love or outrage, irrelevant to the agency of man. "The advancement of learning at the expense of man," Nietzsche wrote, "is the most pernicious thing in the world."

Exactly what is the moral obligation of the University as a corporate body? It is no use telling us now, as we were told recently by Richard Hofstadter, that while individual members of the University may voice conviction, the University as a public institution is bound to strict neutrality. Mr. Kerr demolished that argument for all time. It is no less neutral to oppose society than to support it, to refuse a place to military service than to credit it.

Neutrality is only conceivable with isolation. Nothing in the public realm can fail, at specific points, to aid or undermine established power. Man's existence is only possible through action, which requires the selection of choices and the foreclosure of others. One cannot, in all instances, avoid choice; the only hope is to choose responsibly, in light of the largest understanding and the most humane commitment.

As the University is rooted in the world, it must, at given moments, choose a public course. The liberal contention that the University should refrain from criticism is an expression of "preferential neutralism," a transparently hypocritical device for the maintenance of continued service.

Of course, it is not the corporate function of the University to speak to every public issue, nor even to the vast majority of prevailing social concerns. The fundamental purpose of the University does not encompass any specific policy in regard to most contemporary matters. In its public pronouncement and corporate activity, the University should refrain from endorsing particular views in the overwhelming number of cases. But when the University's support is solicited by established agencies of power, it must decide if the services requested of it violate its defining purpose, and reject them if they do. And so, it is also obligated to protest when society has undertaken to violate, in regard either to the University itself or to humanity at large, values that the University is specifically charged to honor.

To discover the public function of a University one must begin with its internal imperative—the gathering of a community of scholars in devotion to disinterested knowledge. Such, at least, is the traditional wisdom. But it is not adequate to our time.

John Stuart Mill wrote for an age in which the distinction between pure and applied research was largely valid. The man of science could pursue his theory in the general expectation that it would not be employed to endanger mankind. Today the distinction between pure and applied science is disappearing with the growth of a state power so imperious and technologically competent that it can transform the most esoteric knowledge into techniques of terror.

Science has itself contributed to the creation of that state machinery which now makes the enterprise of science hazardous. It has done so because it has lacked responsibility for its growth. It is too late now to fall back on the platitudes of academic freedom; no biochemist can be sure that in pursuing the structure of an enzyme he is not perfecting a lethal form of warfare. This government will have to be disarmed before the clear and present danger now subverting thought can be dissolved. Until men of knowledge act to change the world, they cannot claim the unrestricted right to understand it.

But what is the obligation of those members of the University whose knowledge cannot be technologized? To answer this question we must answer another. What is the true nature of the University?

The University is the institutionalized embodiment of the life of the dialogue; that is, of communal inquiry. Dialogue is rooted in the fact that men are imperfect and perfectible. Comprehensive knowledge is not given to man in an instant. It is the elaboration of history. Nor is it given to any single man; it is the cooperative achievement of a human community. Dialogue cannot be perfected unless it is free, and the basis of rational freedom is the self-determination of imperfect reason by its own ideal. It is freeing because it liberates intelligence from matter that is extraneous or destructive of is inherent purpose—knowledge.

A mind in pursuit of knowledge is one in which the various facets of awareness are active, cumulative, and mutually relevant, wherein observation, inference, imagination, and evaluative judgment inform each other in a cumulative achievement. It is a process which depends upon creativity—the capacity to construct new alternatives. To this end the University cultivates the arts, whose function is not merely to act as a critical interpreter of experience, but to manifest to us, through concrete works, those ideal possibilities of existence of which we were previously unaware. Whatever the differences between art and discursive reason, they share a common enterprise: they cultivate the human spirit, which is the capacity of man to transcend his present context for the sake of a more comprehensive, articulate, and worthy vision of himself. That vision, in all its forms, is culture, which it is the obligation of the University to honor and protect.

The peculiar alienation of the intellectual leads him to pursue culture as an abstract end. He becomes blind to the simple fact that there is no knowledge independent of the "knowings" of individual men, nor any realm of art or science separate from the creations of actual, concrete human beings. What the University is meant to house and celebrate is not a detached domain of lifeless categories, but the spiritual existence of man, in which those categories live and take their meaning.

What is the obligation of the University in a world in which one nation is reducing the people of another to the most primitive functions of its existence; when the very rudiments of civilization are being extinguished and the orders of life upon which reason grows are being destroyed by systematic violence? In such circumstances it is the obligation of the University to rebel against the violation of man and align itself in public witness with humanity.

Today, the University is required to condemn the government of the United States for its barbaric crusade against the life and spirit of the people of Vietnam. A university that will not speak for man, whatever tasks it continues to perform, has ceased to be a human enterprise.

The University can deny its times because, like any human agency, it is not wholly absorbed in its social context. It has a special capacity to transcend its social constraints because it embodies a tradition of intellectual diversity and articulate criticism and because, of all human functions, thought is the most difficult to curtail. But while the University is uniquely promising, it is also uniquely threatened by the pressures of ideology to which we have already referred. The University is in constant tension between its ideal critical capacity and the powers of secular service that delimit its hope. Therefore, while the protest movement is centered in the University, the activity of protest is not central to the University.

It is possible to act to change the world because we are not totally imminent in it; but it is necessary for us to change the world because we do not very much transcend it. Here is the point of truth in the conception of the multiversity. The sheer understanding that society is corrupt does not place one outside corruption. For we do not experience social existence at a distance, we ingest it. The act by which the University affirms its humanity and denies American barbarism does not constitute the cure of the University.

It may be, as Hegel has noted, that the hand that inflicts the wound is the hand that cures it. But it does so only through an anguished labor. One cannot throw off all he has been made in the density of the social world with a simple shrug of the understanding. Plato knew this truth two thousand years ago. We are still bound by it. The University has been molded by current powers and we have been formed and malformed in our turn. The alienation of society has become our apathy and fragmentation; its anti-intellectualism and glorification of technology, our play at neutralism in an inversion of ends and means; its crude devotion to wealth and power, our imbalance and intellectual prostitution.

To reconstitute one's self is for a man to remake the world in which he is defined. To know what we might become is not a simple act of the intellect; it requires that we engage in such committed action as can destroy the deforming boundaries of our lives. So, action and thought require each other, inform each other, and complete each other. The obligation imposed on the intellectual, as it is imposed on any one man, is not merely to speak against the world but to refashion it.

It is not a violation of the purpose of a university that some part of its activity serve society; but the University must determine through its own critical agency that the society it is to serve is a place in which the spirit of man may be nurtured and advanced.

The University is at this moment an ideological institution, a mask for systematic dominance and privilege. But as Marx noted: "The call for men to abandon their illusions about their condition is a call for men to abandon a condition which requires illusion." A free and human community of scholars can only flourish when the multitudinous communities of the exploited, the wretched, and the brutalized peoples of the earth have broken the bonds of their subservience and established themselves as men of full stature. To participate in the projection and the making of that world is the responsibility of the intellectual.

The Economic Basis of the New Left
Ernest Mandel

Ernest Mandel (1924-   ) is an economist from Belgium. Among his books are *Europe Versus America;* (1970) *Fifty Years of World Revolution, 1917-1967*, (1970) and *Marxist Economic Theory* (1969).

Today, profound forces are working to undermine the social and economic equilibrium which has reigned in the United States for more than 25 years, since the big depressions of 1929-32 and of 1937-38. Some of these are forces of an international character, linked with the national liberation struggles of the peoples exploited by American imperialism—above all the Vietnamese Revolution. But from the point of view of Marxist method, it is important in the first place to stress those forces which are at work inside the system itself. This essay will attempt to isolate six of these forces—six historic contradictions which are now destroying the social equilibrium of the capitalist economy and bourgeois order of the United States.

From Ernest Mandel, "Where Is American Going?" *New Left Review*, No. 54 (March-April 1969), pp. 3-15. Reprinted by permission.

THE DECLINE OF UNSKILLED LABOUR AND THE SOCIAL ROOTS OF BLACK RADICALIZATION

American society, like every other industrialized capitalist country, is currently in the throes of an accelerated process of technological change. The third industrial revolution—summarized in the catchword 'automation'—has by now been transforming American industry for nearly two decades. The changes which this new industrial revolution has brought about in American society are manifold. During the fifties, it created increased unemployment. The annual growth-rate of productivity was higher than the annual growth-rate of output, and as a result there was a tendency to rising structural unemployment even in times of boom and prosperity. Average annual unemployment reached 5,000,000 by the end of the Republican administration.

Since the early sixties, the number of unemployed has, however, been reduced somewhat (although American unemployment statistics are very unreliable). It has probably come down from an average of 5,000,000 to an average of 3,500,000 to 4,000,000: these figures refer to structural unemployment, and not to the conjunctural unemployment which occurs during periods of recession. But whatever may be the causes of this temporary and relative decline in structural unemployment, it is very significant that one sector of the American population continues to be hit very hard by the development of automation: the general category of unskilled labour. Unskilled labour jobs are today rapidly disappearing in US industry. They will in the future tend to disappear in the economy altogether. In absolute figures, the number of unskilled labour jobs in industry has come down from 13,000,000 to less than 4,000,000, and probably to 3,000,000, within the last 10 years. This is a truly revolutionary process. Very rarely has anything of the kind happened with such speed in the whole history of capitalism. The group which has been hit hardest by the disappearance of unskilled jobs, is, of course, the black population of the United States.

The rapid decline in the number of unskilled jobs in American industry is the nexus which binds the growing negro revolt, especially the revolt of negro youth, to the general socio-economic framework of American capitalism. Of course it is clear, as most observers have indicated, that the acceleration of the negro revolt, and in particular the radicalization of negro youth in the fifties and early sixties, has been closely linked to the development of the colonial revolution. The appearance of independent states in Black Africa, the Cuban Revolution with its radical suppression of racial discrimination, and the development of the Vietnam War, have been powerful subjective and moral factors in accelerating the Afro-American explosion in the USA. But we must not overlook the objective stimuli which have grown out of the inner development of American capitalism itself. The long post-war boom and the explosive progress in agricultural productivity were the first factors in the massive urbanization and proletarization of the Afro-Americans: the Northern ghettoes grew by leaps and bounds. Today, the average rate of unemployment among the black population is double what it is among the white population, and the average rate of unemployment among *youth* is double what it is among adults, so that the average among the black youth is nearly four times the general average in the country. Up to 15 or 20 per cent of the young black workers are unemployed: this is a percentage analogous to that of the Great Depression. It is sufficient to look at these figures to understand the social and material origin of the black revolt.

It is important to stress the very intimate inter-relationship between this high rate of unemployment among black youth and the generally scandalous state of education for black people in the ghettoes. This school system produces a large majority of drop-outs precisely at the moment when unskilled jobs are fast disappearing. It is perfectly clear under these conditions why black nationalists feel so strongly about the problem of community control over black schools—a problem which in New York and elsewhere has become a real crystallizing point for the black liberation struggle.

THE SOCIAL ROOTS OF THE STUDENT REVOLT

The third industrial revolution can be seen at one and the same time as a process of *expulsion* of human labour from traditional industry, and of tremendous *influx* of industrial labour into all other fields of economic and social activity. Whereas more and more people are replaced by machines in industry, activities like agriculture, office administration, public administration and even education become industrialized—that is, more and more mechanized, streamlined and organized in industrial forms.

This leads to very important social consequences. These may be summed up by saying that, in the framework of the third industrial revolution, manual labour is expelled from production while intellectual labour is reintroduced into the productive process on a gigantic scale. It thereby becomes to an every-increasing degree alienated labour—standardized, mechanized, and subjected to rigid rules and regimentation, in exactly the same way that manual labour was in the first and second industrial revolutions. This fact is very closely linked with one of the most spectacular recent developments in American society: the massive student revolt, or, more correctly, the growing radicalization of students. To give an indication of the scope of this transformation in American society, it is enough to consider that the United States, which at the beginning of this century was still essentially a country exporting agricultural products, today contains fewer farmers than students. There are today in the United States 6,000,000 students, and the number of farmers together with their employees and family-help has sunk below 5,500,000. We are confronted with a colossal transformation which upsets traditional relations between social groups, expelling human labour radically from certain fields of activity, but reintroducing it on a larger scale and at a higher level of qualification and skill in other fields.

If one looks at the destiny of the new students, one can see another very important transformation, related to the changes which automation and technological progress have brought about in the American economy. Twenty or thirty years ago, it was still true that the students were in general either future capitalists, self-employed or agents of capitalism. The majority of them became either doctors, lawyers, architects, and so on or functionaries with managerial positions in capitalist industry or the State. But today this pattern is radically changed. It is obvious that there are not 6,000,000 jobs for capitalists in contemporary American society: neither for capitalists or self-employed professionals, nor for agents of capitalism. Thus a great number of present-day students are not future capitalists at all, but future salary-earners, in teaching, public administration and at various technical levels in industry and the economy. Their status will be nearer that of the industrial worker than that of management. For meanwhile, as a result of automation, the difference of status between the technician and the skilled worker is rapidly diminishing. US society is moving towards a situation in which most of the skilled workers for whom there remain jobs in industry will have to have a higher or semi-higher education. Such a situation already exists in certain industries even in countries other than the United States—Japanese shipbuilding is a notorious example.

The university explosion in the United States has created the same intense consciousness of alienation among students as that which is familiar in Western Europe today. This is all the more revealing, in that the material reasons for student revolt are much less evident in the United States than in Europe. Overcrowding of lecture halls, paucity of student lodgings, lack of cheap food in restaurants and other phenomena of a similar kind play a comparatively small role in American universities, whose material infrastructure is generally far superior to anything that we know in Europe. Nevertheless, the consciousness of alienation resulting from the capitalist form of the university, from the bourgeois structure and function of higher education and the authoritarian administration of it, has become more and more widespread. It is a symptomatic reflection of the changed social position of the students today in society.

American students are thus much more likely to understand general social alienation, in other words to become at least potentially anti-capitalist, than they were 10 or 15 years ago. Here the similarity with developments in Western Europe is striking. As a rule, political mobilization on the US campus started with aid to the black population within the United States, or solidarity with liberation movements in the Third World. The first political reaction of American students was an anti-imperialist one. But the logic of anti-imperialism has led the student movement to understand, at least in part, the necessity of anticapitalist struggle, and to develop a socialist consciousness which is today widespread in radical student circles.

AUTOMATION, TECHNICIANS AND THE HIERARCHICAL STRUCTURE OF THE FACTORY

The progress of automation has also had another financial and economic result, which we cannot yet see clearly in Europe, but which has emerged as a marked tendency in the United States during the sixties. Marxist theory explains that one of the main special effects of automation and the present technological revolution is a shortening of the life-cycle of fixed capital. Machinery is now generally replaced every four or five years, while it used to be replaced every ten years in classical capitalism. Looking at the phenomenon from the perspective of the operations of big corporations, this means that there is occurring a shift of the centre of their gravity away from problems of *production* towards problems of *reproduction*.

The real bosses of the big corporations no longer mainly discuss the problems of how to organize production: that is left to lower-echelon levels of the hierarchy. The specific objective in which they are interested is how to organize and to ensure reproduction. In other words, what they discuss is future plans: plans for replacing the existing machinery, plans for financing that replacement, new fields and locations for investment, and so on. This has given the concentration of capital in the United States a new and unforeseen twist. The process of amalgamation during the last few years has not predominantly consisted in the creation of monopolies in certain branches of industry, fusing together automobile, copper or steel trusts, or aviation factories. It has instead been a movement towards uniting apparently quite *unconnected* companies, operating in completely heteroclite fields of production. There are some classical examples of this process, widely discussed in the American financial press, such as the Xerox-CIT merger, the spectacular diversification of the International Telephone and Telegraph Corporation, or the Ling-Temco-Vought empire, which recently bought up the Jones and Loughlin Steel Corporation.

What this movement really reflects is the growing pre-occupation with 'pure' problems of accumulation of capital. That is to say, the imperative today is to assemble enough capital and then to diversify the investment of that capital in such a way as to minimize the risks of structural or conjunctural decline in this or that branch—risks which are very great in periods of fast technological change. In other words, the operation of the capitalist system in the United States today shows in a very clear way what Marxists have always said (and what only economists in the Soviet Union and some of their associates in East European countries and elsewhere are forgetting today), namely that real cost reduction and income maximization is impossible if profitability is reckoned only at plant level. In fact, it is a truth which every big American corporation understands, that it is impossible to have maximum profitability and economic rationality at plant level, and that it is even impossible to achieve it at the level of a *single branch of industry*. That is why the prevailing capitalist tendency in the USA is to try to combine activities in a number of branches of production. The type of financial empire which is springing up as a result of this form of operation is a fascinating object of study for Marxists.

But the more Big Capital is exclusively pre-occupied with problems of capital accumulation and reproduction, the more it leaves plant management and organization of production to lower-echelon experts, and the more the smooth running of the economy must clash with the survival of private property and of the hierarchical structure of the factory. The absentee factory-owners and money-juggling financiers divorced from the productive process are not straw men. They retain ultimate power—the power to open or to close the plant, to shut it in one town and relaunch it 2,000 miles away, to suppress by one stroke of their pens 20,000 jobs and 50 skills acquired at the price of long human efforts. This power must seem more and more arbitrary and absolute in the eyes of the true technicians who precisely do *not* wield the decisive power, that of the owners of capital. The higher the level of education and scientific knowledge of the average worker-technician, the more obsolete must become the attempts of both capitalists and managers to maintain the hierarchical and authoritarian structure of the plant, which even contradicts the logic of the latest techniques—the need for flexible co-operation within the factory in the place of a rigid chain of command.

THE EROSION OF REAL WAGE INCREASES THROUGH INFLATION

Since the beginning of the sixties and the advent of the Kennedy Administration, structural unemployment has gone down and the rate of growth of the American economy has gone up. This shift has been generally associated with an increased rate of inflation in the American economy. The concrete origins and source of this inflation are to be located not only in the huge military establishment—although, of course, this is the main cause—but also in the vastly increased indebtedness of the whole American society. Private debt has accelerated very quickly; in the last 15 years it has gone up from something like 65 per cent to something like 120 per cent of the internal national income of the country, and this percentage is rising all the time. It passed the $1,000,0000,000 (thousand billion) mark a few years ago, in 1966, and is continually rising at a quicker rate than the national income itself. The specific price behaviour of the monopolistic and oligopolistic corporations, of course, interlocks with this inflationary process.

This is not the place to explore the technical problems of inflation. But it should be emphasized that the result of these inflationary tendencies, combined with the Vietnam war, has been that, for the first time for over three decades the growth of the real disposable income of the American working class has stopped. The highest point of that disposable real income was reached towards the end of 1965 and the beginning of 1966. Since then it has been going down. The downturn has been very slow—probably less than 1 per cent per annum. Nevertheless it is a significant break in a tendency which has continued practically without interruption for the last 35 years. This downturn in the real income of the workers has been the result of two processes: on the one hand inflation, and on the other a steep increase in taxation since the beginning of the Vietnamese war. There is a very clear and concrete relation between this halt in the rise of the American working class's real income, and the growing impatience which exists today in American working class circles with the US Establishment as such, whose distorted reflection was partly to be seen in the Wallace movement.

It is, of course, impossible to speak at this stage of any political opposition on the part of the American working class to the capitalist system as such. But if American workers accepted more or less easily and normally the integration of their trade union leadership into the Democratic Party during the long period which started with the Roosevelt Administration, this acceptance was a product of the fact that their real income and material conditions, especially their social security, improved during that period. Today that period seems to be coming to an end. The current stagnation of proletarian real income means that the integration of the trade union bureaucracy into the bourgeois Democratic Party is now no longer accepted quite so easily as it was even four years ago. This was evident during the Presidential Election campaign of 1968. The UAW leadership organized their usual special convention to give formal endorsement to the Democratic candidates, Humphrey and Muskie. This time they got a real shock. Of the thousand delegates who normally come to these conventions, nearly one half did not show up at all. They no longer supported the Democratic Party with enthusiasm. They had lost any sense of identification with the Johnson Administration. All the talk about welfare legislation, social security, medicare and the other advantages which the workers had gained during the last four years was largely neutralized in their eyes by the results of inflation and of increased taxation on their incomes. The fact was that their real wages had stopped growing and were even starting to decline a little.

It is well known that dollar inflation in the United States has created major tensions in the world monetary systems. Inside the USA, there is now a debate among different circles of the ruling class, the political personnel of the bourgeoisie, and the official economic experts, as to whether to give priority to restoring the US balance of payments, or to maintaining the present rate of growth. These two goals seem to be incompatible. Each attempt to stifle inflation completely, to re-establish a very stable currency, can only be ensured by deflationary policies which create unemployment—and probably unemployment on a considerable scale. Each attempt to create full employment and to quicken the rate of growth inevitably increases inflation and with it the general loss of power of the currency. This is the dilemma which confronts the new Republican administration today as it confronted Johnson yesterday. It is impossible to predict what course Nixon will choose, but it is quite possible that his economic policy will be closer to that of the Eisenhower Administration than to that of the Kennedy-Johnson Administrations.

A group of leading American businessmen, who form a council of business advisors with semi-official standing, published a study two weeks before the November 1968 election which created a sensation in financial circles. They stated bluntly that in order to combat inflation, at least 6 per cent unemployment was needed. These American businessmen are far more outspoken than their British counterparts, who are already happy when there is talk about 3 per cent unemployment. Unemployment of 6 per cent in the United States means about 5,000,000 permanently without work. It is a high figure compared to the present level, to the level under 'normal' conditions, outside of recessions. If Nixon should move in that direction, in which the international bankers would like to push him, the American bourgeoisie will encounter increased difficulty in keeping the trade-union movement quiescent and ensuring that the American workers continue to accept the integration of their union bureaucracy into the system, passively submitting to both bosses and union bureaucrats.

THE SOCIAL CONSEQUENCES OF PUBLIC SQUALOR

There is a further consequence of inflation which will have a growing impact on the American economy and especially on social relations in the United States. Inflation greatly intensifies the contradiction between 'private affluence' and 'public squalor'. This contradiction has been highlighted by liberal economists like Galbraith, and is today very striking for a European visiting the United States. The extent to which the public services in that rich country have broken down is, in fact, astonishing. The huge budget has still not proved capable of maintaining a minimum standard of normally functioning public services. In late 1968, the *New York Times Magazine*, criticizing the American postal services, revealed that the average letter travels between Washington and New York more slowly today than it did a hundred years ago on horseback in the West. In a city like New York street sweeping has almost entirely disappeared. Thoroughfares are generally filthy: in the poorer districts, streets are hardly ever cleaned. In the richer districts, the burgers achieve clean streets only because they pay private workers out of their own pockets to sweep the streets and keep them in more or less normal conditions. Perhaps the most extraordinary phenomenon, at any rate for the European, is that of certain big cities in the South-West, like Houston or Phoenix, which have half a million inhabitants or more and yet do not have any public transport system *whatsoever*: not a broken-down system—just no system at all. There are private cars and nothing else—no buses, no trams, no subways, nothing.

The contradiction between private affluence and public squalor has generally been studied from the point of view of the consumer, and of the penalties or inconveniences that it imposes on the average citizen. But there is another dimension to this contradiction which will become more and more important in the years to come. This is its impact on what one could call the 'producers', that is to say of the people who are employed by public administration.

The number of these employees is increasing very rapidly. Public administration is already the largest single source of employment in the United States, employing over 11,000,000 wage earners. The various strata into which these 11,000,000 can be divided are all chronically underpaid. They have an average income which is lower than the income of the equivalent positions in private industry. This is not exceptional; similar phenomena have existed or exist in many European countries. But the results—results which have often been seen in Europe during the last 10 or 15 years—are now for the first time appearing on a large scale in the United States.

Public employees, who in the past were outside the trade-union movement and indeed any form of organized social activity, are today becoming radicalized at least at the union level. They are organizing, they are agitating, and they are demanding incomes at least similar to those which they could get in private industry. In a country like the United States, with the imperial position it occupies on a world scale, the vulnerability of the social system to any increase in trade-union radicalism by public employees is very great. A small example will do as illustration. In New York recently both police and firemen were, not officially but effectively, on strike—at the same time. They merely worked to rule, and thereby disorganized the whole urban life of the city. Everything broke down. In fact, for six days total traffic chaos reigned in New York. Drivers could park their cars anywhere without them being towed away. (Under normal conditions, between two and three thousand cars are towed away by the police each day in New York.) For those six days, with motorists free to park where they liked, the town became completely blocked after an hour of morning traffic—just because the police wanted a 10 per cent rise in wages.

The economic rationale of this problem needs to be understood. It is very important not to see it simply as an example of mistaken policy on the part of public administrators or capitalist politicians, but rather as the expression of basic tendencies of the capitalist system. One of the main trends of the last 25 or 30 years of European capitalism has been the growing socialization of all indirect costs of production. This constitutes a very direct contribution to the realization of private profit and to the accumulation of capital. Capitalists increasingly want the State to pay not only for electrical cables and roads, but also for research, development, education, and social insurance. But once this tendency towards the socialization of indirect costs of production gets under way, it is obvious that the corporations will not accept large increases in taxation to finance it. If they were to pay the taxes needed to cover all these costs, there would in fact be no 'socialization'. They would continue to pay for them privately, but instead of doing so directly they would pay indirectly through their taxes (and pay for the administration of these payments too). Instead of lessening the burden, such a solution would in fact increase it. So there is an inevitable institutionalized resistance of the corporations and of the capitalist class to increasing taxes up to the point where they would make possible a functional public service capable of satisfying the needs of the entire population. For this reason, it is probable that the gap between the wages of public employees and those of private workers in the United States will remain, and that the trend towards radicalization of public employees—both increased unionization and even possibly political radicalization—will continue.

Moreover, it is not without importance that a great number of university students enter public administration—both graduates and so-called drop-outs. Even today, if we look at the last four or five years, many young people who were student leaders or militants three or four years ago are now to be found teaching in the schools or working in municipal social services. They may lose part of their radical consciousness when they take jobs; that is the hope not only of their parents but also of the capitalist class. But the evidence shows that at least part of their political consciousness is preserved, and that there occurs a certain infiltration of radicalism from the student sector into the teaching body—especially in higher education—and into the various strata of public administration in which ex-students become employed.

THE IMPACT OF FOREIGN COMPETITION

The way in which certain objective contradictions within the United States economy have been slowly tending to transform the subjective consciousness of different groups of the country's population—negroes, especially negro youth; students; technicians; public employees—has now been indicated. Inflation has begun to disaffect growing sections of the working class. But the final, and most important, moment of a Marxist analysis of US imperial society today has not yet been reached—that is the threat to American capitalism now posed by international competition.

Traditionally, American workers have always enjoyed much higher real wages than European workers. The historical causes for this phenomenon are well known. They are linked with the shortage of labour in the United States, which was originally a largely empty country. Traditionally, American capitalist industry was able to absorb these higher wages because it was practically isolated from international competition. Very few European manufactured goods reached the United States, and United States industry exported only a small part of its output. Over the last 40 years, of course, the situation has slowly changed. American industry has become ever more integrated into the world market. It participates increasingly in international competition, both because it exports more and because the American domestic market is rapidly itself becoming the principal sector of the world market, since the exports of all other capitalist countries to the United States have been growing rapidly. Here a major paradox seems to arise. How can American workers earn real wages which are between two and three times higher than real wages in Western Europe, and between four and five times higher than real wages in Japan, while American industry is involved in international competition?

The answer is, of course, evident. These higher wages have been possibly because United States industry has operated on a much higher level of productivity than European or Japanese industry. It has enjoyed a productivity gap, or as Engels said of British industry in the 19th century, a *productivity monopoly* on the world market. This productivity monopoly is a function of two factors: higher technology, and economy of scale—that is a much larger dimension of the average factory or firm. Today, both of these two causes of the productivity gap are threatened. The technological advance over Japan or Western Europe which has characterized

American imperialism is now disappearing very rapidly. The very trend of massive capital export to the other imperialist countries which distinguishes American imperialism, and the very nature of the so-called 'multi-national' corporation (which in nine cases out of ten is in reality an American corporation), diffuses American technology on a world scale, thus equalizing technological levels at least among the imperialist countries. At the same time, it tends, of course, to increase the gap between the imperialist and the semi-colonial countries. Today, one can say that only in a few special fields such as computers and aircraft does American industry still enjoy a real technological advantage over its European and Japanese competitors. But these two sectors, although they may be very important for the future, are not decisive for the total export and import market either in Europe or in the United States, nor will they be decisive for the next 10 or 20 years. So this advantage is a little less important than certain European analysts have claimed.

If one looks at other sectors, in which the technological advantage is disappearing or has disappeared—such as steel, automobiles, electrical appliances, textiles, furniture, or certain types of machinery—it is evident that a massive invasion of the American market by foreign products is taking place. In steel, something between 15 and 20 per cent of American consumption is today imported from Japan and Western Europe. The Japanese are beginning to dominate the West Coast steel market, and the Europeans to take a large slice of the East Coast market. It is only in the Mid-West, which is still the major industrial region of the United States, that imported steel is not widely used. But with the opening of the St. Lawrence seaway, even there the issue may be doubtful in the future. Meanwhile, automobiles are imported into the United States today at a rate which represents 10-15 per cent of total annual consumption. This proportion too could very quickly go up to 20-25 per cent. There is a similar development in furniture, textiles, transistor radios and portable television sets; shipbuilding and electrical appliances might be next.

So far, the gradual disappearance of the productivity differential has created increased competition for American capitalism in its own home market. Its foreign markets are seriously threatened or disappearing in certain fields like automobiles and steel. This, of course, is only the first phase. If the concentration of European and Japanese industry starts to create units which operate on the same scale as American units, with the same dimensions as American corporations, then American industry will ultimately find itself in an impossible position. It will then have to pay three times higher wages, with the same productivity as the Europeans or the Japanese. That would be an absolutely untenable situation, and it would be the beginning of a huge structural crisis for American industry.

Two examples should suffice to show that this is not a completely fantastic perspective. The last merger in the Japanese steel industry created a Japanese corporation producing 22,000,000 tons of steel a year. In the United States, this would make it the second biggest steel firm. On the other hand, in Europe the recent announcement that Fiat and Citroen are to merge by 1970 has created an automobile corporation producing 2,000,000 cars a year; this would make it the third largest American automobile firm, and it would move up into second place, overtaking Ford, if the momentum of its rate of growth, compared with the current rate of growth in the American industry, were maintained for another three or four years.

These examples make it clear that it is possible for European and Japanese firms, if the existing process of capital concentration continues, to attain not only a comparable technology but also comparable scale to that of the top American firms. When they reach that level, American workers' wages are certain to be attacked, because it is not possible in the capitalist world to produce with the same productivity as rivals abroad and yet pay workers at home two or three times higher wages.

THE WAGE DIFFERENTIALS ENJOYED BY AMERICAN WORKERS

The American ruling class is becoming increasingly aware that the huge wage differential which it still grants its workers is a handicap in international competition. Although this handicap has not yet become a serious fetter, American capitalists have already begun to react to it in various ways over the past few years.

The export of capital is precisely designed to counteract this wage differential. The American automobile trusts have been investing almost exclusively in foreign countries, where they enjoy lower wages and can therefore far more easily maintain their share of the world market, with cars produced cheaply in Britain or Germany, rather than for higher wages inside the United States. Another attempt to keep down the growth of real wages was the type of incomes policy advocated by the Kennedy and Johnson administrations—until 1966, when it broke down as a result of the Vietnam war. A third form of counteraction has been an intensification of the exploitation of labour—in particular a speed-up in big industry which has produced a structural transformation of the American working class in certain fields. This speed-up has led to a work rhythm that is so fast that the average adult worker is virtually incapable of keeping it up for long. This has radically lowered the age structure in certain industries, such as automobiles or steel. Today, since it is increasingly difficult to stay in plants (under conditions of speed-up) for 10 years without becoming a nervous or physical wreck, up to 40 per cent of the automobile workers of the United States are young workers. Moreover, the influx of black workers in large-scale industry has been tremendous as a result of the same phenomenon, since they are physically more resistant. Today, there are percentages of 35, 40 or 45 per cent black workers in some of the key automobile factories. In Ford's famous River Rouge plant, there are over 40 per cent black workers; in the Dodge automobile plant in Detroit, there are over 50 per cent. These are still exceptional cases—although there are also some steel plants with over 50 per cent black workers. But the average employment of black workers in United States industry as a whole is far higher than the demographic average of 10 per cent: it is something like 30 per cent.

None of these policies has so far had much effect. However, if the historic moment arrives when the productivity gap between American and West European and Japanese industry is closed, American capitalism will have absolutely no choice but to launch a far more ruthless attack on the real wage levels of American workers than has occurred hitherto in Western Europe, in the various countries where a small wage differential existed (Italy, France, West Germany, England and Belgium, at different moments during the sixties). Since the wage differential between Europe and America is not a matter of 5, 10, or 15 per cent, as it is between different Western European countries, but is of the order of 200-300 per cent, it is easy to imagine what an enormous handicap this will become when productivity becomes comparable, and how massive the reactions of American capitalism will then be.

It is necessary to stress these facts in order to adopt a Marxist, in other words a materialist and not an idealist approach to the question of the attitudes of the American working class towards American society. It is true that there is a very close inter-relation between the anti-communism of the Establishment, the arms expenditure which makes possible a high level of employment, the international role of American imperialism, the surplus profits which the latter gets from its international investments of capital, and the military apparatus which defends these investments. But one thing must be understood. The American workers go along with this whole system, not in the first place because they are intoxicated by the ideas of anti-communism. They go along with it because it has been capable of delivering the goods to them over the last 30 years. The system has been capable of giving them higher wages and a higher degree of social security. It is this fact which has determined their acceptance of anti-communism, and not the acceptance of anti-communism, and not the acceptance of anti-communism which has determined social stability. Once the system becomes less and less able to deliver the goods, a completely new situation will occur in the United States.

Trade-union consciousness is not only negative. Or, to formulate this more dialectically, trade-union consciousness is in and by itself socially neutral. It is neither reactionary nor revolutionary. It becomes reactionary when the system is capable of satisfying trade-union demands. It creates a major revolutionary potential once the system is no longer capable of satisfying trade-union demands. Such a transformation of American society under the impact of the international competition of capital is today knocking at the door of US capitalism.

The liberation struggles of the peoples of the Third World, with their threat to American imperialist investment, will also play an important role in ending the long socio-economic equilibrium of American capitalism. But they do not involve such dramatic and immediate economic consequences as the international competition of capital could have, if the productivity gap were filled.

As long as socialism or revolution are only ideals preached by militants because of their own convictions and consciousness, their social impact is inevitably limited. But when the ideas of revolutionary socialism are able to unite faith, confidence and consciousness with the immediate material interest of a social class in revolt—the working class, then their potential becomes literally explosive. In that sense, the political radicalization of the working class, and therewith socialism, will become a practical proposition in the United States within the next 10 or 15 years, under the combined impact of all these forces which have been examined here. After the black workers, the young workers, the students, the technicians and the public employees, the mass of the American workers will put the struggle for socialism on the immediate historical agenda in the United States. The road to revolution will then be open.

A Revolution in Values
Herbert Marcuse

Herbert Marcuse (1898-   ), one of the intellectual leaders of the New Left, taught at Brandeis University for several years and is currently Professor of Philosophy at the University of California at San Diego. Among his major works are *Reason and Revolution* (1941), *Eros and Civilization* (1955), and *One-Dimensional Man* (1964).

At the beginning, I have to say briefly what I mean by values in this context. I mean norms and aspirations which motivate the behavior of social groups in the process of satisfying their needs, material as well as cultural, and in defining their needs. In this sense, values are not a matter of personal preference; they express the exigencies of the established production relations and the established pattern of consumption. However, and this is decisive, at the same time, values express the possibilities inherent in but repressed by the productivity of the established society. Let me give you a few very familiar examples of this two-fold character of values: on the one hand, to be bound and confined to the existing social system, on the other hand, to transcend it by aiming at possibilities still denied by the system. For example, the value of honor in feudal society expresses, first of all a basic exigency of feudalism; namely, the requirements of a hierarchy of domination and dependence founded on direct personal relationships assured not only by force but also by the sanctity of contracts. The value of loyalty, proclaimed in a society of oppression and inequality, was idealized, sublimated, in the great court epics, the romances, the court ceremonial of the time, but it would be nonsense to say that heroes like Tristan, Percival, and others are nothing but feudal knights and vassals, that their ideals, adventures, and conflicts do not transcend the feudal society; they certainly do. In and above the feudal framework, we find universal human possibilities, promises, sufferings and happiness.

Similarly, the values of liberty and equality express first of all the exigencies of the capitalist mode of production, namely, free competition among relative equals, free wage labor, exchange of equivalents regardless of race, status, and so on. But, at the same time the same values project better forms of human association, still unrealized possibilities. The same ambivalence we have in another of the decisive values characteristic of the modern period, namely, the concept of work as calling and vocation. Work is a necessity for the entire adult life, and in most cases an unpleasant necessity; still, or precisely because of it, work is said to be the vocation of man sanctioned by religion. Now, for the vast majority of the population work has always been dehumanizing, painful, alienated labor, that is, an activity in which a human being cannot develop and satisfy his or her own individual faculties and capabilities. At the same time, this concept of work as calling and vocation projects

A speech delivered at a conference on science, technology, and values in February 1972 at the University of South Florida, Tampa, Fla.

a very different attitude and position of work in life; namely, the self-realization of a human being in creative work.

After these preliminary and very sketchy definitions, I would like to discuss two main aspects of my theme, namely, the role of values in social change and the contemporary revolution of values as an unprecedented transformation. Let me start by taking the Marxian theory of how a transformation of values takes place. Socially effective new values replace the established ones if and when they express the interest of an advancing, ascending class in the struggle against the existing ruling class. But, the new values articulate the particular class interests in a general form, claiming that the class interest is at the same time the universal interest and in this way, class-determined values assume the form of a universal truth. This is the ideological character of values. Values are ideological inasmuch as they abstract from their restriction or denial in reality. In capitalist society, liberty and equality remain abstract, partial liberty and equality—a privilege. But the very same ideology becomes a material force in the process of change as soon as it begins to impell political action on a mass scale aiming at the full realization of the distorted and denied values.

Now, it is important to notice that the Marxian conception does not mean a simple chronological sequence, namely, first basic change in the class relations, then a revolution in values. To say that the new values of socialism can only be the products of new social and economic institutions is vulgar, not dialectical materialism. Rather the articulation of new social values almost invariably *precedes* the institutionalization of new class relations and of a new mode of production. Examples abound in history; I shall mention only two: the Enlightenment prior to the French Revolution, and socialist theory itself. This situation illuminates the role of the intelligentsia in the process of social change, which I shall discuss subsequently. The transformation of values is not merely the ideological reflex of the social structure. A radical transformation rather articulates radically new historical possibilities, forces not yet incorporated into the process of social change. An intellectual, "cultural" revolution precedes social revolution, projects the latter, is the catalyst of the latter.

The transition from an established value system or an established value hierarchy to another one is a dialectical process. Thus, the bourgeois ideology cancels the feudal contract relations by generalizing this relation in the idea of the social contract which binds all members of society while submitting all of them, in very different ways, to the overriding laws of the exchange economy. Similarly, socialism is to cancel the abstract and exploitative structure behind the bourgeois ideology of liberty and equality, and to make work truly a vocation, namely, the self-realization of the individual in an association with free human beings. The translation of the ideology into reality is to take place in the revolutionary action of the proletariat. How does this conception apply to the situation in the advanced capitalist countries today?

Today's cultural revolution (and I speak only of the cultural revolution in the West) involves a transformation of values which strikes at the entirety of the established culture, material as well as intellectual. This attack on the entire traditional system of values finds its peak in the rejection of the Performance Principle. According to this principle, everyone has to earn his living in alienating but socially necessary performances, and one's reward, one's status in society will be determined by this performance (the work-income relation). The rejection of the

Performance Principle also rejects the notion of progress which has up to now characterized the development of western civilization, namely, progress as increasingly productive exploitation and mastery of nature, external and human, a progress which has turned out to be self-propelling destruction and domination. Note that this rejection of the Performance Principle does not only strike at the principle governing the existing capitalist society, but at any society which maintains the subjection of man to the instruments of his labor. Now as against this Performance Principle, the cultural revolution calls for an end to this domination, for freedom and solidarity as a quality of the human existence, for the abolition of a society which condemns the vast majority of its members to live their lives as a means for earning a living rather than as end in itself.

At this point, a warning against any false romanticism. There can be no such thing as a total abolition of alienation. Dialectical materialism recognizes the inexorable objectivity of nature, of matter, the inexorable struggle of man with nature confronting the human subject and limiting its freedom no matter in what form of society. It is not the question of abolishing alienation altogether but abolishing what I might call surplus alienation, namely the alienation exacted by the existing society in the interest of maintaining and enlarging the status quo. This surplus alienation has been the soil on which quantitative progress has taken place; it has sustained the separation of intellectual from manual labor, the need and the growing need for dehumanizing, parasitarian and destructive work, the need for repression; it has wasted and polluted the available resources—technical, natural and human. Quantitative progress now could, and should, turn into quality: a new mode of life which would free the potentialities of man and nature by negating the established system of exploitation and its values. This transformation of values would not only invalidate the existing political and economic institutions, it would also make for a new morality, for new relations between the sexes and generations, for a new relation between man and nature.

The scope of these tendencies and their radical character assume a new force at the present stage of capitalist development. In all preceding revolutions of values these demands remained largely abstract, marginal; they kept "above" an order of social as well as instinctual repression which was in itself rational and legitimate as long as it really developed the productive forces. To date, however, this organization of society is becoming incompatible not only with further progress but also with the very survival of mankind as a human race. And accordingly, today's revolution of values no longer proceeds within the established continuum of quantitative progress, but it tends to break this continuum. It is a *qualitative leap* into the possibility of an essentially different way of life.

Let me try merely to enumerate the main aspects of this break with, and transcendence beyond the established continuum. The foundation and the aim would still be the shift from self-propelling productivity to collectively controlled production for freely developing individual needs: socialism. It implies the shift from utility values to aesthetic values, the emergence of a new sensibility, new modes of perception, or experience. Aesthetic values are inherently non-exploitative, non-repressive; their articulation in radical political movements suggest the striving for a change also in the instinctual foundations of civilization. In the last analysis, this tendency would counteract the male aggressiveness of patriarchal civilization and thereby subject more effectively aggressive to erotic energy, to the life instincts. One sees today a widespread rebellion against the domineering values of virility, heroism and force, invoking the images of society which may bring about the end of violence.

This is the historical and psychological depth dimension of the Women's Liberation Movement. It does not yet seem conscious of its truly subversive radical potential, which could propel a decisive transformation of the entire material and intellectual culture, could reduce repression, and provide the psychological, instinctual foundation for a less aggressive Reality Principle.

The ascendence of new radical values is more than a merely ideological revolution; rather it tends to become a material force generated by the very dynamics of advanced capitalist society and foreshadowing the internal weakening, perhaps even disintegration of this society. This ideological revolution, which is all but a reversal of values, reflects a new historical stage of social development, namely, the stage where society has achieved the satisfaction of basic needs for the great majority of its members while sustaining oppression and misery at home and abroad. This society must, under the pressure for enlarged capital accumulation, incessantly create and stimulate needs over and above the needs of subsistence, in other words cultural and luxury needs. Thereby, this society is invalidating the legitimacy of perpetuating profitable repression. The attained level of the productivity of labor would allow the reduction of working time required for the reproduction of society to a minimum and thus eliminate the necessity of full-time alienated labor—but full-time alienated labor is the foundation of the system. It is undermined by the constant production of goods and services which are superfluous in terms of subsistence. Spending one's life in "earning a living," life as a means rather then as an end-in-itself: this mode of existence becomes evermore blatantly unproductive, obsolete, irrational—rational only for the maintenance of the status quo. Under these conditions, demands are generated for a radically different social division and organization of labor, for the abolition of the work-income relation: "transcendent" needs of freedom which cannot be satisfied within the framework of institutions based on the rule of Performance Principle.

Corresponding to this stage of development, a new pattern of social change is gradually emerging, namely, the possibility of a revolution on the grounds of satisfied basic needs and unsatisfied transcendent needs. It would be a revolution under the pressure of the vital need for self-determination, the need for joy, for no longer being an instrument of the ever-present apparatus. This is not simply the well-known pattern of rising expectations, better offerings from the available "cake", but rather the awareness of goals subverting the established hierarchy and priority of values and aiming at a new rationality, new sensibility, new morality.

Now how does this revolution of values manifest itself today as a material force, as radical social ferment? Here, I can only indicate the most conspicuous features of this process. First, we have in this country some sort of "Keynesianism with a vengeance". Max Weber characterized the spirit of capitalism as "inner-wordly asceticism", the drive to save and save and save, to invest and to invest in order to produce more and more profit, work, and to accept even the lowest and most inhuman work as "calling", as the vocation of man. Today, we see the negation of this principle: the urge to spend, and the revolt against prevalues of production; work discipline and responsibility are weakening; people question effectively the necessity for life-long alienation.

Secondly, and related to the trend just discussed, there is a pervasive deterioration of the commodity world itself, of the quality of goods and services, and a recurring disruption of the process of production in a more than "normal" way: wildcat strikes, strikes against the entire organization of work and not only for higher wages and better working conditions. A high rate of absenteeism prevails, and individual and group sabotage are frequent. And in this general climate, the ecology drive articulates the need for a new relation between man and nature as his life environment—a drive which, if sustained and extended, can become a political force, striking at the very institutions which create the perpetuate pollution.

Behind all this is the awareness, the feeling that one can live as a human being without running in the rat race, without performing dehumanizing jobs, the awareness of the repressive and destructive impact of the "consumer society". Given the structure and organization of advanced capitalism, it is no wonder that the new values are not carried by one ascending class in its struggle against the ruling class. These values do not express the immediate interests of any specific class. They are, at the present stage, still carried by non-integrated groups among the youth, the women, the black and brown population, the young workers, the intelligentsia.

They are minorities; they are by themselves no revolutionary groups, nor can they in any sense replace the working class as the basis of radical social change. But they are indispensable today, the sole catalysts of change, and they articulate needs which are in reality the needs of the entire underlying population. And, if and when the working class becomes the carrier of revolution, it will be a very different class, in which the blue collar labor will only be a minority, a class which will include large strata of middle classes, and in which intellectual work will play an increasing role.

This trend accentuates the importance of the colleges and universities in the process of change. The students, far from being merely a privileged elite without a material base, are in fact the potential *cadres* of the existing as well as the future society. The construction of a free society, the abolition of poverty the world over, the reduction of necessary but inhuman work to a minimum of time, the rebuilding of towns, the restoration of the countryside, the control of disease, of the birth rate—these tasks require a high degree of scientific progress, also in the humanities and social sciences! The progressive elimination of violence, the emancipation of the senses, far from implying a rejection of reason and rationality, demand a new and more rational rationality, a new and more rational reason, capable of organizing and developing also non-instrumentalist, non-utilitarian, non-repressive goals. The question arises whether there is not some surplus aggressiveness and violence in the established science and technology, in their very structure, perhaps the reflex and at the same time the stimulus of the service of science and technology to destructive social powers. Can we, in any sense, rationally speculate on a change, not only in the application of science but also in its direction and method? A change perhaps generated by an entirely new experience of nature, a new relation to nature and to man? The ascent of aesthetic values as non-violent, non-aggressive values suggest at least the possibility of a different formation of scientific concepts, a different direction of scientific abstraction; a more concrete, more sensuous, more qualitative science and technology, including a science of the imagination, as a creative faculty of human beings.

A few words in conclusion. The tendencies which I have tried to sketch here draw into the process of change the instinctual structure itself, the senses, minds and bodies of men and women; they enlarge the scope of the potential revolution.

It seems that the established society is fully aware of the scope and depth of the challenge. The power structure answers with intensified, legal and extra-legal repression, with the organization of the preventive counter-revolution, preventive because no successful revolution has preceded it in the advanced industrial countries. Under these circumstances, the prospects are not very exhilarating. The initiative today is with the forces of repression. There is no historical law according to which capitalism will inevitably be followed by socialism. The socialist tradition itself has always recognized and retained the alternative: either a free and human society, socialism, or a long period of civilized barbarism, a society entirely in the hands of an omnipresent and all-powerful administration and management—some kind of neofascism. I believe that it is not too late. I think that barbarism, neofascist barbarism, can still be fought. If it is not fought today, it may be too late because we know of no case where a fascist regime, once established, has been defeated from within. So it is not yet too late, but if this generation doesn't fight it, it may very well be too late.

The Disintegration of the New Left
Christopher Lasch

Christopher Lasch (1932-   ) is a professor at Northwestern University. Among his books are *The American Liberals and the Russian Revolution* (1962), *The New Radicalism in America* (1965), and *The Agony of the American Left* (1969).

An interminable war in Indochina; the revolutionary movement elsewhere in disarray; the American left fragmented and driven onto the defensive; Nixon acting belatedly but with apparent success to disarm his opponents; public services in decline; the quality of public discussion lower than ever; demoralization and drift on every side—the political scene has seldom looked more dreary. Only three years ago the glacial rigidity of American politics appeared to be breaking up. Even habitual pessimists proclaimed a "great thaw." Columbia, Paris, the dumping of Johnson seemed so many proofs that the diverse strands making up the new left had finally coalesced as a movement, a political force.

Now it appears that the new left, even in the moment of its apparent triumphs, had already passed the peak of its influence. The Chicago convention was an end rather than a beginning. The nomination of Humphrey and, even more important, the smooth handing-on of the war from a Democratic to a Republican administration showed how limited was the left's capacity to influence national events; while the government emerged from the turmoil of '68 slightly shaken but

From Christopher Lasch, "Can the Left Rise Again?" *The New York Review of Books*, Vol. 17 (October 21, 1971), p. 36. Reprinted with permission from *The New York Review of Books*. Copyright © 1971 by New York Review, Inc.

capable of carrying on a hateful war, of intimidating or outflanking its critics, and even—as recent events have shown—of acting with decisiveness and imagination.

The collapse of the new left became unmistakable in 1969 with the split in SDS, the emergence of the Weathermen, and the virtual disappearance of the antiwar movement. The Chicago trial, the Spock case, the Berrigan affair, and the harassment of the Panthers forced radicals on the defensive and obliged them to expend their energies on self-preservation. Meanwhile the assassination of Martin Luther King and Robert Kennedy removed the foremost leaders of an aspiring liberal resurgence, while the failure of the McCarthy campaign solidified the defeat of left-leaning liberals.

Throughout the Sixties, there had been a reciprocal relation between Kennedy liberalism and the new left, easily overlooked by radicals who insist that the left thrives on repression. If the radical opposition widened the space available to respectable dissent and forced some establishment politicians to the left (the growing radicalism of Robert Kennedy himself being the clearest example), it is also true that the new left was helped into being in the first place by the new sense of expectancy introduced into American politics by John F. Kennedy, whatever his intentions, and kept alive by his brother.

The advent of Nixon, Agnew, and Mitchell coincided with the dissipation of the moral energies of the black movement (briefly revived—a last gasp—after the death of King), the collapse of the antiwar movement, the sudden decline of campus militancy after Cambodia, and the spread of a new mood of uncertainty and resignation.

The degree of its dependence on the surrounding political environment reveals the failure of the American left to develop an autonomous life. The new left either refused or was unable to learn much from its predecessors, even from their mistakes, and in the end paid heavily for its indifference to the past. Conceived in many ways as a direct repudiation of the old left, it rejected not only the dogma and sectarian factionalism of the old left but whatever might have been gained from a more sympathetic understanding of its history. Too often the new left confused dogma with ideas and tried to live without them, preferring pure intentions to clear thinking. When it turned out after all that the movement needed an "analysis," many elements of the new left embraced Marxism in its most rigid and sterile forms, or Third World revolutionary doctrines quite inapplicable to the US, and began to engage in sectarian polemics as pointless and trivial as those of the 1930s.

The absence of continuity in American radicalism—in American life generally—made it possible for the radicals of the Sixties to discover all over again the existence of oppression and exploitation, the power of the ruling class, and the connection between capitalism and foreign wars. In their excitement, they quickly proceeded from reformist to revolutionary ideas, not only leaving most of their followers behind but glossing over a host of difficulties—both tactical and theoretical—that were inherent in the adoption of revolutionary goals. It should at least have been treated as an open question whether classical conceptions of revolution, deriving from a conjunction of historical circumstances not likely to recur, have any meaning in an advanced industrial society.

A major theoretical problem for the new left was precisely to work out a new conception of social reconstruction, in other words to formulate new ideas about revolution itself instead of being content with unanalyzed images from the past. In the absence of any real analysis of the concept or its applicability to contemporary

American life, "revolution" quickly became the emptiest of clichés and was used indiscriminately by radicals, liberals, conservatives, advertising men, and the media, usually to describe changes that were nonexistent.

Useless as the word soon became, it had important effects on those who continued to take it seriously. Consider its influence on the antiwar movement. As soon as the leaders of the movement realized that the Indochina war could not be attributed simply to diplomatic bungling but had roots in the social structure of advanced capitalism (roots which have yet, however, to be fully explained), they began to insist that this recognition be immediately embodied in the movement's practice. This at least seemed to be the intention of the much publicized transition "from dissent to resistance," announced in 1966-1967, although it was not always clear whether this slogan implied an escalation of strategy or merely more militant forms of civil disobedience. (Even in the latter case, however, the almost unavoidable tendency was to justify new sacrifices by the announcement of revolutionary objectives.)

In any case, "from dissent to resistance" was a misleading slogan for a movement that would continue to depend on "dissenters" for much of its effectiveness. Even as a tactic, "resistance" led the antiwar movement into attacks not only against the war but, increasingly, against the entire apparatus of military-corporate domination both at home and abroad, while at the same time the adoption of an "anti-imperialist" perspective unavoidably narrowed the movement's ideological appeal and its base of support. A dangerous dispersion of energies followed from decisions made by the antiwar movement in 1966 and 1967—decisions that arose not so much from calculation of their political consequences as from the need to make an adequate response to the rising militancy of the young, to the agony of the choices confronting men eligible for the draft, to the atrocity of the war.

The history of the student movement in many ways paralleled that of the antiwar movement, if indeed their histories can be disentangled. After the student left discovered the university's links to the war machine and the corporations, it needed to develop an analysis of higher education that would simultaneously explain why the university had become the center of opposition to the war. An analysis that treated the university simply as an agency of oppression could not explain why so many students had apparently resisted brainwashing and consistently took positions more critical of American society than those taken by other citizens. The problem confronting the student movement was to expose and attack the university's "complicity" in war and exploitation without forgetting that it was precisely the relative independence of the universities (or, more accurately, of the colleges of arts and science), together with the fact that they were at least formally committed to values directly counter to those of industrial capitalism, that made them a good ground on which to fight.

The adoption of revolutionary points of view did nothing to clarify these issues. It encouraged on the one hand a misplaced class analysis of the university itself, in which student "proletarians" confront a ruling class made up of administrators and faculty, and on the other hand a preoccupation with the "real" problems outside academic life, especially those of the working class, which led student activists to abandon the attempt to reform the university and in many cases to leave academic life altogether. These positions, however much they differed from one another, shared an unwillingness to confront the difficulty of explaining the university's relation to society or the relation of students to the class structure as a whole.

Were students to be regarded as future members of an oppressive bourgeoisie, whose defection from this class and rejection of "bourgeois life styles" therefore constituted the first stage of the "cultural revolution" called for by Abbie Hoffman? Or were they apprentices to a new kind of technical intelligentsia, in which case student rebellion might be considered, in Norman Birnbaum's phrase, as an anticipatory strike of the work force? These questions concealed an even more fundamental issue: had the class structure of industrial society changed in such important ways as to render much of traditional Marxism obsolete? The inability of the "Marxist" left to answer these questions helps to explain the rapid growth of a left based on youth culture, on "liberated life styles," which at least takes a clear position in favor of the first of these hypotheses, and which is prepared to interpret even a change of costume as a "revolutionary act"—thereby reducing the complexities of revolutionary action to an absolute minimum.

"Marxism-Leninism" had something of the same effect on the Black Panthers as it had on SDS. It widened the split between political and cultural radicals. It also widened the split between liberals and the left, although in the case of the black movement this split had already become irreconcilable by 1966 and was precipitated not by the adoption of explicitly revolutionary objectives but by the revival of militant black nationalism.

The advocates of black power did not at first regard themselves as revolutionaries. For some time they remained indifferent to socialism or Marxist ideology. Their criticism of the civil rights movement went deeper than anything that could be summed up in the formula "revolution vs. reform." They attacked the whole idea of integration as a social goal. Arguing that the genuinely distinctive features of the culture of American blacks had been wholly overlooked by the civil rights movement, they held up, by implication, the goal of a culturally pluralistic democracy in place of the homogenized society toward which civil rights agitation seemed destined to lead. In some ways their conception was similar to the vision of a "transnational America" advanced by Randolph Bourne and other cultural radicals during the First World War and later taken up by the Harlem renaissance.

The idea of cultural pluralism was, to be sure, only a single strain in the movement for black power. The movement also split from the civil rights movement over tactical issues: expulsion of whites, willingness to use violence. By insisting on the connection between black politics and black culture, however, the advocates of black power broke decisively with the civil rights movement and the liberalism of the early Sixties (which regarded culture as a matter of private choice, hence as something falling outside the domain of politics), while at the same time anticipating many of the themes of the later new left.

Unfortunately the black power movement did not succeed in working out a political program that incorporated its insights into black culture. Self-determination for the ghetto was all too clearly exposed to the criticism that it would perpetuate poverty under a more dignified name. Without an adequate politics, cultural nationalism tended to lapse back into political quiescence and into the religious fantasies from which, among other sources, it had originally sprung.

The political activists, on the other hand, in the process of distinguishing themselves from "reactionary" cultural nationalists like Ron Karenga, tended to lose sight of cultural issues altogether. The Panthers' "revolutionary nationalism" provided a purely verbal resolution of the difficulty. Even the political ideas of the Panthers, which at first promised to unite elements of the Marxist tradition with a recognition of the need for decentralization and "community control," degenerated into a vague summons, reminiscent of the late Thirties and early Forties, for a "united front against war and fascism," as the exigencies of self-defense forced the Panthers into an alliance with elements of the old left.

. . . When the makeshift radicalism of the early Sixties proved incapable of giving strategic direction to the movement, it gave way to "Marxism-Leninism," the most easily available leftist ideology. Old leftists emerged from their obscurity and offered ideological advice. It did not matter that they themselves were rudely repudiated; the prestige of their ideological tradition overcame generational barriers. By the late Sixties, two varieties of Leninism had emerged—an old-fashioned economic determinism mindful of "objective conditions" and stressing the need (as PL contended) for the left to place itself under the guidance of the proletariat, and an extreme voluntarism that treated revolution as a pure act of will and never tired of intoning the meaningless slogan of Che: "The duty of the revolutionary is to make the revolution." The adherents of the two positions, equally addicted to a belief in the decisive role of political vanguards, contended for mastery of what remained of the left.

Bored or repelled by their polemics, the new left constituency broke into fragments—"new politics" people, peaceniks, Catholic anarchists, feminists, Trotskyists, cultural radicals of one sort or another. The revolutionary fervor of the later Sixties had raised the usual euphoric expectations which, subsiding, left a familiar residue of disenchantment. Cultural and political radicalism, briefly joined in a period of rising political hopes, split apart, the political radicals increasingly absorbed in their ideological pronouncements, the cultural radicals denouncing all politics as a snare and a delusion.

Deprived of its political basis, the youth "culture"—the vaguely defined revolt against affluence still led, in so far as it is led at all, by Jerry Rubin and Abbie Hoffman—has turned sour and ugly, even as it spreads downward through the generations. Very young adolescents—precocious fugitives from respectability, prematurely hardened tramps and migrants—are now appropriating the forms of cultural revolt, but with little understanding of the political content which formerly gave to the rebellion of youth such moral power as it had.

Long hair, ragged clothing, rock, drugs, a contempt for the authority of the past—these persist as the outward trappings of alienation but are emptied of their political core. The claim of alienated youth to represent society's embattled conscience is correspondingly diminished. Formerly the uneasiness and disgust with which the liberal middle class confronted the youth culture was tempered not only by a wish to believe, as good Americans, that idealism and moral purity are always on the side of youth, but by the undeniable seriousness underlying the movement, which manifested itself as political courage.

To many young people today, however, the risks once associated with radical action seem to have gone for nothing; even the very recent past appears remote and "irrelevant." The political struggle appears lost—has already, in fact, become incomprehensible—and in its place appears a new cynicism and toughness, a suspiciousness extending even to brothers, and a casual acceptance of crime and violence—feebly justified as "ripping off the system"—as a means of survival. These tendencies are naturally strengthened by the willingness even of many middle-class liberals to countenance severe repression, as the moral claims of the youth culture grow more and more attenuated. Desperate and bitter, brutalized by drugs and police, the youth culture sinks into the underworld and becomes increasingly indistinguishable from the lumpenproletariat.

There are signs, however, that many of those who were demoralized and disoriented by the collapse of the political left and the degeneration of the cultural revolt—including some of the cultural radicals themselves—are once again finding their way back to political action. Some of the academic dropouts have returned to school, with the hope of changing the professions from within. Having tried to survive as independent activists or intellectuals, they are rediscovering the importance of institutional ties. Professional work and organizations turn out to be not purely imprisoning; they also provide some minimal support for the creative use of one's talents, together with the necessary fellowship of one's peers. Nor are the professions completely closed to innovation, as many radicals had supposed. The old guards are still entrenched, but the number of dissidents is growing.

All the professions, even medicine, are in ferment. Ralph Nader has uncovered among young lawyers an unexpected devotion to public concerns. Young architects are challenging urban renewal, young teachers the stultified schools. Biologists and physicists are debating whether they have an ethical obligation to concern themselves with the uses to which scientific discoveries are put. So far little has come of all this, although Nader's activities have done more to publicize certain specific evils of corporate power than all Democratic politicians put together. Two or three years ago, all these efforts would have been dismissed as well-meaning reformism.

Revolutionary rhetoric, however, though it still thrills the media, no longer commands the terrified respect of the left, the revolutionaries having all too obviously failed to revolutionize even their own lives. Besides, many of the present-day reformers are themselves former revolutionaries, graduates of SDS, and cannot be intimidated or impressed by the ostentatious display of revolutionary manhood. They have no illusions about reform, but neither are they without hope. Is it possible that these stirrings in the professions foreshadow a more general movement of people at their work, trying to turn their work into something at once more satisfying and less deleterious in its social effects—a new kind of labor movement?

Whether the present collapse of the left signifies the beginning of another long interlude of political stagnation—an interlude American society can scarcely afford—or whether it proves to be only a temporary setback depends in part on whether we can assimilate the experience of the Sixties and profit from it. We need sober historical guidance to these events. In place of that, publishers offer a flood of books on student rebellion, the "counter-culture," the "black revolution," and women's liberation—books more or less indistinguishable from one another in the haste with which they are thrown together, in the shrillness with which they compete for attention, and in their inability to say anything that is not already worn from overuse.

.   .   .

By no means do I intend to suggest that the alternative lies in a revival of trade union strategies, such as is currently being advocated by certain doctrinaire Marxists under the guise of spreading "revolutionary consciousness" to the working class. Trade union politics demands higher wages and better working conditions for auto workers, for example, without asking about the social consequences of the unlimited production of automobiles. Wage demands reinforce the capitalist premise that everything has its price and help to sustain the illusion that the deterioration of the public environment is somehow unrelated to the policies of "private" corporations. The flight of industry to the suburbs leaves urban neighborhoods impoverished and contributes to the so-called crisis of the cities, but the working class, so long as it views that crisis from traditional trade union perspectives, has no way of explaining it except to blame everything on the government, the blacks, outside agitators, or the general decline of morals.

"Citizen politics" as defined by Walzer avoids these pitfalls by concentrating on issues that affect the community as a whole. But it is no better able than trade unionism to show the *connection* between conditions at work and deteriorating neighborhoods, schools, and public services. Neither amateur activists nor old-time trade unionists challenge the fatal split between home and work—the system under which people are in effect compensated for loss of dignity and autonomy at work by increased leisure and higher wages to spend on consumer goods and leisure-time activities. It is because work is seen merely as a means to something else, instead of an intrinsically satisfying and necessary activity, that people no longer concern themselves with its social consequences.

The auto worker who drives long distances to work along choked highways, under polluted skies, suffers directly from the social consequences of the automobile. But his union does not concern itself with those consequences or with the corporate policies that help to bring them about; nor does the worker dream that he himself might have something to say about what use is made of the cars he produces, or about better ways to produce less harmful cars. To him the production of cars is his means of support, nothing more. The civic-minded conservationist and amateur reformer, on the other hand, tend to forget that the production of cars is, among other things, people's means of support; they think solely of the car's effect on the "environment."

What seems to be needed, then, is a fusion of community politics and trade union politics—two dissident traditions that have increasingly grown apart. The product of this fusion would not be simply a new unionism or a new kind of community organizing but a new form of politics altogether, centered on the factory—and on the research and development laboratory, the intellectual assembly line, the professions, the media—but always heedful of work in its larger social implications.

As we have already seen, it is precisely because the "working conditions" in the modern university in some ways approximate those of the more highly developed sectors of modern industry, and because the underlying issue raised by student politics within the university—the social uses of knowledge—mirrors the overriding issue for society as a whole, that the student movement of the Sixties can be regarded as anticipating, perhaps even as a preparation for, whatever the new politics will be in the Seventies and Eighties.

If we think of the problem of radical politics as that of combining styles of action inherited from the labor movement with a determination to see work in its relation to all phases of community life, we ought to be able to learn something from the career of Saul Alinsky. When he turned to community organizing in the late Thirties, Alinsky consciously borrowed techniques he had learned in the labor movement. A new political type emerged—the professional organizer, whose constiteunts are not workers but citizens.

.   .   .

Alinsky describes the organizer's work with a candor verging on cynicism. He stresses the need for the organizer to keep himself discreetly in the background. "Much of the time, . . . the organizer will have a pretty good idea of what the community should be doing," but if he tries to prevail through the force of his own arguments the community will reject him as an outside agitator. Instead he uses "guided questioning" and learns to rely on "skillful and sensitive role-playing." Alinsky anticipates and disarms the objection:

Is this manipulation? Certainly, just as a teacher manipulates, and no less, even a Socrates. As time goes on and education proceeds, the leadership becomes increasingly sophisticated. . . . [The organizer's job] becomes one of weaning the group away from dependency upon him. Then his job is done.

To those who would argue that Alinsky proposes merely to give his clients the illusion of deciding for themselves he can reply that it is only by means of this illusion, artfully encouraged in the initial stages of organization, that exploited people overcome the habit of deference and feelings of helplessness engendered by the vastness and impenetrability of modern society.

It may be further objected that the poor ought to furnish their own leadership from the beginning. Why should they rely on outside organizers at all? Shouldn't they oppose to their oppressors not the slick expertise of the organizer but the strength and dignity of their own ways? These objections, in Alinsky's view, betray the middle-class reformer's inclination to romanticize the poor, although he realizes that poor people themselves may seize on these ideas in order to explain their own inaction. He sees the poor—like all people—as normally lazy and uncurious even about their own oppression, preferring the safety of known misery to the uncertainty of action. At the same time they are embarrassed by their failure to act, especially in the presence of an organizer, and appeal to middle-class rhetoric about "cultural identity" in order to excuse it. A conversation between Alinsky and a group of Canadian Indians shows how this self-deception works.

Indians: *Well, we can't organize.*
[Alinsky:] *Why not?*
Indians: *Because that's a white man's way of doing things. . . . You see, if we organize, that means getting out and fighting the way you are telling us to do and that would mean that we would be corrupted by the white man's culture and lose our own values.*

Alinsky comments:

It was quite obvious what was happening since I could see from the way the Indians were looking at each other they were thinking: "So we invite this white organizer from south of the border to come up here and he tells us to get organized. . . . What must be going through his mind is: 'What's wrong with you Indians that you have been sitting around here for a couple of hundred years now and you haven't organized to do these things?' "

Because the new left so often ignores such self-deception or unwittingly encourages it, Alinsky impatiently condemns much of the radicalism of the Sixties. The new left, he says, valued the purity of its principles more than practical results. Instead of taking the poor as they are, it romanticized and at the same time patronized them. It spoke in abstractions about the class struggle, instead of confronting the immediate issues that matter to the poor: jobs, inflation, discrimination, violence in the streets. "If the real radical finds that having long hair sets up psychological barriers to communication and organization, he cuts his hair."

These criticisms accurately expose many of the weaknesses of the new left, but they do not necessarily leave us with a workable alternative. For one thing, Alinsky exaggerates the effectiveness of his own methods. He speaks of "bringing to heel" one of the Chicago department stores and of engineering the "downfall" of Eastman Kodak, when all he means is that these companies made certain concessions to organized pressure from blacks. Alinsky's habit of setting himself limited objectives causes him to overestimate the importance of their achievement.

No doubt it is tactically necessary for the organizer "to convert the plight into a problem," but the problem should not be allowed to obscure the underlying plight. To personalize the adversary, as Alinsky urges again and again, is, moreover, to regress to a more primitive level of political awareness. It is important to insist on the concrete as against empty slogans and abstractions, but this does not mean that every general question can be dissolved in a discussion of tactics.

Although Alinsky's organization has often concerned itself indirectly with job discrimination and other matters pertaining to people's work, it is mainly concerned with citizens and consumers. Currently Alinsky is attempting to organize middle-class stockholders to use their proxies against corporate policies that lead to pollution and despoliation of the environment. In Rochester Alinsky persuaded Kodak stockholders to assign their proxies to FIGHT or to come to stockholders' meetings and vote against Eastman's discriminatory hiring policies. He now argues that this tactic should be used on a wider scale. "The way of proxy participation," he believes, "could mean the democratization of corporate America"—nothing short of a "revolution." A more "revolutionary" strategy, however, would attempt to put the corporations under the control not of the stockholders, but of those who work in them. The community organizer thinks of his constituents almost automatically as consumers. This is at once his strength and his weakness.

In *Reveille for Radicals*, written in 1946, Alinsky attacked the labor unions for dealing with the worker only as a worker, instead of keeping "clearly in mind the obvious and true picture of the worker who votes, rents, consumes, breeds, and participates in every avenue of what we call life." Whatever was fruitful in Alinsky's subsequent career sprang from this initial insight. At the same time, the shift from union politics to community organizing precluded the possibility of describing industrial society in class terms. Alinsky had to reject a socialist orientation in favor of neo-populism—the "people" against the "tycoons."

Like many radicals of the late Thirties and early Forties, Alinsky rejected the stupidities of American socialism, by that time almost exclusively identified with the Communist party, only to fall into a Deweyite celebration of democracy as process. "The objective is never an end in itself," he wrote in *Reveille*. What mattered was "the passionate desire of all human beings to feel that they have personally contributed to the creation and the securing of any objective they desire." Having divested his movement of any suspicion of "ideology," having substituted "citizens" for "workers" and interests for classes, and having exalted process over objectives, Alinsky was free to define "participation" itself as the objective of community organization—of politics in general.

Alinsky's attack on the new left overlooks the degree to which this exaltation of participation, which his own career did so much to identify with American radicalism, not only was a major influence on the early new left ideas of "participatory democracy" and "community organizing" but helped to mislead young radicals and to prepare the way for subsequent disappointments. Instead of providing a historical explanation for those features of the new left that he dislikes—its cult of revolutionary purity, its infatuation with failure, its dogmatism—Alinsky psychologizes about them, characteristically attributing these failings to bourgeois affluence and generational revolt. But the sectarianism of the later new left, as I have already suggested, might better be seen as a consequence of the poverty of its early ideas—and notably of its own obsession with participation as an end in its own right.

Clearly this criticism does not apply to Saul Alinsky, who is nothing if not a professional; indeed his professionalism accurately defines the limits of his belief in participation as an end in itself. For the left as a whole, however, belief in the intrinsic value of participation has no such limits. Its distrust of professionalism does not rest merely on a healthy disrespect for "experts" or on an awareness of the ways in which the concept of professionalism has been progressively debased (not least in the academic professions, where it has become synonymous with timid pedantry and a pose of "scientific objectivity"). It reflects an intellectual orientation which, pushed to its furthest extreme, scorns not only professionalism but the "work ethic" itself, on the grounds that spontaneous and sensuous enjoyment of life is the only genuine form of participation in its pleasures, while submission to a discipline is inherently "alienating."

.   .   .

It is obvious that all institutions in American life are not equally democratic. "Private" corporations, academic or industrial, are not even formally democratic in their organization, unlike the state. Before arguing that they should be, according to Dahl, one must consult the "principle of competence," according to which authority should be exercised by those who are best qualified to exercise it and who understand the consequences of their decisions. To insist on democracy in the operating room or on the bridge of an ocean liner would be madness for patients and passengers. The argument for democracy in the state therefore depends on the proposition that "the ordinary man is more competent than anyone else to decide when and how much he shall intervene on decisions he feels are important to him." In order for this argument to apply also to the university or the private corporation, it must be shown that these institutions, although in most cases nominally private, actually embody political power, are intertwined with the state, and are public in everything but name.

For the idea of "participatory democracy," while it may have served initially as a necessary corrective to the bureaucratic centralism so long associated with parties of the left, rapidly degenerated into political primitivism, the old dream of a primary democracy without factions or parties—in other words, of a political community without politics.

.   .   .

For all his tactical realism, Alinsky shares with the early new left a disposition to dismiss ideas and programs as "ideological." Again and again he tells us that ideas are merely a cloak for self-interest, that action takes precedence over understanding, and that the objective of political action is "never an end in itself" but a means of rousing people "to a higher degree of participation." No one can deny that the size and complexity of modern societies have given rise to feelings of powerlessness or that apathy has become a political issue in its own right. It is dangerous, however, to equate democracy with participation and to encourage the belief that it is possible for people to take part directly in every decision that "affects their lives." Efforts to implement these beliefs end by integrating people more securely than ever into structures in which, whether they are controlled by the existing powers or by demagogues of the left, popular control is strictly an illusion.

The mystique of participation has had a profoundly misleading influence on recent American radicalism. It is a symptom of the general malaise of modern culture that watching a play, reading a poem, or getting an education are defined as passive and spectatorial, inherently inferior in the quality of their emotional satisfaction to acting in a play, writing a poem, or simply "living." The notion that education and "life," art and "reality," understanding and action are radically opposed derives ultimately from the opaqueness of the structures in which we live and from a despair of understanding them.

Official propaganda encourages this belief as assiduously as the so-called "counter-culture," which in this respect (as in many others) merely reflects prevailing values—or, more accurately, takes them more literally than they are taken by the ruling class. Thus although the cult of participation encourages among other things a distrust of professionalism, the institutions of American society continue to be operated by professionals. It is only the left which, both in its politics and in its culture, clings to the illusion that competence is equally distributed among people of good intentions and regards any attempt to uphold professional standards as a betrayal of democracy.

.   .   .

Still another development that may have wide-ranging political implications is the revival of the "woman question." Worker control of the corporation would require a change not only in attitudes toward work but in attitudes toward leisure, consumption, and domestic life. It is now generally recognized that the privatized, mother-centered family is one of the bastions of the consumer economy. No institution more clearly embodies the separation between work and the rest of life, and no institution, not even the corporation itself, illustrates so specifically the bad effects of this separation.

The precarious political and economic stability that was re-established after the Great Depression rested as heavily on a rehabilitation of domesticity, mildly challenged during the Twenties and Thirties by the new sexual freedom and the appearance of a new type of "career woman," as it did on military spending. The arrangement whereby private consumption compensates for loss of autonomy at work, and for the absence of a vigorous public and communal life, depended on a new sentimentalization of the family, in which the nineteenth-century cult of domesticity was refurbished with images of the suburb as a refuge from the city.

An attack on suburbia—as banal at times as the reality it sought to describe—characterized the new left from the beginning. Recently there has been added to it a more pointed and specific attack on the family. At its worst, this new feminism merely makes explicit one of the tendencies that was implicit in the old—repudiation of men, a heightening of the sex war. At its best, it provides the clearest perspective from which to view the degradation of work into a meaningless routine and the hollowness of the pleasures that are offered in its place. Radical women perceive that the demand for equal access to jobs and equal pay often means very boring work and low pay, while domestic life, far from having been enriched by its isolation from work, has been steadily impoverished. It is more and more difficult to recognize in the contemporary family — although of course everyone knows exceptions to the general pattern—the description of bourgeois domesticity provided by Max Horkheimer in 1941 as the last defense of a rich and autonomous inner life against the encroachments of the mass society.

The middle class family, though it has frequently been an agency of obsolescent social patterns, has made the individual aware of other potentialities than his labor or vocation opened to him. As a child, and later as a lover, he saw reality not in the hard light of its practical biddings but in a distant perspective which lessened the force of its commandments. This realm of freedom, which originated outside the workshop, was adulterated with the dregs of all past cultures, yet it was man's private preserve in the sense that he could there transcend the function society imposed upon him by way of its division of labor.

Today family life increasingly exists in a vacuum and has become vacuous. This fact in many ways sums up the contemporary plight.

What will emerge from the new criticism of the family is not yet clear. Whether the latest wave of feminism leaves a more lasting mark than earlier waves depends on its ability to associate criticism of the family with a criticism of other institutions, particularly those governing work. If the attack on the family results merely in the founding of rural communes, it will offer no alternative either to the isolated family or to the factory, since in many ways the rural commune simply caricatures the new domesticity, re-enacting the flight to nature and the search for an isolated and emotionally self-sufficient domestic life. To be sure, it reunites the family with work, but with a kind of primitive agricultural labor which is itself marginal. The "urban commune," in which the members work outside, avoids these difficulties, but it is not clear that it is more than a dormitory—in particular, it is not clear whether it can successfully raise children.

Lately there has been a tendency for the attack on the family, like so many other fragments of the new left, to degenerate into a purely cultural movement, one aimed not so much at institutional change as at abolishing "male chauvinism." I have already criticized the illusion that a "cultural revolution," a change of heart, can serve as a substitute for politics. Here it is necessary only to add that the criticism applied with special force to feminism, since the peculiar strength of this movement is precisely its ability to dramatize specific connections between culture and politics—between the realm of production on the one hand and education, child-rearing, and sexual relations on the other.

It ought to be recognized, for example, that large numbers of women will not be able to enter the work force, except by slavishly imitating the careers of men, unless the nature of work undergoes a radical change. The entire conflict between "home and career" derives from the subordination of work to the relentless demands of industrial productivity. The system that forces women (and men also) to choose between home and work is the same system that demands early specialization and prolonged schooling, imposes militarylike discipline in all areas of work, and forces not only factory workers but intellectual workers into a ruthless competition for meager rewards. At bottom, the "woman question" is indistinguishable from what used to be known as the social question.

It would be foolishly optimistic to conclude from the existence of the woman's movement, the student movement, and the black movement, and from growing signs of uneasiness among professional and technical workers in various strata of the population, that the basis for a "new politics" already exists. These movements are no more than portents; they exist, moreover, in isolation from each other. If we have learned anything from the Sixties, it is that the "system" is much less vulnerable than many radicals had supposed. The realization of its strength can become an occasion for premature despair or for renewed attempts to create a radical coalition.

Sexual Politics
Kate Millet

Kate Millet (1934-   ), professor, author, feminist leader, is generally known as the "principal theoretician" of the woman's liberation movement. She wrote *Sexual Politics* (1970).

In introducing the term "sexual politics," one must first answer the inevitable question "Can the relationship between the sexes be viewed in a political light at all?" The answer depends on how one defines politics.[1] This essay does not define the political as that relatively narrow and exclusive world of meetings, chairmen, and parties. The term "politics" shall refer to power-structured relationships, arrangements whereby one group of persons is controlled by another. By way of parenthesis one might add that although an ideal politics might simply be conceived of as the arrangement of human life on agreeable and rational principles from whence the entire notion of power *over* others should be banished, one must confess that this is not what constitutes the political as we know it, and it is to this that we must address ourselves.

The following sketch, which might be described as "notes toward a theory of patriarchy," will attempt to prove that sex is a status category with political implications. Something of a pioneering effort, it must perforce be both tentative and imperfect. Because the intention is to provide an overall description, statements must be generalized, exceptions neglected, and subheadings overlapping and, to some degree, arbitrary as well.

The word "politics" is enlisted here when speaking of the sexes primarily

[1] The American Heritage Dictionary's fourth definition is fairly approximate: "methods or tactics involved in managing a state or government." *American Heritage Dictionary* (New York: American Heritage and Houghton Mifflin, 1969). One might expand this to a set of stratagems designed to maintain a system. If one understands patriarchy to be an institution perpetuated by such techniques of control, one has a working definition of how politics is conceived in this essay.

because such a word is eminently useful in outlining the real nature of their relative status, historically and at the present. It is opportune, perhaps today even mandatory, that we develop a more relevant psychology and philosophy of power relationships beyond the simple conceptual framework provided by our traditional formal politics. Indeed, it may be imperative that we give some attention to defining a theory of politics which treats of power relationships on grounds less conventional than those to which we are accustomed.[2] I have therefore found it pertinent to define them on grounds of personal contact and interaction between members of well-defined and coherent groups: races, castes, classes, and sexes. For it is precisely because certain groups have no representation in a number of recognized political structures that their position tends to be so stable, their oppression so continuous.

In America, recent events have forced us to acknowledge at last that the relationship between the races is indeed a political one which involves the general control of one collectivity, defined by birth, over another collectivity, also defined by birth. Groups who rule by birthright are fast disappearing, yet there remains one ancient and universal scheme for the domination of one birth group by another—the scheme that prevails in the area of sex. The study of racism has convinced us that a truly political state of affairs operates between the races to perpetuate a series of oppressive circumstances. The subordinated group has inadequate redress through existing political institutions, and is deterred thereby from organizing into conventional political struggle and opposition.

Quite in the same manner, disinterested examination of our system of sexual relationship must point out that the situation between the sexes now, and throughout history, is a case of phenomenon Max Weber defined as *herrschaft*, a relationship of dominance and subordinance.[3] What goes largely unexamined, often even unacknowledged (yet is institutionalized nonetheless) in our social order, is the birthright priority whereby males rule the females. Through this system a most ingenious form of "interior colonization" has been achieved. It is one which tends moreover to be sturdier than any form of segregation, and more rigorous than class stratification, more uniform, certainly more enduring. However muted its present appearance may be, sexual dominion obtains nevertheless as perhaps the most pervasive ideology of our culture and provides is most fundamental concept of power.

This is so because our society, like all other historical civilizations, is a patriarchy.[4] The fact is evident at once if one recalls that the military, industry,

[2] I am indebted here to Ronald V. Samson's *The Psychology of Power* (New York: Random House, 1968) for his intelligent investigation of the connection between formal power structures and the family and for his analysis of how power corrupts basic human relationships.

[3] "Domination in the quite general sense of power, i.e. the possibility of imposing one's will upon the behavior of other persons, can emerge in the most diverse forms." In this central passage of *Wirtschaft und Gesellschaft* Weber is particularly interested in two such forms: control through social authority ("patriarchal, magisterial, or princely") and control over economic force. In patriarchy as in other forms of domination "that control over economic goods, i.e. economic power, is a frequent, often purposively willed, consequence of domination as well as one of its most important instruments." Quoted from Max Rheinstein's and Edward Shil's translation of portions of *Wirtschaft und Gesellschaft* entitled *Max Weber on Law in Economy and Society* (New York: Simon and Schuster, 1967), pp. 323-24.

[4] No matriarchal societies are known to exist at present. Matrilineality, which may be, as some anthropologists have held, a residue or a transitional stage of matriarchy, does not constitute an exception to patriarchal rule, it simply channels the power held by males through female descent:— e.g. the Avunculate.

technology, universities, science, political office, and finance—in short, every avenue of power within the society, including the coercive force of the police, is entirely in male hands. As the essence of politics is power, such realization cannot fail to carry impact. What lingers of supernatural authority, the Deity, "His" ministry, together with the ethics and values, the philosophy and art of our culture—its very civilization—as T. S. Eliot once observed, is of male manufacture.

If one takes patriarchal government to be the institution whereby that half of the populace which is female is controlled by that half which is male, the principles of patriarchy appear to be two fold: male shall dominate female, elder male shall dominate younger. However, just as with any human institution, there is frequently a distance between the real and the ideal; contradictions and expectations do exist within the system. While patriarchy as an institution is a social constant so deeply entrenched as to run through all other political, social, or economic forms, whether of caste or class, feudality or bureaucracy, just as it pervades all major religions, it also exhibits great variety in history and locale. In democracies,[5] for example, females have often held no office or do so (as now) in such minuscule numbers as to be below even token representation. Aristocracy, on the other hand, with its emphasis upon the magic and dynastic properties of blood, may at times permit women to hold power. The principle of rule by elder males is violated even more frequently. Bearing in mind the variation and degree in patriarchy—as say between Saudi Arabia and Sweden, Indonesia and Red China—we also recognize our own form in the U.S. and Europe to be much altered and attentuated by the reforms described in the next chapter.

IDEOLOGICAL

Hannah Arendt[6] has observed that government is upheld by power supported either through consent or imposed through violence. Conditioning to an ideology amounts to the former. Sexual politics obtains consent through the "socialization" of both sexes to basic patriarchal polities with regard to temperament, role, and status. As to status, a pervasive assent to the prejudice of male superiority gaurantees superior status in the male, inferior in the female. The first item, temperament, involves the formation of human personality along stereotyped lines of sex category ("masculine" and "feminine"), based on the needs and values of the dominant group and dictated by what its members cherish in themselves and find convenient in subordinates: aggression, intelligence, force, and efficacy in the male; passivity, ignorance, docility, "virtue," and ineffectuality in the female. This is complemented by a second factor, sex role, which decrees a consonant and highly elaborate code of conduct, gesture and attitude for each sex. In terms of activity, sex role assigns domestic service and attendance upon infants to the female, the rest of human achievement, interest, and ambition to the male. The limited role allotted the female tends to arrest her at the level of biological experience. Therefore, nearly all that can be described as distinctly human rather than animal activity (in their

[5] Radical democracy would, of course, preclude patriarchy. One might find evidence of a general satisfaction with a less than perfect democracy in the fact that women have so rarely held power within modern "democracies."

[6] Hannah Arendt, "Speculations on Violence," *The New York Review of Books*, Vol. XII No. 4, February 27, 1969, p. 24.

own way animals also give birth and care for their young) is largely reserved for the male. Of course, status again follows from such an assignment. Were one to analyze the three categories one might designate status as the political component, role as the sociological, and temperament as the psychological—yet their interdependence is unquestionable and they form a chain. Those awarded higher status tend to adopt roles of mastery, largely because they are first encouraged to develop temperaments of dominance. That this is true of caste and class as well is self-evident.

BIOLOGICAL

Patriarchal religion, popular attitude, and to some degree, science as well[7] assumes these psycho-social distinctions to rest upon biological differences between the sexes, so that where culture is acknowledged as shaping behavior, it is said to do no more than cooperate with nature. Yet the temperamental distinctions created in patriarchy ("masculine" and "feminine" personality traits) do not appear to originate in human nature, those of role and status still less.

. . .

Not only is there insufficient evidence for the thesis that the present social distinctions of patriarchy (status, role, temperament) are physical in origin, but we are hardly in a position to assess the existing differentiations, since distinctions which we know to be culturally induced at present so outweigh them. Whatever the "real" differences between the sexes may be, we are not likely to know them until the sexes are treated differently, that is alike. And this is very far from being the case at present. Important new research not only suggests that the possibilities of innate temperamental differences seem more remote than ever, but even raises questions as to the validity and permanence of psycho-sexual identity. In doing so it gives fairly concrete positive evidence of the overwhelmingly *cultural* character of gender, i.e., personality structure in terms of sexual category.

What Stoller and other experts define as "core gender identity" is now thought to be established in the young by the age of eighteen months. This is how Stoller differentiates between sex and gender:

Dictionaries stress that the major connotation of sex *is a biological one, as for example, in the phrases* sexual relations *or the* male sex. *In agreement with this, the word* sex *in this work will refer to the male or female sex and the component biological parts that determine whether one is a male or a female; the word* sexual *will have connotations of anatomy and physiology. This obviously leaves tremendous areas of behavior, feelings, thoughts and fantasies that are related to the sexes and yet do not have the primarily biological connotations. It is for some of these psychological phenomena that the term* gender *will be used: one can speak of the male sex or the female sex, but one can also talk about masculinity and feminity and not necessarily be implying anything about anatomy or physiology. Thus, while* sex *and* gender *seem to common sense inextricably bound together, one purpose of this study will be to confirm the fact that the two realms (sex and gender) are not inevitably bound in anything like a one-to-one relationship, but each may go into quite independent ways.*[8]

[7] The social, rather than the physical sciences are referred to here. Traditionally, medical science had often subscribed to such beliefs. This is no longer the case today, when the best medical research points to the conclusion that sexual stereotypes have no bases in biology.

[8] Robert J. Stoller, *Sex and Gender* (New York, Science House, 1968), from the preface, pp. viii–ix.

In cases of genital malformation and consequent erroneous gender assignment at birth, studied at the California Gender Identity Center, the discovery was made that it is easier to change the sex of an adolescent male, whose biological identity turns out to be contrary to his gender assignment and conditioning—through surgery—than to undo the educational consequences of years, which have succeeded in making the subject temperamentally feminine in gesture, sense of self, personality and interests. Studies done in California under Stoller's direction offer proof that gender identity (I am a girl, I am a boy) is the primary identity any human being holds—the first as well as the most permanent and far-reaching. Stoller later makes emphatic the distinction that sex is biological, gender pyschological, and therefore cultural: "*Gender* is a term that has psychological or cultural rather than biological connotations. If the proper terms for sex are "male" and "female", the corresponding terms for gender are "masculine" and "feminine"; these latter may be quite independent of (biological) sex."[9] Indeed, so arbitrary is gender, that it may even be contrary to physiology: ". . . although the external gentalia (penis, testes, scrotum) contribute to the sense of maleness, no one of them is essential for it, not even all of them together. In the absence of complete evidence, I agree in general with Money, and the Hampsons who show in their large series of intersexed patients that gender role is determined by postnatal forces, regardless of the anatomy and physiology of the external genitalia."[10]

SOCIOLOGICAL

Patriarchy's chief institution is the family. It is both a mirror of and a connection with the larger society; a patriarchal unit within a patriarchal whole. Mediating between the individual and the social structure, the family effects control and conformity where political and other authorities are insufficient.[11] As the fundamental instrument and the foundation unit of patriarchal society the family and its roles are prototypical. Serving as an agent of the larger society, the family not only encourages its own members to adjust and conform, but acts as a unit in the government of the patriarchal state which rules its citizens through its family heads. Even in patriarchal societies where they are granted legal citizenship, women tend to be ruled through the family alone and have little or no formal relation to the state.[12]

As co-operation between the family and the larger society is essential, else both would fall apart, the fate of three patriarchal institutions, the family, society, and the state are interrelated. In most forms of patriarchy this has generally led to the granting of religious support in statements such as the Catholic precept that "the father is head of the family," or Judaism's delegation of quasi-priestly authority to

---

[9] *Ibid.*, p. 9.

[10] *Ibid.*, p. 48.

[11] In some of my remarks on the family I am indebted to Goode's short and concise analysis. See William J. Goode, *The Family* (Englewood Cliffs, New Jersey, Prentice-Hall, 1964).

[12] Family, society, and state are three separate but connected entities: women have a decreasing importance as one goes from the first to the third category. But as each of the three categories exists within or is influenced by the overall institution of patriarchy, I am concerned here less with differentiation than with pointing out a general similarity.

the male parent. Secular governments today also confirm this, as in census practices of designating the male as head of household, taxation, passports etc. Female heads of household tend to be regarded as undesirable; the phenomenon is a trait of poverty or misfortune. The Confucian prescription that the relationship between ruler and subject is parallel to that of father and children points to the essentially feudal character of the patriarchal family (and conversely, the familial character of feudalism) even in modern democracies. . . .[13]

CLASS

It is in the area of class that the castelike status of the female within patriarchy is most liable to confusion, for sexual status often operates in a superficially confusing way within the variable of class. In a society where status is dependent upon the economic, social, and educational circumstances of class, it is possible for certain females to appear to stand higher than some males. Yet not when one looks more closely at the subject. This is perhaps easier to see by means of analogy: a black doctor or lawyer has higher social status than a poor white sharecropper. But race, itself a caste system which subsumes class, persuades the latter citizen that he belongs to a higher order of life, just as it oppresses the black professional in spirit, whatever his material success may be. In much the same manner, a truck driver or butcher has always his "manhood" to fall back upon. Should this final vanity be offended, he may contemplate more violent methods. The literature of the past thirty years provides a staggering number of incidents in which the caste of virility triumphs over the social status of wealthy or even educated women. In literary contexts one has to deal here with wish-fulfillment. Incidents from life (bullying, obscene, or hostile remarks) are probably another sort of psychological gesture of ascendancy. Both convey more hope than reality, for class divisions are generally quite impervious to the hostility of individuals. And yet while the existence of class division is not seriously threatened by such expressions of enmity, the existence of sexual hierarchy has been re-affirmed and mobilized to "punish" the female quite effectively.

The function of class or ethnic mores in patriarchy is largely a matter of how overtly displayed or how loudly enunciated the general ethic of masculine supremacy allows itself to become. Here one is confronted by what appears to be a paradox: while in the lower social strata, the male is more likely to claim authority on the strength of his sex rank alone, he is actually obliged more often to share power with the women of his class who are economically productive; whereas in the middle and upper classes, there is less tendency to assert a blunt patriarchal dominance, as men who enjoy such status have more power in any case.[14]

It is generally accepted that Western patriarchy has been much softened by the concepts of courtly and romantic love. While this is certainly true, such influence has also been vastly overestimated. In comparison with the candor of "machismo" or oriental behavior, one realizes how much of a concession traditional chivalrous behavior represents—a sporting kind of reparation to allow the subordinate female

---

[13] J. K. Folsom makes a convincing argument as to the anomalous character of patriarchal family systems within a democratic society. See Joseph K. Folsom *The Family and Democratic Society* (New York: John Wiley, 1934, 1943).

[14] Goode, *op cit.*, p. 74.

certain means of saving face. While a palliative to the injustice of woman's social position, chivalry is also a technique for disguising it. One must acknowledge that the chivalrous stance is a game the master group plays in elevating its subject to pedestal level. Historians of courtly love stress the fact that the raptures of the poets had no effect upon the legal or economic standing of women, and very little upon their social status.[15] As the sociologist Hugo Beigel has observed, both the courtly and the romantic versions of love are "grants" which the male concedes out of his total powers.[16] Both have had the effect of obscuring the patriarchal character of Western culture and in their general tendency to attribute impossible virtues to women, have ended by confining them in a narrow and often remarkably conscribing sphere of behavior. It was a Victorian habit, for example, to insist the female assume the function of serving as the male's conscience and living the life of goodness he found tedious but felt someone ought to do anyway.

The concept of romantic love affords a means of emotional manipulation which the male is free to exploit, since love is the only circumstance in which the female is (ideologically) pardoned for sexual activity. And convictions of romantic love are convenient to both parties since this is often the only condition in which the female can overcome the far more powerful conditioning she has received toward sexual inhibition. Romantic love also obscures the realities of female status and the burden of economic dependency. As to "chivalry," such gallant gesture as still resides in the middle classes has degenerated to a tired ritualism, which scarcely serves to mask the status situation of the present.

Within patriarchy one must often deal with contradictions which are simply a matter of class style. David Riesman has noted that as the working class has been assimilated into the middle class, so have its sexual mores and attitudes. The fairly blatant male chauvinism which was once a province of the lower class or immigrant male has been absorbed and taken on a certain glamour through a number of contemporary figures, who have made it, and a certain number of other working-class male attitudes, part of a new, and at the moment, fashionable life style. So influential is this working-class ideal of brute virility (or more accurately, a literary and therefore middle-class version of it) become in our time that it may replace more discreet and "gentlemanly" attitudes of the past.[17]

One of the chief effects of class within patriarchy is to set one woman against another, in the past creating a lively antagonism between whore and matron, and in the present between career woman and housewife. One envies the other her "security" and prestige, while the envied yearns beyond the confines of respectability for what she takes to be the other's freedom, adventure, and contact

[15] This is the gist of Valency's summary of the situation before the troubadours, acknowledging that courtly love is an utter anomaly: "With regard to the social background, all that can be stated with confidence is that we know nothing of the objective relationships of men and women in the Middle Ages which might conceivably motivate the strain of love-poetry which the troubadours developed." Maurice Valency, *In Praise of Love* (Macmillan, New York, 1958), p. 5.

[16] Hugo Beigel, "Romantic Love," *The American Sociological Review*, Vol. 16, 1951, p. 331.

[17] Mailer and Miller occur to one in this connection, and Lawrence as well. One might trace Rojack's very existence as a fictional figure to the virility symbol of Jack London's Ernest Everhard and Tennessee William's Stanley Kowalski. That Rojack is also literate is nothing more than an elegant finish upon the furniture of his "manhood" solidly based in the hard oaken grain of his mastery over any and every "broad" he can better, bludgeon, or bugger.

with the great world. Through the multiple advantages of the double standard, the male participates in both worlds, empowered by his superior social and economic resources to play the estranged women against each other as rivals. One might also recognize subsidiary status categories among women: not only is virtue class, but beauty and age as well.

ECONOMIC AND EDUCATIONAL

One of the most efficient branches of patriarchal government lies in the agency of its economic hold over its female subjects. In traditional patriarchy, women, as non-persons without legal standing, were permitted no actual economic existence as they could neither own nor earn in their own right. Since women have always worked in patriarchal societies, often at the most routine or strenuous tasks, what is at issue here is not labor but economic reward. In modern reformed patriarchal societies, women have certain economic rights, yet the "woman's work" in which some two thirds of the female population in most developed countries are engaged is work that is not paid for.[18] In a money economy where autonomy and prestige depend upon currency, this is a fact of great importance. In general, the position of women in patriarchy is a continuous function of their economic dependence. Just as their social position is vicarious and achieved (often on a temporary or marginal basis) through males, their relation to the economy is also typically vicarious or tangential.

Since education and economy are so closely related in the advanced nations, it is significant that the general level and style of higher education for women, particularly in their many remaining segregated institutions, is closer to that of Renaissance humanism than to the skills of mid-twentieth-century scientific and technological society. Traditionally patriarchy permitted occasional minimal literacy to women while higher education was closed to them. While modern patriarchies have, fairly recently, opened all educational levels to women,[19] the kind and quality of education is not the same for each sex. This difference is of course apparent in early socialization, but it persists and enters into higher education as well. Universities, once places of scholarship and the training of a few professionals, now also produce the personnel of a technocracy. This is not the case with regard to women. Their own colleges typically produce neither scholars nor

[18] Sweden is an exception in considering housework a material service rendered and calculable in divorce suits etc. Thirty-three to forty per cent of the female population have market employment in Western countries: this leaves up to two thirds out of the market labor force. In Sweden and the Soviet Union that figure is lower.

[19] We often forget how recent an event is higher education for women. In the U.S. it is barely one hundred years old; in many Western countries barely fifty. Oxford did not grant degrees to women on the same terms as to men until 1920. In Japan and a number of other countries universities have been open to women only in the period after World War II. There are still areas where higher education for women scarcely exists. Women do not have the same access to education as do men. The Princeton Report stated that "although at the high school level more girls than boys receive grades of "A," roughly 50% more boys than girls go to college." *Princeton Report to the Alumni on Co-Education* (pamphlet), Princeton, J.J. 1968, p. 10. Most other authorities give the national ratio of college students as two males to one female. In a great many countries it is far lower.

professionals nor technocrats. Nor are they funded by government and corporations as are male colleges and those co-educational colleges and universities whose primary function is the education of males. . . .

In keeping with the inferior sphere of culture to which women in patriarchy have always been restricted, the present encouragement of their "artistic" interests through study of the humanities is hardly more than an extension of the "accomplishments" they once cultivated in preparation for the marriage market. Achievement in the arts and humanities is reserved, now, as it has been historically, for males. Token representation, be it Susan Sontags' or Lady Murasaki's, does not vitiate this rule.

FORCE

We are not accustomed to associate patriarchy with force. So perfect is its system of socialization, so complete the general assent to its values, so long and so universally has it prevailed in human society, that it scarcely seems to require violent implementation. Customarily, we view its brutalities in the past as exotic or "primitive" custom. Those of the present are regarded as the product of individual deviance, confined to pathological or exceptional behavior, and without general import. And yet, just as under other total ideologies (racism and colonialism are somewhat analogous in this respect) control in patriarchal society would be imperfect, even inoperable, unless it had the rule of force to rely upon, both in emergencies and as an ever-present instrument of intimidation.

Historically, most patriarchies have institutionalized force through their legal systems. For example, strict patriarchies such as that of Islam, have implemented the prohibition against illegitimacy or sexual autonomy with a death sentence. In Afghanistan and Saudi Arabia the adulteress is still stoned to death with a mullah presiding at the execution. Execution by stoning was once common practice through the Near East. It is still condoned in Sicily. Needless to say there was and is no penalty imposed upon the male correspondent. Save in recent times or exceptional cases, adultery was not generally recognized in males except as an offense one male might commit against another's property interest. . . .

Excepting a social license to physical abuse among certain class and ethnic groups, force is diffuse and generalized in most contemporary patriarchies. Significantly, force itself is restricted to the male who alone is psychologically and technically equipped to perpetrate physical violence.[20] Where differences in physical strength have become immaterial through the use of arms, the female is rendered innocuous by her socialization. Before assault she is almost universally defenseless both by her physical and emotional training. Needless to say, this has the most far-reaching effects on the social and psychological behavior of both sexes.

.   .   .

[20] Vivid exceptions come to mind in the wars of liberation conducted by Vietnam, China, etc. But through most of history, women have been unarmed and forbidden to exhibit any defense of their own.

ANTHROPOLOGICAL: MYTH AND RELIGION

Evidence from anthropology, religious and literary myth all attests to the politically expedient character of patriarchal convictions about women. One anthropologist refers to a consistent patriarchal strain of assumption that "woman's biological differences set her apart ... she is essentially inferior," and since "human institutions grow from deep and primal anxieties and are shaped by irrational psychological mechanisms ... socially organized attitudes toward women arise from basic tensions expressed by the male."[21] Under patriarchy the female did not herself develop the symbols by which she is described. As both the primitive and the civilized worlds are male worlds, the ideas which shaped culture in regard to the female were also of male design. The image of women as we know it is an image created by men and fashioned to suit their needs. These needs spring from a fear of the "otherness" of woman. Yet this notion itself presupposes that patriarchy has already been established and the male has already set himself as the human norm, the subject and referent to which the female is "other" or alien. Whatever its origin, the function of the male's sexual antipathy is to provide a means of control over a subordinate group and a rationale which justifies the inferior station of those in a lower order, "explaining" the oppression of their lives.

The feeling that woman's sexual functions are impure is both world-wide and persistent. One sees evidence of it everywhere in literature, in myth, in primitive and civilized life. It is striking how the notion persists today. The event of menstruation, for example, is a largely clandestine affair, and the psycho-social effect of the stigma attached must have great effect on the female ego. There is a large anthropological literature on menstrual taboo; the practice of isolating offenders in huts at the edge of the village occurs throughout the primitive world. . . .

Primitive peoples explain the phenomenon of the female's genitals in terms of a wound, sometimes reasoning that she was visited by a bird or snake and mutilated into her present condition. Once she was wounded, now she bleeds. Contemporary slang for the vagina is "gash." The Freudian description of the female genitals is in terms of a "castrated" condition. The uneasiness and disgust female genitals arouse in patriarchal societies is attested to through religious, cultural, and literary proscription. In preliterate groups fear is also a factor, as in the belief in a castrating *vagina dentata*. The penis, badge of the male's superior status in both preliterate and civilized patriarchies, is given the most crucial significance, the subject both of endless boasting and endless anxiety. . . .

The Pandora myth is one of two important Western archetypes which condemn the female through her sexuality and explain her position as her well-deserved punishment for the primal sin under whose unfortunate consequences the race yet labors. Ethics have entered the scene, replacing the simplicities of ritual, taboo, and mana. The more sophisticated vehicle of myth also provides official explanations of sexual history. In Hesiod's tale, Zeus, a rancorous and arbitrary father figure, in sending Epimetheus evil in the form of female genitalia, is actually chastising him

[21] H. R. Hays, *The Dangerous Sex, the Myth of Feminine Evil* (New York: Putnam, 1964). Much of my summary in this section is indebted to Hays's useful assessment of cultural notions about the female.

for adult heterosexual knowledge and activity. In opening the vessel she brings (the vulva or hymen, Pandora's "box") the male satisfies his curiosity but sustains the discovery only by punishing himself at the hands of the father god with death and the assorted calamities of postlapsarian life. The patriarchal trait of male rivalry across age or status line, particularly those of powerful father and rival son, is present as well as the ubiquitous maligning of the female.

The myth of the Fall is a highly finished version of the same themes. As the central myth of the Judeo-Christian imagination and therefore of our immediate cultural heritage, it is well that we appraise and acknowledge the enormous power it still holds over us even in a rationalist era which has long ago given up literal belief in it while maintaining its emotional assent intact.[22] This mythic version of the female as the cause of human suffering, knowledge, and sin is still the foundation of sexual attitudes, for it represents the most crucial argument of the patriarchal tradition in the West.

The Israelites lived in a continual state of war with the fertility cults of their neighbors; these latter afforded sufficient attraction to be the source of constant defection, and the figure of Eve, like that of Pandora, has vestigial traces of a fertility goddess overthrown. There is some, probably unconscious, evidence of this in the Biblical account which announces, even before the narration of the fall has begun—"Adam called his wife's name Eve; because she was the mother of all living things." Due to the fact that the tale represents a compilation of different oral traditions, it provides two contradictory schemes for Eve's creation, one in which both sexes are created at the same time, and one in which Eve is fashioned later than Adam, an afterthought born from his rib, peremptory instance of the male's expropriation of the life force through a god who created the world without benefit of female assistance.

The tale of Adam and Eve is, among many other things, a narrative of how humanity invented sexual intercourse. Many such narratives exist in preliterate myth and folk tale. Most of them strike us now as delightfully funny stories of primal innocents who require a good deal of helpful instruction to figure it out. There are other major themes in the story: the loss of primeval simplicity, the arrival of death, and the first conscious experience of knowledge. All of them revolve about sex. Adam is forbidden to eat of the fruit of life or of the knowledge of good and evil, the warning states explicitly what should happen if he tastes of the latter: "in that day that thou eatest thereof thou shalt surely die." He eats but fails to die (at least in the story), from which one might infer that the serpent told the truth.

But at the moment when the pair eat of the forbidden tree they awake to their nakedness and feel shame. Sexuality is clearly involved, though the fable insists it is only tangential to a higher prohibition against disobeying orders in the matter of another and less controversial appetite—one for food. Róheim points out that the Hebrew verb for "eat" can also mean coitus. Everywhere in the Bible "knowing" is

---

[22] It is impossible to assess how deeply embedded in our consciousness is the Eden legend and how utterly its patterns are planted in our habits of thought. One comes across its tone and design in the most unlikely places, such as Antonioni's film *Blow-Up*, to name but one of many striking examples. The action of the film takes place in an idyllic garden, loaded with primal overtones largely sexual, where, prompted by a tempter with a phallic gun, the female again betrays the male to death. The photographer who witnesses the scene reacts as if he were being introduced both to the haggard knowledge of the primal scene and original sin at the same time.

synonymous with sexuality, and clearly a product of contact with the phallus, here in the fable objectified as a snake. To blame the evils and sorrows of life—loss of Eden and the rest—on sexuality, would all too logically implicate the male, and such implication is hardly the purpose of the story, designed as it is expressly in order to blame all this world's discomfort on the female. Therefore it is the female who is tempted first and "beguiled" by the penis, transformed into something else, a snake. Thus Adam has "beaten the rap" of sexual guilt, which appears to be why the sexual motive is so repressed in the Biblical account. Yet the very transparency of the serpent's universal phallic value shows how uneasy the mythic mind can be about its shifts. Accordingly, in her inferiority and vulnerability the woman takes and eats, simple carnal thing that she is, affected by flattery even in a reptile. Only after this does the male fall, and with him, humanity—for the fable has made him the racial type, whereas Eve is a mere sexual type and, according to tradition, either expendable or replaceable. And as the myth records the original sexual adventure, Adam was seduced by woman, who was seduced by a penis. "The woman whom thou gavest to be with me, she gave me of the fruit and I did eat" is the first man's defense. Seduced by the phallic snake, Eve is convicted for Adam's participation in sex.

Adam's curse is to toil in the "sweat of his brow," namely the labor the male associates with civilization. Eden was a fantasy world without either effort or activity, which the entrance of the female, and with her sexuality, has destroyed. Eve's sentence is far more political in nature and a brilliant "explanation" of her inferior status. "In sorrow thou shalt bring forth children. And thy desire shall be to thy husband. And he shall rule over thee." Again, in the Pandora myth, a proprietary father figure is punishing his subjects for adult heterosexuality. It is easy to agree with Róheim's comment on the negative attitude the myth adopts toward sexuality: "Sexual maturity is regarded as a misfortune, something that has robbed mankind of happiness ... the explanation of how death came into the world."[23]

What requires further emphasis is the responsibility of the female, a marginal creature, in bringing on this plague, and the justice of her suborned condition as dependent on her primary role in this original sin. The connection of woman, sex, and sin constitutes the fundamental pattern of western patriarchal thought thereafter.

PSYCHOLOGICAL

The aspects of patriarchy already described have each an effect upon the psychology of both sexes. Their principal result is the interiorization of patriarchal ideology. Status, temperament, and role are all value systems with endless psychological ramifications for each sex. Patriarchal marriage and the family with its ranks and division of labor play a large part in enforcing them. The male's superior economic position, the female's inferior one have also grave implications. The large quantity of guilt attached to sexuality in patriarchy is overwhelmingly placed upon the female, who is, culturally speaking, held to be the culpable or the

[23] Géza Róheim, "Eden," *Psychoanalytic Review*, Vol. XXVII, New York, 1940. See also Theodor Reik, *The Creation of Woman*, and the account given in Hays, *op. cit.*

more culpable party in nearly any sexual liaison, whatever the extenuating circumstances. A tendency toward the reification of the female makes her more often a sexual object than a person. This is particularly so when she is denied human rights through chattel status. Even where this has been partly amended the cumulative effect of religion and custom is still very powerful and has enormous psychological consequences. Woman is still denied sexual freedom and the biological control over her body through the cult of virginity, the double standard, the prescription against abortion, and in many places because contraception is physically or psychically unavailable to her. . . .

Ideology of the Family
Juliet Mitchell

Juliet Mitchell (1937-   ) is the author of *Woman's Estate* (1971). She has taught English at the University of Reading, England, and is active in the Women's Liberation Movement in England.

The family as the first form of social organization, has clearly undergone many changes with the advance of the economic methods of production which have always necessitated more and more elaborate social formations to accompany them. In her article "A Woman's Work Is Never Done"[1] Peggy Morton points out that under early capitalism the main economic task of the family was to produce large numbers of children for the new industrial jobs which demanded enormous numbers of workers; but under advanced capitalism, labor-intensive industry gives way to capital-intensive and quality rather than quantity of workers is what is required. The family adapts itself accordingly:

Profits depend more and more on the efficient organization of work and on the "self-discipline" of the workers rather than simply on speed-ups and other direct forms of increasing the exploitation of the workers. The family is therefore important both to shoulder the burden of the cost of higher education, and to carry out the repressive socialization of children. The family must raise children who have internalized hierarchical social relations, who will discipline themselves and work efficiently without constant supervision. . . . Women are responsible for implementing most of this socialization.[2]

I agree with Peggy Morton that the way the family is evolving produces an increased number of contradictions for the woman within it. As there is, likewise, a contradiction within the sector of sexuality alone. However, there is also a further

[1] Peggy Morton: "A Woman's Work Is Never Done," *Leviathan*, vol. II, no. 1.
[2] *Ibid.*, p. 34.

crucial contradiction not just within the family, but between it and the social organization that surrounds it. For though the family *has changed* since its first appearance, it *has also remained*—not just an idealist concept but as a crucial ideological and economic unit with a certain rigidity and autonomy despite all its adaptations.

Pre-capitalist society flourishes on individual private property—the peasant has his bit of land, the artisan his tools. Capitalist organization of work deprives the individual of his private property and takes all the separate pieces of private property (land, tools, etc.), pools them, and makes the newly accumulated wealth the private property of a few—the capitalists. The appropriation of individual private property necessitates a form of social organization of the property (men have to get together to work it) which is simultaneously denied: the mass of men get together to work it, but what they produce and how they produce it is taken by the "few" as their own personal private property. However, individual private property for the mass of the people does continue side by side with this new process—it continues in the family. Engels traced the origin of the oppression of women to the demand for individual private property: women had to be "owned," faithful to marriage to produce an heir for the inheritance of this individual private property. But perhaps more interesting than the "origin" of the oppression is its maintenance, as Marx and Engel's analyses of other issues demonstrate. In every revolution (whether from tribalism to feudalism, feudalism to capitalism, capitalism to socialism) the new ruling class, in order to overcome the old ruling class has to *appear* to represent the vast majority of the people in a society (only in the last instance is this *actually* the case): it doesn't, therefore, appear as a particular "class" but as the whole society:

For each new class which puts itself in the place of one ruling before it, is compelled, simply in order to achieve its aims, to represent its interests as the common interest of all the members of society, i.e., employing an ideal formula to give its ideas the form of universality and to represent them as the only rational and universally valid ones. The class which makes a revolution appears from the beginning not as a class but as the representative of the whole of society, simply because it is opposed to a class. It appears as the whole mass of society confronting a single ruling class. . . Every new class, therefore, achieves its domination only on a broader basis than that of the previous ruling class . . .[3]

It is in representing this limited "class" interest as the general, universal interest, that "ideas" play such an important part. Emergent capitalist society in confronting and overcoming feudal society has to appear to offer what the majority want—this naturally takes the form of an idealization of what the previous socio-economic system offered as its basis in, inevitably, a totally un-ideal manner. The ideas and desires of all people are conditioned by what they have: they simply want it bigger and better. To put this concretely—the peasant masses of feudal society had individual private property; their ideal was simply more of it. Capitalist society seemed to offer more because it stressed the *idea* of individual private property in a new context (or in a context of new ideas). Thus it offered individualism (an old value) plus the apparently new means for its greater realization—freedom and equality (values that are conspicuously absent from feudalism). However, the only place where this ideal could be given an apparently concrete base was in the

[3] Karl Marx: *The German Ideology*, 1845-6, *Collected Works*, vol. I, iv, pp. 35-7.

maintenance of an old institution: the family. Thus the family changed from being the economic basis of individual private property under feudalism to being the focal point of the *idea* of individual private property under a system that banished such an economic form from its central mode of production—capitalism. In actually owning things, privately and individually, the bourgeois family gives reality to this idea. For the rest, it remains an ideal desire—the possible fulfillment of which is an inducement to work in a manner at loggerheads with it. The working class work socially in production for the private property of a few capitalists *in the hope of* individual private property for themselves and their families.

But, of course, the ruling-class interests that pose, in the first place, as universal interests, increasingly decline into "mere idealizing phrases, conscious illusions and deliberate deceits. ... But the more they are condemned as falsehoods, and the less they satisfy the understanding, the more dogmatically they are asserted and the more deceitful, moralizing and spiritual becomes the language of established society."[4] Such a state of affairs perfectly describes that of individual private property and its embodiment, the family, towards the end of the nineteenth century in England. During the twentieth century, feudalism having been firmly overcome and capitalism entrenched, the basic ideology remains, but has naturally become more flexible in order to maintain its hold of the reins.

This is not to reiterate the notion that the family had an economic function under feudalism and today under capitalism has only an ideological one. Such a notion misrepresents the specific relationship here between the economic and the ideological and it is further in danger of being interpreted to mean that the family is unnecessary, a part of some con-job. The quotation above which treats ideology from a moral perspective can induce this attitude. There is nothing less "real" or "true" or important about the ideological than there is about the economic. Both determine our lives. In any case, the function of the family is not simply one or the other, it is both: it has an economic and ideological role under capitalism. Roughly, the economic role is the provision of a certain type of productive labor force and of the arena for massive consumption. This is specifically capitalistic. This economic function interacts with the ideology requisite to produce the missing ideals of peasant, feudal society; a place *equally* and *freely* to enjoy individual private property. This ideology which looks backwards for its rationale is, nevertheless, crucial for the present: without it people might hanker back to the past as a "golden age;" once Utopianism of any sort occurs, after looking backwards, it is liable to look forwards and thus endanger the status quo. The family, thus, embodies the most conservative concepts available: it rigidifies the past ideals and presents them as the present pleasures. By its very nature, it is there to prevent the future. No wonder revolutionaries come up with the vulgar desperation: abolish the family—it does seem *the* block to advance, *the* means of preserving a backwardness that even capitalism makes feel redundant, though, of course, it is essential to it.

This task of ideology to capture and preserve the ideals that arose from a past reality explains, at least in this context, the degree of separation that exists between the ideological superstructure and the economic basis. The ideological construct seems to be less variable, to preserve itself across revolutionary changes in the mode of production. It seems that the values of the present-day family are appropriate to

---

[4] *Ibid.*, p. 27. Actually this language remains on the terrain it is attacking—it is ideological language, moral and descriptive rather than analytical. It is, however, elegantly appropriate here.

peasant production. But it is the function of the ideology precisely to give this sense of continuity in progress. The dominant ideological formation is not separable from the dominant economic one, but, while linked, it does have a certain degree of autonomy and its own laws. Thus the ideology of the family can remain: individualism, freedom and equality; (at home you're "yourself"), while the social and economic reality can be very much at odds with such a concept. The contradictions between the ideological intentions of the family and its socio-economic base do not mean that we say the former is false. Quite the contrary, as its meshes draw tighter we protest on behalf of the ideology: "I can't say a thing without you getting at me. . . . I'm not free to think my own thoughts. . . . I've got nothing I can call my own. . . ."

Of course, the ideological concept of the family embodies a paradox which reflects the contradiction between it and the dominant, capitalist method of organizing production. As I have already mentioned, this method of organizing involves social production (a mass of "team" of workers), and the family provides the relief from the confiscation of this social production by apparently offering individual private property. Now the same contradiction is today contained within the family itself. The family is the most fundamental (the earliest and most primitive) form of social organization. When, under capitalism, it was made to embody as an ideal, what had been its economic function under feudalism, a chronic contradiction took place. What had hitherto been a *united* unit within the overall diversified social structure became, because of changing social conditions, a *divided* one. The peasant family works together for itself—it *is* one. The family and production are homogeneous. But the members of a working-class family work separately, for different bosses in different places and, though the family interest unites them, the separation of their place and conditions of their work fragments, perforce, that unity. Part of the function of the ideology of the family under capitalism is to preserve this unity in the face of its essential break-up. However, in doing this, it ties itself in knots. The social nature of work under capitalism fragments the unitary family; thereby it enforces the social nature of the family itself.

The peasant family owned its individual private property as the family's; but ideological individualism under capitalism cannot relate to a social group (even one as small as the modern family); it must, because it counterposes this to social work, relate to the individual. It is almost as though the family has got smaller and smaller in order to make itself "one," in a desperate struggle against the disparity of its members in the outside world. Under capitalism, each member of the family is supposed to be "an individual," it is not the family unit that is individualized. No wonder there are tensions. Each is supposed to be for the other, but every encounter—school, college, work—makes him for himself alone. It is this contradiction between an ideology of the privacy and individuation of the family and its basic social nature, which capitalism by its social organization of work has brought into play, that underlies the psychic problems documented (in England) in the works of the psychiatrists Laing, Esterson, and Cooper. Each member wants to be an individual—but it is the family itself that is supposed to be "individual" . . . "Mary's not like my other children, she's always been different . . . she's got a mind of her own and will go places . . . she's so stubborn, that's why things went wrong and I've brought her to you, doctor. . . ." The woman's task is to hold on to the unity of the family while its separate atoms explode in different directions.

It seems possible that within this dual contradiction lies the eventual dissolution of the "family," a future already visible within the conditions of capitalism. The social nature of production restores the family to its social form—a social group of individuals. Restores it, in fact, to something like the days before it was a family in little more than the biological sense. But this is only "something like;" final forms bear a misleading resemblance to postulated original forms—the difference is the entire intervening social development, and the difference between the social groups prior to the private-interest family, and social groups after it, is the difference between "golden age" primitive communism and revolutionary communism. It is too late for one and high time for the other. Meanwhile, the self-contradictory ideology of the family, which preserves the individualism of the unit only in the increasingly disruptive individualism of its members, both retards and hastens the day.

PSYCHOANALYSIS AND THE FAMILY

The Women's Liberation Movement must have a complex reaction to the nuclear family. It must concentrate on separating out the structures—the woman's roles—which are oppressively fused into it. It must fragment its unity.

To do this, we have to examine the concrete role and nature of today's family from within. We have to see precisely what function it serves at all levels. Yet simultaneously we have to see it as a *relatively* constant unit in relation to the entire course of social history. As such, it has a certain autonomy and inflexibility, whatever the stage of economic development of the society as a whole. This is because, in part, it clearly belongs to the ideological superstructure and always has done—even when this coincided with its economic function, as it did with the peasant family: [At the temple] "people came to burn incense and offer prayers for good fortune, abundant crops, *and many children* [emphasis added] ."[5]
And . . .

[. . . *in pre-revolutionary China] very interesting and significant was the factor of family size. The landlords and rich peasants averaged more than five persons per household, the middle peasants fewer than five, the poor peasants, between three and three and a half, the hired laborers about three. . . . Those without land or with very small holdings were often unable even to marry. If they did marry they were unable to hold their families together, lost more children to disease and famine, had to sell children, or even sell wives, and thus had households about half the size.*

If the landholdings of the pre-revolutionary period were calculated on the basis of the number of families rather than per capita, the concentration of wealth in the hands of the landlords and rich peasants was more marked. On that basis—a very realistic one for China, where the traditional emphasis has always been on the family rather than on the individual—the landlords and rich peasants, with only 5 per cent of the families, controlled 31 per cent of the land. . . .[6]

Today, the ideological function clearly still relates to the economic function—

[5] William Hinton: *op. cit.*, p. 20.
[6] *Ibid.*, p. 28. This makes two of my points at once—the coincidence of economic need and ideological attitude and the feudal stress on the *individual family*—rather than the capitalist stress on the individual person.

though both have changed at different rates and an important dislocation has resulted.

If we undertake only the first analysis, the meaning of the family, or of women's roles, we get sociology—the type of research that has littered the academic bookshelves of the Anglo-Saxon world (significantly) in the last decade. If we study only the place of the family within capitalist society, we get mere idealism for we fall into the trap of seeing it as an abstract concept:

The family, which is at first the only social relationship, becomes later, when increased needs create new social relations and the increased population new needs, a subordinate one . . . and must then be treated and analysed according to the existing empirical data, not according to the "concept of the family." [7]

Yes and no. A political study of the family, crucial to the development of the Women's Liberation Movement, involves the double approach: both the empirical data and the structure and importance of the ideological concept: the family itself in its "conceptual" unitary form.

The Family "Makes" the Woman. We are concerned primarily with the implications of the capitalist family for the woman enmeshed within it. On one level, women in today's family, are the main repositories for what are coming to seem the screaming illusions of our society: freedom, equality, individuality. "My wife and I are equals" is the correlate of "the two sides of industry." "Equality" and "sides" suggest a faint line drawn down the *middle*. In both cases there is a topside and a bottom side, an unequal division of labor and an unequal division of profits—to put it mildly.

The family is a stronghold of what capitalism needs to preserve but actually destroys: private property and individualism. The housewife-mother is the guardian and representative of these. She is a backward, conservative force—and this is what her oppression means. She is forced to be the stone in the stream. Her work is private and *because it is private*, and for no other reason, it is unsupervised. This is the source of that complacent "Your time's your own, you are your own boss' mystifying build-up that housewives are given. For every process of production that involves combined social forces and cooperation (enforced or voluntary) also requires superintendence or direction; it is only *isolated* labor that is free from this need. The "freedom" of the housewife is her isolation.

The Effects of Oppression. Working alone, grappling with the vestiges of individual property, women in the family are used to deflect the tide and implications of social labor. Out of the increasingly numerous contradictions of their position, a sense of their oppression is growing ever stronger. From this can come the revolutionary impulse to overthrow it. But we must not neglect the marks that oppression has left us with.

Just as, on the one hand, it is crucial that we are never guilty of underestimating the potential of women, so we must never neglect to be aware of the difficulties of our position. In a different context (that of military struggle) Mao called going it alone and underestimating the difficulties "Left Sectarianism" and underestimating one's potential and fearing to struggle "Right Opportunism." On the one hand, we

---

[7] *The German Ideology: op. cit.*, pp. 18-19.

have to dare to struggle, dare to win: on the other, we have to treat the struggle seriously. In the Women's Liberation Movement we have (at least in the United States), made the initial move possible, but if we don't correctly estimate the difficulties we will be guilty of "Left Sectarianism"—a voluntarism that will be at least a temporary death knell.

The difficulties that confront us are not just the opposition of the system we are confronting, but also its influence. It is this latter difficulty that I think we are in danger of ignoring. The conditions of our oppression *do* condition us. And we have to assess the weakness of women as a political force in order *not* to succumb to it. The Women's Liberation Movement is directed at all women—we have to know what we are asking.

What does our oppression within the family *do* to us women? It produces a tendency to small-mindedness, petty jealousy, irrational emotionality and random violence, dependency, competitive selfishness and possessiveness, passivity, a lack of vision and conservatism. These qualities are *not* the simple produce of male chauvinism, nor are they falsely ascribed to women by a sexist society that uses 'old women' as a dirty term. *They are the result of the woman's objective conditions within the family*—itself embedded in a sexist society. You cannot inhabit a small and backward world without it doing something to you. Peasants, as a potential revolutionary force, present comparable problems. Their whole life having been based on personal struggles for a little land and beating each other's prices in the market-place, makes revolutionary solidarity hard for them and the tendency to divisive and selfish seizure of individual gain, a difficult one to combat. Women, likewise, have always competed for the best men, the nicest home, the most successful kids; it is hard for them to come together as a socialized political force when the conditions of their lives are set to exclude this possibility. The working class is the revolutionary class under capitalism, because it engages in *socially* organized work, in this society in an antagonistic form which in turn makes clear to it that it must overthrow this form to release its social potential—socialism. This does not mean that oppressed peoples have no revolutionary potential—their oppression guarantees that. But the nature of the oppression does determine some of the difficulties of their struggle.

Though "women are wonderful" and "Black is beautiful" are crucial elements in the "dare to struggle, dare to win" stage, they must go hand in hand with a knowledge of what our oppression has done to retard us. It is in understanding this latter aspect that radical feminism seems to me to fall down. If men are the oppressors rather than, say, men in particular roles, such as father and husband, acting as agents of the objective oppression, then all we have to do is to overturn these oppressed characteristics and we will be liberated. The struggle would be much easier—because it is impossible. To say that women have none (or need have none) of the above-listed negative feminine characteristics is moralism not politics. And it is engaging battle on the terrain of moralism: "There have never been any great women artists. . . . Yes, there have, you just didn't notice them or you never let us be. . . . I dedicate this book to my wife without whose stoical patience and endless assistance . . . shut up." Well, that's alright as rhetoric, and rhetoric and anger have their place—but that place is political strategy, not in place of strife.

Suggested Readings

Brown, Norman, *Life Against Death* (London: Routledge & Kegan Paul Ltd., 1959).

Cohn-Bendit, Daniel, *Obsolete Communism* (New York: McGraw-Hill Book Company, 1969).

Gorz, Andre, *Strategy for Labor (Boston: The Beacon Press, Inc., 1969).*

Kolakowski, Leszek, *Toward a Marxist Humanism* (New York: Grove Press, Inc., 1969).

Long, Priscilla, *The New Left* (Boston: Porter Sergent, 1970).

Marcuse, Herbert, *Eros and Civilization* (Boston: The Beacon Press, Inc., 1955).

Marcuse, Herbert, *One-Dimensional Man* (Boston: The Beacon Press, Inc., 1964).

Oglesby, Carl, *The New Left Reader* (New York: Grove Press, Inc., 1969).

Third-World Ideologies

INTRODUCTION

It is the people of Africa, Asia, and Latin America who constitute the Third World. They are the people of color: black, yellow, and brown. The people of Europe and North America constitute the other two worlds. The emergence of the Third World is one of the most important political events of our time. The people of this world seek to free themselves from domination by Europe and North America. Just as the empires of Spain and Portugal in Latin America were overthrown during the nineteenth century, so the Third World seeks to overthrow the power of the other two worlds. It is the colonialism, direct and indirect, political and economic that the Third World finds oppressive. This is even true of the third-world people in the United States, who think of their relationship to whites as that of colonials. They play the same subsidiary political, economic, and social role in the United States as the black, yellow, and brown people played in the Third World; thus the Third World is both a place and a people. It is the black, yellow, and brown people of Africa, Asia, and Latin America who are among the oppressed.

The Third World struggles everywhere to overthrow these colonialisms. It should not be surprising to find that these oppressed try to think their way through to an independent political philosophy before, during, and after their struggle for political independence. The oppressors are racists. The oppressed are indoctrinated to feel inferior. The only way they can successfully obtain dignity and the feeling of human worth is by developing a political philosophy that affirms their own dignity and worth. In the United States the most seriously oppressed third-world groups are the Blacks, Indians, and Chicanos. The following essays exhibit ideological expressions of each of these three groups.

The ideology of the Black Panther Party shows the Marxist influence, but it mainly comes through the writings of the African Marxist Franz Fanon, who attacks traditional Marxist-Leninism "for its narrow preoccupation with Europe and the affairs and salvation of White Folks, while lumping all third world peoples into the category of *Lumpenproletariat* and then forgetting them there. . . ." Cleaver sees the blacks as the *Lumpenproletariat* and he characterizes them as "all those who have no secure relationship or vested interest in the means of production and the institutions of the capitalist society." Cleaver argues that the working class is the Right Wing while the *Lumpenproletariat* is the Left Wing. Hence the *Lumpenproletariat* must even take sides against the working class and create their own rebellion.

Deloria's essay represents the social-political ideology of the American Indian. In contrast to the belief in rugged individualism of the conservatives, the American Indian wants and has a society structured differently. To be a person one must become a member of a tribe, for it is only this type of social organization that is suited to the nurturing of the kind of self that is appropriate to changing cultural trends.

Paz and Contreras state the social-cultural ideology of the Chicano. They each state the problems facing a person who is trying to find his identity when he has origins in one culture but is forced to find his place in another culture. Just as Deloria contended that the person could only find his identity in a social unit, so Contreras and Paz maintain that the search for a personal identity is a collective endeavor.

In the Third World outside the United States, we find a very heavy influence of Marxism. Except for a few oil kingdoms there is scarcely a single nation that has the capital to develop any sort of economic system except a socialist one. Few of the countries are communist but nearly all of them are socialist.

Che Guevara's doctrines were very influential in Latin America. He not only wanted political revolution, but he, as well as Mao, tried to construct a new society from which new men would emerge. This concept of the new man is important in the Third World and will continue to be so. President Senghor of Senegal develops a socialist humanism that is a combination of Marx and de Chardin, and he attempts to develop a new definition of man—Marxist with a mystical twist.

Senghor argues that African socialism must proceed slowly. He finds that giving priority to heavy industry or agrarian reform has created difficulties. He established the following as priorities: infrastructure, rural economy, processing industry, heavy industry—in line with reasonable requirements and his countries realities. It is not a purely socialistic economy, but a very heavy part of the budget goes to health, housing, and education.

The Chinese communists see themselves as strict Marxist-Leninists, but they do address themselves to the creation of the new man. Their political writings may seem to be somewhat confessional but they are determined that philosophy has often been very abstract and not applicable to individuals; the Maoists are determined to be concrete in their philosophy and have it be applicable to individual lives.

Ideology of the Black Panther Party

Eldridge Cleaver

Eldridge Cleaver (1935–) has been one of the leaders of the Black Panther Party. He now lives in exile in Algeria. He wrote the well-known *Soul on Ice* (1967).

We have said: the ideology of the Black Panther Party is the historical experience of Black people and the wisdom gained by Black people in their 400 year long struggle against the system of racist oppression and economic exploitation in Babylon, interpreted through the prism of the Marxist-Leninist analysis by our Minister of Defense, Huey P. Newton.

However, we must place heavy emphasis upon the last part of that definition— *"interpreted . . . by our Minister of Defense.' . . .* The world of Marxism–Leninism has become a jungle of opinion in which conflicting interpretations, from Right Revisionism to Left Dogmatism, foist off their reactionary and blind philosophies as revolutionary Marxism-Leninism. Around the world and in every nation people, all who call themselves Marxist-Leninists, are at each other's throats. Such a situation presents serious problems to a young party, such as ours, that is still in the process of refining its ideology.

When we say that we are Marxist-Leninists, we mean that we have studied and understood the classical principles of scientific socialism and that we have adapted these principles to our own situation for ourselves. However, we do not move with a closed mind to new ideas or information. At the same time, we know that we must rely upon our own brains in solving ideological problems as they relate to us.

For too long Black people have relied upon the analyses and ideological perspectives of others. Our struggle has reached a point now where it would be absolutely suicidal for us to continue this posture of dependency. No other people in the world are in the same position as we are, and no other people in the world can get us out of it except ourselves. There are those who are all too willing to do our thinking for us, even if it gets us killed. However, they are not willing to follow through and do our dying for us. If thoughts bring about our deaths, let them at least be our own thoughts, so that we will have broken, once and for all, with the flunkeyism of dying for every cause and every error—except our own.

One of the great contributions of Huey P. Newton is that he gave the Black Panther Party a firm ideological foundation that frees us from ideological flunkeyism and opens up the path to the future—a future to which we must provide new ideological formulations to fit our ever changing situation.

Much—*most*—of the teachings of Huey P. Newton are unknown to the people because Huey has been placed in a position where it is impossible for him to really communicate with us. And much that he taught while he was free has gotten

From pamphlet published by Ministry of Information, Black Panther Party, San Francisco, 1967.

distorted and watered down precisely because the Black Panther Party has been too hung up in relating to the courts and trying to put on a good face in order to help lawyers convince juries of the justice of our cause. This whole court hang-up has created much confusion.

For instance, many people confuse the Black Panther Party with the Free Huey Movement or the many other mass activities that we have been forced to indulge in in order to build mass support for our comrades who have gotten captured by the pigs. We are absolutely correct in indulging in such mass activity. But we are wrong when we confuse our mass line with our party line.

Essentially, what Huey did was to provide the ideology and the methodology for organizing the Black Urban Lumpenproletariat. Armed with this ideological perspective and method, Huey transformed the Black Lumpenproletariat from the forgotten people at the bottom of society into the vanguard of the proletariat.

There is a lot of confusion over whether we are members of the Working Class or whether we are Lumenproletariat. It is necessary to confront this confusion, because it has a great deal to do with the strategy and tactics that we follow and with our strained relations with the White radicals from the oppressor section of Babylon.

Some so-called Marxist-Leninists will attack us for what we have to say, but that is a good thing and not a bad thing because some people call themselves Marxist-Leninists who are the downright enemies of Black people. Later for them. We want them to step boldly forward, as they will do—blinded by their own stupidity and racist arrogance—so that it will be easier for us to deal with them in the future.

We make these criticisms in a fraternal spirit of how some Marxist-Leninists apply the classical principles to the specific situation that exists in the United States because we believe in the need for a unified revolutionary movement in the United States, a movement that is informed by the revolutionary principles of scientific socialism. Huey P. Newton says that "power is the ability to define phenomena and make it act in a desired manner." And we need power, desperately, to counter the power of the pigs that now bears so heavily upon us.

Ideology is a comprehensive definition of a status quo that takes into account both the history and the future of that status quo and serves as the social glue that holds a people together and through which a people relate to the world and other groups of people in the world. The correct ideology is an invincible weapon against the oppressor in our struggle for freedom and liberation.

Marx defined the epoch of the bourgeoisie and laid bare the direction of the Proletarian future. He analyzed Capitalism and defined the method of its doom: VIOLENT REVOLUTION BY THE PROLETARIAT AGAINST THE BOURGEOIS STATE APPARATUS OF CLASS OPPRESSION AND REPRES-SION. REVOLUTIONARY VIOLENCE AGAINST THE COUNTER-REVOLUTIONARY CLASS VIOLENCE PERPETRATED THROUGH THE SPECIAL REPRESSIVE FORCE OF THE ARMED TENTACLES OF THE STATE.

This great definition by Marx and Engels became the mightiest weapon in the hands of oppressed people in the history of ideology. It marks a gigantic advance for all mankind. And since Marx's time, his definition has been strengthened, further elaborated, illumined, and further refined.

But Marxism has never really dealt with the United States of America. There have been some very nice attempts. People have done the best that they know how.

However, in the past, Marxist-Leninists in the United States have relied too heavily upon foreign, imported analyses and have seriously distorted the realities of the American scene. We might say that the Marxism-Leninism of the past belongs to the gestation period of Marxism-Leninism in the United States, and that now is the time when a new, strictly American ideological synthesis will arise, springing up from the hearts and souls of the oppressed people inside Babylon, and uniting these people and hurling them mightily, from the force of their struggle, into the future. The swiftly developing revolution in America is like the gathering of a mighty storm, and nothing can stop that storm from finally bursting, inside America, washing away the pigs of the power structure and all their foul, oppressive works. And the children of the pigs and the oppressed people will dance and spit upon the common graves of these pigs.

There are some Black people in the United States who are absolutely happy, who do not feel themselves to be oppressed, and who think that they are free. Some even believe that the President wouldn't lie, and that he is more or less an honest man; that Supreme Court decisions were almost written by god in person; that the Police are Guardians of the Law; and that people who do not have jobs are just plain lazy and good-for-nothing and should be severely punished. These are like crabs that must be left to boil a little longer in the pot of oppression before they will be ready and willing to relate. But the overwhelming majority of Black people are uptight, know that they are oppressed and not free; and they wouldn't believe Nixon if he confessed to being a pig; they don't relate to the Supreme Court or any other court; and they know that the racist pig cops are their sworn enemies. As for poverty, they know what it is all about.

These millions of Black people have no political representation, they are unorganized, and they do not own or control any of the natural resources; they neither own nor control any of the industrial machinery, and their daily life is a hustle to make it by any means necessary in the struggle to survive.

Every Black person knows that the wind may change at any given moment and that the Lynch Mob, made up of White members of the "Working Class," might come breathing down his neck if not kicking down his door. It is because of these factors that when we begin to talk about being Marxist-Leninists, we must be very careful to make it absolutely clear just what we are talking about.

On the subject of racism, Marxism-Leninism offers us very little assistance. In fact, there is much evidence that Marx and Engels were themselves racists—just like their White brothers and sisters of their era, and just as many Marxist-Leninists of our own time are also racists. Historically, Marxism-Leninism has been an outgrowth of European problems and it has been primarily preoccupied with finding solutions to European problems.

With the founding of the Democratic People's Republic of Korea in 1948 and the People's Republic of China in 1949, something new was injected into Marxism-Leninism, and it ceased to be just a narrow, exclusively European phenomenon. Comrade Kim Il Sung and Comrade Mao Tse-tung applied the classical principles of Marxism-Leninism to the conditions in their own countries and thereby made the ideology into something useful for their people. But they rejected that part of the analysis that was not beneficial to them and had only to do with the welfare of Europe.

Given the racist history of the United States, it is very difficult for Black people to comfortably call themselves Marxist-Leninists or anything else that takes its name from White people. It's like praying to Jesus, a White man. We must emphasize the fact that Marx and Lenin didn't invent Socialism. They only added their contributions, enriching the doctrine, just as many others did before them and after them. And we must remember that Marx and Lenin didn't organize the Black Panther Party. Huey P. Newton and Bobby Seale did.

Not until we reach Fanon do we find a major Marxist-Leninist theoretician who was primarily concerned about the problems of Black people, wherever they may be found. And even Fanon, in his published works, was primarily focused on Africa. It is only indirectly that his works are beneficial to Afro-Americans. It is just easier to relate to Fanon because he is clearly free of that racist bias that blocks out so much about the Black man in the hands of Whites who are primarily interested in themselves and the problems of their own people. But even though we are able to relate heavily to Fanon, he has not given us the last word on applying the Marxist-Leninist analysis to our problems inside the United States. No one is going to do this for us because no one can. We have to do it ourselves, and until we do, we are going to be uptight.

We must take the teachings of Huey P. Newton as our foundation and go from there. Any other course will bring us to a sorry and regrettable end.

Fanon delivered a devastating attack upon Marxism-Leninism for its narrow preoccupation with Europe and the affairs and salvation of White folks, while lumping all third world peoples into the category of the Lumpenproletariat and then forgetting them there; Fanon unearthed the category of the Lumpenproletariat and began to deal with it, recognizing that vast majorities of the colonized people fall into that category. It is because of the fact that Black people in the United States are also colonized that Fanon's analysis is so relevant to us.

After studying Fanon, Huey P. Newton and Bobby Seale began to apply his analysis of colonized people to Black people in the United States. They adopted the Fanonian perspective, but they gave it a uniquely Afro-American content.

Just as we must make the distinctions between the mother country and the colony when dealing with Black people and White people as a whole, we must also make this distinction when we deal with the categories of the Working Class and the Lumpenproletariat.

We have, in the United States, a "Mother Country Working Class" and a "Working Class from the Black Colony." We also have a Mother Country Lumpenproletariat and a Lumpenproletariat from the Black Colony. Inside the Mother Country, these categories are fairly stable, but when we look at the Black Colony, we find that the hard and fast distinctions melt away. This is because of the leveling effect of the colonial process and the fact that all Black people are colonized, even if some of then occupy favored positions in the schemes of the Mother Country colonizing exploiters.

There is a difference between the problems of the Mother Country Working Class and the Working Class from the Black Colony. There is also a difference between the Mother Country Lumpen and the Lumpen from the Black Colony. We have nothing to gain from trying to smooth over these differences as though they don't exist, because they are objective facts that must be dealt with. To make this point clear, we have only to look at the long a bitter history of the struggles of Black Colony Workers fighting for democracy inside Mother Country Labor Unions.

Historically, we have fallen into the trap of criticizing mother country labor unions and workers for the racism as an explanation for the way they treat Black workers. Of course, they are racist, but this is not the full explanation.

White workers belong to a totally different world than that of Black workers. They are caught up in a totally different economic, political, and social reality, and on the basis of this distinct reality, the pigs of the power structure and treacherous labor leaders find it very easy to manipulate them with Babylonian racism.

This complex reality presents us with many problems, and only through proper analysis can these problems be solved. The lack of a proper analysis is responsible for the ridiculous approach to these problems that we find among Mother Country Marxist-Leninists. And their improper analysis leads them to advocate solutions that are doomed to failure in advance. The key area of the confusion has to do with falsely assuming the existence of one All-American Proletariat; one All-American Working Class; and one All-American Lumpenproletariat.

O.K. We are Lumpen. Right on. The Lumpenproletariat are all those who have no secure relationship or vested interest in the means of production and the institutions of capitalist society. That part of the "Industrial Reserve Army" held perpetually in reserve; who have never worked and never will; who can't find a job; who are unskilled and unfit; who have been displaced by machines, automation, and cybernation, and were never "retained or invested with new skills;" all those on Welfare or receiving State Aid.

Also the so-called "Criminal Element," those who live by their wits, existing off that which they rip off, who stick guns in the faces of businessmen and say "stick'em up," or "give it up!" Those who don't even want a job, who hate to work and can't relate to punching some pig's time clock, who would rather punch a pig in the mouth and rob him than punch that same pig's time clock and work for him, those whom Huey P. Newton calls "the illegitimate capitalists." In short, all those who simply have been locked out of the economy and robbed of their rightful social heritage.

But even though we are Lumpen, we are still members of the Proletariat, a category which theoretically cuts across national boundaries but which in practice leaves something to be desired.

CONTRADICTIONS WITHIN THE PROLETARIAT OF THE USA

In both the Mother Country and the Black Colony, the Working Class is the Right Wing of the Proletariat, and the Lumpenproletariat is the Left Wing. Within the Working Class itself, we have a major contradiction between the Unemployed and the Employed. And we definitely have a major contradiction between the Working Class and the Lumpen.

Some blind so-called Marxist-Leninists accuse the Lumpen of being parasites upon the Working Class. This is a stupid charge derived from reading too many of Marx's footnotes and taking some of his offhand scurrilous remarks for holy writ. In reality, it is accurate to say that the Working Class, particularly the American Working Class, is a parasite upon the heritage of mankind, of which the Lumpen has been totally robbed by the rigged system of Capitalism which in turn, has thrown the majority of mankind upon the junkheap while it buys off a percentage with jobs and security.

The Working Class that we must deal with today shows little resemblance to the

Working Class of Marx's day. In the days of its infancy, insecurity, and instability, the Working Class was very revolutionary and carried forward the struggle against the bourgeoisie. But through long and bitter struggles, the Working Class has made some inroads into the Capitalist system, carving out a comfortable niche for itself. The advent of Labor Unions, Collective Bargaining, the Union Shop, Social Security, and other special protective legislation has castrated the Working Class, transforming it into the bought-off Labor Movement—a most un-revolutionary, reformist minded movement that is only interested in higher wages and more job security. The Labor Movement has abandoned all basic criticism of the Capitalist system of exploitation itself. The George Meanys, Walter Reuthers, and A. Phillip Randolphs may correctly be labelled traitors to the proletariat as a whole, but they accurately reflect and embody the outlook and aspirations of the Working Class. The Communist Party of the United States of America, at its poorly attended meetings, may raise the roof with its proclamations of being the Vanguard of the Working Class, but the Working Class itself looks upon the Democratic Party as the legitimate vehicle of its political salvation.

As a matter of fact, the Working Class of our time has become a new industrial elite, resembling more the chauvanistic elites of the selfish craft and tradeguilds of Marx's time than the toiling masses ground down in abject poverty. Every job on the market in the American Economy today demands as high a complexity of skills as did the jobs in the elite trade and craft guilds of Marx's time.

In a highly mechanized economy, it cannot be said that the fantastically high productivity is the product solely of the Working Class. Machines and computers are not members of the Working Class, although some spokesmen for the Working Class, particularly some Marxist-Leninists, seem to think like machines and computers.

The flames of revolution, which once raged like an inferno in the heart of the Working Class, in our day have dwindled into a flickering candle light, only powerful enough to bounce the Working Class back and forth like a ping pong ball between the Democratic Party and the Republican Party every four years, never once even glancing at the alternatives on the Left.

WHO SPEAKS FOR THE LUMPENPROLETARIAT?

Some Marxist-Leninists are guilty of that class egotism and hypocrisy often displayed by superior classes to those beneath them on the social scale. On the one hand, they freely admit that their organizations are specifically designed to represent the interests of the Working Class. But then they go beyond that to say that by representing the interests of the Working Class, they represent the interest of the Proletariat as a whole. This is clearly not true. This is a fallacious assumption based upon the egotism of these organizations and is partly responsible for their miserable failure to make a revolution in Babylon.

And since there clearly is a contradiction between the right wing and the left wing of the Proletariat, just as the right wing has created its own organizations, it is necessary for the left wing to have its form of organization to represent its interests against all hostile classes—including the Working Class.

The contradiction between the Lumpen and the Working Class is very serious because it even dictates a different strategy and set of tactics. The students focus their rebellions on the campuses, and the Working Class focuses its rebellions on the factories and picket lines. But the Lumpen finds itself in the peculiar position of being unable to find a job and therefore is unable to attend the Universities. The Lumpen has no choice but to manifest its rebellion in the University of the Streets.

It's very important to recognize that the streets belong to the Lumpen, and that it is in the streets that the Lumpen will make their rebellion.

One outstanding characteristic of the liberation struggle of Black people in the United States has been that most of the activity has taken place in the streets. This is because, by and large, the rebellions have been spearheaded by Black Lumpen.

It is because of Black people's lumpen relationship to the means of production and the institutions of the society that they are unable to manifest their rebellion around those means of production and institutions. But this does not mean that the rebellions that take place in the streets are not legitimate expressions of an oppressed people. These are the means of rebellion left open to the Lumpen.

The Lumpen have been locked outside of the economy. And when the Lumpen does engage in direct action against the system of oppression, it is often greeted by hoots and howls from the spokesmen of the Working Class in chorus with the mouthpieces of the bourgeoisie. These talkers like to put down the struggles of the Lumpen as being "spontaneous" (perhaps because they themselves did not order the actions!), "unorganized," and "chaotic and undirected." But these are only prejudiced analyses made from the narrow perspective of the Working Class. But the Lumpen moves anyway, refusing to be straight-jacketed or controlled by the tactics dictated by the conditions of life and the relationship to the means of production of the Working Class.

The Lumpen finds itself in the position where it is very difficult for it to manifest its complaints against the system. The Working Class has the possibility of calling a strike against the factory and the employer and through the mechanism of Labor Unions they can have some arbitration or some process through which its grievances are manifested. Collective bargaining is the way out of the pit of oppression and exploitation discovered by the Working Class, but the Lumpen has no opportunity to do any collective bargaining. The Lumpen has no institutionalized focus in Capitalist society. It has no immediate oppressor except perhaps the Pig Police with which it is confronted daily.

So that the very conditions of life of the Lumpen dictates the so-called spontaneous reactions against the system, and because the Lumpen is in this extremely oppressed condition, it therefore has an extreme reaction against the system as a whole. It sees itself as being bypassed by all of the organizations, even by the Labor Unions, and even by the Communist Parties that despise it and look down upon it and consider it to be, in the words of Karl Marx, the father of Communist Parties, "The Scum Layer of the Society". The Lumpen is forced to create its own forms of rebellion that are consistent with its condition in life and with its relationship to the means of production and the institutions of society. That is, to strike out at all the structures around it, including at the reactionary Right Wing of the Proletariat when it gets in the way of revolution.

The faulty analyses which the ideologies of the Working Class have made, of the true nature of the Lumpen, are greatly responsible for the retardation of the development of the revolution in urban situations. It can be said that the true revolutionaries in the urban centers of the world have been analyzed out of revolution by some Marxist-Leninists.

WHAT WE WANT, WHAT WE BELIEVE (OCTOBER 1966 BLACK PANTHER PARTY PLATFORM AND PROGRAM)

1. We want freedom. We want power to determine the destiny of our Black Community.

We believe that black people will not be free until we are able to determine our destiny.

2. We want full employment for our people.

We believe that the federal government is responsible and obligated to give every man employment or a guaranteed income. We believe that if the white American businessmen will not give full employment, then the means of production should be taken from the businessmen and placed in the community so that the people of the community can organize and employ all its people and give a high standard of living.

3. We want an end to the robbery by the capitalist of our Black Community.

We believe that this racist government has robbed us and now we are demanding the overdue debt of forty acres and two mules. Forty acres and two mules were promised 100 years ago as restitution for slave labor and mass murder of black people. We will accept the payment in currency which will be distributed to our many communities. The Germans are now aiding the Jews in Israel for the genocide of the Jewish people. The Germans murdered six million Jews. The American racist has taken part in the slaughter of over fifty million black people; therefore, we feel that this is a modest demand that we make.

4. We want decent housing, fit for shelter of human beings.

We believe that if the white landlords will not give decent housing to our black community, then the housing and the land should be made into cooperatives so that our community, with government aid, can build and make decent housing for its people.

5. We want education for our people that exposes the true nature of this decadent American society. We want education that teaches us our true history and our role in the present-day society.

We believe in an educational system that will give to our people a knowledge of self. If a man does not have knowledge of himself and his position in society and the world, then he has little chance to relate to anything else.

6. We want all black men to be exempt from military service.

We believe that Black people should not be forced to fight in the military service to defend a racist government that does not protect us. We will not fight and kill other people of color in the world who, like black people, are being victimized by the white racist government of America. We will protect ourselves from the force and violence of the racist police and the racist military, by whatever means necessary.

7. We want an immediate end to Police Brutality and Murder of black people.

We believe we can end police brutality in our black community by organizing black self-defense groups that are dedicated to defending our black community from racist police oppression and brutality. The Second Amendment to the Constitution of the United States gives a right to bear arms. We therefore believe that all black people should arm themselves for self-defense.

8. We want freedom for all black men held in federal, state, county and city prisons and jails.

We believe that all black people should be released from the many jails and prisons because they have not received a fair and impartial trial.

9. We want all black people when brought to trial to be tried in court by a jury of their peer group or people from their black communities, as defined by the Constitution of the United States.

We believe that the courts should follow the United States Constitution so that black people will receive fair trials. The 14th Amendment of the U.S. Constitution gives a man a right to be tried by his peer group. A peer is a person from a similar economic, social, religious, geographical, environmental, historical and racial background. To do this the court will be forced to select a jury from the black community from which the black defendant came. We have been, and are being tried by all-white juries that have no understanding of the "average reasoning man" of the black community.

10. We want land, bread, housing, education, clothing, justice and peace. And as our major political objective, a United Nations-supervised plebiscite to be held throughout the black colony in which only black colonial subjects will be allowed to participate, for the purpose of determining the will of black people as to their national destiny.

When, in the course of human events, it becomes necessary for one people to dissolve the political bands which have connected them with another, and to assume, among the powers of the earth, the separate and equal station to which the laws of nature and nature's God entitle them, a decent respect to the opinions of mankind requires that they should declare the causes which impel them to the separation.

We hold these truths to be self-evident, that all men are created equal; that they are endowed by their Creator with certain unalienable rights; that among these are life, liberty, and the pursuit of happiness. That, to secure these rights, governments are instituted among men, deriving their just powers from the consent of the governed; that, whenever any form of government becomes destructive of these ends, it is the right of the people to alter or to abolish it, and to institute a new government, laying its foundation on such principles, and organizing its powers in such form, as to them shall seem most likely to effect their safety and happiness. Prudence, indeed, will dictate that governments long established should not be changed for light and transient causes; and, accordingly, all experience hath shown, that mankind are more disposed to suffer, while evils are sufferable, than to right themselves by abolishing the forms to which they are accustomed. But, when a long train of abuses and usurpations, pursuing invariably the same object, evinces a design to reduce them under absolute despotism, it is their right, it is their duty, to throw off such government, and to provide new guards for their future security.

Black Panther Party Platform
Bobby Seale

Bobby Seale (1941-   ) is a California leader of the Black Panther Party. He lives in California, and he has published many pamphlets on the Black Movement.

Every member of the BLACK PANTHER PARTY throughout this country of racist America must abide by these rules as functional members of this party. CENTRAL COMMITTEE members, CENTRAL STAFFS, and LOCAL STAFFS, including all captains subordinate to either national, state, and local leadership of the BLACK PANTHER PARTY will enforce these rules. Length of suspension or other disciplinary action necessary for violation of these rules will depend on national decisions by national, state or state area, and local committees and staffs where said rule or rules of the BLACK PANTHER PARTY WERE VIOLATED.

Every member of the party must know these verbatim by heart. And apply them daily. Each member must report any violation of these rules to their leadership or they are counter-revolutionary and are also subjected to suspension by the BLACK PANTHER PARTY.

The rules are:

1. No party member can have narcotics or weed in his possession while doing party work.

2. Any party member found shooting narcotics will be expelled from this party.

3. No party member can be DRUNK while doing daily party work.

4. No party member will violate rules relating to office work, general meetings of the BLACK PANTHER PARTY, and meetings of the BLACK PANTHER PARTY ANYWHERE.

5. No party member will USE, POINT, or FIRE a weapon of any kind unnecessarily or accidentally at anyone.

6. No party member can join any other army force other than the BLACK LIBERATION ARMY.

7. No party member can have a weapon in his possession while DRUNK or loaded off narcotics or weed.

8. No party member will commit any crimes against other party members or BLACK people at all, and cannot steal or take from the people, not even a needle or a piece of thread.

9. When arrested BLACK PANTHER MEMBERS will give only name, address, and will sign nothing. Legal first aid must be understood by all Party members.

10. The Ten-Point Program and platform of the BLACK PANTHER PARTY must be known and understood by each Party member.

11. Party Communications must be National and Local.

12. The 10-10-10-program should be known by all members and also understood by all members.

13. All Finance officers will operate under the jurisdiction of the Ministry of Finance.

14. Each person will submit a report of daily work.

15. Each Sub-Division Leader, Section Leaders, and Lieutenants, Captains must submit Daily reports of work.

16. All Panthers must learn to operate and service weapons correctly.

17. All leadership personnel who expel a member must submit this information to the Editor of the Newspaper, so that it will be published in the paper and will be known by all chapters and branches.

18. Political Education Classes are mandatory for general membership.

19. Only office personnel assigned to respective offices each day should be there. All others are to sell papers and do Political work out in the community, including Captains, Section Leaders, etc.

20. COMMUNICATIONS—all chapters must submit weekly reports in writing to the National Headquarters.

21. All Branches must implement First Aid and/or Medical Cadres.

22. All Chapters, Branches and components of the BLACK PANTHER PARTY must submit a monthly Financial Report to the Ministry of Finance, and also the Central Committee.

23. Everyone in a leadership position must read no less than two hours per day to keep abreast of the changing political situation.

24. No chapter or branch shall accept grants, poverty funds, money or any other aid from any government agency without contacting the National Head-quarters.

25. All chapters must adhere to the policy and the ideology laid down by the CENTRAL COMMITTEE of the BLACK PANTHER PARTY.

26. All branches must submit weekly reports in writing to their respective Chapters.

POINTS OF ATTENTION

1. Speak politely.
2. Pay fairly for what you buy.
3. Return everything you borrow.
4. Pay for anything you damage.
5. Do not hit or swear at people.
6. Do not damage property or crops of the poor, oppressed masses.
7. Do not take liberties with women.
8. If we ever have to take captives do not ill-treat them.

MAIN RULES OF DISCIPLINE

1. Obey orders in all your actions.
2. Do not take a single needle or a piece of thread from the poor and oppressed masses.
3. Turn in everything captured from the attacking enemy.

Political Ideology of the New American Indian
Vine Deloria

Vine Deloria (1934-   ) has been active in Indian affairs in the United States for many years. Recently he engaged in law studies to further this activity. Among his publications are *Red Man in the New World* (1971); *Custer Died for Your Sins* (1969); and *We Talk, You Listen* (1970).

A century ago whites broke the Fort Laramie Treaty with the Sioux so they could march into the Black Hills and dig gold out of the ground. Then they took the gold out of the Black Hills, carried it to Fort Knox, Kentucky, and buried it in the ground. Throughout the Midwest, Indians were forced off their lands because whites felt that the Indians didn't put the lands to good use. Today most of this land lies idle every year while the owners collect a government check for not planting anything. Wilderness was taken because "no one" lived there and cities were built in which no one could live.

      .   .   .

Again, last summer, a noted female anthropologist presented a scholarly paper to the effect that Indians drink to gain an identity. Anyone who has ever seen Indians would laugh at the absurdity of this idea. It is unquestionably the other way. Indians first ask what your name is, then what your tribe is. After these preliminaries you are sometimes asked to have a drink. Drinking is only the confirmation of a friendship already established by the fact that you belong to a specific tribe. If we acted the way anthropologists describe us, we would get lousy stinking drunk, THEN DECIDE WHAT TRIBE WE WANTED TO BELONG TO, and finally choose a surname for ourselves.

All of these things have set me wondering if there isn't a better way to distinguish between the Indian mood, life style, and philosophy, and that of the non-Indian. It is very difficult to do. Non-Indians are descended from a peculiar group of people. The first group thought they were sailing off the edge of the world and probably would have had we not pulled them ashore. Their successors spent years traveling all over the continent in search of the Fountain of Youth and the Seven Cities of Gold. They didn't even know how to plant an ear of corn when they arrived on these shores. So the non-Indian is pretty set in his ideas and hard to change.

      .   .   .

Trying to communicate is an insurmountable task, however, since one cannot skip readily from another way of life to the conceptual world of the non-tribal person. The non-tribal person thinks in a linear sequence, in which A is the foundation of B, and C always follows. The view and meaning of the total event is rarely understood by the non-tribal person, although he may receive more objective information concerning any specific element of the situation. Non-tribals can measure the distance to the moon with unerring accuracy, but the moon remains an impersonal object to them without personal relationships that would support or illuminate their innermost feelings.

Tribal society is of such a nature that one must experience it from the inside. It is holistic, and logical analysis will only return you to your starting premise none the wiser for the trip. Being inside a tribal universe is so comfortable and reasonable that it acts like a narcotic. When you are forced outside the tribal context you become alienated, irritable, and lonely. In desperation you long to return to the tribe if only to preserve your sanity. While a majority of Indian people today live in the cities, a substantial number make long weekend trips back to their reservations to spend precious hours in their own land with their people.

The best method of communicating Indian values is to find points at which issues appear to by related. Because tribal society is integrated toward a center and non-Indian society is oriented toward linear development, the process might be compared to describing a circle surrounded with tangent lines. The points at which the lines touch the circumference of the circle are the issues and ideas that can be shared by Indians and other groups. There are a great many points at which tangents occur, and they may be considered as windows through which Indians and non-Indians can glimpse each other. Once this structural device is used and understood, non-Indians, using a tribal point of view, can better understand themselves and their relationship to Indian people.

The problem is complicated by the speed of modern communications media. It floods us with news that is news because it is reported as news. Thus, if we take a linear viewpoint of the world, the sequence of spectacular events creates the impression that the world is going either up- or downhill. Events become noted more for their supportive or threatening aspects than for their reality, since they fall into line and do not themselves contain any means of interpretation. When we are unable to absorb the events reported to us by the media, we begin to force interpretations of what the world really means on the basis of what we have been taught rather than what we have experienced.

Indian people are just as subject to the deluge of information as are other people. In the last decade most reservations have come within the reach of television and computers. In many ways Indian people are just as directed by the electric nature of our universe as any other group. But the tribal viewpoint simply absorbs what is reported to it and immediately integrates it into the experience of the group. In many areas whites are regarded as a temporary aspect of tribal life and there is unshakable belief that the tribe will survive the domination of the white man and once again rule the continent. Indians soak up the world like a blotter and continue almost untouched by events. The more that happens, the better the tribe seems to function and the stronger it appears to get. Of all the groups in the modern world Indians are best able to cope with the modern situation. To the non-Indian world, it does not appear that Indians are capable of anything. The flexibility of the tribal viewpoint enables Indians to meet devastating situations and survive. But this flexibility is seen by non-Indians as incompetency, so that as the non-Indian struggles in solitude and despair he curses the Indian for not coveting the same disaster.

In 1969, non-Indians began to rediscover Indians. Everyone hailed us as their natural allies in the ancient struggle they were waging with the "bad guys." Conservatives embraced us because we didn't act uppity, refused to move into their neighborhoods, and didn't march in *their* streets. Liberals loved us because we were the most oppressed of all the peoples who had been oppressed, and besides we generally voted Democratic.

Blacks loved us because we objected to the policies of the Department of the Interior (we would probably object if we had set the damn thing up ourselves) which indicated to them that we were another group to count on for the coming revolution. I attended one conference last fall at which a number of raging militants held forth, giving their views on the upcoming revolt of the masses. In a fever pitch they described the battle of Armageddon in which the "pigs" would be vanquished and the meek would inherit the earth (or a reasonable facsimile thereof). When asked if he supported the overthrow of the establishment, an old Sioux replied, "not until we get paid for the Black Hills." Needless to say, revolutionaries have not been impressed with the Indian fervor for radical change.

Hippies proudly showed us their beads and, with a knowing smile, bid us hello in the Navajo they had learned while passing through Arizona the previous summer. We watched and wondered as they paraded by in buckskin and feathers, anxiously playing a role they could not comprehend. When the Indians of the Bay area occupied Alcatraz, the hippies descended on the island in droves, nervously scanning the horizon for a vision of man in his pristine natural state. When they found that the tribesmen had the same organizational problems as any other group might have, they left in disappointment, disillusioned with "Indianism" that had existed only in their imaginations.

For nearly a year, the various minority and power groups have tried to get Indians to relate to the social crisis that plagues the land. Churches have expended enormous sums creating "task forces" of hand-picked Indians to inform them on the national scope of Indian problems. They have been disappointed when Indians didn't immediately embrace violence as a technique for progress. Government agencies have tried to understand Indians in an urban context that no longer has validity for even the most stalwart urbanite. Conservationists have sought out Indians for their mystical knowledge of the use of land. It has been an exciting year.

There is no doubt in my mind that a major crisis exists. I believe, however, that it is deeper and more profound than racism, violence, and economic deprivation. American society is undergoing a total replacement of its philosophical concepts. Words are being emptied of old meanings and new values are coming in to fill the vacuum. Racial antagonisms, inflation, ecological destruction, and power groups are all symptoms of the emergence of a new world view of man and his society. Today thought patterns are shifting from the traditional emphasis on the solitary individual to as yet unrelated definitions of man as a member of a specific group.

This is an extremely difficult transition for any society to make. Rather than face the situation head-on, people have preferred to consider social problems as manifestations of a gap between certain elements of the national community. The most blatant example of this attitude is to speak of the "generation gap." Other times it is categorized as a racial problem—the white racist power structure against the pure and peace-loving minority groups. We know that this is false. In those programs where blacks have dominated they have been as racist against Indians as they claim whites have been against them. Behind every movement is the undeniable emergence of the group as a group. Until conceptions of the nature of mass society are enlarged and accepted by the majority of people there will be little peace in this society.

. . .

Much of the emphasis of recent years has been toward the realization of power by segments of the minority communities. Power has been defined in a number of ways, and where it has not been defined, activism has been substituted for power itself. Thus decibel level has often passed for elucidation and voluminous slogan-izing has replaced articulation of ideas.

In 1966, a number of us in the Indian field advanced "Red Power" as a means of putting the establishment on. We were greatly surprised when newspapermen began to take us seriously and even more so when liberals who had previously been cool and unreceptive began to smile at us in conferences. But the militant medium was quick to overtake us. Consequently I was approached one day in a Midwestern city by a group of young Indians who asked for my permission to break windows. Red Power had arrived!

The very concept of power has been so debilitated in recent years that it now seems incongruous to speak of mere power when the younger and more aggressive people are threatening to burn everything down. Yet power cannot be understood outside of its social-political context. When merged together, the social and political aspects ultimately become historical-religious concepts describing movement by a particular group of people toward a particular destiny. Few members of racial minority groups have realized that inherent in their peculiar experience on this continent is hidden the basic recognition of their power and sovereignty.

. . .

Because discrimination has been based upon group identity, it has been through group action that progress has been made toward making the political structure more flexible. Or, in the case of Indian tribes, group action by coalitions of tribes have enabled the Indian community to withstand the incredible pressures brought to bear on them. When one reverses the powerlessness of the minority groups and begins to affirm the handicaps suffered by minority groups as positive aspects of their place in American society, the emergence of certain concepts becomes quite clear.

Powerlessness becomes potential for power within certain limits using certain techniques. Scapegoat identity becomes sovereignty of the group and freedom from oppression because of race, color, or culture becomes a positive identity which can be fulfilled rather than a hurdle to be overcome. This is the threat over and above the burning and looting which frightens all white Americans. When the position of the minority groups is viewed in its philosophical and conceptual positive sense, then it is clear that ONLY minority groups can have an identity which will withstand the pressures and the tidal waves of the electric world. ONLY minority groups have within themselves the potential for exercise of power. And ONLY minority groups have the vision of freedom before them. For this reason, at Woodstock in 1969, the disenchanted white youth proclaimed themselves a new minority group.

While merely announcing the formation of a new minority group does not make it so, yet the willingness to identify as a separate and distinct group in the face of four centuries of Western European tradition on this continent and two centuries of persecution of minority groups by the United States government indicates that something lasting may be afoot. The next few years may well tell whether white society itself will break apart into irreconcilable groups, or whether the present movement by youth is another fad to fill the leisure of affluence.

Much of the significance of group movement today is that leadership within the respective groups is taking the reverse side of the coin of discrimination and emphasizing the positive side of discriminatory concepts. But far too few leaders are willing to realize the philosophical implications of the reversal. In many cases they are using derogatory terms tagged on their group years ago by an uneducated white majority as proofs of racism inherent in the white man, rather than using the stone rejected by the builders to form a new edifice.

Persecution of a group because it is a group is the negative side of that group's existence. And such values have validity only when the persecuting majority has a united front. In today's white world no such front exists. It therefore seems unfair and a method of copping out to continually call on minority groups to fight white racism. Such efforts merely polarize whites against minority groups without taking into account the need of minority groups to solidify themselves for positive and aggressive action.

In order to validate the persecution of a group, the persecutors must in effect recognize the right of that group to be different. And if the group is different in a lasting sense, then it can be kept as a scapegoat for the majority. It also suffers with respect to its deviations—blacks as to color, Indians and Mexicans as to culture. The question is then posed as to how far the deviations fall short of the white norm and how far they indicate the basic solidity and validity of the group.

Implicit in the sufferings of each group is the acknowledgment of the sovereignty of the group. It is this aspect—sovereignty—which has never been adequately used by minority groups to their own advantage. Perhaps many cannot conceive of sovereignty outside of a territory within which they can exercise their own will. But with the present scene strewn with victims of violence, many of the victims intruders of the turf of the local communities, this cannot be the case.

More to the point, perhaps, is the fact that legal issues have always been presented in the singular—is such and such a violation of the basic rights of the individual? Thus the attention of the minority groups has been drawn away from their rights and power as a group to a quicksand of assimilationist theories which destroy the power of the group to influence its own future, when that future is dominated by continued persecution of individuals because of their group membership.

Tactical efforts of minority groups should be based upon the concept of sovereignty. Only in this manner can they hope to affect policies which now block them from full realization of the nature and extent of their problems. And the history of intergroup relations is littered with examples of the recognition, no matter how implicit, of the sovereignty of minority groups.

Any leader in a minority-group community will inevitably have it thrown at him that he "doesn't represent all the (blacks, Indians, Mexicans, etc.)." Why should he? What is it in the mind of whites, sympathetic and hostile, that demands that the leadership in a minority community represent ALL the people in that community when the questioner represents NONE of his community? Even under the most rudimentary reading of the Constitution, only a majority is required for whites to represent themselves. Yet an absolute majority is always required of minority groups in order for them to have a valid opinion.

This demand is a recognition of the fundamental sovereignty of the group. It basically states that the group is foreign and autonomous, whether it actually is or not, and that whites can have no dealing with a segment of that community on the chance that they will take the wrong group and find themselves in trouble. This recognition of the basic integrity of the minority-group community has been used in a negative sense to play politics within the group and neutralize them. It should now be seen in a positive sense as an affirmation, in spite of the flowery phrases of equality and unity, of the basic position of the group as a sovereign, autonomous nation which must be treated as an equal entity to the federal and state governments.

When sovereignty is combined with power on behalf of the community, then it becomes apparent that power is manifested in a major way by the willingness to enter into agreements between communities. Without formalized agreements or treaties, there is no way that two communities can work together if one community insists on recognizing the sovereignty of the other, even though it denies the abstract validity of the other as a sovereign community.

Sovereignty and power go hand in hand in group action. One cannot exist without the other, although either can be misused to the detriment of the other. Thus power without a concept of responsibility to a sovereign group is often ruthlessness in disguise. Thus the attempt by foundations and churches to "give" power to the powerless has resulted in the creation and support of demagogues and not the transfer of power, since power cannot be given and accepted.

The responsibility which sovereignty creates is oriented primarily toward the existence and continuance of the group. As such, it naturally creates a sense of freedom not possible in any other context. Freedom has traditionally meant an absence of restrictions. The fact that passports are not needed to go from state to state is often cited as an example of the freedoms which we have in this country that are not present in other nations.

This is too naïve to hold much water, however. If freedom is to be defined in counterdistinction to oppression, then people are free to the extent that they do not feel immediate oppression or they do not recognize alternatives to oppression. In this sense a failure to enforce laws would be as valid as an absence of laws itself. This is the sense of individual group freedom shared by the early hippies. The refusal to follow traditional norms was considered a breakthrough for freedom of the group.

In the years since the massive hippie migrations to the Haight and other centers of the acid culture, the power structure has become aware of the irresponsibility toward laws and has cracked down on the youth. Thus the initial freedom of the hippie was due more toward a lack of energy on the part of the Establishment than to the discovery of a new way of life by the hippies.

With the emergence of the Woodstock Nation and the absolute failure of the police to enforce laws against them during the festival, people are becoming optimistic about the creation of a lasting culture of the new minority group. This cannot be unless the individuals articulating the sovereignty of the new group find within their own understanding the necessity to be responsible to the group itself. If this is developed, then the freedom which sovereignty can give will emerge within the group.

The freedom of sovereignty is based upon the passage beyond traditional stumbling blocks of Western man. It is existence beyond the problem of identity and power conflicts. Buffy Sainte-Marie has a classic phrase to characterize this freedom. She says that an Indian doesn't have to dress or act like an Indian because he already is one. This is the freedom of sovereignty without which sovereignty itself cannot exist.

In certain areas of action in the minority groups and post-hippie movement such freedom currently exists. Many people are fellow-sympathizers without putting on the costume of the hippie of yesterday or the nationalist of today. They fully share the mores and ideas of the group without finding it necessary to conform to the outward aspects of dress and action in order to claim identity.

For a long time liberals held this pattern of freedom within their community. A man might not necessarily have to participate in activities of the liberal community so long as he raised his voice and exerted his individual strength on behalf of his beliefs when the crisis came. It was during the later days of the civil rights movement that this aspect of liberalism was destroyed. People demanded that everyone go all the way in everything or be tagged racists. Thus the sovereignty of the liberal community was destroyed because the freedom beyond the identity crisis was denied to people.

One of the chief weaknesses of the Indian community has been its absolute freedom. Like the liberal freedom described above, Indian people were free to participate according to their own sense of responsibility. In massing to prevent an invasion of rights, Indians were often able to come up with a very meager fighting force because the cause was not attractive enough. No individual was forced to participate in any course of action since he was freed from allegiance to abstractions.

Freedom in this context begins with certain tribal assumptions which are not questioned, since they would not provide answers capable of articulation. An Indian never questions whether or not he is an Indian. The query he faces is *what kind* of Indian. And this is the same question now facing individuals of other groups which affirmed the sovereignty of their group.

Living beyond the identity question channels behavior patterns into a tacit acknowledgment of the customs of the group. Thus the problem of law and order which plagues urbanized Western society does not have the fear potential and impact in sovereign groups. Competition is limited to group values and has the welfare of the people as a group as its reference point. To impose restrictions from outside and define freedom in that manner would undercut the values of the group.

The contemporary struggle between the younger and older generations may be a manifestation of the clash between two understandings of freedom. While the older generation still suffers from nightmares of its European past where arbitrary exercise of police powers created a rigid society and persecutions, it can only conceive of freedom as a lack of restrictions imposed from outside the group. Its only choice to maintain a relatively safe existence is to grasp power and manipulate it for the benefit of those who are acceptable in that particular generation.

Youth and minority groups conceive of freedom as an unfilled potential of being. They despise rules and regulations which compress the individual into a state of fear and conformity. The difference is easy to see. The older generation tries to be "good," that is, it wants to live without a police record and with plenty of recommendations. Youth tries to "be," that is, to express what it feels as a result of being a person. Therefore police records and acceptance by society are nice but not really relevant to the question of freedom.

The way of youth and minority groups is the more difficult path of the two. It is ultimately dependent upon the existence of the group and its ability to use its power constructively. There is thus great danger that immoral use of group power or unwitting compromise will destroy the sovereignty of the group and dissipate the power, thus turning fundamental freedoms into licentiousness.

At this stage in history it is vitally important that power movements, insofar as they do represent movements towards sovereignty, are viewed in that light. The unreasonable fear which affirmation of sovereignty creates when it is not understood is not worth the effort. Globally, efforts to assert sovereignty have been universally interpreted as a gigantic plot against Western man. Thus the Vietnam civil war has become an insidious Communist movement of global import. People feel that unless the Vietcong are stopped in the Mekong Delta, they will soon invade Westchester County. Patriots of the old order volunteer for Vietnam stating that they would rather stop the Communists over there than in Disneyland.

From the lack of understanding of the movement toward sovereignty of numerous nation groups comes the understanding of the world which again recognizes the enemy as a sovereign group. Thus Communism is viewed as a massive and monolithic threat against all that is decent. From this premise, every disturbance regardless of its original motivation, is lumped into the universal conspiracy.

This viewpoint is destructive in every aspect. It allows a "cowboy-and-Indian" interpretation, the good guys of peaceful settlement against the bad guys of the uprising, of every major event. . . .

The natural result of this type of conflict is the opposition of abstract mythology against events of the real world. Events are not understood in their own context, but they are categorized according to preconceived interpretations of the world. When this situation is combined with the optimistic conception of history as "progress" which has been the standard of distinction used by Western man, the result is truly demonic and frightening. Western man thus is creating his own barbaric tribes which, when faced with continual alienation and misunderstanding, desire nothing more than the total destruction of Western society. . . .

Among the other dissident groups splitting from American society, the most publicized are the hippie alumni. They had, by summer of 1969, become the largest group of new landowners in northern New Mexico. Deserting the urban slums and desiring to create a new type of life in rural areas, hundreds of former flower children came to New Mexico to set up independent communes. The movement has spread and now some communes have been established in the eastern United States in the forested areas of New England. But these are dwarfed by the development of urban communes and pads.

In almost every case the movement is toward withdrawal and establishment of sovereign groups. With corresponding development of internal customs of each group and new religious practices, the establishment of the new minority group will be complete. It will remain only for them to begin to exercise their untouched power as a group on the political processes of the nation, and then they will have achieved almost total independence and the freedom which sovereignty and independence can give. . . .

The trend toward independence by minority, ethnic, and youth groups appears to be just starting. The days of power movements and demonstrations may be over. If so, the nature of the problem of dissident groups and cultural rebels is much more serious than middle-class America realizes. The basic message of demonstrations was that the demonstrators "cared" enough to protest. They had not yet reached the necessity to affirm their sovereignty as a group and to use that sovereignty as a means of withdrawal and boycott.

Now, it appears, traditional Western culture has become largely irrelevant to the needs of a substantial number of people. They would rather fight it out on behalf of their own communities than make any further attempts to conform or reach a cultural compromise with the impotent mythologies of Western man. Oppressive measures will undoubtedly increase, since the power structure now sees an opportunity to crush some of the movements following their withdrawal.

It is absolutely vital to the continuance of any semblance of society for the recognition of groups as groups to be acknowledged. In this way, as groups split off from their allegiance to traditional myths, they will still have a status within the Constitutional framework that will not prove abrasive to other groups or to those people who continue to adhere to the traditional myths.

Unless society can find a means of integrating the rights of groups with the broader and more abstract rights of individuals, it will succeed in creating its own barbarians who will eventually destroy it. Oppressive legislation, once written into law, will come back to haunt the very people who wrote the laws. The sovereignty of tribalistic-communal groups is more than the conglomerate of individual desires writ large. It is a whole new way of adjusting to the technology which dominates life in this century.

If society refuses to adjust to what it has created, it cannot gain the upper hand over developments which are not integrated into a consistent understanding of the world and which have, by almost everyone's agreement, turned man into the object of events which take away from him the power over his world. Sovereignty is dangerous only to the extent that it follows traditional modes of social change which are merely adjustments of the basic structure and not changes at all.

This is not to say that no alternatives can be created by society which will neutralize present developments. Society is basically an expression of Western man. As such, it can at any time revert to traditional hidden forms of social organization which are contained in the historical experience of Western European man. Simple reversion to tribal forms by dissidents against Western cultural forms does not guarantee that the movement will not go beyond tribalism, McLuhan not withstanding, to an ancient feudalistic form which would be more comfortable for the descendants of King Arthur and Charlemagne.

The present situation is thus fraught with desperate alternatives. The question is whether or not the current movements can struggle through the problems now facing them to achieve a new type of society, or whether at the last minute they will relapse into traditional European forms and mankind will be doomed to repeat the history of Western man in a new setting.

. . .

We have two antithetical ideas of the individual in today's society. One stems directly from the ideas held in the founding days of the Republic. At that time people assumed that a person, given free will and the right to exercise it, would generally make the correct decisions for himself and for his community. The voting franchise was thus considered to be the best method of arriving at a determination of the desires of the community at large, since any decisions made would be the result of the conscious and intelligent decisions of a number of responsible people.

This concept was more than optimistic. We have seen in practice that each person makes decisions according to his own good and hopes that somehow society will arrive at a wise and just decision in its deliberations. Unless a political movement is triggered by a charismatic political leader, society generally limps along postponing fundamental decisions because a majority of people want small adjustments and not major changes in their lives.

One theory of individualism has risen in recent years and is best characterized by the saying "do your thing." It indicates a complete freedom of movement for the individual person without regard to social goals and political movements. The remarkable thing is that the latter form of individualism has proven to be catalytic, whereas the more traditional understanding of the individual has produced stagnation and inability to comprehend mass movements.

Indians have always been the utmost individualists, but American society has failed to absorb them in its mainstream and there has been a continual warfare between the Indian tribes and the rest of society over this question. Yet the extreme individualism of the Indian has made it appear as if he would be suited above all to enter into the American social and political system. People are stunned to find that Indians totally reject American political ideology and concepts of equality, all the while being unable to reach any kind of conclusion within their own tribes as to programs and policies.

The vital difference between Indians in their individualism and the traditional individualism of Anglo-Saxon America is that the two understandings of man are built on entirely different premises. White America speaks of individualism on an economic basis. Indians speak of individualism on a social basis. While the rest of America is devoted to private property, Indians prefer to hold their lands in tribal estate, sharing the resources in common with each other. Where Americans conform to social norms of behavior and set up strata for social recognition, Indians have a free-flowing concept of social prestige that acts as a leveling device against the building of social pyramids.

Thus the two kinds of individualism are diametrically opposed to each other, and it would appear impossible to reconcile one with the other. Where the rich are admired in white society, they are not particularly welcome in Indian society. The success in economic wars is not nearly as important for Indians as it is for whites, since the sociability of individuals with each other acts as a binding tie in Indian society.

It is thus very important to understand the advent of the hippie and his subsequent influence on American life styles. The hippie, like the Indian, does not depend upon economic competition for his identity. He is more relaxed, more sociable, less worried about material goods, and more concerned with creating a community of others who share his interests and values. Youth of today fall into all grades of commitment to the new life style. Broadway shows reflect the new mode of life, books and magazines and underground newspapers chronicle it, and popular music spreads it abroad like a raging forest fire. Clothing and hair styles are creeping forward into age groups that formerly rejected out of hand a change in values.

The important thing about the hippie, and one thing that has certainly been missed by older commentators, is that the release from economic competition has created the necessity to derive a new identity based on other than economic criteria. Thus some of the most active and enthusiastic people in the new movement have been children of affluent homes that have not had to face economic competition. Born into the good life, they have been at a loss for identity since

392 / Third-World Ideologies

early childhood, and they have been the first generation that has been able to examine itself purely on the basis of feelings and experiences.

Older people have been horrified because their children have rejected out of hand the riches and power that they have spent so much time accumulating. They grew up in the Depression, where a lack of economic power meant relegation to a long line of unemployed, broken, status-less people. Thus the older generation promptly sought and in many cases achieved a position of economic power in which they could express their identity as a person without suffering the demeaning indignity of being another man in a long line or another number in an endless list of numbers.

The generation gap is more than an age difference in many ways. It reflects a difference in views of the world. The younger generation sees the world as inhabited by persons who must in some way relate to each other. The older generation understands the world as an economic jungle where, without allies, the individual is crushed by forces beyond his control. If the world of economic reality is destroyed, then the older generation will lose identities that it has struggled all its life to achieve. If there is continued economic definition of man, then the younger generation will feel hopelessly trapped with identities it does not accept or understand.

The ideological basis of society is thus shifting every year as the older generation dies off and the younger generation becomes more radical in its search for itself. . . .

When competition becomes freed from its economic foundation, as it has been in the Indian tribes, then life takes on a whole new aspect. Status depends upon the manner in which a person contributes to his community. Knowledge for knowledge's sake becomes an irrelevant assertion, because it does not directly contribute to the elevation of people within the group. It becomes much more important that a person be wise and enter into the decisions of the group than that he know a great number of facts. Science is the handmaiden of economics because it creates tools by which men can climb the economic ladder, but it is useless in a noneconomic society because it is an abstraction of life.

Eliminating economic competition from a society thus creates a change of great dimensions. Wisdom with respect to the immediate situation is much more valuable than is the ability to consume and dispense great gobs of knowledge. Depth rather than breadth characterizes the tribal society. In the younger generation we can already see a rabid devouring of esoteric works in search of wisdom, and their poetry reflects a more sophisticated understanding of life than does the work of previous generations. Dylan's poetry, for example, caricatures the procedures by which the older generation operates, warning the youth that this is ephemeral and perhaps a charade that may fascinate but also entrap.

The outrageous clothing worn by young people emphasizes the "beautiful" aspect of their lives. It corresponds in many ways to Indian war-bonnet vanity and the desire to demonstrate acceptance by the group and honored status. It is no accident that many hippies wear beads and buckskin, because these combine simplicity of economic origin with advertisement of personal worth. Beads are extraneous to clothing, yet they become an integral part of personality.

The contemporary movement toward communes also emphasizes tribalistic life and is not competitive in economic terms. The concept of massing great stores of wealth runs counter to the demand that a person be respected in his group because of what he is. For that reason Charlie Manson's charisma was much more important than his ability to provide an economic base for his "family." As communes gather, the standard of living is defined by the group and not by outside forces. Thus communes can exist because they provide an understanding of togetherness which then defines economic reality. The older generation views it differently, feeling that economic considerations come first and neighborhoods form on that basis. Thus the suburbs are settled according to economic ability to provide and not sociability of people. Families are isolated in the suburbs because all they have in common is a bank balance of a certain size and the ability to keep it replenished.

.   .   .

The tribal-communal way of life, devoid of economic competition, views land as the most vital part of man's existence. It is THEIRS. It supports them, tells them where they live, and defines for them HOW they live. Land does not have the simple sentimentality of purple mountains majesty or the artificial coloring of slides taken by tourists. It is more than a passing fancy to be visited on a vacation and forgotten. Rather it provides a center of the universe for the group that lives on it. As such, the people who hold land in this way always have a home to go to. Their identity is secure. They live with it and do not abstract themselves from it and live off it.

.   .   .

The Woodstock Nation is thus the result of a feeling of humanity shared by a substantial number of people. In a sense it did represent a gathering of the tribes in the same way that the old Sioux nation, in the days before the white men came, met every year near Bear Butte in northwestern South Dakota, to visit, exchange presents, and renew the existence of the tribe. . . .

Identity derived from economic status will probably be with us to some degree for a great while. It serves as a means of distinguishing between people and in turn promotes economic growth necessary to keep society operating. That is, it is not all bad and has proven useful to all Americans in a number of ways. The real problem is that we have passed the point of no return with respect to economics. Machines and computers are now so efficient that they are eliminating the ability and opportunity of most people to compete economically. Whether we like it or not we have undertaken to remove ourselves from the economic equation that was designed to support American society.

Already conservatives are talking about the guaranteed annual income, and the major part of American industry is on subsidy or economic existence guaranteed by government support. Without the ability or necessity to compete economically as a means of distinguishing between individuals, society must necessarily change to another form of identity-formation. This is what the younger generation has largely done and it happens to coincide with tribalistic forms already present in Indian tribes. Thus social movement, after four centuries of economic determinism, is reverting to pre-Columbian expression, although modified by contemporary technology.

With machines producing an overabundance of wealth, the primary task of people will be to consume what is produced, lest the system break apart by overproduction. Agriculture already has broken apart, with large areas held out of production, and the result has been the breakdown of rural society. Suicides range higher in those rural areas where affluence and support appears to be greatest, because the people have not yet adjusted to the vacuum created by the absence of economic competition. . . .

Whether we like it or not, the movement is steadily in one direction. The best that we can do is to open up as many options as possible so that the polarization of groups and group values does not freeze movements into violent confrontations. This would mean dropping traditional ideas and getting behind them to discover what we think we have been trying to do. Persecution of one group for smoking pot while another group destroys itself via nicotine and alcohol is a refusal to face reality. Subsidization of large farms while quibbling over pennies in food stamps is ridiculous. Authorizing supersonic transport planes while cutting education budgets is absurd. . . .

The "do-your-thing" doctrine of youth presents the ultimate challenge to American society, for it challenges society to expand its conception of the individual beyond the field of economics. It creates criteria by which a total sense of person and humanity can be defined. "Doing-your-thing" speaks of what a man IS, not what he HAS. In this type of change Indians are far ahead of the rest of society and may be steadily pulling away from the rest of the pack. Hence the absurdity of studies on how to bring Indians into the mainstream when the mainstream is coming to the tribe. . . .

Chicano Ideology
Octavio Paz

Octavio Paz (1914-   ) is a Mexican writer and diplomat. Among his books are *Claude Levi-Strauss: An Introduction* (1970), *Selected Poems* (1958), and *The Labyrinth of Solitude: Life and Thought in Mexico* (1961).

All of us, at some moment, have had a vision of our existence as something unique, untransferable and very precious. This revelation almost always takes place during adolescence. Self-discovery is above all the realization that we are alone: it is the opening of an impalpable, transparent wall—that of our consciousness—between the world and ourselves. It is true that we sense our aloneness almost as soon as we are born, but children and adults can transcend their solitude and forget themselves in games or work. The adolescent, however, vacillates between infancy and youth, halting for a moment before the infinite richness of the world. He is astonished at the fact of his being, and this astonishment leads to reflection: as he leans over the river of his consciousness, he asks himself if the face that appears there, disfigured by the water, is his own. The singularity of his being, which is pure sensation in children, becomes a problem and a question.

Much the same thing happens to nations and peoples at a certain critical moment

From *The Labyrinth of Solitude: Life and Thought in Mexico* by Octavio Paz (New York: Grove Press, Inc., 1963). Reprinted by permission of Grove Press, Inc. Translated by Lysander Kemp. Copyright © 1961 by Grove Press, Inc.

in their development. They ask themselves: What are we, and how can we fulfill our obligations to ourselves as we are?

. . .

Something of the same sort characterizes the Mexicans you see in the streets. They have lived in the city for many years, wearing the same clothes and speaking the same language as the other inhabitants, and they feel ashamed of their origin; yet no one would mistake them for authentic North Americans. I refuse to believe that physical features are as important as is commonly thought. What distinguishes them, I think, is their furtive, restless air: they act like persons who are wearing disguises, who are afraid of a stranger's look because it could strip them and leave them stark naked. When you talk with them, you observe that their sensibilities are like a pendulum, but a pendulum that has lost its reason and swings violently and erratically back and forth. This spiritual condition, or lack of a spirit, has given birth to a type known as the *pachuco*. The *pachucos* are youths, for the most part of Mexican origin, who form gangs in Southern cities; they can be identified by their language and behavior as well as by the clothing they affect. They are instinctive rebels, and North American racism has vented its wrath on them more than once. But the *pachucos* do not attempt to vindicate their race or the nationality of their forebears. Their attitude reveals an obstinate, almost fanatical will-to-be, but this will affirms nothing specific except their determination—it is an ambiguous one, as we will see—not to be like those around them. The *pachuco* does not want to become a Mexican again; at the same time he does not want to blend into the life of North America. His whole being is sheer negative impulse, a tangle of contradictions, an enigma. Even his very name is enigmatic: *pachuco*, a word of uncertain derivation, saying nothing and saying everything. It is a strange word with no definite meaning; or, to be more exact, it is charged like all popular creations with a diversity of meanings. Whether we like it or not, these persons are Mexicans, are one of the extremes at which the Mexicans can arrive.

. . .

The *pachuco* tries to enter North American society in secret and daring ways, but he impedes his own efforts. Having been cut off from his traditional culture, he asserts himself for a moment as a solitary and challenging figure. He denies both the society from which he originated and that of North America. When he thrusts himself outward, it is not to unite with what surrounds him but rather to defy it. This is a suicidal gesture, because the *pachuco* does not affirm or defend anything except his exasperated will-not-be. He is not divulging his most intimate feelings: he is revealing an ulcer, exhibiting a wound. A wound that is also a grotesque, capricious, barbaric adornment. A wound that laughs at itself and decks itself out for the hunt. The *pachuco* is the prey of society, but instead of hiding he adorns himself to attract the hunter's attention. Persecution redeems him and breaks his solitude: his salvation depends on his becoming part of the very society he appears to deny. Solitude and sin, communion and health become synonymous terms.

This is not the moment to analyze our profound sense of solitude, which alternately affirms and denies itself in melancholy and rejoicing, silence and sheer noise, gratuitous crimes and religious fervor. Man is alone everywhere. But the solitude of the Mexican, under the great stone night of the high plateau that is still inhabited by insatiable gods, is very different from that of the North American, who wanders in an abstract world of machines, fellow citizens and moral precepts. In the Valley of Mexico man feels himself suspended between heaven and earth, and he oscillates between contrary powers and forces, and petrified eyes, and devouring mouths. Reality—that is, the world that surrounds us—exists by itself here, has a life of its own, and was not invented by man as it was the United States. The Mexican feels himself to have been torn from the womb of this reality, which is both creative and destructive, both Mother and Tomb. He has forgotten the word that ties him to all those forces through which life manifests itself. Therefore he shouts or keeps silent, stabs or prays, or falls asleep for a hundred years.

Our solitude has the same roots as religious feelings. It is a form of orphanhood, an obscure awareness that we have been torn from the All, and an ardent search: a flight and a return, an effort to re-establish the bonds that unite us with the universe.

Nothing could be further from this feeling than the solitude of the North American. In the United States man does not feel that he has been torn from the center of creation and suspended between hostile forces. He has built his own world and it is built in his own image: it is his mirror. But now he cannot recognize himself in his inhuman objects, nor in his fellows. His creations, like those of an inept sorcerer, no longer obey him. He is alone among his works, lost—to use the phrase by José Gorostiza—in a "wilderness of mirrors."

When I arrived in the United States I was surprised above all by the self-assurance and confidence of the people, by their apparent happiness and apparent adjustment to the world around them. This satisfaction does not stifle criticism, however, and the criticism is valuable and forthright, of a sort not often heard in the countries to the south, where long periods of dictatorship have made us more cautious about expressing our points of view. But it is a criticism that respects the existing systems and never touches the roots. I thought of Ortega y Gasset's distinction between uses and abuses, in his definition of the "revolutionary spirit." The revolutionary is always a radical, that is, he is trying to correct the uses themselves rather than the mere abuses of them. Almost all the criticisms I heard from the lips of North Americans were of the reformist variety: they left the social or cultural structures intact and were only intended to limit or improve this or that procedure. It seemed to me then, and it still does, that the United States is a society that wants to realize its ideals, has no wish to exchange them for others, and is confident of surviving, no matter how dark the future may appear. I am not interested in discussing whether this attitude is justified by reason and reality; I simply want to point out that it exists. It is true that this faith in the natural goodness of life, or in its infinite wealth of possibilities, cannot be found in recent North American literature, which prefers to depict a much more somber world; but I found it in the actions, the words and even the faces of almost everyone I met.[1]

On the other hand, I heard a good deal of talk about American realism and also about American ingenuousness, qualities that would seem to be mutually exclusive. To us a realist is always a pessimist. And an ingenuous person would not remain so for very long if he truly contemplated life realistically. Would it not be more

---

[1] These lines were written before the public was clearly cognizant of the danger of universal annihilation made possible by nuclear weapons. Since then the North Americans have lost their optimism but not their confidence, a confidence based on resignation and obstinacy. The truth is that although many people talk about the danger, secretly no one believes—no one wants to believe—that it is real and immediate.

accurate to say that the North American wants to use reality rather than to know it? In some matters—death, for example—he not only has no desire to understand it, he obviously avoids the very idea. I met some elderly ladies who still had illusions and were making plans for the future as if it were inexhaustible. Thus they refuted Nietzsche's statement condemning women to an early onset of skepticism because "men have ideals but women only have illusions." American realism, then, is of a very special kind, and American ingenuousness does not exclude dissimulation and even hypocrisy. When hypocrisy is a character trait it also affects one's thinking, because it consists in the negation of all the aspects of reality that one finds disagreeable, irrational or repugnant.

In contrast, one of the most notable traits of the Mexican's character is his willingness to contemplate horror: he is even familiar and complacent in his dealings with it. The bloody Christs in our village churches, the macabre humor in some of our newspaper headlines, our wakes, the custom of eating skull-shaped cakes and candies on the Day of the Dead, are habits inherited from the Indians and the Spaniards and are now an inseparable part of our being. Our cult of death is also a cult of life, in the same way that love is a hunger for life and a longing for death. Our fondness for self-destruction derives not only from our masochistic tendencies but also from a certain variety of religious emotion.

And our differences do not end there. The North Americans are credulous and we are believers; they love fairy tales and detective stories and we love myths and legends. The Mexican tells lies because he delights in fantasy, or because he is desperate, or because he wants to rise above the sordid facts of his life; the North American does not tell lies, but he substitutes social truth for the real truth, which is always disagreeable. We get drunk in order to confess; they get drunk in order to forget. They are optimists and we are nihilists—except that our nihilism is not intellectual but instinctive, and therefore irrefutable. We are suspicious and they are trusting. We are sorrowful and sarcastic and they are happy and full of jokes. North Americans want to understand and we want to contemplate. They are activists and we are quietists; we enjoy our wounds and they enjoy their inventions. They believe in hygiene, health, work and contentment, but perhaps they have never experienced true joy, which is an intoxication, a whirlwind. In the hubbub of a fiesta night our voices explode into brilliant lights, and life and death mingle together, while their vitality becomes a fixed smile that denies old age and death but that changes life to motionless stone.

What is the origin of such contradictory attitudes? It seems to me that North Americans consider the world to be something that can be perfected, and that we consider it to be something that can be redeemed. Like their Puritan ancestors, we believe that sin and death constitute the ultimate basis of human nature, but with the difference that the Puritan identifies purity with health. Therefore he believes in the purifying effects of asceticism, and the consequences are his cult of work for work's sake, his serious approach to life, and his conviction that the body does not exist or at least cannot lose—or find—itself in another body. Every contact is a contamination. Foreign races, ideas, customs, and bodies carry within themselves the germs of perdition and impurity. Social hygiene complements that of the soul and the body. Mexicans, however, both ancient and modern, believe in communion and fiestas: there is no health without contact. Tlazolteotl, the Aztec goddess of filth and fecundity, of earthly and human moods, was also the goddess of steam baths, sexual love and confession. And we have not changed very much, for Catholicism is also communion.

These two attitudes are irreconcilable, I believe, and, in their present form, insufficient. . . .

The North American system only wants to consider the positive aspects of reality. Men and women are subjected from childhood to an inexorable process of adaptation; certain principles, contained in brief formulas, are endlessly repeated by the press, the radio, the churches and the schools, and by those kindly, sinister beings, the North American mothers and wives. A person imprisoned by these schemes is like a plant in a flowerpot too small for it: he cannot grow or mature. This sort of conspiracy cannot help but provoke violent individual rebellions. Spontaneity avenges itself in a thousand subtle or terrible ways. The mask that replaces the dramatic mobility of the human face is benevolent and courteous but empty of emotion, and its set smile is almost lugubrious: it shows the extent to which intimacy can be devastated by the arid victory of principles over instincts. The sadism underlying almost all types of relationships in contemporary North American life is perhaps nothing more than a way of escaping the petrifaction imposed by that doctrine of aseptic moral purity. The same is true of the new religions and sects, and the liberating drunkenness that opens the doors of "life." It is astonishing what a destructive and almost physiological meaning this word has acquired: to live means to commit excesses, break the rules, go to the limit (of what?), experiment with sensations. The act of love is an "experience" (and therefore unilateral and frustrating). But it is not to my purpose to describe these reactions. It is enough to say that all of them, like their Mexican opposites, seem to me to reveal our mutual inability to reconcile ourselves to the flux of life.

A study of the great myths concerning the origin of man and the meaning of our presence on earth reveals that every culture—in the sense of a complex of values created and shared in common—stems from the conviction that man the intruder has broken or violated the order of the universe. He has inflicted a wound on the compact flesh of the world, and chaos, which is the ancient and, so to speak, *natural* condition of life, can emerge again from this aperture. The return of "ancient Original Disorder" is a menace that has obsessed every consciousness in every period of history. Hölderlin expresses in several different poems his dread of the great empty mouth of chaos with its fatal seduction for man and the universe:

> . . . if, beyond the straight way,
> The captive Elements and the ancient
> Laws of the Earth break loose
> Like maddened horses. And then a desire to return
> To chaos rises incessantly. There is much
> To defend, and the faithful are much needed.[2]

The faithful are much needed because there is *much to defend*. Man collaborates actively in defending universal order, which is always being threatened by chaos. And when it collapses he must create a new one, this time his own. But exile, expiation and penitence should proceed from the reconciliation of man with the universe. Neither the Mexican nor the North American has achieved this reconciliation. What is even more serious, I am afraid we have lost our sense of the very meaning of all human activity, which is to assure the operation of an order in which knowledge and innocence, man and nature are in harmony. If the solitude of

---

[2] *Reif sind, in Feuer getaucht. . . .*

the Mexican is like a stagnant pool, that of the North American is like a mirror. We have ceased to be springs of living water. . . .

The Chicano's Search for Identity
Hilario H. Contreras

Hilario H. Contreras (1930-   ) has written many articles about the Chicano movement.

The most human faculty of man is the awareness of his existence as a distinct person who exists in the continum of the past, the present and the future and who, with a sense of self-determination, plans and shapes his own fate.

Self-awareness is the most immediate of our experiences; it can't be compared with any other experience, and, because it can't be experienced except from the one single vantage point of subjectivity, it is quite elusive. And yet, it is the most fundamental fact of our life. Paradoxically, one becomes keenly aware of one's self in the morbid states of depersonalization, when a person suddenly feels strange to himself—an experience well known to many members of minority groups in Anglo-American society. Only when the feeling of identity is disrupted do we become aware of our existence.

We realize that it is the same person who played on the floor as an infant, was praised, loved, and also scolded by his parents, who quarreled with his brothers and sisters, who went to school, who chose an occupation or profession, who married and had children. This feeling of *continuity in an emotionally undisturbed person* is not interrupted and starts quite early in life. Beyond this there is no memory because remembering presupposes the existence of an *ego* which has the feeling of some kind—no matter how vague—of identity.

The preservation of an undisturbed feeling of identity depends on a continuously progressive, integrative process during the distinct phases of personality development: infancy, early childhood, adolescence, early adulthood and adulthood, each characterized by biologically determined changes in the person's physical, emotional, and intellectual capacity.

Each new phase of development is considered an identity-crisis requiring new integrative tasks to include the changing libidinal forces and the *changing expectations of the environment* upon the growing individual into a harmonious unit which is perceived as a distinct *self*.

In adolescence such an identity-crisis is very noticeable: a yet emotionally unprepared ego has to cope with the impact of the biologically reinforced sexual

From Hilario Contreras, "The Chicano's Search for Identity." *Con Safos*, Vol. 2, No. 5.

impulses that are symptomatic of puberty. Suddenly a mature body, almost overnight, is entrusted to an inexperienced ego. At the same time, the adolescent is confronted with an environment which considers him almost an adult. And has new expectations of him. From lack of experience, the adolescent feels most insecure.

Such transitory identity-crises during the process of ego maturation are easily overcome *under stable external conditions* to be found only in countries with old civilizations. In the United States of America, on the other hand, cultural traditions, in a strict sense, do not exist. The only behavioral demands American society makes on the individual citizen is conformity to the life pattern of the Anglo majority. And it is exactly at this point where the identity-crises of members of minority groups have been provoked.

The constant influx of foreign-born parents has been a consistent feature of the American scene, a factor that has been recognized by such anthropologists as Margaret Mead as a particular danger to psychological maturation. Second-generation children, especially among European immigrants, can't take their parents as models of accepted *Anglo behavior*. They must experiment by trying to imitate their Anglo peers who, in the majority of cases, hesitate to accept them completely and never let them forget that *your parents speak English with a foreign accent*!

In the case of Chicanos we can't speak of immigrants, because historically speaking, it is the Anglos who have immigrated into the states of Texas, New Mexico, Colorado, Arizona and California. And instead of *adjusting* to the prevalent indio-hispano civilization, they colonized the native population and treated them as *racially inferior and second-class citizens*. As a consequence of that shameless confiscation of the American Southwest by the Anglo immigrants, *the personal and racial identity of the Chicano*, during the last century, has been seriously and constantly threatened.

The Chicano child does not have to wait for the advent of puberty to undergo the ordinary identity-crisis caused by sudden physical maturation without emotional preparedness. His ego identity is already threatened when he enters Elementary School where the English language is compulsory and where he is given to understand that Spanish is a *foreign, un-American* idiom which he must forget in order to think, talk and behave like and Anglo-American, in order to be—not accepted, but rather—*tolerated* by his Anglo teachers and fellow-pupils. Thus, at the age of six, the Chicano child is precipitated into the worst identity-crisis that can happen to a person at such an early age. The impact of the crudely condescending attitude of Anglo teachers on the helpless Chicano child can be of traumatic intensity and become the cause of a life-long, severe identity-crisis with all its psychological complications resulting in *dropping-out* at a pre-puberty age, in delinquency, and drug-addiction, and all the other symptoms of emotional insecurity.

In order to understand the magnitude of the average Chicano's loss of identity, one must compare the characteristics of the centuries old Mexican civilization with those of Anglo-American society. I intentionally use the term *society*, because the United States of America confuses the instruments of civilization with civilization itself. A people may possess all the gadgets of civilization such as banks, industrial enterprise, newspapers, radio, television, washing machines and garbage disposals and yet remain uncivilized; whereas so-called primitive peoples, such as many American and Mexican Indian tribes and certain *backward* oriental peoples, might have none of these gadgets and yet be highly civilized. The Chicano, whose identity has been continually threatened, instinctively recognizes the Anglo society's lack of genuine civilization, not to speak of a lack of *culture*—culture which is an exaltation of the human spirit, *el alma*, the soul of a people.

Anglo-American society, or shall we say, the American Way of Life, is based on a soulless philosophy which may be called *economism*; it interprets the purpose of human life in terms of the production, acquisition and distribution of wealth. The French economist, Michel Chevalier (1806-1879), who visited the United States early in the 19th century, said that "American society has the morale of an army on the march;" the morale of the looter. The German economist, Theodor Luddecke, defined *Americanism* as "the economic instinct raised in all departments of private and public life to its highest power." Whenever the U.S. has undertaken to *help* underdeveloped peoples, it never has concerned itself with beauty, intellect or spiritual values, but it has concerned itself with better material living conditions. This is called the pursuit of happiness. And, although the Anglo immigrants conquered and occupied and industrialized all the land between the Atlantic and the Pacific oceans, they have not found happiness.

The Chicano, who does not conceive of *culture* as the pursuit of material happiness, noticed quite early that the center of the Anglo-American's life was an empty waste similar to the continental wilderness he had so greedily colonized. Of a real *inner* life, despite the often exaggerated religious and sociological enthusiasm, the Anglo possesses only a ready-made cliche. Most of his science, art and sophisticated amusement came straight from Europe. The best American writers always dreamed of something America did not offer. They often died abroad of severed roots, or remained to suffer and blaspheme. The American mass-man never found happiness and began to confuse it with *fun*. Although the great Mexican poet and thinker, Octavio Paz speaks of the *Labyrinth of Solitude* in the Mexican psyche, he is well aware of the psyche, he is well aware of the psychological loneliness of the average Anglo-American who more and more, manifests this in psycho-neurotic symptoms. The purely materialistic ambition of the *pioneer* survives in contemporary Anglo thinking: "Better a new continent—or a new planet—to conquer and colonize than an empty mind to fill!"

The tragedy of the Anglo-American's *lack* of identity is final, while the Chicano's *loss* of cultural identity is only temporary. What was lost can be regained. When we speak of the *cultural heritage* of the Chicano, we should think mainly in psychological terms. The Mexican, in contrast to the Anglo, has always been what the social psychologist, David Riesman, calls an *inner-directed* person.

According to Riesman, the inner-directed person is one who possesses a well-defined stable internal organization of principles and values which govern his behavior. This gives such a person a relative independence from the changing attitudes and expectations of others. It goes hand-in-hand with a feeling of identity, as with a person who takes himself for granted and is not disturbed by constant doubts about his goals, values and internal problems, and is not constantly occupied in comparing himself to others. Such a person's attention can be fully absorbed by goals and strivings toward causes which lie outside of him; he can afford the luxury of healthy extroversion, devotion to things beyond his personal concerns. He can successfully incorporate and integrate *traditional cultural values* with his own individual propensities. He does not need to be preoccupied with the ways of a good life; these were given to him through identifications with parents and peers, each corresponding to his chronological and emotional age. He acquired them during a relatively undisturbed process of mental growth.

The so-called *other-directed* person is typified by the modern Anglo-American. He is constantly challenged to make adjustments; in fact, his life is spent in finding his place; he can never accept himself as he is; he does not know who he is, since his self was never crystallized. Because he remains a problem to himself, he must constantly watch others. All his cues come from outside. He has none of his own. He is always on the go, always searching without ever knowing what he is after. His energies are absorbed by *the continuous, never-ending problem of adjustment*, because no adjustment he makes is supposed to last for long in the restless Anglo society. Because of his social mobility, he continuously changes his jobs, his occupation, his marriages and his social environment. He depends more than the inner-directed person on chance and opportunities. Because his life does not follow a design which is the expression of a *traditional value system* modified by his unique self, there is less continuity in his self-awareness. Today he is this and tomorrow something else, not only in his occupation but in his own personality.

The arduous job of adjusting to an ever-changing human environment consumes all of his energies. Consequently, there is little left for creativity, for solid relationships, for devotion to causes that lie outside of himself. *His principal occupation is to get along with others.* Neurotic or psychotic disintegration of personality is only one of the outcomes of this constant unsuccessful struggle to find a balance between a lacking identity and a changing environment. This is the reason why the other-directed Anglo is not capable of cultivating cultural values, and, even less, of identifying with a distinct cultural group. All he is able to identify with are the colorless masses whose sole purpose of life is the amassing of wealth for the mere sake of doing so. In Anglo-American society the human individual is reduced to a cog in the social machinery. For such a society the uniqueness of the individual is useless; hence, it prefers to deal with him in terms of a *social role* and not in terms of the development of a *distinct* personality with the capacity to realize unique potentialities.

The instinctive protest of the Chicano against such a society is caused by its emphasis on *adjustment* and utility instead of creativity, the polar opposite of adjustment. To be creative means to produce something which is not yet in existence; adjustment means to accept and to conform with what is already here.

The Chicano knows that the nearer man comes to acquiring wealth, the more he undermines the foundations of a meaningful existence in which materialistic goals are not ultimate aims *but only means by which he can remain human*. Therefore, in order to regain and retain his cultural identity, the Chicano protests not only against exposing his children to teachers who believe that the English language and the white race are God's gift to the world, but chiefly against an *other-directed* society whose members have no identity of their own and will never be able to acquire one unless they realize that the human spirit, *el alma*, alone creates culture. The *primitive* Indian's distrust of the white man's machines and his computerized society stems from an ancient, inherently instinctual truth that happiness does not come from the possession of things, but from self-knowledge, from realizing the union of the individual self with the cosmic self. Or, as Jesus said to the Pharises: "The kingdom of heaven cometh not with observation . . . It is neither here, nor there; for behold, the kingdom of heaven is *with you* . . . !"

Modern psychology would express this by speaking of an *integrated personality*, of a person who knows his real identity that embraces everything created and uncreated. Man as a spiritual being goes beyond organized religion, beyond dogma and creeds. Although the Chicano knows that the body has to be fed, housed and clothed, he feels his identity with the spirit and declares with pride: *Por mi raza habla el espiritu*!

The Ideology of the New Man
Ernesto Che Guevara

Ernesto Che Guevara (1927-1967) was a leader in the Cuban communist movement. Among his writings are *Che Guevara Speaks* (1967), *Complete Bolivian Diaries of Che Guevara and Other Captured Documents* (1968), *On Vietnam and World Revolution* (1965), *Socialism and Man* (1969), and *Venceremos.* (1966).

Dear Comrade:

I am finishing these notes while traveling through Africa, moved by the desire to keep my promise, although after some delay. I should like to do so by dealing with the topic that appears in the title. I believe it might be of interest to Uruguayan readers.

It is common to hear how capitalist spokesmen use as an argument in the ideological struggle against socialism the assertion that such a social system, or the period of building socialism upon which we have embarked, is characterized by the extinction of the individual for the sake of the state. I will make no attempt to refute this assertion on a merely theoretical basis, but will instead establish the facts of the Cuban experience and add commentaries of a general nature. I shall first broadly sketch the history of our revolutionary struggle both before and after taking power.

As we know, the exact date of the beginning of the revolutionary actions which were to culminate on January 1, 1959, was July 26, 1953. A group of men led by Fidel Castro attacked the Monada military garrison in the province of Oriente, in the early hours of the morning of that day. The attack was a failure. The failure became a disaster and the survivors were imprisoned, only to begin the revolutionary struggle all over again, once they were amnestied.

During this process, which contained only the first seeds of socialism, man was a basic factor. Man—individualized, specific, named—was trusted and the triumph or failure of the task entrusted to him depended on his capacity for action.

Then came the stage of guerrilla warfare. It was carried out in two different environments: the people, an as yet unawakened mass that had to be mobilized, and its vanguard, the guerrilla, the thrusting engine of mobilization, the generator of

From Speech, Havana, Cuba, 1963.

revolutionary awareness and militant enthusiasm. This vanguard was the catalyst which created the subjective condition necessary for victory. The individual was also the basic factor in the guerrilla, in the framework of the gradual proletarianization of our thinking, in the revolution taking place in our habits and in our minds. Each and every one of the Sierra Maestra fighters who achieved a high rank in the revolutionary forces has to his credit a list of noteworthy deeds. It was on the basis of such deeds that they earned their rank.

It was the first heroic period in which men strove to earn posts of greater responsibility, of greater danger, with the fulfillment of their duty as the only satisfaction. In our revolutionary educational work we often return to this instructive topic. The man of the future could be glimpsed in the attitude of our fighters.

At other times of our history there have been repetitions of this utter devotion to the revolutionary cause. During the October Crisis and at the time of the hurricane Flora, we witnessed deeds of exceptional valor and self-sacrifice carried out by an entire people. One of our fundamental tasks from the ideological standpoint is to find the way to perpetuate such heroic attitudes in everyday life.

The revolutionary government was established in 1959 with the participation of several members of the "sell-out" bourgeoisie. The presence of the rebel army constituted the guarantee of power as the fundamental factor of strength.

Serious contradictions arose which were solved in the first instance in February 1959, when Fidel Castro assumed the leadership of the government in the post of Prime Minister. This process culminated in July of the same year with the resignation of President Urrutia in the face of mass pressure.

With clearly defined features, there now appeared in the history of the Cuban Revolution a personage which will systematically repeat itself: the masses.

This multifacetic being is not, as it is claimed, the sum total of elements of the same category (and moreover, reduced to the same category by the system imposed upon them) and which acts as a tame herd. It is true that the mass follows its leaders, especially Fidel Castro, without hesitation, but the degree to which he has earned such confidence is due precisely to the consummate interpretation of the people's desires and aspirations, and to the sincere struggle to keep the promises made.

The mass participated in the agrarian reform and in the difficult undertaking of the management of the state enterprises; it underwent the heroic experience of Playa Girón; it was tempered in the struggle against the groups of bandits armed by the CIA; during the October Crisis it lived one of the most important definitions of modern times, and today it continues the work to build socialism.

Looking at things from a superficial standpoint, it might seem that those who speak of the submission of the individual to the state are right; with incomparable enthusiasm and discipline, the mass carries out the tasks set by the government whatever their nature: economic, cultural, defense, sports, etc. The initiative generally comes from Fidel or the high command of the revolution: it is explained to the people, who make it their own. At times local experiences are taken up by the party and the government and are thereby generalized, following the same procedure.

However, the state at times makes mistakes. When this occurs, the collective enthusiasm diminishes palpably as a result of a quantitative diminishing that takes place in each of the elements that make up the collective, and work becomes paralyzed until it finally shrinks to insignificant proportions; this is the time to rectify.

This is what happened in March 1962 in the presence of the sectarian policy imposed on the party by Anibal Escalante.

This mechanism is obviously not sufficient to ensure a sequence of sensible measures; what is missing is a more structured relationship with the mass. We must improve this connection in the years to come, but for now, in the case of the initiatives arising on the top levels of government, we are using the almost intuitive method of keeping our ears open to the general reactions in the face of the problems that are posed.

Fidel is a past master at this; his particular mode of integration with the people can only be appreciated by seeing him in action. In the big public meetings one can observe something like the dialogue of two tuning forks whose vibrations summon forth new vibrations each in the other. Fidel and the mass begin to vibrate in a dialogue of growing intensity which reaches its culminating point in an abrupt ending crowned by our victorious battle cry.

What is hard to understand for anyone who has not lived the revolutionary experience is that close dialectical unity which exists between the individual and the mass, in which both are interrelated, and the mass, as a whole composed of individuals, is in turn interrelated with the leader.

Under capitalism certain phenomena of this nature can be observed with the appearance on the scene of politicians capable of mobilizing the public, but if it is not an authentic social movement, in which case it is not completely accurate to speak of capitalism, the movement will have the same life span as its promoter or until the rigors of capitalist society put an end to popular illusions. Under capitalism man is guided by a cold ordinance which is usually beyond his comprehension. The alienated human individual is bound to society as a whole by an invisible umbilical cord: the law of value. It acts upon all facets of his life, shaping his road and his destiny.

The laws of capitalism, invisible and blind for most people, act upon the individual without his awareness. He sees only the broadness of horizon that appears infinite. Capitalist propaganda presents it in just this way, and attempts to use the Rockefeller case (true or not) as a lesson in the prospects for success. The misery that must be accumulated for such an example to arise and the sum total of baseness contributing to the formation of a fortune of such magnitude do not appear in the picture, and the popular forces are not always able to make these concepts clear. (It would be fitting at this point to study how the workers of the imperialist countries gradually lose their international class spirit under the influence of a certain complicity in the exploitation of the dependent countries and how this fact at the same time wears away the militant spirit of the masses within their own national context, but this topic is outside the framework of the present note.)

In any case we can see the obstacle course which may apparently be overcome by an individual with the necessary qualities to arrive at the finish line. The reward is glimpsed in the distance and the road is solitary. Furthermore, it is a race of wolves: He who arrives does so only at the expense of the failure of others.

I shall now attempt to define the individual, the actor in this strange and moving drama that is the building of socialism, in his twofold existence as a unique being and a member of the community.

I believe that the simplest approach is to recognize his unmade quality: he is an unfinished product. The flaws of the past are translated into the present in the individual consciousness and constant efforts must be made to eradicate them. The process is twofold: On the one hand society acts upon the individual by means of direct and indirect education, while on the other hand the individual undergoes a conscious phase of self-education.

The new society in process of formation has to compete very hard with the past. This makes itself felt not only in the individual consciousness, weighed down by the residues of an education and an upbringing systematically oriented toward the isolation of the individual, but also by the very nature of this transition period, with the persistence of commodity relations. The commodity is the economic cell of capitalist society: As long as it exists, its effects will make themselves felt in the organization of production and therefore in man's consciousness.

Marx's scheme conceived of the transition period as the result of the explosive transformation of the capitalist system torn apart by its inner contradictions: Subsequent reality has shown how some countries, the weak limbs, detach themselves from the imperialist tree, a phenomenon foreseen by Lenin. In those countries capitalism has developed sufficiently to make its effects felt upon the people in one way or another, but it is not its own inner contradictions that explode the system after exhausting all of its possibilities. The struggle for liberation against an external oppressor, the misery which has its origin in foreign causes, such as war, whose consequences make the privileged classes fall upon the exploited, the liberation movements aimed at overthrowing neocolonial regimes, are the customary factors in this process. Conscious action does the rest.

In these countries there still has not been achieved a complete education for the work of society, and wealth is far from being within the reach of the masses through the simple process of appropriation. Underdevelopment and the customary flight of capital to "civilized" countries make impossible a rapid change without sacrifices. There still remains a long stretch to be covered in the building of the economic base, and the temptation to follow the beaten paths of material interest as the lever of speedy development is very great.

There is a danger of not seeing the forest because of the trees. Pursuing the chimera of achieving socialism with the aid of the blunted weapons left to us by capitalism (the commodity as the economic cell, profitability and individual material interest as levers, etc.), it is possible to come to a blind alley. And the arrival there comes about after covering a long distance where there are many crossroads and where it is difficult to realize just when the wrong turn was taken. Meanwhile, the adapted economic base has undermined the development of consciousness. To build communism, a new man must be created simultaneously with the material base.

That is why it is so important to choose correctly the instrument of mass mobilization. That instrument must be fundamentally of a moral character, without forgetting the correct use of material incentives, especially those of a social nature.

As I already said, in moments of extreme danger it is easy to activate moral incentives: To maintain their effectiveness, it is necessary to develop a consciousness in which values acquire new categories. Society as a whole must become a huge school.

The broad characteristics of the phenomenon are similar to the process of formation of capitalist consciousness in the system's first stage. Capitalism resorts to force, but it also educates people in the system. Direct propaganda is carried out by those who are entrusted with the task of explaining the inevitability of a class regime, whether it be of divine origin or due to the imposition of nature as a mechanical entity. This placates the masses, who see themselves oppressed by an evil against which it is not possible to struggle.

This is followed by hope, which differentiates capitalism from the previous caste regimes that offered no way out. For some the caste formula continues in force: The obedient are rewarded by the *post mortem* arrival in other wonderful worlds where the good are requited, and the old tradition is continued. For others, innovation: The division in classes is a matter of fate, but individuals can leave the class to which they belong through work, initiative, etc. This process, and that of self-education for success, must be deeply hypocritical: It is the interested demonstration that a lie is true.

In our case, direct education acquires much greater importance. Explanations are convenient because they are genuine; subterfuges are not needed. It is carried out through the State's educational apparatus in the form of general, technical, and ideological culture, by means of bodies such as the Ministry of Education and the party's information apparatus. Education takes among the masses, and the new attitude that it praised tends to become habit; the mass gradually takes it over and exerts pressure on those who have still not become educated. This is the indirect way of educating the masses, as powerful as the other, structured, one.

But the process is a conscious one: The individual receives the impact of the new social power and perceives that he is not completely adequate to it. Under the influence of the pressure implied in indirect education, he tries to adjust to a situation that he feels to be just and whose lack of development has kept him from doing so thus far. He is educating himself.

We can see the new man who begins to emerge in this period of the building of socialism. His image is as yet unfinished. In fact it will never be finished, since the process advances parallel to the development of new economic forms. Discounting those whose lack of education makes them tend toward the solitary road, toward the satisfaction of their ambitions, there are others who, even within this new picture of over-all advances, tend to march in isolation from the accompanying mass. What is important is that people become more aware every day of the need to incorporate themselves into society and of their own importance as motors of that society.

The institutionality of the Revolution has still not been achieved. We are seeking something new that will allow a perfect identification between the government and the community as a whole, adapted to the special conditions of the building of socialism and avoiding to the utmost the commonplaces of bourgeois democracy transplanted to the society in formation (such as legislative houses, for example). Some experiments have been carried out with the aim of gradually creating the institutionalization of the Revolution, but without too much hurry. We have been greatly restrained by the fear that any formal aspect might make us lose sight of the ultimate and most important revolutionary aspiration: to see man freed from alienation.

Notwithstanding the lack of institutions, which must be overcome gradually, the masses now make history as a conscious aggregate of individuals who struggle for the same cause. In spite of the apparent standardization of man in socialism, he is more complete; his possibilities for expressing himself and making himself heard in the social apparatus are infinitely greater, in spite of the lack of a perfect mechanism to do so.

It is still necessary to accentuate his conscious, individual and collective, participation in all the mechanisms of direction and production and associate it with the idea of the need for technical and ideological education, so that the individual will realize that these processes are closely interdependent and their advances are parallel. He will thus achieve total awareness of his social being, which is equivalent to his full realization as a human being, having broken the chains of alienation.

This will be translated concretely into the reappropriation of his nature through freed work and the expression of his own human condition in culture and art.

In order for it to develop in culture, work must acquire a new condition; man as commodity ceases to exist, and a system is established that grants a quota for the fulfillment of social duty. The means of production belong to society, and the machine is only the front line where duty is performed. Man begins to free his thought from the bothersome fact that presupposed the need to satisfy his animal needs by working. He begins to see himself portrayed in his work and to understand its human magnitude through the created object, through the work carried out. This no longer involves leaving a part of his being in the form of labor power sold, which no longer belongs to him; rather it signifies an emanation from himself, a contribution to the life of society in which he is reflected, the fulfillment of his social duty.

We are doing everything possible to give work this new category of social duty and to join it to the development of technology, on the one hand, which will provide the conditions for greater freedom, and to voluntary work on the other, based on the Marxist concept that man truly achieves his full human condition when he produces without being compelled by the physical necessity of selling himself as a commodity.

It is clear that work still has coercive aspects, even when it is voluntary: Man has still not transformed all the coercion surrounding him into conditioned reflexes of a social nature, and in many cases he still produces under the pressure of the environment (Fidel calls this moral compulsion). He is still to achieve complete spiritual recreation in the presence of his own work, without the direct pressure of the social environment but bound to it by new habits. That will be communism.

The change in consciousness does not come about automatically, just as it does not come about automatically in the economy. The variations are slow and not rhythmic; there are periods of acceleration, others are measured and some even involve a retreat.

We must consider, as we have pointed out previously, that we are not before a pure transition period such as that envisioned by Marx in the "Critique of the Gotha Program," but rather a new phase not foreseen by him: the first period in the transition to communism or in the building of socialism.

Elements of capitalism are present within this process, which takes place in the midst of violent class struggle. These elements obscure the complete understanding of the essence of the process.

If to this be added the scholasticism that has held back the development of Marxist philosophy and impeded the systematic treatment of the period, whose political economy has still not been developed, we must agree that we are still in diapers. We must study all the primordial features of the period before elaborating a more far-reaching economic and political theory.

The resulting theory will necessarily give preeminence to the two pillars of socialist construction: the formation of the new human being and the development of technology. We still have a great deal to accomplish in both aspects, but the delay is less justifiable as far as the conception of technology as the basis is concerned: Here, it is not a matter of advancing blindly, but rather of following for a sizable stretch the road opened up by the most advanced countries of the wrold. This is why Fidel harps so insistently on the necessity of the technological and scientific formation of all of our people and especially of the vanguard.

.   .   .

The error of mechanical realism has not appeared (in Cuba), but rather the contrary. This is so because of the lack of understanding of the need to create a new human being who will represent neither nineteenth-century ideas nor those of our decadent and morbid century. it is the twenty-first-century man whom we must create, although this is still a subjective and unsystematic aspiration. This is precisely one of the basic points of our studies and work; to the extent that we make concrete achievements on a theoretical base or vice versa, that we come to broad theoretical conclusions on the basis of our concrete studies, we will have made a valuable contribution to Marxism-Leninism, to the cause of mankind.

.   .   .

I should now like to explain the role played by the personality, the man as the individual who leads the masses that make history. This is our experience, and not a recipe.

Fidel gave impulse to the Revolution in its first years, he has always given it leadership and set the tone, but there is a good group of revolutionaries developing in the same direction as Fidel and a large mass that follows its leaders because it has faith in them. It has faith in them because these leaders have known how to interpret the longings of the masses.

It is not a question of how many kilograms of meat are eaten or how many times a year someone may go on holiday to the seashore or how many pretty imported things can be bought with present wages. It is rather that the individual feels greater fulfillment, that he has greater inner wealth and many more responsilibities. In our country the individual knows that the glorious period in which it has fallen to him to live is one of sacrifice; he is familiar with sacrifice.

The first came to know it in the Sierra Maestra and wherever there was fighting; later we have known it in all Cuba. Cuba is the vanguard of America and must make sacrifices because it occupies the advance position, because it points out to the Latin American masses the road to full freedom.

Within the country, the leaders have to fulfill their vanguard role; and it must be said with complete sincerity that in a true revolution, to which you give yourself completely without any thought for material retribution, the task of the vanguard revolutionary is both magnificent and anguishing.

Let me say, with the risk of appearing ridiculous, that the true revolutionary is guided by strong feelings of love. It is impossible to think of an authentic revolutionary without this quality. This is perhaps one of the great dramas of a leader; he must combine an impassioned spirit with a cold mind and make painful decisions without flinching. Our vanguard revolutionaries must idealize their love for the people, for the most hallowed causes, and make it one and indivisible. They cannot descend, with small doses of daily affection, to the terrain where ordinary men put their love into practice.

The leaders of the Revolution have children who do not learn to call their father with their first faltering words; they have wives who must be part of the general sacrifice of their lives to carry the Revolution to its destination; their friends are strictly limited to their comrades in revolution. There is no life outside the Revolution.

In these conditions the revolutionary leaders must have a large dose of humanity, a large dose of a sense of justice and truth, to avoid falling into dogmatic extremes, into cold scholasticism, into isolation from the masses. They must struggle every day so that their love of living humanity is transformed into concrete deeds, into acts that will serve as an example, as a mobilizing factor.

The revolutionary, ideological motor of the Revolution within his party, is consumed by this uninterrupted activity that ends only with death, unless construction be achieved on a worldwide scale. If his revolutionary eagerness becomes dulled when the most urgent tasks are carried on a local scale, and if he forgets about proletarian internationalism, the revolution that he leads ceases to be a driving force and it sinks into a comfortable drowsiness which is taken advantage of by imperialism, or irreconcilable enemy, to gain ground. Proletarian internationalism is a duty, but it is also a revolutionary need. This is how we educate our people.

That immense multitude is ordering itself; its order responds to an awareness of the need for order; it is no longer a dispersed force, divisible in thousands of fractions shot into space like the fragments of a grenade, trying by any and all means, in a fierce struggle with their equals, to achieve a position that would give them support in the face of an uncertain future.

We know that we have sacrifices ahead of us and that we must pay a price for the heroic fact of constituting a vanguard as a nation. We, the leaders, know that we must pay a price for having the right to say that we are at the head of the people that is at the head of America.

Each and every one of us punctually pays his share of sacrifice, aware of being rewarded by the satisfaction of fulfilling our duty, aware of advancing with everyone toward the new human being who is to be glimpsed on the horizon.

Allow me to attempt to come to some conclusion.

We socialists are more free because we are more fulfilled: We are more fulfilled because we are more free.

The skeleton of our complete freedom is formed, but it lacks the protein substance and the draperies. We will create them.

Our freedom and its daily sustenance are the color of blood and swollen with sacrifice.

Our sacrifice is a conscious one: It is in payment for the freedom we are building.

The road is long and in part unknown; we are aware of our limitations. We will make the twenty-first-century man; we ourselves.

We will be tempered in daily actions, creating a new human being with a new technology.

The personality plays the role of mobilization and leadership in so far as it incarnates the highest virtues and aspirations of the people and does not become detoured.

The road is opened up by the vanguard group, the best among the good, the party.

The basic raw material of our work is the youth: In it we place our hopes and we are preparing it to take the banner from our hands.

If this faltering letter has made some things clear, it will have fulfilled my purpose in sending it.

Accept our ritual greetings, as a handshake or an "Ave Maria Purisïma."

Patria o muerte

Ideology of African Socialism
Léopold Sédar Senghor

Léopold Sédar Senghor (1906-   ) is a Senegalese poet and President of the Republic of Senegal. He is the author of *On African Socialism* (1964), *Selected Poems* (1964), and several monographs on Pierre Teilhard de Chardin, Gaston Berger, and St. John Perse.

In the respective programs of our former parties, all of us used to proclaim our attachment to socialism. This was a good thing, but it was not enough. Most of the time, we were satisfied with stereotyped formulas and vague aspirations, which we called scientific socialism—as if socialism did not mean a return to original sources. Above all, we need to make an effort to rethink the basic texts in the light of Negro African realities.

The antifederalists have accused us of being atheists, Marxists, and of outlawing religion. Though this smacks of propaganda, it poses a fundamental question. Can we integrate Negro African cultural values, especially religious values, into socialism? We must answer that question once and for all with an unequivocal "Yes."

We are not "Marxists" in the sense given the word today, in so far as Marxism is presented as atheistic metaphysics, a total and totalitarian view of the world, a *Weltanschauung*. In this sense, Marx himself once said: "As for me, I am not a Marxist." We are socialists. In other words, we shall exclude neither Marx nor Engels from our sources; we shall start from their works as from those of the "utopian socialists," and we shall add to these sources the works of their successors and commentators. But we shall retain only the method and the ideas: the method, which can help us to analyze our situation; the ideas, which can help us to solve our problems.

We shall start from Marx and Engels. Whatever their limitations, their inadequacies, or their errors, they, more than all others, revolutionized political and economic thought of the nineteenth century. . . .

We may wonder, first of all, whether the socialism, the economics of Marx, is really "scientific." Yes and no. *No*, if one means by science the exact knowledge

From Léopold Sédar Senghor, *African Socialism*, translated by Mercer Cook (New York: American Society of African Culture, 1959); reprinted by permission of Praeger Publishers, Inc.

and formation of economic facts in laws which permit one to foresee and to organize a balanced economy. *Yes*, if science is defined as comprehension of the real, if it consists of deciphering the complexities basic to economic facts, especially man's reactions to these facts, and if its aim is to unveil "the economic law of motion of modern society."

So we must not seek in Marx—not even in *Capital*—an exposé of economic laws. Considering them more or less as contingent "appearances," Marx was not interested in them. Moreover, he went so far as to predict changes that have not occurred.

In *Conflit du Siècle*, Fritz Sternberg has analyzed almost all the changes that have taken place in economic, social, and political reality since the publication of *Capital*. They are impressive and have been listed by other writers. In our résumé of Marx's theories, we have skipped over most of them, and we shall now mention only a few, while noting the recent studies made in France by the Autonomous Socialist Party:

1. The class struggle is much more complex than Marx thought. In fact, the working class is not a simple reality. Moreover, it is diminishing while the several categories of salaried workers with dissimilar interests are increasing.

2. The peasants, whom Marx considered more or less impervious to revolutionary ferment and dedicated "to the stupidity of rural life," have belied his judgment in underdeveloped countries.

3. The theory of capitalist concentration has not been verified by the facts. On the contrary, the number of small and medium-sized businesses continues to grow in Western European countries.

4. Though periodic economic crises have not ceased, they are becoming rarer, and we cannot reasonably foresee a general cataclysm ending the capitalist system, which is adjusting to economic and social evolution.

5. "Socialism" has not triumphed, as Marx predicted, in the industrial nations of Western Europe, but in the underdeveloped nations of Eastern Europe and Asia.

By excessive simplification of the theory class struggle—a more precise translation of *Klassenkampf* would be a "class war"—Marx overestimated the role of the determinism of things and underestimated man's freedom and the organizing power of the capitalist state. In fact, thanks to trade-union activity and a more enlightened middle class, the capitalistic state, by policy of intervention and rational organization, has been able progressively to reduce the surplus value. This surplus value, reduced by more equitable taxation, has permitted the productive investments of the postwar era and the institution of social security. Marx advocated social legislation; in his opinion, it would lead to increased unemployment, bitter class antagonism, and, finally, to the revolution. However, social reforms have produced quite the opposite effects.

We may also observe, in passing, that he did not pay enough attention to the role of cooperatives, as preached by the utopian socialists. We know that these have proved their worth in the Scandinavian socialist democracies. Thus, a will to reform has replaced—in Western labor unions—the will to revolt. In the Communist countries, the "dictatorship of the proletariat," contrary to the teachings of Marx, has made the state an omnipotent, soulless monster, has stifled the natural freedoms of the human being, and has dried up the sources of art, without which life is not worth living.

One final word on this point. In Marx's day, colonialism was just beginning. He could not foresee its universal development during the second half of the nineteenth century. He spoke, of course, about "the modern theory of colonization,"[1] but merely in the etymological sense of the word. He had in mind only European colonization of the United States. Moreover, his macroeconomic theory, his almost blind confidence in proletarian generosity and conscience prevented him from anticipating the opposition that would develop between colonizing and colonized countries, between the well fed and the famished. It is a fact, now commonplace, that the standard of living of the European masses has been able to rise only at the expense of the standard of living of the masses in Asia and Africa. The economy of European nations consists fundamentally of selling manufactured products to underdeveloped countries at high prices and buying raw materials from them at the lowest possible cost. And I am not talking about the United States. The problem is different in France, but if the prices paid for raw materials in African countries are supported, it it no less true that French prices are generally the highest in Western Europe. This compensates for that. In a word, the European proletariat has profited from the colonial system; therefore, it has never really—I mean effectively—opposed it.

There we have a series of facts that we must think about, we men from underdeveloped countries, we men inspired by socialism. We must not consider Marx as an economist like Keynes, but as a sociologist, a philosopher. This is something that would have astonished the founder of "scientific socialism," since he refrained from "philosophizing." And yet his thought remains that of a philosopher. Beyond the economic "appearances," it dives into the human reality that causes them. For the *factual* view of things, Marx substitutes a profound insight into human needs. His is a new humanism, new because it is *incarnate.*

Humanism, *philosophy of humanism*, rather than economics—this is the basic character, the positive contribution of Marxian thought. As we said earlier, Marx does not formulate economic facts; he defines "the economic law of motion of modern society," which is a social "tendency" rather than a law. In his analysis, he advances by *postulates* and theories which explain the facts. . . .

FOR AN AFRICAN TYPE OF SOCIALISM

Let us recapitulate Marx's positive contributions. They are: the philosophy of humanism, economic theory, dialectical method. To these we may add trade unionism, planning, and also federalism and cooperation, which come to us from the French idealistic socialists: Saint Simon, Proudhon, and Fourier—to name only the outstanding ones.

Thus, we are not Communists. Does this mean that we shall practice anti-Communism? Certainly not. Anti-Communism, the "witch hunt," can have but one result: increased tension between East and West and a continuation of the Cold War at the obvious risk of unleashing a third global conflict, from which humanity would not recover. We are not Communists for a theoretical reason. Lenin's definition of matter proceeds from a one-sided concept, from a purely materialistic and deterministic postulate. At the beginning of *Anarchy and Socialism*, Stalin goes

[1] *Capital*, IV, 314-28.

even further: "Marxism is not only a theory of socialism, it is a definitive view of the world, a philosophical system."

We are not Communists for a practical reason. The anxiety for human dignity, the need for freedom—man's freedom, the freedoms of collectivities—which animate Marx's thought and provide its revolutionary ferment—this anxiety and this need are unknown to Communism, whose major deviation is Stalinism. The "dictatorship of the proletariat," which was to be only temporary, becomes the dictatorship of the party and state by perpetuating itself. "The Soviet Union," said Mamadou Dia on his return from Moscow, "has succeeded in building socialism, but at the sacrifice of religion, of the soul."

The paradox of socialistic construction in Communist countries—in the Soviet Union at least—is that it increasingly resembles capitalistic construction in the United States, the American way of life, with high salaries, refrigerators, washing machines, and television sets. And it has less art and freedom of thought. Nevertheless, we shall not be won by a regime of liberal capitalism and free enterprise. We cannot close our eyes to segregation, although the government combats it; nor can we accept the elevation of material success to a way of life.

We stand for a middle course, for a *democratic socialism* which goes so far as to integrate spiritual values, a socialism which ties in with the old ethical current of the French socialists. Historically and culturally, we belong to the current. Besides, the French socialists—from Saint Simon to the Léon Blum of *A l'Echelle humaine*—are not so utopian as they are reputed to be. In so far as they are idealists, they fulfill the requirements of the Negro African soul, the requirements of men of all races and countries. *Not by Bread Alone*—this is the title of a novel by Dudintsev, a citizen of the Soviet Union, and the Russians read this book avidly. Khrushchev was not mistaken: "De-Stalinization was imposed by the people by the thirst for freedom, the hunger for spiritual nourishment."

Concluding his report on the German Democratic Republic [East Germany], Michel Bosquet writes: "But when I ask him [the head of a labor union] what the workers demand, he replies: 'Today they want TV sets and motorcycles. When they get them, they will demand a shorter work week. And then? . . . I can only answer for myself. What I would like, what I miss, is more good literature.' "[2] This fact is not unrelated to a phenomenon observed in America: the appeal of the contemplative life, as a reaction against the surrounding machinism. Among American Catholics, the proportion of priests to laity is one of the highest in the world.

This thirst for freedom, this hunger for spiritual nourishment, strengthened by the moral tradition of French socialism, explains why numerous French Marxists in recent years have shunned Stalinism and even Communism: Henri Lefebvre, Pierre Fougeyrollas, and Edgar Morin, among others, who have stated their reasons lately in sorrowful but lucid volumes.[3] The major reason, common to all of them, is that the Party has come to submerge the individual under the collectivity, the person under the class, to hide reality behind the screen of ideology. If we reflect about these cases, we shall discover that not only Marxism but Marx himself is "called to question"—except perhaps by Lefebvre. For, if the person is submerged, it is

[2] *L'Express*, June 4, 1959, p. 24.
[3] Cf. Lefebvre, *La Somme et le reste* (La Nef de Paris); Fougeyrollas, *Le Marxisme en question* (Editions du Seuil); Morin, *Autocritique* (Julliard).

because Marx did not pay sufficient attention to the "natural determination"—namely, the *nation*—that is not effaced by class.

Marx underestimated political and national idealism, which, born in France upon the ruins of provincial fatherlands with the Revolution of 1789, won over the world. "Justice," Marx writes, "humanity, liberty, equality, fraternity, independence. If the creater of scientific sociology return to this earth, he would historical and political questions, prove absolutely nothing." I repeat: independence. If the creator of scientific sociology returned to this earth, he would perceive with amazement that these "chimeras," as he called them, and above all the concept of *nation*, are living realities in the twentieth century.

What is left of the 1789 Revolution? A political doctrine and technique, accepted nowadays even by the devout. . . . From Marxism there will surely remain an economic doctrine and technique, inasmuch as they do not contradict the teachings of Christianity and Islam—far from it.

But a third revolution is taking place, as a reaction against capitalistic and Communistic materialism—one that will integrate moral, if not religious, values with the political and economic contributions of the two great revolutions. In this revolution, the colored peoples, including the Negro African, must play their part; they must bring their contribution to the construction of the new planetary civilization. As Aimé Césaire says: "They will not come empty-handed to the rendezvous of give-and-take." Between the two world wars, Paul Morand observed: "The Negroes have rendered an enormous service to America. But for them, one might have thought that men could not live without a bank account and a bathtub."

FOR A STRONG FEDERAL DEMOCRACY

Our democracy will be *federal*. . . . We do not need to remind you that local diversities, with their complementary qualities, will enrich the federation. Conversely, the federation will preserve those diversities. The decentralized federal structure will be extended, within the framework of the federal state, to regional and communal collectivities, even into economic and social areas. The Yugoslavian structures, adapted to our realities, will, in this instance, serve as a model.

Thus we shall fill the dangerous void now existing between the federal state and the village. Our leaders are bored with their freedom from responsibility. Even when they fill this void by the political formation of militants, they tend to devote their activity to contention over slogans. Regional and communal assemblies, among others, would give them a practical opportunity to exercise their responsibilities. A revolution remains ideological, therefore ineffective, so long as it is not translated into concrete action which, by transforming the structure, raises the standard of living and culture of the citizens. . . .

A federal democracy, yes . . . but a strong democracy. As the Secretary General suggests in his report, it is a question of avoiding two dangers: on the one hand, fascist dictatorship, which one observes in the antifederalist states; on the other hand, governmental instability, which was common in France during the Third and Fourth Republics. Both deviations are signs of weakness; in the long run they provoke the revolt of the people and the disintegration of the state.

The Federation of Mali, like the federated states, will be a democracy.[4] The electoral law will continue to be impartial . . . not a law of circumstance, cut to the measure of the government or the majority party. Freedom of opinion, speech, press, assembly, and association is guaranteed by the constitutions of Mali and the federated states—in the antifederalist states also. But, with us, these freedoms do not exist only on paper; they are effectively enjoyed and will continue to be so. Above all, the right of *free settlement* of the citizens will be assured, whether or not they were born in Mali. A democratic policy pays dividends; in addition, it conforms to our humanitarian ideal. Already, public opinion in black Africa and France is grateful to us. This is excellent propaganda for Mali.

The rights of the minority, of the opposition, will therefore be respected in Mali. They will find their natural and legal limits in the rights of the majority, the popular will, which is sovereign; in other words, in the rights of the nation-state. For we are a quasi nation, as Francois Perroux says.

The stability of the executive is guaranteed by our constitutions. We need to assure it in actual political practice. It is necessary that governments govern, that they, along with the legislative assemblies, take the initiative of making laws within the framework of the doctrine and program of the majority party. Governments must apply the law firmly, and legislative assemblies must check on the action of the government. It is necessary that the party (congress, executive committee, and officers) have the final word in matters of control. Yet, to be effective, the various controls will be general and *a posteriori*. Meddling and harassing controls would not work. Here again, we shall avoid two dangers: granting government action a blank check, and taking away the executive power. The controls must be political, not technical.

Let us return to the rights of the opposition. Their role, certainly, is to criticize. But "criticism" means critical spirit, not spirit of criticism, systematic carping. In a democracy, criticism must be constructive and serve the general, not factional, interest. At any rate, one cannot grant the opposition more rights than the majority enjoys. The law also applies to the opposition, which is likewise required to observe it. Under the control of the majority party, the governments will take all necessary steps to curb demagogic opposition. They will not tolerate violations of the law, appeals to illegality or to violence, whether the pretexts be religious or racial. This is the democratic sense that we attach to the "dictatorship of the proletariat."

---

[4] In August, 1960, after this report was made, the Federation of Mali separated into its component parts, Senegal and the Sudan (which took the name of the Republic of Mali).—Ed.

What Is "Negritude"?

Paradoxically, it was the French who first forced us to seek its essence, and who then showed us where it lay . . . when they enforced their policy of assimilation and thus deepened our despair. . . . Earlier, we had become aware within ourselves that assimilation was a failure; we could assimilate mathematics or the French language, but we could never strip off our black skins or root out black souls. And so we set out on a fervent quest for the "holy grail": our collective soul. And we came upon it.

It was not revealed to us by the "official France" of the politicians who, out of self-interest and political conviction, defended the policy of assimilation. Its whereabouts was pointed out to us by that handful of free-lance thinkers—writers, artists, ethnologists, and prehistorians—who bring about cultural revolutions in France. It was, to be quite precise, our teachers of ethnology who introduced us to the considerable body of work already achieved in the understanding of Africa, by the University of Oxford.

What did we learn from all those writers, artists, and teachers? That the early years of colonization and especially, even before colonization, the slave trade had ravaged black Africa like a bush fire, wiping out images and values in one vast carnage. That Negroid civilization had flourished in the Upper Paleolithic Age, and that the Neolithic revolution could not be explained without them. That their roots retain their vigor and would one day produce new grass and green branches. . . .

Negritude is the *whole complex of civilized values—cultural economic, social, and political—which characterize the black peoples*, or, more precisely, the Negro-African world. All these values are essentially informed by intuitive reason, because this sentient reason, the reason which comes to grips, expresses itself emotionally, through that self-surrender, that coalescence of subject and object; through myths, by which I mean the archetypal images of the collective soul; and, above all, through primordial rhythms, synchronized with those of the cosmos. In other words, the sense of communion, the gift of mythmaking, the gift of rhythm, such are the essential elements of Negritude which you will find indelibly stamped on all the works and activities of the black man. . . .

In opposition to European racialism, of which the Nazis were the symbol, we set up an "antiracial racialism." The very excesses of Nazism, and the catastrophes it engendered, were soon to bring us to our senses. Such hatred, such violence, above all, such weeping and such shedding of blood produced a feeling of revulsion. It was so foreign to our continent's genius: our *need to love*. And then the anthropologists taught us that there is no such thing as a pure race: Scientifically speaking—races do not exist. They went one better and forecast that, with a mere 200 million people, we would in the end disappear as a "black race," through miscegenation. At the same time, they did offer us some consolation. "The focal points of human development," wrote Teilhard de Chardin in 1939, "always seem to coincide with the points of contact and anastomosis of several nerve paths"—that is, in the

Excerpts from a speech delivered by Senghor at Oxford University in October, 1961; reprinted, by permission, from *West Africa*, November 4, 1961.

ordinary man's language, of several races. If, then, we were justified in fostering the values of Negritude and arousing the energy slumbering within us, it must be in order to pour them into the mainstream of cultural miscegenation (the biological process taking place spontaneously). They must flow toward the meeting point of all humanity; they must be our contribution to the civilization of the universal.

Biological miscegenation, then, takes place spontaneously, provoked by the very laws which govern life, and in the face of all policies of apartheid. It is a different matter in the realm of culture. Here, we remain wholly free to cooperate or not, to provoke or prevent the synthesis of cultures. This is an important point. For, as certain biologists point out, the psychological mutations brought about by education are incorporated in our genes and are then transmitted by heredity. Hence the major role played by culture.

Seen within this prospect of the civilization of the universal, the colonial policies of Great Britain and France have proved successful complements to each other, and black Africa has benefited. The policies of the former tended to reinforce the traditional native civilization. As for France's policy, although we have often reviled it in the past, it too ended with a credit balance, through forcing us actively to assimilate European civilization. This fertilized our sense of Negritude. Today, our Negritude no longer expresses itself as opposition to European values, but as a *complement* to them. Henceforth, its militants will be concerned, as I have often said, *not to be assimilated, but to assimilate*. They will use European values to arouse the slumbering values of Negritude, which they will bring as their contribution to the civilization of the universal.

Nevertheless, we still disagree with Europe: not with its values any longer (with the exception of capitalism), but with its theory of the civilization of the universal. . . . In the eyes of the Europeans, the 'exotic civilizations" are static in character, being content to live by means of archetypal images, which they repeat indefinitely. The most serious criticism is that they have no idea of the *pre-eminent dignity of the human person*. My reply is this: Just as much as black Africa, Europe and its North American offspring live by means of archetypal images. For what are free enterprise, democracy, and Communism but *myths*, around which hundreds of millions of men and women organize their lives? Negritude itself is a myth (I am not using the word in any pejorative sense), but a living, dynamic one, which evolves with its circumstances into a form of humanism. Actually, our criticism of the [European] thesis is that it is monstrously antihumanist. For if European civilization were to be imposed, unmodified, on all peoples and continents, it could only be by force. That is its first disadvantage. A more serious one is that it would not be *humanistic*, for it would cut itself off from the complementary values of the greater part of humanity. As I have said elsewhere, it would be a universal civilization; it would not be the civilization of the univeral.

Our revised Negritude is humanistic. I repeat, it welcomes the complementary values of Europe and the white man, and, indeed, of all other races and continents. But it welcomes them in order to fertilize and reinvigorate its own values, which it then offers for the construction of a civilization which shall embrace all mankind. The neohumanism of the twentieth century stands at the point where the paths of all nations, races, and continents cross, "where the four winds of the spirit blow."

The Ideology of Non-violence
Mohandas K. Gandhi

Mohandas K. Gandhi (1869-1948) was a lawyer who devoted his life to "experiments with truth," in which he tried to improve the lot of Indians in South Africa, untouchables in India, and Indian subjects of the British colonial regime. His advocacy of nonviolence as an action of the brave won the attention of the late Martin Luther King, Jr. Gandhi wrote an autobiography, but most of his other articles were speeches and newspaper columns, which have been collected in *Non-violence in Peace and War* and *Satyagraha.* Publication of his complete works is now in progress.

MY TASK

426. In the past, non-co-operation has been deliberately expressed in violence to the evil doer. I am endeavouring to show to my countrymen that violent non-co-operation only multiplies evil and that as evil can only be sustained by violence, withdrawal of support of evil requires complete abstention from violence. Non-violence implies voluntary submission to the penalty or non-co-operation with evil.—*YI*, 23-3-22, 168.

427. I am not a visionary. I claim to be a practical idealist. The religion of non-violence is not meant merely for the *rishis*[1] and saints. It is meant for the common people as well. Non-violence is the law of our species as violence is the law of the brute. The spirit lies dormant in the brute and he knows no law but that of a physical might. The dignity of man requires obedience to a higher law—to the strength of the spirit.

I have therefore ventured to place before India the ancient law of self-sacrifice. For, *satyagraha*[2] and its off-shoots, non-co-operation and civil resistance, are nothing but new names for the law of suffering. The *rishis*, who discovered the law of non-violence in the midst of violence, were greater geniuses than Newton. They were themselves greater warriors than Wellington. Having themselves known the use of arms, they realized their uselessness and taught a weary world that its salvation lay not through violence but through non-violence.—*YI*, 11-8-20, *Tagore* 712. . . .

MORAL EQUIVALENT OF WAR

439. Up to the year 1906, I simply relied on appeal to reason. I was a very industrious reformer. I was a good draftsman, as I always had a close grip of facts

From *Selections from Gandhi*, 2nd edition, edited by Nirmal Kumar Bose, Navajivan Publishing House, 1957, pp. 149, 153-154, 156-157, 158-159, 163-167, and 170-172. They are reprinted here by permission of the Navajivan Trust, Copyright © 1957 the Navajivan Trust.

[1] [Holy Hindu sages, saints, or inspired poets. Ed.]
[2] [This has been variously rendered into English as love-force, truth-force, or soul-force. Ed.]

which in its turn was the necessary result of my meticulous regard for truth. But I found that reason failed to produce an impression when the critical moment arrived in South Africa. My people were excited; even a worm will and does sometimes turn—and there was talk of wreaking vengeance. I had then to choose between allying myself to violence or finding out some other method of meeting the crisis and stopping the rot and it came to me that we should refuse to obey legislation that was degrading and let them put us in jail if they liked. Thus came into being the moral equivalent of war. I was then a loyalist, because, I implicitly believed that the sum total of the activities of the British Empire was good for India and for humanity. Arriving in England soon after the outbreak of the war I plunged into it and later when I was forced to go to India as a result of the pleurisy that I had developed, I led a recruiting campaign at the risk of my life, and to the horror of some of my friends. The disillusionment came in 1919 after the passage of the Black Rowlatt Act and the refusal of the Government to give the simple elementary redress of proved wrongs that we had asked for. And so, in 1920, I became a rebel. Since then the conviction has been growing upon me, that things of fundamental importance to the people are not secured by reason alone but have to be purchased with their suffering. Suffering is the law of human beings; war is the law of the jungle. But suffering is infinitely more powerful than the law of the jungle for converting the opponent and opening his ears, which are otherwise shut, to the voice of reason. Nobody has probably drawn up more petitions or espoused more forlorn causes than I and I have come to this fundamental conclusion that if you want something really important to be done you must not merely satisfy the reason, you must move the heart also. The appeal of reason is more to the head but the penetration of the heart comes from suffering. It opens to the inner understanding in man. Suffering is the badge of the human race, not the sword.—*YI*, 5-11-31, 341.

THE ESSENCE OF NON-VIOLENCE

440. (1) Non-violence is the law of the human race and is infinitely greater than and superior to brute force.

(2) In the last resort it does not avail to those who do not possess a living faith in the God of Love.

(3) Non-violence affords the fullest protection to one's self-respect and sense of honour, but not always to possession of land or movable property, though its habitual practice does prove a better bulwark than the possession of armed men to defend them. Non-violence in the very nature of things is of no assistance in the defence of ill-gotten gains and immoral acts.

(4) Individuals and nations who would practice non-violence must be prepared to sacrifice (nations to the last man) their all except honour. It is therefore inconsistent with the possession of other people's countries, i.e. modern imperialism which is frankly based on force for its defence.

(5) Non-violence is a power which can be wielded equally by all—children, young men and women or grown-up people, provided they have a living faith in the God of Love and have therefore equal love for all mankind. When non-violence is accepted as the law of life it must pervade the whole being and not be applied to isolated acts.

(6) It is a profound error to suppose that whilst the law is good enough for individuals it is not for the masses of mankind.—*H*, 5-9-36, 236. . . .

WHY THEN NOT KILL THOSE WHO OPPRESS MANKIND?

446. No human being is so bad as to be beyond redemption, no human being is so perfect as to warrant his destroying him whom he wrongly considers to be wholly evil.—*YI*, 26-3-31, 49.

447. A *satyagrahi* must never forget the distinction between evil and the evil-doer. He must not harbour ill-will or bitterness against the evil person, however unrelieved his evil might be. For it is an article of faith with every *satyagrahi* that there is no one so fallen in this world but can be converted by love. A *satyagrahi* will always try to overcome evil by good, anger by love, untruth by truth, *himsa* by *ahimsa*.[3] There is no other way of purging the world of evil.—*YI*, 8-8-29, 263.

ABSENCE OF HATRED

448. I hold myself to be incapable of hating any being on earth. By a long course of prayerful discipline, I have ceased for over forty years to hate anybody. I know this is a big claim. Nevertheless, I make it in all humility. But I can and do hate evil wherever it exists. I hate the system of government that the British people have set up in India. I hate the ruthless exploitation of India even as I hate from the bottom of my heart the hideous system of untouchability for which millions of Hindus have made themselves responsible. But I do not hate the domineering Englishmen as I refuse to hate the domineering Hindus. I seek to reform them in all the loving ways that are open to me. My non-co-operation has its roots not in hatred, but in love. My personal religion peremptorily forbids me to hate anybody.—*YI*, 6-8-25, 272.

449. We can only win over the opponent by love, never by hate. Hate is the subtlest form of violence. We cannot be really non-violent and yet hate in us.—*H*, 17-8-34, 212. . . .

NON-VIOLENT RESISTANCE

457. My goal is friendship with the whole world and I can combine the greatest love with the greatest opposition to wrong.—*YI*, 10-3-20, *Tagore*, 139.

458. Non-violence is 'not a resignation from all real fighting against wickedness.' On the contrary, the non-violence of my conception is a more active and real fight against wickedness than retaliation whose very nature is to increase wickedness. I contemplate, a mental and therefore a moral opposition to immoralities. I seek entirely to blunt the edge of the tyrant's sword, not by putting up against it a sharper-edged weapon, but by disappointing his expectation that I would be offering physical resistance. The resistance of the soul that I should offer would elude him. It would at first dazzle him and at last compel recognition from him, which recognition would not humilitate him but would uplift him, it may be urged that this is an ideal state. And so it is.—*YI*, 8-10-25, 346, *cf*. 133, 386, 426, 551. . . .

---

[3] [*Himsa* is the causing of pain or death from anger or selfishness or with the intention to injure. To refrain from doing this is *ahimsa*. Ed.]

LIMITATIONS OF VIOLENCE

478. Hitherto I have given historical instances of bloodless non-co-operation. I will not insult the intelligence of the reader by citing historical instances of non-co-operation combined with violence, but I am free to confess that there are on record as many successes as failures in violent non-co-operation.—*YI*, 4-8-20, *Tagore*, 320.

479. Revolutionary crime is intended to exert pressure. But it is the insane pressure of anger and ill-will. I contend that non-violent acts exert pressure far more effective than violent acts, for that pressure comes from goodwill and gentleness.—*YI*, 26-12-24, 420.

480. I do not blame the British. If we were weak in numbers as they are, we too would perhaps have resorted to the same methods as they are now employing. Terrorism and deception are weapons not of the strong but of the weak. The British are weak in numbers, we are weak in spite of our numbers. The result is that each is dragging the other down. It is common experience that Englishmen lose in character after residence in India and that Indians lose in courage and manliness by contact with Englishmen. This process of weakening is good neither for us two nations, nor for the world.—*YI*, 22-9-20, *Tagore*, 1092.

481. I object to violence because when it appears to do good, the good is only temporary; the evil it does is permanent. I do not believe that the killing of even every Englishman can do the slightest good to India. The millions will be just as badly off as they are today, if someone made it possible to kill off every Englishman tomorrow. The responsibility is more ours than that of the English for the present state of things. The English will be powerless to do evil if we will but be good. Hence my incessant emphasis on reform from within.—*YI*, 21-5-25, 178.

482. Good brought through force destroyed individuality. Only when the change was effected through the persuasive power of non-violent non-co-operation, i.e. love, could the foundation of individuality be preserved, and real, abiding progress be assured for the world.—*H*, 9-3-47, 58.

483. History teaches us that those who have, no doubt with honest motives, ousted the greedy by using brute force against them, have in their turn become a prey to the disease of the conquered.—*YI*, 6-5-26, 164.

TO THE REVOLUTIONARY

484. Those whom you seek to depose are better armed and infinitely better organized than you are. You may not care for your own lives, but you dare not disregard those of your countrymen who have no desire to die a martyr's death.—*YI*, 25-12-24, 428.

485. From violence done to the foreign ruler, violence to our own people whom we may consider to be obstructing the country's progress is an easy natural step. Whatever may have been the result of violent activities in other countries and without reference to the philosophy of non-violence, it does not require much intellectual effort to see that if we resort to violence for ridding society of the many abuses which impede our progress, we shall add to our difficulties and postpone the day of freedom. The people unprepared for reform because unconvinced of their necessity will be maddened with rage over their coercion, and

will seek the assistance of the foreigner in order to retaliate. Has not this been happening before our eyes for the past many years of which we have still painfully vivid recollections?—*YI*, 2-1-30, 4.

486. I hold that the world is sick of armed rebellions. I hold too that whatever may be true of other countries, a bloody revolution will not succeed in India. The masses will not respond. A movement in which masses have no active part can do no good to them. A successful bloody revolution can only mean further misery for the masses. For it would be still foreign rule for them. The non-violence I teach is active non-violence of the strongest. But the weakest can partake in it without becoming weaker. They can only be the stronger for having been in it. The masses are far bolder today than they ever were. A non-violent struggle necessarily involves construction on a mass scale. It cannot therefore lead to *tamas*[4] or darkness or inertia. It means a quickening of the national life. That movement is still going on silently, almost imperceptibly, but none the less surely.

I do not deny the revolutionary's heroism and sacrifice. But heroism and sacrifice in a bad cause are so much waste of splendid energy and hurt the good cause by drawing away attention from it by the glamour of the misused heroism and sacrifice in a bad cause.

I am not ashamed to stand erect before the heroic and self-sacrificing revolutionary because I am able to pit an equal measure of non-violent men's heroism and sacrifice untarnished by the blood of the innocent. Self-sacrifice of one innocent man is a million times more potent than the sacrifice of a million men who die in the act of killing others. The willing sacrifice of the innocent is the most powerful retort to insolent tyranny that has yet been conceived by God or man.—*YI*, 12-2-25, 60.

NON-VIOLENCE THE SWIFTER WAY

487. The spiritual weapon of self-purification, intangible as it seems, is the most potent means of revolutionizing one's environment and loosening external shackles. It works subtly and invisibly; it is an intense process though it might often seem a weary and long-drawn process, it is the straightest way to liberation, the surest and quickest and no effort can be too great for it. What it requires is faith—an unshakable mountainlike faith that flinches from nothing.

488. You need not be afraid that the method of non-violence is a slow long-drawn out process. It is the swiftest the world has seen, for it is the surest.—*YI*, 30-4-25, 153.

489. India's freedom is assured if she has patience. That way will be found to be the shortest even though it may appear to be the longest to our impatient nature. The way of peace insures internal growth and stability.—*YI*, 20-5-26, 184.

NON-VIOLENCE ALSO THE NOBLER WAY

490. I am more concerned in preventing the brutalization of human nature than in the prevention of the sufferings of my own people. I know that people who

---

[4] [The darkness, inertia, or dullness that constitutes one of the three primal qualities or elements of matter according to Sankhya philosophy. Ed.]

voluntarily undergo a course of suffering raise themselves and the whole of humanity; but I also know that people who become brutalized in their desperate efforts to get victory over their opponents or to exploit weaker nations or weaker men, not only drag down themselves but mankind also. And it cannot be a matter of pleasure to me or anyone else to see human nature dragged to the mire. If we are all sons of the same God and partake of the same divine essence, we must partake of the sin of every person whether he belongs to us or to another race. You can understand how repugnant it must be to invoke the beast in any human being, how much more so in Englishmen, among whom I count numerous friends. I invite you all to give all the help that you can in the endeavour that I am making.–*YI*, 29-10-31, 325.

491. The doctrine of violence has reference only to the doing of injury by one to another. Suffering injury in one's own person is on the contrary of the essence of non-violence and is the chosen substitute for violence to others. It is not because I value life low that I can countenance with joy thousands voluntarily losing their lives for *satyagraha*, but because I know that it results in the long run in the least loss of life and what is more, it enobles those who lose their lives and morally enriches the world for their sacrifice.–*YI*, 8-10-25, 345.

492. The method of passive resistance is the clearest and safest, because, if the cause is not true, it is the resisters, and they alone, who suffer.–*Nat.* 305.

493. Passive resistance is an all-sided sword; it can be used anyhow; it blesses him who uses it and him against whom it is used.–*IHR*, 48.

494. The beauty of *satyagraha*, of which non-co-operation is but a chapter, is that it is available to either side in a fight; that it has checks that automatically work for the vindication of truth and justice for that side, whichever it may be, that has truth justice in preponderating measure. It is as powerful and faithful a weapon in the hands of the capitalist as in that of the labourer. It is as powerful in the hands of the government, as in that of the people, and will bring victory to the government, if people are misguided or unjust, as it will win the battle for the people if the government be in the wrong. Quick disorganization and defeat are bound to be the fate of bolstered up cases and artificial agitations, if the battle is fought with *satyagraha* weapons. Suppose the people are unfit to rule themselves, or are unwilling to sacrifice for a cause, then, no amount of noise will bring them victory in non-co-operation.–*YI*, 23-6-20, *Tagore*, 42. . . .

CAN AGGRESSION BE STOPPED BY NON-VIOLENCE?

498. *Q.* How could a disarmed neutral country allow other nations to be destroyed? But for our army which was waiting ready at our frontier during the last war we should have been ruined.

A. At the risk of being considered a visionary or a fool I must answer this question in the only manner I know. It would be cowardly of a neutral country to allow an army to devastate a neighbouring country. But there are two ways in common between soldiers of war and soldiers of non-violence, and if I had been a civilian of Switzerland and a President of the Federal State what I would have done would be to refuse passage to the invading army by refusing all supplies. Secondly, by re-enacting a Thermopylae in Switzerland, you would have presented a living wall of men and women and children and invited the invaders to walk over your corpses. You may say that such a thing is beyond human experience and endurance, I say that it is not so. It was quite possible. Last year in Gujarat, women stood *lathi*[5] charges unflinchingly and in Peshawar thousands stood hails of bullets without resorting to violence. Imagine these men and women staying in front of an army requiring a safe passage to another country. The army would be brutal enough to walk over them, you might say. I would then say you will still have done your duty by allowing yourselves to be annihilated. An army that dares to pass over the corpses of innocent men and women would not be able to repeat that experiment. You may, if you wish, refuse to believe in such courage on the part of the masses of men and women; but then you would have to admit that non-violence is made of sterner stuff. It was never conceived as a weapon of attack, but of the stoutest hearts.

Q. Is it open to a soldier to fire in the air and avoid violence?

A. A soldier who having enlisted himself flattered himself that he was avoiding violence by shooting in the air did no credit to his courage or to his creed of non-violence. In my scheme of things, such a man would be held guilty of untruth and cowardice both—cowardice in that in order to escape punishment he enlisted, and untruth in that he enlisted to serve as soldier and did not fire as expected. Such a thing discredits the cause of waging war against war. The war-resisters have to be like Caesar's wife—above suspicion. Their strength lies in absolute adherence to the morality of the question.—*YI*, 31-12-31, 427.

499. Indeed the weakest State can render itself immune from attack if it learns the art of non-violence. But a small State, no matter how powerfully armed it is, cannot exist in the midst of a powerful combination of well-armed States. It has to be absorbed by or be under the protection of one of the members of such a combination.—*H*, 7-10-39, 293.

500. Whatever Hitler may ultimately prove to be, we know what Hitlerism has come to mean. It means naked, ruthless force reduced to an exact science and worked with scientific precision. In its effect it becomes almost irresistible.

Hitlerism will never be defeated by counter-Hitlerism. It can only breed superior Hitlerism raised to n[th] degree. What is going on before your eyes is the demonstration of the futility of violence as also of Hitlerism.

What will Hitler do with his victory? Can he digest so much power? Personally he will go as empty-handed as his not very remote predecessor Alexander. For the Germans he will have left not the pleasure of owning a mighty empire but the burden of sustaining its crushing weight. For they will not be able to hold all the conquered nations in perpetual subjection. And I doubt if the Germans of future generations will entertain unadulterated pride in the deeds of which Hitlerism will be deemed responsible. They will honour Herr Hitler as a genius, as a brave man, a matchless organizer and much more. But I should hope that the Germans of the future will have learnt the art of discrimination even about their heroes. Anyway I think it will be allowed that all the blood that has been spilled by Hitler has added not a millionth part of an inch to the world's moral stature.

As against this imagine the state of Europe today if the Czechs, the Poles, the Norwegians, the French and the English had all said to Hitler: 'You need not make your scientific preparation for destruction. We will meet your violence with non-violence. You will therefore be able to destroy our non-violent army without

---

[5] [A weapon used by police for riot control. Ed.]

tanks, battleships and airships.' It may be retorted that the only difference would be that Hitler would have got without fighting what he has gained after a bloody fight. Exactly. The history of Europe would then have been written differently. Possession might (but only might) have been taken under non-violent resistance, as it has been taken now after perpetration of untold barbarities. Under non-violence, only those would have been killed who had trained themselves to be killed, if need be, but without killing anyone and without bearing malice towards anybody. I dare say that in that case Europe would have added several inches to its moral stature. And in the end I expect it is moral worth that will count. All else is dross.—*H*, 22–6–40, 172.

On "Let a Hundred Flowers Blossom"

Mao Tse-tung

Mao Tse-tung (1893-   ) is Chairman of the Communist Party of the People's Republic of China and the leader of some 700 million Chinese. His numerous writings include *New Democracy* (1944), *The Fight for a New China* (1945), and *Quotations from Chairman Mao Tse-tung* (1966).

"Let a hundred flowers blossom, let a hundred schools of thought contend" and "long-term coexistence and mutual supervision"—how did these slogans come to be put forward? They were put forward in the light of China's specific conditions, on the basis of the recognition that various kinds of contradictions still exist in socialist society, and in response to the country's urgent need to speed up its economic and cultural development. Letting a hundred flowers blossom and a hundred schools of thought contend is the policy for promoting the progress of the arts and the sciences and a flourishing socialist culture in our land. Different forms and styles in art should develop freely and different schools in science should contend freely. We think that it is harmful to the growth of art and science if administrative measures are used to impose one particular style of art or school of thought and to ban another. Questions of right and wrong in the arts and sciences should be settled through free discussion in artistic and scientific circles and through practical work in these fields. They should not be settled in summary fashion. A period of trial is often needed to determine whether something is right or wrong. Throughout history, new and correct things have failed at the outset to win recognition from the majority of people and have had to develop by twists and turns in struggle. Often correct and good things have first been regarded not as fragrant flowers but as poisonous weeds. Copernicus' theory of the solar system

From *Five Articles by Chairman Mao Tse-tung,* (Peking: Foreign Language Press, 1968).

and Darwin's theory of evolution were once dismissed as erroneous and had to win through over bitter opposition. Chinese history offers many similar examples. In a socialist society, conditions for the growth of the new are radically different from and far superior to those in the old society. Nevertheless, it still often happens that new, rising forces are held back and rational proposals constricted. Moreover, the growth of new things may be hindered in the absence of deliberate suppression simply through lack of discernment. It is therefore necessary to be careful about questions of right and wrong in the arts and sciences, to encourage free discussion and avoid hasty conclusions. We believe that such an attitude can help to ensure a relatively smooth development of the arts and sciences.

People may ask, since Marxism is accepted as the guiding ideology by the majority of the people in our country, can it be criticized? Certainly it can. Marxism is scientific truth and fears no criticism. If it did, and if it could be overthrown by criticism, it would be worthless. In fact, aren't the idealists criticizing Marxism every day and in every way? Aren't those who harbour bourgeois and petty-bourgeois ideas and do not wish to change—aren't they also criticizing Marxism in every way? Marxists should not be afraid of criticism from any quarter. Quite the contrary, they need to temper and develop themselves and win new positions in the teeth of criticism and in the storm and stress of struggle. Fighting against wrong ideas is like being vaccinated—a man develops greater immunity from disease as a result of vaccination. Plants raised in hot-houses are unlikely to be sturdy. Carrying out the policy of letting a hundred flowers blossom and a hundred schools of thought contend will not weaken but strengthen the leading position of Marxism in the ideological field.

What should our policy be towards non-Marxist ideas? As far as unmistakable counter-revolutionaries and saboteurs of the socialist cause are concerned, the matter is easy: we simply deprive them of their freedom of speech. But incorrect ideas among the people are quite a different matter. Will it do to ban such ideas and deny them any opportunity for expression? Certainly not. It is not only futile but very harmful to use summary methods in dealing with ideological questions among the people, with questions concerned with man's mental world. You may ban the expression of wrong ideas, but the ideas will still be there. On the other hand, if correct ideas are pampered in hot-houses without being exposed to the elements or immunized from disease, they will not win out against erroneous ones. Therefore, it is only by employing the method of discussion, criticism and reasoning that we can really foster correct ideas and overcome wrong ones, and that we can really settle issues.

The Identity and Struggle of the Aspects of a Contradiction

When we understand the universality and the particularity of contradiction, we must proceed to study the problem of the identity and struggle of the aspects of a contradiction.

Identity, unity, coincidence, interpenetration, interpermeation, interdependence (or mutual dependence for existence), interconnection or mutual co-operation—all these different terms mean the same thing and refer to the following two points: first, the existence of each of the two aspects of a contradiction in the process of the development of a thing presupposes the existence of the other aspect, and both aspects coexist in a single entity; second, in given conditions, each of the two contradictory aspects transforms itself into its opposite. This is the meaning of identity.

Lenin said:

Dialectics is the teaching which shows how opposites can be and how they happen to be (how they become) identical—under what conditions they are identical, transforming themselves into one another,—why the human mind should take these opposites not as dead, rigid, but as living, conditional, mobile, transforming themselves into one another.

What does this passage mean?

The contradictory aspects in every process exclude each other, struggle with each other and are in opposition to each other. Without exception, they are contained in the process of development of all things and in all human thought. A simple process contains only a single pair of opposites, while a complex process contains more. And in turn, the pairs of opposites are in contradiction to one another. That is how all things in the objective world and all human thought are constituted and how they are set in motion.

This being so, there is an utter lack of identity or unity. How then can one speak of identity or unity?

The fact is that no contradictory aspect can exist in isolation. Without its opposite aspect, each loses the condition for its existence. Just think, can any one contradictory aspect of a thing or of a concept in the human mind exist independently? Without life, there would be no death; without death, there would be no life. Without "above," there would be no "below;" without "below," there would be no "above." Without misfortune, there would be no good fortune: without good fortune, there would be no misfortune. Without facility, there would no difficulty; without difficulty, there would be no facility. Without landlords, there would be no tenant-peasants; without tenant-peasants, there would be no landlords. Without the bourgeoisie, there would be no proletariat; without the proletariat, there would be no bourgeoisie, Without imperialist oppression of nations, there would be no colonies or semi-colonies; without colonies or

From *Five Articles by Chairman Mao Tse-tung* (Peking: Foreign Language Press, 1968).

semi-colonies, there would be no imperialist oppression of nations. It is so with all opposites; in given conditions, on the one hand they are opposed to each other, and on the other they are interconnected, interpenetrating, interpermeating and interdependent, and this character is described as identity. In given conditions, all contradictory aspects possess the character of non-identity and hence are described as being in contradiction. But they also possess the character of identity and hence are interconnected. This is what Lenin means when he says that dialectics studies "how *opposites* can be . . . *identical*." How then can they be identical? Because each is the condition of the other's existence. This is the first meaning of identity.

But is it enough to say merely that each of the contradictory aspects is the condition for the other's existence, that there is identity between them and that consequently they can coexist in a single entity? No, it is not. The matter does not end with their dependence on each other for their existence; what is more important is their transformation into each other. That is to say, in given conditions, each of the contradictory aspects within a thing transforms itself into its opposite, changes its position to that of its opposite. This is the second meaning of the identity of contradiction.

Why is there identity here, too? You see, by means of revolution the proletariat, at one time the ruled, is transformed into the ruler, while the bourgeoisis, the erstwhile ruler, is transformed into the ruled and changes its position to that originally occupied by its opposite.

On New Democracy

Thus the numerous types of state system in the world can be reduced to three basic kinds according to the class character of their political power: (1) republics under bourgeois dictatorship; (2) republics under the dictatorship of the proletariat; and (3) republics under the joint dictatorship of several revolutionary classes.

The first kind comprises the old democratic states. To-day, after the outbreak of the second imperalist war, there is hardly a trace of democracy in many of the capitalist countries, which have come or are coming under the bloody militarist dictatorship of the bourgeoisie. Certain countries under the joint dictatorship of the landlords and the bourgeoisie can be grouped with this kind.

The second kind exists in the Soviet Union, and the conditions for its birth are ripening in capitalist countries. In the future, it will be the dominant form throughout the world for a certain period.

The third kind is the transitional form of state to be adopted in the revolutions of the colonial and semi-colonial countries. Each of these revolutions will necessarily have specific characteristics of its own, but these will be minor variations on a general theme. So long as they are revolutions in colonial or semi-colonial countries, their state and governmental structure will of necessity be basically the same, *i.e.*, a new-democratic state under the joint dictatorship of several anti-imperialist classes. In present-day China, the anti-Japanese united front

From *On New Democracy* (Peking: Foreign Language Press, 1967).

represents the new-democratic state under the joint dictatorship of several anti-imperialist classes. It is anti-Japanese and anti-imperialist; it is also a united front, an alliance of several revolutionary classes.

Communism is at once a complete system of proletarian ideology and a new social system. It is different from any other ideology or social system, and is the most complete, progressive, revolutionary and rational system in human history. The ideological and social system of feudalism has a place only in the museum of history. The ideological and social system of capitalism has also become a museum piece in one part of the world (in the Soviet Union), while in other countries it resembles "a dying person who is sinking fast, like the sun setting beyond the western hills," and will soon be relegated to the museum. The communist ideological and social system alone is full of youth and vitality, sweeping the world with the momentum of an avalanche and the force of a thunderbolt. The introduction of scientific communism into China has opened new vistas for people and has changed the face of the Chinese revolution. Without communism to guide it, China's democratic revolution cannot possibly succeed, let alone move on to the next stage. This is the reason why the bourgeois die-hards are so loudly demanding that communism be "folded up." But it must not be "folded up," for once communism is "folded up," China will be doomed. The whole world today depends on communism for its salvation, and China is no exception. . . .

Combat Liberalism

We stand for active ideological struggle because it is the weapon for ensuring unity within the Party and the revolutionary organizations in the interest of our fight. Every Communist and revolutionary should take up this weapon.

But liberalism rejects ideological struggle and stands for unprincipled peace, thus giving rise to a decadent, philistine attitude and bringing about political degeneration in certain units and individuals in the Party and the revolutionary organizations.

Liberalism manifests itself in various ways.

To let things slide for the sake of peace and friendship when a person has clearly gone wrong, and refrain from principled argument because he is an old acquaintance, a fellow townsman, a schoolmate, a close friend, a loved one, an old colleague or old subordinate. Or to touch on the matter lightly instead of going into it thoroughly, so as to keep on good terms. The result is that both the organization and the individual are harmed. This is one type of liberalism.

To indulge in irresponsible criticism in private instead of actively putting forward one's suggestions to the organization. To say nothing to people to their faces but to gossip behind their backs, or to say nothing at a meeting but to gossip afterwards. To show no regard at all for the principles of collective life but to follow one's own inclination. This is a second type.

To let things drift if they do not affect one personally; to say as little as possible

From *Five Articles by Chairman Mao Tse-tung* (Peking: Foreign Language Press, 1968).

while knowing perfectly well what is wrong, to be worldly wise and play safe and seek only to avoid blame. This is a third type.

Not to obey orders but to give pride of place to one's own opinions. To demand special consideration from the organization but to reject its discipline. This is a fourth type.

To indulge in personal attacks, pick quarrels, vent personal spite or seek revenge instead of entering into an argument and struggling against incorrect views for the sake of unity or progress or getting the work done properly. This is a fifth type.

To hear incorrect views without rebutting them and even to hear counter-revolutionary remarks without reporting them, but instead to take them calmly as if nothing had happened. This is a sixth type.

To be among the masses and fail to conduct propaganda and agitation or speak at meetings or conduct investigations and inquiries among them, and instead to be indifferent to them and show no concern for their well-being, forgetting that one is a Communist and behaving as if one were an ordinary non-Communist. This is a seventh type.

To see someone harming the interests of the masses and yet not feel indignant, or dissuade or stop him or reason with him, but to allow him to continue. This is an eighth type.

To work half-heartedly without a definite plan or direction; to work per-functorily and muddle along—"So long as one remains a monk, one goes on tolling the bell." This is a ninth type.

To regard oneself as having rendered great service to the revolution, to pride oneself on being a veteran, to disdain minor assignments while being quite unequal to major tasks, to be slipshod in work and slack in study. This is a tenth type.

To be aware of one's own mistakes and yet make no attempt to correct them, taking a liberal attitude towards oneself. This is an eleventh type.

We could name more. But these eleven are the principal types.

They are all manifestations of liberalism.

Liberalism is extremely harmful in a revolutionary collective. It is a corrosive which eats away unity, undermines cohesion, causes apathy and creates dissension. It robs the revolutionary ranks of compact organization and strict discipline, prevents policies from being carried through and alienates the Party organizations from the masses which the Party leads. It is an extremely bad tendency.

Liberalism stems from petty-bourgeois selfishness, it places personal interests first and the interests of the revolution second, and this gives rise to ideological, political and organizational liberalism.

People who are liberals look upon the principles of Marxism as abstract dogma. They approve of Marxism, but are not prepared to practise it or to practise it in full; they are not prepared to replace their liberalism by Marxism. These people have their Marxism, but they have their liberalism as well—they talk Marxism but practise liberalism; they apply Marxism to others but liberalism to themselves. They keep both kinds of goods in stock and find a use for each. This is how the minds of certain people work.

Liberalism is a manifestation of opportunism and conflicts fundamentally with Marxism. It is negative and objectively has the effect of helping the enemy; that is why the enemy welcomes its preservation in our midst. Such being its nature, there should be no place for it in the ranks of the revolution.

We must use Marxism, which is positive in spirit, to overcome liberalism, which is negative. A Communist should have largeness of mind and he should be staunch and active, looking upon the interests of the revolution as his very life and subordinating his personal interests to those of the revolution; always and everywhere he should adhere to principle and wage a tireless struggle against all incorrect ideas and actions, so as to consolidate the collective life of the Party and strengthen the ties between the Party and the masses; he should be more concerned about the Party and the masses than about any individual, and more concerned about others than about himself. Only thus can he be considered a Communist.

Freedom Through Dictatorship of the People

Our general subject is the correct handling of contradictions among the people. For convenience's sake, let us discuss it under twelve sub-headings. Although reference will be made to contradictions between ourselves and our enemies, this discussion will center mainly on contradictions among the people.

TWO DIFFERENT TYPES OF CONTRADICTIONS

Never has our country been as united as it is today. The victories of the bourgeois-democratic revolution and the socialist revolution, coupled with our achievements in socialist construction, have rapidly changed the face of old China. Now we see before us an even brighter future. The days of national disunity and turmoil which the people detested have gone forever. Led by the working class and the Communist party, and united as one, our 600 million people are engaged in the great work of building socialism. Unification of the country, unity of the people, and unity among our various nationalities—these are the basic guarantees for the sure triumph of our cause. However, this does not mean that there are no longer any contradictions in our society. It would be naive to imagine that there are no more contradictions. To do so would be to fly in the face of objective reality. We are confronted by two types of social contradictions—contradictions between ourselves and the enemy and contradictions among the people. The two types of contradictions are totally different in nature . . . .

In the conditions existing in China today, what we call contradictions among the people include the following:

Contradictions within the working class, contradictions within the peasantry, contradictions within the intelligentsia, contradictions between the working class and the peasantry, contradictions between the working class and the peasantry on the one hand and the intelligentsia on the other, contradictions between the working class and other sections of the working people on the one hand the national

From *Four Articles by Chairman Mao Tse-tung,* (Peking: Foreign Language Press, 1968).

bourgeoisie on the other, contradictions within the national bourgeoisie, and so forth. Our People's Government is a government that truly represents the interests of the people and serves the people, yet certain contradictions do exist between the Government and the masses. These include contradictions between the interests of the state, collective interests and individual interests; between democracy and centralism; between those in positions of leadership and the led, and contradictions arising from the bureaucratic practices of certain state functionaries in their relations with the masses. All these are contradictions among the people; generally speaking, underlying the contradictions among the people is the basic identity of the interests of the people. . . .

Ours is a people's democratic dictatorship, led by the working class and based on the worker-peasant alliance. What is this dictatorship for? Its first function is to suppress the reactionary classes and elements and those exploiters in the country who range themselves against the socialist revolution, to suppress all those who try to wreck our socialist construction; that is to say, to solve the contradictions between ourselves and the enemy within the country—for instance, to arrest, try and sentence certain counter-revolutionaries, and for a specified period of time deprive landlords and bureaucrat-capitalists of their right to vote and freedom of speech—all this comes within the scope of our dictatorship. To maintain law and order and safeguard the interests of the people, it is likewise necessary to exercise dictatorship over robbers, swindlers, murderers, arsonists, hooligans and other scoundrels who seriously disrupt social order.

The second function of this dictatorship is to protect our country from subversive activities and possible aggression by the external enemy. Should that happen, it is the task of this dictatorship to solve the external contradiction between ourselves and the enemy. The aim of this dictatorship is to protect all our people so that they can work in peace and build China into a socialist country with a modern industry, agriculture, science and culture.

Who is to exercise this dictatorship? Naturally, it must be the working class and the entire people led by it. Dictatorship does not apply in the ranks of the people. The people cannot possibly exercise dictatorship over themselves; nor should one section of them oppress another section. Lawbreaking elements among the people will be dealt with according to law, but this is different in principle from using the dictatorship to suppress enemies of the people. What applies among the people is democratic centralism. Our constitution lays it down that citizens of the People's Republic of China enjoy freedom of speech, of the press, of assembly, of association, of procession, of demonstration, of religious belief and so on. Our constitution also provides that state organs must practice democratic centralism and must rely on the masses, that the personnel of state organs must serve the people. Our socialist democracy is democracy in the widest sense, such as it not to be found in any capitalist country. Our dictatorship is known as the people's democratic dictatorship, led by the working class and based on the worker-peasant alliance. That is to say, democracy operates within the ranks of the people, while the working class, uniting with all those enjoying civil rights, the peasantry in the first place, enforces dictatorship over the reactionary classes and elements and all those who resist social transformation and oppose socialist construction. By civil rights, we mean political freedom and democratic rights.

But this freedom is freedom with leadership, and this democracy is democracy under centralized guidance, not anarchy. Anarchy does not conform to the interests or wishes of the people.

Certain people in our country were delighted when the Hungarian events took place. They hoped that something similar would happen in China, that thousands upon thousands of people would demonstrate in the streets against the People's Government. Such hopes ran counter to the interests of the masses and therefore could not possibly get their support. In Hungary, a section of the people deceived by domestic and foreign counter-revolutionaries made the mistake of resorting to acts of violence against the People's Government, with the result that both the state and the people suffered for it. The damage done to the country's economy in a few weeks of rioting will take a long time to repair.

There were other people in our country who took a wavering attitude toward the Hungarian events because they were ignorant about the actual world situation. They felt that there was too little freedom under our people's democracy and that there was more freedom under Western parliamentary democracy. They ask for the adoption of the two-party system of the West, where one party is in office and the other out of office. But this so-called two-party system is nothing but a means of maintaining the dictatorship of the bourgeoisie; under no circumstances can it safeguard the freedom of the working people. As a matter of fact, freedom and democracy cannot exist in the abstract; they only exist in the concrete.

In a society where there is class struggle the exploiting classes are free to exploit the working people while the working people have no freedom from being exploited; where there is democracy for the bourgeoisie, there can be no democracy for the proletariat and other working people. In some capitalist countries, the Communist parties are allowed to exist legally, but only to the extent that they do not endanger the fundamental interests of the bourgeoisie; beyond that, they are not permitted legal existence.

Those who demand freedom and democracy in the abstract regard democracy as an end and not a means. Democracy sometimes seems to be an end, but it is in fact only a means. Marxism teaches us that democracy is part of the superstructure and belongs to the category of politics. That is to say, in the last analysis is serves the economic base. The same is true of freedom. Both democracy and freedom are relative, not absolute, and they come into being and develop under specific historical circumstances. . . .

This is how things stand today: The turbulent class struggles waged by the masses on a large scale characteristic of the revolutionary periods have, in the main, concluded, but class struggle is not entirely over. While the broad masses of the people welcome the new system, they are not yet quite accustomed to it. Government workers are not sufficiently experienced and should continue to examine and explore ways of dealing with questions relating to specific policies.

In other words, time is needed for our socialist system to grow and consolidate itself, for the masses to get accustomed to the new system, and for Government workers to study and acquire experience. It is imperative that at this juncture we raise the question of distinguishing contradictions among the people from contradictions between ourselves and the enemy, as well as the question of the proper handling of contradictions among the people, so as to rally the people of all nationalities in our country to wage a new battle—the battle against nature—to develop our economy and culture, enable all our people to go through this transition period in a fairly smooth way, make our new system secure, and build up our new state.

Suggested Readings

I. United States

Betts, Robert, *Ideology of Blackness* (Boston, D.C.: Heath & Company, 1969).

Foner, Philip S., Ed., *The Black Panthers Speak* (Philadelphia: J. B. Lippincott Co., 1970).

Hanke, L., *Aristotle and the American Indians* (London: Hollis & Carter, 1959).

Jackson, George, *Soledad Brothers* (New York: Bantam Books, 1968).

Leiden, Carl, and Karl M. Schmitt, *The Politics of Violence* (Englewood Cliffs, N.J.: Prentice-Hall, Inc., 1968).

McEvoy, James, and Abraham Miller, Eds., *Black Power and Student Rebellion* (Belmont, Calif.: Wadsworth Publishing Co., Inc., 1969).

Mason, Philip, *Race Relations* (New York: Oxford University Press, Inc., 1970).

II. Abroad

Aquilor, Luis, *Marxism in Latin America* (New York: Alfred A. Knopf, Inc., 1968).

Debray, Regis, *Revolution in the Revolution* (New York: Grove Press, Inc., 1967).

Fann, K. T., *The Chinese Cultural Revolution* (New York: Grove Press, Inc., 1968).

Fann, K. T., and Donald C. Hodges, Eds., *Readings in U.S. Imperialism* (Boston: Porter Sargent, 1971).

Fanon, F., *The Wretched of the Earth* (London: MacGibbon and Kee, 1965).

Lavan, George, *Che Guevara Speaks* (New York: Grove Press, Inc., 1967).

Marquard, L., *The Peoples and Policies of South Africa*, 2nd ed. (New York: Oxford University Press, Inc., 1960).

Nkrumah, Kwame, *Consciencism* (New York: Modern Reader Paperbacks, 1964).

North, Robert C., *Chinese Communism* (New York: McGraw-Hill Book Company, 1970).

Anarchism, Neoanarchism, and Counterculture

INTRODUCTION

The first concern of anarchists has always been the abolition of the state. There have been advocates of several different means of achieving this end. These means have ranged from the general strike, to the use of terror, assassinations, and so on, to the formation of self-sufficient cooperative communities or communes. All these elements are discussed in this section. The first selection serves as a historical and conceptual introduction to anarchism; the Kropothin selection is both a critique of the state and its authority and the affirmation of cooperative or communal institutions.

Anarchism has its contemporary adherents. Most of these adherents form what can be called neoanarchist or countercultural movements. These are discussed in the contributions of Roszak and Lerner. Although anarchism and counterculture do not precisely coincide, Lerner, in his essay, has catalogued the many points of similarity which place the latter in the anarchist tradition. These are, among others, the rejection of mainstream society and culture and the desire to break out, the acceptance of violence as a tactic, the repudiation of majoritarianism, extreme moral individualism, a radical critique of the technological state, asceticism, and the move toward primitive communal simplicity in life style. The counterculture, in Lerner's eyes, consists of a convergence of life styles, ideas, and political patterns of behavior which have their roots in classical anarchism and which form a common opposition to establishment culture and its values. Whereas the older forms of anarchism tended to be antitheoretical, the new movement tends to reject "formal ideologies" even more explicitly. Its orientation must be extracted from its art and from its actions.

We can see that a central theme of all anarchist ideology prevails among contemporary representatives. It is a preoccupation with individualism Also stressed in the new movement, as well as the old, is a disinterest in systematic

437

political theory and ideology—which itself takes on the form of a nonprogrammatic ideology—and a deemphasis on political organization. Finally, there is the belief that the revolution must come in men's minds before it can be realized in a new social order. "There will be a qualitative transformation, a new living, life giving revelation, a new heaven and a new earth, a young and mighty world. . . ."

Since programmatic Marxism has failed to produce a free and cooperative society in the West and since it has led to the dictatorship of the party and state socialism in Eastern Europe, the Anarchist typically calls for a return to political first principles. This involves the rejection of Marxist ideology and practice, a greater commitment to individuality and self-reliance, but a disavowal of "possessive individualism and competition."

The final defense of anarchism must be that it is not a closed ideological system. It can grow and is flexible in terms of practice and in meeting human needs. According to its advocates, it is superior to the dominant form of socialist ideology (Marxism-Leninism) because it is freer to innovate. These are the basic ideological values that motivated the early anarchists and they equally sustain the neoanarchist and counterculturalist movements of the present.

The Theory of Anarchism
Irving Louis Horowitz

Irving Louis Horowitz (1929-   ) is Professor of Sociology of Rutgers University. He is the author of many books, including *Claude Helvetius* (1954) and *Radicalism and the Revolt Against Reason* (1961). He also edited *Power, Politics and People and Sociology and Pragmatism* (1969), *The New Sociology*; and *The Anarchists* (1964).

NATURAL MAN AND POLITICAL MAN

From its historical beginnings a linguistic ambiguity resides in what the term "anarchism" signifies. The ambiguity is not exclusively a failing of language. It is a consequence of the claims and counterclaims, currents and crosscurrents that necessarily plague a social movement dedicated to "propaganda of the deed" and "scientific liberation from political myth" simultaneously. The anarchists are theorists and terrorists, moralists and deviants, and above all, political and anti-political.

If we examine the matter from a purely definitional viewpoint, we find the concept of anarchy raising up two contrasting visions. On one hand, it describes a negative condition, that which is unruly or disorganized, that which is not controlled or controllable. Sociologists might say that a condition of anarchy prevails when any event is unstructured or lacking in norms, such as spontaneous crowd behavior. These negative connotations of anarchism have penetrated the scientific literature no less than the popular literature. Nonetheless, there is also a popular positive notion of anarchy as conscious rebellion. What is entailed is a view of anarchy as "un-rule" because normal rule systems are unnecessary and superfluous in the governing of normal men. The phenomenon of altruism, or self-sacrifice of personal ambitions, indicates that spontaneous behavior is not synonymous with irrational behavior. We are thus confronted with a negative concept of anarchy as a condition of unruliness in contrast to a positive view of anarchy as the superfluity of rules.

Anarchist negation is embodied by an event, or an agency of events, such as the group, which rejects external pressures in the form of adjustment to a context of prevailing norms or superimposed rules. Conversely, positive anarchism, anarchy as affirmation, means the "internalization" of rules to such a high degree as to do away with the need for external constraint altogether. This ambiguity in anarchism has as its theoretical underpinning an idealization of natural man in contrast and in opposition to civilized man.

One of the confusions, at least, is not so much the work of anarchism as of the commentators on anarchism who consider it to be exclusively a historical movement or a political organism. Some historians see the demise of anarchism in 1914, or with the absorption of anarchist ideals by social reformers and the awakening of "social conscience" in the middle classes.[1] Others consider anarchist ideas to have been absorbed by mass union and political movements.[2] And still others place the final death agony of anarchism in 1939, with the collapse of the Spanish Republic.[3] What seems to bind the historical school is a consensus that, however fuzzy the beginnings of anarchism might have been, there is no question about its definite terminal point. The plain truth is that as a historical force, anarchism never had much of a reality. When Bakunin spoke of three thousand anarchists in Lyons, he considered this an extraordinary achievement. And even in Republican Spain, the anarchist "organization," *Federación Anarquista Ibérica*, could claim only a fractional (and factional) membership.

What characteristically distinguishes anarchism from other radical movements is precisely the low premium placed on immediate political success, and the high premium placed on the fashioning of a "new man" in the womb of the old society. The great Italian anarchist, Errico Malatesta, who bridges 19th- and 20th-century European thought as few of his peers did, put the matter directly:

Our belief is that the only way of emancipation and of progress is that all shall have the liberty and the means of advocating and putting into practice their ideas—that is to say, anarchy. Thus, the more advanced minorities will persuade and draw after them the more backward by the force of reason and example.[4]

The classical anarchists, Bakunin, Malatesta, Sorel, Kropotkin, have a shared consensus in anarchism as a "way of life" rather than as a "view of the future."

[1] Barbara W. Tuchman, "The Anarchists," *The Atlantic.* Vol. 211, No. 5 (May, 1963), pp. 91-110.
[2] G. D. H. Cole, *Socialist Thought: Marxism and Anarchism, 1850-1890.* London: Macmillan & Co. Ltd., 1954, pp. 315-60.
[3] George Woodcock, *Anarchism: A History of Libertarian Ideas and Movements.* Cleveland and New York: The World Publishing Co., 1962, esp. pp. 393-8.
[4] Errico Malatesta, in *Le Réveil* (1906), as quoted in G. D. H. Cole, *op. cit.*, pp. 356-7.

What is offered is a belief in "natural man" as more fundamental and historically prior to "political man."

Civilization is viewed as a series of impediments and obstructions preventing the natural man from realizing himself. This represents an inversion of Hobbes' doctrine of the "war of every man against every man." In Hobbes, the Leviathan exists for the exclusive purpose of curbing "the solitary, poor, nasty, brutish, and short" character of natural man. From the anarchist standpoint, Rousseau's doctrine of the natural goodness of man is only a partial solution to the problems presented in Hobbes' view of human nature. For whether man is "good" or "brutish" is less important to the anarchist than what men do to preserve their inner core. Rousseau shares with the power theorists the idea that self-preservation requires men to contract out their private rights. The Rousseau paradox is that to gain survival entails a loss of humanity. Rights are swallowed up by obligations. The State absorbs Civil society. Natural man is outflanked and outmaneuvered by society.

The anarchist rebuttal to this line of reasoning is that to make a contract, which is an involuntary act to begin with, is really to compromise the natural man. If man is really good, then the purpose of life, in contrast to the purpose of politics, ought to be the restoration of the natural condition of human *relations* at whatever level of human *development* thus far achieved. This is not exclusively a matter of internalizing felt needs, but no less, a form of shedding that which is superfluous and unnecessary. Intrinsic to anarchism is an asceticism and an ascetic mood. One finds the anarchist as a historical figure to be a person very close to "natural" values and "fundamental" living conditions. Their attitudes toward matters of food, shelter, sexuality, and the generalized expression of human needs in the social economy are simply that all needs can be satisfied once the "natural laws of society" shed the impediments of civilization. This sublime faith in the natural in contrast to the social accounts to a considerable degree for the central peculiarity of anarchism—the absence of a well worked-out commitment to economic development.

Precisely because economics in its advanced form must necessarily cope with problems of affluence, consumer and producer demands, distribution of goods, allocation of natural resources, etc., the anarchist tends to consider economic prognostication as catering to both the impossible (because prediction is unfeasible for future social systems) and the unnecessary (since any "rational" economy would center on "production for use"). Even in its specifically economic form, such as in the work of Pierre Joseph Proudhon, anarchism makes little attempt to chart the contours of a rational economy. Proudhon's critique of property relations is everything Marx said it was: abstract, grandiose in statement, and rhetorical in content. Piecework is described as the "deprivation of the soul," machinery becomes the "protest against homicidal labor," and economic history as such becomes a "sequence of ideas."[5] Even those later figures, like Bakunin and Kropotkin, who accepted the main contours of socialist economics, did so more as an instrument by which the restoration of the feudal workshop could be achieved rather than as a guide to the study of economic realities.

There is a perennial tension between the naturalistic character of anarchism and

[5] Pierre Joseph Proudhon, *What Is Property: An Inquiry into the Principles of Right and of Government*. New York: Humboldt Publishing Co., 1891; and *Système des contradictions économiques ou philosophie de la misère*. Paris: Guillaumin, 1846. In contrast, see the critique of Karl Marx, *The Poverty of Philosophy* (1847). New York: International Publishers, 1935.

its emergent participation in socialist currents. On frankly moral grounds the anarchists opposed the stratification of men into classes. Social classes violate the natural equality of men in their psychological-biological characteristics. Anarchism tends to distinguish wage laborers from factory owners in terms of the moral properties of work rather than the alienative features of class relations. A strong pietistic religious element is present: work is good, idleness is evil; the poor are noble while the rich are sinful. Men are naturally equal, while they are socially stratified. Real and legitimate differences are obscured by social position and by family property. Anarchist man sees differences in terms of the quality of mind of each person, the degree of self-realization and self-fulfillment, and the extent of socialization. Capitalist man is the accommodating man: solicitous when profits are at stake, brutal when workers are at stake, cruel when the social system is at stake.

The anarchist image of life is in terms of a moral drama, a drama in which individuals are pitted against social systems. It is little wonder, then, that the anarchist has an apocalyptic attitude toward social classes. Abolish class relations, and the natural man will come to fructification. This attitude toward classes is comparable to the approach that nudists take to clothing. Eliminate clothing, and all people will immediately perceive the absurdity of clothing, as well as its harmful psychological by-products, such as repression and guilt. So, too, runs the anarchist argument. Abolish social classes, and the absurdity of class distinctions will immediately become manifest. The absurd by-products of the class system—oppression of the poor by the rich, impoverishment of the many on behalf of the few, etc.—will give way to the new dawning. Just how this process will install an economy of abundance and distributive justice becomes a matter for future generations to discuss. Just as it would be metaphysics to discuss the problems that would occur in a world of naked people, so too, the anarchist holds the socialists to be metaphysicians for attempting to anticipate the problems as well as the contours of a society without exploitation and an economy without classes.

This tension between "naturalism" and "socialism" is also present in the anarchist stance toward politics. The whole world of politics is itself an embodiment of authority, of arbitrary power. At some level the definition of politics in necessarily linked to the exercise or restraint of power. The whole concept of politics has as its perfect social expression superordination and subordination, just as in the previous illustration the whole notion of economics has as its basis, mastery and slavery. Once again then, the reason the anarchists take an antipolitical position, not simply against certain forms of politics, but against the content of politics as such, is that the notion of superordination and subordination, resting as it does on a social concept to justify power, is a superfluity, a civilized manner for expressing the social fact of inequality. The point of view of most anarchists is that the doctrine of self-interest arises only at that point when the interests of society are schismatic or bifurcated. When it is seen or felt that the self is something other than the society, only at that point does hedonism become a force.

The political doctrines of anarchism are totalistic. They are anti-egoistic, because egoism is an expression of civilization. It is antifatalist, because fatalism violates individual liberty. The propensity of natural man is voluntary association based on the practice of mutual aid. The concept of mutual aid, while sharing many properties of altruism, differs from the latter since altruism implies conscious surrender of self in an egotistical milieu. Mutual aid is socially systematized.

There is no longer any psychology of egotism in anarchist society, and therefore altruism cannot have a psychological base. One wouldn't perform an altruistic act. One performs social acts at all levels—whether in defense of self or on behalf of other persons. Psychology as a division among men will be broken down in the anarchist world. There will then be a possibility of a truly human association that at the same time overcomes the distinction between the public and the private.

This utilitarian "mutual aid" aspect of anarchism is dominant and fully expressed from Godwin to Tolstoy. It was particularly suitable as the ultimate expression of the plight of the modern peasantry. Collectivist anarchism departs from this social stress to the idea of the individual's war against the state as a form of self-preservation. The ever-enlarged scope of bureaucratic domination has led anarchism to emphasize the need to survive under the pressures and censures of society.

What characterizes contemporary anarchism, as contrasted with earlier forms, is the highly personal nature of the revolt against authority. There might very well be a sense in which the anarchism of intellectuals is a very special variant of anarchism. It possesses three distinguishing qualities: (1) emphasis on individual responses, on the "politics of truth"; (2) rejection of professionalism and departmental academicism; and (3) belief in the sanctity of the "private life." In the intellectual's powerful sense of the distinction between public and private, which D. H. Lawrence in particular has pointed out, and the image of the fighting private intellectual there is perhaps an anomic kind of anarchism, if one may speak of *anomie* in this connection.

In its classical model, the notion of the fighting romantic against the world is antithetical to anarchism as a theory, but quite in keeping with the "deviant" psychological characteristics of the anarchists as people. The anarchist as a person tends to be highly deviant, closely allied to the criminal sectors in European society, and to the *lumpenproletariat* in the United States, the tramps, hoboes, and rummies. While the anarchist does not define himself as a criminal (criminality is seen as a form of lower-class egotism—excusable rather than practicable) he does not consider the criminal, as does the bourgeois, to be "an enemy of society." Indeed, they have close dealings since anarchists have at times hired out as professional criminals to commit assassinations and bank robberies in Italy and Spain. But the anarchist who steals does not do so for his own self-interest. He carefully allocates funds making very sure that nothing is used for creature comforts. He will kill, but he is very careful not to harm anyone who is innocent from the viewpoint of the class struggle. He will cajole, but not for the purpose of keeping the reigns of power. The goal, however ill-defined, is all-important. And the means used in its attainment (the overthrow of the state and of the class system) are moral in virtue of these aims. Therefore, the means used are conditioned only by the question of efficiency of realizing the ends. No ethic is attached to them. Clearly, the anarchist is not a pragmatist. He does not accept the idea that there is a means-ends continuum. The purposes of violence determine its good or its evil character—and not the fact of violence as such. The dichotomization gives to the anarchist the appearance of criminality, while distinguishing his essence. It also provides for a life-style that is often awkward and difficult to manage—since he must work with egotists while maintaining his altruism; and cooperate with derelicts while urging a "new man" theory of social change; and he must oppose totalitarianism in theory while maintaining authoritarian personality traits in his personal habits and behavior.

The fundamental development of anarchism as a social agency for change and as an intellectual mood reached full expression in the nineteenth century. It is not inconsequential to take note of the philosophical climate and technological level surrounding this development. The philosophical point of view underlying classical anarchism is not so much Hegel's dialectics as it was Kant's ethics. The only true morality that the anarchist would recognize is one in which there would no longer be a distinction between what is done for one's self and what is done for others.

A derivative of this is the antitechnological claims of anarchism. These turn out to be fundamentally petty bourgeois or peasant. The notion of community was very strong in utopian varieties of community life. Small-scale farming and small-scale industry, where there was indeed intimacy and rapport between the people at work, where work itself was an organizing principle and a viable one, were a vital principle of life writ large. This combination of the technology of the small factory and the small farm, combined as it was with this highly rationalistic Kantian image of what a moral man defines the communal obligation to be, reveals the anarchist as antitechnological in his stance just as previously he is described as antipolitical and anti-economic. He is total in his commitment to a social ethic in which the personality is part and parcel of that social view. And the alienation of men from the sources of their labor, and from the machine directly, violates this social ethic. The fact that anarchism in its most distilled form is the idea of the brotherhood of man and the *naturalness* of this equality, any separatist movement, such as nationalism or racialism, that has imaginary pressures from the exploiting strata of every state has to be sharply opposed. The main evil of nationalism is not solely that it breeds wars, but that it does so because nationalism is *unnatural*. Civilization sets up arbitrary differentiations so that national distinctions intensify and exaggerate factors making for conflict: patriotic gore, class animus, racial purity. They are unreal and susceptible to dissolution and alteration. Their only reality derives from the power relations that are caused by class domination and legal rationalization.

The philosophic stance of anarchism is juxtaposed against the power relations of society. Anarchism is a commitment to the idea of nature, to the belief that nature is an "essence," while society is an "accident." It stands in contrast to the idea of existence because the concept of existence, as it has unfolded in both Marxist and Existentialist thought, involves problems of revolution, of change in terms of other men, in terms of a fundamental theory of the redistribution of power, in terms of the redistribution of wealth rather than the notion of wealth as such. So that the difference between socialism and anarchism is primarily a difference between those who would abolish the forms of social relations as they now exist, and those who would abolish the content of all hitherto existing class society. The socialist has ultimate visions of future society through the redistribution of power, property, etc. The anarchist sees any such compromise as stillborn and doomed to perpetuate in new form the same divisions that have riven society historically. For the anarchist, the root of the problem is society; for the socialist, the root of the problem is class. This helps explain, in addition to the fierce personality clashes, the bitterness between socialists and anarchists. Their philosophical and ideological premises differ despite the superficial acceptance by both of a communal economy. It is shallow to say that the difference between anarchists and socialists is tactical, i.e., that socialists would postpone the abolition of the state while the anarchists want to abolish the state now. What underlies this tactical difference are contrasting theories of human nature.

Anarchists regard socialists as corrupted by the political structure since they accept the premises of the bourgeois state: order, constitutional limits, parliamentary procedure, etc., in order to wrest power. By failing to destroy power, they are corrupted by it and perpetuate the state they are pledged to overthrow. The anarchist assumption is that to better civilization is a subtle form of corruption, of self-delusion. What is required is abolition, not improvement. Not even the word "revolution" really encompasses the anarchist idea. Revolution is the idea of the radical change in the forms of life. The anarchist notion of abolition is more profoundly radical in its implications because of the distinctions between contamination through the acceptance of the forms of civilization and regeneration through the breaking of such civilized forms. The socialist changes society, leaving inherited civilization intact. He reforms its worst abuses. His arguments are for a higher development of civilization. The anarchist rejects the inherently constricting and corrupting nature of civilization and demands total reconstruction of the human condition. It means to annihilate sociological, economic, and political features of human life that we have come to consider fixed. The practical socialist claims no more than the right to humanize and equalize the power structure. The impractical anarchist claims to do no less than liquidate State power as such.

Law and Authority
Peter Kropotkin

Peter Kropotkin (1842-1921) was a Russian revolutionary anarchist who escaped from prison in Russia and lived mainly in England. He wrote extensive defenses of anarchism. After the Revolution he returned to Russia but was greatly disturbed by the "law and authority" that he saw developing there.

I

"When ignorance reigns in society and disorder in the minds of men, laws are multiplied, legislation is expected to do everything, and each fresh law being a fresh miscalculation, men are continually led to demand from it what can proceed only from themselves, from their own education and their own morality." It is no revolutionist who says this, not even a reformer. It is the jurist, Dalloy, author of the collection of French law known as *Répertoire de la Legislation*. And yet, though these lines were written by a man who was himself a maker and admirer of law, they perfectly represent the abnormal condition of our society.

In existing States a fresh law is looked upon as a remedy for evil. Instead of themselves altering what is bad, people begin by demanding a *law* to alter it. If the road between two villages is impassable, the peasant says:—"There should be a law

First published as a pamphlet from Freedom Press, London, 1886.

about parish roads." If a park-keeper takes advantage of the want of spirit in those who follow him with servile observance and insults one of them, the insulted man says, "There should be a law to enjoin more politeness upon park-keepers." If there is stagnation in agriculture or commerce, the husbandman, cattle-breeder, or corn speculator argues, "It is protective legislation we require." Down to the old clothesman there is not one who does not demand a law to protect his own little trade. If the employer lowers wages or increases the hours of labor, the politician in embryo exclaims, "We must have a law to put all that to rights." In short, a law everywhere and for everything! A law about fashions, a law about mad dogs, a law about virtue, a law to put a stop to all the vices and all the evils which result from human indolence and cowardice.

We are so perverted by an education which from infancy seeks to kill in us the spirit of revolt, and to develop that of submission to authority; we are so perverted by this existence under the ferrule of a law, which regulates every event in life—our birth, our education, our development, our love, our friendship—that, if this state of things continues, we shall lose all initiative, all habit of thinking for ourselves. Our society seems no longer able to understand that it is possible to exist otherwise than under the reign of law, elaborated by a representative government and administered by a handful of rulers. And even when it has gone so far as to emancipate itself from the thralldom, its first care has been to reconstitute it immediately. "The Year 1 of Liberty" has never lasted more than a day, for after proclaiming it men put themselves the very next morning under the yoke of law and authority.

Indeed, for some thousands of years, those who govern us have done nothing but ring the changes upon "Respect for law, obedience to authority." This is the moral atmosphere in which parents bring up their children, and school only serves to confirm the impression. Cleverly assorted scraps of spurious science are inculcated upon the children to prove necessity of law; obedience to the law is made a religion; moral goodness and the law of the masters are fused into one and the same divinity. The historical hero of the schoolroom is the man who obeys the law, and defends it against rebels.

Later when we enter upon public life, society and literature, impressing us day by day and hour by hour as the water-drop hollows the stone, continue to inculcate the same prejudice. Books of history, of political science, of social economy, are stuffed with this respect for law. Even the physical sciences have been pressed into the service by introducing artificial modes of expression, borrowed from theology and arbitrary power, into knowledge which is purely the result of observation. Thus our intelligence is successfully befogged, and always to maintain our respect for law. The same work is done by newspapers. They have not an article which does not preach respect for law, even where the third page proves every day the imbecility of that law, and shows how it is dragged through every variety of mud and filth by those charged with its administration. Servility before the law has become a virtue, and I doubt if there was ever even a revolutionist who did not begin in his youth as the defender of law against what is generally called "abuses," although these last are inevitable consequences of the law itself. . . .

To understand this [worship of law], we must transport ourselves in imagination into the eighteenth century. Our hearts must have ached at the story of the atrocities committed by the all-powerful nobles of that time upon the men and women of the people before we can understand what must have been the magic influence upon the peasant's mind of the words, "Equality before the law, obedience to the law without distinction of birth or fortune." He who until then had been treated more cruelly than a beast, he who had never had any rights, he who had never obtained justice against the most revolting actions on the part of a noble, unless in revenge he killed him and was hanged—he saw himself recognized by this maxim, at least in theory, at least with regard to his personal rights, as the equal of his lord. Whatever this law might be, it promised to affect lord and peasant alike; it prolaimed the equality of rich and poor before the judge. The promise was a lie, and to-day we know it; but at that period it was an advance, a homage to justice, as hypocrisy is a homage rendered to truth. This is the reason that when the saviors of the menaced middle class (the Robespierres and the Dantons) took their stand upon the writings of the Rousseaus and the Voltaires, and proclaimed "respect for law, the same for every man," the people accepted the compromise; for their revolutionary impetus had already spent its force in the contest with a foe whose ranks drew closer day by day; they bowed their neck beneath the yoke of law to save themselves from the arbitrary power of their lords.

The middle class has ever since continued to make the most of this maxim, which with another principle, that of representative government, sums up the whole philosophy of the bourgeois age, the nineteenth century. It has preached this doctrine in its schools, it has propagated it in its writings, it has moulded its art and science to the same purpose, it has thrust its beliefs into every hole and corner—like a pious Englishwoman, who slips tracts under the door—and it has done all this so successfully that today we behold the issue in the detestable fact that men who long for freedom begin the attempt to obtain it by entreating their masters to be kind enough to protect them by modifying the laws which these masters themselves have created!

But times and tempers are changed. Rebels are everywhere to be found who no longer wish to obey the law without knowing whence it comes, what are its uses, and whither arises the obligation to submit to it, and the reverence with which it is encompassed. The rebels of our day are criticizing the very foundations of society which have hitherto been held sacred, and first and foremost amongst them that fetish, law.

The critics analyze the sources of law, and find there either a god, product of the terrors of the savage, and stupid, paltry and malicious as the priests who vouch for its supernatural origin, or else, bloodshed, conquest by fire and sword. They study the characteristics of law, and instead of perpetual growth corresponding to that of the human race, they find its distinctive traits to be immobility, a tendency to crystallize what should be modified and developed day by day. They ask how law has been maintained, and in its service they see the atrocities of Byzantinism, the cruelties of the inquisition, the tortures of the middle ages, living flesh torn by the lash of the executioner, chains, clubs, axes, the gloomy dungeons of prisons, agony, curses, and tears. In our own days they see, as before, the axe, the cord, the rifle, the prison; on the one hand, the brutalized prisoner, reduced to the condition of a caged beast by the debasement of his whole moral being, and on the other, the judge, stripped of every feeling which does honor to human nature, living like a visionary in a world of legal fictions, revelling in the infliction of imprisonment and death, without even suspecting, in the cold malignity of his madness, the abyss of degradation into which he has himself fallen before the eyes of those whom he condemns.

They see a race of law-makers legislating without knowing what their laws are about; today voting a law on the sanitation of towns, without the faintest notion of hygiene, tomorrow making regulations for the armament of troops, without so much as understanding a gun; making laws about teaching and education without ever having given a lesson of any sort; or even an honest education to their own children; legislating at random in all directions, but never forgetting the penalties to be meted out to ragamuffins, the prison and the galleys, which are to be the portion of men a thousand times less immoral than these legislators themselves.

Finally, they see the jailer on the way to lose all human feeling, the detective trained as a blood-hound, the police spy despising himself; "informing," metamorphosed into a virtue; corruption, erected into a system; all the vices, all the evil qualities of mankind countenanced and cultivated to insure the triumph of law.

All this we see, and, therefore, instead of inanely repeating the old formula, "Respect the law," we say, "Despise law and all its attributes!" In place of the cowardly phrase, "Obey the law," our cry is "Revolt against all laws!"

Only compare the misdeeds accomplished in the name of each law with the good it has been able to effect, and weigh carefully both good and evil, and you will see if we are right.

II

Relatively speaking, law is a product of modern times. For ages and ages mankind lived without any written law, even that graved in symbols upon the entrance stones of a temple. During that period, human relations were simply regulated by customs, habits and usages, made sacred by constant repetition, and acquired by each person in childhood, exactly as he learned how to obtain his food by hunting, cattle-rearing or agriculture.

All human societies have passed through this primitive phase, and to this day a large proportion of mankind have no written law. Every tribe has its own manners and customs; customary law, as the jurists say. It has social habits, and that suffices to maintain cordial relations between the inhabitants of the village, the members of the tribe or community. . . .

Two distinctly marked currents of custom are revealed by analysis of the usages of primitive people.

As man does not live in a solitary state, habits and feelings develop within him which are useful for the preservation of society and the propagation of the race. Without social feelings and usages, life in common would have been absolutely impossible. It is not law which has established them; they are anterior to all law. Neither is it religion which has ordained them; they are anterior to all religions. They are found amongst all animals living in society. They are spontaneously developed by the very nature of things, like those habits in animals which men call instinct. They spring from a process of evolution, which is useful, and, indeed, necessary, to keep society together in the struggle it is forced to maintain for existence. Savages end by no longer eating one another because they find it in the long run more advantageous to devote themselves to some sort of cultivation than to enjoy the pleasure of feasting upon the flesh of an aged relative once a year. Many travelers have depicted the manners of absolutely independent tribes, where laws and chiefs are unknown, but where the members of the tribe have given up stabbing one another in every dispute, because the habit of living in society has ended by developing certain feelings of fraternity and oneness of interest, and they prefer appealing to a third person to settle their differences. The hospitality of primitive peoples, respect for human life, the sense of reciprocal obligation, compassion for the weak, courage, extending even to the sacrifice of self for others which is first learnt for the sake of children and friends, and later for that of members of the same community—all these qualities are developed in man anterior to all law, independently of all religion, as in the case of the social animals. Such feelings and practices are the inevitable results of social life. Without being, as say priests and metaphysicians, inherent in man, such qualities are the consequence of life in common.

But side by side with these customs, necessary to the life of societies and the preservation of the race, other desires, other passions, and therefore other habits and customs, are evolved in human association. The desire to dominate others and impose one's own will upon them; the desire to seize upon the products of the labor of a neighboring tribe; the desire to surround oneself with comforts without producing anything, while slaves provide their master with the means of procuring every sort of pleasure and luxury—these selfish, personal desires give rise to another current of habits and customs. The priest and the warrior, the charlatan who makes a profit out of superstition, and after freeing himself from the fear of the devil cultivates it in others; and the bully, who procures the invasion and pillage of his neighbors that he may return laden with booty and followed by slaves. These two, hand in hand, have succeeded in imposing upon primitive society customs advantageous to both of them, but tending to perpetuate their domination of the masses. Here profiting by the indolence, the fears, the inertia of the crowd, and thanks to the continual repetition of the same acts, they have permanently established customs which have become a solid basis for their own domination.

For this purpose, they would have made use, in the first place, of that tendency to run in a groove, so highly developed in mankind. In children and all savages it attains striking proportions, and it may also be observed in animals. Man, when he is at all superstitious, is always afraid to introduce any sort of change into existing conditions; he generally venerates what is ancient. "Our fathers did so and so; they got on pretty well; they brought you up; they were not unhappy; do the same!" the old say to the young every time the latter wish to alter things. The unknown frightens them, they prefer to cling to the past even when that past represents poverty, oppression and slavery.

It may even be said that the more miserable a man is, the more he dreads every sort of change, lest it may make him more wretched still. Some ray of hope, a few scraps of comfort, must penetrate his gloomy abode before he can begin to desire better things, to criticize the old ways of living, and prepare to imperil them for the sake of bringing about a change. So long as he is not imbued with hope, so long as he is not freed from the tutelage of those who utilize his superstition and his fears, he prefers remaining in his former position. If the young desire any change, the old raise a cry of alarm against the innovators. Some savages would rather die than transgress the customs of their country because they have been told from childhood that the least infraction of established routine would bring ill-luck and ruin the whole tribe. Even in the present day, what numbers of politicians, economists, and would-be revolutionists act under the same impression, and cling to a vanishing past. How many care only to seek for precedents. How many fiery innovators are mere copyists of bygone revolutions.

The spirit of routine, originating in superstition, indolence, and cowardice, has in all times been the mainstay of oppression. In primitive human societies it was cleverly turned to account by priests and military chiefs. They perpetuated customs useful only to themselves, and succeeded in imposing them on the whole tribe. So long as this conservative spirit could be exploited so as to assure the chief in his encroachments upon individual liberty, so long as the only inequalities between men were not the work of nature, and these were not increased a hundred-fold by the concentration of power and wealth, there was no need for law and the formidable paraphernalia of tribunals and ever-augmenting penalties to enforce it.

But as society became more and more divided into two hostile classes, one seeking to establish its domination, the other struggling to escape, the strife began. Now the conqueror was in a hurry to secure the results of his actions in a permanent form, he tried to place them beyond question, to make them holy and venerable by every means in his power. Law made its appearance under the sanction of the priest, and the warrior's club was placed at its service. Its office was to render immutable such customs as were to the advantage of the dominant minority. Military authority undertook to ensure obedience. This new function was a fresh guarantee to the power of the warrior; now he had not only mere brute force at his service; he was the defender of law.

If law, however, presented nothing but a collection of prescriptions serviceable to rulers, it would find some difficulty in insuring acceptance and obedience. Well, the legislators confounded in one code the two currents of custom of which we have just been speaking, the maxims which represent principles or morality and social union wrought out as a result of life in common, and the mandates which are meant to ensure external existence to inequality. Customs, absolutely essential to the very being of society, are, in the code, cleverly intermingled with usages imposed by the ruling caste, and both claim equal respect from the crowd. "Do not kill," says the code, and hastens to add, "And pay tithes to the priest." "Do not steal," says the code, and immediately after, "He who refuses to pay taxes, shall have his hand struck off."

Such was law; and it has maintained its two-fold character to this day. Its origin is the desire of the ruling class to give permanence to customs imposed by themselves for their own advantage. Its character is the skillful commingling of customs useful to society, customs which have no need of law to insure respect, with other customs useful only to rulers, injurious to the mass of the people, and maintained only by the fear of punishment.

Like individual capital, which was born of fraud and violence and developed under the auspices of authority, law has no title to the respect of men. Born of violence and superstition, and established in the interests of consumer, priest and rich exploiter, it must be utterly destroyed on the day when the people desire to break their chains. . . .

III

. . . The great [French] Revolution began the demolition of this framework of law, bequeathed to us by feudalism and royalty. But after having demolished some portions of the ancient edifice, the Revolution delivered over the power of law-making to the bourgeoisie, who, in their turn, began to raise a fresh framework of laws intended to maintain and perpetuate middle-class domination among the masses. Their parliament makes laws right and left, and mountains of law accumulate with frightful rapidity. But what *are* all these laws at bottom?

The major portion have but one object—to protect private property, i.e., wealth acquired by the exploitations of man by man. Their aim is to open out to capital fresh fields for exploitation, and to sanction the new forms which that exploitation continually assumes, as capital swallows up another branch of human activity, railways, telegraphs, electric light, chemical industries, the expression of man's thought in literature and science, etc. The object of the rest of these laws is fundamentally the same. They exist to keep up the machinery of government which serves to secure to capital the exploitation and monopoly of the wealth produced. Magistrature, police, army, public instruction, finance, all serve one God—capital; all have but one object—to facilitate the exploitation of the worker by the capitalist. Analyze all the laws passed and you will find nothing but this.

The protection of the person, which is put forward as the true mission of law, occupies an imperceptible space among them, for, in existing society, assaults upon the person directly dictated by hatred and brutality tend to disappear. Nowadays, if anyone is murdered, it is generally for the sake of robbing him; rarely because of personal vengeance. But if this class of crimes and misdemeanors is continually diminishing, we certainly do not owe the change to legislation. It is due to the growth of humanitarianism in our societies, to our increasingly social habits rather than to the prescriptions of our laws. Repeal tomorrow every law dealing with the protection of the person, and tomorrow stop all proceedings for assault, and the number of attempts dictated by personal vengeance and by brutality would not be augmented by one single instance.

It will perhaps be objected that during the last fifty years, a good many liberal laws have been enacted. But, if these laws are analyzed, it will be discovered that this liberal legislation consists in the repeal of the laws bequeathed to us by the barbarism of preceding centuries. Every liberal law, every radical program, may be summed up in these words,—abolition of laws grown irksome to the middle-class itself, and return and extension to all citizens of liberties enjoyed by the townships of the twelfth century. The abolition of capital punishment, trial by jury for all "crimes" (there was a more liberal jury in the twelfth century), the election of magistrates, the right of bringing public officials to trial, the abolition of standing armies, free instruction, etc., everything that is pointed out as an invention of modern liberalism, is but a return to the freedom which existed before church and king had laid hands upon every manifestation of human life.

Thus the protection of exploitation directly by laws on property, and indirectly by the maintenance of the State is both the spirit and the substance of our modern codes, and the one function of our costly legislative machinery. But it is time we gave up being satisfied with mere phrases, and learned to appreciate their real significance. The law, which on its first appearance presented itself as a compendium of customs useful for the preservation of society, is now perceived to be nothing but an instrument for the maintenance of exploitation and the domination of the toiling masses by rich idlers. At the present day its civilizing mission is *nil*; it has but one object,—to bolster up exploitation.

This is what is told us by history as to the development of law. Is it in virtue of this history that we are called upon to respect it? Certainly not. It has no more title to respect than capital, the fruit of pillage. And the first duty of the revolution will be to make a bonfire of all existing laws as it will of all titles to property.

IV

The millions of laws which exist for the regulation of humanity appear upon investigation to be divided into three principal categories: protection of property, protection of persons, protection of government. And by analyzing each of these three categories, we arrive at the same logical and necessary conclusion: *the uselessness and hurtfulness of law.*

Socialists know what is meant by protection by property. Laws on property are not made to guarantee either to the individual or to society the enjoyment of the produce of their own labor. On the contrary, they are made to rob the producer of a part of what he has created, and to secure to certain other people that portion of the produce which they have stolen either from the producer or from society as a whole. When, for example, the law establishes Mr. So-and-So's right to a house, it is not establishing his right to a cottage he has built for himself, or to a house he has erected with the help of some of his friends. In that case no one would have disputed his right. On the contrary, the law is establishing his right to a house which is *not* the product of his labor; first of all because he has had it built for him by others to whom he has not paid the full value of their work, and next because that house represents a social value which he could not have produced for himself. The law is establishing his right to what belong to everybody in general and to nobody in particular. The same house built in the midst of Siberia would not have the value it possesses in a large town, and, as we know, that value arises from the labor of something like fifty generations of men who have built the town, beautified it, supplied it with water and gas, fine promenades, colleges, theatres, shops, railways and roads leading in all directions. Thus by recognizing the right of Mr. So-and-So to a particular house in Paris, London or Rouen, the law is unjustly appropriating to him a certain portion of the produce of the labor of mankind in general. And it is precisely because this appropriation and all other forms of property bearing the same character are a crying injustice, that a whole arsenal of laws and a whole army of soldiers, policemen and judges are needed to maintain it against the good sense and just feeling inherent in humanity.

Half our laws,—the civil code in each country,—serves no other purpose than to maintain this appropriation, this monopoly for the benefit of certain individuals against the whole of mankind. Three-fourths of the causes decided by the tribunals are nothing but quarrels between monopolists—two robbers disputing over their booty. And a great many of our criminal laws have the same object in view, their end being to keep the workman in a subordinate position towards his employer, and thus afford security for exploitation.

As for guaranteeing the product of his labor to the producer, there are no laws which even attempt such a thing. It is so simple and natural, so much a part of the manners and customs of mankind, that law has not given it so much as a thought. Open brigandage, sword in hand, is no feature of our age. Neither does one workman ever come and dispute the produce of his labor with another. If they have a misunderstanding they settle it by calling in a third person, without having recourse to law. The only person who exacts from another what that other has produced, is the proprietor, who comes in and deducts the lion's share. As for humanity in general, it everywhere respects the right of each to what he has created, without the interposition of any special laws.

As all the laws about property which make up thick volumes of codes and are the delight of our lawyers have no other object than to protect the unjust appropriation of human labor by certain monopolists, there is no reason for their existence, and, on the day of the revolution, social revolutionists are thoroughly determined to put an end to them. Indeed, a bonfire might be made with perfect justice of all laws bearing upon the so-called "rights of property," all title-deeds, all registers, in a word, of all that is in any way connected with an institution which will soon be looked upon as a blot in the history of humanity, as humiliating as the slavery and serfdom of past ages.

The remarks just made upon laws concerning property are quite as applicable to the second category of laws; those for the maintenance of government, i.e., constitutional law.

It again is a complete arsenal of laws, decrees, ordinances, orders in council, and what not, all serving to protect the diverse forms of representative government, delegated or usurped, beneath which humanity is writhing. We know very well—anarchists have often enough pointed out in their perpetual criticism of the various forms of government—that the mission of all governments, monarchical, constitutional, or republican, is to protect and maintain by force the privileges of the classes in possession, the aristocracy, clergy and traders. A good third of our laws—and each country possesses some tens of thousands of them—the fundamental laws on taxes, excise duties, the organization of ministerial departments and their offices, of the army, the police, the church, etc., have no other end than to maintain, patch up, and develop the administrative machine. And this machine in its turn serves almost entirely to protect the privileges of the possessing classes. Analyze all these laws, observe them in action day by day, and you will discover that not one is worth preserving.

About such laws there can be no two opinions. Not only anarchists, but more or less revolutionary radicals also, are agreed that the only use to be made of laws concerning the organization of government is to fling them into the fire.

The third category of law still remains to be considered; that relating to the protection of the person and the detection and prevention of "crime." This is the most important because most prejudices attach to it; because, if law enjoys a certain amount of consideration, it is in consequence of the belief that this species of law is absolutely indispensable to the maintenance of security in our societies. These are laws developed from the nucleus of customs useful to human communities, which have been turned to account by rulers to sanctify their own domination. The authority of the chiefs of tribes, of rich families in towns, and of the king, depended upon their judicial functions, and even down to the present day, whenever the necessity of government is spoken of, its function as supreme judge is the thing implied. "Without a government men would tear one another to pieces," argues the village orator. "The ultimate end of all government is to secure twelve honest jurymen to every accused person," said Burke.

Well, in spite of all the prejudices existing on this subject, it is quite time that anarchists should boldly declare this category of laws as useless and injurious as the preceding crime.

First of all, as to so-called "crimes"—assaults upon persons—it is well known that two-thirds, and often as many as three-fourths, of such "crimes" are instigated by the desire to obtain possession of someone's wealth. This immense class of so-called "crimes and misdemeanors" will disappear on the day on which private property ceases to exist. "But," it will be said, "there will always be brutes who will attempt the lives of their fellow citizens, who will lay their hands to a knife in every quarrel, and revenge the slightest offense by murder, if there are no laws to restrain and punishments to withhold them." This refrain is repeated every time the right of society *to punish* is called in question.

Yet there is one fact concerning this head which at the present time is thoroughly established; the severity of punishment does not diminish the amount of crime. Hang, and, if you like, quarter murderers, and the number of murders will not decrease by one. On the other hand, abolish the penalty of death, and there will not be one murder more; there will be fewer. Statistics prove it. But if the harvest is good, and bread cheap, and the weather fine, the number of murders immediately decreases. This again is proved by statistics. The amount of crime always augments and diminishes in proportion to the price of provisions and the state of the weather. Not that all murders are actuated by hunger. That is not the case. But when the harvest is good, and provisions are at an obtainable price, and when the sun shines, men, lighter-hearted and less miserable than usual, do not give way to gloomy passions, do not from trivial motives plunge a knife into the bosom of a fellow creature.

Moreover, it is also a well known fact that the fear of punishment has never stopped a single murderer. He who kills his neighbor from revenge or misery does not reason much about consequences; and there have been few murderers who were not firmly convinced that they should escape prosecution.

Without speaking of a society in which a man will receive a better education, in which the development of all his faculties, and the possibility of exercising them, will procure him so many enjoyments that he will not seek to poison them by remorse—even in our society, even with those sad products of misery whom we see today in the public houses of great cities—on the day when no punishment is inflicted upon murderers, the number of murders will not be augmented by a single case. And it is extremely probable that it will be, on the contrary, diminished by all those cases which are due at present to habitual criminals, who have been brutalized in prisons.

We are continually being told of the benefits conferred by law, and the beneficial effect of penalties, but have the speakers ever attempted to strike a balance between the benefits attributed to laws and penalties, and the degrading effect of these penalties upon humanity? Only calculate all the evil passions awakened in mankind by the atrocious punishments formerly inflicted in our streets! Man is the cruelest animal upon earth. And who has pampered and developed the cruel instincts unknown, even among monkeys, if it is not the king, the judge, and the priests, armed with law, who caused flesh to be torn off in strips, boiling pitch to be poured into wounds, limbs to be dislocated, bones to be crushed, men to be sawn asunder to maintain their authority? Only estimate the torrent of depravity let loose in human society by the "informing" which is countenanced by judges, and paid in hard cash by governments, under pretext of assisting in the discovery of "crime." Only go into the jails and study what man becomes when he is deprived of freedom and shut up with other depraved beings, steeped in the vice and corruption which oozes from the very walls of our existing prisons. Only remember that the more these prisons are reformed, the more detestable they become. Our model modern penitentiaries are a hundred-fold more abominable than the dungeons of the middle ages. Finally, consider what corruption, what depravity of mind is kept up among men by the idea of obedience, the very essence of law; of chastisement; of authority having the right to punish, to judge irrespective of our conscience and the esteem of our friends; of the necessity for executioners, jailers, and informers—in a word, by all the attributes of law and authority. Consider all this, and you will assuredly agree with us in saying that a law inflicting penalties is an abomination which should cease to exist.

Peoples without political organization, and therefore less depraved than ourselves, have perfectly understood that the man who is called "criminal" is simply unfortunate; that the remedy is not to flog him, to chain him up, or to kill him on the scaffold or in prison, but to help him by the most brotherly care, by treatment based on equality, by the usages of life among honest men. In the next revolution we hope that this cry will go forth:

"Burn the guillotines; demolish the prisons; drive away the judges, policemen and informers—the impurest race upon the face of the earth; treat as a brother the man who has been led by passion to do ill to his fellow; above all, take from the ignoble products of middle-class idleness the possibility of displaying their vices in attractive colors; and be sure that but few crimes will mar our society."

The main supports of crime are idleness, law and authority; laws about property, laws about government, laws about penalties and misdemeanors; and authority, which takes upon itself to manufacture these laws and to apply them.

No more laws! No more judges! Liberty, equality, and practical human sympathy are the only effectual barriers we can oppose to the anti-social instincts of certain among us.

Technocracy's Children
Theodore Roszak

Theodore Roszak (1933-   ) was born in Chicago. He received his Ph.D. in history from Princeton University in 1958. In addition to *The Making of a Counter Culture* (1968-1969), he has published *The Dissenting Academy* (1968).

The struggle of the generations is one of the obvious constants of human affairs. One stands in peril of some presumption, therefore, to suggest that the rivalry between young and adult in Western society during the current decade is uniquely critical. And yet it is necessary to risk such presumption if one is not to lose sight of our most important contemporary source of radical dissent and cultural innovation. For better or worse, most of what is presently happening that is new, provocative, and engaging in politics, education, the arts, social relations (love, courtship, family, community), is the creation either of youth who are profoundly, even fanatically, alienated from the parental generation, or of those who address themselves primarily to the young. It is at the level of youth that significant social criticism now looks for a responsive hearing as, more and more, it grows to be the common expectation that the young should be those who act, who make things happen, who take risks, who generally provide the ginger. It would be of interest in its own right that the age-old process of generational disaffiliation should now be transformed from a peripheral experience in the life of the individual and the family into a major lever of radical social change. But if one believes, as I do, that the alienated young are giving shape to something that looks like the saving vision our endangered civilization requires, then there is no avoiding the need to understand and to educate them in what they are about.

The reference of this book is primarily to America, but it is headline news that generation antagonism has achieved international dimensions. Throughout the West (as well as in Japan and parts of Latin America) it is the young who find themselves cast as the only effective radical opposition within their societies. Not all the young, of course: perhaps only a minority of the university campus population. Yet no analysis seems to make sense of the major political upheavals of the decade other than that which pits a militant minority of dissenting youth against the sluggish consensus-and-coalition politics of their middle-class elders. This generation dichotomy is a new fact of political life, one which the European young have been more reluctant to accept than their American counterparts. The heirs of an institutionalized left-wing legacy, the young radicals of Europe still tend to see themselves as the champions of "the people" (meaning the working class) against the oppression of the bourgeoisie (meaning, in most cases, their own parents). Accordingly, they try valiantly to adapt themselves to the familiar patterns of the past. They reach out automatically along time-honored ideological lines to find allies—to the workers, the trade unions, the parties of the left . . . only to discover that these expected alliances strangely fail to materialize and that they stand alone and isolated, a vanguard without a following.

In Germany and Italy the major parties of the left opposition have allowed themselves to be co-opted into the mainstream of respectable politicking—perhaps even to the point of joining governing coalitions. Despite the fact that German students (less than 5 per cent of whom come from working-class families) risk the wrath of the police to crusade beneath banners bearing the names of Rosa Luxemburg and Karl Liebknecht, the backlash their street politics produces is as sharp among the workers as the bourgeoisie. When Berlin students demonstrate against the war in Vietnam, the trade unions respond (as in February 1968) with counter-demonstrations supporting Washington's version of "peace and freedom" in Southeast Asia.

In Britain, the Aldermaston generation and its disillusioned successors have long since had to admit that the Labour Party, angling always for the now decisive middle-class vote, is little more than Tweedledum to the Tories' Tweedledee. As for the British working class, the only cause that has inspired a show of fighting spirit on its part during the sixties (other than the standard run of wages and demarcation grievances) is the bloody-minded cry to drive the colored immigrants from the land.

In France, the battle-scarred students of the May 1968 Rebellion have had to watch the much-mellowed CGT and PC conniving to function as President de Gaulle's labor lieutenants in the maintenance of responsible, orderly government against the menace of "anarchy" in the streets. If the students march by rebellious thousands to the barricades, their cautious parents march in behalf of the status quo by the tens of thousands and vote by the millions for the general and the managerial elite he has recruited from the Ecole *polytechnique* for the purpose of masterminding the new French affluence. Even the factory workers who swelled the students' ranks from thousands to millions during the early stages of the May 1968 General Strike seem to have decided that the essence of revolution is a bulkier pay envelope.

Over and again it is the same story throughout Western Europe: the students may rock their societies; but without the support of adult social forces, they cannot overturn the established order. And that support would seem to be nowhere in sight. On the contrary, the adult social forces—including those of the traditional left—are the lead-bottomed ballast of the status quo. The students march to the Internationale, they run up the red flag, they plaster the barricades with pictures of Marxist heroes old and new ... but the situation they confront stubbornly refuses to yield to a conventional left-right analysis. Is it any wonder that, in despair, some French students begin to chalk up the disgruntled slogan *"Je suis marxiste, tendance Groucho"* ("I'm a Marxist of the Groucho variety")? At last they are forced to admit that the entrenched consensus which repels their dissent is the generation phenomena which French and German young have begun to call "daddy's politics."

If the experience of the American young has anything to contribute to our understanding of this dilemma, it stems precisely from the fact that the left-wing of our political spectrum has always been so pathetically foreshortened. Our young are therefore far less adept at wielding the vintage rhetoric of radicalism than their European counterparts. But where the old categories of social analysis have so little to tell us (or so I will argue here), it becomes a positive advantage to confront the novelty of daddy's politics free of outmoded ideological preconceptions. The result may then be a more flexible, more experimental, though perhaps also a more seemingly bizarre approach to our situation. Ironically, it is the American young, with their underdeveloped radical background, who seem to have grasped most clearly the fact that, while such immediate emergencies as the Vietnam war, racial injustice, and hard-core poverty demand a deal of old-style politicking, the paramount struggle of our day is against a far more formidable, because far less obvious, opponent, to which I will give the name "the technocracy"—a social form more highly developed in America than in any other society. The American young have been somewhat quicker to sense that in the struggle against *this* enemy, the conventional tactics of political resistance have only a marginal place, largely limited to meeting immediate life-and-death crises. Beyond such front-line issues, however, there lies the greater task of altering the total cultural context within which our daily politics takes place.[1]

.   .   .

[1] For a comparison of American and European student radicalism along the lines drawn here, see Gianfranco Corsini, "A Generation Up in Arms," *The Nation*, June 10, 1968.

Daniel Cohn-Bendit and his spontaneous revolutionaries in France are something of an exception to what I say here about the young European radicals. Cohn-Bendit's anarchist instincts (which greatly riled the old-line leftist student groups during the May 1968 troubles) provide him with a healthy awareness of "the bureaucratic phenomenon" in modern industrial society and of the way in which it has subtly eroded the revolutionary potential of the working class and of its official left-wing leadership. He therefore warns strongly against "hero-worshiping" the workers. But even so, he continues to conceive of "the people" as the workers, and of the workers as the decisive revolutionary element, the students functioning only as their allies and sparkplugs. This leads him to the conclusion that the subversion of the status quo

By the technocracy, I mean that social form in which an industrial society reaches the peak of its organizational integration. It is the ideal men usually have in mind when they speak of modernizing, up-dating, rationalizing, planning. Drawing upon such unquestionable imperatives as the demand for efficiency, for social security, for large-scale co-ordination of men and resources, for ever higher levels of affluence and ever more impressive manifestations of collective human power, the technocracy works to knit together the anachronistic gaps and fissures of the industrial society. The meticulous systematization Adam Smith celebrated in his well-known pin factory now extends to all areas of life, giving us human organization that matches the precision of our mechanistic organization. So we arrive at the era of social engineering in which entrepreneurial talent broadens its province to orchestrate the total human context which surrounds the industrial complex. Politics, education, leisure, entertainment, culture as a whole, the unconscious drives, and even, as we shall see, protest against the technocracy itself: all these become the subjects of purely technical scrutiny and of purely technical manipulation. The effort is to creat a new social organism whose health depends upon its capacity to keep the technological heart beating regularly. In the words of Jacques Ellul:

Technique requires predictability and, no less, exactness of prediction. It is necessary, then, that technique prevail over the human being. For technique, this is a matter of life and death. Technique must reduce man to a technical animal, the king of the slaves of technique. Human caprice crumbles before this necessity; there can be no human autonomy in the face of technical autonomy. The individual must be fashioned by techniques, either negatively (by the techniques of understanding man) or positively (by the adaptation of man to the technical framework), in order to wipe out the blots his personal determination introduces into the perfect design of the organization. [2]

In the technocracy, nothing is any longer small or simple or readily apparent to the non-technical man. Instead, the scale and intricacy of all human activities—political, economic, cultural—transcends the competence of the amateurish citizen and inexorably demands the attention of specially trained experts. Further, around this central core of experts who deal with large-scale public necessities, there grows up a circle of subsidiary experts who, battening on the general social prestige of technical skill in the technocracy, assume authoritative influence over even the most seemingly personal aspects of life: sexual behavior, child-rearing, mental health, recreation, etc. In the technocracy everything aspires to become purely technical, the subject of professional attention. The technocracy is therefore the regime of experts—or of those who can employ the experts. Among its key institutions we find the "think-tank," in which is housed a multi-billion-dollar brainstorming industry that seeks to anticipate and integrate into the social planning quite simply everything on the scene. Thus, even before the general public

need not await a total cultural transformation, but can be pulled off by "insurrectional cells" and "nuclei of confrontation" whose purpose is to set an example for the working class. See Daniel and Gabriel Cohn-Bendit, *Obsolete Communism: The Left-Wing Alternative* (New York: McGraw-Hill, 1969), especially the keen analysis of the working partnership between "empiricist-positivist" sociology and technocratic manipulation, pp. 35-40.

[2] Jacques Ellul, *The Technological Society*, trans. John Wilkinson (New York: A. A. Knopf, 1964), p. 138. This outrageously pessimistic book is thus far the most global effort to depict the technocracy in full operation.

has become fully aware of new developments, the technocracy has doped them out and laid its plans for adopting or rejecting, promoting or disparaging.[3]

Within such a society, the citizen, confronted by bewildering bigness and complexity, finds it necessary to defer on all matters to those who know better. Indeed, it would be a violation of reason to do otherwise, since it is universally agreed that the prime goal of the society is to keep the productive apparatus turning over efficiently. In the absence of expertise, the great mechanism would surely bog down, leaving us in the midst of chaos and poverty. As we will see in later chapters, the roots of the technocracy reach deep into our cultural past and are ultimately entangled in the scientific world-view of the Western tradition. But for our purposes here it will be enough to define the technocracy as that society in which those who govern justify themselves by appeal to technical experts who, in turn, justify themselves by appeal to scientific forms of knowledge. And beyond the authority of science, there is no appeal.

Understood in these terms, as the mature product of technological progress and the scientific ethos, the technocracy easily eludes all traditional political categories. Indeed, it is characteristic of the technocracy to render itself ideologically invisible. Its assumptions about reality and its values become as unobtrusively pervasive as the air we breathe. While daily political argument continues within and between the capitalist and collectivist societies of the world, the technocracy increases and consolidates its power in both as a trans-political phenomenon following the dictates of industrial efficiency, rationality, and necessity. In all these arguments, the technocracy assumes a position similar to that of the purely neutral umpire in an athletic contest. The umpire is normally the least obtrusive person on the scene. Why? Because we give our attention and passionate allegiance to the teams, who compete within the rules; we tend to ignore the man who stands above the contest and who simply interprets and enforces the rules. Yet, in a sense, the umpire is the most significant figure in the game, since he alone sets the limits and goals of the competition and judges the contenders.

The technocracy grows without resistance, even despite its most appalling failures and criminalities, primarily because its potential critics continue trying to cope with these breakdowns in terms of antiquated categories. This or that disaster is blamed by Republicans on Democrats (or vice versa), by Tories on Labourities (or vice versa, by French Communists on Gaullists (or vice versa), by Maoists on Revisionists (or vice versa). But left, right, and center, these are quarrels between technocrats or between factions who subscribe to technocratic values from first to last. The angry debates of conservative and liberal, radical and reactionary touch everything except the technocracy, because the technocracy is not generally perceived as a political phenomenon in our advanced industrial societies. It holds the place, rather, of a grand cultural imperative which is beyond question, beyond discussion.

When any system of politics devours the surrounding culture, we have totalitarianism, the attempt to bring the whole of life under authoritarian control. We are bitterly familiar with totalitarian politics in the form of brutal regimes which achieve their integration by bludgeon and bayonet. But in the case of the

---

[3] For a report on the activities of a typical technocratic brain trust, Herman Kahn's Hudson Institute, see Bowen Northrup's "They Think for Pay" in *The Wall Street Journal,* September 20, 1967. Currently, the Institute is developing strategies to integrate hippies and to exploit the new possibilities of programmed dreams.

technocracy, totalitarianism is perfected because its techniques become progressively more subliminal. The distinctive feature of the regime of experts lies in the fact that, while possessing ample power to coerce, it prefers to charm conformity from us by exploiting our deep-seated commitment to the scientific world-view and by manipulating the securities and creature comforts of the industrial affluence which science has given us.

So subtle and so well rationalized have the arts of technocratic domination become in our advanced industrial societies that even those in the state and/or corporate structure who dominate our lives must find it impossible to conceive of themselves as the agents of a totalitarian control. Rather, they can easily see themselves as the conscientious managers of a munificent social system which is, by the very fact of its broadcast affluence, incompatible with any form of exploitation. At worst, the system may contain some distributive inefficiencies. But these are bound to be repaired . . . in time. And no doubt they will be. Those who gamble that either capitalism or collectivism is, by its very nature, incompatible with a totally efficient technocracy, one which will finally eliminate material poverty and gross physical exploitation, are making a risky wager. It is certainly one of the oldest, but one of the weakest radical arguments which insists stubbornly that capitalism is *inherently* incapable of laying golden eggs for everyone.

The great secret of technocracy lies, then, in its capacity to convince us of three interlocking premises. They are:

1. That the vital needs of man are (contrary to everything the great souls of history have told us) purely technical in character. Meaning: the requirements of our humanity yield wholly to some manner of formal analysis which can be carried out by specialists possessing certain impenetrable skills and which can then be translated by them directly into a congeries of social and economic programs, personnel management procedures, merchandise, and mechanical gadgetry. If a problem does not have such a technical solution, it must not be a *real* problem. It is but an illusion . . . a figment born of some regressive cultural tendency.
2. That this formal (and highly esoteric) analysis of our needs has now achieved 99 per cent completion. Thus, with minor hitches and snags on the part of irrational elements in our midst, the prerequisites of human fulfillment have all but been satisfied. It is this assumption which leads to the conclusion that wherever social friction appears in the technocracy, it must be due to what is called a "breakdown in communication." For where human happiness has been so precisely calibrated and where the powers that be are so utterly well intentioned, controversy could not possibly derive from a substantive issue, but only from misunderstanding. Thus we need only sit down and reason together and all will be well.
3. That the experts who have fathomed our heart's desires and who alone can continue providing for our needs, the experts who *really* know what they're talking about, all happen to be on the official payroll of the state and/or corporate structure. The experts who count are the certified experts. And the certified experts belong to headquarters.

One need not strain to hear the voice of the technocrat in our society. It speaks strong and clear, and from high places. For example:

Today these old sweeping issues have largely disappeared. The central domestic problems of our time are more subtle and less simple. They relate not to basic clashes of philosophy or ideology, but to ways and means of reaching common goals—to research for sophisticated solutions to complex and obstinate issues. . . .

What is at stake in our economic decisions today is not some grand warfare of rival ideologies which will sweep the country with passion, but the practical management of a modern economy. What we need are not labels and cliches but more basic discussion of the sophisticated and technical questions involved in keeping a great economic machinery moving ahead. . . .

I am suggesting that the problems of fiscal and monetary policy in the Sixties as opposed to the kinds of problems we faced in the Thirties demand subtle challenges for which technical answers—not political answers—must be provided.[4]

Or, to offer one more example, which neatly identifies elitist managerialism with reason itself:

Some critics today worry that our democratic, free societies are becoming overmanaged. I would argue that the opposite is true. As paradoxical as it may sound, the real threat to democracy comes, not from overmanagement, but from undermanagement. To undermanage reality is to not keep free. It is simply to let some force other than reason shape reality. That force may be unbridled emotion; it may be greed, it may be aggressiveness; it may be hatred; it may be ignorance; it may be inertia; it may be anything other than reason. But whatever it is, if it is not reason that rules man, then man falls short of his potential.

Vital decision-making, particularly in policy matters, must remain at the top. This is partly, though not completely, what the top is for. But rational decision-making depends on having a full range of rational options from which to choose, and successful management organizes the enterprise so that process can best take place. It is a mechanism whereby free men can most efficiently exercise their reason, initiative, creativity and personal responsibility. The adventurous and immensely satisfying task of an efficient organization is to formulate and analyze these options.[5]

Such statements, uttered by obviously competent, obviously enlightened leadership, make abundantly clear the prime strategy of the technocracy. It is to level life down to a standard of so-called living that technical expertise can cope with—and then, on that false and exclusive basis, to claim an intimidating omnicompetence over us by its monopoly of the experts. Such is the politics of our mature industrial societies, our truly *modern* societies, where two centuries of aggressive secular skepticism, after ruthlessly eroding the traditionally transcendent ends of life, has concomitantly given us a proficiency of technical means that now oscillates absurdly between the production of frivolous abundance and the production of genocidal munitions. Under the technocracy we become the most scientific of societies; yet, like Kafka's K., men throughout the "developed world"

[4] John F. Kennedy, "Yale University Commencement Speech," New York *Times*, June 12, 1962, p. 20.

[5] From Robert S. McNamara's recent book *The Essence of Security* (New York: Harper & Row, 1968) pp. 109-10. In the present generation, it is second- and third-level figures like McNamara who are apt to be the technocrats par excellence: the men who stand behind the official facade of leadership and who continue their work despite all superficial changes of government. McNamara's career is almost a paradigm of our new elitist managerialism: from head of Ford to head of the Defense Department to head of the World Bank. The final step will surely be the presidency of one of our larger universities or foundations. Clearly it no longer matters *what* a manager manages; it is all a matter of juggling vast magnitudes of things: money, missiles, students. . . .

become more and more the bewildered dependents of inaccessible castles wherein inscrutable technicians conjure with their fate. True, the foolproof system again and again bogs down in riot or apathetic rot or the miscalculations of overextended centralization; true, the chronic obscenity of thermonuclear war hovers over it like a gargantuan bird of prey feeding off the bulk of our affluence and intelligence. But the members of the parental generation, storm-tossed by depression, war, and protracted war-scare, cling fast to the technocracy for the myopic sense of prosperous security it allows. By what right would they complain against those who intend only the best, who purport to be the agents of democratic consensus, and who invoke the high rhetorical sanction of the scientific world view, our most unimpeachable mythology? How does one take issue with the paternal beneficence of such technocratic Grand Inquisitors? Not only do they provide bread aplenty, but the bread is soft as floss: it takes no effort to chew, and yet is vitamin-enriched.

To be sure, there are those who have not yet been cut in on the material advantages, such as the "other Americans" of our own country. Where this is the case, the result is, inevitably and justifiably, a forceful, indignant campaign fixated on the issue of integrating the excluded into the general affluence. Perhaps there is an exhausting struggle, in the course of which all other values are lost sight of. But, at least (why should we doubt it?), all the disadvantaged minorities are accommodated. And so the base of the technocracy is broadened as it assimilates its wearied challengers. It might almost be a trick, the way such politics works. It is rather like the ruse of inveigling someone you wish to capture to lean all his weight on a door you hold closed . . . and then, all of a sudden, throwing it open. He not only winds up inside, where you want him, but he comes crashing in full tilt.

In his analysis of this "new authoritarianism," Herbert Marcuse calls our attention especially to the technocracy's "absorbent power": its capacity to provide "satisfaction in a way which generates submission and weakens the rationality of protest." As it approaches maturity, the technocracy does indeed seem capable of anabolizing every form of discontent into its system.

Let us take the time to consider one significant example of such "repressive desublimation" (as Marcuse calls it). The problem is sexuality, traditionally one of the most potent sources of civilized man's discontent. To liberate sexuality would be to create a society in which technocratic discipline would be impossible. But to thwart sexuality outright would create a widespread, explosive resentment that required constant policing; and, besides, this would associate the technocracy with various puritanical traditions that enlightened men cannot but regard as superstitious. The strategy chosen, therefore, is not harsh repression, but rather the *Playboy* version of total permissiveness which now imposes its image upon us in every slick movie and posh magazine that comes along. In the affluent society, we have sex and sex galore—or so we are to believe. But when we look more closely we see that this sybaritic promiscuity wears a special social coloring. It has been assimilated to an income level and social status available only to our well-heeled junior executives and the jet set. After all, what does it cost to rent these yachts full of nymphomaniacal young things in which our playboys sail off for orgiastic swimming parties in the Bahamas? *Real* sex, we are led to believe, is something that goes with the best scotch, twenty-seven-dollar sunglasses, and platinum-tipped shoelaces. Anything less is a shabby substitute. Yes, there is permissiveness in the technocratic society; but it is only for the swingers and the big spenders. It is the reward that goes to reliable, politically safe henchmen of the status quo. Before our would-be playboy can be an assembly-line seducer, he must be a loyal employee.

Moreover, *Playboy* sexuality is, ideally, casual, frolicsome, and vastly promiscuous. It is the anonymous sex of the harem. It creates no binding loyalties, no personal attachments, no distractions from one's primary responsibilities—which are to the company, to one's career and social position, and to the system generally. The perfect playboy practices a career enveloped by noncommittal trivialities: there is no home, no family, no romance that divides the heart painfully. Life off the job exhausts itself in a constant run of imbecile affluence and impersonal orgasms.

Finally, as a neat little dividend, the ideal of the swinging life we find in *Playboy* gives us a conception of femininity which is indistinguishable from social idiocy. The woman becomes a mere playmate, a submissive bunny, a mindless decoration. At a stroke, half the population is reduced to being the inconsequential entertainment of the technocracy's pampered elite.

As with sexuality, so with every other aspect of life. The business of inventing and flourishing treacherous parodies of freedom, joy, and fulfillment becomes an indispensable form of social control under the technocracy. In all walks of life, image makers and public relations specialists assume greater and greater prominence. The regime of experts relies on a lieutenancy of counterfeiters who seek to integrate the discontent born of thwarted aspiration by way of clever falsification. Thus:

We call it "education," the "life of the mind," the "pursuit of the truth." But it is a matter of machine-tooling the young to the needs of our various baroque bureaucracies: corporate, governmental, military, trade union, educational.

We call it "free enterprise." But it is a vastly restrictive system of oligopolistic market manipulation, tied by institutionalized corruption to the greatest munitions boondoggle in history and dedicated to infantilizing the public by turning it into a herd of compulsive consumers.

We call it "creative leisure": finger painting and ceramics in the university extension, tropic holidays, grand athletic excursions to the far mountains and the sunny beaches of the earth. But it is, like our sexual longings, an expensive adjunct of careerist high-achievement: the prize that goes to the dependable hireling.

We call it "pluralism." But it is a matter of the public authorities solemnly affirming everybody's right to his own opinion as an excuse for ignoring anybody's troubling challenge. In such a pluralism, critical viewpoints become mere private prayers offered at the alter of an inconsequential conception of free speech.

We call it "democracy." But it is a matter of public opinion polling in which a "random sample" is asked to nod or wag the head in response to a set of prefabricated alternatives, usually related to the *faits accompli* of decision makers, who can always construe the polls to serve their own ends. Thus, if 80 per cent think it is a "mistake" that we ever "went into" Vietnam, but 51 per cent think we would "lose prestige" if we "pulled out now," then the "people" have been "consulted" and the war goes on with their "approval."

We call it "debate." But it is a matter of arranging staged encounters between equally noncommittal candidates neatly tailored to fit thirty minutes of prime network time, the object of the exercise being to establish an "image" of competence. If there are interrogators present, they have been hand-picked and their questions rehearsed.

We call it "government by the consent of the governed." But even now, somewhere in the labyrinth of the paramilitary agencies an "area specialist" neither you nor I elected is dispatching "special advisors" to a distant "trouble-spot" which will be the next Vietnam. And somewhere in the depths of the oceans a submarine commander neither you nor I elected is piloting a craft equipped with firepower capable of cataclysmic devastation and perhaps trying to decide if—for reasons neither you nor I know—the time has come to push the button.

It is all called being "free," being "happy," being the Great Society.

From the standpoint of the traditional left, the vices of contemporary America we mention here are easily explained—and indeed too easily. The evils stem simply from the unrestricted pursuit of profit. Behind the manipulative deceptions there are capitalist desperados holding up the society for all the loot they can lay hands on.

To be sure, the desperados are there, and they are a plague of the society. For a capitalist technocracy, profiteering will always be a central incentive and major corrupting influence. Yet even in our society, profit taking no longer holds its primacy as an evidence for organizational success, as one might suspect if for no other reason than that our largest industrial enterprises can now safely count on an uninterrupted stream of comfortably high earnings. At this point, considerations of an entirely different order come into play among the managers, as Seymour Melman reminds us when he observes:

The "fixed" nature of industrial investment represented by machinery and structures means that large parts of the costs of any accounting period must be assigned in an arbitrary way. Hence, the magnitude of profits shown in any accounting period varies entirely according to the regulations made by the management itself for assigning its "fixed" charges. Hence, profit has ceased to be the economists' independent measure of success or failure of the enterprise. We can define the systematic quality in the behavior and management of large industrial enterprises not in terms of profits, but in terms of their acting to maintain or to extend the production decision power they wield. Production decision power can be gauged by the number of people employed, or whose work is directed, by the proportion of given markets that a management dominates, by the size of the capital investment that is controlled, by the number of other managements whose decisions are controlled. Toward these ends profits are an instrumental device—subordinated in given accounting periods to the extension of decision power.[6]

Which is to say that capitalist enterprise now enters the stage at which large-scale social integration and control become paramount interests in and of themselves: the corporations begin to behave like public authorities concerned with rationalizing the total economy. If profit remains an important lubricant of the system, we should recognize that other systems may very well use different lubricants to achieve the same end of perfected, centralized organization. But in so doing they still constitute *technocratic* systems drawing upon their own inducements.

In the example given above of *Playboy* permissiveness, the instruments used to integrate sexuality into industrial rationality have to do with high income and extravagant merchandizing. Under the Nazis, however, youth camps and party courtesans were used for the same integrative purpose—as were the concentration camps, where the kinkier members of the elite were rewarded by being allowed free exercise of their tastes. In this case, sexual freedom was not assimilated to income

[6] Seymour Melman, "Priorities and the State Machine," *New University Thought*, Winter 1966-67, pp. 17-18.

level or prestige consumption, but to party privilege. If the communist regimes of the world have not yet found ways to institutionalize sexual permissiveness, it is because the party organizations are still under the control of grim old men whose puritanism dates back to the days of primitive accumulation. But can we doubt that once these dismal characters pass from the scene—say, when we have a Soviet version of Kennedy-generation leadership—we shall hear of topless bathing parties at the Black Sea resorts and of orgiastic goings-on in the *dachias*? By then the good apparatchiks and industrial commissars will also acquire the perquisite of admission to the swinging life.

It is essential to realize that the technocracy is not the exclusive product of the old devil capitalism. Rather, it is the product of a mature and accelerating industrialism. The profiteering could be eliminated; the technocracy would remain in force. The key problem we have to deal with is the paternalism of expertise within a socioeconomic system which is so organized that it is inextricably beholden to expertise. And, moreover, to an expertise which has learned a thousand ways to manipulate our acquiescence with an imperceptible subtlety.

Anarchism and the American Counterculture
Michael Lerner

Michael Lerner (1945-   ) is a research assistant at Yale University.

Nine years ago George Woodcock surveyed the "ghost of the historical anarchist movement" and concluded that there was "no reasonable likelihood of a renaissance." History showed that "the movements which fail to take the chances it offers them are never born again." Seven years later, when identifiably anarchist tendencies re-emerged in the youth movements in England and Holland, Woodcock wondered "whether I had been rash in so officiously burying the historic anarchist movement." He decided that he had not been rash because of the differences between the new anarchists and the old. The new anarchists represented no "knock in the coffin" but "a new manifestation of the [anarchist] idea."

Woodcock described the new anarchists as "militant pacifists" who had "forgotten Spain and had no use for the old romanticism of the *dinamitero* and the *petroleuse.*" He pointed to the difference between the old days when one "joined" an anarchist party and the current situation in which the young "*became*" anarchists. Finally, Woodcock discerned no obvious signs of an anarchist revival in the United States.[1]

ANARCHISM RENASCENT

It was not only the professional observer of radical and anarchist movements who did not foresee what was in the making in America. A whole school of political observers, sociologists, and political scientists forecast at the start of the 1960s a convergence of political systems, an end of ideology, and a decrease in the salience of political issues as technicians of government assumed control. For all these people the emergence of the first American youth movement, massive and militant, with the children they had raised as they wrote their predictions in its ranks, was probably the biggest surprise of the decade. If black militance was also unforeseen, it was more easily explicable in familiar neo-Marxist metaphors than the aspirations of youth. One could still try to argue that the decisive fact was that a "student class" seven million strong had exceeded some critical mass on the campuses. But the pioneers of LSD—Ken Kesey and his Pranksters—and the hippies, street people, and flower children fit uncomfortably into Marxist categories. And it was they who were leading the students in building what Roszak has aptly named the "counter-culture."[2]

Blacks wanted "in;" once-Marxist theorists understood that. Hippies, less understandably, wanted "out." They showed no ambition to battle for control of American capitalism and to make it serve the working class. They spoke in embarrassingly utopian terms of changing people's minds—attributable, doubtless, to their drug excesses. Drug-induced or not their words were indistinguishable from those of anarchists as dissimilar as Tolstoy and Bakunin who thought that the revolution had to be in men's minds. "There will be a qualitative transformation, a new living, life-giving revelation, a new heaven and a new earth, a young and mighty world," Bakunin wrote, a vision that the songs of the counter-culture described precisely.

How would the transformation of minds be effected? The Beatles gave an early, widely disseminated answer—"All You Need Is Love." Some historic anarchists might have agreed. But this answer set the youth culture far from Bakunin, who had concluded: "Let us put our trust in the eternal spirit which destroys and annihilates only because it is the unsearchable and eternally creative source of all life."[3] Those words still would not ring true in the counter-culture today. But the interesting point is that many of the young are moving ever closer to Bakunin's

---

[1] In "Anarchism Revisited," *Commentary*, August 1968, George Woodcock reviews the analysis he made in his major study. *Anarchism*, New York, World, 1962; Meridian edition, 1967. Although Woodcock saw no "obvious" anarchist revival in the United States, he agreed with Jack Newfield (*A Prophetic Minority*, New York, New American Library, 1966) that anarchism was an important influence in the new radical thought of 1966-67. Yet the quiet anarchist influence on intellectual currents that Woodcock had in mind is very different from the explicit and often violent manifestations of the anarchist idea and practice that have emerged in the past two years.

[2] Theodore Roszak, *The Making of Counter Culture*, New York, Anchor, 1969, has written a pioneering but flawed study of the counter-culture. The problem is that his dislike of drugs, violence and even rock music impinges upon his perspective—he denounces what he does not like often without providing a careful analysis of the phenomena. Thus Ken Kesey and Timothy Leary are blamed for leading young people into drugs, while neither they nor the drug phenomenon are adequately analysed. Violence in the counter-culture is, similarly, deplored without being examined.

[3] Woodcock, *Anarchism*, p. 151.

view than to the love tactics espoused a few years ago. For the espousal of a neo-anarchist world view by intelligent young people in the historical situation of the 1960s seemed *prima facie* even less likely than the emergence of the youth culture itself.

Woodcock's observations provide a useful guide for dating the speed with which anarchism as a potent if often unlabelled force in the America counter-culture has developed and matured. He wrote in August 1968, just before the role of the Yippies at the Chicago police riot catapulted Abbie Hoffman, Yippie leader and author of *Revolution for the Hell of It*, to national prominence. The growing acceptance of violent tactics can also be dated from the period of Chicago, Nixon's election, and the battle over People's Park in Berkeley. There is even an ironic hint of change in organizational structure: only a few months ago Abbie Hoffman suggested that his friends should consider forming a more formal party complete with membership cards. The rash of bombing and burning of buildings testifies that the *dinamitero* and the *petroleuse* are not forgotten. Whatever the utility of Woodcock's distinction between social movements resurrected and reincarnated, the new American anarchista have begun to resemble their forebears in depth and detail.

Some of the most significant similarities between the new anarchism and the old seem to include the new acceptance of violence, the rejection of majoritarianism, the insistence on the moral responsibility of the individual, the radical critique of the technological state, the asceticism towards property, and the desire to simplify life.[4] The next three sections of this essay attempt to describe this nucleus of anarchist tendencies as it has re-emerged in the counter-culture. The fifth section suggests some psychosocial factors in the specific American situation that may help to account for the re-emergence of anarchist tendencies.

A caveat before proceeding: this description and analysis is highly problematic. My views, while often stated unequivocally, are just what they seem—views; moreover, I hold other more sceptical views that often prevail over those described here. But I am an American youth as well as an academic, and though I am uncomfortable either as a participant or as an unengaged observer, I feel the arguments for the new anarchism to be persuasive to an important part of me—an important fragment of my identity. Take as an example the analysis of personal violence advanced in what follows: by turns I see it from different personal perspectives as psychologically sophistic and socially perilous or as psychologically accurate and socially important, as an intellectual game or as potentially prophetic. Since in childhood, adolescence and perhaps youth, games often prophesy, the analysis may be both playful and serious. In any case, it seemed valuable as an aid to understanding the ethos of the new anarchism to let the sympathetic fragment of me speak without burdening the product with predictable "tough minded" criticisms that readers, according to their predilections, may provide.

Before proceeding to the discussion of violence I should say what I mean by "counter-culture." Counter-culture, as currently used, refers to norms and patterns of behaviour, emerging institutions (such as rock festivals and communes), and beliefs and artistic traditions that have coalesced to provide an opposing alternative to the cultural templates of the main culture. It is a term that can be broadly applied to radical students, hippies, motor cycle gangs, the homosexual Gay Power

---

[4] *Ibid.*, Woodcock suggests that these were important elements in historical anarchism.

movement, women's liberation groups, the Maoist Revolutionary Youth Movement factions, the Black Panthers, Puerto Rican Young Lords, and lower class white Patriots. Though all of these groups join in opposition to the main culture, I will use counter-culture in its narrower sense below, as it refers to a *core coalition* of "hippies" and the groups closest to them. Thus by counter-culture I mean the people who are living in the mountains and woods in California, Vermont, Oregon, New Mexico and elsewhere, the street people of New York and Berkeley, the mystics, the people whose lives centre on drugs and/or music, the commune dwellers, those who have given up professions for crafts, and the political action hippies such as the Yippies, the Crazies, the Molotov Cocktail Party, and the Motherfuckers. To this one would have to add those deprecatingly referred to, for want of a better term as "life-style people"—the musicians, artists, students, and people proudly without occupational identity who populate counter-culture communities. The marginal groups that I would include as part of this core coalition are the cyclists who move in and out of hippie communities, some of the antidraft resisters, and the Revolutionary Youth Movement I—the Weathermen. The Weathermen constitute a useful marginal case: whereas they regard themselves as Marxist, they resemble the political action hippies in their activities and outlook more than they resemble their friends in the more traditionally Marxist Revolutionary Youth Movement II. I would tend to exclude from this "core coalition" the Panthers, Young Lords and Patriots, some of the more traditional McCarthy and Vietnam summer activists, and the large body of students who smoke a little marijuana or dress a little hip but who have made no basic commitment to the values that the core coalition—for all its many divergencies—shares.

The core coalition is conscious of its centrality in the counter-culture and I think would be identified as central by others both inside and outside the broader collection of oppositional groups. I suspect one would also find a hiatus between the identification that members of the core coalition make with each other and the broader identification they have with the other oppositional groups. And I do not think it is an artifact of my classification but, rather, a significant empirical fact, that it is this 'core coalition' in the counter-culture that most closely resembles the historic anarchists.

ANARCHIST VIOLENCE

The most startling new resemblance between the counter-culture anarchists and the historic anarchists is the increasingly widespread acceptance of violence as a tactic. It is simply no longer true that the new anarchists are militant pacifists with no use for "the old romanticism of the *dinamitero* and the *petroleuse*."

Discerning increasing *acceptance* of violence is different from predicting that widespread utilization of violent tactics will necessarily follow from their acceptance. People are no longer shocked by talk and instances of violent political action, but there is a step from there to initiation of violence. Sporadic bombing and burning has already started in California, which has for years led the nation in these developments; now there are bombings of large corporate headquarters in New York as well. Whether the inititation of violence on a large scale will come next is something I do not think we can foresee.

The acceptance of violence is expressed in the counter-culture in characteristic ways. There are few written arguments for violence. One way new anarchists continue to differ from the old is in their indifference to formal ideology and written position papers (thus in one ironic sense they are proving the end-of-ideology theorists right). There are exceptions to the general indifference to formal ideology at the margins of the counter-culture. Revolutionary Youth Movement adherents—both the Weathermen and the opposing faction—write out their views, as do a generally older group of contributors to the *New York Review of Books*, who recently discussed the wisdom of antidraft groups continuing to turn themselves in to the police after raids on draft centres. For the rest, the acceptance of violence is expressed in talk, action, film, and music. Timothy Leary has accurately described the rock musicians as the true prophets of the counter-culture. To hear vividly expressed the way in which the mood of the rock musicians (and their listeners) has changed, one need only listen to Mick Jagger of the Rolling Stones sing "Street Fighting Man," or the Steve Miller Band sing "Space Cowboy:"

> Let me tell you people that I've found a new way
> And I'm tired of all this talk about love . . . .
> You back-room schemers, star-struck dreamers
> Better find something new to say;
> It's the same old story, same old song
> And you've got some heavy dues to pay . . . .
> . . . I've been travelling through space
> Since the moment I first realized
> What all you fast-talking cats would do if you could
> I'm ready for the final surprise. . . .

Jagger, the Steve Miller Band, and groups such as the Jefferson Airplane, MC 5, the Doors, and Steppenwolf have come a long way from the Beatles' "All You Need Is Love." The Beatles made one attempt to stem the turn towards violence with a cautionary song called "Revolution" which says in part: "But when you talk about destruction—Don't you know that you can count me out." But even the Beatles were ambivalent, for after the word "out" comes a whisper hissed "*in!*" And the augurs seem to be that soon Jagger and the Steve Miller Band will seem tame. There is a new band called "Up" that plays with bayonets attached to the necks of its guitars.

The turn towards violence is not the only politically significant development in the counter-culture since the Chicago confrontations. Another important trend that has mixed significance for the turn towards violence is the movement of many radicals and hippies out of the cities and into communes in the country. The move to the country started well before 1969 and was partly a response to dissatisfaction with the cities. But its accelerating course also shares with the new acceptance of violence a common genesis, the deep sense of frustration at the intractability of the main culture that developed with the death of Robert Kennedy, the defeat of Eugene McCarthy, events in Chicago, Nixon's election, the multiple indictments and jail sentences facing Movement leaders, and the Telegraph Avenue battle that marked the demise of the People's Park in Berkeley. There were two main responses to these signals of this beginning of what Abbie Hoffman warned would be a period of oppression. Some wished to stay and fight; others wished to move out and find the freedom to create the lives they wanted for themselves. Some even combined the two impulses by describing the move to the country as a necessary preface to a guerrilla offensive.

On the one hand the move to the country may decrease the likelihood of any real or large-scale guerrilla action in the cities growing out of the new acceptance of violence as a tactic. On the other hand, the life-style and convictions of many who have moved to the country and those who want to keep the cities as a base reinforce each other, and reinforce the acceptance of violence. In dress there is a similarity between the new backwoodsman and the new guerrilla. In action there is a relationship between the woodsman's acceptance of physical violence and the guerrilla's espousal of political violence. The two tendencies will reinforce each other most explicitly, of course, if one of the next moves of the legal authorities is a widespread crackdown on rural communes.

Many people in both New York and Berkeley are talking as though preparing for violence. Some groups, such as the Motherfuckers in the East Village in New York, have organized patrols to protect hippies from police harassment. Far more widespread is the toughness with which people are dressing—and this should be distinguished from the *mocking* adaptation of military and police uniforms by flower people that is still in evidence. The Weathermen, who take their name from Bob Dylan's line, "You don't need to be a weatherman to see which way the wind blows," have begun to fling themselves against the police armed with sticks and chains and they are by no means as universally disavowed by the young as newspaper columnists would have one believe. The rumours that they plan to use guns next are not greeted with horror. On college campuses one hears admiring stories, perhaps partly true and largely apocryphal, of white Vietnam veterans becoming guerrillas in the North Dakota badlands, supplying themselves with arms by stealing trucks from army convoys. No film is more admired than Gillo Pontecorvo's "Battle of Algiers," which convincingly recreates a terroristic, suicidal and ultimately successful urban guerrilla movement. One could multiply examples but the point is clear: whatever else differentiates the new anarchists from the old, the often romantic attachment to violence has reappeared.

Since this new acceptance of violence is likely to be condemned everywhere except where it is accepted within the counter-culture, let us look—if only to understand it better—at some of its characteristically anarchist qualities. But first note that one important thing has changed: very few of the new anarchists either wish to or believe they can destroy the state completely. What they hope to achieve by violence is either a fundamental modification of the state or (and this is more true of the commune dwellers) the *de facto* right of counter-culture communities to control their own affairs at a local level.

Some of the young who are "into violence" have that clear predilection for physical assault that characterized a number of historical anarchists and—more generally—the self-selected storm troopers of every social movement. There are those who like to break heads, either as Weathermen or as policemen. Yet at the Berkeley campus of the University of California, one has a different feeling about the grim young men who warn motorists not to leave their cars in the pay parking lot that now stands where the community-built People's Park once stood. The story of People's Park tells something of the kind of scenario that increases acceptance of violence. In brief, street people and students turned some cleared land owned by the university into a very creative park. The university, to re-establish its "conveniently forgotten" deed to the land, surrounded it with a chainlink fence, bulldozed it flat, and defended it with the aid of police. The defence of the bulldozed lot was bloody; several deputies have since been indicted for their treatment of students and street people. The university, which plans to build on the land eventually, then could find no one willing to touch the land except a parking-lot company, to which it leased the lot on terms that made it almost a gift. Now the young people picket the lot with signs advising motorists—"Park at Your Own Risk." The licence numbers of those who park in the lot despite the warning are listed on bulletin boards under the caption "Actions Speak Louder Than Words."

The reader of these broadsides is being invited to bomb the cars: in one sense the grim young men are no longer militant pacifists. Yet if you ask these advocates of local terrorism about their view of modern war, many still reject it unequivocally. When it comes to opposing a reactionary and repressive state government, however, they believe that they must turn to violence to secure the kind of community they once fought peaceably for or else give up the quest. As Tolstoy said of Kropotkin: "His arguments in favour of violence do not seem to me the expression of his opinions, but only of his fidelity to the banner under which he has served so honestly all his life."[5]

Two further anarchist characteristics of much counter-culture violence are the scale on which violence is undertaken and the view of the violent act of rebellion as somehow sacred. It is well known that when violence becomes the policy of opposed groups there almost inevitably results an escalation in its savagery. Yet in no case can the violence planned by the new anarchists become the technological violence of the bomber pilot who flies miles above a country he may never have set foot in and releases bombs of terrible power and sophistication without feeling either anger or deep personal conviction. The pattern of violence predominant now in the counter-culture is reflected by the Weathermen who—like everyone else in the country—have access to guns. Yet more may be involved than a calculus of penalties when they attack the police with clubs and chains instead of guns, often expecting to be arrested and prepared to take blows just as they give them. Their medieval assaults resemble in their physical immediacy the jousts that Norman Mailer once proposed New York should hold in Central Park.

It can be argued that the recovery of the capacity for aggression on this insistently personal scale in the counter-culture is not, as some have wishfully thought, some aberrant development, but rather may be related to the recovery of the capacity for love, the lifting of various repressions, the recovery of the wish for primitive community, and so forth. In such a state a man may wish to stop inflicting constant small violence upon his woman, himself, and his friends, and may attempt to push the aggression outwards—perhaps the way primitive man did—fighting back against the enforcers of state justice instead of accepting their commands as a necessary price of civilization. An extreme and pathological example will show the "transvaluation of values" in respect to violence that has taken place in the counter-culture: Charles Manson, who is alleged to have ordered the murder of Sharon Tate and her friends, is not *utterly* condemned by many I have spoken to. More recently, in fact, he has become a hero and symbol of revolt for some of the Weathermen groups. These people are not surprised, in particular, that his girls loved him, and that however crazy he was and however indefensible his alleged act, his violence and the gentleness of which the girls so often spoke were "out front."

[5] Woodcock, *Anarchism*, p. 223.

The Weathermen and Charles Manson are the extremes. Everywhere in the counter-culture one finds people who are seeking to get back in touch with their capacity to shout, hit, face physical danger with courage, and feel. In many less destructive forms the recovery of the capacity for aggression on a human scale is a pressing concern. In California there are the cyclists, the serious admirers of Che Guevara, the new backwoodsmen, and the devotees of karate and other "martial arts."

It is not difficult to see how the task of integrating the acceptance of violence into one's life becomes a somehow sacred task. "Ritualistic" murders and the explicitly sacred violence of karate are clear examples of the fact that this transformation of violence from profane to sacred does indeed take place. There is a subtler sense of sacred mission in the violence of the Weathermen, the terrorism in "The Battle of Algiers," and more generally in the violence of the Arab commandos, who have become widely admired.

It is easy and perhaps wise to query critically any sanctification of violence. But before dismissing the new anarchist violence on these grounds one should inquire whether the way they make *their* violence sacred differs from the practice of the main culture. Robert Lifton, suggesting that nuclear technology has eroded the symbolic continuities that make men feel meaningfully connected with a past and with a future, has argued that men often deify the power that destroyed their old continuities. He discerns a religion of nuclearism in which people come to worship in some sense the awesome weapons that destroyed the old "magical" guarantees that their lives had significance, much as Indians and Africans worshipped the "white man's magic" that was more powerful than their own.[6] We even give to nuclear holocausts a name similar to that given to the God of the early Hebrews—thus Herman Kahn wrote a book called *Thinking About The Unthinkable.*

The middle and upper classes in the dominant culture have lost touch with personal violence. They bring up children out of touch with and neurotically afraid of their own anger. They are urged to accept surrogate violence—football, jets, nuclear weaponry—while advertising defines surrogate sex and surrogate lives that they may come in touch with through the use of the advertised preparations, potions, and charms. The characteristic of the main culture that the counter-culture has rejected most emphatically in its transvaluation of values is the acceptance of surrogate (or endlessly delayed) gratification. As part of this pattern, the religion of nuclearism and the Sunday ritual of watching the violence of televised football are rejected and the feelings of sacredness are returned to acts of personal violence. This may not be a long step forward in some ways, particularly since personal violence can so easily escalate into technological violence regardless of whether the societal inequities protested against will be reduced by the escalation. Most would judge the return to personal violence as a step backward from any standpoint. But in other ways personal violence—if boundaries of its sacred sphere and non-lethal ritualization of its enactment become better defined—may be a more satisfying and less dangerous persuasion than the nuclearism that has tried to replace it.

Whether or not this argument holds, it remains true that historically anarchists such as Bakunin saw something akin to the sacred in the violent response of

[6] Robert Lifton, informal remarks at the Wellfleet Psychohistorical Conference, 1969.

individuals to governmental oppression or dispossession, and this vision has returned in the counter-culture today.[7]

[7] The discussion above stressed the positive aspects of personal violence, such as the personal consequences of getting back in touch with anger. The potential danger of personal violence for the polity must be mentioned as well. By readily accessible techniques, the angry anarchist can move from clubs to bombs. There is increasing evidence of a trend in this direction in New York and California. Bombs are, of course, very much in the anarchist tradition. Yet their use allows one to move away from violence as an expression of personal anger towards violence as a dispassionate policy. When violence becomes policy and technology allows physical and emotional remove, the *personal* values of getting back in touch with the physical expression of hostility are sacrificed.

To *understand* the bombings it is important to recognize that to bomb buildings may be a sign of the psychological well-being of the bomber as easily as it is a sign of pathological hostility projected into the public sphere. One could suggest, only partly ironically, that the bombers may be young radicals who genuinely discovered "the meaning of meaning it" in their commitment to radical social change. Strong object relationships, the quest for competence, and capacity for realistic appraisal of the situation may have indicated to them that emotionally fulfilling personal violence was an impotent weapon against societal oppression. Though as members of the counter-culture they may have valued the immediate gratification that personal violence brings, they found the gratification lessened by the realization that personal violence became fantasy posturing—what Robert Brustein has called "revolution as theatre". They could not resign themselves to ivory tower dreaming as academics, guerrilla theatre playing at revolution, or retreat into fantasy. Thus they adopt what the main culture always urged—capacity for sublimation and delayed gratification. They become willing to behave "appropriately," to bomb (though they find this behaviour intrinsically less satisfying than regressive personal violence) in the realistic quest for a broader societal good.

And yet they find themselves caught up in the process anarchists have always objected to: techniques of violence—technology—transform not only the weapons but also the fighters. Aggression that once served personal needs is transformed by realistic perception of the impotence of personal violence into a personally unsatisfying, brutalizing and depersonalized activity. This technological violence only brings gratification to the sublimated wish inasmuch as the technique successfully achieves the policy objectives.

Nor can one deny the psychological well-being of bombers on the grounds that they utterly misperceive the effects of bombing in the existing situation. I think they utterly misperceive its effects, which I think may well be disastrous. But though I may fear a right-wing reaction, the terrorists can guess that the Nixon Administration will over-react to a limited number of bombings and that the country will be radicalized by distaste for the Administration response. Though the odds may favour the first scenario, to expect or hope that the second is accurate is not delusional or crazy in any clinical sense.

What the observation that the bombers may not be crazy at all underlines is the fact that what is arguably healthy for some individuals may be disastrous for the society. Bombing may be an "appropriate" extension of their commitment, yet others from no less valid a perspective can judge that it is a terrible error. The bombings fit the anarchist tradition but suggest an anarchist dilemma. For to bomb is to move away from personal towards technological violence; the technological means compromise the anarchist's personal and societal ends. This dilemma exists whatever one's view of the bombings may be.

Suggested Readings

Apter, David, E., and James Joll, *Anarchism Today* (New York: Doubleday & Company, Inc., 1972).

Bakunin, Mikhail, *The Political Philosophy of Bakunin* (New York: The Free Press, 1953).

Goodman, Paul, and Percival Goodman, *Communitas* (Chicago: University of Chicago Press, 1947).

Hoffman, Robert, *Anarchism* (New York: Atherton Press, Inc., 1970).

Illich, Ivan, *Celebration of Awareness* (New York: Doubleday & Company, Inc., 1969).

Joll, James, *The Anarchists* (London: Eyre and Spottiswoode, Ltd., 1964).

Keniston, Kenneth, *Young Radicals* (New York: Harcourt Brace and Jovanovich, Inc., 1968).

Krimerman, L. I., and L. Perry, *Patterns of Anarchy* (Garden City, N.Y.: Doubleday & Company, Inc., 1966).

Kropotkin, Peter, *Mutual Aid* (Boston: Extending Horizons Books), 1955.

Read, Herbert, *Anarchy and Order* (London: Faber & Faber, Ltd., 1954).

Read, Herbert, *Poetry and Anarchism* (London: Freedom Press, 1948).

Roszak, Theodore, *The Making of a Counter Culture* (Garden City, N.Y.: Doubleday & Company, Inc., 1969).

Sorel, Georges, *Reflections on Violence* (New York: P. Smith, 1941).

Woodcock, George, *Anarchism* (Cleveland: Meridian Books, 1962).

Woodcock, George, and Ivan Avakumovia, *The Anarchist Prince: A Biographical Study of Peter Kropotkin* (New York: T. V. Boardman, 1950; Kraus Reprint, 1970).

The End of Ideology

INTRODUCTION

Among many social and political scientists it came to be thought in the 1950s and early 1960s that the age of ideologies had come to an end. This belief seems to have grown out of a particular method of study conjoined with a particular way of looking at the world. This perspective involved several elements. First, it was postulated that societies be conceived as systems having varying capacities to adapt to fringe and minor internal disturbances. Second, it was laid down that most if not all societies in the contemporary world were systems of this type. The United States was the paradigm of this conception. As a society it had overcome the tensions and contradictions that had threatened stability in the past. To most onlookers it appeared to be rapidly adapting to social problems of past decades through its response to the civil rights movement (integration), by its high standards of living and full employment, by means of economic expansion, and by a general accommodation it had reached with communist countries in a move toward coexistence. The society was stabilized, the peace was achieved. The Western democracies and even the Soviet Union appeared to be following this pattern of stabilization.

On this view there was little concern with the conflicting political ideologies that had guided masses and parties of the past. In fact, political parties closely resembled each other; there was little to choose between them. Ideologies in this context played only an insignificant role in society, if any at all. The political scientists who took up this approach were far less interested in knowing the mechanisms of social change than they were in discovering the mechanisms of social equilibrium that would ensure continued stability. Thus their conception of society was not dynamic; it was functional and integrative. The normative function of such an approach is the perpetuation of stability by means of identifying the mechanisms of accommodation and equilibration.

By the mid-1960s unforeseen developments had thrown societies (especially in the West) into chaos. The rise of the new left in West Germany, the radicalization of students all over the world, the revolt of the ethnic minorities in the cities and the burnings in the inner cities, widespread assassination of political leaders, mass demonstrations against the war in Indo-China, the sudden rise of Marxist,

Maoist, and Marxist-Leninist parties, draft resistance, political trials, and later economic collapse, the revolt of prison populations, civil war in Ireland, in general the rise and clash of new and old ideologies—the war of political ideas was resumed, the society and those who had believed that the age of ideology had ended fell into disarray. The two articles in this section consider the debate between those who proclaimed the "end of ideology" and their critics, who assert that "the-end-of-ideology" thesis is no more than a variant of liberal or conservative ideology.

The End of Ideology
Daniel Bell

Daniel Bell (1919-   ) received his B.S. from City College of New York and the Ph.D. from Columbia University. He has been Professor of Sociology at Harvard University from 1969 until present. Author of *Work and Its Discontents* (1956), *The New American Right* (1955), and *The Radical Right* (1963).

There have been few periods in history when man felt his world to be durable, suspended surely, as in Christian allegory, between chaos and heaven. In an Egyptian papyrus of more than four thousand years ago, one finds: ". . . impudence is rife . . . the country is spinning round and round like a potter's wheel . . . the masses are like timid sheep without a shepherd . . . one who yesterday was indigent is now wealthy and the sometime rich overwhelm him with adulation." The Hellenistic period as described by Gilbert Murray was one of a "failure of nerve;" there was "the rise of pessimism, a loss of self-confidence, of hope in this life and of faith in normal human effort." And the old scoundrel Talleyrand claimed that only those who lived before 1789 could have tasted life in all its sweetness.

This age, too, can add appropriate citations—made all the more wry and bitter by the long period of bright hope that preceded it—for the two decades between 1930 and 1950 have an intensity peculiar in written history: world-wide economic depression and sharp class struggles; the rise of fascism and racial imperialism in a country that had stood at an advanced stage of human culture; the tragic self-immolation of a revolutionary generation that had proclaimed the finer ideals of man; destructive war of a breadth and scale hitherto unknown; the bureaucratized murder of millions in concentration camps and death chambers.

For the radical intellectual who had articulated the revolutionary impulses of the past century and a half, all this has meant an end to chiliastic hopes, to millenarianism, to apocalyptic thinking—and to ideology. For ideology, which once was a road to action, has come to be a dead end.

Whatever its origins among the French *philosophes*, ideology as a way of translating ideas into action was given its sharpest phrasing by the left Hegelians, by Feuerbach and by Marx. For them, the function of philosophy was to be critical, to rid the present of the past. ("The tradition of all the dead generations weighs like a nightmare on the brain of the living," wrote Marx.) Feuerbach, the most radical of all the left Hegelians, called himself Luther II. Man would be free, he said, if we could demythologize religion. The history of all thought was a history of progressive disenchantment, and if finally, in Christianity, God had been transformed from a parochial deity to a universal abstraction, the function of criticism—using the radical tool of alienation, or self-estrangement—was to replace theology by anthropology, to substitute Man for God. Philosophy was to be directed at life, man was to be liberated from the "specter of abstractions" and extricated from the bind of the supernatural. Religion was capable only of creating "false consciousness." Philosophy would reveal "true consciousness." And by placing Man, rather than God, at the center of consciousness, Feuerbach sought to bring the "infinite into the finite."

If Feuerbach "descended into the world," Marx sought to transform it. And where Feuerbach proclaimed anthropology, Marx, reclaiming a root insight of Hegel, emphasized History and historical contexts. The world was not generic Man, but men; and of men, classes of men. Men differed because of their class positions. And truths were class truths. All truths, thus, were masks, or partial truths, but the real truth was the revolutionary truth. And this real truth was rational.

Thus a dynamic was introduced into the analysis of ideology, and into the creation of a new ideology. By demythologizing religion, one recovered (from God and sin) the potential in man. By the unfolding of history, rationality was revealed. In the struggle of classes, true consciousness, rather than false consciousness, could be achieved. But if truth lay in action, one must act. The left Hegelians, said Marx, were only *littérateurs*. (For them a magazine was "practice.") For Marx, the only real action was in politics. But action, revolutionary action as Marx conceived it, was not mere social change. It was, in its way, the resumption of all the old millenarian, chiliastic ideas of the Anabaptists. It was, in its new vision, a new ideology.

Ideology is the conversion of ideas into social levers. Without irony, Max Lerner once entitled a book "Ideas Are Weapons." This is the language of ideology. It is more. It is the commitment to the consequences of ideas. When Vissarion Belinsky, the father of Russian criticism, first read Hegel and became convinced of the philosophical correctness of the formula "what is, is what ought to be," he became a supporter of the Russian autocracy. But when it was shown to him that Hegel's thought contained the contrary tendency, that dialectically the "is" evolves into a different form, he became a revolutionary overnight. "Belinsky's conversion," comments Rufus W. Mathewson, Jr., "Illustrates an attitude toward ideas which is both passionate and myopic, which responds to them on the basis of their immediate relevances alone, and inevitably reduces them to tools."

What gives ideology its force is its passion. Abstract philosophical inquiry has always sought to eliminate passion, and the person, to rationalize all ideas. For the ideologue, truth arises in action, and meaning is given to experience by the "transforming moment." He comes alive not in contemplation, but in "the deed." One might say, in fact, that the most important, latent, function if ideology is to tap emotion. Other than religion (and war and nationalism), there have been few forms of channelizing emotional energy. Religion symbolized, drained away, dispersed emotional energy from the world onto the litany, the liturgy, the sacraments, the edifices, the arts. Ideology fuses these energies and channels them into politics.

But religion, at its most effective, was more. It was a way for people to cope with the problem of death. The fear of death—forceful and inevitable—and more, the fear of violent death, shatters the glittering, imposing momentary dream of man's power. The fear of death, as Hobbes pointed out, is the source of conscience; the effort to avoid violent death is the source of law. When it was possible for people to believe, really believe, in heaven and hell, then some of the fear of death could be tempered or controlled; without such belief, there is only the total annihilation of the self.

It may well be that with the decline in religious *faith* in the last century and more, this fear as total annihilation, unconsciously expressed, has probably increased. One may hypothesize, in fact, that here is a cause of the breakthrough of the irrational, which is such a marked feature of the changed moral temper of our time. Fanaticism, violence, and cruelty are not, of course, unique in human history. But there was a time when such frenzies and mass emotions could be displaced, symbolized, drained away, and dispersed through religious devotion and practice. Now there is only this life, and the assertion of self becomes possible—for some even necessary—in the domination over others.[1] One can challenge death by emphasizing the omnipotence of a movement (as in the "inevitable" victory of communism), or overcome death (as did the "immortality" of Captain Ahab) by bending others to one's will. Both paths are taken, but politics, because it can institutionalize power, in the way that religion once did, becomes the ready avenue for domination. The modern effort to transform the world chiefly or solely through politics (as contrasted with the religious transformation of the self) has meant that all other institutional ways of mobilizing emotional energy would necessarily atrophy. In effect, sect and church became party and social movement.

A social movement can rouse people when it can do three things: simplify ideas, establish a claim to truth, and, in the union of the two, demand a commitment to action. Thus, not only does ideology transform ideas, it transforms people as well. The nineteenth-century ideologies, by emphasizing inevitability and by infusing passion into their followers, could compete with religion. By identifying inevitability with progress, they linked up with the positive values of science. But more important, these ideologies were linked, too, with the rising class of intellectuals, which was seeking to assert a place in society.

The differences between the intellectual and the scholar, without being invidious, are important to understand. The scholar has a bounded field of

[1] The Marquis de Sade, who, more than any man, explored the limits of self-assertion, once wrote: "There is not a single man who doesn't want to be a despot when he is excited . . . he would like to be alone in the world . . . any sort of equality would destroy the despotism he enjoys then." de Sade proposed, therefore, to canalize these impulses into sexual activity by opening universal brothels which could serve to drain away these emotions. de Sade, it should be pointed out, was a bitter enemy of religion, but he understood well the latent function of religion in mobilizing emotions.

knowledge, a tradition, and seeks to find his place in it, adding to the accumulated, tested knowledgy of the past as to a mosaic. The scholar, qua scholar, is less involved with his "self." The intellectual begins with *his* experience, *his* individual perceptions of the world, *his* privileges and deprivations, and judges the world by these sensibilities. Since his own status is of high value, his judgments of the society reflect the treatment accorded him. In a business civilization, the intellectual felt that the wrong values were being honored, and rejected the society. Thus there was a "built-in" compulsion for the free-floating intellectual to become political. The ideologies, therefore, which emerged from the nineteenth century had the force of the intellectuals behind them. They embarked upon what William James called "the faith ladder," which in its vision of the future cannot distinguish possibilities from probabilities, and converts the latter into certainties.

Today, these ideologies are exhausted. The events behind this important sociological change are complex and varied. Such calamities as the Moscow Trials, the Nazi-Soviet pact, the concentration camps, the suppression of the Hungarian workers, form one chain; such social changes as the modification of capitalism, the rise of the Welfare State, another. In philosophy, one can trace the decline of simplistic, rationalistic beliefs and the emergence of new stoic-theological images of man, e.g. Freud, Tillich, Jaspers, etc. This is not to say that such ideologies as communism in France and Italy do not have a political weight, or a driving momentum from other sources. But out of all this history, one simple fact emerges: for the radical intelligentzia, the old ideologies have lost their "truth" and their power to persuade.

Few serious minds believe any longer that one can set down "blueprints" and through "social engineering" bring about a new utopia of social harmony. At the same time, the older "counter-beliefs" have lost their intellectual force as well. Few "classic" liberals insist that the State should play no role in the economy, and few serious conservatives, at least in England and on the Continent, believe that the Welfare State is "the road to serfdom." In the Western world, therefore, there is today a rough consensus among intellectuals on political issues: the acceptance of a Welfare State; the desirability of decentralized power; a system of mixed economy and of political pluralism. In that sense, too, the ideological age has ended.

And yet, the extraordinary fact is that while the old nineteenth-century ideologies and intellectual debates have become exhausted, the rising states of Asia and Africa are fashioning new ideologies with a different appeal for their own people. These are the ideologies of industrialization, modernization, Pan-Arabism, color, and nationalism. In the distinctive difference between the two kinds of ideologies lies the great political and social problems of the second half of the twentieth century. The ideologies of the nineteenth century were universalistic, humanistic, and fashioned by intellectuals. The mass ideologies of Asia and Africa are parochial, instrumental, and created by political leaders. The driving forces of the old ideologies were social equality and, in the largest sense, freedom. The impulsions of the new ideologies are economic development and national power.

And in this appeal, Russia and China have become models. The fascination these countries exert is no longer the old idea of the free society, but the new one of economic growth. And if this involves the wholesale coercion of the population and the rise of new elites to drive the people, the new repressions are justified on the ground that without such coercions economic advance cannot take place rapidly enough. And even for some of the liberals of the West, "economic development" has become a new ideology that washes away the memory of old disillusionments.

It is hard to quarrel with an appeal for rapid economic growth and modernization, and few can dispute the goal, as few could ever dispute an appeal for equality and freedom. But in this powerful surge—and its swiftness is amazing—any movement that instates such goals risks the sacrifice of the present generation for a future that may see only a new exploitation by a new elite. For the newly-risen countries, the debate is not over the merits of Communism—the content of that doctrine has long been forgotten by friends and foes alike. The question is an older one: whether new societies can grow by building democratic institutions and allowing people to make choices—and sacrifices—voluntarily, or whether the new elites, heady with power, will impose totalitarian means to transform their countries. Certainly in these traditional and old colonial societies where the masses are apathetic and easily manipulated, the answer lies with the intellectual classes and their conceptions of the future.

Thus one finds, at the end of the fifties, a disconcerting caesura. In the West, among the intellectuals, the old passions are spent. The new generation, with no meaningful memory of these old debates, and no secure tradition to build upon, finds itself seeking new purposes within a framework of political society that has rejected, intellectually speaking, the old apocalyptic and chiliastic visions. In the search for a "cause," there is a deep, desperate, almost pathetic anger. The theme runs through a remarkable book, *Convictions*, by a dozen of the sharpest young Left Wing intellectuals in Britain. They cannot define the content of the "cause" they seek, but the yearning is clear. In the U.S. too there is a restless search for a new intellectual radicalism. Richard Chase, in his thoughtful assessment of American society, *The Democratic Vista*, insists that the greatness of nineteenth-century America for the rest of the world consisted in its radical vision of man (such a vision as Whitman's), and calls for a new radical criticism today. But the problem is that the old politico-economic radicalism (pre-occupied with such matters as the socialization of industry) has lost its meaning, while the stultifying aspects of contemporary culture (e.g., television) cannot be redressed in political terms. At the same time, American culture has almost completely accepted the avant-garde, particularly in art, and the older academic styles have been driven out completely. The irony, further, for those who seek "causes" is that the workers, whose grievances were once the driving energy for social change, are more satisfied with the society than the intellectuals. The workers have not achieved utopia, but their expectations were less than those of the intellectuals, and the gains correspondingly larger.

The young intellectual is unhappy because the "middle way" is for the middle-aged, not for him; it is without passion and is deadening. Ideology, which by its nature is an all-or-none affair, and temperamentally the thing he wants, is intellectually devitalized, and few issues can be formulated any more, intellectually, in ideological terms. The emotional energies—and needs—exist, and the question of how one mobilizes these energies is a difficult one. Politics offers little excitement. Some of the younger intellectuals have found an outlet in science or university pursuits, but often at the expense of narrowing their talent into mere technique; others have sought self-expression in the arts, but in the wasteland the lack of content has meant, too, the lack of the necessary tension that creates new forms and styles.

Whether the intellectuals in the West can find passions outsides of politics is moot. Unfortunately, social reform does not have any unifying appeal, nor does it give a younger generation the outlet for "self-expression" and "self-definition" that it wants. The trajectory of enthusiasm has curved East, where, in the new ecstasies for economic utopia, the "future" is all that counts.

And yet, if the intellectual history of the past hundred years has any meaning—and lesson—it is to reassert Jefferson's wisdom (aimed at removing the dead hand of the past, but which can serve as a warning against the heavy hand of the future as well), that "the present belongs to the living." This is the wisdom that revolutionists, old and new, who are sensitive to the fate of their fellow men, rediscover in every generation. "I will never believe," says a protagonist in a poignant dialogue written by the gallant Polish philosopher Leszek Kolakowski, "that the moral and intellectual life of mankind follows the law of economics, that is by saving today we can have more tomorrow; that we should use lives now so that truth will triumph or that we should profit by crime to pave the way for nobility."

And these words, written during the Polish "thaw," when the intellectuals had asserted, from their experience with the "future," the claims of humanism, echo the protest of the Russian writer Alexander Herzen, who, in a dialogue a hundred years ago, reproached an earlier revolutionist who would sacrifice the present mankind for a promised tomorrow: "Do you truly wish to condemn all human beings alive today to the sad role of caryatids . . . supporting a floor for others some day to dance on? . . . This alone should serve as a warning to people: an end that is infinitely remote is not an end, but if you like, a trap; an end must be nearer—it ought to be, at the very least, the labourer's wage or pleasure in the work done. Each age, each generation, each life has its own fullness. . . ."

The End of Ideology and the Ideology of the End of Ideology

Alasdair MacIntyre

Alasdair C. MacIntyre (1924-   ) is a Professor of Philosophy. He has taught at Oxford University, University of Essex, and Brandeis University. He now teaches at Boston University and is Dean of the College of Liberal Arts. Among his books are *Difficulties in Christian Belief* (1959), *Marxism: An Interpretation* (1963), *New Essays in Philosophical Theology* (1955), *Marxism and Christianity* (1968), *The Religious Significance of Atheism* (1969), *Secularization and Moral Change* (1967), and *Against the Self-Images of the Age* (1971).

The 1950s were a decade of immoderate claims made on behalf of what its defenders took to be moderation. Apocalyptic salutations hailed the arrival of the mixed economy guided by what was alleged—quite falsely—to be Keynesian economic theory; messianic value was attached to the politics of social democracy. As in earlier apocalyptic and messianic moments, it was proclaimed intemperately that nothing but the sober truth was at last being told. The core of this prophesying was the "end-of-ideology" thesis, first advanced by Edward Shils at a Congress of Cultural Freedom meeting in 1954 and later endorsed and developed by Daniel Bell and Seymour Martin Lipset. The central message of this thesis was that in the advanced industrial societies of the West, ideology was at an end because fundamental social conflict was at an end.

In the view maintained by advocates of this thesis, there were no longer any social roots for a politics which proposed a revolutionary transformation of the social order. There might still be Utopian visions of a social order in which the ills of the existing order had been done away—and Daniel Bell at least was anxious to stress the continuing relevance of Utopian vision, provided that it was treated as vision and not as something else; but practical politics must now be a matter of pragmatic compromise with an agreed framework of basic and even not so basic values. This agreed framework depended upon a consensus which had been arrived at by means of the institutions of the welfare state and of the economic and political domestication of the working class. Those rival and competing interests which had been allowed expression within the official political order would therefore no longer breed disruptive conflict; and the presentation of ideological world views which might guide and inform a politics of passionate conflict would henceforth be out of place in the advanced industrial societies.

That the end-of-ideology thesis was a diagnosis which expressed something real and important about those societies in the 1950s is undeniable. The political apathy, for instance, to which its protagonistts pointed (and which Lipset, for example, took to be a precondition of the stability of democratic political orders) was not an illusion. Moreover, the proliferation of similar theses among political

From Alasdair MacIntyre, *Against the Self Images of the Age* (New York: Schocken Books, Inc., 1971), pp. 3-11.

philosophers and political scientists is itself to some degree evidence of a general frame of mind. Shils in Chicago, Lipset in California, Bell in New York found allies in J. L. Talmon in Jerusalem, who proclaimed that the ideological theorists of the eighteenth and nineteenth centuries—and especially Rousseau and Marx—were the progenitors of the totalitarian politics of the twentieth century (the equation of ideological theorizing with totalitarian politics is a central theme in most of these writers); in Sir Isaiah Berlin at Oxford, who identified a belief in "positive liberty" (to be found in Rousseau and Hegel) as a prime source of totalitarian evils; and in Norman Cohn, who saw in the millenarians of the Middle Ages and the sixteenth century the predecessors of modern Utopians, identifying the source of both movements in the psychological disorders—and probably the paranoia—of the individuals concerned. The end-of-ideology thesis, therefore, was part of a general intellectual landscape. Moreover, it found a counterpart in the avowed beliefs of those engaged in politics. The writings of Anthony Crosland and John Strachey espouse what is plainly the same basic standpoint.

If therefore the sheer weight of this agreement is evidence that the end-of-ideology thesis expressed something implicitly or explicitly recognized by many perceptive observers of the 1950s, it still remains to ask wehther the end-of-ideology thesis diagnosed correctly the nature of that to which it was sensitive. On this point three initial observations are in order. The first is that when such writers were themselves Marxists, or post-Marxists, none were unwilling to declare their allegiance in Cold War terms, and it is therefore pertinent to ask whether they may not have confused the local demise of Marxist ideology with the local demise of ideology. To ask this question suggests that we ought to inquire whether these authors had freed themselves from the influence of Marxism to quite the extent which they believed they had. For their thesis appears to be that it is because what they take to be profound social changes have occurred that ideology is no longer possible, In their view of the causal sequence—for which none of these writers seems to argue explicitly—it is possible to perceive the ghosts of the Marxist concepts of basis and superstructure. For otherwise, surely they might have taken more seriously the possibility that it was because ideology was not what it was, that social and political conflict was not what *it* was, rather than vice versa.

I deliberately used in the last sentence the neutral expression "because ideology was not what it was," in order to lead on to the suggestion that, in fact, the end-of-ideology theorists had misconstrued their situation in two related ways. They were right to see that in the 1950s ideology was not what it was; and they were right also to relate this fact to the lessening of social conflict. But not only did they confuse the exhaustion of Marxism with the exhaustion of ideology, they failed to entertain one crucial alternative possibility: namely, that the end-of-ideology thesis, far from marking the end of ideology, was itself a key expression of the ideology of the time and place where it arose. Here again there is a strong reminiscence of classical Marxism. For Marx saw Marxism as having an independence of existing social structures and hence an objectivity which rescued it from the relativity of ideological thought which he diagnosed in his opponents. It was, of course, only in the Communist future, when the social roots of ideological thinking had been finally destroyed, that ideology would finally wither away. But Marxism offers an anticipation of this apocalyptic culmination. This surely is the ancestor of that muted apocalypticism in Bell and Lipset which surrounds the announcement of the end of ideology.

To make good the thesis that the end-of-ideology thesis was itself part of an ideology, and was thus also self-refuting, it is necessary to be clear about what we ought to understand by the expression "ideology." Shils, Bell, and Lipset are all astonishingly brief in their exposition; since I wish to make use of this notion not merely to criticize the end-of-ideology thesis, but for other independent purposes, I shall have to discuss this point at somewhat greater length.

I take any ideology to have three key features. The first is that it attempts to delineate certain general characteristics of nature or society or both, characteristics which do not belong only to particular features of the changing world which can be investigated only by empirical inquiry. So for Christianity the God-created and God-maintained character of the world is just such a characteristic; so for Marxism the laws of dialectical change are such a characteristic. Two closely related queries can always be raised about this feature of an ideology: What is the status of statements about these general characteristics and how do we show such statements to be true or false? And what is the relationship between the truth or falsity of such statements and the truth or falsity of scientific or historical claims about the character of empirically investigable processes and events? How for Christianity are claims about divine providence related to claims about historical events in first-century Palestine? How for Marxism are claims about the dialectic related to claims about the wage levels of the working class under industrial capitalism?

The second central feature of any ideology is an account of the relationship between what is the case and how we ought to act, between the nature of the world and that of morals, politics, and other guides to conduct. That is to say, I am making it a defining property of an ideology that it does not merely tell us how the world is *and* how we ought to act, but is concerned with the bearing of the one upon the other. This involves a concern, explicit or implicit, with the status of statements of moral rules and of statements expressing evaluations.

This latter concern, like the concern with the status of statements about the nature of things, shows that a good deal of what I have characterized as ideology not only overlaps with the proper concerns of philosophy, it *is* philosophy. So that philosophical inquiry is always liable to be a solvent of ideological conviction and commitment by arriving at conclusions incompatible with the positions of a particular ideology. Likewise, the dominance of a particular ideology may limit or inhibit philosophical inquiry. I do not refer only or most importantly to the use of policemen by those who are not only ideologically committed but also politically powerful to threaten or abolish free inquiry. For what I shall treat as the third defining property of an ideology is that it is not merely believed by the members of a given social group, but believed in such a way that it at least partially defines for them their social existence. By this I mean that its concepts are embodied in, and its beliefs presupposed by, some of these actions and transactions, the performance of which is characteristic of the social life of that group. The relatively noncommittal word "group" is used advisedly, for it is itself a matter for ideological debate how ideologies come to exercise such hold as they do upon social life. There is a Christian account of why Christians are Christians and the heathens are not; and there is a Marxist account of why Marxists are Marxists and the heathens are not. It is for this reason that a good deal of ideology not only overlaps with the proper concerns of sociology, but *is* sociology; and hence, sociological inquiry, like philosophical inquiry, is liable to be a solvent of ideological conviction and also to be limited or inhibited by the dominance of particular ideologies.

This potentiality of conflict between any dominating or even aspiring ideology, and both philosophy and sociology, is not merely a source of tension. Rather, it is one of the signs, although only one of the signs, that an ideology is living and not dead, that it should actually breed conflict both with the philosophy and with the empirical science of its day. Conversely, any situation in which an ideology has no problems of conflict with philosophy or human or natural science is characteristically a sign, not that the ideology in question has triumphantly solved the intellectual problems of the age, but rather that the ideology has become empirically vacuous and has won its freedom from conflict at the cost of becoming empirically and perhaps practically empty.

That this is true of Christianity as it now exists I have argued in two essays in *The Religious Significance of Contemporary Atheism*,[1] and I shall not repeat the argument here, especially as the germ of that argument is to be found in "God and the Theologians."[2] But it is important to stress that it is not just the character of Christianity or just the character of contemporary society, but rather the coincidence of certain features of these two changing characters that has rendered Christianity ideologically vacuous. The attempt to maintain the values and the credibility of Christianity in the intellectual and moral climate of, for example, contemporary Britain has led to a vacuity that was not present when Christians such as Karl Barth or Dietrich Bonhoeffer or Franz Jaegstaetter defined their faith in words and action by contrast with and against Nazi mythology.

An ideology may of course be empirically vacuous, because it is held in such a way that is unfalsifiable, and yet not be practically vacuous. So it is with psychoanalytic doctrine in a certain social milieu at the present time. In the cultural desert created by the prejudices of the liberal intelligentsia of New York or of the Californian cities, the questioning of the scientific pretensions of psychoanalysis is restricted almost entirely to those concerned with the philosophy of science. The therapeutic needs of such aids perhaps make intelligible the extraordinary situations whereby a theory that is certainly no better confirmed—and perhaps not as well confirmed—as witchcraft or astrology should have gained the credence that it has.

Finally, at this point we ought to note that the same doctrine can, during its history, experience vicissitudes as a result of which it alters its ideological character, both in respect to its relevance and vacuity and in respect to the liberating or oppressive character of its social effects. This is peculiarly true of both Christianity and Marxism. But in the advanced industrial societies of the West at least, although it may be dangerous to misunderstand why Christianity and Marxism are for the most part impotent, it is far more dangerous to rest this misunderstanding on the kind of endorsement of the status quo involved in the end-of-ideology thesis.

The ideological character of that thesis is most clearly apparent in Lipset's version of it in *Political Man*. The key notions which carry ideological weight are those of the conflicting interests which have been domesticated within the welfare state and that of the political consensus which provides the framework for that domestication. The key empirical contention is that a large measure of nonparticipation in active political decision-making promotes democratic and peaceful political and social processes, while widespread participation tends to go hand in hand with totalitarianism and authoritarianism. About these notions and this contention the following needs to be said: first, that the crucial question is how an

[1] With Paul Ricoeur (New York: Columbia University Press, 1967).

[2] See pp. 12-26. (*Against the Self Images of the Age*, from which this selection was taken. Ed.)

interest is defined and how it is identified. Lipset and Bell, when they speak of the welfare state, clearly have in mind the recognition of trade unions either in their own right or through social-democratic parties as an interest which the political decision-makers must consult. But what about the recipients of welfare? Do they or ought they to constitute an interest with a distinctive political voice? What is quite clear is that the processes of formal democracy can coexist with the recognition of certain institutionalized interests, while the distribution of power and of the goods of which power determines the recipients remains radically unequal and radically unjust. The continuous rediscovery of and indeed the continuous re-creation of poverty in advanced societies ought to make this fact central to any political analysis.

Consensus is a concept correlative to that of interest. The question of which interests are recognized and acknowledged and the question of whose voice is heard in the consensus are the same question. It is not, of course, the case that those whose wants are not recognized and acknoweledge as an interest by the established political consensus do not have their needs considered in the course of political decision-making; they may constitute an object of acute concern, especially when they create problems for their decision-makers. If the problems they create are sufficiently intractable, then the attempt will be made to give the problem-makers an institutionalized voice *within* the consensus. So at any given time there will be two types of politics possible: one, the politics of those within; the other, the politics of those excluded. The end-of-ideology thesis is one ideology of those concerned with legitimating only the former.

This exercise is underpinned by the selection of facts and by lack of conceptual awareness. The selection of facts is a matter of the type and the range of variables studied. Lipset never considers the type of nonparticipation in decision-making—which in fact prevails in totalitarian and authoritarian states and organizations as a counterexample to his thesis—with the consequence, that either his thesis must be construed as false or his use of "participation" so loose and undefined as to be useless for his own express purposes. But above all, Lipset never considers how the evaluation and selection of the facts not only results in a political commitment (as Charles Taylor has argued in his paper on "Neutrality and Political Science"[3] and as Lipset himself acknowledges when he writes that "democracy [he means the parliamentary democracy of the West] is not only or even primarily a means through which different groups can attain their ends or seek the good society; it is the good society itself in operation" *Political Man*, p. 403), but arises from a critical standpoint which is not only methodological but also ideological. The Lipset-Bell vision of the world is informed by a view of rationality which makes liberal, pragmatic man the paradigm of rationality. Hence, the antithesis is framed between the reasonable, empirical approach of the proponents of the end-of-ideology thesis and the partisan passions of *les idéologues* (this deprecating sense of ideology was first used by Napoleon). Now rationality may be and, as I shall argue in a later essay, is one. But what are rational goals for those within the concensus to lay down, explicitly or implicitly, for those outside the consensus are not rational goals for those outside the consensus to lay down for themselves, if only because of the force of that always to be remembered truism that not only in the end, but even in

[3] In *Philosophy, Politics, and Society*, Third Series, edited by P. Laslett and W. G. Runciman (Oxford: Blackwell; New York: Barnes & Noble, 1967).

the relatively short run, nobody can know what an agent wants better than the man himself. Every restriction upon the right of men to speak for themselves in this respect involves either some unjustified claim that others can know better than they what they want, or some claim that their wants are irrelevant, perhaps because what they want is not what is good for them. Hence, the democratic claim of Jefferson or of Robespierre is the necessary political counterpart of any moral regard for human wants.

The ideological antithesis of Jefferson or Robespierre is Burke, and it is no accident that the antithesis between a politics of interests and a politics of ideology is as at home in Burke's writings as it is in those of Bell or Lipset. What Burke failed to see is what Bell and Lipset fail to see: that the costs of consensus are paid by those excluded from it. It is noteworthy that neither Bell in *The End of Ideology*, nor Lipset in *Political Man* or even in his much later article on "Anglo-American Society," in the *International Encyclopaedia of the Social Sciences* sees the place of the blacks in advanced societies as posing a radical question mark. Of them we may say what Michelet said of the Irish when he reproved the English: "Sitting at your ease on the corpse of Ireland ... be good enough to tell us: did your revolution of interests not cost more blood than our revolution of ideas?" (The Irish were for a long time the blacks of the British Isles.) The central polarity of advanced industrial societies is that between minorities who cannot solve their problems and majorities who cannot even face them. One instrument which is of importance in their avoidance-behavior (the behavior which elected Mr. Nixon to the Presidency) is the largely implicit belief that all problems are piecemeal and detailed, to be confronted by an empirical and pragmatic approach and that the transformation of society as a whole is an ideological will o' the wisp. But just this is the belief explicitly articulated and defended by the end-of-ideology thesis. It is thus not merely an ideology, but one that lacks any liberating power.

When I speak of the end of the end of ideology I do not mean of course to dwell merely on the fact that the end-of-ideology thesis is itself ideological. For while the end-of-ideology thesis was sensitive to a widespread mood in the 1950s among not only intellectuals, but also students, it proved to be highly discordant with the mood of intelligentsia of the 1960s when social conflict was at its most intense in the advanced societies in the institutions of higher education. What was notable was, of course, not the birth of new ideologies, but a romanticism which sometimes disclaimed any coherent ideology and sometimes constructed an amalgam of ideological fragments to use for its own purposes. This confrontation of middle-aged pragmatism and youthful romanticism, of a pragmatic insistence on the detailed and the empirical and a passionate attachment to vague and large ideological critiques, is misleadingly characterized as a generational conflict, even if it was in fact accompanied by such conflict. For such a characterization misses the symbiotic character of the phenomenon; the pragmatism of the attitude involved in the end-of-ideology thesis leaves precisely those whom it seeks to educate vulnerable to almost any ideological appeal by its failure to criticize social wholes. Each party to this dispute provides the other with an opponent made in precisely the required image. The children of those who define social reality in technocratic, bureaucratic, and academic terms aspire to a definition of human reality which will escape all institutional constraints. The implicit nihilism of so much student attack on institutions is the natural outcome of the defense of the institutions of the status quo as the only possible ones.

It is partly because of this connection that the end-of-ideology thesis still deserves attention. Those who wish to remake society are under an obligation to learn to frame alternative institutions that will escape the crushing polarities of the present. This is a political task. To perform it in a minimally adequate way it will be a necessary preliminary to understand how we can escape ideological deformation by the social order in which we live. One version of that deformation is to allow the fear of 1984 to revive the politics which glorified 1688.

Suggested Readings

Aron, Raymond, *The Opium of the Intellectuals* (New York: W. W. Norton & Company, Inc., 1962).

Bell, Daniel, Ed., *The End of Ideology* (New York: The Free Press, 1960).

Bottomore, T. B., *Critics of Society* (New York: Pantheon Books, Random House, 1968).

Bottomore, T. B., "Conservative Man," *New York Review of Books*, Vol. 15, No. 6 (October 1970).

Lipset, Seymore, *Political Man* (Garden City, N.Y.: Doubleday & Company, Inc., 1960).

Truitt, Willis H., "Emerging Ideologies," *Diogenes*, Vol. 73, 70-87 (Spring 1971).

INDEX

INDEX